Derived Equivalence Rules

16. **Commutativity of $\vee$ (COMM$\vee$)** $A \vee B \leftrightarrow B \vee A$

17. **Commutativity of & (COMM&)** $A \mathbin{\&} B \leftrightarrow B \mathbin{\&} A$

18. **Associativity of $\vee$ (ASSC$\vee$)** $(A \vee B) \vee C \leftrightarrow A \vee (B \vee C)$

19. **Associativity of & (ASSC&)** $(A \mathbin{\&} B) \mathbin{\&} C \leftrightarrow A \mathbin{\&} (B \mathbin{\&} C)$

20. **Distribution $\vee$/& (DIST$\vee$/&)** $A \vee (B \mathbin{\&} C) \leftrightarrow (A \vee B) \mathbin{\&} (A \vee C)$

21. **Distribution &/$\vee$ (DIST&/$\vee$)** $A \mathbin{\&} (B \vee C) \leftrightarrow (A \mathbin{\&} B) \vee (A \mathbin{\&} C)$

22. **Contraposition (CONTR)** $A \supset B \leftrightarrow {\sim}B \supset {\sim}A$

23. **Conditional equivalence (CE)** $A \supset B \leftrightarrow {\sim}A \vee B$

24. **Biconditional equivalence (BE)**
    $A \equiv B \leftrightarrow (A \mathbin{\&} B) \vee ({\sim}A \mathbin{\&} {\sim}B)$
    $A \equiv B \leftrightarrow (A \supset B) \mathbin{\&} (B \supset A)$

25. **Exportation (EXP)** $(A \mathbin{\&} B) \supset C \leftrightarrow A \supset (B \supset C)$

26. **Idempotence of $\vee$ (IDEM$\vee$)** $A \leftrightarrow A \vee A$

27. **Idempotence of & (IDEM&)** $A \leftrightarrow A \mathbin{\&} A$

28. **DeMorgan's laws (DEM)**
    ${\sim}(A \vee B) \leftrightarrow {\sim}A \mathbin{\&} {\sim}B$
    ${\sim}(A \mathbin{\&} B) \leftrightarrow {\sim}A \vee {\sim}B$

29. **Absorption (ABS)** $A \supset B \leftrightarrow A \supset (A \mathbin{\&} B)$

30. **Tautology & (TAUT&)** $A \leftrightarrow A \mathbin{\&} (B \vee {\sim}B)$

31. **Tautology $\vee$ (TAUT$\vee$)** $A \vee (B \vee {\sim}B) \leftrightarrow (B \vee {\sim}B)$

32. **Contradiction & (CON&)** $A \mathbin{\&} (B \mathbin{\&} {\sim}B) \leftrightarrow (B \mathbin{\&} {\sim}B)$

33. **Contradiction $\vee$ (CON$\vee$)** $A \leftrightarrow A \vee (B \mathbin{\&} {\sim}B)$

34. **Double negation equivalence (DNE)** $A \leftrightarrow {\sim}{\sim}A$

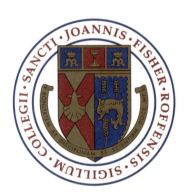

Lavery Library

St. John Fisher
College
Rochester, New York

From Logic to Computing

From Logic to Computing

Robert P. McArthur
Colby College

Philosophy Editor: Kenneth King
Editorial Assistants: Karen Jones, Michelle L. Palacio
Production Editors: Harold P. Humphrey, Karen Garrison
Designer: Carolyn Deacy
Print Buyer: Karen Hunt
Copy Editor: Stephanie Prescott
Illustrator: Marilyn Krieger
Compositor: Omegatype Typography, Inc.
Cover: Harry Voigt

Printed in the United States of America   19
1 2 3 4 5 6 7 8 9 10—95 94 93 92 91

Library of Congress Cataloging-in-Publication Data

McArthur, Robert P., 1944–
    From Logic to computing / Robert P. McArthur.
        p.   cm.
    Includes index.
    ISBN 0–534–13320–7
    1. Computer Science. 2. Logic, Symbolic and mathematical.
I. Title
QA76.M365   1991
004'.01'5113—dc20   90–35858
                                                       CIP

Contents

*More difficult or optional sections.

Preface

Primarily, this is a logic book. It provides a survey of the fundamental principles of deductive logic in order to impart an understanding of logical theory and to foster increased skills in using logic. As students learn the fundamentals of deductive logic, however, they are close to having mastered the fundamentals of the computer as well. So this book is also about computers. Computers are logic machines in two senses: their electronic design follows basic logical principles, and their programs are based on logical principles too. Given the importance of the computer in our time, and the essential connection between logic and computers, it seems sensible, *and interesting*, to study the two together.

Obviously computers are everywhere; they are involved in almost every facet of our lives. In the age of information technology, we are constantly exposed to so much information that conventional methods for its storage, organization, retrieval, and production are hopelessly inadequate. Libraries are too big for paper card catalogues, there are too many airplanes in the air for humans alone to keep track of, and many factories could not function without computers to monitor production. Even the various stock markets are entirely dependent on computers, as is much of contemporary medicine and art. Computers are increasingly used to assist in important decisions, even to make decisions, in some sense, of great significance. These decisions affect actions on battlefields, in operating rooms, at nuclear power plants, in government agencies, and in corporate conference rooms. In short, computer technology is worth knowing something about because we are all so dependent upon it now and will be even more so in the future.

The book is arranged in two parts. Part 1, *Logic*, covers the standard array of deductive logic topics. Students will learn why some reasoning is correct and other reasoning is faulty, and will come to be skilled at telling one from the other. Along the way, at various key points, the ties between logic and computers will begin to appear. (After all, students shouldn't have to wait until part 2 before beginning to see the connections.) Part 2, *Computing*, shows how the logic studied in part 1 is embedded in the very heart of all computers. Starting with the basic circuits of which computers are composed, the discussion covers several simplified examples of computing devices at work. One of these examples is actually a full computer. The principles that allow computers to run programs are discussed, as well as the principles that limit what computers can do—now or ever.

The main feature of part 1 is an unusual breadth of coverage of the components of deductive logic. Statement logic is developed with due attention to the subtleties of ordinary language statements and arguments. The full range of logical properties and relations is stressed, although *validity* is given pride of place, as it deserves. In addition to full truth tables and shortcuts, both Richard Jeffrey's truth trees and Fitch-style natural deduction rules are presented. When methods that yield algorithms appear, they are noted, and exercises are included that challenge the student to work out algorithms for various purposes. Several sections on the relation between data sets and answering questions are included. The resolution method for statement logic (SL) is also covered. As you can tell, computers are never very far from view, even when fairly standard logical topics are covered.

One important use of derivation skills is in simplifying circuits; circuits are covered in chapter 10. The first step in designing a circuit is to develop a table of inputs and outputs that has the form of a truth table. The Post-paraphrase technique of representing truth tables by SL statements is included in section 2.3. The derivation rules in chapter 4 include equivalences that are especially useful in simplification problems such as TAUT and CON (see endpapers). In addition, a novel procedure called *equivalence derivations* is included. This procedure allows direct proof that one statement is equivalent to another; only equivalence rules are used in such derivations.

The chapters on predicate logic also stress ordinary language. Truth trees appear again and again, as do natural deduction and resolution. Showing that truth trees and resolution do not provide algorithms for determining validity for predicate logic leads to an introduction to the limits on mechanized reasoning. But the monadic fragment of predicate logic (later discussed as a Boolean system) is shown to permit algorithmic methods. In order to be able to discuss the conditions under which statements involving quantifiers are true and false, the notion of *substitutional interpretation* of the quantifiers is used. This treatment permits a simple extension of the truth tables and valuations from the chapters on statement logic to the complexities of predicate logic. Substitutional renderings of the quantifiers also are a natural complement to the truth tree method for predicate logic and provide a useful foundation to the clausal quantification forms that the resolution rules require.

Although included in part 2, a chapter on Boolean systems ties together both the logic of statements and a fragment of the logic of predicates and sets the scene for the grand synthesis when logical circuits and binary numerical representation are later covered. A chapter on numerical systems fully covers the binary and hexadecimal systems and the underlying principles of numerical representation in general. Most treatments of circuitry in logic courses are very superficial. Chapter 12 includes four extended examples of computing devices so that students can come to understand how pervasive logic is in computing. An optional section provides an instruction set for a standard microprocessor.

Algorithms and their efficiency are treated in chapter 11, although sections of chapter 11 could as well be used as early as chapter 3. The ties between what is computable and how algorithms are developed for specific purposes are explored. Turing machines are fully discussed, and the decision problem for predicate logic is given a separate section.

The essential connections between the chapters in parts 1 and 2 are the prevalence of logical principles and the fundamental role played by true/false, **1/0**, and on/off; the binary states behind statement logic, predicate logic (under the substitutional view), Boolean set theory, the binary numerical system, and computer circuitry and machine code. Truth tables are one of the simplest aspects of logic, but properly understood, they are also the key to the most technologically advanced computers.

Although I believe that an understanding, at least at the level of logic, of how electronic computers work is vital, the text includes no electronics except an optional section on chips. I have arranged the discussion so that an elementary series of electronics demonstrations could accompany the discussion, but that would be an enhancement and is by no means required. Throughout the development of this book I have had in mind an audience of interested students from the liberal arts and social science. I have assumed neither a particular aptitude with quantitative materials nor a knowledge of computers. My aims are to some extent missionary; I want to help the student who is not technologically sophisticated understand the soul of computing through logic.

There is too much material here for a one-semester course. But instructors and readers will vary in their background, interests, and goals. So the sections and chapters are somewhat independent. It is possible to plot a variety of courses through the book, and I am sure others will think of novel ways of ordering and combining topics to suit their particular needs. In order to serve a wide range of interests, I have tried to be inclusive rather than exclusive, but I have also tried to link everything together so that coherence persists through whatever array of topics is chosen. Sections and exercises that are marked with an asterisk are either side issues or more difficult than the bulk of the material.

This project developed through a grant from Colby College and the Alfred Sloan Foundation as part of the New Liberal Arts Program. The aim of that program, I hope, is exemplified here: to encourage an understanding and appreciation of technology by generalists. I owe thanks to James Adams of the Program on Values, Technology, Science, and Society of Stanford University for gracious hospitality during a sabbatical year. I would also like to acknowledge my debt to the following individuals: the students in my Philosophy 258 class, especially Brad Olson; Bangs L. Tapscott of the University of Utah for his wonderful Ophir software, and the publisher's reviewers who made many helpful suggestions: Robert Burch, Texas A&M

University; David J. Cole, University of Minnesota, Duluth; Donald R. Keyworth, Drake University; Alexander Rosenberg, University of California, Riverside; and Ken Warmbrod, University of Manitoba. Additional thanks to Laura Senier who learned logic by working most of the problems, and Shannon McArthur for tolerance and patient support. Ken King deserves more than just thanks for an extraordinary job of editorial and friendly encouragement.

With great gratitude and fondness I dedicate this book to my logic teacher, Hugues Leblanc.

Robert P. McArthur
Waterville, Maine

I

Logic

1

Reasoning

*A*ll science begins with observation, with noticing that the familiar world has features that can be gathered together under a few general concepts. From such concepts come the formulation of theory and laws, and, finally, a science emerges. As a first step on your path to learning about the science of logic, we will pay close attention in this chapter to a few examples of reasoning. From these we will move on to a survey of some basic logical terms and general concepts that will be used throughout the book.

1.1 FOUR EXAMPLES OF REASONING

We will begin with several examples of reasoning.

The case of David and Daphne   David is late for a meeting and can't find his car keys. Daphne, seeing his distress, offers to help. She says: "You had your keys when you came home last night, so did you leave them on the hall table?"

"No," replies David.

"Then you must have put them on the dresser in the bedroom or left them in your coat pocket," suggests Daphne.

"Well, I can't find them on the dresser; I have looked over and over."

And they move simultaneously to the closet to check the coat pocket.

The case of Stephen   Although not much of a student, Stephen regularly attends class and takes careful notes. Reading over his class notes for the exam, he discovers a statement made by the teacher on the first day of classes:

"No one will receive an A in this course unless he comes to every class."

Stephen realizes, with pounding pulse, that he hasn't missed a single day; he figures he will get an A after all.

The Smith triplets[1]   The three Smith brothers—James, John, and William—are identical triplets; no one but their mother can tell them apart just by looking at them. They are different in some ways, however, because while William *always* tells the truth, his brothers James and John *always* lie. Suppose you meet one of the Smiths and want to know whether it is John, who owes you money. Which of the following questions might you ask to ascertain whether or not you were talking to John and not one of his brothers?

a. Are you James Smith?

b. Are you John Smith?

c. Are you William Smith?

The babies and crocodiles   Lewis Carroll (the author of *Alice in Wonderland*) poses this question in his logic book:[2] What follows logically from the following three statements?

a. Babies are illogical.

b. Nobody is despised who can manage a crocodile.

c. Illogical persons are despised.

Carroll's answer is 'Babies cannot manage crocodiles'.[3]

These four examples all involve reasoning. And to reason is to employ logic. But not all reasoning is good and not all employments of logic are successful. Thus, it is useful to be able to tell good reasoning from the bad, both to

---

[1]This example is from Raymond Smullyan, *To Mock a Mockingbird* (New York: Harper and Row, 1985), p. 9. This and the other Smullyan books are a gold mine of logic puzzles.

[2]Lewis Carroll, *Symbolic Logic*, ed. W. W. Bartley, III (New York: Charles N. Potter, 1977), p. 160.

[3]When *talking about* rather than *using* a statement, the statement will always be enclosed in single quotes, unless it is displayed on a separate line, or displayed in italics or bold face type. The same practice will also be followed for words, phrases, and symbols. Direct quotation, however, which is a special case of talking about a sentence, will receive the customary double quotes. The important distinction between using and mentioning allows us to differentiate, for example, saying that the house is on fire and saying that (the sentence) 'The house is on fire' has five words. It is also the way we distinguish references to numerals like *III* (Roman), 3 (decimal), and **111** (binary) from the number 3.

improve our own reasoning skills and to know when others have gone wrong or reasoned well. So what about David and Daphne? She is attempting to help find the keys by first figuring out where they might be and then eliminating possibilities until only one remains. How has she done? Surely you will agree that her logic is correct, assuming that she is right about the possible locations of the keys (the hall table, the bedroom dresser, the coat pocket). She and David have agreed that the keys must be in one of three places and have eliminated two; so they conclude that the keys are in the third place—the coat pocket—and hurry to check their conclusion. We might note that if they do not find the keys in the pocket, then they were wrong about there being only three possible locations; there must be a fourth! Keep this case in mind; we will come back to David and Daphne later on.

Unlike Daphne, Stephen does not get high marks for astute reasoning. He has misconstrued his teacher's remark. The teacher threatened her students to make them more conscientious about attending, but Stephen thinks the teacher promised the class a reward for perfect attendance. Perhaps the problem is the word 'unless,' which can be tricky, as we will discover as we go along. Of course Stephen is not confused about the actual words the teacher used; after all he wrote them down faithfully. His problem lies in knowing how that fateful sentence applies to his perfect attendance. Stephen thinks the teacher's statement implies that if someone has attended every class, then he or she will receive an A in the course. But the teacher has said only that *if* a person is to get an A, then he or she must have attended every class, not the other way around. There is a crucial difference between these two, so Stephen has no guarantee that he will receive an A. Note the difference:

(a) If someone has attended every class, then he or she will receive an A in the course.

(b) If a person is to get an A, then he or she must have attended every class.

To solve the puzzle about the Smith triplets, we need to ask a question that John will answer differently from both of his brothers. Let's take each of the possibilities in turn. If you ask (b), "Are you John Smith?" here are the possible answers:

James: "Yes."   (since he lies)

John: "No."   (since he also lies)

William: "No."   (since he tells the truth)

So from question (b), you will know that you are talking to James— if the answer is yes—but you can not know whether you are talking to John, because both he and his brother William will answer no. Note that all three brothers answer yes to question (c), "Are you William Smith?" James and John both lie and say yes, and William tells the truth and answers yes. So we cannot differentiate them with question (c). Thus, question (a)—"Are you James Smith?"—is correct, since only John answers yes to this question.

In the fourth example, we see how inventive Lewis Carroll was with logic problems. (We will look at some of his classics in later chapters.) But how in this case did he arrive at his answer? He reasoned something like this: Statement (a), 'Babies are illogical', says that babies are illogical people, and statement (c), 'Illogical persons are despised', says that illogical people are despised. From those two statements he concludes that *babies are despised*. (This is one of the hidden conclusions Carroll leaves to his readers to discover.) Then, since statement (b), 'Nobody is despised who can manage a crocodile', says that people who *can* manage crocodiles are not despised, he concludes that those who are despised cannot manage crocodiles. Therefore, since babies are despised, it follows that babies cannot manage crocodiles.

Although the Lewis Carroll example seems simple, it contains some of the complexities we will be studying throughout the book. Here is a summary of his reasoning:

Premise (a) Babies are illogical. = Babies are illogical people.

Premise (c) Illogical persons are despised. = Illogical people are despised.

From premises (a) and (c) it follows that

(d) Babies are despised.

From premise (b):

(b) Nobody is despised who can manage a crocodile.

= People who can manage crocodiles are not despised.

it follows that

(e) Those who are despised cannot manage crocodiles.

Finally, (d) and (e) are themselves used as premises from which the conclusion follows:

(f) Babies cannot manage crocodiles.

All four examples illustrate logical principles that we shall study in some detail. In particular, we will want to understand the **principles of correct reasoning and their applications,** which is the primary subject matter of logic. Correct logical principles are at work in three of these four examples, in every case but that of the hapless Stephen. These principles allow us to move from the known to the unknown, from evidence to its consequences. But in addition to their role in the discovery of new information, logical principles also allow us to demonstrate that a particular chain of reasoning is either correct or faulty. This is their role in **proofs**—determining whether one statement or claim does or does not follow from another. When, for example, we checked Stephen's reasoning and we found it wanting, we were also applying some of the basic logical principles we will study.

Various methods for substantiating that reasoning in a particular case is correct or incorrect will be studied in the next six chapters. Then we will see how the same logical principles are at the heart of computers and computing.

EXERCISES 1.1

Try your hand at the following logic problems and puzzles. Don't worry if some seem too difficult to solve at this point. By the time you have finished chapter 6, you will think of them as routine.

1. Read the following paragraph and then answer questions a–d.

   In order to graduate from XYZ College, a student must have compiled 120 credit hours and must have a grade point average of at least 2.0. A student must have taken at least 8 credit hours in each of the three academic divisions: humanities, social sciences, natural sciences. In addition, a student must have taken a freshman seminar, satisfied the language requirement by demonstrating intermediate level competence, and completed a major. Students can demonstrate intermediate level competence in a foreign language either by taking three semesters of a language or by scoring at least 56 on the College Board Achievement Test.

   a. Must all students take a freshman seminar?

   b. If Bill scored a 56 on a language achievement test and has completed a major, what else does he need to do to graduate?

   c. If Mary is a physics major, do her physics credits (she has 40) fulfill the natural science requirement?

   d. Explain the reasoning that lead you from the information to each of your answers.

2. What conclusion follows from the statements in each of the following groups?[4]

   a. All those who subscribe to the *Times* are educated.
      No hedgehogs can read.
      Those who cannot read are not educated.

---

[4]Carroll, *Symbolic Logic*, p. 162.

b. Ducks never waltz.
No officers ever decline to waltz.
All my poultry are ducks.

c. Promise-breakers are not trustworthy.
Wine-drinkers are very communicative.
One can always trust a very communicative person.

d. Everyone who is sane can do logic.
No lunatics are fit to serve on a jury.
None of your sons can do logic.
(Note: lunatic = not sane)

e. No interesting poems are unpopular among people of real taste.
No modern poetry is free from affectation.
All your poems are on the subject of soap bubbles.
No affected poetry is popular among people of real taste.
No ancient poem is on the subject of soap bubbles.

*3. **The towers of Hanoi problem** This ancient problem is said to have originated in a monastery in Tibet. There are three pegs (towers), and rings of different sizes are to be moved from peg to peg. The rules are these:

a. Rings are moved one at a time from one peg to another peg.

b. A larger ring is *never* to be placed on top of a smaller ring.

Suppose the three pegs are labeled A, B, and C and there are three rings initially on peg A. Describe, in the shortest number of steps, how to move the three rings so that they are all on peg B. (Handy notation: let $X \rightarrow Y$ represent the action of moving the top ring from peg X to peg Y. Hint: you will need to use peg C in the process.)

Next, try the problem with four rings on peg A to be moved to peg B.

You may be interested to know that there is a legend that the original Tibetan version involved sixty-four rings initially on one of the pegs. The inventors of the problem said that the world would come to an end when all sixty-four rings had been moved, according to the rules, to another peg.[5]

*4. **The missionaries and cannibals problem** Three missionaries and three cannibals seek to cross a river. A boat is available that can hold two people and can be navigated by any combination of missionaries and cannibals involving one or two people. If at any time the missionaries on either bank of the river or en route on the river are outnumbered by the cannibals, the cannibals will engage in their characteristic activity

---

[5]From David Harel, *Algorithmics: The Spirit of Computing* (Reading, MA: Addison-Wesley, 1987), p. 32.

and do away with the missionaries. The problem is to find the simplest schedule of crossings that will permit all of the missionaries and cannibals to cross the river safely.[6]

1.2 KEY TERMS AND FUNDAMENTAL CONCEPTS

Statements

In actual use, logical principles can be applied in many different ways. In the case of Daphne and David, for example, Daphne reasons by asking David *questions* and at the end moves toward the closet to find the keys. But as we reconstructed her acts we put them in terms of relations between certain *statements*. We say that she first arrives at the claim that

(1) The keys are on the hall table, or on the dresser, or in the coat pocket.

It is important to grasp that there are many ways to record what Daphne used as her first step in reasoning. This is because the same statement can be made in several different ways, using different words or even different languages. But however it is expressed, we should be clear that **a statement is a claim about how things are.** As such, it is either **true** or **false,** depending on whether things are as the statement says. Some statements are made in unstatementlike ways: They may seem to ask a question ("Do you always dress so sloppily?"), or they may involve pointing and screeching to indicate that the rope from which I am hanging is about to break. In addition, what appears to be a statement may actually not be, as in playacting, for example, or in the polite reply of "Very well, thank you" to the standard greeting "How are you today?"

Since statements make claims about how things are, two or more sentences, or other equivalent linguistic forms, amount to one and the same statement if they make the very same claim about the world. Thus, the opening statements by Daphne concerning the three possible locations of the keys could have been phrased in any of the following ways:

(1) There are three places the keys might be: the hall table, the dresser, and the coat pocket.

(2) The keys are in the coat pocket, or they are on the hall table or the dresser.

(3) The keys are on the hall table, or, if not, they are on the dresser or in the coat pocket.

Despite variations in wording, all three of these sentences make essentially the same claim about the whereabouts of the keys.

---

[6]This version of the problem is adapted from Michael R. Genesereth and Nils J. Nilsson, *Logical Foundations of Artificial Intelligence* (San Mateo, CA: Morgan Kaufmann, 1987), p. 8.

The recognition that statements can be made in various ways is absolutely critical for logic. In the process of studying logical theory, we will learn just how a statement can be made by means of different sentences. As we will see, logical theory begins with such fundamental observations about language and thought and then provides principles that give a deeper understanding of those fundamental observations as well as a means of extending them to a vastly wider field.

Before moving on, let's look at yet another example of statements, this time from Lewis Carroll. We noted earlier that Carroll's statement

Nobody is despised who can manage a crocodile

makes the same statement as

All people who can manage crocodiles are not despised.

(We could also drop the 'all' and just say 'People who can manage crocodiles are not despised'.) Suppose someone challenges us about this claim; how might we defend it? We would have to show that exactly the same features of the world are depicted by both sentences. We might argue that the first asserts that nobody, that is, *no person,* who can manage a crocodile is despised. Now we don't know from this statement that there actually are any such crocodile managers, but if there are any, they are surely not despised. So, if a person, say Alice, can manage crocodiles, then she is not despised, and if another person, Bill, can manage crocodiles, then he is not despised, and if Cathy can manage crocodiles, then she is not despised, and if Deborah can manage crocodiles, then she is not despised, and so on for all people. And the simplest way to record this general claim about all people is just to assert 'All people who can manage crocodiles are not despised', which is what we wanted.[7]

In the last paragraph we employed a common logical strategy: we looked at simpler claims about the world in order to better understand the general statement at issue. This sort of move might be called **reductive analysis,** and it is an essential feature of all the logic we will study. In reductive analysis, we break complex statements down into simpler statements in order to understand what claims about the world are actually being made. In Daphne's initial statements, we featured the three simpler claims 'the keys are on the table', 'the keys are on the dresser', and 'the keys are in the coat pocket'. And in the Lewis Carroll statement concerning crocodile managers, we mentioned a potentially long list of claims about specific people. We will have much more to say about reductive analysis in the later chapters.

---

[7]This way of understanding general statements is called the 'substitutional interpretation' and will be studied in detail in chapters 6 and 7.

Arguments

To return to Daphne's astute reasoning, recall that her second move was to ascertain that the keys were not on the hall table, thus eliminating a possibility. Next she found that the keys weren't on the dresser either, so another possibility disappeared. Only one remained, and she hurried to the closet to search the coat pocket. It is convenient to refer to such chains of reasoning as **arguments.** In an argument someone intends to move from a group of statements, called **premises,** to another statement, called the **conclusion,** which is supposedly supported by the premises. The qualification 'supposedly' is important here because not all arguments do, in fact, correctly lead from premises to conclusion; Stephen's argument is an example. Stephen incorrectly believed that his conclusion 'If I went to every class meeting, then I will get an A in the course' followed logically from the premise asserted by his teacher: 'No one will get an A in this course unless he attends every class.'

Daphne's reasoning, reconstructed using standard argument form, might look like this:

> The keys are on the hall table, or the keys are on the dresser, or the keys are in the coat pocket.
>
> The keys are not on the hall table.
>
> The keys are not on the dresser.
> _____
> The keys are in the coat pocket.

Note that the premises are listed as separate sentences above the horizontal line; the conclusion appears below the line. You should note that the statement listed above as the conclusion—'The keys are in the coat pocket'—was not actually spoken in any part of the exchange between David and Daphne. We include this statement as the conclusion of the argument as we reconstruct their reasoning, even though we gain a somewhat *idealized* version as a result. We will have more to say about the depiction of arguments later on in this section.

We can indicate the argument behind Stephen's reasoning as follows:

> No one will get an A in this course unless he or she attends every class.
> _____
> If I went to every class meeting, then I will get an A in the course.

The premise is his instructor's statement to the class; the conclusion is what Stephen believes (hopes!) the statement implies. Once again, the instructor or Stephen may not have ever said the exact words in the conclusion or even consciously had that exact thought. Yet it seems quite certain that 'If I went to every class meeting, then I will get an A in the course', is a correct formulation of the conclusion he erroneously drew as his hopes for an A rose.

There is little doubt how the Lewis Carroll example should be depicted, since it was presented more or less in standard argument form. Here it is again:

Babies are illogical.

Nobody is despised who can manage a crocodile.

Illogical persons are despised.

Babies cannot manage crocodiles.

From the standpoint of logic, a *good* argument, in the sense employed here, is one in which the premises completely support the conclusion. All of the reasoning we shall study, hence all of the arguments we shall investigate, are **deductive;** that is, the conclusion is supposed to follow *with certainty* from the premises, as in the example above from Lewis Carroll.

On the other hand, reasoning in which only *probability* is claimed for the conclusion, based on the premises, is called **inductive.** Here is an example:

Most birds fly.

Tweety is a bird.

Tweety flies.

Note that Tweety might be a penguin, or an ostrich, or somehow disabled. So the conclusion should not be claimed as certain when both premises are asserted as true. The study of this kind of reasoning is usually known as inductive logic and lies outside the scope of this book.

What the author of a deductive argument intends is usually indicated by means of the words he or she uses, and we detect arguments by attending to a set of verbal clues. There are characteristic ways of marking statements as premises and as conclusions. Here are lists of some of the common premise and conclusion *indicators* that are often used in conjunction with deductive arguments.

Conclusion indicators	**Premise indicators**
Thus	Since
So	Because
Consequently	On account of
In conclusion	Given that
Therefore	In that
Hence	In as much as
It follows that	For
As a result	Assuming
Implies that	
We may conclude	

In identifying arguments, it is important to distinguish between instances in which a conclusion is clearly said to follow from one or more premises and instances in which only a statement is made. Consider the following case:

> Smith will have to act as secretary for the meeting because Jones cannot be here today and no one else takes careful notes.

The word 'because' is used to indicate that the statements that come next are the basis for the claim that Smith will have to act as secretary. Hence, in this short passage we have an argument, which might be displayed as follows:

> Jones cannot be here today.
>
> No one else takes as careful notes as Smith.
> _____
> Smith will have to act as secretary for the meeting.

'Because' serves to indicate that both of the statements

> Jones cannot be here today

and

> No one else takes as careful notes as Smith

are asserted as *true*, and that the statement

> Smith will have to act as secretary for the meeting

logically follows from these two statements.

Compare this case with the assertion

> If Jones cannot be here today, then Smith will have to act as secretary.

This statement does *not* state that Jones is not here today but rather sets up what we will call a *conditional* by use of the 'If . . . then' construction. This is a *statement*, which is true or false, not an argument in which one statement is said to follow from another. Changing the wording slightly, however, results in an argument:

> Jones cannot be here today; therefore Smith will have to act as secretary.

The word 'therefore' serves to indicate that a conclusion follows. And in this case we do have the *assertion* that Jones cannot be here today.

The task of detecting and reconstructing arguments from ordinary language can be very complicated. Exercises that provide some practice will be found at the end of this section.

Validity

Any deductive argument is **valid** if its conclusion follows with certainty from its premises. We will maintain that deductive arguments are valid, if at all, because of the *structure* of their premises and conclusions, and the point of the reductive analysis that we will study in later chapters is to reveal the crucial features of this structure.

We would concede that in some arguments, however, the premise or premises support the conclusion with certainty simply because of the *meanings* of the key terms involved and, seemingly, not because of any structural relations. The following is such a case:

Jim is a bachelor.

Jim is unmarried.

The relation between premise and conclusion here is entirely due to the meaning of the word 'bachelor' as an 'unmarried male'. Fortunately we can express such arguments in terms of our structural concept of deductive validity by supplying an extra premise that spells out the linguistic connections:[8]

Jim is a bachelor.

All bachelors are unmarried males.

Jim is unmarried.

Validity is the key logical concept, so further discussion is warranted. We said that validity is a property of arguments that results from the structure of their component statements—the premises and the conclusion. An argument is valid when the conclusion could not be false if the premises are true; this is what is meant by the conclusion following *with certainty* from the premises. To illustrate this point, remember that in the case of David and Daphne we allowed for the possibility that they might not find the keys in the coat pocket, but only if one of the initial assumptions (premises) is incorrect. If they don't find the keys, the validity of their argument is unaffected, but they know that at least one premise is false. Thus, a valid

---

[8]For other views on this issue, see, for example, Max Black, *The Labyrinth of Language* (New York: New American Library, 1969), pp. 103–105 and Terry Winograd and Fernando Flores, *Understanding Computers and Cognition* (Reading, MA: Addison-Wesley, 1987).

argument can have a factually false conclusion, but only if one or more of its premises is false as well. If all premises are true, the conclusion must be true as well.

The following distinctions are vital: in a *valid* argument, the truth of the premises guarantees the truth of the conclusion, but the conclusion may be false if at least one premise is. However, a true conclusion does not necessarily indicate a valid argument. Finally, an argument that is valid *and* has true premises is said to be **sound,** and the conclusion of a sound argument is sure to be true as well.

Contrast the case of Stephen. Here the premise of his argument is true (let us suppose), but the conclusion is false: Stephen will not get an A. But, you might object, suppose Stephen gets an A for another reason, say a mix-up in the grade book. Is the argument now valid just because the conclusion is true? The answer is that the argument is still invalid (i.e., not valid) despite the true conclusion. What is missing is the relation between the premise and conclusion that makes the truth of the premise a *guarantee* of the truth of the conclusion.

Here are some further examples of these points:

1. A valid argument with a false premise but a true conclusion:

   All generals are short.

   Napolean was a general.
   _____

   Napolean was short.

2. A valid argument with a false conclusion:

   France and Zambia are in Africa.
   _____

   France is in Africa.

3. A sound argument (true premises and valid):

   If the battery is dead, then the car will not start.
   _____

   If the car starts, then the battery is not dead.

The Greek philosopher and scientist Aristotle, over 2300 years ago, was the first to recognize that deductive validity and invalidity were principally a matter of the structure or form of the premises and conclusion.[9] This was an important discovery, for it conferred on the subject of logic the essential

_____

[9]His logical works are collected under the title *The Organon*. The standard edition is published by Oxford University Press (1931).

feature in the development in any science: *generality.* What Aristotle noticed is that once a certain argument has been determined to be valid, say the classic

(a) All humans are mortal

Socrates is human
_____

Socrates is mortal

then it follows that other arguments of similar structure, or **logical form,** as we shall say, are valid as well. So,

(b) All students were supposed to pay the deposit by March 20.

Sue is a student.
_____

Sue was supposed to pay the deposit by March 20.

It is fairly easy to see why these two arguments are said to have the same form. The first premise in each has the form:

All A are B

where A in the first is 'human' and in the second is 'student', and B in the first is 'mortal' and in the second is 'supposed to pay the deposit by March 20'. The second premise has the form:

a is A

where a is a proper name ('Socrates', 'Sue'). The conclusion in each case is, of course,

a is B

Putting these together we have as the common logical form of both arguments:

All A are B

a is A
_____

a is B

Since validity is a matter of form or structure, all arguments with this same form are valid, no matter what is substituted for A, B, and a. As a further illustration, try constructing an argument substituting 'people who rake leaves' for A and 'people who work hard' for B and your name for a.

You may have noticed two things in this discussion of logical form. First, if you are looking for ways to challenge the claim that argument (b) above is valid, you might have protested that perhaps Sue is not the kind of student who was supposed to pay a deposit. Perhaps she goes to the local high school and only college students are to pay the deposit. This objection calls forth a convention that we will follow throughout the book. We assume that all of the words in a single argument are used in the same sense; so 'student' in the first premise of argument (b) means the same as 'student' in the second premise. There is nothing sneaky about this convention. The context in which we are speaking (or writing) often requires us to nail down exactly what we mean. This is clear with regard to pronouns like 'she', for example. If someone says 'She is over by the door and she is getting pretty angry', you will naturally assume that 'she' in both occurrences refers to the same person. If a different meaning is intended, some way of so indicating is required (such as parenthetical remarks). Hence, in the course of an argument, the same words are presumed to have the same meaning; if words change their meaning or reference, some explicit indication or qualification must be given.

A second issue requiring clarification is that there is some fiddling with the grammar of the original statements in the arguments to get everything to come out smoothly. For example the phrase *'were* supposed to pay the deposit by March 20' in the first premise of argument (b) and the phrase *'was* supposed to pay the deposit by March 20' in the conclusion are both represented by *B* in the formal version of the argument. The legitimacy of such fiddles will be fully discussed in chapter 5; for now it is important to notice that we take 'All students were supposed to pay the deposit by March 20' to mean something like 'Every student is a person who was supposed to pay the deposit by March 20', so the conclusion is strictly taken to be 'Sue is a person who was supposed to pay the deposit by March 20'. But the manner we used to express this conclusion is less stilted than this and sounds more like ordinary English.

Here is another obviously valid argument:

(c) The keys are on the table or the dresser.

They are not on the table.
_____

They are on the dresser.

We may represent the logical form of the argument in the following way:

T or *D*

not *T*
_____

D

where T means 'the keys are on the table', D means 'the keys are on the dresser', and *not* T means 'the keys (i.e., 'they') are not on the table'. Now look at this next argument:

(d) Everybody may have cookies or ice cream.

You, Peter, may not have ice cream.

You may have cookies.

Is argument (d) of the same form as argument (c)? There are obvious similarities between the two arguments—the use of 'or' in the first premise, the negative second premise—but there are differences as well. The first premise of argument (d) is a *general statement* about what everybody can have (at a children's party, let's suppose); the second denies ice cream to Peter (say, because of his allergy). But the logical form of the first premise of argument (c) consists of two independent clauses joined by 'or'. Note the difference:

Everybody may have cookies or ice cream.

The keys are on the table, or the keys are on the dresser.

So, despite some similarity, the arguments are different in form, and the validity of the first does not in itself guarantee the validity of the second. However, as it turns out, the second argument is valid too.

Summary

To summarize, here is a list of the most important terms discussed in this chapter along with brief definitions.

Logic   The study of the principles of correct reasoning.

Statement   A claim about how things are in the world. Statements are true or false, depending upon whether the claim matches reality or not. A statement can be made through a variety of different sentences. A statement can also be made through actions like pointing or screeching. The analysis of statements into the simpler statements on which they depend is called **reductive analysis.**

Argument   A group of statements some of which (the **premises**) are offered in support for the other (the **conclusion**).

Deductive argument   An argument in which the conclusion is presented as following with certainty from the premises.

Inductive argument   An argument in which the conclusion is supported with some degree of probability by the premises.

Valid argument   A (deductive) argument in which the truth of all of the premises guarantees the truth of the conclusion.

Sound argument   An argument that is valid and has true premises.

EXERCISES 1.2

1. Which of the following passages contain arguments? For each passage that does, identify its premises and conclusion.

   a. All humans are animals; therefore, all animals are human.

   b. Since Cleveland is a large city in Ohio, it is sure to be included in the new bill because all large Ohio cities are covered by the legislation.

   c. If David had lost his keys, then they would not have been in his coat pocket.

   d. Yesterday I went to the movies with my friend. We then went out for ice cream and later stopped by another friend's house. All in all, it was a dull day.

   e. If Shem had no sons or daughters, he had no descendants. But he had descendants, so he must have had sons or daughters.

2. Identify the premises and conclusion of each of the following arguments.

   a. Since all humans are mortals and Socrates is a human, then Socrates is a mortal.

   b. If all humans are mortal, then Socrates is mortal. So not all humans are mortal since Socrates is immortal.

   c. All students are unhappy this week. Hence John is happy this week since he isn't a student.

   d. Many of my friends are home at night, but John must be at work because his job requires him to work at night.

   e. To solve a problem, a person needs an understanding of the terms involved and the correct tools. If a problem is posed in a language not understood, then the terms will not be understood. If the correct problem-solving tools are missing, then the problem will not be solved. So if a person has the tools and understands the terms of a problem, then he or she will be able to solve it.

3. Determine whether the following assertions are true or false. If the sentence is false, state why.

   a. All valid arguments have true conclusions.

   b. Any argument with true premises and a true conclusion is valid.

   c. Two different sentences never can be used to make the same statement.

   d. All statements are expressed by words.

   e. All declarative sentences spoken or written by people are statements.

   f. Sound arguments have true conclusions.

   g. All valid arguments are sound.

   h. All invalid arguments have false conclusions.

*4. Try writing out a set of instructions for (1) recognizing whether a passage contains an argument, and (2) identifying the conclusion of the argument. Test the adequacy of your instructions by giving them to a friend who has never studied logic and ask him or her to pick out arguments from a newspaper and identify their conclusions using only your instructions.

Statement Logic: Fundamentals

*T*his chapter provides the basic apparatus for our study of the logic of statements. As we have already discussed, the validity of an argument is a matter of its *form* or structure. We can reveal that logical form by employing a number of symbolic devices that enable us to symbolize ordinary English statements and arguments in a logical language called **statement logic**, or SL. The resources of SL provide a means for the precise characterization of validity and allow the development of several techniques for testing arguments; these matters will be taken up in chapters 3 and 4.

The study of SL has another purpose that will be clear in part 2 of this book. The logical principles that lie behind the validity of arguments will turn out to be embedded in the very design of all computers and in the programs they run.

2.1 CONJUNCTION, DISJUNCTION, AND NEGATION: 'AND', 'OR', AND 'NOT'

When we try to understand the conditions under which certain statements are true or false, we often find that their truth depends upon the truth or falsehood of other statements. Here is an example we have already seen of this sort of dependence:

(1) James *and* John are liars.

Here *both* of the statements 'James is a liar' *and* 'John is a liar' have to be true for statement (1) to be true; if either James or John is not a liar, the statement is, of course, false.

Another type of dependence is exemplified by a second example from the last chapter:

> (2) The keys are on the table *or* the dresser.

It is obvious that the truth of this statement depends on whether at least one of the following statements is true:

> (3) The keys are on the table.

> (4) The keys are on the dresser.

If either of these is true, then the initial statement is true; otherwise, if both (3) and (4) are false, then the initial statement (2) is false.

Perhaps the simplest case of the dependence of one statement upon another is in the presence of negation. A statement like

> (5) The keys are *not* on the table.

clearly can be true only if statement (3) is false, and is false only if (3) is true.

The particular type of dependence between statements we will study in this chapter involves statements that can be understood as **components** of other statements. In the case of (2), 'The keys are on the table or the dresser', we will say that it is **composed** of the simpler statements (3) and (4). This composition can be readily displayed if statement (2) is paraphrased as follows:

> (6) The keys are on the table or the keys are on the dresser.

Here, the presence of the simpler statements is quite evident. To see this composition in the case of negation, think of statement (5) as

> (7) It is not the case that the keys are on the table.

Again, the simpler statement 'The keys are on the table' is literally a component of the statement (7). The same sort of paraphrase of statement (1) also reveals its components:

> (8) James is a liar and John is a liar.

Since it is the logical *form* of statements and, eventually, of arguments, that is of paramount importance, as was discussed in the last chapter, it will be convenient to adopt a standard notation for representing the form of statements. To do this, we will use capital letters *A*, *B*, *C*, etc., called **statement letters**, to represent the component statements, and we will use other symbols called **logical statement connectives** to take the place of the 'or', 'it is not the case that', and 'and' in the preceding examples.

The particular symbols that are used as logical statement connectives are fairly standard and have standard names. Here they are with examples and standard ways to read them:[1]

Conjunction: &	Example: *A & B*	Read: *A* and *B*
Disjunction: $\lor$	Example: *A* $\lor$ *B*	Read: *A* or *B*
Negation: ~	Example: ~*A*	Read: not *A*

A compound statement made from the disjunction symbol $\lor$ is called a **disjunction** (sometimes **disjunctive statement**), and its two components are called its **disjuncts.** A compound statement made from the conjunction connective is called a **conjunction (conjunctive statement),** and its components are called its **conjuncts.** So in *T* $\lor$ *D*, the entire statement is a disjunction and *T* and *D* are its disjuncts; in *J & H*, the statement is a conjunction and *J* and *H* are its conjuncts.

By means of just the notation introduced so far, it is possible to depict the logical form of a variety of statements. For example, using *J* for 'James is a liar' and *H* for 'John is a liar', the compound statement (1), 'James and John are liars', is

J & H

Using *T* for 'The keys are on the table' and *D* for 'The keys are on the dresser', the form of statement (2), 'The keys are on the table or the dresser', is

T $\lor$ *D*

What we have done in each of these cases is to find the simpler statements on which the truth or falsehood of the original depends. Then we have given these simpler statements capital letters as designations. Next we have chosen the appropriate statement connective for the particular dependency relation involved: the conjunction symbol, &, in the first case; the disjunction symbol, $\lor$, in the second. In these two now-familiar cases, it is fairly easy to see that conjunction fits the first and disjunction the second.

Negation, disjunction, and conjunction are often called **truth-functional connectives** to underscore the fact that the truth or falsehood of the state-

---

[1]See section 2.5 for the other commonly used symbols for the statement connectives.

ments in which they appear depends entirely on, or is a function of, the truth or falsity of the component statements joined by these connectives. Statements that can be considered to have a logical form in which such connectives are involved are sometimes called **truth-functional compound statements**. The simpler statements joined by the connectives are called **truth functional components**.

Based on this classification, we take a statement like

Jack and Jill went up the hill

to be a truth-functional compound of its two truth-functional components:

Jack went up the hill.

Jill went up the hill.

But the statement

All men are mortal

is *not* a truth-functional compound statement, even though it is general and depends upon a great many facts for its truth. This may well seem odd, so a word of explanation should be helpful.[2] At this point we are looking at a certain kind of truth dependency, in fact, the very simplest kind (as we will see). The only compounds that we currently acknowledge are those that can be construed to depend directly on simpler component statements in the three ways we have so far indicated: as a negation of another statement, as a disjunction of two statements, or as a conjunction of two statements. This is as much reductive logical analysis as we can do, so far. All statements that are not amenable to this truth-functional analysis are, for us, noncompound, no matter how complicated they may, in fact, be. Needless to say, we will dramatically enlarge the scope of our logical operations before too long, but, even so, there will still be interesting statements (from a logical point of view) that we will not yet be ready to confront. Logical theory is an ongoing discipline with a great deal of active research at its frontiers.

The simplest way to understand the particular nature of truth dependency of the conjunction, disjunction, and negation connectives is to display the possibilities in what is called a **truth table**. A truth table is simply a schematic representation of all the possible states of truth (**T**) and falsehood (**F**) for a (truth-functional) compound statement in terms of the possible

---

[2]In chapter 6 we will discuss how such general statements can be understood in terms of a large number of simpler statements, but the analysis will be much more complex than it is here.

truth-values (**T** or **F**) of its component statements. The truth tables for the truth-functional statement connectives, then, are as follows:[3]

Negation

A	~A
T	F
F	T

Disjunction

A	B	A ∨ B
T	T	T
T	F	T
F	T	T
F	F	F

Conjunction

A	B	A & B
T	T	T
T	F	F
F	T	F
F	F	F

This is the standard method for depicting truth tables that will be used throughout this book. The possible truth-values (**T** or **F**) are listed in vertical columns under statement letters or combinations of statement letters and connectives. The columns to the left of the vertical rule are for the *components*; the column to the right of the rule is for the *compound*. The columns of truth-values under the components always follow a certain order. In the far-left column under **A** are two **T**'s followed by two **F**'s; in the next column, under **B**, **T** and **F** alternate, beginning with **T**. A brief inspection of the horizontal rows reveals that all possible combinations of truth-values are given for the components **A** and **B**: both true, one true, the other false, both false, etc. Learning this standard pattern will make remembering the various truth tables easier and will allow quick comparisons. We will later see enlargements of the pattern, but they too will follow the same principles as the tables above.

For each particular combination of truth-values of the components, the table depicts the corresponding truth-value of the compound itself. In the table for negation, for example, a negated statement is **T** in the case that its component is **F**, and vice versa. In the case of a disjunction compound, the compound statement is **T** in every case except when both components are **F**. And in a conjunction, the compound is **T** only when both compounds are also **T**.

Thus far we have been using 'statement' and other terms somewhat loosely to more easily explain the fundamental concepts of statement logic.

---

[3]From this point on, **boldface** letters **A**, **B**, **C**, and **D** are used to represent *any* statement, whether compound or not; other letters will be used to represent particular statements. For example, the symbolic representation *J* & *H* ('James and John are liars') might be represented by the general pattern **A**, since it is a statement, or by **A** & **B** since it is a conjunction.

But at this point some refinements are in order. We already have the barest outline of a logical language: we have some symbols—capital letters and the three connectives—and we have fragments of an informal grammar or set of rules for correct usage. For example, you will probably recognize that the combination of symbols & & **A** has no intelligibility. Furthermore, meanings have been given to the symbols. The three connectives are defined by their respective truth tables, and the capital letters function as statements.

In any case, the rudimentary language of logic is meant to parallel some parts of English (and other natural languages), namely the parts in which statements are made. But there is no exact equivalency between the logical language and English. The logical language is very narrow and precise, whereas English, or any other natural language, is flexible and somewhat imprecise. It might be useful to think of our logical language as a partial *model* of English. Like models of other kinds (e.g., toy trains), it shares some important features but lacks others. For example, both toy trains and real trains run on tracks, but toy train tracks are lightweight, bend easily, and are supported by plastic crosspieces, whereas the steel in real train tracks is very strong, and the tracks are nailed with large spikes to wooden railroad ties.

An important consideration to remember is that while some English statements may well be truth-functional, our logical connectives are not meant to be exact translations of or shorthand for the English words 'and', 'or', and 'not'. Rather, the logical connectives—the symbols ~, &, and ∨— serve the functions that these words sometimes perform in establishing an explicit relationship of truth dependency between a compound statement and what we have called its components. To put this point another way, the formula *J & H* represents only *the truth-functional logical form* of the English statement 'James and John are liars'. Any tone or texture that the speaker intends, in addition to the truth-functional relationship, is ignored in the logical form.

Consider again the truth tables for disjunction and conjunction:

Disjunction

A	B	A ∨ B
T	T	T
T	F	T
F	T	T
F	F	F

Conjunction

A	B	A & B
T	T	T
T	F	F
F	T	F
F	F	F

Sometimes in English 'or' is taken to mean 'either but not both', as in 'You may take the car *or* I will drive you'. But, as the first row in the truth table for disjunction reveals, we understand a statement of the form **A** ∨ **B** to be true if both **A** and **B** are true. Thus, the logical sense of disjunction is sometimes called **inclusive** because it allows for the inclusion of the truth of both disjuncts. We will talk about the *exclusive* sense of 'or' later (see section 2.5).

There is also a common interpretation of 'and' in English other than the one depicted by the truth table for conjunction. We sometimes say 'George went home and went to bed' and we mean that *first* George went home, and *second* he went to bed. Our truth table does not capture this sequential sense of 'and' because, in our terms, if **A** & **B** is true, then so will be **B** & **A** (the symbol &, in other words, is *commutative*). In the sequential sense, 'and' is not commutative; it would be a very different statement to say 'George went to bed and then went home'.

To realize the full potential of the symbolic apparatus, we use a punctuation device, namely parentheses, that allows the statement connectives to be employed in more complex combinations. The use of parentheses in this manner is illustrated by the following pair of logical statements:

~A ∨ B   ~(A ∨ B)

The first of these is a disjunction whose left disjunct is the negated statement ~**A** and whose right disjunct is the statement **B**. The second is a negated disjunction; that is, the entire disjunction is negated. The two compounds are clearly different. Any statement with the form ~**A** ∨ **B** is true if **B** is true; but in the statement of the form ~(**A** ∨ **B**), **B** must be false. The only way to differentiate between these situations is through the use of parentheses, which group the symbols and indicate the **scope** of the connectives. We will adopt the convention of minimum scope; connectives operate on the smallest units punctuation allows.

So if we want to represent 'Pamela and Quentin won't both pass the course', we use *P* for 'Pamela will pass the course' and *Q* for 'Quentin will pass the course' and symbolize the statement as follows:

~(P & Q)

If we had written ~*P* & *Q* instead, we would have symbolized 'Pamela won't pass the course and Quentin will', which is a quite different statement. The parentheses around *P* & *Q* indicate that the *entire conjunction* is negated.

Expanding on this example, consider 'Pamela and Quentin will pass the course, or Robert will not'. Let *R* be 'Robert will pass the course'. The correct symbolization is:

(P & Q) ∨ ~R

Without parentheses, the symbolic statement would be ambiguous. It isn't clear what P & $Q \lor \sim R$ might mean. Placing the parentheses around the disjunction yields

P & $(Q \lor \sim R)$

which depicts 'Pamela will pass and either Quentin will also pass or Robert won't'. Again, these two statements make quite different claims. The first says that Pamela and Quentin's fortunes are linked: they either both pass or Robert doesn't. The second, on the other hand, says that Pamela will definitely pass, but either Quentin will or Robert won't.

To see more clearly the difference that punctuation makes, here are the truth tables for the two sets of statements:

P	Q	P & Q	$\sim(P$ & $Q)$
T	T	T	F
T	F	F	T
F	T	F	T
F	F	F	T

P	Q	$\sim P$	$\sim P$ & Q
T	T	F	F
T	F	F	F
F	T	T	T
F	F	T	F

Note that the truth table pattern expands to accomodate these more complicated examples. The components are listed in increasing complexity from left to right, and the full statement occupies the far-right column. It is immediately evident from a comparison of the far-right columns of the two tables that the use of parentheses changes the truth dependency of the statement. $\sim(P$ & $Q)$ is true in the second, third, and fourth rows, whereas $\sim P$ & Q is true only in the third row.

To compare statements with three components P, Q, and R we need a more extensive truth table. The truth tables we have used so far have had either one statement letter and two rows or two statement letters and four rows. With three statement letters as components, how many rows are needed? The answer is easily computed: there are exactly two possibilities (**T** or **F**) for each statement letter, so for two statement letters there are 2×2 ($= 4$) possibilities, and for three statement letters there are $2 \times 2 \times 2 (= 8)$ possibilities. We can generalize this relationship by noting that the number of possibilities increases as exponents of 2: $2^1 = 2$; $2^2 = 4$; $2^3 = 8$. Thus, to construct any truth table, follow this general rule:

Truth Table Rule *A truth table for* n *different statement letters will have* 2^n *rows.*

The truth tables for $(P \& Q) \lor \sim R$ and for $P \& (Q \lor \sim R)$ will look like this:

P	Q	R	$\sim R$	P & Q	$(P \& Q) \lor \sim R$
T	T	T	F	T	T
T	T	F	T	T	T
T	F	T	F	F	F
T	F	F	T	F	T
F	T	T	F	F	F
F	T	F	T	F	T
F	F	T	F	F	F
F	F	F	T	F	T

P	Q	R	$\sim R$	$Q \lor \sim R$	$P \& (Q \lor \sim R)$
T	T	T	F	T	T
T	T	F	T	T	T
T	F	T	F	F	F
T	F	F	T	T	T
F	T	T	F	T	F
F	T	F	T	T	F
F	F	T	F	F	F
F	F	F	T	T	F

Inspection of these two tables reveals that the statements vary in their truth-value in the sixth and eighth rows; again, parentheses make a difference (especially to Pamela!).

To more precisely analyze the truth-conditions of compound symbolic statements, we need to make a few distinctions about the construction of truth tables. First, every compound statement, no matter how complicated, has just one **major connective**. This is the connective that has the greatest scope in the statement, the one that links together the largest component or components of the statement. Some illustrations are:

Statement	Major connective
(1) $P \lor (Q \mathbin{\&} R)$	$\lor$
(2) $(P \lor Q) \mathbin{\&} R$	$\&$
(3) $\sim(P \lor \sim Q)$	$\sim$
(4) $(P \lor Q) \mathbin{\&} (P \lor \sim R)$	$\&$
(5) $\sim[\sim(P \lor \sim Q) \mathbin{\&} R]^4$	$\sim$

The statement or statements that the major connective symbol connects are its **immediate components**. The immediate components in the examples above are:

Statement	Immediate component(s)
(1) $P \lor (P \mathbin{\&} R)$	P, $P \mathbin{\&} R$
(2) $(P \lor Q) \mathbin{\&} R$	$P \lor Q$, R
(3) $\sim(P \lor \sim Q)$	$P \lor \sim Q$
(4) $(P \lor Q) \mathbin{\&} (P \lor \sim R)$	$P \lor Q$, $P \lor \sim R$
(5) $\sim[\sim(P \lor \sim Q) \mathbin{\&} R]$	$\sim(P \lor \sim Q) \mathbin{\&} R$

The analysis of a statement into its immediate components and then their components, and so on, is a good example of the reductive analysis we spoke of in the last chapter. One way to depict the relations of components to compounds within a statement is by means of a **grammatical tree**, whose *trunk* is at the top, above its *branches*. Here are the grammatical trees for the statements above:

(1) $P \lor (Q \mathbin{\&} R)$

---

[4]We will often use brackets like [ ] or ⟦ ⟧ in place of parentheses to make symbolic expressions easier to read.

(2) $(P \lor Q) \& R$

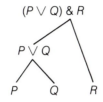

```
        (P ∨ Q) & R
         /‾‾‾‾‾
     P ∨ Q
     /\
    P   Q       R
```

(3) $\sim(P \lor \sim Q)$

```
     ~(P ∨ ~Q)
         |
      P ∨ ~Q
      /‾‾‾
     /      ~Q
    /        \
   P          Q
```

(4) $(P \lor Q) \& (P \lor \sim R)$

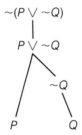

```
      (P ∨ Q) & (P ∨ ~R)
       /‾‾‾‾‾‾‾‾‾
   P ∨ Q          P ∨ ~R
    /\              /\
   /  \            /   ~R
  /    \          /     \
 P      Q        P       R
```

(5) $\sim[\sim(P \lor \sim Q) \& R]$

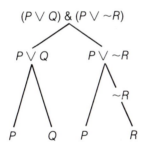
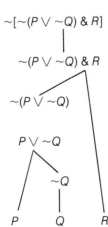

```
   ~[~(P ∨ ~Q) & R]
          |
     ~(P ∨ ~Q) & R
      /‾‾‾‾‾‾
   ~(P ∨ ~Q)
       |
     P ∨ ~Q
      /‾
     /   ~Q
    /     |
   P      Q        R
```

As you can see, the branches of the tree record immediate componenthood; the working out of the tree continues until only unnegated statement letters are left at the bottom of each branch. The complete list of components of any given statement can easily be retrieved from a statement tree by just listing all of the statements occurring anywhere in the tree. It is easiest to work line by line from the bottom of the tree to the top; that way the list of components will match the initial statement at the top of the truth table. For example, the complete list of components of (5), $\sim[\sim(P \vee \sim Q) \& R]$ is

P, Q, R, $\sim Q$, $P \vee \sim Q$, $\sim(P \vee \sim Q)$, $\sim(P \vee \sim Q) \& R$

Since the truth-value of any truth-functional compound statement directly depends upon the truth-values of its components, being able to identify the components is a very important skill.

Once you are able to determine all of the components of a statement, constructing its truth table, even for fairly complicated ones like those above, is a routine matter. Here is a step-by-step guide using the truth table for statement (5): $\sim[\sim(P \vee \sim Q) \& R]$.

Constructing Truth Tables

Step 1   Determine the number of rows by counting the *different* statement letters ($= n$) in the initial statement and determining the value of 2^n. In this case, we have three statement letters, P, Q, and R, so we will have 8 ($= 2^3$) rows.

Step 2   Write the statement letters on a horizontal line, then list the components as if you were moving upwards through the statement tree. At the far right, write the statement itself. Here is the result:

P Q R $\sim Q$ $P \vee \sim Q$ $\sim(P \vee \sim Q)$ $\sim(P \vee \sim Q) \& R$ $\sim[\sim(P \vee \sim Q) \& R]$

Step 3   Under the n statement letters, write the appropriate truth-values for the 2^n rows. To do this most simply, begin in the far-left column by listing one-half the number of rows $\frac{2^n}{2}$ of **T**'s followed by an equal number of **F**'s (four apiece, in the example below). In each column to the right, the number of sequential **T**'s and **F**'s is halved until a single **T** and **F** alternate under the final statement letter. Draw a vertical line to complete the array.

Here is the result of this process. Note that all possible combinations of truth-values to the statement letters are found in the array.

P	Q	R	$\sim Q$	$P \vee \sim Q$	$\sim(P \vee \sim Q)$	$\sim(P \vee \sim Q) \& R$	$\sim[\sim(P \vee \sim Q) \& R]$
T	T	T					
T	T	F					
T	F	T					
T	F	F					
F	T	T					
F	T	F					
F	F	T					
F	F	F					

Notice the pattern that emerges in folowing step 3. The far-left column contains an equal number of **T**'s and **F**'s, and in the far-right column, single **T**'s and **F**'s alternate. There are distinct advantages in following a definite pattern when constructing truth tables, so *we will always construct truth tables in this manner.*

Step 4 Calculate the truth-value of each statement for each row of the table, working from left to right.

Here are the first four rows of truth-values:

P	Q	R	$\sim Q$	$P \vee \sim Q$	$\sim(P \vee \sim Q)$	$\sim(P \vee \sim Q) \& R$	$\sim[\sim(P \vee \sim Q) \& R]$
T	T	T	F	T	F	F	T
T	T	F	F	T	F	F	T
T	F	T	T	T	F	F	T
T	F	F	T	T	F	F	T
F	T	T					
F	T	F					
F	F	T					
F	F	F					

It is easier to keep track if you *place the truth-value of a statement under its major connective*, as above. The **T** or **F** under the major connective of the initial statement is its truth-value on that row, i.e., its truth-value given that particular assignment of truth-values to its statement letters. For example, on the first row, $\sim[\sim(P \vee \sim Q) \& R]$ is **T** when P is **T**, Q is **T**, and R is **T**. Fill out the rest of the table as an exercise.

Summary

Here are the key terms and concepts that have been discussed in this section.

Truth-value   A statement's truth-value is either true (**T**) or false (**F**).

Statement connective   A means of forming compound statements out of other statements. The **immediate component(s)** of a compound statement are the statement(s) from which it is directly formed by means of a single connective.

Truth-functional compound   A statement whose truth-value depends entirely upon the truth-values of its components. The statement connectives found in truth-functional compounds are **truth-functional connectives**.

Truth table   A table displaying the truth-values of a statement and the truth-values of its components. If a statement is composed from n statement letters, there will be 2^n rows in its truth table.

Grammatical tree   A means of systematically displaying the various components of a compound statement by means of branching lines. Immediate components are listed directly below a compound statement, and at the bottom of each branch is a statement letter.

The following truth-functional connectives have been discussed so far:

Negation   Symbol: $\sim$
Example: *It is not the case that* the keys are on the table.
Truth table:

A	~A
T	F
F	T

Disjunction   Symbol: $\vee$
Example: The keys are on the table, *or* the keys are on the dresser.
Immediate components are called **disjuncts**.

Truth table:

A	B	A ∨ B
T	T	T
T	F	T
F	T	T
F	F	F

Conjunction   Symbol: &
Example: The keys are on the table, *and* the keys are on the dresser.
Immediate components are called **conjuncts**.
Truth table:

A	B	A & B
T	T	T
T	F	F
F	T	F
F	F	F

EXERCISES 2.1

1. Which of the following statements could be considered truth-functional compounds and which could not? Indicate immediate components and the nature of the connective in those you deem truth-functional.

   a. The keys are on the dresser, and the grocery list is as well.

   b. James isn't able to tell the truth.

   c. All whales migrate for the winter.

   d. William and John are good students.

   e. Someday, all nations will be at peace.

   f. Either Mary or Sue will win the election.

   g. I won't go, but he will.

   h. Neither rain nor snow shall keep these tireless servants from their appointed rounds.

i. Pamela and Quincy will both pass the test.

j. Pamela and Quincy won't both pass the test.

k. This form is incomplete.

l. Either switch X or switch Y is open, or the circuit will be off.

2. Using *P* for 'Pamela will pass the test' and *Q* for 'Quincy will pass the test' and *R* for 'Rachel will be disappointed', give a symbolic version of each of the following:

a. Rachel will not be disappointed.

b. Either Rachel will be disappointed or Pamela will pass the test.

c. Both Pamela and Quincy fail the test.

d. Pamela passes the test but Quincy fails.

e. Pamela will pass the test, and either Quincy fails or Rachel will be disappointed.

f. Either Pamela and Quincy both fail the test, or Rachel will be disappointed.

g. Pamela and Quincy won't both pass the test.

h. Pamela and Quincy won't both fail the test.

*i. Exactly one of Pamela and Quincy will fail the test.

(We will have more to say about translations like this in section 2.5.)

3. Construct a grammatical tree for each of the following.

a. $P \lor (Q \,\&\, {\sim}R)$

b. ${\sim}(P \lor (Q \,\&\, {\sim}R))$

c. ${\sim}(Q \lor P) \,\&\, (R \lor S)$

d. ${\sim}[P \lor (Q \lor (R \,\&\, S))] \,\&\, P$

e. $[{\sim}(P \,\&\, Q) \lor S] \,\&\, [(P \,\&\, Q) \lor (S \lor (T \,\&\, S))]$

4. Construct a truth table for each of the following.

a. ${\sim}(P \,\&\, Q)$	b. ${\sim}P \lor {\sim}Q$
c. ${\sim}(P \lor Q)$	d. ${\sim}P \,\&\, {\sim}Q$
e. $P \lor (Q \lor R)$	f. $(P \lor Q) \lor R$
g. $P \,\&\, (Q \,\&\, R)$	h. $(P \,\&\, Q) \,\&\, R$
i. $P \,\&\, (Q \lor R)$	j. $(P \,\&\, Q) \lor (P \,\&\, R)$
k. $P \lor (Q \,\&\, R)$	l. $(P \lor Q) \,\&\, (P \lor R)$

What similarities do you notice between the pairs on each line (a and b, c and d, etc.)?

*5. This problem requires a knowledge of the binary numerical system, which, if you need to review (or have never seen it), you will find in section 8.3 of chapter 8. Using **1** for **T** and **0** for **F**, show how to construct the truth table array of all possible truth-values for any number n of statement letters by beginning with $2^n - 1$ in binary notation and counting down to 0. (Hint: begin with truth tables for one statement letter, then two, then three, etc.)

2.2 CONDITIONAL AND BICONDITIONAL: 'IF . . . THEN', AND 'IF AND ONLY IF'

The two other common truth-functional connectives that we will discuss in this section are the **conditional** and the **biconditional**.

The symbol ⊃ (called the 'horseshoe') is the connective for the truth-functional conditional. Its truth table follows:

	A	B	A ⊃ B
(1)	T	T	T
(2)	T	F	F
(3)	F	T	T
(4)	F	F	T

Notice that any statement of the form **A ⊃ B** is true *except* when **A** is true and **B** is false (row (2)). Because of this, the truth table for **A ⊃ B** fairly closely matches a very important use of 'if . . . then' and equivalent forms in ordinary language. Note, for example, that the statement

If the keys are not on the table, *then* they are on the dresser

seeks to *exclude* the possibility that the keys are not on the table and are not on the dresser (which would be the second row of the truth table).

In any conditional **A ⊃ B**, **A** is called the **antecedent** and **B** is called the **consequent**.

There are four important logical facts about 'if . . . then' statements that the above truth table adequately represents:

1. *Modus ponens*

2. Contraposition

3. Necessary and sufficient conditions

4. 'Not . . . or' and 'if . . . then'

Let's look at each of these in turn.

Modus ponens   Medieval logicians recognized the importance of this valid argument type and named it *modus ponens*.

If the current is on, the switch is broken.

The current is on.

The switch is broken.

The key to the argument form is, of course, the 'if . . . then' statement in the first premise. Now remember that the conclusion 'The switch is broken' cannot be false when both premises are true; that is the requirement of validity. This requirement is upheld if the argument form is symbolized as:

$C \supset S$

C

S

Here, for reference, is the truth table for $C \supset S$

	C	S	$C \supset S$
(1)	T	T	T
(2)	T	F	F
(3)	F	T	T
(4)	F	F	T

If $C \supset S$ is true, then according to the truth table, either C is false (third and fourth rows of the truth table) or S is true (first and third rows). But since C is the second premise of the argument, if it is true, then S can only be true (as in first row of the truth table). So rendering the 'if . . . then' statement by $\supset$ satisfies the validity conditions of *modus ponens* type arguments.

Contraposition   This is another term from the medieval textbooks. The contrapositive of a conditional 'if **A** then **B**' has the form 'if not **B** then not **A**'. If the first statement is true, so is the second (its contrapositive), and vice versa. For example, if someone says 'If it is 7 PM, then it is time for MacNeil-Lehrer' ($E \supset M$), it would be equally true to say: 'If it is not time for MacNeil-Lehrer, then it isn't 7 PM' ($\sim M \supset \sim E$). The relation between an 'if . . . then' statement and its contrapositive is preserved by the truth table for the symbol $\supset$ as shown below

	E	M	$E \supset M$	$\sim E$	$\sim M$	$\sim M \supset \sim E$
(1)	T	T	T	F	F	T
(2)	T	F	F	F	T	F
(3)	F	T	T	T	F	T
(4)	F	F	T	T	T	T

As you can see, the columns under $E \supset M$ and its contrapositive $\sim M \supset \sim E$ are identical.

Necessary and Sufficient Conditions   In a simple flashlight, the battery must be charged in order for the flashlight to work properly. That is, having a charged battery is a *necessary* condition of a working flashlight. But it would be a mistake to conclude that just because the battery is fresh, the flashlight will work. Although a necessary condition, a charged battery is not *sufficient*. To work, a flashlight needs more than a good battery; it needs a working light bulb and unimpaired circuitry (including the switch). All of these conditions together are sufficient for a working flashlight.

To take another example, a teacher might say: 'If you get *this* problem right, you'll get an A for the quiz!' The teacher has made a correct answer to that one problem into a sufficent condition for an A in the quiz, no matter what else you may do. But there may be other ways to get an A, so just because getting the problem right is sufficient for an A, it may not be necessary.

Necessary and sufficient conditions are often expressed by means of 'if . . . then' statements like the following (note the use of the contrapositive):

Necessity   If the flashlight is working,then the batteries must be charged.

(or)   If the batteries aren't charged, the flashlight won't work.

Sufficiency   If you solve the problem, then you'll get an A for the quiz.

Often a sufficient condition is indicated by 'if' used as follows:

That window will break *if* you poke it with that stick.

When we cite sufficient conditions, as in the preceding, we often emphasize the consequent by saying it first.

Necessary conditions can also be indicated by means of 'only if', as in:

It rains *only if* there are clouds in the sky.

The use here of 'only' gives a clearer suggestion of the necessity of clouds for rain than would be conveyed by 'If it rains, then there are clouds in the sky,' even though both express the same statement.

We should pause to remember Stephen, the so-so student from chapter 1. Recall that Stephen took a threat for a promise when he remembered that his teacher said, "No one will receive an A in this course unless he comes to every class." Another way of capturing Stephen's folly is to think of him as having confused the following two statements:

Stephen will get an A *if* he attends every class (i.e., $C \supset A$).

Stephen will get an A *only if* he attends every class (i.e., $A \supset C$).

(C: Stephen attends every class; A: Stephen gets an A.)

The first statement cites a sufficient condition for an A—which the teacher did not commit to—and the second cites only a necessary condition. Perhaps the clearest way of all to indicate necessity is by the contrapositive:

If Stephen doesn't attend every class, he won't get an A.

These examples indicate that 'if . . . then' statements are generally *not* reversible. The truth of 'if **A** then **B**' does not guarantee the truth of 'if **B** then **A**.' The truth table for the connective $\supset$ also matches this requirement. As the rows (2) and (3) clearly show, truth-functional conditionals cannot, in general, be reversed.

'Not . . . Or' and 'If . . . Then'   A final feature of 'if . . . then' statements is that they are often equivalent to statements involving 'not' and 'or'. Consider the following pairs, for example:

Either that's not Tom or he's been on a diet.

If that's Tom, he's been on a diet.

Either you stop that, or you'll get hurt.

If you don't stop that, you'll get hurt.

The statements in both pairs are readily interchangeable. If the statements in each pair are symbolized as disjunctions and conditionals, respectively, we can show how this interchange might look. The truth tables for $\sim$**A** $\vee$ **B** and **A** $\supset$ **B** are exactly the same:

A	B	$\sim$A	A $\supset$ B	$\sim$A $\vee$ B
T	T	F	T	T
T	F	F	F	F
F	T	T	T	T
F	F	T	T	T

This lengthy demonstration shows that the four basic logical features of 'if . . . then' statements that we have discussed are adequately captured by the truth-functional conditional. However, there remains an air of paradox about the conditional connective because statements like the following are also true when symbolized with $\supset$:

(a) If you have a dollar in your pocket, then 2 + 2 = 4.

(b) If the moon is made of green cheese, then 2 + 2 = 5.

The reason can be seen by again noting the truth table for $\supset$:

	A	B	A $\supset$ B
(1)	T	T	T
(2)	T	F	F
(3)	F	T	T
(4)	F	F	T

Rows (1) and (3) guarantee that any truth-functional conditional is true *whenever its consequent is true,* no matter what the antecedent says. Thus, symbolized truth-functionally, statement (a) would be true. And, rows (3) and (4) guarantee that any truth-functional statement will be true *whenever its antecedent is false,* no matter what the consequent says. Hence, as a truth-functional conditional, statement (b) is true.

So what other alternatives might there be? As it turns out, we can explore two other options for symbolizing 'if . . . then' statements: (1) use a different truth table to define $\supset$ or (2) declare all 'if . . . then' statements to be outside of the logic of truth-functional connectives. The first option is easily dismissed. If we are going to use a truth table to define 'if . . . then' as a connective, then the only possibility is the one above. No other table would preserve the four logical features we have discussed. The features that most people find odd about the conditional truth table are that in any statement of the form **A** ⊃ **B**, if **A** is false, the conditional is true no matter what **B** is (third and fourth rows), and if **B** is true, the conditional is true no matter what **A** is (first and third rows). But as we have seen, it is these very rows that allow for contraposition and preserve the distinction between necessary and sufficient conditions. And the entire table must be as it is if 'if . . . then' and 'not . . . or' are to be equivalent.

What of the second option, that all 'if . . . then' statements are really outside truth-functional logic altogether? It is certainly the case that *some* 'if . . . then' English statements are not truth-functional; here are two examples of candidates:

If Hitler had invaded England, Germany would have won the war.

If Susan continues to work around asbestos, she will surely contract cancer.

The first is a contrary-to-fact, subjunctive, hypothetical statement. Its truth depends upon a host of facts about how the Second World War was waged in Europe. Note that since 'Hitler invaded England' is false, the entire statement would be true if it were considered a truth-functional conditional. But so too would be 'If Hitler had invaded Bolivia, Germany would have won the war' and any other statement that begins 'If Hitler had invaded X, then . . . ' in which X is some country he didn't actually invade.[5] The second statement posits a *causal relation* between working around asbestos and contracting cancer; but cause-and-effect relations are not adequately represented by the truth-functional conditional either. The truth of a causal statement is not simply a question of the truth-value of its components, but a question of a general relationship between events of certain types.

From the undeniable fact that there is quite a bit of 'if . . . then' logic that is not representable in truth-functional terms, it would be hasty to conclude that all 'if . . . then' statements are not truth-functional. The approach taken here is that the truth-functional analysis of 'if . . . then' statements using the connective ⊃ reveals important logical principles that are very useful in understanding correct reasoning, just as a model (like a toy train) can reveal important features of the larger reality. Unfortunately, we will occasionally find an odd consequence as a result, but these will be more trivial than harmful. For those who are still troubled by the truth table for

---

[5]An illuminating book on the logic of such statements is David Lewis, *Counterfactuals* (Cambridge: Harvard University Press, 1973.) On other approaches, see W. L. Harper, R. Stalnaker, and G. Pierce, *Ifs* (Boston: D. Reidel, 1981).

the truth-functional conditional ⊃, it will be helpful to think that the sense of 'if . . . then' being dealt with here is that which is exactly interchangeable with 'not . . . or'.

Our fifth truth-functional connective is the **biconditional**, so named because it works like a double conditional. The connective appears in statements like 'It will rain tomorrow *if and only if* the jet stream shifts'. The symbol is ≡ and the truth table is

A	B	A ≡ B
T	T	T
T	F	F
F	T	F
F	F	T

Note that **A** ≡ **B** is true only if **A** and **B** have the same true-value; that is, if both are true or both are false. To see why the name 'biconditional' applies, notice the final column of the truth table for (**A** ⊃ **B**) & (**B** ⊃ **A**):

A	B	A ⊃ B	B ⊃ A	(A ⊃ B) & (B ⊃ A)
T	T	T	T	T
T	F	F	T	F
F	T	T	F	F
F	F	T	T	T

The table shows that the truth-functional biconditional is like a double conditional. The connective ≡ permits a good representation of many uses of 'if and only if' and 'just in case' in English. Sometimes a biconditional is also said to depict necessary *and* sufficient conditions; that is, **A** if **B** (= **B** ⊃ **A**) *and* **A** only if **B** (= **A** ⊃ **B**), which would normally indicate that **B** is both necessary and sufficient for **A**. For example, paper will burn if and only if both heat and oxygen are present. Heat and oxygen by themselves are necessary; together, they are sufficient.

The conditional and biconditional connectives may occur along with the other truth-functional connectives. We will have more to say in section 2.4 about how complex, ordinary language statements and arguments are symbolized; for now, here are just two examples.

(1) If the keys are not on the table or the dresser, then they are in the coat pocket.

In symbols: $\sim(T \lor D) \supset P$

where T is 'The keys are on the table'.
D is 'The keys are on the dresser'.
P is 'The keys are in the coat pocket'.

(2) William tells the truth if and only if both John and James are liars.

In symbols: $W \equiv (H \,\&\, J)$

where W is 'William tells the truth'.
H is 'John is a liar'.
J is 'James is a liar'.

Since both the conditional and the biconditional connectives require two immediate components, they function in grammatical trees just like conjunction and disjunction. This is a grammatical tree for the first statement above:

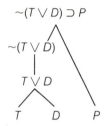

You now have the essential constituents of the logical language we will call SL for "statement logic." SL uses capital letters, called statement letters, and the five truth-functional statement connectives: $\sim$, $\lor$, $\&$, $\supset$, and $\equiv$. For punctuation, parentheses ( ) and [ ] are used. The statement connectives are defined by their respective truth tables.

Although not much has been said about it so far, we have already applied a minimal grammar to SL expressions. Certain combinations of SL symbols make sense, and other combinations are senseless, e.g. G ($\lor$ &. We can tidy up this informal understanding by means of the following rules that define what counts as an *SL statement*:

---

1. *If **A** is a statement letter, then **A** is an SL statement.*
2. *If **A** and **B** are SL statements, then (**A** $\lor$ **B**) is an SL statement.*
3. *If **A** and **B** are SL statements, then (**A** & **B**) is an SL statement.*
4. *If **A** and **B** are SL statements, then (**A** $\supset$ **B**) is an SL statement.*
5. *If **A** and **B** are SL statements, then (**A** $\equiv$ **B**) is an SL statement.*
6. *If **A** is an SL statement, then $\sim$**A** is an SL statement.*
7. *All SL statements may be formed by repeated application of these rules.*

These rules exactly match our use of statement trees (with parentheses dropped). Note that the bottom line of a statement tree consists of just statement letters (which are obviously statements). The next line up counts as a statement because its components are statements, the next line up from that is a statement because its components are statements, and so on.

The following examples show just how these seven rules do precisely define what counts as an SL statement.

(a) $(J \& H) \vee (\sim T \& \sim S)$

(b) $\sim(W \equiv (H \& J)$

To be an SL statement, (a) must be a disjunction of SL statements, according to rule 2. Thus, the focus shifts to the components $(J \& H)$ and $(\sim T \& \sim S)$. According to rule 3, $(J \& H)$ is an SL statement, and $(\sim T \& \sim S)$ is an SL statement if both $\sim T$ and $\sim S$ are. According to rule 6, both are indeed SL statements. By working through the components of (a), we have shown that it is an SL statement. Now look at the grammatical tree for (a). As has become our practice, outer parentheses may be dropped from SL statements unless doing so would lead to any confusion.

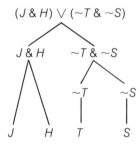

We see that the grammatical tree provides the same analysis of (a) as an SL statement; all entries on each line of the tree must be SL statements.

When we try to do the same analysis on (b) we discover that $\sim(W \equiv (H \& J)$ is an SL statement if, according to rule 6, $W \equiv (H \& J)$ is. But, according to rule 5, $(W \equiv (H \& J)$ is an SL statement only if W is and $(H \& J$ is. But $(H \& J$ is *not* an SL statement because it is missing a right parenthesis. So (b) is not an SL statement. Here is an attempted statement tree for (b):

$\sim(W \equiv (H \& J)$
|
$W \equiv (H \& J$ ←

W ?

The tree shows the problem exactly: the right parenthesis is missing in the second line.

We refer to SL statements that do not contain any connectives as **atomic statements** and to those that do contain one or more connectives as **compound statements**. Note that atomic statements are just statement letters. We also say that an argument whose premises and conclusion are SL statements is an **SL argument**. Finally, the four boldface capital letters **A**, **B**, **C**, and **D** represent *statement variables*; they are used to generally stand in for statements, whether atomic or compound.

For the rest of this chapter and in the next two we will explore the logic of ordinary English statements and arguments by means of the apparatus of SL. In chapters 6 and 7 we will expand the resources of SL and learn another logical language, PL, or predicate logic, which will provide tools for even deeper logical analysis.

Summary

Here is a summary of the two connectives and the other important concepts introduced in this section.

Conditional   Symbol: $\supset$

Example: *If* the keys are not on the table, *then* the keys are on the dresser. Immediate components of **A** $\supset$ **B**: **A** is the antecedent; **B** is the consequent.
Truth table:

A	B	A $\supset$ B
T	T	T
T	F	F
F	T	T
F	F	T

Biconditional   Symbol: $\equiv$
Example: The keys are on the table *if and only if* the keys are on the dresser.
Truth table:

A	B	A $\equiv$ B
T	T	T
T	F	F
F	T	F
F	F	T

Necessary condition X is a necessary condition for Y if Y cannot take place without X. Example: 'The flashlight will work only if the battery is charged'.

Sufficient condition X is a sufficient condition for Y if the presence of X is enough to guarantee the presence of Y. Example: 'You will get an A in this quiz if you get this problem right'.

SL   Short for "statement logic", the language that permits symbolization of the logical form of ordinary English statements that can be considered truth-functional.

Atomic SL statement   An SL statement that does not contain any connectives (e.g., a sentence letter).

Compound SL statement   An SL statement that contains at least one statement connective. Each compound SL statement can be classified in terms of its **major connective**.

SL argument   An argument made up of SL statements.

EXERCISES 2.2

1. Symbolize the following statements in SL notation:
   a. If John plays, then the game will go on all night.
   b. If John doesn't play, then the game will go on all night.
   c. Mary will go if Sue goes.
   d. Mary will go only if Sue goes.
   e. Mary will go if and only if Sue goes.
   f. If Sue doesn't go, then Mary will go only if Jim goes.
   g. If Al is asleep and breakfast isn't ready, then Dave and Ethel will be late for school.

   (See Exercises 2.4 for additional translation problems.)

2. Construct grammatical trees for each of the following.
   a. $(P \vee Q) \supset (R \equiv S)$
   b. $\sim(R \supset S) \, \& \, T$
   c. $T \equiv \sim(Q \, \& \, (P \vee T))$

3. Create a grammatical tree and a truth table for each of the following.
   a. $(P \vee Q) \supset Q$
   b. $\sim P \supset Q$
   c. $\sim(P \supset \sim Q)$
   d. $P \supset (P \, \& \, Q)$
   e. $(P \, \& \, Q) \supset R$

    f. $P \supset (Q \supset R)$

    g. $\sim P \equiv \sim Q$

    h. $\sim P \equiv Q$

    i. $P \equiv \sim Q$

    j. $\sim(P \equiv Q)$

    k. $(P \& Q) \vee (\sim P \& \sim Q)$

4. This exercise is based on the following information:

   Current flowing through a wire is interrupted by an open switch but will continue to flow when the switch is closed. A wire on which two switches are found will have current flowing provided that both switches are closed.

   a. Based on the above, formulate three conditionals that are true.

   b. Formulate two conditionals that are false.

   c. What is a necessary condition for current flowing through a wire?

   d. Is your answer to *c* also a sufficient condition? Explain.

   e. What is a sufficient condition of current *not* flowing through a wire?

5. Show that each of the expressions in exercise 2.2.2 is an SL statement.

6. Why isn't $\sim[(P \& Q) \vee (\sim P \& \sim Q) \& (P \equiv \sim Q)]$ an SL statement?

*7. Another way of determining whether a symbolic expression is an SL statement is to replace all statement letters with numbers, all negations with a minus sign ($-$) and all other connectives with a plus sign ($+$). Try and formulate a set of rules for how such a procedure might work. To test your rules, ask a friend who doesn't know any logic to apply them to a few cases. (Hint: there will be a problem with parentheses, so you will need a separate rule to determine if the expression has the right number of parentheses.)

*2.3 TRUTH-FUNCTIONAL STATEMENT COMPOSITION[6]

You have been introduced to five truth-functional statement connectives so far; those for negation, disjunction, conjunction, conditional and biconditional. The negation connective attaches to a single statement to form a compound; the others join two statements together. Negation might be said to be a *one-place connective*, while disjunction, conjunction, conditional, and biconditional are *two-place connectives*.

    In theory, negation is not the only possible one-place, truth-functional connective. To see that there are others, just think of all the possible truth tables we can construct for compound statements containing only one state-

---

[6]Although independent of the remainder of chapter 2, this section is important background for chapter 10 (Logical Circuits).

ment letter, say **A**. There are the following four possibilities, labelled c_1, c_2, c_3, and c_4.

A	c_1	c_2	c_3	c_4
T	T	T	F	F
F	T	F	T	F

The third possible table, c_3, is, of course, that for negation. The others do not have any normal English equivalents, except that c_2 is the truth table for 'It is true that . . .'. But if we wanted to find statements for the others, we can do so with just the resources we already have available, using two-place connectives. That is, we can easily form compounds of a single statement letter **A** that will have the four possible truth tables. Here they are:

A	A ∨ ~A	A ∨ A	~A	A & ~A
T	T	T	F	F
F	T	F	T	F

We can also look at two-place connectives from a similar point of view and ask what the other possibilities may be. We have identified four two-place connectives: there are twelve other possibilities.[7]

The possible truth tables for two-place, truth-functional connectives are tabulated as follows (the corresponding connectives we have already identified are placed above):

		∨				⊃		≡	&
A	B	c_1	c_2	c_3	c_4	c_5	c_6	c_7	c_8
T	T	T	T	T	T	T	T	T	T
T	F	T	T	T	T	F	F	F	F
F	T	T	T	F	F	T	T	F	F
F	F	T	F	T	F	T	F	T	F

---

[7]Recall that for *n* statement letters there will be 2^n rows in the truth table for any *one* manner of forming a compound from them. So there will be 2^{2^n} of possible ways of forming all such truth tables.

A	B	c_9	c_{10}	c_{11}	c_{12}	c_{13}	c_{14}	c_{15}	c_{16}
T	T	F	F	F	F	F	F	F	F
T	F	T	T	T	T	F	F	F	F
F	T	T	T	F	F	T	T	F	F
F	F	T	F	T	F	T	F	T	F

As before, c_1, c_2, c_3, etc. are used for the various possible truth tables connectives might have.

Four of the possible sixteen two-place connectives are, of course, the familiar conjunction (c_8), disjunction (c_2), conditional (c_5) and biconditional (c_7). Several others are so common that they could easily be given similar official status:

Exclusive disjunction (c_{10})   This truth table represents the strong or exclusive sense of *or*, as in '**A** *or* **B**, *but not both*'. Some texts use the special symbol $\veebar$ for exclusive disjunction.

Neither . . . nor (c_{15})   This truth table is some times called *joint denial*. It represents the sense of '*neither* **A** *nor* **B**', that is, **A** is false and **B** is false too. Joint denial is sometimes symbolized as $\downarrow$, called the 'fell swoop' or 'dagger'.

Not both (c_9)   This truth table is sometimes called *alternative denial*. It represents the sense of '*not both* **A** and **B**'. Alternative denial also has its own special symbol, |, known as the 'Sheffer stroke'.[8]

Even though we have introduced only four official two-place connectives, it is nevertheless possible to formulate a symbolic expression for any of the sixteen possible truth tables. In fact, we can capture every one of them using only the three connectives $\sim$, $\vee$, and &. Here are versions of each of the sixteen possible connectives from the above table expressed with just these three connectives:

c_1: $(A \vee \sim A) \vee B$

c_2: $A \vee B$

c_3: $A \vee \sim B$

---

[8]The logic of joint denial and alternative denial is based on the work of H. M. Sheffer. See W. V. Quine, *Methods Of Logic*, 3rd ed. (New York: Holt, Rinehart & Winston, 1972), pp. 18, 74. In chapter 10, we will study electronic networks that correspond to these last three two-place connectives. They are called XOR, NOR, and NAND, respectively.

c_4: **(A & B) $\lor$ (A & ~B)**

c_5: **~A $\lor$ B**   (conditional)

c_6: **(A & B) $\lor$ (~A & B)**

c_7: **(~A $\lor$ B) & (A $\lor$ ~B)**   (biconditional)

c_8: **A & B**

c_9: **~(A & B)**   (alternative denial)

c_{10}: **(A $\lor$ B) & ~(A & B)**   (exclusive disjunction)

c_{11}: **(A & ~B) $\lor$ (~A & ~B)**

c_{12}: **A & ~B**   (negated conditional)

c_{13}: **(~A & B) $\lor$ (~A & ~B)**

c_{14}: **~A & B**

c_{15}: **~A & ~B**   (joint denial)

c_{16}: **(A & ~A) & B**

(Note: these are not the only possible renderings, nor are they necessarily the simplest. See below.)

We have already encountered statements that, when expressed symbolically, involve three statement letters, and it is easy to construct even more complicated statements, such as,

> If the keys are not on the table or on the dresser, then either they are in the coat pocket, or they were left at the office and they were stolen.
>
> In symbols: $(\sim T \,\&\, \sim D) \supset [P \lor (L \,\&\, S)]$

Each statement, no matter how complex, when expressed in terms of truth-functional connectives has a corresponding truth table. Using the general rules for constructing such tables (discussed in section 2.2), once we have a symbolic statement, we can find an appropriate truth table. But what about the reverse? Can we find a symbolic expression for *any* truth table, no matter how many statement letters are involved?

The answer is yes, and the proof was an important discovery of the logician Emil Post in 1921.[9] What Post showed was that corresponding to any truth table for any number of statement letters, there is a symbolic expression that uses only the three connectives ~, $\lor$ and &. Needless to say, these expressions become rather lengthy when large numbers of statement letters are involved. But the procedure is fairly simple; in fact, if you look back at the symbolic expressions for the two-place connectives c_4, c_6,

---

[9]The version of Post's discovery that follows is from Hugues Leblanc and William A. Wisdom, *Deductive Logic*, 2nd ed. (New York: Allyn and Bacon, 1976). For the full proof, see pp. 246–248.

and c_{11}, you have already seen examples of how Post's metho
two statement letters.

Remember how truth tables work: no matter how many staten.
are involved, the table has essentially the same form. Suppose, for e
there are five statement letters, **A** through **E**; the first five rows of u.
side of the table would look like this (the full table has $2^5 = 32$ rows):

A	B	C	D	E	...
T	T	T	T	T	
T	T	T	T	F	
T	T	T	F	T	
T	T	T	F	F	
T	T	F	T	T	

Recall that with five statement letters, the first column will have sixteen **T**'s
and sixteen **F**'s (i.e., $2^5/2$), the next will have eight **T**'s, eight **F**'s, eight **T**'s,
and eight **F**'s, the third column will repeat groups of four **T**'s and four **F**'s,
and so on. And, according to the rules, the same kind of pattern will be
found in truth tables for one hundred statement letters, with 2^{100} rows!

When *all* the possible truth tables for a certain number n of statement
letters are displayed using the same format we used above, the first table
will be a column of all **T**'s (e.g., c_1 above), and the final table will be a column
of all **F**'s (e.g., c_{16} above). These two tables are easy to represent symbolically.
Suppose the n statement letters in the table are A_1, A_2, A_3, ..., A_n; just
use for the first column:

A$_1$ V ~A$_1$ V A$_2$ V A$_3$ V ... V A$_n$ [10]

For the last column, use:

A$_1$ & ~A$_1$ & A$_2$ & A$_3$ & ... & A$_n$

Since A_1 V ~A_1 is a disjunct in the first statement, and A_1 V ~A_1 will always
be true, the statement cannot be false. With A_1 & ~A_1 as a conjunct in the
second statement, the statement can only be false, since A_1 & ~A_1 is always
false. If you look back at the table of all possible truth tables for two-place
connectives, you will see that this is how the first (c_1) and last (c_{16}) columns
were rendered.

---

[10] The usual parentheses are omitted here for easy reading. They can be quite simply restored.

Each of the other truth table columns will contain some **T**'s and some **F**'s. Such columns can be represented by forming the column's **Post paraphrase**. The procedure is this: When a **T** occurs in the column under the connective, we form a *conjunction* that corresponds to that row. Suppose in the fragment of the full truth table for five statement letters, a **T** is found in the second row of the column marked * as follows:

A	B	C	D	E	*	
T	T	T	T	T	F	
T	T	T	T	F	T	←
T	T	T	F	T		
T	T	T	F	F		
T	T	F	T	T		

Then the corresponding conjunction is formed by conjoining the statement letters that are **T** and the negation of the statement letters that are **F** as follows:

A & B & C & D & ~E   (*corresponding conjunction* for second row)

To continue the example, suppose there is another **T** in the fourth row:

A	B	C	D	E	*	
T	T	T	T	T	F	
T	T	T	T	F	T	
T	T	T	F	T	F	
T	T	T	F	F	T	←
T	T	F	T	T		

The corresponding conjunction for the fourth row would be:

A & B & C & ~D & ~E

No matter how many statement letters may be involved in a truth table, such corresponding conjunctions can easily be constructed for any row which is **T**.

To form the Post paraphrase of a column, all of the *conjunctions* that correspond to rows with **T**'s in the column are connected by disjunctions. Look back at columns c_4, c_6, and c_{11} in the full table for two statement letters. Then look at the symbolic expressions that are listed; these are examples of Post paraphrases. Suppose the column marked * in the table for five statement letters has **T**'s *only* in the second and fourth rows. Then the Post paraphrase of that column would be:

(A & B & C & D & ~E) ∨ (A & B & C & ~D & ~E)
   (second row)   (fourth row)

that is, the disjunction of the corresponding conjunction of each row that is **T** in the column.

The reason this method works is that in forming the Post paraphrase of the column we are forming a statement that is sure to be true only in those rows that are **T**. Since the components of the disjunction are conjunctions, all of them will be false in the other rows, and so the disjunction itself will be false as well. For example, here is an evaluation of the Post paraphrase for the values in the first row of the column for * above.

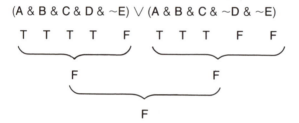

The Post paraphrase method is entirely general, so by using it a symbolic statement that uses only the connectives ~, ∨, and &, can be constructed for *any* column in *any* truth table, for any number of statement letters.

The method may not give the simplest possible statement, however. Note that if the method were used for c_3 in the table for two statement letters, i.e.,

A	B	c_3
T	T	T
T	F	T
F	T	F
F	F	T

it would produce as the Post paraphrase:

(A & B) ∨ (A & ~B) ∨ (~A & ~B)

instead of the vastly simpler **A ∨ ~B**.

We will have more to say later about the important problem of simplifying these Post paraphrases (see chapter 10, section 10.4).

A consequence of Post's discovery is that we have considerable expressive redundancy in our five official statement connectives; we could easily make do with just ~, ∨, and &, no matter how complicated a statement may be. An even more startling consequence is that we actually could make do with just *two* of our statement connectives, and we have two choices as to which pair at that! The basis for this claim is that we can express any conjunction by means of negation and disjunction, and we can express any disjunction by means of negation and conjunction. To see this, here are two sets of truth tables. The first presents conjunction in terms of negation and disjunction:

A	B	A & B	~(~A ∨ ~B)
T	T	T	T
T	F	F	F
F	T	F	F
F	F	F	F

The second presents disjunction in terms of negation and conjunction:

A	B	A ∨ B	~(~A & ~B)
T	T	T	T
T	F	T	T
F	T	T	T
F	F	F	F

What these two tables mean is that *any* disjunction or conjunction can be replaced by the other if negations and parentheses are employed as indicated. In particular, any Post paraphrase can be rewritten in terms of just two connectives: either ~ and ∨ or ~ and &. The result is an ungainly beast, but the theoretical point is all that is at issue here. For example, the Post paraphrase of the truth table we called *, for five statement letters, is given below, together with two alternative forms, each of which uses just two connectives.

Original: (A & B & C & D & ~E) ∨ (A & B & C & ~D & ~E)

In terms of ~ and &: ~[~(A & B & C & D & ~E) & ~(A & B & C & ~D & ~E)]

In terms of ~ and ∨:
 ~(~A ∨ ~B ∨ ~C ∨ ~D ∨ ~~E) ∨ ~(~A ∨ ~B ∨ ~C ∨ ~~D ∨ ~~E)[11]

Now recall that special symbols were mentioned for both joint denial, ↓ (the dagger or fell swoop), and alternative denial, | (the Sheffer stroke), and that these connectives can be expressed in terms of our official connectives as follows:

Joint denial: A ↓ B   Expressed as: ~A & ~B

Alternative denial: A | B   Expressed as: ~A ∨ ~ B

Since we can use either negation and conjunction *or* negation and disjunction to represent any truth-function, we have also established that any truth-functional compound can be represented by means of only *one* connective, and we can choose either | or ↓ . The easiest way to show this is to demonstrate that all five of our official connectives can be expressed solely in terms of either | or ↓ .

Negation	~A
dagger	A ↓ A
Sheffer stroke	A	A
Conjunction	A & B
dagger	(A ↓ A) ↓ (B ↓ B)
Sheffer stroke	(A	B)	(A	B)
Disjunction	A ∨ B
dagger	(A ↓ B) ↓ (A ↓ B)
Sheffer stroke	(A	A)	(B	B)
Conditional	A ⊃ B
dagger	[(A ↓ A) ↓ B] ↓ [(A ↓ A) ↓ B]
Sheffer stroke	A	(B	B)
Biconditional	A ≡ B
dagger	[[(A ↓ B) ↓ (A ↓ B)] ↓ (A ↓ B)] ↓ [[(A ↓ B) ↓ (A ↓ B)] ↓ (A ↓ B)]
Sheffer stroke	[[A	(B | B)]	[(A | A)	B]]	[[A	(B | B)]	[(A | A)	B]]

The ability to express any truth-functional relationship in terms of the dagger and the Sheffer stroke might seem to be of purely theoretical interest at this point, but in chapter 10 we will investigate physical manifestations of

---

[11]A number of intermediary steps have been omitted.

connectives as they function in computer circuits. The ability to use a version of the dagger or the Sheffer stroke in place of other connectives has proved of great importance in computer circuitry design.

Summary

In summary, this section has presented a version of **Post's theorem** that all truth-functional compounds of n statement letters can be represented by means of just the connectives $\sim$, $\vee$, and &. We discussed a method that employs **Post paraphrases** to construct a symbolic expression of any truth table. We also showed that, in fact, either of the following pairs, $\sim$ and $\vee$, or $\sim$ and &, would also serve, as would the single connectives for **joint denial** $\downarrow$ and for **alternative denial** $|$.

EXERCISES 2.3

1. Try to find other symbolic statements to represent each of the columns in the full truth table for one statement letter.

2. Try to find other symbolic statements to represent each of the columns in the full truth table for two statement letters.

3. How many possible truth tables are there for compounds of three statement letters? Of four?

4. Formulate a set of instructions for systematically constructing the full truth table of all possible compounds of n statement letters.

5. Using the instructions in 4, write the truth table for the second-to-the-last column in the full truth table of all compounds of three statement letters.

6. Construct the Post paraphrase for the truth table in 5 and show that the statement indeed has this truth table.

7. Rewrite the following statements just in terms of $\sim$ and &.

    a. $\sim P \supset Q$

    b. $P \equiv (Q \vee \sim R)$

    c. $\sim(P \vee (Q \supset R))$

8. Rewrite the three statements just in terms of $\sim$ and $\vee$.

9. Rewrite the three statements just in terms of $|$.

10. Rewrite the three statements just in terms of $\downarrow$.

2.4 TURNING ENGLISH INTO SYMBOLS

To be able to investigate the validity of actual arguments, we have to employ the symbolic apparatus of SL. This means that we have to capture accurately the logical form of ordinary language statements and arguments by means of statement letters and truth-functional connectives. Unlike other parts of logical theory, the question of how to properly represent the logical form of a statement in English, or any other natural language, does not have a simple answer. Subtleties in the use of language abound, and they often impinge on logical relationships.

Here are some hints on how our five connectives can be used in representations of ordinary language statements.

Negations There are a variety of negating devices in English, but they all serve to indicate that something isn't true. In SL, we understand that 'something' to be the immediate component statement. All of the following, in which *J* stands for 'Jim will pass', can be thought of as negations.

Jim won't pass:	$\sim J$
It isn't the case that Jim will pass:	$\sim J$
It is false that Jim will pass:	$\sim J$
Jim won't fail:	$\sim\sim J$ (note: 'fail' = 'won't pass')

Conjunction The nature of a truth-functional conjunction is that both immediate components are asserted as true. So the following statements can safely be represented as conjunctions. In addition to *J* for 'Jim will pass', we will use *H* for 'Harriett will pass'.

Harriett and Jim will both pass:	$J \& H$
Jim will pass, but Harriett won't:	$J \& \sim H$
Although Harriett will pass, Jim won't:	$H \& \sim J$
Neither Jim nor Harriett will pass:	$\sim J \& \sim H$
Jim passes as does Harriett:	$J \& H$
Harriett will pass; however, Jim won't:	$H \& \sim J$
Harriett won't pass; Jim will	$\sim H \& J$

In the last case, there is no English word to indicate the conjunction; a semicolon, however, serves the same purpose.

One question that often arises concerning conjunctions is how to distinguish between one conjunctive statement and two (or more) separate statements. Given the truth table for the conjunctive connective, the answer to the question is that there is no real difference between the two, except, perhaps, in matters of emphasis. For example, in arguing for the innocence of her client an attorney might assert the following:

Stevens was sick that night, and so he stayed at his office. We know he was at his office, since his front door never opened. And if he stayed at his office, he couldn't have been at the restaurant.

How many statements has she made here? We could safely say that she has made three, basing our claim on the number of sentences. But notice that the break between the second sentence and the third is entirely arbitrary and, when the sentences are spoken, will probably not be noticed. Further, the first and second sentences could have been joined into one by a semicolon, and the first sentence could have been broken into two short sentences. We could correctly symbolize the passage as three separate claims corresponding to the sentences:

$S \& O$
$O \& \sim F$
$O \supset \sim R$

or we could symbolize like this (eliminating the redundant second O):

S
O
$\sim F$
$O \supset \sim R$

or we could tie everything together into one grand conjunction:

$[(S \& O) \& (O \& \sim F)] \& (O \supset \sim R)$

From a logical point of view, there is no difference among these three approaches to the passage.

Disjunction We understand a disjunction to assert that either of two statements is true. It is important to note that whether there is a possibility that both might also be true is often essential to the correct understanding of 'or' in English. Our official disjunctive connective $\lor$ represents what is sometimes called **inclusive disjunction**, meaning that it is possible that both disjuncts are true (recall the first row of the truth table for $\lor$). The stronger **exclusive disjunction** denies that possibility, as in 'Taxpayers will use either form 1040 or form 1040EZ'. The Internal Revenue Service does not mean to include the possibility that some taxpayers will use both; it is one or the other. We can symbolically represent exclusive disjunction by adding the rider 'but not both' as an additional conjunct. This and other common expressions for disjunction are listed below.

Jim or Harriett will pass but not both: $(J \lor H) \& \sim (J \& H)$

One or the other will pass: $J \lor H$

Only one will pass: $(J \lor H) \& \sim (J \& H)$

At most one will pass: $\sim J \lor \sim H$ [or $\sim (J \& H)$]

Both won't pass: $\sim J \lor \sim H$

Either Jim won't pass or Harriett will: $\sim J \lor H$

Conditional In the truth-functional representation of the conditional, a conditional statement explicitly excludes the possibility that the antecedent is true while the consequent is false. Thus the sense of a statement of the form $A \supset B$ is essentially the same as $\sim(A \ \& \sim B)$ or as $\sim A \lor B$. Counterfactual hypothetical statements and causal statements are at best inadequately rendered as truth-functional conditionals. Here are some common patterns for which the conditional is a reasonable rendering.

If Jim passes, then Harriett won't pass:	$J \supset \sim H$
Jim will pass if Harriett passes:	$H \supset J$
Jim will pass only if Harriett passes:	$J \supset H$
If Harriett passes, Jim will too:	$H \supset J$
When Jim passes, Harriett passes:	$J \supset H$
As long as Harriett doesn't pass, Jim will:	$\sim H \supset J$
Jim will pass unless Harriett passes:	$\sim H \supset J$

'Unless' can be tricky. (Remember Stephen's difficulty from chapter 1.) Representing 'Jim will pass unless his headache returns' as $\sim R \supset J$ interprets the statement to mean that if the headache doesn't return, then Jim definitely will pass. But what if the headache does return? There are two possibilities. The weak understanding of 'unless' allows for both the headache to return and Jim to pass. Sometimes 'unless' carries a stronger suggestion, as in 'Jim will pass unless the headache returns, *in which case he won't*'. In such a case, 'unless' conveys an *exclusive* sense of disjunction, and would be treated as 'Jim will pass or the headache returns, but not both', i.e., $(J \lor R) \ \& \sim(J \ \& \ R)$. When in doubt as to what was intended (the usual case), perhaps the best way to treat it is as above, $\sim R \supset J$, or just as a simple *disjunction* of the two immediate statement components, i.e., as $J \lor R$, which has exactly the same truth table.

Since most people stumble over 'unless', the recommended course is to always replace it with a disjunction.

Biconditional The majority of biconditionals in English are obvious because they use 'if and only if' or 'just in case'. However, sometimes just 'if' or 'only if' is intended to convey biconditionality. The context, however, usually makes this clear. A cautionary note is in order, however, about straying very far from the actual words used. Suppose Stephen's teacher had said,

You will get an A only if you attend all lectures.

If he were allowed to correctly treat his teacher's statement as a biconditional, he would get the A after all. That is, suppose his teacher's statement is symbolized as

$G \equiv L$

(*G* for 'You will get an A'; *L* for 'You attend all lectures'.)

Since Stephen did attend all the lectures, he would get his A. But surely his teacher did not intend to say this. What this shows is that, as always, good judgment should accompany all attempts to interpret what someone has said.

Symbolizing more complicated statements is simply a matter of building up from simpler parts, like doing a grammatical tree in reverse. Remember that the connective with the largest scope is the major connective; its truth table is the truth table for the statement as a whole. Statement letters should always represent simple (i.e., non-truth-functional compound) statements. Here are a few sample cases as illustration:

A. It is just not the case that if Sean gets ice cream, then Fiona will too.

   Step 1   Choose representative statement letters:

   S: 'Sean gets ice cream'.

   F: 'Fiona gets ice cream'.

   Step 2   Symbolize the inner statement:

   It is just not the case that ($S \supset F$).

   Step 3   Finish the job:

   $\sim(S \supset F)$

B. Perkins will go up the mast if the mainsail is torn and the wind dies down.

   Step 1   *P*: 'Perkins will go up the mast'.
   M: 'The mainsail is torn'.
   W: 'The wind dies down'.

   Step 2   Perkins will go up the mast if (M & W).

   Step 3   (M & W) $\supset$ Perkins will go up the mast.

   Step 4   (M & W) $\supset P$.

C. Either Jim and Harriett will pass, or Ted and Sarah won't.

   Step 1   *J*: 'Jim will pass'.
   H: 'Harriett will pass'.
   T: 'Ted will pass'.
   S: 'Sarah will pass'.

Step 2 $(J \& H)$ or $(\sim T \& \sim S)$

Step 3 $(J \& H) \vee (\sim T \& \sim S)$

D. Exactly one of Jim, Harriett, and Ted will pass.

Step 1 Same as above.

Step 2 $[J \& (\sim H \& \sim T)] =$ 'Jim passes and the others don't'.

$[H \& (\sim J \& \sim T)] =$ 'Harriett passes and the others don't'.

$[T \& (\sim J \& \sim H)] =$ 'Ted passes and the others don't'.

Step 3 $[J \& (\sim H \& \sim T)] \vee [[H \& (\sim J \& \sim T)] \vee [T \& (\sim J \& \sim H)]]$

Capturing the logical form of *arguments* is just more of the same once one has sorted out the conclusion and premises. It is often helpful in this task to remember the words and phrases that are commonly used as premise and conclusion indicators. Here again are the examples we discussed in chapter 1:

Conclusion indicators	**Premise indicators**
Thus	Since
So	Because
Consequently	On account of
In conclusion	Given that
Therefore	In that
Hence	In as much as
It follows that	For
As a result	Assuming
Implies that	
We may conclude	

The following are two sample arguments. To represent their logical form, we first must identify the conclusion and the premises, and then translate all statements into symbolic expressions. Again we will proceed in steps.

A. If the dormitory is not built by September, some students will have to be in temporary housing. But if some students will be in temporary housing, then fees will have to be reduced. And if fees are reduced, the dormitory will not be built by September. So the dormitory will not be ready in September.

Step 1 The conclusion is 'The dormitory will not be ready in September'. (conclusion indicator 'so')

Step 2 The premises are the first three statements.

Step 3 D: 'The dormitory will be ready in September'.

T: 'Some students will be in temporary housing'.

R: 'Fees will have to be reduced'.

Step 4 First premise: $\sim D \supset T$

Step 5 Second premise: $T \supset R$

Step 6 Third premise: $R \supset \sim D$

Step 7 Conclusion: $\sim D$

Step 8 Logical form of the entire argument:

$\sim D \supset T$

$T \supset R$

$R \supset \sim D$

———————

$\sim D$

B. Oklahoma and Villanova will not play one another in the second round. For they would play in the second round if and only if Oklahoma wins its first round and Villanova beats Georgetown. And if Villanova wins against Georgetown and beats Oklahoma, then it plays Michigan. But Villanova will not play Michigan, and Oklahoma will not win its first round.

Step 1 The premises all follow the occurrence of 'for' (a premise indicator).

Step 2 The conclusion then is: 'Oklahoma and Villanova will not play one another in the second round.'

Step 3 O: 'Oklahoma and Villanova will play one another in the second round'.

W: 'Oklahoma wins its first round'.

V: 'Villanova beats Georgetown'.

K: 'Villanova beats Oklahoma'.

M: 'Villanova plays Michigan'.

Step 4 First premise: $O \equiv (W \& V)$

Step 5   Second premise: $(V \& K) \supset M$

Step 6   Third premise: $\sim M \& \sim W$

Step 7   Conclusion: $\sim O$

Step 8   Logical form of entire argument:

$$O \equiv (W \& V)$$
$$(V \& K) \supset M$$
$$\sim M \& \sim W$$
$$\overline{\sim O}$$

The next chapter will present several methods for evaluating arguments; we will come back to these two arguments as part of that discussion.

Summary

This section has covered the translation of statements in English into symbolic SL expressions that reveal their logical form. In deciding on a correct translation, it is important to understand the consequences of alternative translations. In complicated translations work in small pieces and then connect the pieces together, like working grammatical trees in reverse. Arguments can be symbolized only after their premises and conclusions are recognized. The **premise indicator** and **conclusion indicator** words and phrases that were listed will assist you in this process.

EXERCISES 2.4

1. For each of the following SL expressions, make up an ordinary-sounding English statement for which it is a reasonable symbolic translation. Indicate what each of the statement letters abbreviates.

   a. $\sim P \supset Q$
   b. $T \lor (Q \supset \sim P)$
   c. $\sim (P \& \sim R)$
   d. $(P \& R) \supset \sim S$
   e. $R \supset (P \lor Q)$
   f. $P \equiv (R \& S)$
   g. $\sim P \lor (S \& \sim R)$
   h. $\sim P \equiv \sim Q$

2. Symbolize the following using the suggested notation. *P*: 'Peter plays'; *T*: 'Tanya plays'; *H*: 'Helen studies'; *R*: 'Roger studies'.

   a. Peter will play if Tanya plays.

   b. Either Tanya won't play or Peter will.

   c. If Peter plays, then Tanya won't.

   d. Helen won't study if Tanya plays.

   e. Unless Tanya plays, Peter won't play.

   f. Roger will study only if Helen will.

   g. If Peter or Tanya plays and Helen studies, then Roger will study.

3. Symbolize each of the following; indicate what your statement letters abbreviate. If you think a statement is vague or ambiguous, indicate why.

   a. The world is a nasty place, but I like it anyway.

   b. If Sam drinks, everybody drinks.

   c. Neither Oklahoma nor Kansas won the tournament.

   d. If John says he is telling the truth then he is a liar, but if William says that he is telling the truth, he probably is.

   e. No more than one of Peter, Ruth, and Helen did it.

   f. "If neither the dependent nor the dependent's spouse is required to file, but they file a joint return to get a refund of all tax withheld, then you may claim him (or her) if the other four tests are met." (*Instructions for Form 1040*, Internal Revenue Service)

   g. "Consider yourself single if on December 31 you were unmarried or separated from your spouse and you do not qualify for another filing status." (*ibid*.)

   h. If both inputs are high, the AND gate gives a high output; otherwise, the output is low.

   i. If either input is high, the OR gate gives a high output; if both inputs are low, the output is low.

4. For each of the following arguments, find the premises and the conclusion and give the symbolic logical form of the argument. Indicate what each of your statement letters abbreviates.

   a. If I spend the summer at home, I can get a job only if I have a car. But if I spend the summer at the Cape, either I get a job there or my parents will have to support me. But my parents won't support me and I won't have a car. So I guess I'll be working at the Cape this summer.

   b. If his chances of getting into medical school are not to be diminished, Jim will take the course pass/fail or he will not do poorly. For if the course is difficult, Jim will take it pass/fail. But if the course is not difficult, he will take it for a letter grade. If he takes it for a letter grade and does poorly, his GPA will be lowered. If his GPA is lowered, his chances at getting into medical school will be diminished.

*2.5 ALTERNATIVE NOTATION SYSTEMS

There are a number of alternative symbols for the five statement connectives of SL. In general, notation for the logical connectives and a number of mathematical operation symbols can be grouped into two general systems. We have been using an **infix** system, which places the connective *between* its immediate components. Thus, we symbolize 'John and William are foolish' as J & W, placing the & symbol roughly where the English 'and' occurs. In mathematics, placing the arithmetical operations of addition, subtraction, etc. between the two *operands*, e.g. 2 + 4, is similarly an infix notation. The second system is **outfix** notation, which places the connective or operation symbol either before or after the immediate components (operands). Negation, of course, is always an outfix symbol.

The principal outfix logical notation is called **Polish notation** after its originator Jan Lucasiewicz, an important logician of the post-World War I period.[12] In Polish notation, capital letter symbols are used for each of the five connectives, and lowercase letters are used as sentence letters. The connective symbols are:

Disjunction	A
Conjunction	K
Negation	N
Conditional	C
Biconditional	E

Lower case letters p, q, r, etc. are used as statement letters. The Polish system symbolizes statements *without* the use of parentheses, because the connective precedes its component(s). Here are some examples:

Infix notation	**Polish notation**
$P \& Q$	$K\,p\,q$
$P \lor Q$	$A\,p\,q$
$P \supset (Q \equiv R)$	$C\,p\,E\,q\,r$
$\sim(R \lor S)$	$N\,A\,r\,s$
$\sim R \lor (S \equiv \sim T)$	$A\,N\,r\,E\,s\,N\,t$

---

[12]See A. N. Prior, *Formal Logic* (Oxford: Oxford University Press, 1955) for details.

Polish notation takes some getting used to, but it makes perfectly good sense and has the advantage of avoiding parentheses without ambiguity in long, complex expressions. It is also immediately clear which connectives are major and which subsidiary, so truth tables are quite easy to work out in this system. Some calculator manufacturers use a variant called **reverse Polish notation** to enter data for computation. In the reverse form, the connective or operator *follows*, rather than precedes the components or operands.

As we will see in chapter 12, when we study an electronic calculator, there are very good reasons to prefer reversed *outfix* notation systems for numerical data and operation symbols. For example, the expression 4 × 8 in reverse outfix notation is 4 8 × and the expression 2 × ((43 + 14) − 21) would appear in reverse outfix notation as:

2 43 14 + 21 − ×

If you have used a pocket calculator, you will know that this computation usually requires several stages that are held in memory. But with reverse outfix notation, the entire calculation can be entered at once.

Other symbols commonly used in *infix notational systems* are given in the following table:

Name	Symbol used in this text	Alternatives
Disjunction	A ∨ B	(no alternatives)
Conjunction	A & B	AB, A ∧ B, A · B
Negation	~A	− A, ¬A, $\overline{A}$
Conditional	A ⊃ B	A \ B, A → B
Biconditional	A ≡ B	A ↔ B

EXERCISES 2.5

1. Symbolize each of the following in Polish notation:

   a. $\sim P \supset Q$

   b. $T \vee (Q \supset \sim P)$

   c. $\sim (P \ \& \sim R)$

   d. $(P \ \& \ R) \supset \sim S$

   e. $R \supset (P \vee Q)$

   f. $P \equiv (R \ \& \ S)$

   g. $\sim P \vee (S \ \& \sim R)$

   h. $\sim P \equiv \sim Q$

3

Statement Logic: Validity

*T*his chapter gives a precise characterization of *validity*, the key logical concept. Along the way we will also study various other logical properties and relations for SL statements. By the end of the chapter you will know three methods—and their limitations—for testing arguments for validity, and you will have learned how to apply these methods to the task of answering questions based upon sets of information.

3.1 VALUATIONS

Before we can study a precise characterization of validity and other logical properties and relations involving SL statements, we need to review several preliminary concepts. Recall that each symbolic SL statement has a *truth table*, which is just a display of all possible combinations of truth-values of the component atomic statements and a tabulation of the truth-value of the statement in each case. Across each row of the truth table, then, are the particular truth-values for each atomic component of the given statement. Such assignments of truth-values are called **valuations**. Here is a general definition of this term:

Valuation A **valuation** *is the result of matching* one *of the two truth-values, true (T) or false (F), with each of a group of atomic SL statements.*

As an example, look at the third row in the truth table for the statement $P \vee ((Q \supset \sim R) \equiv S)$:

P	Q	R	S	T	$\sim R$	$Q \supset \sim R$	$(Q \supset \sim R) \equiv S$	$P \vee ((Q \supset \sim R) \equiv S)$
T	T	T	F	T	F	F	T	T

The valuation represented by this row in the truth table is

P	Q	R	S	T
T	T	T	F	T

that is, the assigned truth-value of P, Q, R, and T is **T**, and the assigned truth-value of S is **F**. On this valuation, the statement $P \vee ((Q \supset \sim R) \equiv S)$ is, as the table shows, true.

It will often be useful to be able to refer to particular valuations; the lowercase Greek letters α (alpha) and β (beta), sometimes with subscripts (α_1), will be used for this purpose. A particular valuation may be as simple as a match of a truth-value with a single statement letter or as complex as the match of truth-values with all possible statement letters. The range of any given valuation will be explicitly stated or will be clear from the context.

Since truth tables are by this point fairly familiar, it may be easiest to remember that a valuation of the atomic components of a statement is represented by a row of **T**'s and **F**'s underneath the statement letters that are components of the statement. For example, here are the first two rows in a truth table involving four statement letters.

	P	Q	R	S	. . .
α:	T	T	T	T	
β:	T	T	T	F	

Valuation α matches the truth-value 'true' with all of the four statement letters; valuation β matches 'true' with P, Q, and R, and matches 'false' with S. In general, **an atomic SL statement A is true** on a valuation α just in case α matches 'true' (**T**) with A; **an atomic SL statement A is false** on a valuation α

just in case α matches 'false' (**F**) with A. So, P, Q, and R are all true on both α and β, whereas S is true on α and false on β.

Utilizing the notion of valuation, we can summarize the conditions under which an SL statement is true or false:

---

*An SL statement is **true** on any valuation α of its atomic components (and possibly other atomic statements) just in case:*

1. *If the statement is atomic, α matches it with **T**;*
2. *If it is a negation, $\sim$**A**, α matches **A** with **F**;*
3. *If it is a conjunction **A** & **B**, α matches both **A** and **B** with **T**;*
4. *If it is a disjunction **A** $\vee$ **B**, α matches either **A** or **B** with **T**;*
5. *If it is a conditional **A** $\supset$ **B**, α either matches **A** with **F** or **B** with **T**;*
6. *If it is a biconditional **A** $\equiv$ **B**, both **A** and **B** have the same truth-value on α.*

*If a statement is not true on α, then it is **false** on α.*

The advantage of this compact definition of the truth-conditions for SL statements is that every possible SL statement is covered by the six conditions. As we saw in chapter 2, such definitions allow a complex case to be handled in terms of its simpler subcases. To see this, let's figure out the truth-value of the SL statement

$$R \equiv [W \vee (S \supset \sim P)]$$

on the following valuation

	P	R	W	S	Q
α_1:	T	F	F	T	T

Note that α_1 gives a truth-value to the atomic statement Q, which is *not* a component of the compound statement in question; since that portion of the valuation is irrelevant to the truth-value of the statement we are evaluating, we ignore it. The statement is a biconditional, since the biconditional symbol is its major connective. Thus, the truth-value of $R \equiv [W \vee (S \supset \sim P)]$ depends on whether $W \vee (S \supset \sim P)$ is **F** on α_1, since R is **F** on α_1. Now $W \vee (S \supset \sim P)$ is a disjunction, so the truth-value of $W \vee (S \supset \sim P)$ depends on whether either W or $S \supset \sim P$ is **T** on α_1. Since W is **F**, we must evaluate $S \supset \sim P$. Since both S and P are **T**, $S \supset \sim P$ is **F** on α_1. So $W \vee (S \supset \sim P)$ is **F**, and, so, the entire statement $R \equiv [W \vee (S \supset \sim P)]$ is **T**, since its immediate components are both **F**, and hence the statement is true on α_1.

So far we have spoken of the truth-value of specific statements on valuations, but now we will generalize a bit and talk about the truth-value of a number of statements on a particular valuation. Clearly, a statement **A** can have a truth-value on a valuation α if and only if α matches truth-values with every one of **A**'s atomic components; otherwise the truth-value of **A** would be *undefined* on valuation α. To facilitate the discussion of the truth-values of several statements on valuations, we will use the notion of a valuation of the atomic components of a **set** of statements.[1] We take a set to be a collection of any number of objects, and we allow for the possibility, which may seem odd at first, that a set may not have any members. Such a set is called the **null** or **empty set**. The sets of principal interest here, however, will be sets of statements like the following:

$$\{P, Q \vee R, R \equiv [W \vee (S \supset \sim P)]\}$$

Sets are customarily designated either by specifying some property that all members of the set have, e.g., 'The set of all SL statements appearing on this page' or by a list of the members of the set, as displayed above. When a list is used, the members are separated by commas and the list is enclosed in curved brackets (sometimes called 'set brackets'). An empty set might be indicated by means of { }, that is, a set without any members.

If a valuation α matches truth-values with *all* of the atomic components of the members of a set of statements, then every member of the set will clearly have a truth-value on α. Such a valuation can be represented as a row in the truth table for all of the atomic components of the members of the set. For example, valuation α_1 above gives truth-values to all of the atomic components of the members of the set that was listed $\{P, Q \vee R, R \equiv [W \vee (S \supset \sim P)]\}$. Thus, each member has a truth-value on α_1:

Member statement	Truth-value on α_1
P	true
$Q \vee R$	true
$R \equiv [W \vee (S \supset \sim P)]$	true

Given the relation between truth table rows and valuations, it should be clear that the number of possible different valuations to n atomic statements is 2^n.

---

[1]Sets are extensively discussed in chapter 8.

Summary

In this section we have discussed the notion of **valuation**, which is a matching of truth-values with atomic components. Using these valuations, we defined the truth-conditions for all SL statements.

We also saw how members of a **set** of statements might have truth-values on a valuation providing that all of the atomic components of the members of the set are given truth-values on that valuation.

EXERCISES 3.1

1. Determine the truth-value of each of the following statements on a valuation on which P and Q are **T**, and R and S are **F**.

   a. $P \vee (Q \& R)$

   b. $P \equiv (R \equiv S)$

   c. $\sim S \vee (Q \supset R)$

   d. $\sim [R \vee (Q \vee S)]$

   e. $P \vee [\sim P \vee (Q \supset R)]$

   f. $R \& [P \supset (S \vee Q)]$

   g. $[R \equiv (S \& P)] \vee Q$

2. Is there some shortcut available when evaluating the truth-value of statements like a, c, e, and g above? Is there a shortcut available when evaluating the truth-value of statements like f above?

*3. Suppose we are using only the connectives $\vee$ and $\sim$ (which are adequate to represent all SL statements, as was shown in section 2.3). In place of truth tables, one can think about these two connectives in terms of a set of rules that use two special letters, t and f. The rules for each connective are:

$$\vee \text{ rules: } t \vee t = t \qquad \sim \text{ rules: } \sim t = f$$
$$t \vee f = t \qquad \qquad \sim f = t$$
$$f \vee t = t$$
$$f \vee f = f$$

Based on these rules, try to formulate a set of instructions that would allow someone ignorant of logic to determine the truth-value of an SL statement on any valuation, so long as the statement contains only the two connectives $\sim$ and $\vee$. Try your instructions out on a friend to be sure that they work. There is a hint in a footnote, but first try the problem without looking at the hint.[2]

---

[2]Hint: The instructions should begin by substituting the letter t for any statement letter true on the valuation, and the letter f for any statement letter false on the valuation.

3.2 VALIDITY AND OTHER LOGICAL PROPERTIES AND RELATIONS

In chapter 1 we said that an argument is **valid** if and only if its conclusion cannot be false when all of its premises are true. Consider the following SL argument:

Either that is Peter or Quentin.

It isn't Quentin.

So it must be Peter.

In symbols:

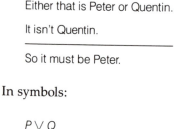

$P \lor Q$

$\sim Q$

P

According to the general definition of validity, if this argument is valid, then under any circumstances that the premises 'Either that is Peter or Quentin' $(P \lor Q)$ and 'It isn't Quentin' $(\sim Q)$ are true, the conclusion 'It must be Peter' (P) must be true as well.

We can put this another way, using the notion of valuations that was introduced in the previous section, and give a precise definition of **validity** for SL arguments:

Validity An SL argument is **valid** just in case any valuation on which all of its premises are true also makes its conclusion true.

Truth tables provide a straightforward procedure for determining whether an argument is valid or not once the argument has been put into symbols. We call this procedure, outlined below, the **truth table test for validity**.

Steps in the Truth Table Test for Validity

1. Determine the atomic components of the premises and the conclusion.
2. Write them in a horizontal row, followed by the premises of the argument, and, last, the conclusion.
3. Draw a line underneath this row of statements.

4. Formulate the truth table, and calculate the truth value of the premises and conclusion for each row.[3]

5. Find the rows in the table (if any) in which the conclusion is **F**.

6. Is there a **T** under every premise in any such row?

7. If the answer is yes, the argument is not valid (i.e., it is invalid).

8. If there are no rows in which the conclusion is **F**, or the answer to step 6 is no, the argument is valid.

Here is the truth table for the argument above:

P	Q	$P \lor Q$	$\sim Q$	P
T	T	T	F	T
T	F	T	T	T
F	T	T	F	F*
F	F	F	T	F*

Note that even though the conclusion P is an atomic component, it is listed again at the end of the table. Doing this bit of extra work makes finding the rows in which the conclusion is false much easier. The rows in which the conclusion P is **F** are marked with a *. In neither of them are both premises **T**, so the argument is *valid*.

The truth table test has several important features. First, it is clearly a *formal test* of validity. That is, any argument having the same *form* as the one above will clearly also be valid; the particular statements or statement letters that compose the argument are not important. Only the arrangement of the statements and connectives matters for validity. To see this point clearly, just rewrite the argument using 'Sue gets an A in Physics' for P and 'Her parents will be angry' for Q and try the truth table test on the symbolic version of the new argument.

Another important feature of the truth table method to test validity is that it is **mechanical**: for any SL argument, the instructions can be followed, one by one, *by rote*, and a definite answer to the question of validity will result in a predictable and finite number of steps. These instructions can be called an **algorithm** (the official name for such mechanical procedures) for deter-

---

[3]This set of instructions does not require you to write down the *components* of each statement being evaluated in the truth table, as we did in chapter 2. Truth tables become long and complex if all components are entered, but you might do this anyway until you are skilled at working truth tables for more than one statement.

mining validity in SL. This is not the first algorithm that has appeared in this book; can you think of another?

The study of algorithms is of vital importance to logic and to computing, and chapter 11 will discuss algorithms in detail. At this point, it is only necessary for you to notice that the truth table test does have the essential algorithmic characteristic and to compare it to a nonalgorithmic procedure, for example, translating from English into SL symbols. Despite the various hints that were given about translation, a great deal of judgment is still required to correctly represent the logical form of a statement or argument in SL. The formulation of an algorithm for English-to-SL translation is a subject of intense study in linguistics and computer science. As yet, however, there is no such algorithm.[4]

The only possible complication in applying the truth table test for validity is the rather staggering recordkeeping involved in working out truth tables for more than three or four statement letters. Since many arguments have numerous statement letters, we will discuss other methods of testing for validity later on. But the instructions given above apply in precisely the same manner no matter how complicated a truth table may be. For example, here is an argument, involving three statement letters, which was discussed at the end of chapter 2.

$\sim D \supset W$

$W \supset R$

$R \supset \sim D$

___

$\sim D$

D	R	W	$\sim D \supset W$	$W \supset R$	$R \supset \sim D$	$\sim D$
T	T	T	T	T	F	F*
T	T	F	T	T	F	F*
T	F	T	T	F	T	F*
T	F	F	T	T	T	F*
F	T	T	T	T	T	T
F	T	F	F	T	T	T
F	F	T	T	F	T	T
F	F	F	F	T	T	T

___

[4]See, for example, Terry Winograd and Fernando Flores, *Understanding Computers and Cognition* (Reading, Mass.: Addison-Wesley, 1987).

The rows in which the conclusion ~D is **F** are marked with an *. Scanning them reveals that in the fourth row, all of the premises are *T* and the conclusion is **F**. So, the argument is *invalid*.

You will be given an opportunity to try your hand at the truth table test in the exercises.

You may have wondered about the parenthetical phrase 'if any' in instruction 5 in the algorithm for testing validity through truth tables. This phrase suggests that, on some occasions, a conclusion will not ever be false, no matter what the truth-value of the premises of the argument. The class of SL statements that share this trait of never being false is very important. Such a statement is called a **tautology**, and can be defined in terms of valuation:

Tautology An SL statement is a **tautology** *just in case it is true on every valuation of its atomic components.*

Perhaps the classic tautology is the statement of the form **A** $\lor$ **~A**, which even the ancient logicians recognized. It and two other classics are listed below, with their historic titles:

(1) **A** $\lor$ **~A**   the law of excluded middle

(2) **A** $\supset$ **A**   the law of identity

(3) **~(A & ~A)**   the law of noncontradiction

Tautologies may seem particularly magical since they are true just because of the way in which they are constructed. But ordinary language versions are entirely without informational value. Take the simple statement 'It will rain'. Such a statement might be very informative, especially if you are planning a picnic or to go to the beach. But

It will either rain or it won't

is unhelpful in any circumstance. This statement is true every day, everywhere. It covers all possible cases, as its truth table shows:

P	P $\lor$ ~P
T	T
F	T

The other tautologies, (2) and (3), are no better at providing information. 'If Peter is coming, then he is coming', certainly doesn't say much about whether he is coming or not. And 'It is not both the case that Peter is coming and he isn't' won't take one very far, unless someone else has fallen into a contradiction (see below).

Even though tautologies are devoid of content and, therefore, are trivial statements, finding tautologies can be an important enterprise because of the close relationship between tautologies and valid arguments. To facilitate the search, one uses truth tables. Any statement that comes out **T** in every row of its truth table is a tautology. Here are truth tables for two statements as illustrations of this method:

P	Q	$(\sim P \,\&\, \sim Q) \equiv \sim(P \lor Q)$
T	T	T
T	F	T
F	T	T
F	F	T

The statement $(\sim P \,\&\, \sim Q) \equiv \sim(P \lor Q)$ is a tautology because its truth table shows that it is not false on any valuation.

P	Q	$(P \supset Q) \equiv (Q \supset P)$
T	T	T
T	F	F
F	T	F
F	F	T

In this case, the statement $(P \supset Q) \equiv (Q \supset P)$ is clearly *not a tautology* since it is **F** on two rows of the truth table.

The opposite of a tautology is a **contradiction**. We can formally define this concept as follows:

Contradiction *An SL statement is a **contradiction** just in case it is false on every valuation of its atomic components.*

Not surprisingly, any statement of the form **A** & ~**A** is a contradiction. On a truth table, if a statement is **F** on every row, it is a contradiction.

There is one possiblity remaining for SL statements: those that are neither tautologies nor contradictions. Such statements are said to be **contingent**.

Contingent Statements An SL statement is *contingent* just in case it is true on at least one valuation of its atomic components and false on at least one other.

Scanning the truth table reveals contingency; look for a **T** row *and* an **F** row, as in the following statement.

P	Q	R	(P & Q) ∨ ~R
T	T	T	T
T	T	F	T	←
T	F	T	F	←
T	F	F	T
F	T	T	F
F	T	F	T
F	F	T	F
F	F	F	T

Most ordinary statements people actually make are contingent; they can be true or false. Their truth-value is thus a function of how things are rather than how the statement is logically constructed. Note that all atomic statements are thus contingent, as are their negations.

An important logical relation that holds between statements is **truth-functional equivalence**. For ease of use we shorten this term to 'equivalence' or 'SL equivalence', but we will always mean 'equivalent in the truth-functional sense'. Two SL statements are equivalent when they have the same truth-table, that is, when they are true or false under the same circumstances. A precise definition of equivalence is

---

Equivalence Two statements are SL *equivalent* if they have the same truth-value on every valuation.

Statements that are equivalent are interchangeable from a logical point of view, so the concept of equivalence is a powerful notion. We have skirted around equivalence in several previous discussions. For example, during the discussion of the conditional **A** ⊃ **B**, it was pointed out that it has the same truth table as both ~**A** ∨ **B** and ~(**A** & ~**B**). To be more precise, we can now say that such statements are equivalent.

If **A** and **B** are equivalent statements, then the statement **A** ≡ **B** is a tautology; that is, **A** and **B** have the same truth conditions, so they will have the same truth-value on any valuation. Thus, when **A** and **B** are equivalent, every valuation will make the biconditional **A** ≡ **B** true. This fact has led some writers to refer to the biconditional connective as 'equivalence'. But to do so mixes categories; the biconditional forms compound statements out of its components whereas equivalence is a relation between statements. For example:

(a) Paper will burn just in case sufficient heat and oxygen are present.

(b) 'It can't not rain tomorrow' is equivalent to 'It will rain tomorrow'.

To test for equivalence using a truth table, a table is assembled with the two statements side by side. If the two statements have exactly the same column of **T**'s and **F**'s under them, they are equivalent; if they differ, even in a single row, they are not equivalent. Here are two tables: the first for equivalent statements, the second for two statements that are not equivalent:

P	*Q*	*P* & *Q*	~(~*Q* ∨ ~*P*)
T	T	T	T
T	F	F	F
F	T	F	F
F	F	F	F

P & *Q* and ~(~*Q* ∨ ~*P*) are equivalent

P	*Q*	*P* ⊃ *Q*	*Q* ⊃ *P*	
T	T	T	T	
T	F	F	T	←
F	T	T	F	←
F	F	T	T	

P ⊃ *Q* and *Q* ⊃ *P* are *not* equivalent

Note that all tautologies are logically equivalent to each other, since all tautologies are true on every valuation to their atomic components. Hence the two tautologies

$$P \supset (Q \supset P) \qquad R \supset (S \supset R)$$

are equivalent, even though they involve different statement letters. They will both come out true on any valuation to the atomic statements P, Q, R, and S. Similarly, all contradictions are equivalent as well.

You may well wonder whether the relation of truth-functional equivalence between statements captures the notion of sameness of meaning. This question brings us again to the ways in which the logical principles we are studying are like a model of related principles in ordinary language. For there is a sense in which, for example, the two statements below have the same meaning:

Either you clean your room or you can't go to the movies.

If you have permission to go to the movies, then you have cleaned your room.

There is also a sense in which they don't. The emphasis in the first statement is different from that in the second; the first sounds like an order, the second is rather more descriptive and neutral. But we ignore these shadings when we translate into SL notation; their SL versions *are* equivalent (i.e., $C \lor {\sim}M$ and $M \supset C$, respectively). Thus, we are not saying that all statements that would be represented in SL as tautologous necessarily have the same meaning in English. It would be clearly be odd to say that 'Either it will rain or it won't' and 'Either Mary had her hair cut or she didn't' have the same meaning. But we do say that, in a logical sense, they are equivalent.

A number of SL equivalences are particularly useful to know, and we will make use of them over and over. The relationships listed below hold for any statements **A**, **B**, and **C** and, because of this generality, they are sometimes called **logical laws.**

1. Commutation: $(A \lor B) \equiv (B \lor A)$
   $(A \,\&\, B) \equiv (B \,\&\, A)$

2. Association: $[(A \lor B) \lor C] \equiv [A \lor (B \lor C)]$
   $[(A \,\&\, B) \,\&\, C] \equiv [A \,\&\, (B \,\&\, C)]$

3. Distribution: $[A \lor (B \,\&\, C)] \equiv [(A \lor B) \,\&\, (A \lor C)]$
   $[A \,\&\, (B \lor C)] \equiv [(A \,\&\, B) \lor (A \,\&\, C)]$

4. Double Negation Equivalence: ${\sim}{\sim}A \equiv A$

5. Contraposition: $(A \supset B) \equiv ({\sim}B \supset {\sim}A)$

6. Conditional Equivalence: $(A \supset B) \equiv ({\sim}A \lor B)$

7. Biconditional Equivalence: $(A \equiv B) \equiv [(A \supset B) \,\&\, (B \supset A)]$
   $(A \equiv B) \equiv [(A \,\&\, B) \lor ({\sim}A \,\&\, {\sim}B)]$

8. Exportation: $[(A \& B) \supset C] \equiv [A \supset (B \supset C)]$

9. Idempotence: $A \equiv (A \vee A)$
$A \equiv (A \& A)$

10. DeMorgan's Laws: $\sim(A \vee B) \equiv (\sim A \& \sim B)$
$\sim(A \& B) \equiv (\sim A \vee \sim B)$

11. Absorption: $(A \supset B) \equiv [A \supset (A \& B)]$

A few comments on this list may be helpful. As you can see, many of them convey basic facts about the operations of the connectives involved. Order makes no difference when $\vee$ or & is the only connective; such connectives are said to be commutative and associative (like the operations of addition and multiplication). When applied to a single statement, disjunction and conjunction do not add anything; that is the idempotence property. The distribution principle and DeMorgan's laws show how the two connectives function together. And we commented earlier that conditionals may well be thought of as 'not . . . or' disjunctions and we noted the 'double conditional' feature of the biconditional. The conditional and biconditional principles record these facts. The double negation law contains the essential fact about negation; it reverses the truth-value of its immediate component, so applying it twice returns one to the starting point.

Summary

In summary, we introduced a number of logical properties and relations in this section: **validity, tautology, contradiction, contingent statement**, and **equivalence**.

We also discussed the **truth table test** to determine whether SL arguments are valid, and whether the other logical properties and relations hold. The test was formulated as an **algorithm** in the case of validity, that is, as a mechanical procedure that produces an answer in a predictable and finite number of steps.

We also presented a list of important logical equivalences in the form of logical laws that will be found over and over through the rest of the book.

EXERCISES 3.2

1. By means of truth tables, decide whether the following are valid or invalid.

   a. $P \supset \sim Q$

   $Q \supset \sim P$
   _____
   $P \equiv Q$

b. $Q \lor R$

$\sim Q$

R

c. $\sim(H \equiv R)$

$\sim H$

$\sim R$

d. $Q \& R$

$Q \lor \sim R$

Q

2. Check each of the following pairs to determine whether the statements are equivalent or not. Use truth tables.

a. $P \equiv Q$ $(P \& Q) \lor (\sim P \& \sim Q)$

b. $P \supset (Q \supset R)$ $(P \& Q) \supset R$

c. $P \supset Q$ $P \supset (P \& Q)$

d. $\sim(P \lor Q)$ $\sim P \& \sim Q$

3.3 THE SHORTCUT TEST AND TWO MORE LOGICAL PROPERTIES AND RELATIONS

The Shortcut Method

Since doing long truth tables is tedious, there is a **shortcut method** that can be used to determine whether statements are tautologies and whether arguments are valid. If we are testing a statement to see whether it is a tautology, all we are interested in is whether it *could be false* on any valuation, or row, of a truth table. As soon as we find that it can be false, we don't need the rest of the table; we don't need to investigate other valuations. On the other hand, if we could eliminate the possibility that the statement could be false, then it is clear that the statement is a tautology and we don't need the entire table. Out of such considerations comes the shortcut method.

You should know in advance that the shortcut method has, occasionally, no particular advantage over a full truth table; the structure of the statement (or statements in the case of arguments) determines its effectiveness. But here is a case where it works very well:

$P \supset (Q \supset \sim P)$

To determine by the shortcut method whether this statement is a tautology, we systematically search out the valuation (if any) on which the statement is false. Since the statement is a conditional, if it were false, then the antecedent P would have to be true and the consequent $Q \supset \sim P$ would have to be false, according to the truth-conditions for conditional statements, i.e.,

P	$\supset$	$(Q \supset \sim P)$
T	F	F

Is this a possibility? If so, since P is true, we know that $\sim P$ is false. Given that, the conditional $Q \supset \sim P$ could be false if Q were true.

P	$\supset$	$(Q$	$\supset$	$\sim P)$
T	F	T	F	F

And so we have found a valuation on which the statement is false, as follows:

P	Q	$P \supset (Q \supset \sim P)$
T	T	F

Thus, the statement is *not* a tautology. And we don't need to look at the remaining three rows of the truth table.

Here is another case:

$[P \supset (Q \supset R)] \supset [(P \& Q) \supset R]$

Any valuation of P, Q, and R that makes this statement false makes the antecedent $P \supset (Q \supset R)$ true and the consequent $(P \& Q) \supset R$ false (since the statement is a conditional).

$[P \supset (Q \supset R)]$	$\supset$	$[(P \& Q) \supset R]$
T	F	F

According to the truth-conditions for the conditional, P & Q is true and R false if $(P \mathbin{\&} Q) \supset R$ is false. So both P and Q are true.

P	Q	R	$[P \supset (Q \supset R)] \supset [(P \mathbin{\&} Q) \supset R]$				
T	T	F	T	F	T	F F	

But if P and Q are true and R is false, then the antecedent $P \supset (Q \supset R)$ is also false, and, hence, the whole statement is true.

P	Q	R	$[P \supset (Q \supset R)] \supset [(P \mathbin{\&} Q) \supset R]$				
T	T	F	T X̷ T	F F̷	T	F F	
			F	T			

Since there is no valuation on which $[P \supset (Q \supset R)] \supset [(P \mathbin{\&} Q) \supset R]$ is false, *it is a tautology.*

As you can see, the method works very well if the major connective is a conditional because there is only one case in which conditionals are false (true antecedent, false consequent). So too with disjunctions. But two cases immediately emerge for biconditionals, and three for conjunctions, so ruling out the possibility of a falsifying valuation becomes more difficult. On the other hand, if you manage to find a falsifying assignment, you can easily verify that the statement is false in this case, and the method will surely have saved some time. Be forewarned: to be able to use the shortcut method effectively, you really have to know the truth tables for the connectives.

When the shortcut method is applied to SL *arguments*, we look for a valuation on which the premises are all true and the conclusion is false. If successful, we have shown the argument to be invalid; if we fail, the argument is valid. As an example, let's take the following case from the end of chapter 2.

$O \equiv (W \mathbin{\&} V)$

$(V \mathbin{\&} K) \supset M$

$\sim M \mathbin{\&} \sim W$

$\sim O$

We are looking for a valuation of the atomic components K, O, M, V, and W on which the conclusion, $\sim O$, is false (and hence O is true) and all the premises are true.

K	O	M	V	W	$O \equiv W \,\& V)$	$(V \,\& K) \supset M$	$\sim M \,\& \sim W$	$\sim O$
?	?	?	?	?	T	T	T	F

Note that immediately it is clear that since O is true on such an assignment, W and V have to be true as well from the first premise.

K	O	M	V	W	$O \equiv (W \,\& V)$	$(V \,\& K) \supset M$	$\sim M \,\& \sim W$	$\sim O$
?	T	?	T	T	T	T	T	F

Discovering the truth-values for O, W, and V is just the kind of breakthrough that helps in the shortcut method. Now substitute those values in the other statements and see what happens; do they remain true? Note that the last premise, $\sim M \,\& \sim W$ cannot be true if W is true, and the second premise could be true or false, depending upon K and M.

K	O	M	V	W	$O \equiv (W \,\& V)$	$(V \,\& K) \supset M$	$\sim M \,\& \sim W$	$\sim O$
?	T	?	T	T	T	T	~~T~~	F
							F	

Even if both K and M were false, making the second premise true, the third premise cannot be true because of W.

K	O	M	V	W	$O \equiv (W \,\& V)$	$(V \,\& K) \supset M$	$\sim M \,\& \sim W$	$\sim O$
F	T	F	T	T	T	T	~~T~~	F
							F	

Thus, there is no possible valuation on which the premises are all true and the conclusion is false. Thus, the argument is *valid*.

Working through the shortcut method teaches quite a bit about validity. You can actually see why an argument is valid (if it is) by finding the points at which the falsehood of the conclusion conflicts with the assumption of the simultaneous truth of the premises. Here is another illustration, from the exercises in chapter 2:

> If I spend the summer at home, I can get a job only if I have a car. But if I spend the summer at the Cape, either I get a job there or my parents will have to support me. But my parents won't support me and I won't have a car. So I guess I'll be working at the Cape this summer.

The argument can be symbolized as follows:

$S \supset (E \supset C)$

$J \supset (D \lor P)$

$\sim P \mathbin{\&} \sim C$

_____

D

S:	I spend the summer at home
E:	I get a job at home
C:	I have a car
J:	I spend the summer at the Cape
P:	My parents will have to support me
D:	I get a job at the Cape

We begin by assuming that the conclusion D is false and the premises are all true on some valuation. This requires that both P and C are *false* because of the third premise $\sim P \mathbin{\&} \sim C$. Thus, we know that $D \lor P$ has to be false; hence, if the second premise $J \supset (D \lor P)$ is to be true on the valuation, J will have to be false. Now the question becomes: can $S \supset (E \supset C)$ be true on such a valuation? The answer is yes; just make either E or S (or both) false. So we have found a valuation on which the premises are true and the conclusion is false. Such assignments are called **counterexamples** to the argument.

The counterexample

C	D	E	J	P	S
F	F	F	F	F	F

Since working out the full truth table would have involved 64 lines (2^6), the shortcut method has obviously saved a great deal of work.

Consistency

Another important logical property, this time of *sets of statements*, is **consistency**.[5] The idea behind consistency is that all of the statements in a set can be true at the same time; they don't conflict with each other. Here is a more precise definition.

Consistency A set of SL statements is **consistent** just in case there is a valuation of all of the atomic components of the members of the set on which all members of the set are true. A set for which there is no such valuation is said to be **inconsistent**.

A few words about inconsistency. It is sometimes tempting to think that there always will be two members of an inconsistent set that directly contradict one another. That is, there will be a statement **A** and its negation ~**A** somewhere in an inconsistent set. Although such a set would be inconsistent, there are other patterns of inconsistency as well. For example, the set

$\{P \supset (Q \,\&\, R), P \supset \,\sim R, P\}$

is inconsistent. But there is no *direct* contradiction present. If this isn't clear to you, try to find a valuation of which all members of the set are true (a truth table will be found below).

Furthermore, it is not *simply* the presence of negation that makes a set inconsistent. For example, if the atomic statement P were removed from the above set, it would be a *consistent set*, even though it would still contain a statement with a negated component.

It is easy to show, however, that if none of the statements in a set of SL statements contain negated components, then the set will be consistent. To see this, imagine, in general, what such negation-free sets would look like. They consist of statement letters, and compounds of statement letters made with the four connectives $\supset$, &, $\vee$, and $\equiv$. Recall that the top row of any truth table assigns all **T**'s to the statement letters. And all two-place compounds of atomic statements are **T** in the top row; so, for any statements **A** and **B**,

A	B	A $\vee$ B	A & B	A $\supset$ B	A $\equiv$ B
T	T	T	T	T	T

---

[5]If you are unfamiliar with the basic theory of sets, or with the concept of an empty set, see chapter 8.

All negation-free compounds of true statements are **T**, even for the most complex statements. This same analysis clearly extends to sets in which more than one statement is involved. Since all of the members of a negation-free set are true on a valuation of **T** of all atomic components of its members, such a set is clearly consistent. Consequently, without occurrences of negation, a set will be consistent; but even when negation does occur, the set may still be consistent.

Inconsistency is a particularly important concept in information systems. When new information is added to an existing set of statements, or **data set**, as these are sometimes called, there is a danger that the *result* will be inconsistent. For example, suppose a data set consists of the following statements:

(1) John isn't eligible if he hasn't passed his courses.

(2) If John plays, then he must be in good standing.

(3) If John plays, then he has been issued a uniform.

(4) John has not been issued a uniform.

Now suppose the following statements are added to the above set:

(5) Either John plays or he withdraws from the university.

(6) Mary Smith is the team coach.

(7) Seventy students went out for the team.

(8) John did not withdraw from the university.

The set consisting of statements (1) through (4) is consistent, as is the set consisting of statements (5) through (8). However, the combined set containing statements (1) through (8) is inconsistent (see exercise 3.2.5). When confronted with an inconsistent set, it may be desirable to pare down the set until a *consistent kernel* or *subset* is reached. We can be assured that there will always be such a consistent kernel in any inconsistent set, although the kernel might be so small as to be practically useless.[6]

The worst such situation would be a set composed entirely of contradictions. The presence of any contradictory statement in a set will render the set inconsistent, of course, since contradictions are not true on any valuation. If a set consists entirely of contradictions, then the consistent kernel will be the result of extracting *every* member of the set. We would be left with the *empty set*, which is consistent by default.[7]

---

[6]A method for finding consistent kernels is found in section 3.4; also see section 3.5.

[7]Later on we will say that all *inconsistent* sets entail contradictions; since the empty set does not, it is also consistent in this sense by default. How a set without members satisfies the definition of consistency that all members are true on at least one valuation will be explained in chapter 6 when we study the truth-conditions of general statements.

A set can be tested for consistency by means of truth tables in an obvious manner. The table is built from all atomic components of all member statements, in the above case P, Q, and R. The member statements are listed in a line and then the table is worked out. If there is a row (i.e., a valuation) on which all members of the set are true, then the set is *consistent*. If there is no such row, then the set is *inconsistent*.

P	Q	R	$P \supset (Q \& R)$	$P \supset {\sim}R$	P
T	T	T	T	F	T
T	T	F	F	T	T
T	F	T	F	F	T
T	F	F	F	T	T
F	T	T	T	T	F
F	T	F	T	T	F
F	F	T	T	T	F
F	F	F	T	T	F

Clearly, this set is inconsistent; on every row at least one member is **F**.

Often the shortcut method is simpler. To work it, assume all members to be true and see whether a valuation emerges. If so, the set is consistent; if not, as in the case above, then the set is inconsistent.

There are two classes of arguments that, although they are valid, do not add anything to what we already know. The first class consists of arguments with tautologies as conclusions. As previously noted, tautologies cannot be false, so any argument with a tautologous conclusion is therefore valid, since there is no valuation on which the premises are all true and the conclusion is false. For example, any argument having the form

A_1

A_2

A_3

.

.

$B \lor {\sim}B$

is valid, no matter what statements A_1, A_2, A_3, . . . may be, because any statement of the form $B \lor {\sim}B$ is a tautology. Since tautologies lack informative content, as noted earlier, there isn't anything to learn from such arguments. Nevertheless, according to the definition of validity, they are valid.

A second class of unhelpful (but all too common) valid arguments consists of those with inconsistent premises. Since the premises cannot be true together, there is no possible way that the premises will be all true when the conclusion is false. The conclusion of an argument with inconsistent premises could even be a contradiction, and the argument would nonetheless be valid. In fact, this is how inconsistency is sometimes described: a set of statements is said to be inconsistent just in case an argument with those statements as premises and a contradiction like P & $\sim P$ as a conclusion would be valid. In other words, if we discover that an argument with a contradiction as a conclusion is valid, then we know that the premises of that argument form an inconsistent set.

Here is an example of an argument with inconsistent premises:

If John plays then he has been issued a uniform.

Either John plays or he withdraws from the university.

John has not been issued a uniform and he did not withdraw from the university.

John isn't playing.

This argument is valid because the premises cannot all be true, and if the conclusion were changed to 'John isn't playing and he is playing' (a contradiction) or to the irrelevant 'The moon is made of green cheese', the argument would remain valid.

Entailment

Finally, another way to talk about the relation between the premises and conclusion of a valid argument is to say that the set of the premises **entails** the conclusion. This important logical relation is defined in SL as follows:

Entailment *A set of SL statements* $\{A_1, A_2, A_3, \ldots, A_n\}$ ***entails*** *an SL statement B just in case there is no valuation on which B is false and all of the statements* $A_1, A_2, A_3, \ldots, A_n$ *are true. (Note: the set represented as* $\{A_1, A_2, A_3, \ldots, A_n\}$ *may be empty; in that case n would be 0.)*

Thus, if an SL argument is valid, its premises entail its conclusion, and if a set of statements entails a statement, then the corresponding argument— with the statements from the set as premises and the entailed statement as conclusion—is valid.

Although as we defined it, an *argument* must have at least one premise (and, of course, a conclusion), a set that entails a statement may be empty. This curious-sounding situation can occur when a statement is a tautology.

Every set entails any tautology, and all tautologies are even entailed by the empty set! So *entailment* is, one might say, the parent concept under which validity falls. Validity is a property of arguments; entailment is a relation between a (possibly) empty set and a statement; the set of the premises of valid arguments entail their conclusions.

We can test for entailment, just as we can for validity and invalidity, by means of either truth tables or the shortcut method. Either way, we seek to know whether all the members of the set can be true on a valuation (i.e., a row of a truth table) on which the statement in question is false. If this can be the case, then the purported entailment does not hold; if such cannot be the case, then the set entails the statement.

To look at a specific case, consider again the set from the previous section:

$$\{P, Q \vee R, R \equiv [W \vee (S \supset \sim P)]\}$$

We may ask whether this set entails the statement

$$R \supset (W \vee \sim S)$$

To find out, we seek a *counterexample*; if none exists, the entailment holds. As was the case in the discussion of validity, a counterexample is a valuation or row of a truth table on which the three statements in the set P, $Q \vee R$, and $R \equiv [W \vee (S \supset \sim P)]$ are true, and the statement $R \supset (W \vee \sim S)$ is false. Following the shortcut method, we can systematically search out the possibility of a counterexample by supposing that there is a valuation on which $R \supset (W \vee \sim S)$ is false. This would require that R is true and that $W \vee \sim S$ is false. But then W would be false and S would be true. When these truth-values are applied to $R \equiv [W \vee (S \supset \sim P)]$, it turns out that this statement can be true only on such a valuation if $\sim P$ is true. But then P would be false. In order for $R \supset (W \vee \sim S)$ to be false, then at least one of the statements in the set would have to be false as well. Thus, the entailment holds; there is no counterexample.

Summary

We introduced a **shortcut method** for testing arguments for validity that consists of a systematic search for a **counterexample**, that is, a valuation on which the premises are true and the conclusion is false. The shortcut method is not mechanical, like the truth table method, but it usually saves time. We also showed the method applicable to testing for other logical properties and relations.

Several new concepts were also introduced in this section:

A set of SL statements is **consistent** just in case all members of the set are true on some valuation of all of the atomic components of the members of the set.

A set of SL statements $\{A_1, A_2, A_3, \ldots, A_n\}$ **entails** a statement **B** just in case there is no valuation on which **B** is false and all of the statements $A_1, A_2, A_3, \ldots, A_n$ are true. (Note: the set may be empty.)

We discussed several important facts, summarized below, concerning the connections between the SL logical properties and relations; others will be covered in the exercises.

1. If

   A_1

   A_2

   A_3

   .

   A_n
   —
   B

   is a valid argument, for statements $A_1, A_2, A_3, \ldots, A_n$ and **B**, then the set $\{A_1, A_2, A_3, \ldots, A_n\}$ entails **B**.

2. If a set of statements is inconsistent, then the conjunction of the members of the set is a contradiction.

3. If any member of a set is a contradiction, then the set is inconsistent.

4. The negation of a tautology is a contradicton, and vice versa.

5. If a set of statements is inconsistent, then the set entails every statement.

6. If a set of statements entails a statement and its negation, then that set is inconsistent.

7. If a set of statements $\{A_1, A_2, A_3, \ldots, A_n\}$ entails **B**, then a statement having the form:

   $$(A_1 \,\&\, A_2 \,\&\, A_3 \,\&\, \ldots \,\&\, A_n) \supset B$$

   is a tautology.

8. Every tautology is entailed by every set of statements.

9. If an argument has inconsistent premises, then it is valid.

10. A valid argument with a contradiction as a conclusion has inconsistent premises.

11. If a set **S** entails a statement **A**, then any set containing all the members of **S** also entails **A**.

12. If an argument is valid, the set containing the premises and the negation of the conclusion is inconsistent.

Take particular note of this final fact; it forms the basis of the truth tree method for testing for validity, which we will study in the next section.

EXERCISES 3.3

1. Use the shortcut method to determine whether the following are valid. (If you want more practice, try the shortcut method on Exercises 3.2.1 and 3.2.2.)

   a. $P \supset (Q \lor R)$

      $R \supset S$

      _____

      $P \lor S$

   b. $P \equiv (Q \mathbin{\&} S)$

      Q

      _____

      $P \supset S$

   c. $\sim(R \lor S) \mathbin{\&} P$

      $\sim P \lor S$

      _____

      R

   d. Q

      R

      _____

      $R \supset \sim R$

   e. If his chances of getting into medical school are not to be diminished, Jim will take the course pass/fail or he will not do poorly. For if the course is difficult, Jim will take it pass/fail. But if the course is not difficult, he will take it for a letter grade. If he takes it for a letter grade and does poorly, his GPA will be lowered. If his GPA is lowered, his chances at getting into medical school will be diminished.

2. Using the shortcut method, determine whether the following are tautologies:

   a. $P \supset (P \lor Q)$

   b. $(P \lor Q) \equiv (Q \lor P)$

   c. $(P \lor Q) \mathbin{\&} (Q \lor P)$

   d. $[P \supset (Q \supset \sim R)] \supset [R \supset (P \supset \sim Q)]$

   e. $\sim(P \mathbin{\&} Q) \mathbin{\&} P$

   f. $(P \supset Q) \mathbin{\&} (P \supset \sim Q)$

   g. $(Q \supset P) \mathbin{\&} (\sim Q \supset P)$

   h. $[(P \supset \sim Q) \mathbin{\&} \sim P] \supset Q$

   i. $P \supset (P \supset P)$

3. Are the following sets consistent? Use truth tables or the shortcut method.

   a. $\{P \vee Q, \sim Q, P \supset \sim P\}$

   b. $\{P \vee (Q \& R), R \supset P, \sim Q\}$

   c. $\{\sim(P \vee Q), P \& Q\}$

   d. $\{\sim(P \supset \sim P), \sim(Q \supset \sim Q), \sim(P \vee Q)\}$

4. Show that the set of statements (1) through (8) on p. 89 is inconsistent. Find a consistent kernel containing statements from both original sets, and give a valuation on which the members of the kernel are all true.

5. Give reasons why each of the following is true:

   a. If a set of statements is inconsistent, then the conjunction of the members of the set is a contradiction.

   b. If a set of statements is inconsistent, then the set entails every statement.

   c. If a set of statements $\{A_1, A_2, A_3, \ldots, A_n\}$ entails B, then the statement $(A_1 \& A_2 \& A_3 \& \ldots \& A_n) \supset B$ is a tautology.

   d. If an argument is valid, the set containing the premises and the negation of the conclusion is inconsistent.

3.4 TRUTH TREES

Once you have constructed even a single truth table for three or more statement letters, you know the principal shortcoming of the method: truth tables are tedious. But, as we have seen, truth tables do provide a mechanical procedure for the determination of all of the SL logical properties and relations, so their virtues are not to be lightly dismissed. The shortcut method, on the other hand, saves time in most cases, but it is not algorithmic.[8]

In this section we will study a technique that retains the virtues of truth tables but not, so to speak, their vices. Constructing *truth trees* is an algorithmic method to test for SL validity, tautologies, contradictions, contingency, consistency, and entailment, and it is much less tedious than constructing truth tables and more thorough than using the shortcut method.[9]

The basic idea behind truth trees is that one can search out in a systematic way all of the valuations on which the members of a given set of SL statements are true, if there are any such assignments. If there aren't, then that fact will become quite clear as the method is applied. Either way, truth

---

[8]See chapter 11.

[9]Truth trees were first announced in Richard Jeffrey, *Formal Logic: Its Scope and Limits* (New York: McGraw-Hill, 1967). Jeffrey credits Raymond Smullyan with the original version, and there are other important precursors as well. See Jeffrey's preface for details.

trees pronounce on the consistency or inconsistency of sets of statements. But recall from the last section that all of the SL logical properties and relations (such as validity and entailment) can be defined in terms of consistency and inconsistency; this possibility gives the truth tree method its generality.

Like grammatical trees, truth trees are formed by decomposing compound statements into tree-like structures. However, since the decomposition does not always follow the lines of immediate components, as is the case with grammatical trees, *it will be important to keep the two kinds of trees quite distinct in your mind.* The decomposition in truth trees follows truth dependency or truth-conditions.

In the truth tree method, there are decomposition rules for each connective. The rules are perhaps easiest to understand (and remember) if we refer back to truth tables:

We begin with disjunction:

A	B	A ∨ B
T	T	T
T	F	T
F	T	T
F	F	F

One way to think of the table for disjunction is that there are essentially *two* ways for a statement of the form **A** ∨ **B** to be true: either **A** is true or **B** is true. Thus, the truth of **A** is a sufficient (but nonnecessary) condition for the truth of **A** ∨ **B**, as is the truth of **B** as well. In either case, the other disjunct can have either truth-value. We can display this rule as follows:

A	B	A ∨ B
T	T	T
T	F	T
F	T	T
F	F	F

That there are exactly two ways for a statement of the form **A** $\lor$ **B** to be true is reflected in the table above; the two cases are labeled 1 and 2, and the false case is shaded.

In truth trees we indicate the sufficient conditions for truth by means of *branches*. Each sufficient condition constitutes a separate branch. The truth tree rule for disjunction, then, is this:

Disjunction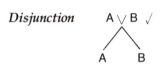

Each branch under a statement thus represents a possible way (i.e., a sufficient condition) in which that statement can be true; that is why the decomposition into branches is said to follow truth dependency. Thus, the left branch represents case 1 in the truth table above, and the right branch indicates case 2.

Next, conjunction. Clearly there is only one way to make a conjunction true: both conjuncts must be true. So, the sufficient condition for the truth of a conjunction is the truth of both conjuncts. By shading the false cases, the truth table for a statement of the form **A** & **B** below reflects this:

A	B	A & B
T	T	T
T	F	F
F	T	F
F	F	F

Thus, the tree rule for a conjunction will have only *one* branch, since there is only one way to make a conjunction true:

Conjunction   A & B $\checkmark$
                   A
                   B

The conditional, like disjunction, can be true in two ways, as this table indicates:

A	B	A ⊃ B
T	T	T
T	F	F
F	T	T
F	F	T

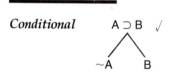

In case 1 the antecedent **A** is false, and in case 2 the consequent **B** is true. As in a disjunction, in case 1 or 2, the other component can have either truth-value, and there is one valuation in common (both true). That a false antecedent or a true consequent is a sufficient condition for the truth of a conditional was discussed in some detail in section 2.2; there we noted the relations with disjunction that are apparent here as well. The truth tree rule for the conditional looks like this:

Conditional   A ⊃ B √

```
      /\
    ~A   B
```

Recall that we have said that a biconditional acts like a double conditional, a conjunction of two conditionals, as reflected in the table below:

A	B	A ≡ B
T	T	T
T	F	F
F	T	F
F	F	T

In case 1 both **A** and **B** are true, and in case 2 both components are false; these are the sufficient conditions for the truth of a biconditional statement.

The tree rule, therefore, is this:

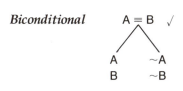

Either branch produces a valuation: the left has both **A** and **B** true, the right has both false.

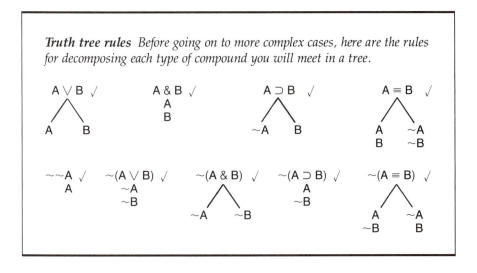

The first thing to notice about the rules is that they are written in general form, so they hold for *any* statements that are conjunctions, disjunctions, etc. This will become clearer as we apply the rules. Second, you will notice a check mark ($\sqrt{}$) next to each compound. When a rule is used to decompose a particular compound statement into the tree, the compound is *checked* to keep track. By checking a statement as we decompose it, we leave reminders that will indicate when a tree is finished.

The second row of rules treats negated compounds. In the first case, the rule for negation of negation, the only possibility is the component without the double negation. The DeMorgan equivalences mentioned in section 3.1 explain the rules for negated disjunction and negated conjunction; a statement of the sort ~(**A** $\lor$ **B**) is treated as though it were ~**A** & ~**B**, and a statement of the sort ~(**A** & **B**) is treated as though it were ~**A** $\lor$ ~**B**.

The negated conditional rule relies on the equivalence between the conditional **A ⊃ B** and ~(**A** & ~**B**), as reflected in the truth conditions for the conditional. That is, a negated conditional could be true only if both the antecedent and the negated consequent were true. Finally, the negated biconditional rule relies on the equivalence between statements of the sort ~(**A ≡ B**) and (**A** & ~**B**) ∨ (~**A** & **B**). A negated biconditional could be true only if the immediate components have *different* truth values.

Now let's see how the rules work when applied to sets containing several statements. We will work in steps through several examples.

Example 1

$\{P \lor Q, P \equiv Q\}$

Step 1   List the statements in the set in a column, and draw a double line underneath the final statement.

(1) $P \lor Q$

(2) $P \equiv Q$
$$\overline{\overline{}}$$

Step 2   Decompose the first statement into the bottom of the tree, and check it. (Note: You can actually choose which statement to decompose first, but we will save strategy hints for later on.) Parenthetically keep track of the source of each statement added to the tree.

(1) $P \lor Q$ √

(2) $P \equiv Q$
$$\overline{\overline{}}$$

(3) P Q (from 1)

Step 3   Decompose the second statement into the bottom of each branch under the statement (note this!), and check it.

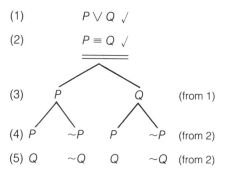

(1) $P \lor Q$ √

(2) $P \equiv Q$ √
$$\overline{\overline{}}$$

(3) P Q (from 1)

(4) P ~P P ~P (from 2)

(5) Q ~Q Q ~Q (from 2)

Step 4 If any branch of the tree contains an atomic statement (i.e., a statement letter) and its negation on separate lines, **close that branch** by putting an X at the bottom of that branch.

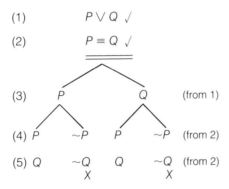

(1)	$P \vee Q$ ✓	
(2)	$P \equiv Q$ ✓	
(3)	P Q	(from 1)
(4)	P $\sim P$ P $\sim P$	(from 2)
(5)	Q $\sim Q$ Q $\sim Q$	(from 2)
	X X	

Step 5 Are there other unchecked compound statements anywhere in the tree on open branches (i.e., branches not closed with X)? If so, repeat steps 1–4 and decompose them. If not, the tree is finished.

As you can see, the tree is built by decomposing each compound statement, in turn, according to the rules. Since the tree is considered to begin with the very first statement at the top and run down the *trunk* to the bottom of each branch, *each initial statement is decomposed into each branch that is not closed*. Once a branch is closed, no additional statements are added to it.

As the tree is built, each open branch represents a sufficient condition of the truth of the statements on the branch; each branch thus allows the reading of one or more valuations in which all statements on that branch are true. Sometimes several branches will represent the same valuation.

In the first example, there are two **open branches** (i.e., branches that are not closed with an X at the end). The far-left branch represents a valuation to the atomic components of members of the set on which both P and Q are true, since both occur on the branch. The other open branch represents the same valuation. Thus, according to the tree, there is exactly one valuation on which both members of the initial set $\{P \vee Q, P \equiv Q\}$ are true: it is the valuation of true to P and to Q.

Example 2

$\{P \supset (Q \vee R), P, \sim Q, R \& P\}$

Step 1 Arrange the statements in a column and draw a double line:

(1) $P \supset (Q \vee R)$

(2) P

(3) ~Q

(4) R & P

====

Step 2 Decompose each compound statement into the tree, closing branches on which atomic statements and their negations are found.

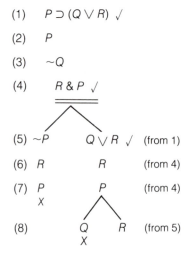

(1) $P \supset (Q \lor R)$ ✓

(2)   P

(3)   ~Q

(4)   R & P ✓
====

(5) ~P $Q \lor R$ ✓   (from 1)

(6) R   R   (from 4)

(7) P   P   (from 4)
    X

(8)   Q   R   (from 5)
             X

Step 3 There are no other compounds to decompose, so the tree is finished.

You should note that, in the above tree, the compound statement $Q \lor R$ resulted in line 5 from the decomposition of the first statement. Since all compounds must be decomposed in order to finish the tree, $Q \lor R$ is decomposed after the initial statements. *Also note that* Q ∨ R *is decomposed only into the branches that run through it, not the other branches.* In the tree there is only one open branch. So, the tree shows that there is exactly one valuation on which all members of the initial set are true: *P* and *R* are true, and *Q* is false.

Example 3

$\{P \supset (Q \,\&\, R), P \supset {\sim}R, P\}$

Step 1   (1) $P \supset (Q \,\&\, R)$

(2) $P \supset {\sim}R$

(3)   P
====

Step 2

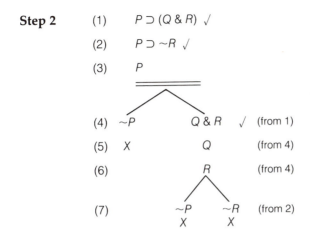

(1) $P \supset (Q \& R)$ √

(2) $P \supset {\sim}R$ √

(3) P

(4) ${\sim}P$ $Q \& R$ √   (from 1)

(5)   X Q (from 4)

(6) R (from 4)

(7) ${\sim}P$ ${\sim}R$ (from 2)
                    X   X

Step 3   There are no compounds left to decompose and every branch is closed; the tree is finished.

In this example you may notice that $Q \& R$ in line 4 is decomposed *before* the second initial statement. In general, *it is always a good strategy to first decompose statements that will not close a branch*. This practice will minimize the number of branches in long trees and save time. In this example, all branches of the tree close, which means there are no possible valuations of the atomic components of the initial set on which all members of the set are true.

Since there are branches open in the trees for the first two examples, we can declare their initial sets **consistent**. In the third example, since all branches closed, the initial set is known to be **inconsistent**. The general application of the truth tree method to questions of consistency and inconsistency can be summarized as follows:

In a truth tree for a set of statements, a **valuation of the atomic components** of the members of the set can be read from any open branch as follows:

1. Assign **T** to atomic statements that occur unnegated on the branch.

2. Assign **F** to atomic statements that occur negated on the branch.

3. Assign *either* **T** or **F** to the other atomic components of the members of the set.

The resulting valuation makes all members of the initial set true.

If the truth tree for a set of statements has one or more open branch, then the set is **consistent,** and a valuation on which the members of the set are all true can be read from any open branch. If the tree has all closed branches, then the set is **inconsistent**.

Since the validity and invalidity of arguments are of principal concern in the study of logic, we want to find ways to use the tree method to make such determinations. Recall from the last section that an argument is *valid* if the set consisting of the premises and the negation of the conclusion is *inconsistent*. This correlation, then, provides the key to using the tree method to test for validity. Beginning with an argument, list the premises and the *negation of the conclusion*. Test this set for consistency; if it is consistent, then the argument is *invalid* and a counterexample can be read from any open branch. If the set is inconsistent, then the argument has been shown to be *valid*.

Here are several examples, worked through step by step:

Example 1

$$P \supset \sim Q$$

$$Q \supset \sim P$$

$$\overline{P \equiv Q}$$

Step 1 List the premises and the *negation of the conclusion*; draw a double line.

(1) $P \supset \sim Q$

(2) $Q \supset \sim P$

(3) $\sim (P \equiv Q)$

Step 2 Construct a truth tree for the set.

(1) $P \supset \sim Q$ √

(2) $Q \supset \sim P$ √

(3) $\sim (P \equiv Q)$ √

Step 3 If the tree has one or more open branches, declare the original argument *invalid*; if the tree has all closed branches, declare the original argument to be *valid*. If invalid, produce a counterexample.

The argument $P \supset \sim Q$

$Q \supset \sim P$

$P \equiv Q$

is *invalid*.

Counterexample:

P	Q
T	F	(left open branch)

Note that although all three of the statements in the set to be tested will cause the tree to branch, the third statement $\sim(P \equiv Q)$ was decomposed first. Another strategy hint, then, is to *decompose biconditionals and negated biconditionals before other compounds that create branches*. The reason is that both biconditional rules put two statements into each branch and maximize the possibility of early closure.

We will more fully discuss the algorithmic nature of the tree method in chapters 7 and 11. For now you should have observed that the method always delivers an answer to the questions of consistency/inconsistency and validity/invalidity in a fixed number of steps according to strict instructions. The strategy hints are not part of the method itself but are aimed at helping you shorten your work a bit. You will always obtain the correct answer by means of a truth tree, no matter what order of decomposition you use.

Example 2

$\sim(R \vee S) \mathbin{\&} P$

$\sim P \vee S$

R

Steps 1 & 2 (1) $\sim(R \vee S) \mathbin{\&} P$ $\checkmark$

(2) $\sim P \vee S$ $\checkmark$

(3) $\sim R$

---

(4) $\sim(R \vee S)$ $\checkmark$ (from 1)

(5)   P   (from 1)

(6)   ~R   (from 4)

(7)   ~S   (from 4)

(8) ~P   S   (from 2)
     X   X

Step 3   The argument

$\sim(R \lor S)\ \&\ P$

$\sim P \lor S$

_____

R

is *valid*.

Example 3

$P \supset (Q \lor R)$

$R \supset S$

_____

$P \lor S$

(1) $P \supset (Q \lor R)$ ✓

(2) $R \supset S$ ✓

(3) $\sim(P \lor S)$ ✓

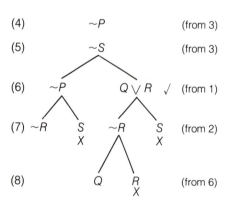

(4)   ~P   (from 3)

(5)   ~S   (from 3)

(6) ~P $Q \lor R$ ✓ (from 1)

(7) ~R   S   ~R   S   (from 2)
         X   X

(8)   Q   R   (from 6)
              X

The argument

$P \supset (Q \lor R)$

$R \supset S$

$P \lor S$

is *invalid*.

Counterexample:

P	Q	R	S
F	T	F	F

A precise statement of the truth tree test for validity is as follows:

Truth Tree Test for Validity *An SL argument with premises* $A_1, A_2, \ldots, A_n$ *and conclusion* **B** *is* ***valid*** *if the truth tree for the set* $\{A_1, A_2, \ldots, A_n, \sim B\}$ *has all closed branches. If one or more branches is open, the argument is* ***invalid*** *and a counterexample can be read from any open branch.*

Since entailment is so closely related to validity, without further ado we can also give its characterization in terms of truth trees.

Entailment *A set of statements* $\{A_1, A_2, \ldots, A_n\}$ ***entails*** *a statement* **B** *in SL just in case the tree for the set* $\{A_1, A_2, \ldots, A_n, \sim B\}$ *has all closed branches.*

If we construct a truth tree for a single statement and find that the tree has *no open branches*, then we know that the statement is a *contradiction*. Recall that when a contradiction is a member of a set, the set is inconsistent because there can be no valuation on which all members of the set are true. However, if a tree for a single statement has one or more open branches, the statement may either be a tautology or a contingent statement. In order to show conclusively that a statement is a tautology, we test its *negation* by means of a tree. If the negation of the statement has a tree with no open branches, then the original statement is, indeed, a tautology. (Recall from the previous section that the negation of a tautology is a contradiction, and vice versa.) The truth tree characterization of these three logical properties of single statements can be given as follows:

Tautology, Contradiction, Contingent Statement An SL statement **A** is a *tautology* just in case the truth tree for {~**A**} has no open branches; **A** is a *contradiction* just in case the truth tree for {**A**} has no open branches; **A** is a *contingent statement* if the truth trees for both {**A**} and {~**A**} have open branches.

To test a statement **A** to determine whether it is a tautology, a contradiction, or a contingent statement may require constructing a tree for both {**A**} and {~**A**}. The question is always which to try first. There is no hard and fast rule here; you have to guess which is most likely to produce a closed tree. Here are a few examples:

Example 1

$P \supset (P \lor Q)$

Step 1   Decide (guess!) which is more promising; to try the tree for the initial statement or its negation. Here we will try the negation because it is a very simple tree.

Step 2   Construct the tree.

(1) ~$(P \supset (P \lor Q))$ √

---

(2) P (from 1)

(3)   ~$(P \lor Q)$ √   (from 1)

(4)   ~P (from 3)

(5)   ~Q (from 3)
            X

Step 3   If all the branches of the tree close, declare the original statement **A** a tautology *if you tested its negation*; declare **A** a contradiction *if you tested **A** itself*. If there is one or more open branch, test the remaining case. If the trees for both {**A**} and {~**A**} have open branches, then declare **A** contingent.

(Declaration:) $P \supset (P \lor Q)$ is a *tautology*.

Note that this method for testing statements remains algorithmic because we are sure to have an answer in a specified number of steps. The guessing in step 1 is to possibly shorten the work. But if we blindly went ahead and first tested the statement itself and, if the tree has open branches, then turned to its negation, we would always come out with the correct answer as a result of either the first tree or the second.

Example 2

$[P \supset (Q \supset \sim R)] \supset [R \supset (P \supset \sim Q)]$

Step 1 Since the statement is a conditional, we will initially test its negation.

Step 2   (1) $\sim[[P \supset (Q \supset \sim R)] \supset [R \supset (P \supset \sim Q)]]$ √

(2) $P \supset (Q \supset \sim R)$ √   (from 1)

(3) $\sim[R \supset (P \supset \sim Q)]$ √   (from 1)

(4) R (from 3)

(5) $\sim(P \supset \sim Q)$ √   (from 3)

(6) P (from 5)

(7) $\sim\sim Q$ (from 5)

(8) $\sim P$ $Q \supset \sim R$ √   (from 2)

(9)   X Q (from 7)

(10) $\sim Q$ $\sim R$ (from 8)
                  X   X

Step 3 $[P \supset (Q \supset \sim R)] \supset [R \supset (P \supset \sim Q)]$ is a *tautology.*

Example 3

$(Q \supset P) \,\&\, (\sim Q \supset P)$

Step 1 Since the statement is a conjunction, we will test it as is.

Step 2 (1) $(Q \supset P) \,\&\, (\sim Q \supset P)$ √

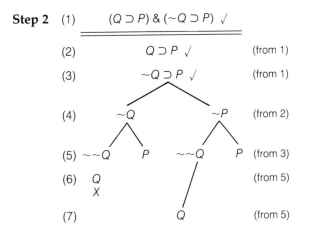

(2) $Q \supset P$ √   (from 1)

(3) $\sim Q \supset P$ √   (from 1)

(4) $\sim Q$ $\sim P$ (from 2)

(5) $\sim\sim Q$ P $\sim\sim Q$ P (from 3)

(6) Q (from 5)
      X

(7) Q (from 5)

Step 3 Since the tree has open branches, we now repeat steps 1 & 2 and construct the tree for the other case, the negation.

(1) $\sim[(Q \supset P) \,\&\, (\sim Q \supset P)]$ √

(2) $\sim(Q \supset P)$ √ $\sim(\sim Q \supset P)$ √   (from 1)

(3) Q $\sim Q$ (from 2)

(4) $\sim P$ $\sim P$ (from 2)

Step 3 (again) Since both trees have open branches, $(Q \supset P) \,\&\, (\sim Q \supset P)$ is a *contingent statement*.

Example 4

$\sim(P \,\&\, \sim Q) \,\&\, \sim(\sim P \lor Q)$

Step 1 Since the statement is a conjunction, we will test it as is.

Step 2 (1) $\sim(P \,\&\, \sim Q) \,\&\, \sim(\sim P \lor Q)$ √

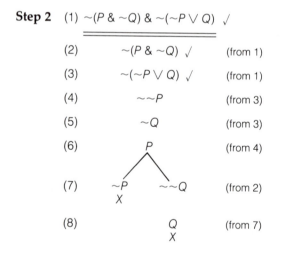

(2) $\sim(P \,\&\, \sim Q)$ √   (from 1)

(3) $\sim(\sim P \lor Q)$ √   (from 1)

(4) $\sim\sim P$ (from 3)

(5) $\sim Q$ (from 3)

(6) P (from 4)

(7) $\sim P$ $\sim\sim Q$ (from 2)
          X

(8) Q (from 7)
                X

Step 3 $\sim(P \,\&\, \sim Q) \,\&\, \sim(\sim P \lor Q)$ is a *contradiction*.

Truth trees are often very useful in testing whether two SL statements are equivalent. The test for equivalence utilizes the negation of the biconditional of the two statements to be tested; if the statements are equivalent, their biconditional must be a tautology, and, hence, the negation of their biconditional is a contradiction. The precise characterization of this test can be given as follows:

Equivalence *Two SL statements* **A** *and* **B** *are* **equivalent** *just in case the truth tree for* {~(**A** ≡ **B**)} *has no open branches.*

We will work through two examples of testing for equivalence.

Example 1 $P \equiv Q$ and $(P \,\&\, Q) \lor (\sim P \,\&\, Q)$

Step 1 Form the negated biconditional of the two statements.

$\sim[(P \equiv Q) \equiv [(P \,\&\, Q) \lor (\sim P \,\&\, Q)]]$

Step 2 Construct a truth tree.

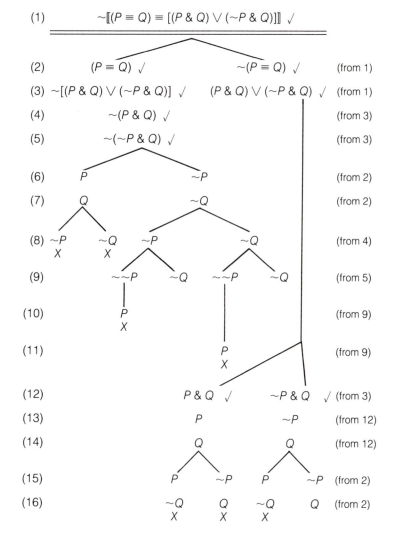

(1)	$\sim[(P \equiv Q) \equiv [(P \,\&\, Q) \lor (\sim P \,\&\, Q)]]$ ✓	
(2)	$(P \equiv Q)$ ✓ $\sim(P \equiv Q)$ ✓	(from 1)
(3)	$\sim[(P \,\&\, Q) \lor (\sim P \,\&\, Q)]$ ✓ $(P \,\&\, Q) \lor (\sim P \,\&\, Q)$ ✓	(from 1)
(4)	$\sim(P \,\&\, Q)$ ✓	(from 3)
(5)	$\sim(\sim P \,\&\, Q)$ ✓	(from 3)
(6)	P $\sim P$	(from 2)
(7)	Q $\sim Q$	(from 2)
(8)	$\sim P$ $\sim Q$ $\sim P$ $\sim Q$	(from 4)
	X X	
(9)	$\sim\sim P$ $\sim Q$ $\sim\sim P$ $\sim Q$	(from 5)
(10)	P	(from 9)
	X	
(11)	P	(from 9)
	X	
(12)	$P \,\&\, Q$ ✓ $\sim P \,\&\, Q$ ✓	(from 3)
(13)	P $\sim P$	(from 12)
(14)	Q Q	(from 12)
(15)	P $\sim P$ P $\sim P$	(from 2)
(16)	$\sim Q$ Q $\sim Q$ Q	(from 2)
	X X X	

Step 3 If there are no open branches, declare the statements *equivalent*; if there is one or more open branches, declare the statements *not equivalent*.

The statements $P \equiv Q$ and $(P \mathbin{\&} Q) \vee (\sim P \mathbin{\&} Q)$ are *not equivalent*.

Example 2

$P \supset (Q \vee R)$ and $(P \supset Q) \vee (P \supset R)$

Steps 1 & 2   (1) $\sim[\![P \supset (Q \vee R)] \equiv [(P \supset Q) \vee (P \supset R)]\!]$ ✓

(2)	$P \supset (Q \vee R)$ ✓ $\sim[P \supset (Q \vee R)]$ ✓	(from 1)
(3)	$\sim[(P \supset Q) \vee (P \supset R)]$ ✓ $(P \supset Q) \vee (P \supset R)$ ✓	(from 1)
(4)	$\sim(P \supset Q)$ ✓	(from 3)
(5)	$\sim(P \supset R)$ ✓	(from 3)
(6)	P	(from 4)
(7)	$\sim Q$	(from 4)
(8)	P	(from 5)
(9)	$\sim R$	(from 5)
(10)	$\sim P$ $Q \vee R$ ✓	(from 2)
	X	
(11)	Q R	(from 10)
	X X	
(12)	P	(from 2)
(13)	$\sim(Q \vee R)$ ✓	(from 2)
(14)	$\sim Q$	(from 13)
(15)	$\sim R$	(from 13)
(16)	$(P \supset Q)$ ✓ $(P \supset R)$ ✓	(from 3)
(17)	$\sim P$ Q $\sim P$ R	(from 16)
	X X X X	

Step 3   The statements $P \supset (Q \vee R)$ and $(P \supset Q) \vee (P \supset R)$ are *equivalent*.

As we have seen, the main function of truth trees is to determine the consistency or inconsistency of sets of SL statements. We have been able to adapt trees to test for validity and the other logical properties and relations because they are conveniently defined in terms of consistency and inconsistency.

Finding Consistent Kernels

Still another task for which trees are useful is to find a consistent **kernel** or **subset** within a set shown to be inconsistent. The method is quite simple; all one does is look for a way to open some closed branch in the tree. Here is an example.

$\{P \supset (Q \& R), P \supset {\sim}R, P\}$

(1) $P \supset (Q \& R)$ ✓

(2) $P \supset {\sim}R$ ✓

(3) P

```
           _____
              /        \
(4)  ~P        Q & R  ✓  (from 1)
      X
(5)                Q       (from 5)
(6)                R       (from 5)
                /     \
(7)        ~P        ~R   (from 2)
            X         X
```

If we can find a way to open a branch, which requires eliminating at least one statement from the initial set, then we have found a consistent kernel of the original set. The newly opened branch does, of course, represent a valuation on which all of the members of the consistent kernel set are true. In the above case, there are several ways to open branches, but perhaps the simplest is to eliminate P from the initial set and thus open the left branch, since the contradiction between P and ${\sim}P$ would, then, no longer be present. Thus, the tree for the resulting kernel set $\{P \supset (Q \& R), P \supset {\sim}R\}$ is the following:

(1) $P \supset (Q \& R)$ ✓

(2) $P \supset {\sim}R$ ✓

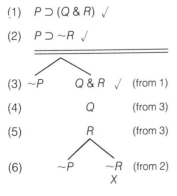

```
           _____
              /        \
(3)  ~P        Q & R  ✓  (from 1)
(4)                Q       (from 3)
(5)                R       (from 3)
                /     \
(6)        ~P        ~R   (from 2)
                      X
```

You might give this question some thought: What are the other consistent kernels of $\{P \supset (Q \,\&\, R), P \supset \sim R, P\}$?[10]

Summary

The truth tree rules and the truth tree tests for the various logical properties and relations were given (see p. 99).

If the truth tree for a set of statement has one or more open branch, then the set is **consistent** and a valuation on which the members of the set are all true can be read from any open branch. If the tree has all closed branches, then the set is **inconsistent**.

In a truth tree for a consistent set of statements, a **valuation** to the atomic components of the members of the set can be read off any open branch by assigning **T** to atomic statements that occur unnegated on the branch, by assigning **F** to atomic statements that occur negated on the branch, and by assigning either **T** or **F** to the other atomic components of the members of the set. The resulting valuation makes all members of the initial set true.

An SL argument with premises $A_1, A_2, \ldots, A_n$ and conclusion **B** is **valid** if the truth tree for the set $\{A_1, A_2, \ldots, A_n, \sim B\}$ has all closed branches. If one or more branches are open, the argument is **invalid** and a counterexample can be read off any open branch.

A set of SL statements $\{A_1, A_2, \ldots, A_n\}$ **entails** a statement **B** just in case the tree for the set $\{A_1, A_2, \ldots, A_n, \sim B\}$ has all closed branches.

An SL statement **A** is a **tautology** just in case the truth tree for $\{\sim A\}$ has no open branches; **A** is a **contradiction** just in case the truth tree for $\{A\}$ has no open branches; **A** is an **SL contingent statement** if the truth trees for *both* $\{A\}$ and $\{\sim A\}$ have open branches.

Two SL statements **A** and **B** are **equivalent** just in case the truth tree for $\{\sim(A \equiv B)\}$ has no open branches.

EXERCISES 3.4

1. By means of truth trees, decide whether the following sets of SL statements are consistent or inconsistent. If the set is consistent, give at least one valuation to the atomic components of its members on which all members of the set are true.

   a. $\{(P \vee Q) \supset \sim R, R \supset P, P \vee Q\}$

   b. $\{\sim(P \vee P) \equiv P\}$

   c. $\{(P \supset Q) \,\&\, (P \supset \sim Q), P\}$

   d. $\{[(P \supset \sim Q) \,\&\, \sim P] \supset Q, \sim(P \,\&\, Q) \,\&\, P\}$

   e. $\{P \,\&\, \sim P, Q \,\&\, \sim Q\}$

   f. $\{(P \,\&\, R) \vee (P \,\&\, Q), \sim(R \,\&\, Q), \sim(P \equiv R)\}$

---

[10]We will further discuss consistent kernels in the next section.

2. For each of the sets in the preceding exercise that you found inconsistent, use the tree to produce a consistent kernel of the original set. (Remember, sometimes the empty set is the only consistent kernel.)

3. Test each of the following arguments for validity by means of trees. If an argument is invalid, provide a counterexample.

   a. $P \vee Q$

      $\sim P \,\&\, S$
      ___
      $Q \,\&\, S$

   b. $\sim W \,\&\, S$

      $W \supset P$
      ___
      $\sim P$

   c. $\sim(P \equiv Q)$

      $\sim P$
      ___
      $Q \vee R$

   d. $R \vee (W \,\&\, P)$

      $\sim P \,\&\, \sim S$

      $R \supset (W \vee Q)$
      ___
      $\sim W \supset Q$

   e. $S \equiv W$

      $W \supset Q$

      $\sim Q$

      $R \supset S$
      ___
      $\sim R$

   f. P

      $Q \supset [P \vee (W \,\&\, \sim S)]$

      $W \supset P$
      ___
      $Q \supset \sim S$

4. In each of the following, symbolize the argument using the suggested notation. Then test the argument for validity by means of a tree. If you find the argument to be invalid, provide a counterexample *in English*.

   a. If Jones is the thief, the jewels are somewhere in his room. If Jones has been to the bank, the jewels are not in his room. So, either Jones has been to the bank or he is the thief. (J, R, B)

b. If England and Ireland play each other in the final, tempers are sure to run high. If Sweden beats France, the final will be boring; if England doesn't play Ireland, the final will be poorly attended. So if the final is not poorly attended, then tempers have run high. [Let E = 'England plays Ireland in the final', let H = 'Tempers run high', let S = 'Sweden beats France', let I = 'Ireland wins over England,' let B = 'The final is boring', let P = 'The final is poorly attended'.

c. The car will run smoothly if and only if it is kept in tune. If the car isn't tuned, then its engine can wear excessively. If the car is kept in tune, its resale price will be higher than average. So, if the car runs smoothly and doesn't have excessive engine wear, then its resale price will be higher than average. (S, K, W, R)

d. The electric company will turn off the power if the bill is not paid on time. The electric bill can be paid only if I find my checkbook. So if the power company turns off the power, I haven't found my checkbook. (P, B, C)

e. The electric company will turn off the power if the bill is not paid on time. The electric bill can be paid only if I find my checkbook. So if I don't find my checkbook, the power will be turned off. (P, B, C)

5. Using truth trees, decide whether the following are tautologies.

a. $P \supset [(P \vee Q) \vee Q]$

b. $(P \supset {\sim}P) \supset {\sim}P$

c. $[P \supset (Q \supset R)] \supset (P \supset Q)$

6. By means of trees check each of the following pairs to determine whether the statements are equivalent or not.

a. $P \equiv {\sim}Q$ and $(P \,\&\, Q) \vee ({\sim}P \,\&\, Q)$

b. $P \supset (Q \supset R)$ and $(P \,\&\, Q) \supset R$

c. $P \supset Q$ and $P \supset (P \,\&\, Q)$

7. For each of the tree rules for negated connectives, explain how the rule reflects the sufficient conditions for the truth of the compound.

*8. Give an argument in terms of truth trees to show that if a compound statement **A** does not have a negation among its connectives, then **A** cannot be a contradiction.

*9. Could the tree procedure be altered so that branches are closed as soon as a *compound* statement **A** and its negation ${\sim}$**A** show up on a branch? If so, explain how.

*10. Explain, in terms of trees, why no statement could be a tautology if its only connectives are & and $\vee$.

*11. We said that the strategy hints are not strictly part of the truth tree method. How might the instructions for constructing trees be revised to incorporate the strategy hints?

3.5 GETTING ANSWERS FROM INFORMATION

In section 3.2 we briefly considered the following set of statements, which we called a data set:

(1) John isn't eligible if he hasn't passed his courses.

(2) If John plays, then he must be in good standing.

(3) If John plays, then he has been issued a uniform.

(4) John has not been issued a uniform.

Suppose you have a question relating to this set of statements which you want answered. Suppose your question is:

Is John playing?

How might you find an answer to this question? By this time you should recognize that the SL principles you have studied in this chapter and in chapter 2 provide you with all the tools you need to find an answer to your question. Supposing that the data set constitutes the reality against which your question is asked, all you need to do is determine whether the set of statements (1) through (4) *entails* the statement

John is playing.

If it does entail the statement, then the answer to your question is obviously yes.

There are two other possibilities we should also consider: the set might entail the negation 'John isn't playing', or the set might not entail either 'John is playing' or its negation. In this case, both would be consistent with the set; that is, if you added either 'John is playing' or 'John isn't playing' the resulting set would be consistent.

In general, then, when a question like 'Is John playing?' is asked relative to a certain set of statements or data, there are three possible answers:

(a) Yes, if the set entails 'John is playing'.

(b) No, if the set entails 'John isn't playing'.

(c) 'Indeterminate', if both 'John is playing' and 'John isn't playing' are consistent with the set.

In the case at hand, we might proceed to find an answer by first symbolizing the statements into SL notation and then testing to see whether the statement 'John is playing' is entailed by the set or not. Here is the set in SL form:

Notation:

E: John is eligible

C: John has passed his courses

P: John plays

G: John is in good standing

U: John has been issued a uniform

Symbolization:

(1) John isn't eligible if he hasn't passed his courses.

$\sim C \supset \sim E$

(2) If John plays then he must be in good standing.

$P \supset G$

(3) If John plays then he has been issued a uniform.

$P \supset U$

(4) John has not been issued a uniform.

$\sim U$

To test whether P ('John is playing') is entailed by the set, we can use any of the three methods covered in this chapter: full truth tables, the shortcut method, or truth trees. We surely want to avoid the full truth table since it will have thirty-two rows ($= 2^5$), and a tree would also be laborious to construct. We can try the shortcut method and consider the members of the set true and the statement P false. We will quickly discover that P is *not entailed by the set* because we will discover a counterexample valuation on which all members of the set and $\sim P$ are true:

C	E	G	P	U
T	T	T	F	F

So far, we know only that the answer is not yes. But we haven't yet answered the question because we haven't determined whether $\sim P$ ('John isn't playing') might be entailed by the set, in which case the answer will be no. So we test for whether $\sim P$ is entailed by the set, and we discover that it is; there is no possible valuation that makes all of the members of the set true and makes $\sim P$ false (i.e., makes P true). Thus, we have discovered that the answer to the original question 'Is John playing?' is no.

Recall that in our earlier discussion of the above data set we combined it with another set of four statements:

(5) Either John plays or he withdraws from the university.

(6) Mary Smith is the team coach.

(7) Seventy students went out for the team.

(8) John did not withdraw from the university.

This set, like the set of statements (1) through (4), is consistent. However, as you showed in exercise 3.2.5, the combined set of statements (1) through (8) is inconsistent. To see the problem that an inconsistent data set causes, recall that *an inconsistent set entails every statement*. Ask a question relative to the combined set, say

Is John eligible?

As before, we take the answer to the question to be yes if the statement

John is eligible.

is entailed by the data set. Since the set is inconsistent, the statement 'John is eligible' will be entailed. But so is every other statement. Relative to this set, the answer to every question is yes, including such questions as

Is the moon made of green cheese?

Is the moon made of chocolate fudge?

Thus, inconsistency is a very undesirable property of a set if it is to be used to produce information.

Finding a consistent kernel of an inconsistent set eliminates the problem caused when every statement is entailed and every question has a positive answer. But it doesn't eliminate all difficulties. Suppose you form the consistent kernel of the set by simply discarding statement (4) 'John has not been issued a uniform'. Now the data set would read

(1) John isn't eligible if he hasn't passed his courses.

(2) If John plays, then he must be in good standing.

(3) If John plays, then he has been issued a uniform.

(5) Either John plays or he withdraws from the university.

(6) Mary Smith is the team coach.

(7) Seventy students went out for the team.

(8) John did not withdraw from the university.

The problem here is that either statement (4) is not true, or one (or more) of the statements among (5) through (8) is not true, since the combined set of statements (1) through (8) is inconsistent. If it happens to be one of the statements among (5) through (8), then our new data set, while consistent, may give *incorrect* answers. The logic will be fine in that the answer will be correct *relative* to the data set, but there is an untruth in the data set that determines those answers. Unless we check the truth of every statement, there is no way to eliminate this problem.

The approach we have taken to the task of answering a simple yes/no question based on a data set is to recast it as a logic problem and use the resources of SL to produce an answer. In the rather simple case we have been discussing, this approach proved effective; we found an answer in a reasonable amount of time.

But most situations in which questions are asked of a data set are far more complicated. For example, suppose you ask your school's registrar whether a particular course, Logic 1, is scheduled for next semester. Your question is:

Is Logic 1 scheduled next semester?

Suppose there are four hundred courses being offered next semester. The data set relative to which you are asking your question then would contain a large number of statements, possibly many more than four hundred, depending upon how it is structured. Clearly, the truth table method or even the truth tree method is a very cumbersome way to determine whether or not the statement

Logic 1 is scheduled next semester

is entailed by the registrar's data set.[11]

To be able to answer questions from large data sets clearly requires quite different methods. Truth tables and truth trees are useful tools for analyzing common arguments because a very limited number of statements are involved. But information processing quickly surpasses the *practical* applications of these methods, even though *theoretically* both truth tables and truth trees could be used to answer any yes/no question of any data set of the sort that can be represented in SL. It just might take a supercomputer several lifetimes to produce an answer. The challenge, then, is to retain the algorithmic features of truth trees and truth tables but to find more efficient ways to use them.

In chapter 4, section 4.3, we will study the *resolution method*, which is widely used in question-answer computer applications and has the two de-

---

[11]Suppose the registrar uses one statement for each course. Then a truth table for this problem would have a minimum of 2^{400} rows.

sirable features we have discussed: it is algorithmic and can be very efficient, even in large data sets.

EXERCISES 3.5

1. Using one of the methods you have studied, answer the questions relative to the following data set:

   (1) Either John plays or he withdraws from the university.

   (2) Mary Smith is the team coach.

   (3) John did not withdraw from the university.

   (4) If seventy students went out for the team, then there will be a cut.

   (5) There will not be a cut if Mary Smith is the coach.

   a. Is John playing?
   b. Will there be a cut?
   c. Did seventy students go out for the team?

2. Can you describe a procedure so that the problem of inconsistent sets will not arise when two data sets are combined?

4

Statement Logic: Inference

All three of the methods presented so far for determining whether arguments are valid are *refutation* methods. In chapters 2 and 3 we looked for counterexamples to the claim of validity: cases in which the premises are true and the conclusion is false. These counterexamples may be a row in a truth table, a truth-value found by the shortcut method, or an open branch on a truth tree. When we fail to find such counterexamples, we say that arguments are valid; otherwise, we say that arguments are invalid.

In this chapter another method of determining the validity of arguments is presented, one that closely parallels the way in which we reason from what we know to what we can infer. Instead of attempting to refute validity, we will be able to *prove* validity directly by showing that a conclusion *follows from* a group of premises. The systems we will study are called **natural deduction** and **resolution**.

4.1 THE BASIC NATURAL DEDUCTION RULES[1]

Many arguments can be shown to be valid merely by inspection and a little thought. For example, recall the case of David and Daphne from chapter 1. A summary of Daphne's reasoning might go as follows:

---

[1]Our presentation of the rules is based on those found in Frederick Fitch, *Symbolic Logic: An Introduction* (New York: The Ronald Press, 1952).

The keys are either on the hall table, or on the dresser, or in the coat pocket. But they are not on the hall table or on the dresser either. So they must be in the coat pocket.

To assess the logic of Daphne's reasoning, we will assume that her premises are true. So, since the keys are not on the hall table, it is clear that they must be either on the dresser or in the coat pocket. But how do we know that the keys are not on the hall table? In the context of Daphne's reasoning, this assumption follows from the second premise, which actually asserts *both* that the keys are not on the hall table *and* that they are not on the dresser. Since the keys are not on the dresser, it follows that they can only be in the coat pocket.

Our reconstruction of Daphne's reasoning involves several familiar inference patterns. First, we assumed that if either of two things is the case and we can eliminate the first, then the second is so. This principle, which we will later call *disjunctive syllogism*, is actually used twice. (Can you find both cases?) The second inference is so obvious you may wonder that we are drawing attention to it: if two assertions are made in a single statement, then both assertions may be thought of as individually following from that joint assertion. When Daphne asserts, 'But they are not on the hall table, or on the dresser either', she is saying that the keys are not on the hall table, *and* the keys are not on the dresser. The pattern of inference of concluding that **B** based on the assertion of **A** *and* **B** is sometimes called *simplification*.

Now let's look at another case, the argument of exercise 3.4.4c:

The car will run smoothly if and only if it is kept in tune. If the car isn't tuned, then its engine can wear excessively. If the car is kept in tune, its resale price will be higher than average. So, if the car runs smoothly and doesn't have excessive engine wear, then its resale price will be higher than average.

To work from the premises to the conclusion, one might reason as follows. Suppose that the car does run smoothly and that it doesn't have excessive engine wear (the antecedent conditions of the conclusion). From the supposition that the car is running smoothly and the first premise, we can infer that the car has been kept in tune. And from the fact that it has been kept in tune and the third premise, it follows that its resale price will be higher than average. Thus, given the initial supposition that the car does run smoothly and that it doesn't have excessive engine wear, we conclude that its resale price will be higher than average. Or, in other words, *if* the car does run smoothly and it doesn't have excessive engine wear, *then* its resale price will be higher than average.

This plausible-sounding reasoning informally involves three different inference patterns. First, that given a biconditional **A** ≡ **B** and also its component **A,** one may infer **B.** The second, closely related, pattern is that given a conditional **A** ⊃ **B** and also its component **A,** one may infer **B.** (This pattern was called *modus ponens* in chapter 2.) A third pattern used is a common form of conditional reasoning: first, *assume* that a certain condition **C** holds, and then *show* that, under that assumption, some other fact **D** may be inferred. Finally, conclude the conditional statement: *if* **C,** *then* **D.**

So far, then, from these two quite ordinary examples of reasoning we have found instances of five different patterns of inference that we use in drawing conclusions from premises. Here they are:

Infer **B** from **A** ∨ **B** and ∼**A.**   (disjunctive syllogism)

Infer **B** from **A** & **B.**   (simplification)

Infer **B** from **A** ≡ **B** and **A.**

Infer **B** from **A** ⊃ **B** and **A.**   (*modus ponens*)

Infer **C** ⊃ **D** from reasoning that shows that **D** follows from the assumption of **C.**

We will return to each of these patterns later on. Of course, we often use other inference patterns as well. We would routinely eliminate the double negatives from 'John is not unmarried' to get the simpler 'John is married'. And we have no hesitation in putting two claims together into one statement, as when we say, 'He likes cheese and he likes fruit' because we know that he likes each one.

The problem is to formulate such rather routine patterns into general rules of inference that will cover all possible cases. That is, we seek a set of rules that will allow us to infer any conclusion that validly follows from a set of premises. Or, to put it the other way, we want a set of rules that will license the inference of statements from sets of statements just in case those statements are *entailed* by that set of statements.

The natural deduction rules that we will use will serve this exact purpose. We will start out with a basic set of eleven rules, and then we will add some more to make the natural deduction system a bit easier to use. Each of the five statement connectives has two rules, one that introduces the connective into a statement and another that eliminates it. Here are the basic eleven rules, grouped by connective (with useful abbreviations in parentheses).[2]

---

[2]The *separation* feature of the rules, that *only* the connective in question appears in premises and conclusion of each rule, was originally formulated by Gerhard Gentzen (who ultimately deserves credit for the origin of truth trees as well). I am thankful to Hugues Leblanc for pointing this out.

Negation rules
 1. **Double negation** *From* ~~*A, we can infer* ***A***. *(DN)*
 2. **Indirect reasoning** *If, on the assumption of a statement* ***A***, *we can infer both some statement* ***B*** *and its negation* ~***B***, *then we can conclude that* ~***A***. *(IR)*

Conjunction rules
 3. **Simplification** *From a conjunction* ***A*** & ***B***, *we can infer* ***A*** *(or* ***B***). *(SIMP)*
 4. **Conjunction** *From statements* ***A*** *and* ***B***, *we can infer* ***A*** & ***B***. *(CONJ)*

Disjunction rules
 5. **Disjunction** *If we have a disjunction* ***A*** ∨ ***B***, *and a statement* ***C*** *follows from both* ***A*** *and from* ***B***, *then we may conclude* ***C***. *(DISJ)*
 6. **Addition** *From* ***A*** *we can infer* ***A*** ∨ ***B*** *(or* ***B*** ∨ ***A***). *(ADD)*

Conditional rules
 7. **Modus ponens** *From* ***A*** *and* ***A*** ⊃ ***B***, *we can infer* ***B***. *(MP)*
 8. **Conditional reasoning** *If on the assumption of a statement* ***A*** *we infer* ***B***, *then we can conclude* ***A*** ⊃ ***B***. *(CR)*

Biconditional rules
 9. **Both ways** *From* ***A*** ≡ ***B*** *and* ***A***, *we may infer* ***B***; *and from* ***A*** ≡ ***B*** *and* ***B***, *we may infer* ***A***. *(BW)*
 10. **Biconditional** *If, on the assumption of* ***A***, ***B*** *can be inferred and on the assumption of* ***B***, ***A*** *can be inferred, then we may conclude* ***A*** ≡ ***B*** *(or* ***B*** ≡ ***A***). *(BICON)*

Reiteration
 11. *Any assumption* ***A*** *may be repeated.* *(R)*
    (Reiteration is a procedural rule that will be important in using the other ten rules.)

These rules will be used in formal **derivations** to show that a certain statement follows logically, or can be legitimately inferred, from a *set* of statements. (Note: this set may contain just one statement, or may even be empty, but more of that later.) Derivations take the form of columns of statements, beginning with the initial statements in the set and ending with the statement that follows from the set. We number each line in a derivation and give a *justification* at each step by citing a rule and the line numbers of the statements involved.

The eleven rules may be divided into two groups: the **absolute rules** and the **assumption rules.** Absolute rules work on one or more statements in a derivation to permit the direct inference of another statement, whereas assumption rules require that some *additional* assumptions be made. The absolute rules are double negation, simplification, conjunction, addition, *modus ponens,* and both ways. We will discuss each of these in turn.

The *double negation* rule says that we can move from a statement of the sort ~~**A,** to **A.** So, we can reason as follows, when ~~**A** is line k of a derivation:

k. | ~~**A**
. | .
. | .
p. | **A**   (DN, k)

Essentially, two negations cancel each other out according to the double negation rule. The schematic derivation above has several features that all natural deduction derivations share. We draw a vertical line at the left of the statements and between the line numbers and the statements. You will see as we go along how such lines allow us to keep track of the various uses of rules in a derivation. Second, each time a statement is inferred from one or more statements in a derivation, a justification is required. Above we use the double negation rule, so the justification is (DN, k), where DN is short-hand for the rule and k is the line number of the statement to which the rule was applied.

Simplification permits us to move from a conjunction to either conjunct:

k. | A & B
. | .
. | .
p. | A   (SIMP, k)

or, alternatively,

k. | A & B
. | .
. | .
p. | B   (SIMP, k)

Conjunction is just the reverse:

k. | A
. |
n. | B
. | .
p. | A & B   (CONJ, k, n)

or,

k. | A
. |
n. | B
. | .
p. | B & A   (CONJ, k, n)

Note that the use of the conjunction rule requires two statements, **A** and **B,** on *separate lines,* so two line numbers are cited in the justification.

Here is an example of how these three rules might be used within a portion of a derivation to infer $P \& R$ from $R \& {\sim}{\sim}P$:

```
4. | R & ~~P
5. | ~~P        (SIMP, 4)
6. | R          (SIMP, 4)
7. | P          (DN, 5)
8. | P & R      (CONJ, 6, 7)
```

The next rule, *addition,* may seem odd at first; you may wonder where **B** comes from, when we move from **A** to **A** $\vee$ **B** (or **B** $\vee$ **A**). The answer is that **B** may be any statement we wish. For example, from 'Sue drives a Buick' we may infer 'Either Sue drives a Buick or Sam is in Malawi'. The first statement guarantees the second, whatever its oddities. In a derivation, the use of this rule looks like this:

```
k. |   A
 . |   .
 . |   .
p. | A ∨ B    (ADD, k)
```

The disjunction can also go the other way in ADD:

```
k. |   A
 . |   .
 . |   .
p. | B ∨ A    (ADD, k)
```

The *modus ponens* rule establishes the most common pattern for deriving a conclusion from a set of statements, including a conditional:

```
k. |   A
 . |   .
n. | A ⊃ B
 . |   .
p. |   B      (MP, k, n)
```

Note that MP requires separate lines for its conditional *and* its antecedent; line numbers for both statements are cited in the justification. Thus, the following patterns are *not* acceptable:

```
k. |   B
 . |
n. | A ⊃ B
 . |   .
p. |   A      (MP, k, n)  IMPROPER!!
```

```
n. | A ⊃ B
 . |   .
p. |   B      (MP, n)  IMPROPER!!
```

The *both ways* rule is, essentially, like *modus ponens* in either direction. It looks like this in a derivation:

$$
\begin{array}{c|l}
\text{k.} & \text{A} \\
\cdot & \\
\text{n.} & \text{A} \equiv \text{B} \\
\cdot & \quad \cdot \\
\text{p.} & \text{B} \qquad (\text{BW, k, n})
\end{array}
$$

or, alternatively,

$$
\begin{array}{c|l}
\text{k.} & \text{B} \\
\cdot & \\
\text{n.} & \text{A} \equiv \text{B} \\
\cdot & \quad \cdot \\
\text{p.} & \text{A} \qquad (\text{BW, k, n})
\end{array}
$$

Again, the order of appearance of the biconditional $\mathbf{A} \equiv \mathbf{B}$ and its immediate component $\mathbf{A}$ (or $\mathbf{B}$) makes no difference, but both statements are required by the rule, and both line numbers are included in the justification.

Next we turn to the *assumption rules:* indirect reasoning, disjunction, conditional reasoning, biconditional, and reiteration. These rules all work on statements that serve as assumptions in a derivation. The first group of assumptions in a derivation are the premises of the argument we are trying to show as valid. These are called *assumptions* because their truth is assumed throughout the derivation. We will mark off assumptions by drawing a line underneath them.

The simplest assumption rule is *reiteration*. This rule allows any statement that is an assumption in a derivation, for example, a statement that is an initial premise, to be rewritten elsewhere in that derivation. The rule is used to move statements from the list of assumptions to the body of the derivation where they may be used. For example, suppose, $\mathbf{A}_1, \mathbf{A}_2, \ldots, \mathbf{A}_n$ are all assumptions of a derivation. Then, where $\mathbf{A}_i$ is one of the assumptions, the reiteration rule works like this:

$$
\begin{array}{c|l}
1. & \mathbf{A}_1 \\
2. & \mathbf{A}_2 \\
\cdot & \\
\text{n.} & \mathbf{A}_n \\
& \overline{\qquad} \\
\cdot & \\
\cdot & \\
\text{p.} & \mathbf{A}_i \qquad (\text{R,i})
\end{array}
$$

Note that a line separates the assumptions from the body of the derivation. All statements in a derivation *except* assumptions must have justifications to indicate their source.

The best way to learn about natural rules and understand their use is by working through some examples, so before going on we will look at a complete derivation. There are two ways derivations come into play: either we are trying to show that the conclusion of some argument really does follow from the premises, or we have a set of statements and we are trying to figure out what those statements might entail. The first kind of case is simpler because the 'target' is already known, so that is where we will start. Pay particular attention to the justification for each line; if you understand that concept, you already have mastered the essentials of natural deduction.

In the first example, we will derive the conclusion Q from the two premises, as follows.

Example 1

$P \equiv Q$

$R \, \& \, P$
___

Q

Step 1 Write the initial statements (assumptions) in a column and draw lines around them as below. (The horizontal line tells us which statements are the premises of the original argument.)

1. $P \equiv Q$
2. $R \, \& \, P$
___
3.

Step 2 Keep in mind the conclusion we are trying to reach, i.e. Q.

Step 3 Each time a rule is invoked, the statement inferred is listed with an appropriate *justification* that cites the rule used on a line or lines.

1.	$P \equiv Q$	
2.	$R \, \& \, P$	
3.	$P \equiv Q$	(R, 1)
4.	$R \, \& \, P$	(R, 2)
5.	P	(SIMP, 4)
6.	Q	(BW, 3, 5)

Since we have reached Q in line 6 by means of the rules, we have shown that Q can be inferred from the premises $P \equiv Q$ and $R \, \& \, P$.

Here is another case:

$P \supset Q$

P
___

$Q \, \& \, P$

The derivation of $Q \& P$ from the two premises $P \supset Q$ and P is as follows:

  1. | $P \supset Q$
  2. | P

  3. | $P \supset Q$ (R, 1)
  4. | P (R, 2)
  5. | Q (MP, 3, 4)
  6. | $Q \& P$ (CONJ, 4, 5)

The other assumption rules work by means of **subsidiary derivations.** We form a subsidiary derivation when we want to make a new assumption and show, by means of the rules, that a certain statement follows in one or more steps from that new additional assumption. Subsidiary derivations must eventually be **discharged** when we no longer need them, so we can get on about the task of the main derivation—showing that some statement follows from the initial set of statements. Forming subsidiary derivations, however, is often the only way we can proceed. It is also important to note that the reiteration rule does allow the rewriting of initial assumptions into subsidiary derivations. But the new assumptions cannot be reiterated into the main derivation—we could prove anything if that were allowed, as the following comparison illustrates:

This derivation demonstrates a *correct* use of reiteration:

  1. | A_1
  2. | A_2
    . |
  n. | A_n

  p. | | B ← new assumption

    . |
  r. | | B (R, p)

But the following type of derivation is *not* permitted:

  1. | A_1
  2. | A_2
    . |
  n. | A_n

  p. | | B

    . |
  r. | B (R, p)   IMPROPER!!

You can see why this attempted use of the reiteration rule cannot be allowed. If it were, we could show, for example, that 'Bill is a fool' follows from 'Today is Tuesday'. The derivation might look like this:

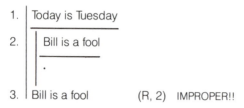

1. | Today is Tuesday
2. | | Bill is a fool
   | | •
3. | Bill is a fool   (R, 2)   IMPROPER!!

The next assumption rule is *indirect reasoning*. In this case, a subsidiary derivation is introduced with the assumption **B** that will lead to the direct contradiction **C** and ~**C**. The intuitive idea behind this rule is that any statement that leads to a direct contradiction must be false; so, if from **B** we get some statement **C** and its negation ~**C**, then we can conclude ~**B**.

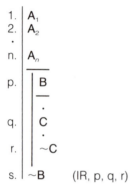

1. | A_1
2. | A_2
   | •
n. | A_n
p. | | B
   | | •
q. | | C
   | | •
r. | | ~C
s. | ~B   (IR, p, q, r)

Note that subsidiary derivations are set off slightly to the right to keep them separate. We are allowed to move back to the main derivation by invoking the indirect reasoning rule and thus *discharging* the assumption of the subsidiary derivation. IR thus requires three lines: the assumption of a statement **B** (line *p*) a statement **C** (line *q*), and its negation ~**C** (line *r*).

Indirect reasoning is often used to great effect in ordinary argumentation. Suppose an opponent is urging the truth of some statement **A**. We might try to refute him or her by arguing that if we *assume* that **A** is true, then a contradiction follows (e.g., some statement and its negation). Having shown this, we then conclude that what our opponent says is *false*. This kind of counterargument is sometimes called *reductio ad absurdum:* reducing the opponent's claim to absurdity. You might also note that the indirect reasoning strategy lies behind the shortcut method and the truth tree method. Recall that, in both cases, we assume the conclusion false and show that a contradiction follows if the argument is valid. In the shortcut method, the contradiction is that the premises are not all true when the conclusion is false, and in trees it is that all branches are closed.

The *disjunction* rule requires *two* subsidiary derivations; it is the most complicated of the natural deduction rules. If, in a derivation, we have the disjunction **B** ∨ **C**, and we want to show that some statement **D** follows, we must show that **D** follows from both side **B** and side **C**. To do this, we *first* make a new assumption of **B** and show that **D** follows; *then* we make another assumption of **C** and show that **D** follows from that assumption as well. *Only after that* can we say that **D** follows from the disjunction **B** ∨ **C**. The use of the disjunction rule in a derivation looks like this:

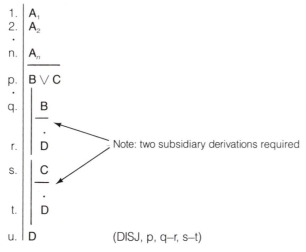

Note: two subsidiary derivations required

The justification for line u is complicated because the disjunction rule has so many requirements. We must have a disjunction **B** ∨ **C** (line p) and a derivation of **D** from **B** (lines q through r) and a derivation of **D** from **C** (lines s through t). Only then can we say that **D** follows from **B** ∨ **C** in the main derivation (line u).

For all its complexity, the disjunction rule does accurately capture what might be called the deductive power of a disjunction. If we know that either of two states of affairs must be so, then to get to a consequence of this fact, we need to show that something further follows from both. Sometimes we use this inference pattern in reverse. Imagine a car mechanic faced with an inoperative interior dome light. He or she might reason that since the light can be turned on by *either* the dashboard switch or the door switch, since it isn't working, *both* switches must be faulty.[3] The reasoning would look something like the following, where S_1 = the dash switch is working; S_2 = the door switch is working; L = the dome light is working:

premise:	$S_1 \supset L$ and $S_2 \supset L$
additional premise:	$\sim L$
final conclusion:	$\sim(S_1 \vee S_2)$ (that is, $\sim S_1$ & $\sim S_2$)

---

[3]The logic of switches is the subject of section 10.1.

The next assumption rule is *conditional reasoning*, which we saw in action at the beginning of this section. Under this rule, when we make an assumption **B** and show that a statement **C** follows we can then conclude that the conditional **B** ⊃ **C** may be inferred in the main derivation.

```
1.  A₁
2.  A₂
.
n.  Aₙ
     ___
p.    | B
      |___
      | .
q.    | C
      | .
r.  B ⊃ C   (CR, p–q)
```

Note that we can assert the conditional **B** ⊃ **C** only on line *r* in the main derivation because we have shown in the *subsidiary* derivation that **C** follows from **B**.

Finally, the *biconditional* rule is just a double application of conditional reasoning. To derive a biconditional, we derive each side from the other in two subsidiary derivations.

```
1.  A₁
2.  A₂
.
n.  Aₙ
     ___
p.    | B
      |___
      | .
q.    | C
      | .
r.    | C
      |___
      | .
s.    | B
t.  B ≡ C   (BICON, p–q, r–s)
```

Now let's look at another example of these rules in action:

Example 2

$H \lor P$

$\sim H$

___

P

Step 1

1. $H \lor P$
2. $\sim H$
   _____
3.

Step 2   We will have to use the disjunction rule to get to the desired conclusion P. The rule says that we may infer a statement that follows from both sides of the disjunction. Obviously P follows from the right disjunct, so the problem is the left. But from H (the left disjunct) and line 2, $\sim H$, it is possible to infer *any* statement by the indirect reasoning rule. But the use of these rules requires several subsidiary derivations. We first reiterate the disjunction and then assume H:

1. $H \lor P$
2. $\sim H$
   _____
3. $H \lor P$ (R, 1)
4. H

Because H is an additional premise, no justification is cited for it; it is put above a line that indicates its role.

Step 3   The next step is to make yet another subsidiary derivation, this time with a premise of $\sim P$ so that we can use indirect reasoning to obtain P from H in the subsidiary inference.

1. $H \lor P$
2. $\sim H$
   _____
3. $H \lor P$ (R, 1)
4. H
5. $\sim P$

Step 4   In the last subsidiary derivation we use the reiteration rule to bring down both H and $\sim H$ under the assumption of $\sim P$:

1. $H \lor P$
2. $\sim H$
   _____
3. $H \lor P$ (R, 1)
4. H
5. $\sim P$
   _____
6. H (R, 4)
7. $\sim H$ (R, 2)

Step 5   Having both a statement and its negation following from the premise of $\sim P$, we can invoke the indirect reasoning rule to conclude $\sim\sim P$ and **discharge** the subsidiary derivation with $\sim P$ as its assumption:

```
1. │ H ∨ P
2. │ ~H
   ├──────
3. │ H ∨ P        (R, 1)
4. │ │ H
   │ ├──────
5. │ │ │ ~P
   │ │ ├──────
6. │ │ │ H        (R, 4)
7. │ │ │ ~H       (R, 2)
8. │ │ ~~P        (IR, 5, 6, 7)
9. │ │ P          (DN, 8)
```

Step 6   After applying the double negation rule to line 8, we have shown that P follows from H. Now we turn to the second half of the disjunction rule to show that P also follows from the right disjunct, which is P itself. We do this with another subsidiary derivation, with P as its assumption:

```
1. │ H ∨ P
2. │ ~H
   ├──────
3. │ H ∨ P        (R, 1)
4. │ │ H
   │ ├──────
5. │ │ │ ~P
   │ │ ├──────
6. │ │ │ H        (R, 4)
7. │ │ │ ~H       (R, 2)
8. │ │ ~~P        (IR, 5, 6, 7)
9. │ │ P          (DN, 8)
   │ │
10.│ │ P
   │ ├──────
11.│ │ P          (R, 10)
```

Step 7   By reiterating P into the subsidiary derivation headed by P, we have shown the obvious fact that P follows from P. So we have satisfied the full terms of the disjunction rule and can now move to the conclusion by discharging both remaining subsidiary derivations:

```
1. │ H ∨ P
2. │ ~H
   ├──────
3. │ H ∨ P        (R, 1)
4. │ │ H
   │ ├──────
5. │ │ │ ~P
   │ │ ├──────
6. │ │ │ H        (R, 4)
7. │ │ │ ~H       (R, 2)
8. │ │ ~~P        (IR, 5, 6, 7)
9. │ │ P          (DN, 8)
   │ │
10.│ │ P
   │ ├──────
11.│ │ P          (R, 10)
12.│ P            (DISJ, 3, 4–9, 10–11)
```

All of this may seem needlessly tedious, since it takes at least twelve steps to show that the simplest argument pattern involving a disjunction is valid! But such is the consequence of using a fairly rigid set of rules. Later on we will relax these rules, and, in fact, we will add the additional rule that **B** may be inferred from **A** $\lor$ **B** and ~**A** (*disjunctive syllogism*). What we have shown above, however, is that such an additional rule is fully consistent with the natural deduction system discussed so far, since we can always obtain statement **B** from statements **A** $\lor$ **B** and ~**A** just by using the basic rules in twelve steps.

Here are additional sample derivations that show how other rules work together:

Example 1

$(G \lor S) \supset V$

$G \equiv \sim P$

$\sim P \,\&\, H$

_____

V

1.	$(G \lor S) \supset V$	
2.	$G \equiv \sim P$	
3.	$\sim P \,\&\, H$	
4.	$\sim P \,\&\, H$	(R, 3)
5.	$\sim P$	(SIMP, 4)
6.	$G \equiv \sim P$	(R, 2)
7.	G	(BW, 5, 6)
8.	$G \lor S$	(ADD, 7)
9.	$(G \lor S) \supset V$	(R, 1)
10.	V	(MP, 8, 9)

The only trick here is the application of the addition rule to line 7. Otherwise, the derivation systematically works toward the goal of isolating V on a separate line. If you attempt to work backward through the original argument to find a derivation strategy, you might reason as follows:

To isolate V we need $G \lor S$ as a line in the derivation. We can obtain $G \lor S$ if we have either disjunct (by ADD). Since G is an immediate component of a biconditional, we could get it as a separate line in the derivation if we had only $\sim P$ (by the BW rule). So we need $\sim P$, which we can get from the third premise by SIMP.

This backward reasoning is often an effective way to find a means of producing a derivation of the conclusion from the premises.

Example 2

$P \supset (G \& W)$

$H \supset E$

$E \supset P$

$H \supset W$

1. | $P \supset (G \& W)$
2. | $H \supset E$
3. | $E \supset P$

---

4. | | H

---

5. | | $H \supset E$ (R, 2)
6. | | H (R, 4)
7. | | E (MP, 5, 6)
8. | | $E \supset P$ (R, 3)
9. | | P (MP, 7, 8)
10. | | $P \supset (G \& W)$ (R, 1)
11. | | $G \& W$ (MP, 9, 10)
12. | | W (SIMP, 11)
13. | $H \supset W$ (CR, 4–12)

In this example, the assumption of H is made at the first opportunity since the conditional conclusion $H \supset W$ is sought. Once this strategy is apparent, the rest of the derivation is straightforward. Note that the subsidiary derivation introduced by the new assumption of H is discharged by means of the conditional reasoning rule.

Example 3

$Q \& \sim Q$

R

1. | $Q \& \sim Q$

2. | | $\sim R$

---

3. | | $Q \& \sim Q$ (R, 1)
4. | | Q (SIMP, 3)
5. | | $\sim Q$ (SIMP, 3)
6. | | $\sim\sim R$ (IR, 2, 5, 6)
7. | R (DN, 6)

This argument owes its validity to the contradictory premise. Using indirect reasoning we can derive any statement from a contradiction. First, assume the *negation* of the statement to be derived—in this case R. Then produce a statement and its negation in that subsidiary derivation. Finally, use the indirect reasoning rule and double negation to conclude. This strategy is often used within the body of some longer derivation when a contradiction can be reiterated or derived under some assumption.

A summary of the basic rules of natural deduction and various strategy hints will be found on pp. 155–157.

EXERCISES 4.1

1. In the following derivations, fill in the missing justification for each line:

a.

1.	$A \supset B$	
2.	$\sim B$	
3.	A	
4.	$A \supset B$	(R, 1)
5.	A	(R, 3)
6.	B	_____
7.	$\sim B$	_____
8.	$\sim A$	_____

b.

1.	$A \supset B$	
2.	$B \supset C$	
3.	A	
4.	$A \supset B$	_____
5.	A	_____
6.	B	(MP, 4, 5)
7.	$B \supset C$	_____
8.	C	_____
9.	$A \supset C$	_____

c.

1. $(A \supset B) \mathbin{\&} (C \supset D)$
2. $A \lor C$
 _____
3. $A \lor C$ _____
4. | A
5. _____
 | A _____
6. | $(A \supset B) \mathbin{\&} (C \supset D)$ _____
7. | $A \supset B$ (SIMP, 6)
8. | B _____
9. | $B \lor D$ _____
10. | C
 _____
11. | $(A \supset B) \mathbin{\&} (C \supset D)$ _____
12. | $C \supset D$ _____
13. | C _____
14. | D _____
15. | $B \lor D$ (ADD, 14)
16. $B \lor D$ _____

d.

1. $P \equiv Q$
2. $\sim Q$
 _____
3. | P
 ___
4. | P _____
5. | $P \equiv Q$ _____
6. | Q _____
7. | $\sim Q$ _____
8. $\sim P$ _____

2. Complete each of the following derivations:

a. Derive: $(A \mathbin{\&} B) \mathbin{\&} C$ from $A \mathbin{\&} (B \mathbin{\&} C)$

1. $A \mathbin{\&} (B \mathbin{\&} C)$
 _____
2. $A \mathbin{\&} (B \mathbin{\&} C)$ (R, 1)
3. A (SIMP, 2)
4. $B \mathbin{\&} C$ (SIMP, 2)

b. Derive: $\sim W$ from $R \supset \sim W$, $R \equiv S$, and S & T.

1. | $R \supset \sim W$
2. | $R \equiv S$
3. | S & T

4. | S & T (R, 3)
5. | S (SIMP, 4)
6. | $R \equiv S$ (R, 2)

c. Derive: $(A \lor B) \lor C$ from $A \lor (B \lor C)$

1. | $A \lor (B \lor C)$

2. | $A \lor (B \lor C)$ (R, 1)
3. | | A

4. | | A (R, 3)
5. | | $A \lor B$ (ADD, 4)
6. | | $(A \lor B) \lor C$ (ADD, 5)

7. | | $B \lor C$

8. | | | B

9. | | | B (R, 8)

4.2 DERIVED RULES

The eleven natural deduction rules form a **logically complete** system, in that they allow the conclusion of every valid argument to be derived from its premises. However, the basic rules are sometimes awkward to use, especially in complicated cases because of the number of steps involved. Therefore, it is helpful to know the additional derivation rules listed below. These additional rules are so common that they too have standard names.

The derived rules fall into two groups. First, **derived inference rules:**

Derived Inference Rules

Modus tollens   From **A** $\supset$ **B** and $\sim$**B**, $\sim$**A** may be inferred. (MT)

1. | $A \supset B$
2. | $\sim B$

3. | | A

4. | | $A \supset B$ (R, 1)
5. | | A (R, 3)
6. | | B (MP, 4, 5)
7. | | $\sim B$ (R, 2)
8. | $\sim A$ (IR, 3, 6, 7)

Hypothetical syllogism   From **A ⊃ B** and **B ⊃ C, A ⊃ C** may be inferred. (HS)

```
1.  | A ⊃ B
2.  | B ⊃ C
    |_____
3.  || A
    ||_____
4.  || A ⊃ B    (R, 1)
5.  || A        (R, 3)
6.  || B        (MP, 4, 5)
7.  || B ⊃ C    (R, 2)
8.  || C        (MP, 6, 7)
9.  | A ⊃ C     (CR, 3–8)
```

Disjunctive syllogism   From **A ∨ B** and **∼A, B** may be inferred. (DS) (See the derivation in section 4.1.)

Constructive dilemma   From **(A ⊃ B) & (C ⊃ D)** and **A ∨ C, B ∨ D** may be inferred. (CD)

```
1.  | (A ⊃ B) & (C ⊃ D)
2.  | A ∨ C
    |_____
3.  | A ∨ C                    (R, 2)
4.  || A
    ||_____
5.  || (A ⊃ B) & (C ⊃ D)      (R, 1)
6.  || A ⊃ B                   (SIMP, 5)
7.  || A                       (R, 4)
8.  || B                       (MP, 6, 7)
9.  || B ∨ D                   (ADD, 8)

10. || C
    ||_____
11. || (A ⊃ B) & (C ⊃ D)      (R, 1)
12. || C ⊃ D                   (SIMP, 11)
13. || C                       (R, 10)
14. || D                       (MP, 12, 13)
15. || B ∨ D                   (ADD, 14)
16. | B ∨ D                    (DISJ, 3, 5–9, 10–15)
```

Derived Equivalence Rules

The second group of rules are the **derived equivalence rules.** Each of these rules will be presented in the form **A ↔ B,** which means that *statement **B** can replace statement **A** anywhere it occurs.*[4] We will show that the statements on either side of the double arrow are *interderivable;* that is, each can be derived from the other. Since the two statements are thus logical equivalents, re-

---

[4]Note that ↔ is not used as an SL connective; it is a special symbol that is read as indicated. Sometimes such symbols are called 'metalogical' because they are used to make statements *about* statements in a logical system like SL. For example, **P ≡ Q** is a statement expressed in SL symbols, whereas **A ↔ B** is a statement *about* SL statements.

placing one with the other in the course of a derivation is permissible. These derived equivalence rules reflect the same SL equivalences that were discussed in section 3.3. Except for the commutativity rules, each equivalence requires two derivations. (Some will be left for you as exercises.)

Commutativity of $\vee$ $A \vee B \leftrightarrow B \vee A$ (COM$\vee$)

1.	$A \vee B$	
2.	$A \vee B$	(R, 1)
3.	A	
4.	A	(R, 2)
5.	$B \vee A$	(ADD, 3)
6.	B	
7.	B	(R, 5)
8.	$B \vee A$	(ADD, 7)
9.	$B \vee A$	(DISJ, 2, 3–4, 6–8)

Commutativity of & $A \,\&\, B \leftrightarrow B \,\&\, A$ (COM&)

1.	$A \,\&\, B$	
2.	$A \,\&\, B$	(R, 1)
3.	A	(SIMP, 2)
4.	B	(SIMP, 2)
5.	$B \,\&\, A$	(CONJ, 4, 3)

Associativity of $\vee$ $(A \vee B) \vee C \leftrightarrow A \vee (B \vee C)$ (ASSC$\vee$)

1.	$(A \vee B) \vee C$	
2.	$A \vee B$	
3.	A	
4.	A	(R, 3)
5.	$A \vee (B \vee C)$	(ADD, 4)
6.	B	
7.	B	(R, 6)
8.	$B \vee C$	(ADD, 7)
9.	$A \vee (B \vee C)$	(ADD, 8)
10.	$A \vee B$	(R, 2)
11.	$A \vee (B \vee C)$	(DISJ, 10, 3–5, 6–9)
12.	C	
13.	C	(R, 10)
14.	$B \vee C$	(ADD, 13)
15.	$A \vee (B \vee C)$	(ADD, 14)
16.	$(A \vee B) \vee C$	(R, 1)
17.	$A \vee (B \vee C)$	(DISJ, 16, 2–11, 12–15)

This derivation may seem to repeat itself several times. But if you pay attention to the subsidiary derivations, all the steps are required by the disjunction rule. The other half of the equivalence, to derive $(A \lor B) \lor C$ from $A \lor (B \lor C)$ is left as exercise 4.2.1l.

Associativity of & $(A \ \& \ B) \ \& \ C \leftrightarrow A \ \& \ (B \ \& \ C)$ (ASSC &)

1.	(A & B) & C	
2.	(A & B) & C	(R, 1)
3.	A & B	(SIMP, 2)
4.	A	(SIMP, 3)
5.	B	(SIMP, 3)
6.	C	(SIMP, 2)
7.	B & C	(CONJ, 5, 6)
8.	A & (B & C)	(CONJ, 4, 7)

(The derivation of $(A \ \& \ B) \ \& \ C$ from $A \ \& \ (B \ \& \ C)$ is left as an exercise.)

Distribution $\lor$/& $A \lor (B \ \& \ C) \leftrightarrow (A \lor B) \ \& \ (A \lor C)$ (DIST $\lor$/&)

1.	A $\lor$ (B & C)	
2.	A	
3.	A	(R, 2)
4.	A $\lor$ B	(ADD, 3)
5.	A $\lor$ C	(ADD, 3)
6.	(A $\lor$ B) & (A $\lor$ C)	(CONJ, 4, 5)
7.	B & C	
8.	B & C	(R, 7)
9.	B	(SIMP, 8)
10.	C	(SIMP, 8)
11.	A $\lor$ B	(ADD, 9)
12.	A $\lor$ C	(ADD, 10)
13.	(A $\lor$ B) & (A $\lor$ C)	(CONJ, 11, 12)
14.	A $\lor$ (B & C)	(R, 1)
15.	(A $\lor$ B) & (A $\lor$ C)	(DISJ, 14, 2–6, 7–13)

(The derivation of $A \lor (B \ \& \ C)$ from $(A \lor B) \ \& \ (A \lor C)$ is left as exercise 4.2.1a.)

Distribution &/∨   **A & (B ∨ C) ↔ (A & B) ∨ (A & C)**   (DIST &/∨)

```
 1.  | A & (B ∨ C)
     |_____
 2.  | A & (B ∨ C)          (R, 1)
 3.  | B ∨ C                (SIMP, 2)
 4.  || B
     ||_____
 5.  || A & (B ∨ C)         (R, 1)
 6.  || A                   (SIMP, 5)
 7.  || B                   (R, 4)
 8.  || A & B               (CONJ, 6, 7)
 9.  || (A & B) ∨ (A & C)   (ADD, 8)

10.  || C
     ||_____
11.  || A & (B ∨ C)         (R, 1)
12.  || A                   (SIMP, 11)
13.  || C                   (R, 10)
14.  || A & C               (CONJ, 12, 13)
15.  || (A & B) ∨ (A & C)   (ADD, 14)
16.  | (A & B) ∨ (A & C)    (DISJ, 3, 4–9, 10–15)
```

(The derivation of **A & (B ∨ C)** from **(A & B) ∨ (A & C)** is left as exercise 4.2.1b.)

Contraposition   **(A ⊃ B) ↔ (~B ⊃ ~A)**   (CONTR)

```
 1.  | A ⊃ B
     |
 2.  || ~B
     ||_____
 3.  || ~B              (R, 2)
 4.  || A ⊃ B           (R, 1)
 5.  || ~A              (MT, 3, 4)
 6.  | ~B ⊃ ~A          (CR, 2–5)
```

(The derivation of **A ⊃ B** from **~B ⊃ ~A** is left as exercise 4.2.1c.)

Conditional equivalence   **(A ⊃ B) ↔ (~A ∨ B)**   (CE)

```
 1.  | A ⊃ B
     |
 2.  || ~(~A ∨ B)
     ||
 3.  ||| ~A
     |||_____
 4.  ||| ~A              (R, 3)
 5.  ||| ~A ∨ B          (ADD, 4)
 6.  ||| ~(~A ∨ B)       (R, 2)
 7.  || ~~A              (IR, 3, 5, 6)
 8.  || A                (DN, 7)
 9.  || A ⊃ B            (R, 1)
10.  || B                (MP, 8, 9)
11.  || ~A ∨ B           (ADD, 10)
12.  || ~(~A ∨ B)        (R, 2)
13.  || ~~(~A ∨ B)       (IR, 2, 11, 12)
14.  | ~A ∨ B            (DN, 13)
```

This derivation incorporates a classic example of the strategy of indirect reasoning. Since there is no way directly to derive $\sim$**A** $\vee$ **B** from **A** $\supset$ **B,** the only option is to assume the negation of what we are trying to derive, i.e., $\sim(\sim$**A** $\vee$ **B**), and attempt to produce a contradiction. We will see this again in the derivation for biconditional equivalence. The derivation of **A** $\supset$ **B** from $\sim$**A** $\vee$ **B** is left as exercise 4.2.1d.

Biconditional equivalence   **A** $\equiv$ **B** $\leftrightarrow$ (**A** & **B**) $\vee$ ($\sim$**A** & $\sim$**B**)   (BE)

1.	A ≡ B	
2.	~[(A & B) ∨ (~A & ~B)]	
3.	A	
4.	A ≡ B	(R, 1)
5.	A	(R, 3)
6.	B	(BW, 4, 5)
7.	A & B	(CONJ, 5, 6)
8.	(A & B) ∨ (~A & ~B)	(ADD, 7)
9.	~[(A & B) ∨ (~A & ~B)]	(R, 2)
10.	~A	(IR, 3, 8, 9)
11.	B	
12.	A ≡ B	(R, 1)
13.	B	(R, 11)
14.	A	(BW, 12, 13)
15.	A & B	(CONJ, 13, 14)
16.	(A & B) ∨ (~A & ~B)	(ADD, 15)
17.	~[(A & B) ∨ (~A & ~B)]	(R, 2)
18.	~B	(IR, 11, 16, 17)
19.	~A & ~B	(CONJ, 10, 18)
20.	(A & B) ∨ (~A & ~B)	(ADD, 19)
21.	~[(A & B) ∨ (~A & ~B)]	(R, 2)
22.	~~[(A & B) ∨ (~A & ~B)]	(IR, 2, 20, 21)
23.	(A & B) ∨ (~A & ~B)	(DN, 22)

(The derivation of **A** $\equiv$ **B** from (**A** & **B**) $\vee$ ($\sim$**A** & $\sim$**B**) is left as exercise 4.2.1e.)

    A second version of biconditional equivalence will also be very useful. It follows from the basic rules for the biconditional.

A ≡ B ↔ (A ⊃ B) & (B ⊃ A)

```
1. | A ≡ B
   |_____
2. || A
   ||_____
3. || A ≡ B              (R, 1)
4. || A                  (R, 2)
5. || B                  (BW, 3, 4)
6. | A ⊃ B               (CR, 2–5)

7. || B
   ||_____
8. || A ≡ B              (R, 1)
9. || B                  (R, 7)
10.|| A                  (BW, 8, 9)
11.| B ⊃ A               (CR, 7–10)
12.| (A ⊃ B) & (B ⊃ A)   (CONJ, 6, 11)
```

(The derivation of **A ≡ B** from **(A ⊃ B) & (B ⊃ A)** is left as exercise 4.2.1f.)

Exportation   **(A & B) ⊃ C ↔ A ⊃ (B ⊃ C)**   (EXP)

```
1. | (A & B) ⊃ C
   |_____
2. || A
   ||_____
3. ||| B
   |||_____
4. ||| (A & B) ⊃ C   (R, 1)
5. ||| A             (R, 2)
6. ||| B             (R, 3)
7. ||| A & B         (CONJ, 5, 6)
8. ||| C             (MP, 4, 7)
9. || B ⊃ C          (CR, 3–8)
10.| A ⊃ (B ⊃ C)     (CR, 2–9)
```

(The derivation of **(A & B) ⊃ C** from **A ⊃ (B ⊃ C)** is left as exercise 4.2.1g.)

Idempotence of ∨   **A ↔ A ∨ A**   (IDEM∨)

```
1. | A
   |____
2. | A        (R, 1)
3. | A ∨ A    (ADD, 2)
```

(The derivation of A from A ∨ A is left as exercise 4.2.1h.)

Idempotence of &   **A ↔ A & A**   (IDEM&)
    (Both derivations are left as exercise 4.2.2a.)

DeMorgan's laws $\sim$(A $\vee$ B) $\leftrightarrow$ $\sim$A & $\sim$B   (DEM).
(Derivation of $\sim$A & $\sim$B is left as exercise 4.2.1i.)

1. | $\sim$A & $\sim$B

2. || A $\vee$ B

3. || $\sim$A & $\sim$B   (R, 1)
4. || $\sim$A   (SIMP, 3)
5. || A $\vee$ B   (R, 2)
6. || B   (DS, 4, 5)
7. || $\sim$B   (SIMP, 3)
8. | $\sim$(A $\vee$ B)   (IR, 2, 6, 7)

Note that we use the derived rule of Disjunctive Syllogism in this derivation, which saves twelve steps!

$\sim$(A & B) $\leftrightarrow$ $\sim$A $\vee$ $\sim$B   (DEM).
(Both derivations are left as exercises 4.2.1j and 4.2.1k.)

Absorption   A $\supset$ B $\leftrightarrow$ A $\supset$ (A & B)   (ABS).
(Both derivations are left as exercise 4.2.2b).

Tautology &   A $\leftrightarrow$ A & (B $\vee$ $\sim$B)[5]   (TAUT&)

1. | A

2. || $\sim$(B $\vee$ $\sim$B)

3. || $\sim$(B $\vee$ $\sim$B)   (R, 2)
4. || $\sim$B & $\sim\sim$B   (DEM, 3)
5. || $\sim$B   (SIMP, 4)
6. || $\sim\sim$B   (SIMP, 4)
7. | $\sim\sim$(B $\vee$ $\sim$B)   (IR, 2, 5, 6)
8. | B $\vee$ $\sim$B   (IR, 2, 5, 6)
9. | A   (R, 1)
10. | A & (B $\vee$ $\sim$B)   (CONJ, 7, 8)

You should note that the contradiction required for the IR rule in line 7 involves the statements $\sim$B (line 5) and its negation $\sim\sim$B (line 6). No additional application of double negation is necessary.

1. | A & (B $\vee$ $\sim$B)

2. | A & (B $\vee$ $\sim$B)   (R, 1)
3. | A   (SIMP, 2)

Tautology $\vee$ A $\vee$ (B $\vee$ $\sim$B) $\leftrightarrow$ (B $\vee$ $\sim$B)   (TAUT$\vee$).
(Both derivations are left as exercise 4.2.2c.)

---

[5]This rule and the next three will be useful in what are later called *equivalence derivations*.

Contradiction $\vee$ $A \leftrightarrow A \vee (B \& {\sim}B)$ (CON$\vee$)

1. | A
   | ―――――――――
2. | $A \vee (B \& {\sim}B)$ (ADD, 1)

1. | $A \vee (B \& {\sim}B)$
2. | | ${\sim}A$
   | | ―――――――――
3. | | $A \vee (B \& {\sim}B)$ (R, 1)
4. | | ${\sim}A$ (R, 2)
5. | | $B \& {\sim}B$ (DS, 3, 4)
6. | | B   (SIMP, 5)
7. | | ${\sim}B$ (SIMP, 5)
8. | ${\sim}{\sim}A$ (IR, 2, 6, 7)
9. | A   (DN, 8)

Contradiction & $A \& (B \& {\sim}B) \leftrightarrow (B \& {\sim}B)$ (CON&).
(Both derivations are left as exercise 4.2.2d.)

Our final equivalence rule is a variant of the basic inference rule, double negation. We already know that any statement **A** may be inferred from ${\sim}{\sim}$**A** by double negation. To go the other way, from **A** to ${\sim}{\sim}$**A**, simply requires assuming ${\sim}$**A** and reiterating both **A** and ${\sim}$**A** into that subsidiary derivation and then concluding ${\sim}{\sim}$**A** by indirect reasoning. Thus, statements **A** and ${\sim}{\sim}$**A** are interderivable. We can make use of this fact in an equivalence rule version of the double negation principle:

Double negation equivalence $A \leftrightarrow {\sim}{\sim}A$ (DNE)

One feature of the derived equivalence rules that makes them very powerful indeed is that they can be used to replace *portions* of statements within derivations. For example, within some derivations, the following replacement can be made by means of DeMorgan's law:

k. | $P \& {\sim}(Q \& R)$
m. | $P \& ({\sim}Q \vee {\sim}R)$ (DEM, k)

The legitimacy of such a step stems from the fact that ${\sim}(Q \& R)$ and ${\sim}Q \vee {\sim}R$ are interderivable, as shown above. Beginning with line *k*, we *could* construct a derivation using only the basic eleven rules, which would result in line *m* (and vice versa). The immediate replacement permitted by De-Morgan's law can thus be thought of as an abbreviation of these (much) longer derivations.

Having the full range of derived rules available dramatically shortens derivations, an advantage that will be very useful in later chapters. Here are several examples of how the rules work together.

Example 1

$P \supset (\sim R \supset Q)$

$R \supset \sim P$

$\sim Q$
_____

$\sim P$

1.	$P \supset (\sim R \supset Q)$	
2.	$R \supset \sim P$	
3.	$\sim Q$	
	_____	
4.	$P \supset (\sim R \supset Q)$	(R, 1)
5.	$(P \& \sim R) \supset Q$	(EXP, 4)
6.	$\sim Q$	(R, 3)
7.	$\sim(P \& \sim R)$	(MT, 5, 6)
8.	$\sim P \lor \sim\sim R$	(DEM, 7)
9.	$\sim P \lor R$	(DN, 8)
10.	$P \supset R$	(CE, 9)
11.	$R \supset \sim P$	(R, 2)
12.	$P \supset \sim P$	(HS, 10, 11)
13.	$\sim P \lor \sim P$	(CE, 12)
14.	$\sim P$	(IDEM $\lor$, 13)

You may be able to find several alternative routes to ~P from these premises. Now that so many rules are available, there are always a number of possible derivations.

Example 2

$(Q \lor R) \supset (Q \supset \sim R)$

$(Q \supset \sim R) \supset (R \supset K)$

$Q \lor R$
_____

$Q \lor K$

1.	$(Q \lor R) \supset (Q \supset \sim R)$	
2.	$(Q \supset \sim R) \supset (R \supset K)$	
3.	$Q \lor R$	
	_____	
4.	$(Q \lor R) \supset (Q \supset \sim R)$	(R, 1)
5.	$(Q \supset \sim R) \supset (R \supset K)$	(R, 2)
6.	$(Q \lor R) \supset (R \supset K)$	(HS, 4, 5)
7.	$Q \lor R$	(R, 3)
8.	$R \supset K$	(MP, 6, 7)
9.	$\sim\sim Q \lor R$	(DNE, 7)
10.	$\sim Q \supset R$	(CE, 9)
11.	$\sim Q \supset K$	(HS, 8, 10)
12.	$\sim\sim Q \lor K$	(CE, 11)
13.	$Q \lor K$	(DNE, 12)

You might note that, in this derivation, before the rule of conditional equivalence could be applied to line 9, the double negation of Q had to be formed. According to the CE rule, $\sim\mathbf{A} \vee \mathbf{B}$ is equivalent to $\mathbf{A} \supset \mathbf{B}$; the negation in the left disjunct is essential and has to be supplied.

Example 3

$(Q \,\&\, R) \equiv S$

$\sim(S \vee \sim Q)$

$\sim R$

1.	$(Q \,\&\, R) \equiv S$	
2.	$\sim(S \vee \sim Q)$	
3.	$\sim(S \vee \sim Q)$	(R, 2)
4.	$\sim S \,\&\, \sim\sim Q$	(DEM, 3)
5.	$\sim S$	(SIMP, 4)
6.	$(Q \,\&\, R) \equiv S$	(R, 1)
7.	$[(Q \,\&\, R) \supset S] \,\&\, [S \supset (Q \,\&\, R)]$	(BICON, 6)
8.	$(Q \,\&\, R) \supset S$	(SIMP, 7)
9.	$\sim(Q \,\&\, R)$	(MT, 5, 8)
10.	$\sim Q \vee \sim R$	(DEM, 9)
11.	$\sim\sim Q$	(SIMP, 4)
12.	$\sim R$	(DS, 10, 11)

Since a negated statement is to be derived, another way of approaching this derivation is to assume R and work toward a contradiction. To illustrate that often several paths lead to the same answer, here is the same conclusion derived another way:

1.	$(Q \,\&\, R) \equiv S$	
2.	$\sim(S \vee \sim Q)$	
3.	R	
4.	$\sim(S \vee \sim Q)$	(R, 2)
5.	$\sim S \,\&\, \sim\sim Q$	(DEM, 4)
6.	$\sim S$	(SIMP, 5)
7.	$(Q \,\&\, R) \equiv S$	(R, 1)
8.	$\sim\sim Q$	(SIMP, 5)
9.	Q	(DN, 8)
10.	R	(R, 3)
11.	$Q \,\&\, R$	(CONJ, 9, 10)
12.	S	(BW, 7, 11)
13.	$\sim R$	(IR, 3, 6, 12)

So far, our use of derivations has been wholly concerned with the inference of a statement from a set of statements. But derivations have other uses as well. By means of derivations, we can directly show that statements are *tautologies*. This is done by deriving the statement without any initial assumptions, that is, from the empty set. To get such a derivation started, some assumption will have to be made and a subsidiary derivation established. So, the assumption rules of inference are especially important to derivations of tautologies. But by the end, that assumption must be discharged. Here are a few examples.

Example 1 $P \supset P$

```
1.  |  | P
       ‾‾‾
2.  |  | P          (R, 1)
3.  |  P ⊃ P        (CR, 1–2)
```

Example 2 $(P \supset Q) \vee (Q \supset P)$

```
 1.  |  |  | ~[(P ⊃ Q) ∨ (Q ⊃ P)]
           ‾‾‾‾‾‾‾‾‾‾‾‾‾‾‾‾‾‾‾‾‾‾‾
 2.  |  |  | ~[(P ⊃ Q) ∨ (Q ⊃ P)]    (R, 1)
 3.  |  |  | ~(P ⊃ Q) & ~(Q ⊃ P)     (DEM, 2)
 4.  |  |  | ~(P ⊃ Q)                (SIMP, 3)
 5.  |  |  | ~(~P ∨ Q)               (CE, 4)
 6.  |  |  | ~~P & ~Q                (DEM, 5)
 7.  |  |  | ~~P                     (SIMP, 6)
 8.  |  |  | P                       (DN, 7)
 9.  |  |  | ~Q ∨ P                  (ADD, 8)
10.  |  |  | Q ⊃ P                   (CE, 9)
11.  |  |  | (P ⊃ Q) ∨ (Q ⊃ P)       (ADD, 10)
12.  |  (P ⊃ Q) ∨ (Q ⊃ P)           (IR, 1, 2, 11)
```

Example 3 $[(P \supset Q) \& (P \supset R)] \supset [P \supset (Q \& R)]$

```
1.  |  |  | (P ⊃ Q) & (P ⊃ R)
           ‾‾‾‾‾‾‾‾‾‾‾‾‾‾‾‾‾‾‾
2.  |  |  | (P ⊃ Q) & (P ⊃ R)                         (R, 1)
3.  |  |  | (~P ∨ Q) & (P ⊃ R)                        (CE, 2)
4.  |  |  | (~P ∨ Q) & (~P ∨ R)                       (CE, 3)
5.  |  |  | ~P ∨ (Q & R)                              (DIST ∨/&, 4)
6.  |  |  | P ⊃ (Q & R)                               (CE, 5)
7.  |  [(P ⊃ Q) & (P ⊃ R)] ⊃ [P ⊃ (Q & R)]           (CR, 1–6)
```

The very same technique can be used to show that a given statement is a *contradiction:* negate the statement and show that the result is a tautology!

To show that a set of statements is *inconsistent,* it suffices to derive some statement *and* its negation from the set. The statements in the set are the initial assumptions of the derivation. The simplest procedure for this is to attempt to derive the negation of some member of the set, since the unnegated statement will be available by rule R when desired. Since inconsistent sets permit the derivations of statements and their negations, we can see why *it is possible to derive any statement from an inconsistent set.* Suppose **S** is the set and **B** and ~**B** are derivable from **S**. Then to derive any statement **A** from **S**, arrange a derivation as follows:

```
1.
2.
 .    members of S
k.
     ─────────────
m.  ‖ ~A

r.  ‖ B
s.  ‖ ~B
t.  ‖ ~~A        (IR, m, r, s)
v.  | A          (DN, t)
```

Two SL statements **A** and **B** are *equivalent* if a statement of the form **A** ≡ **B** is a tautology. In practice, showing that **A** ≡ **B** can be derived without premises involves two subsidiary derivations: **B** is derived from the assumption **A**, and **A** is derived from the assumption **B**. But at various points in later chapters it will be very useful to show *directly* that one SL statement **A** is logically equivalent to another statement **B**. The direct path is to construct what we will call an **equivalence derivation.**

Beginning with some statement **A**, we can show that statement **B** is equivalent by constructing a derivation *that uses only equivalence rules.* Such derivations directly show the equivalence of the two statements. Several examples of this procedure are presented below. We use a *double vertical line* to indicate that the derivation runs up as well as down (that is, the derivation could be turned upside down and each justification shifted down one line), and the initial assumption is not set off from the other statements by the usual line. *The R rule cannot be used here* (since it is an inference rule), and no additional assumptions are permitted.

Example 1⁶ $(P \ \& \ Q) \lor (P \ \& \ {\sim}Q) \equiv P$

```
1.  ‖‖ (P & Q) ∨ (P & ~Q)
2.  ‖‖ P & (Q ∨ ~Q)          (DIST &/∨, 1)
3.  ‖‖ P                      (TAUT&, 2)
```

Notice how this equivalence derivation might be turned upside down. Starting from *P* the first step would be to form *P* & (*Q* ∨ ~*Q*) by the tautology & rule and then move to (*P* & *Q*) ∨ (*P* & ~*Q*) by distribution &/∨. In the upside-down equivalence derivation, the steps are just reversed.

Example 2 ${\sim}[P \lor (Q \ \& \ R)] \equiv [{\sim}(P \lor Q) \lor {\sim}(P \lor R)]$

```
1.  ‖‖ ~[P ∨ (Q & R)]
2.  ‖‖ ~P & ~(Q & R)         (DEM, 1)
3.  ‖‖ ~P & (~Q ∨ ~R)        (DEM, 2)
4.  ‖‖ (~P & ~Q)∨ (~P & ~R)  (DIST &/∨, 3)
5.  ‖‖ ~(P ∨ Q) ∨ (~P & ~R)  (DEM, 4)
6.  ‖‖ ~(P ∨ Q) ∨ ~(P ∨ R)   (DEM, 5)
```

─────────────

⁶This example is the simplification of a Post paraphrase of a truth table for two statement letters. See section 2.3. Equivalence derivations are particularly important in the simplification problems of chapter 10.

Example 3 $[P \lor Q] \equiv [(P \supset Q) \supset Q]$

1.	$P \lor Q$	
2.	$(P \lor Q) \& (Q \lor \sim Q)$	(TAUT, 1)
3.	$(Q \lor P) \& (Q \lor \sim Q)$	(COMM, 2)
4.	$Q \lor (P \& \sim Q)$	(DIST $\lor$/&, 3)
5.	$(P \& \sim Q) \lor Q$	(COMM, 4)
6.	$(\sim\sim P \& \sim Q) \lor Q$	(DNE, 5)
7.	$\sim(\sim P \lor Q) \lor Q$	(DEM, 6)
8.	$\sim(P \supset Q) \lor Q$	(CE, 7)
9.	$(P \supset Q) \supset Q$	(CE, 8)

Two final points. We have used the natural deduction system to show that arguments are valid when we can construct a derivation of the conclusion from the premises. We have also used the system to show that a statement is a tautology or a contradiction, that a set is inconsistent, or that two statements are logically equivalent. In all of these cases we start with the statement to be derived, or the statements to be shown equivalent, and then construct the derivation(s).

The use of the rules, however, *will not* show that a set is consistent, that a statement is contingent, or that an argument is invalid. To show any of these conditions is to show that some derivation *cannot* be completed; but within the natural deduction system we can never be absolutely sure that this is so—the fault may be ours in not having found (yet) the right combination of rules. Of course, if we suspect that a certain argument is invalid, we can construct a truth table or a tree and settle the matter once and for all. But we would then be operating outside of the natural deduction system. This vital difference, plus the fact that applications of the rules require some planning and ingenuity, makes the natural deduction method *nonalgorithmic*. We will have more to say about this in chapter 11.

Finally, natural deduction rules can also be used to *discover* what follows from a given set of statements or what statements are equivalent to a given statement. Each line in a main derivation is a consequent of the set of initial assumptions. Each line in an equivalence derivation is a statement equivalent to the original. Recall the case of Daphne and David; they *discovered* that the keys were in the coat pocket by drawing consequences from their initial set of evidence.

The task of discovery is especially important in the *simplification* problems we will encounter in chapters 10 and 12. In these problems, an SL statement is given and the task is to find an equivalent statement which is simpler, that is, which contains fewer connectives and, possibly, fewer statement letters as well. Since each SL connective will correspond to a portion of an electronic circuit, the simpler the expression, the simpler and cheaper the circuitry. So, simplification problems have a highly significant practical importance in the electronics industry.

Here is an example of a simplification problem for which natural deduction rules and equivalence derivations may be used. Suppose you are asked to find a simpler statement that is the equivalent of

~⟦~(P & Q) ∨ [~P ∨ (P & Q)]⟧[7]

The best strategy is to move the negations inside the parentheses by means of DeMorgan's laws, move things around with the distribution, association, and commutativity rules, and then look for possible applications of the tautology, contradiction, and idempotence equivalence rules, which permit connectives and statement letters to be eliminated.

1.	~⟦(P & Q) ∨ [~P ∨ (P & Q)]⟧	
2.	~(P & Q) & ~[~P ∨ (P & Q)]	(DEM, 1)
3.	~(P & Q) & [~~P & ~(P & Q)]	(DEM, 2)
4.	~(P & Q) & [P & ~(P & Q)]	(DNE, 3)
5.	[~(P & Q) & P] & ~(P & Q)	(ASSC, 4)
6.	[P & ~(P & Q)] & ~(P & Q)	(COMM, 5)
7.	P & [~(P & Q) & ~(P & Q)]	(ASSC, 6)
8.	P & ~(P & Q)	(IDEM, 7)
9.	P & (~P ∨ ~Q)	(DEM, 8)
10.	(P & ~P) ∨ (P & ~Q)	(DIST, 9)
11.	(P & ~Q) ∨ (P & ~P)	(COMM ∨, 10)
12.	P & ~Q	(CON ∨, 11)

As you can see, we were able to simplify dramatically the original statement which has six connectives into a statement with only one. (For more such problems, see exercise 4.2.5.)

Summary

In this section we explained the basic and derived SL natural deduction rules. Here is a convenient summary:

Basic Inference Rules:

1. *Double negation (DN)*   From ~~**A**, we can infer **A**.

2. *Indirect reasoning (IR)*   If on the assumption of a statement **A**, we can infer both some statement **B** and its negation ~**B**, then we can conclude that ~**A**.

3. *Simplification (SIMP)*   From a conjunction **A** & **B**, we can infer **A** (or **B**).

4. *Conjunction (CONJ)*   From statements **A** and **B**, we can infer **A** and **B**.

5. *Disjunction (DISJ)*   If we have a disjunction **A** ∨ **B**, and a statement **C** follows from both **A** and from **B**, then we may conclude **C**.

6. *Addition (ADD)*   From **A** we can infer **A** ∨ **B** (or **B** ∨ **A**).

7. *Modus ponens (MP)*   From **A** and **A** ⊃ **B**, we can infer **B**.

8. *Conditional Reasoning (CR)*   If on the assumption of a statement **A** we can infer **B**, then we can conclude **A** ⊃ **B**.

---

[7]The example is taken from William H. Gothmann, *Digital Electronics*, 2nd ed. (Englewood Cliffs, NJ: Prentice Hall, 1982), p. 91.

9. *Both Ways (BW)*   From **A ≡ B** and **A,** we may infer **B;** and from **A ≡ B** and **B,** we may infer **A.**

10. *Biconditional (BICON)*   If **B** may be inferred from **A,** and **A** may be inferred from **B,** then we may conclude **A ≡ B** (or **B ≡ A**).

11. *Reiteration (R)*   An assumption **A** of a derivation may be repeated in that derivation or in a subsidiary derivation.

Derived Inference Rules

12. *Modus Tollens (MT)*   From **A ⊃ B** and **~B,** we may infer **~A.**

13. *Hypothetical syllogism (HS)*   From **A ⊃ B** and **B ⊃ C, A ⊃ C** may be inferred.

14. *Disjunctive Syllogism (DS)*   From **A ∨ B** and **~ A, B** may be inferred (from **A ∨ B** and **~ B, A** may be inferred).

15. *Constructive Dilemma (CD)*   From **(A ⊃ B) & (C ⊃ D)** and **A ∨ C, B ∨ D** may be inferred.

Derived Equivalence Rules

16. *Commutativity of ∨ (COMM∨)*   **A ∨ B ↔ B ∨ A**

17. *Commutativity of & (COMM&)*   **A & B ↔ B & A**

18. *Associativity of ∨ (ASSC∨)*   **(A ∨ B) ∨ C ↔ A ∨ (B ∨ C)**

19. *Associativity of & (ASSC&)*   **(A & B) & C ↔ A & (B & C)**

20. *Distribution ∨/& (DIST∨/&)*   **A ∨ (B & C) ↔ (A ∨ B) & (A ∨ C)**

21. *Distribution &/∨ (DIST&/∨)*   **A & (B ∨ C) ↔ (A & B) ∨ (A & C)**

22. *Contraposition (CONTR)*   **A ⊃ B ↔ ~B ⊃ ~A**

23. *Conditional equivalence (CE)*   **A ⊃ B ↔ ~A ∨ B**

24. *Biconditional equivalence (BE)*
    A ≡ B ↔ (A & B) ∨ (~A & ~B)
    A ≡ B ↔ (A ⊃ B) & (B ⊃ A)

25. *Exportation (EXP)*   **(A & B) ⊃ C ↔ A ⊃ (B ⊃ C)**

26. *Idempotence of ∨ (IDEM∨)*   **A ↔ A ∨ A**

27. *Idempotence of & (IDEM&)*   **A ↔ A & A**

28. *DeMorgan's laws (DEM)*   **~(A ∨ B) ↔ ~ A & ~B**
    ~(A & B) ↔ ~A ∨ ~ B

29. *Absorption (ABS)*   **A ⊃ B ↔ A ⊃ (A & B)**

30. *Tautology & (TAUT&)*   **A ↔ A & (B ∨ ~B)**

31. *Tautology ∨ (TAUT∨)*   **A ∨ (B ∨ ~B) ↔ (B ∨ ~B)**

32. *Contradiction & (CON&)*   **A & (B & ~B) ↔ (B & ~B)**

33. *Contradiction ∨ (CON∨)*   **A ↔ A ∨ (B & ~B)**

34. *Double negation equivalence (DNE)*   **A ↔ ~~A**

If an SL argument is *valid,* or if a set of statements *entails* a statement, then the conclusion or statement entailed can be derived from the set of premises. If a statement is a *tautology,* it can be derived without any initial assumptions, i.e., from the empty set. If a statement is a *contradiction,* then its negation can be derived as a tautology. If a set of statements is *inconsistent,* then some statement and its negation can be derived from the set. If two statements **A** and **B** are *equivalent,* then **A** ≡ **B** can be derived as a tautology.

In an *equivalence derivation,* a statement **A** is directly shown to be logically equivalent to another statement **B**. Only equivalence rules may be used; no additional assumptions are allowed. The derivation begins with **A** and ends with **B** (or vice versa).

The following strategies are helpful for constructing derivations:

1. *Whenever possible, plan how a derivation might be constructed by working backwards from the conclusion that is sought. Ask yourself at each step: "How could I get this statement?" Then try to fill in the necessary steps.*

2. *When a negated conclusion ~A is sought, begin by assuming A in a subsidiary derivation, and work toward a contradiction so that the rule IR can be used. IR may be used in other cases as well; assume the negation of the conclusion you wish to reach. (This is a good last resort tactic, especially with disjunctive conclusions. But see 4 below.)*

3. *When a conditional A ⊃ B is sought, begin by assuming A and try to show that B follows. Then discharge the subsidiary derivation by using the rule CR.*

4. *When seeking a disjunction A ∨ B, try to get either A or B and then use ADD. When seeking a conjunction A & B, try to get A and B separately, then conjoin them. When seeking a biconditional A ≡ B, try to get both A ⊃ B and B ⊃ A, then use biconditional equivalence.*

5. *Write down a preliminary list of the obvious consequences of the premises; often a strategy for reaching the conclusion will appear in this process. Pay particular attention to the location in the premises of the statement letter components of the conclusion.*

6. *When attempting to show that a statement is a tautology, begin the derivation with an assumption in a subsidiary derivation. You have two choices, either to work towards a conditional by means of conditional reasoning, or to introduce a negation through indirect reasoning.*

7. *The best strategy in constructing equivalence derivations is to push the negations inside the parentheses by means of DeMorgan's laws, move things around with the distribution, association, and commutativity rules, and then look for possible applications of the tautology, contradiction, and idempotence equivalence rules to eliminate statement letters and connectives (especially in simplification problems).*

EXERCISES 4.2

1. Give derivations for each of the following; the use of the rule indicated in parentheses is prohibited.

   a. $\dfrac{(A \lor B)\ \&\ (A \lor C)}{A \lor (B\ \&\ C)}$ (distribution $\lor/\&$)

   b. $\dfrac{(A\ \&\ B) \lor (A\ \&\ C)}{A\ \&\ (B \lor C)}$ (distribution $\&/\lor$)

   c. $\dfrac{\sim B \supset \sim A}{A \supset B}$ (contraposition)

   d. $\dfrac{\sim A \lor B}{A \supset B}$ (conditional equivalence)

   e. $\dfrac{(A\ \&\ B) \lor (\sim A\ \&\ \sim B)}{A \equiv B}$ (biconditional equivalence)

   f. $\dfrac{(A \supset B)\ \&\ (B \supset A)}{A \equiv B}$ (biconditional equivalence)

   g. $\dfrac{A \supset (B \supset C)}{(A\ \&\ B) \supset C}$ (exportation)

   h. $\dfrac{A \lor A}{A}$ (idempotence of $\lor$)

   i. $\dfrac{\sim(A \lor B)}{\sim A\ \&\ \sim B}$ (DeMorgan's laws)

   j. $\dfrac{\sim(A\ \&\ B)}{\sim A \lor \sim B}$ (DeMorgan's laws)

   k. $\dfrac{\sim A \lor \sim B}{\sim(A\ \&\ B)}$ (DeMorgan's laws)

   l. $\dfrac{A \lor (B \lor C)}{(A \lor B) \lor C}$ (associativity of $\lor$)

2. By means of a derivation, prove that each of the following is a tautology; the use of the rule indicated in parentheses is prohibited.

   a. $A \equiv (A\ \&\ A)$ (idempotence of $\&$)

   b. $(A \supset B) \equiv [A \supset (A\ \&\ B)]$ (absorption)

   c. $[A \lor (B \lor \sim B)] \equiv (B \lor \sim B)$ (tautology $\lor$)

   d. $[A\ \&\ (B\ \&\ \sim B)] \equiv (B\ \&\ \sim B)$ (contradiction $\&$)

3. Derive some statement and its negation from each of the following sets.

   a. $\{P \lor Q,\ \sim Q,\ P \supset \sim P\}$

   b. $\{P \lor (Q\ \&\ R),\ R \supset P,\ \sim P,\ \sim Q\}$

   c. $\{\sim(P \lor Q),\ P\ \&\ Q\}$

   d. $\{\sim(P \supset \sim P),\ \sim(Q \supset \sim Q),\ \sim(P \lor Q)\}$

4. Using equivalence derivations, show that each of the following pairs of statements is equivalent.

   a. $P \equiv Q$ and $Q \equiv P$

   b. $\sim(P \& \sim Q)$ and $Q \vee \sim P$

   c. P and $(P \& Q) \vee (P \& \sim Q)$

   d. $P \equiv Q$ and $(\sim P \vee Q) \& (P \vee \sim Q)$

5. Using equivalence derivations, simplify each of the following statements:

   a. $(P \vee Q) \& (P \vee R)$

   b. $[\sim(\sim P \vee Q) \& (R \vee P)] \vee (P \& \sim R)$

   c. $\sim[\sim(P \vee Q) \vee Q]$

   d. $\sim\sim P \vee [P \& (Q \vee \sim Q)]$

   e. $(P \& Q) \vee [\sim(P \& Q) \& R]$

   f. $P \vee [\![Q \vee [(P \& R) \& (\sim P \& R)]]\!]$

   g. $(P \& Q) \vee [(P \& Q) \vee (R \& S)]$

4.3 RESOLUTION

Neither the truth tree method nor natural deduction is particularly well suited to fulfilling the goal of efficiently drawing conclusions from a data set. In this section we look at a method that is based on a single, but powerful, rule of inference known as the **resolution principle.** The important computer language PROLOG is based on resolution.

The resolution method requires that statements be expressed in what is known as **clausal form,** which is similar to some of the representations of SL we studied in section 2.3. First, we call any atomic statement, or negated atomic statement, a **literal.** Literals have already played an important role in the truth tree method; they are the ultimate residue of the application of decomposition rules to construct the branches of a truth tree. Second, we define a **clause** as a set of literals understood to represent their *disjunction.* Thus, in our notation, the clause $\{P, Q, \sim R\}$ represents the SL statement $P \vee Q \vee \sim R$.

Recall that in section 2.3 we showed that the Post paraphrase of any truth table, and, hence of any possible SL statement, could be expressed just using the connectives $\sim$, $\&$, and $\vee$. Further we showed that the form such Post paraphrases take is as a series of disjunctions of conjunctions of atomic statements (i.e., statement letters) and negated atomic statements. For example, the Post paraphrase of a statement of the form $\mathbf{A} \equiv \mathbf{B}$ is $(\mathbf{A} \& \mathbf{B}) \vee (\sim\mathbf{A} \& \sim \mathbf{B})$. As pointed out in section 2.3, even though the Post paraphrase method always produces an equivalent statement, the statements are sometimes much more complicated than they need to be. The simplification question, however, has been postponed to chapter 10.

Also recall that the truth trees can be used to produce a version of a Post paraphrase. If we decompose a noncontradictory statement by means of the tree rules, each open branch on the resulting tree represents a set of truth values on which the initial statement is true; that is, each branch contains a sufficient condition for the truth of the statement. For each open tree, we can form the truth-functionally equivalent **tree associate** of the initial statement by joining the different literals in each *open* branch by means of conjunctions and then joining by disjunction each of these conjunctions. As an example, note the tree for the statement $P \supset (Q \lor (\sim R \& S))$.

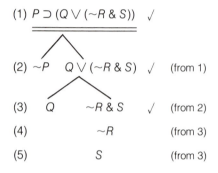

(1) $P \supset (Q \lor (\sim R \& S))$ ✓

(2) $\sim P$ $\quad$ $Q \lor (\sim R \& S)$ ✓ $\quad$ (from 1)

(3) $\quad$ Q $\quad\quad$ $\sim R \& S$ ✓ $\quad$ (from 2)

(4) $\quad\quad\quad\quad\quad$ $\sim R$ $\quad\quad\quad$ (from 3)

(5) $\quad\quad\quad\quad\quad$ S $\quad\quad\quad\quad$ (from 3)

This tree has three open branches. The *tree associate* of the statement $P \supset (Q \lor (\sim R \& S))$ is thus:

$\sim P \lor Q \lor (\sim R \& S)$

SL statements that are expressed in this way, as disjunctions of conjunctions of literals, are sometimes said to be in **disjunctive normal form.** Clearly, if disjunctive normal form were our goal, the tree method would be a particularly good way to produce it. Any statement that is not a contradiction is sure to have an open tree, and the branches represent all possible ways the statement can be true. So the tree associate is sure to be equivalent to the initial statement. For a contradiction, whose tree will, of course, be closed, a statement of the form **A & ~A** will serve as the disjunctive normal form, where **A** is the first statement letter in the statement. (A similar strategy was used in the Post paraphrases.)

Clausal form, however, is essentially **conjunctive normal form,** that is, statements expressed as *conjunctions of disjunctions.* However, there is a simple way of converting statements in disjunctive normal form to conjunctive normal form using repeated applications of the distribution equivalence rule. Recall that the rule is

Distribution $\lor$/&: A $\lor$ (B & C) $\leftrightarrow$ (A $\lor$ B) & (A $\lor$ C)

The procedure is to do an equivalence derivation as below:

1. $\quad \sim\!P \vee (Q \vee (\sim\!R \,\&\, S))$
2. $\quad \sim\!P \vee ((Q \vee \sim\!R) \,\&\, (Q \vee S))$ $\qquad$ (DIST$\vee$/&, 1)
3. $\quad (\sim\!P \vee (Q \vee \sim\!R)) \,\&\, (\sim\!P \vee (Q \vee S))$ $\qquad$ (DIST$\vee$/&, 2)

Hence, $(\sim\!P \vee (Q \vee \sim\!R)) \,\&\, (\sim\!P \vee (Q \vee S))$ is the conjunctive normal form of the original statement $P \supset (Q \vee (\sim\!R \,\&\, S))$.

Of course the conjunctive normal form of any SL statement can be directly produced as well. We can construct an equivalence derivation that systematically replaces connectives in accord with the following general patterns:

A $\supset$ **B** is replaced by $\sim$**A** $\vee$ **B** (i.e., CE)

A $\equiv$ **B** is replaced by ($\sim$**A** $\vee$ **B**) & (**A** $\vee$ $\sim$**B**)

$\sim\!\sim$**A** is replaced by **A** (i.e., DNE)

$\sim$(**A** $\vee$ **B**) is replaced by $\sim$**A** & $\sim$**B** (i.e., DEM)

$\sim$(**A** & **B**) is replaced by $\sim$**A** $\vee$ $\sim$**B** (i.e., DEM)

A $\vee$ (**B** & **C**) is replaced by (**A** $\vee$ **B**) & (**A** $\vee$ **C**) (i.e., DIST$\vee$/&)

So, either by means of trees and then repeated applications of the DIST rule, or by an equivalence derivation directly, any statement can be expressed in conjunctive normal form, as conjunctions of disjunctions of literals.[8] Contradictions can be expressed as **A** & $\sim$**A**, where **A** is the first statement letter in the contradiction; and a tautology can be expressed as **A** $\vee$ $\sim$**A**, where **A** is the first statement letter.

To continue the example, here is the direct equivalence derivation of the conjunctive normal form of $P \supset (Q \vee (\sim\!R \,\&\, S))$.

1. $\quad P \supset (Q \vee (\sim\!R \,\&\, S))$
2. $\quad \sim\!P \vee (Q \vee (\sim\!R \,\&\, S))$ $\qquad$ (CE, 1)
3. $\quad (\sim\!P \vee Q) \vee (\sim\!R \,\&\, S)$ $\qquad$ (ASSC$\vee$, 2)
4. $\quad ((\sim\!P \vee Q) \vee \sim\!R) \,\&\, ((\sim\!P \vee Q) \vee S)$ $\qquad$ (DIST$\vee$/&, 3)
5. $\quad (\sim\!P \vee (Q \vee \sim\!R)) \,\&\, ((\sim\!P \vee Q) \vee S)$ $\qquad$ (ASSC$\vee$, 4)
6. $\quad (\sim\!P \vee (Q \vee \sim\!R)) \,\&\, (\sim\!P \vee (Q \vee S))$ $\qquad$ (ASSC$\vee$, 5)

The clausal form of an SL statement is a *list* of one or more clauses, each of which represents one of the conjuncts of the conjunctive normal form of the statement. So, $P \supset (Q \vee (\sim\!R \,\&\, S))$ expressed in clausal form is

$\{\sim\!P,\ Q,\ \sim\!R\}$
$\{\sim\!P,\ Q,\ S\}$

---

[8]Because of the idempotence rules, we understand a literal itself to count as a disjunction and as a conjunction; P in conjunctive normal form or disjunctive normal form is just P.

The convention used here for clauses is that a *list* represents items that are true; the above list, then, represents the *conjunction* of the two clauses $\{\sim P, Q, \sim R\}$ and $\{\sim P, Q, S\}$.

No member of a set is represented twice in the display of that set; so too in clauses. Therefore, the conjunctive normal form $(P \vee P)$ & $(P \vee \sim Q)$ would be as follows in clausal form:

$\{P\}$
$\{P, \sim Q\}$

Since the idempotence principles hold for $\vee$ and &,

$A \vee A \leftrightarrow A$
$A \,\&\, A \leftrightarrow A$

clauses like $\{P, P, \ldots, P\}$ are simply redundant versions of $\{P\}$. Similarly, the list

$\{P\}$
$\{P\}$
$\{P\}$
etc.

is just a redundant version of the list

$\{P\}$

Finally, given the commutativity of $\vee$, the clause $\{P, \sim Q\}$ is the same as $\{\sim Q, P\}$.

EXERCISES 4.3a

1. Express the following in conjunctive normal form:
   a. $P \supset Q$ d. $\sim(\sim P \equiv Q)$
   b. $P \equiv Q$ e. $(T \supset S) \supset (T \supset R)$
   c. $\sim P \vee (R \,\&\, S)$

2. Express each of the above in clausal form.

3. Express each of the following in clausal form:
   a. $P \vee (P \supset R)$ c. $(P \supset Q) \,\&\, (Q \supset R)$
   b. $\sim(P \equiv Q)$ d. $((P \,\&\, Q) \vee (R \,\&\, \sim S)) \,\&\, S$

*4. How might the Post paraphrase method (section 2.3) be adapted to directly produce an equivalent conjunctive normal form for a statement?

The key element of the resolution method is the resolution rule itself. The basic idea is quite simple: If we know that a statement **A** is true or statement **B** is true, and we know that either **A** is false or **C** is true, then we know that **B** is true or **C** is true. Expressed in the form of an argument, this principle looks like:

A $\vee$ B

~A $\vee$ C
$$\overline{}$$
B $\vee$ C

The official statement of the resolution rule that is used for the resolution method is, however, more general. If we have two clauses that contain a literal **A** and its negation ~**A**, then we can infer the clause that is the union of the two clauses minus both **A** and ~**A**. Here is the general formulation of the resolution rule:

Resolution (Res)

Let $C_1 = \{\ldots, A, \ldots\}$

Let $C_2 = \{\ldots, \sim A, \ldots\}$

$$
\begin{array}{ll}
\text{m.} & C_1 \\
\text{n.} & C_2 \\
& \vdots \\
\text{p.} & C_1 - \{A\} \cup C_2 - \{\sim A\} \quad \text{(Res, m, n)}
\end{array}
$$

There are several features of our statement of the rule worth noting. First, the clauses C_1 and C_2 might not contain literals other than **A** and ~**A**, respectively. Thus the conclusion that follows from them will be an **empty clause,** which we will represent by { }. Second, if the same literal occurs in several clauses, it appears only once in the conclusion. Hence:

$$
\begin{array}{ll}
1. & \{P, Q\} \\
2. & \{\sim P, Q\} \\
\hline
3. & \{Q\} \qquad \text{(Res, 1, 2)}
\end{array}
$$

(Again, this operation is justified by the idempotence principle for $\vee$). We can represent derivations using the resolution rule in the now-familiar manner. However, since the *only* rule is resolution, we mark off the initial assumptions by a horizontal line, but they are not reiterated in the body of the derivation. There will be no subsidiary derivations either, since the natural deduction rules do not apply here.

Many familiar inference patterns have resolution forms. *Modus ponens,* for example, looks like this:

1. {~P, Q}
2. {P}

3. {Q}   (Res, 1, 2)

This is the resolution form of disjunctive syllogism:

1. {P, Q}
2. {~P}

3. {Q}   (Res, 1, 2)

Here is hypothetical syllogism:

1. {~P, Q}
2. {~Q, R}

3. {~P, R}   (Res, 1, 2)

In use, the resolution method permits the derivation of a clause from two or more initial clauses by repeated application of the resolution rule. There may be initial clauses that are not used in an inference, and there may be conclusions drawn from initial clauses or subsequent clauses that are not used in producing the desired conclusion. And some clauses may be used more than once. Here is an example of an initial list of four clauses that lead to the clause containing just ~P:

1. {P}
2. {~P, Q}
3. {~R}
4. {~Q, R}

5. {Q}   (Res, 1, 2)
6. {~Q}   (Res, 3, 4)
7. {~P}   (Res, 2, 6)

Note that the first conclusion, the clause {Q}, has no further role in the derivation, and we really did not need to use initial clause {P} in the derivation at all to obtain the desired conclusion {~P}. You may have noticed, however, that we have produced both {Q} and {~Q} as conclusions, so we could go on to derive the empty clause { } from them in one more step and thus make use of all initial clauses in the derivation of the final conclusion:

8. { }   (Res, 5, 6)

Like the truth tree method, the resolution method can be used to test a list of clauses for inconsistency. We say that *a list of clauses is inconsistent* if the empty clause can be derived from the list of clauses through repeated applications of the resolution rule. Based on the above derivations, the list consisting of

$\{P\}$

$\{\sim P, Q\}$

$\{\sim R\}$

$\{\sim Q, R\}$

is inconsistent.

Since entailment can always be understood in terms of inconsistency (section 3.3), the resolution method can be used to test whether a certain statement is entailed by some set of statements. The procedure is similar to the truth tree method: negate the statement and express it in clausal form; express the initial statements in clausal form; and test whether the empty clause can be derived from the resulting list of clauses. Note that the initial clauses of such a derivation will include the clausal forms of the statements in the set plus the added clausal form of the *negation* of the statement that we are testing to determine whether it is entailed by the set. Thus a derivation of the empty clause is like the production of a closed tree.

A resolution derivation of an empty clause is called a *refutation* derivation. In effect, we are refuting the claim of consistency for the list of clauses when we derive the empty clause. When the negation (in clausal form) of a statement is added to a list of clauses to show that the statement is entailed, the original unnegated statement is called the *goal* of the refutation, and the clause representing its negation is called the *negated goal*.

Here is an example:

$P \equiv (Q \vee R)$

$\sim (P \supset Q)$

_____

R (the goal)

Conjunctive normal forms:

$P \equiv (Q \vee R) = (\sim P \vee Q \vee R) \,\&\, (P \vee \sim Q) \,\&\, (P \vee \sim R)$

$\sim (P \supset Q) = P \,\&\, \sim Q$

Negate conclusion:

$\sim R$ (i.e. the negated goal is $\{\sim R\}$)

Clausal forms:

$\{\sim P, Q, R\}$
$\{P, \sim Q\}$
$\{P, \sim R\}$
$\{P\}$
$\{\sim Q\}$
$\{\sim R\}$

Derivation of { }:

1. | {~P, Q, R}
2. | {P, ~Q}
3. | {P, ~R}
4. | {P}
5. | {~Q}
6. | {~R}   (added)
   |‾‾‾‾‾‾‾‾‾‾
7. | {~P, R}   (Res, 1, 5)
8. | {R}   (Res, 4, 7)
9. | { }   (Res, 8, 6)

Thus we have shown that R follows from the premises $P \equiv (Q \lor R)$ and $\sim(P \supset Q)$.

The resolution method can be used to answer questions from data sets when those data sets are already represented in clausal form (or if we are willing to convert SL statements to clausal form). To obtain an answer to the question of whether R is true based on the following data set,

{~P, Q, R}
{P, ~Q}
{P, ~S}
{P}
{~Q}

we simply *add* the clause {~R} consisting of the negation of R to the data set and try to produce a refutation derivation. If we are successful in deriving the empty clause, then R is true; if the empty clause is not derivable, then R is false (or the truth-value of R is completely independent of the data set). So, is R true?

There is an important difference between the resolution and the natural deduction methods. Because of the addition (ADD) rule, an *infinite* number of statements can be derived from the assumptions of any natural deduction derivation. When the assumptions of a natural deduction derivation are inconsistent, then all possible statements can be derived. There is, however, no version of the addition rule in the resolution method. Furthermore, although a list of inconsistent clauses would entail an *infinite* number of statements in clausal form, the method produces the derivations of only a *finite* number of clausal consequences from any given data set or list of clauses, whether the list is inconsistent or not.

An obvious way of *automating* the resolution method is to instruct a machine to perform all possible applications of the resolution rule to the clauses in some initial list, or data set, and to continue to perform such applications until no more new conclusions are possible. This brute force method works because the number of conclusions that can be derived from any clause is finite, and it is easily implemented because only one rule is involved. The automation might proceed by having the machine simply compare every two clauses in a list and copy any clause that is a conclusion by the resolution rule at the bottom of the list. The list will grow and grow, but when all possible conclusions have been found, including those that use other conclusions, the list will at least come to an end.

Whether we carry out this automated process ourselves or program a machine to do so, we can use certain strategies to make it more efficient.[9] If we are attempting to show, by means of a refutation derivation, that a statement is entailed by a list of clauses, we add the clausal form of the negation of that statement (i.e., the negated goal) to the list and try to derive the empty clause.

Deletion Strategy   Usually there are many more clauses in the data set than are actually needed for the refutation derivation at hand. Therefore, we can eliminate all clauses that contain what are called **pure literals** from further consideration. A pure literal is one whose negation does not occur in any clause in the data set. Pure literals themselves are not used in any application of the resolution rule, and can be safely eliminated from consideration; clauses containing pure literals do not advance us toward the empty clause. The elimination of these clauses cuts down on the number of clauses that must be considered as we work down the list.

A second deletion possibility is all instances of literals and their negations *within* clauses. A clause such as $\{Q, \sim P, P, R\}$ is a tautology in clausal form. Nothing follows from tautologies except other tautologies, so these clauses will not aid us in deriving the empty clause.

Of course, these two kinds of deletions make sense only in refutation derivations, where the desired conclusion is the empty clause. Here is an example of the use of deletion in an automated version of resolution that simply arbitrarily compares clauses and applies the rule whenever possible:

1.	$\{\sim P, Q, R\}$	
2.	$\{Q, \sim Q\}$	
3.	$\{T, \sim S, R\}$	
4.	$\{P\}$	
5.	$\{\sim Q\}$	
6.	$\{\sim R\}$	(added)
7.	$\{Q, R\}$	(Res, 1, 4)
8.	$\{R\}$	(Res, 5, 7)
9.	$\{\sim P, Q\}$	(Res, 1, 6)
10.	$\{Q\}$	(Res, 4, 9)
11.	$\{\sim P, R\}$	(Res, 1, 5)
12.	$\{\sim P\}$	(Res, 6, 11)
13.	$\{Q\}$	(Res, 6, 7)
14.	$\{R\}$	(Res, 4, 11)
15.	$\{\sim P\}$	(Res, 5, 9)
16.	$\{\ \ \}$	(Res, 4, 15)

You will note that even though the deletion strategy saved a few steps, we still have many unnecessary steps because we just arbitrarily found

---

[9] These strategies are from Michael R. Genesereth and Nils J. Nilsson, *Logical Foundations of Artificial Intelligence* (San Mateo, CA: Morgan Kaufmann, 1987), chapter 5.

clauses to which the rule applied. The derivation can actually be performed in as few as three steps, as follows:

1. $\{\sim P, Q, R\}$
2. $\{Q, \sim Q\}$
3. $\{T, \sim S, R\}$
4. $\{P\}$
5. $\{\sim Q\}$
6. $\{\sim R\}$ (added)
---
7. $\{Q, R\}$ (Res, 1, 4)
8. $\{R\}$ (Res, 5, 7)
9. $\{\ \ \}$ (Res, 6, 8)

So, deletion by itself is not a very efficient procedure.

Unit Resolution A clause containing only a single literal is called a **unit clause.** When the resolution rule is applied to pairs of clauses in which at least one clause is a unit clause, the conclusion will be a clause containing a smaller number of literals than one of the initial clauses. For example, applying the resolution rule to the clauses $\{R\}$ and $\{P, \sim Q, T, \sim R, Q\}$ produces the conclusion $\{P, \sim Q, T, Q\}$. When the resolution rule is applied to two-unit clauses, the conclusion will always be an empty clause. Therefore, in trying to derive the empty clause from a list of clauses, it often is very efficient to use only *unit resolution,* which is the restriction of the resolution method to cases where at least one clause is a unit clause. For maximum efficiency, we should prefer applications of the resolution rule to two unit clauses (which produces the empty clause).

An example using the unit-resolution strategy follows:

1. $\{\sim P, Q, R\}$
2. $\{R, \sim Q\}$
3. $\{\sim P, \sim S, R\}$
4. $\{Q\}$
5. $\{\sim R\}$ (added)
---
6. $\{\sim P, Q\}$ (Res, 1, 5)
7. $\{\sim P, \sim S\}$ (Res, 3, 5)
8. $\{\sim Q\}$ (Res, 2, 5)
9. $\{\ \ \}$ (Res, 4, 8)

Since one of the clauses must be a unit clause, we bypass the application of the rule to the clauses in lines 1, 2, and 1, 3, and apply the rule to the clauses in lines 1 and 5. Other applications of the rule to pairs of clauses containing a one-unit clause finally result in $\{Q\}$ and $\{\sim Q\}$ in lines 4 and 8, and the empty clause results. If unit resolution and deletion are combined, several steps could be saved; we would eliminate lines 6 and 7, making the derivation very short indeed. (Note: $\sim P$ and $\sim S$ are pure literals.)

Input Resolution The initial clauses in a resolution derivation may be thought of as the **inputs** of the derivation. It is sometimes efficient to require that all applications of the resolution method in a derivation involve at least one of the inputs, unless opposite unit clauses are available. A simple way to accomplish this is to move from the top down, looking for clauses to which to apply the rule. When we have applied the rule to the first line and every possible clause below it, we then turn to the second line and work down, and so forth. Of course, when opposite clauses appear, we terminate the derivation by producing the empty clause.

Here is our example again, this time using input resolution and deletion; note the number of steps that are saved.

1.	$\{\sim P, Q, R\}$	
2.	$\{Q, \sim Q\}$	
3.	$\{T, \sim S, R\}$	
4.	$\{P\}$	
5.	$\{\sim Q\}$	
6.	$\{\sim R\}$	(added)
7.	$\{Q, R\}$	(Res, 1, 4)
8.	$\{\sim P, R\}$	(Res, 1, 5)
9.	$\{\sim P, Q\}$	(Res, 1, 6)
10.	$\{R\}$	(Res, 4, 8)
11.	$\{\ \ \}$	(Res, 6, 10)

Linear Resolution A particularly efficient way of constructing resolution derivations is to *begin* with the negated goal clause that we have added to the data set. Subsequent applications of the resolution rule either are input resolutions or, when these have been exhausted, are applications to cases in which one clause is the **ancestor** of the other. A clause C_1 is called ancestor of a clause C_2 if C_2 can be traced back through a series of steps to clause C_1. Following this strategy produces a *linear resolution,* which avoids many of the wasteful steps involving conclusions drawn from other conclusions. Linear resolution focuses on the initial clauses and on clauses that are related to one another through ancestry. Note that the initial clauses themselves are ancestors of all clauses that result from them. By setting up the derivation with the negated goal clause at the *top* of the list, we guarantee that the opening applications of the resolution rule involve that clause (assuming that we work from the top down as in input resolution).

Here is our example again, now using the linear resolution strategy (with deletion):

1.	$\{\sim R\}$	(added)
2.	$\{\sim P, Q, R\}$	
3.	$\{Q, \sim Q\}$	
4.	$\{T, \sim S, R\}$	
5.	$\{P\}$	
6.	$\{\sim Q\}$	
7.	$\{\sim P, Q\}$	(Res, 1, 2)
8.	$\{Q\}$	(Res, 5, 7)
9.	$\{\ \ \}$	(Res, 6, 8)

After applying the rule to the added clause and to the first clause we find (line 2), we look for other clauses to match with {~R}. Finding none, we then move to the result of the initial application of the rule (line 7) and try to apply the rule to that clause and to one of its ancestors (i.e., lines 1 and 2). Since that doesn't work, we then find the first unit clause we can (line 5), which then gives us a clause and its opposite. Note how efficiently linear resolution handles this problem.

The utility of combining the above resolution strategies can be seen in the following example.

Show that {Q} follows from the data set:

{~P, R}
{P, Q}
{~R, Q}
{R, S, ~T}
{S}
{~T, R, Q}

We will put the unit clause containing ~Q at the top of the list to further the linear resolution strategy.

1.	{~Q}	(added)
2.	{~P, R}	
3.	{P, Q}	
4.	{~R, Q}	
5.	{R, S, ~T}	
6.	{S}	
7.	{~T, R, Q}	
8.	{P}	(Res, 1, 3)
9.	{~R}	(Res, 1, 4)
10.	{R}	(Res, 2, 8)
11.	{ }	(Res, 9, 10)

The linear resolution strategy had us applying the rule to the negated goal clause and to other input clauses taken in order. Since the rule doesn't apply to the first two clauses, we went to line 3 and applied the rule to obtain {P}. Then we continued and found another application in line 4 to produce {~R}. We could have continued to line 7, but the deletion strategy tells us to ignore the clauses in lines 5, 6, and 7 because they contain the pure literals ~T and S. So our next step was to go to the next input clause (line 2) and apply the rule to it and to a unit clause (line 8) that produced {R}. At that point, the empty clause was within reach.

Since data sets can be very large, using these four strategies will produce answers to questions in many fewer steps than the resolution method might require if no direction at all is established for the application of the rule. In the case above, for example, seven conclusions are produced if the resolution rule is applied generally to the initial clauses.

We will have more to say about the automated use of resolution in chapter 7.

EXERCISES 4.3b

1. Show that the following lists of clauses are inconsistent:

   a. $\{P, Q\}$
      $\{\sim P, Q\}$
      $\{P, \sim Q\}$
      $\{\sim P, \sim Q\}$

   b. $\{P, Q\}$
      $\{\sim Q, \sim R\}$
      $\{R, \sim S\}$
      $\{\sim Q, S\}$
      $\{S\}$
      $\{\sim P, Q\}$

2. Give resolution refutation derivations for each of the following. Note: the negation of the conclusion in some of the following will require more than one clause.

   a. $\dfrac{\sim(A \vee B)}{\sim A \ \& \sim B}$

   b. $\dfrac{A \supset (B \supset C)}{(A \ \& \ B) \supset C}$

   c. $\dfrac{\sim(A \ \& \ B)}{\sim A \vee \sim B}$

   d. $\dfrac{\sim A \vee \sim B}{\sim(A \ \& \ B)}$

   e. $\dfrac{A \vee (B \vee C)}{(A \vee B) \vee C}$

3. By means of the resolution method, show that each of the following sets is inconsistent.

   a. $\{P \vee Q, \sim Q, P \supset \sim P\}$

   b. $\{P \vee (Q \ \& \ R), R \supset P, \sim P, \sim Q\}$

   c. $\{\sim(P \vee Q), P \ \& \ Q\}$

   d. $\{\sim(P \supset \sim P), \sim(Q \supset \sim Q), \sim(P \vee Q)\}$

*4. Provide an example of an efficient use of each of the resolution strategies discussed above.

5

Predicate Logic: Fundamentals

We now turn to a much more powerful logical system, called **predicate logic,** or PL, for short. The development of this system was the crowning glory of late nineteenth and early twentieth century work in logic.[1] We will be able to represent a very large number of inferences in this system; as you will see, many of the most fundamental forms of reasoning are based upon PL principles. The familiar patterns of SL are represented in PL as well. So PL can be thought of as the grand system of logic of which SL is a part.

5.1 NAMES AND PREDICATES

Consider the following intuitively valid argument:

(1) Mary ate pizza.
    _____

    Therefore, someone ate pizza.

If we wanted to symbolize argument (1) in the notation of SL, we would have to use a different statement letter for the premise and the conclusion;

---

[1]See William and Martha Kneale, *The Development of Logic* (London: Oxford University Press, 1962), chapters 8 & 9.

for example *M* for 'Mary ate pizza' and *P* for 'Someone ate pizza'. So the argument in SL would look like this:

M

―

P

As you can see, this SL argument pattern is clearly invalid, as is shown by any valuation that assigns **T** to the statement letter *M* and **F** to the statement letter *P*. Thus, if we are interested in understanding the principles of validity in such arguments as (1) above, we need to go beyond the resources of SL.

To begin, consider these two related statements:

(2) Mary ate pizza.

(3) Sam ate pizza.

Both statements can be thought of as having the *form*

(a) _____ ate pizza

where the blank is to be filled in with some **name,** 'Mary' or 'Sam' for example. It is clear that from statement form (a) we can generate an infinite variety of statements, as many as we have names at our disposal, e.g., 'Fred ate pizza', 'Daphne ate pizza', 'Stephen ate pizza', and on and on. Each of these new statements results from inserting a name into the statement form.

In the statement above, the phrase 'ate pizza' is called the **predicate.**[2] In the case of the statements about Mary and Sam, the predicate denotes a *property* they both share, namely the property of having eaten pizza. Here are some other statements that similarly ascribe properties to individuals:

(4) Jim is a veteran.

(5) Mary has brown shoes.

(6) The table is painted white.

(7) Her book is heavy.

Each of these statements can be divided logically into two components: a name and a predicate. You may well wonder how this division applies to statements like (6) and (7), since they do not contain the names of any

---

[2]This terminology somewhat follows the traditional grammarian's division of sentences into *subject* and *predicate*. However, we will soon look at logical predicates that are not grammatical predicates, and there the analogy breaks down.

people. We are using the term 'name' here in a very general way to mean *any means of denoting an individual thing.* So phrases like 'the table' and 'her book', as well as ones like 'the hot dog I ate last Friday', count as names just as *proper* names like 'Fred' and 'Daphne', since they all serve to indicate specific things.

One way to identify the predicate of a statement like those we have been discussing is to pull the name out; what is left is the predicate. Doing this to the statements listed above results in the following (with blanks replacing names):

Name	Predicate
(2) Mary	_____ ate pizza
(4) Jim	_____ is a veteran
(5) Mary	_____ has brown shoes
(6) the table	_____ is painted white
(7) her book	_____ is heavy

Some statements contain several names; their predicates serve to indicate that some *relation* holds between two or more objects. For example,

(8) Mary and Sam are friends.

(9) The cup is next to the spoon.

(10) The wastebasket is between the door and the table.

(11) Jim loves Sue.

Applying the same technique again of identifying predicates by pulling out the names results in the following:

Names	Predicate
(8) Mary, Sam	_____ and _____ are friends
(9) the cup, the spoon	_____ is next to _____
(10) the wastebasket, the door the desk	_____ is between _____ and _____
(11) Jim, Sue	_____ loves _____[3]

We have seen examples of predicates that take only one name (e.g., '_____ is a veteran'), predicates that take two names (e.g., '_____ is next

---

[3]If you have read section 2.5, you may be reminded here of the way in which reverse outfix notation treats arithmetical operations.

to _____'), and even predicates that take three names ('_____ is between _____ and _____'). Theoretically there is no limit on how many names predicates might take, although, in ordinary English, predicates with more than three names usually seem contrived. For some purposes it will be useful to classify predicates on the basis of how many names they take; we will call predicates that take only one name **monadic** or **one-place** predicates. Those taking two or more names are called **polyadic** or **many-place** predicates, i.e. **two-place, three-place,** etc.

You should note the importance of the *order* of the names in a statement containing a many-place predicate. In (11), 'Jim loves Sue', for example, we would have a very different statement if we wrote 'Sue loves Jim', since the first might be true when the second is false. In (10), 'The wastebasket is between the door and the desk', statements with different truth-values may result from changes in the order of the names, e.g., 'The door is between the wastebasket and the desk'. Of course sometimes changing the order of the names will produce a statement with the *same* truth-value as the original. Two-place predicates that have this property are called **symmetrical.** Some examples of symmetrical predicates are:

_____ is next to _____

_____ equals _____

_____ is the same size as _____

_____ is related to _____

You probably can think of others.

In PL *names* are represented by lowercase letters, largely from the beginning of the alphabet: a, b, c, d, etc. When necessary, we may write these with numerical subscripts, as a_1, a_2, a_3, and so forth. This system gives us the potential of an infinite number of names if we need them (since there are an infinite number of positive integers to use as subscripts). For reasons that will become apparent later on, the letters x, y, and z are *not* used for names. Capital letters are used for *predicates*. We will reserve the boldface capitals **A, B, C,** and **D,** for the special role they played in chapters 2, 3, and 4, namely as variables to stand for any expression whatever. In choosing a capital letter to stand for a predicate, we generally use the first letter of the key word to make it easy to remember what the letter symbolizes. (We ordinarily do this with names as well.) So we would use L for the two-place predicate '_____ loves _____', for example. Other PL notation will be introduced later.

To symbolize PL statements, the longstanding tradition is to write the predicate letter first followed by the name or names *in the order* they appear in the statement. Recall the admonition that the order of the names is significant. Here, for example, are the symbolizations of the ten statements we have already discussed:

	Statement	Symbolization	
(1)	David ate pizza.	*Pa*	(*a*: 'David')
(2)	Daphne ate pizza.	*Pb*	(*b*: 'Daphne')
(3)	Jim is a veteran.	*Vj*	
(4)	Mary has brown shoes.	*Bm*	
(5)	The table is painted white.	*Wt*	
(6)	Her book is heavy.	*Hb*	
(7)	Mary and Sam are friends.	*Fms*	
(8)	The cup is next to the spoon.	*Ncs*	
(9)	The wastebasket is between the door and the table.	*Bwdt*	
(10)	Jim loves Sue.	*Ljs*	

Just to underscore the point about the importance of order, note that while *Fms* above symbolizes 'Mary and Sam are friends', the reversed *Fsm* would symbolize 'Sam and Mary are friends', which is a *different* statement (even if the predicate is symmetrical and the two statements have the same truth value).

PL statements that contain *only* names and predicates are called **atomic statements:** *Ka*, *Vj*, *Fms*, *Bwdt*, and *Ljs* are all atomic PL statements. As the basic building blocks of PL, atomic statements are analogous to the statement letters of SL.

The statement connectives we studied in SL also play an important role in PL. Here are a few examples of how they permit combinations of atomic statements:

(11) If Mary lost her book, then Sam will not be able to use it.

Notation: *L*: '_____ lost her book'
            m: 'Mary'
            U: '_____ will be able to use it'
            s: 'Sam'

Symbolization: *Lm* ⊃ ~*Us*

Note that the statement 'Sam *will not* be able to use it' (~*Us*) is understood to mean 'It is *not* the case that Sam *will* be able to use it' and so is represented as a negation.

(12) John came by train and so did Sue.

Notation: *j*: 'John'
            T: '_____ came by train'
            s: 'Sue'

Symbolization: *Tj* & *Ts*

(13) If Alan doesn't pass the exam, he will have to go to summer school and will not move to Cleveland.

Notation: a: 'Alan'
$\qquad$ P: '_____ passes the exam'
$\qquad$ S: '_____ will go to summer school'
$\qquad$ M: '_____ will move to _____'
$\qquad$ c: 'Cleveland'

Symbolization: $\sim Pa \supset (Sa \,\&\, \sim Mac)$

You may have noticed that there is a certain arbitrariness about our choice of predicates in statements like (13). We could have taken 'Alan doesn't pass the exam' to contain a *two-place* predicate '_____ passes _____' and the two names 'Alan' and 'the exam'. The phrase 'the exam' does indicate a particular examination and so it could count as a name as we here use the term. For some purposes, this more elaborate logical analysis could be important; for others we might just as well use the one-place predicate '_____ passes the exam' as above. Usually the decision about how to symbolize a particular statement will depend on the context in which the statement occurs.

Summary

We have in this section identified **names** as words or phrases that are used in statements to indicate particular persons, places, or things. Some common categories of names are:

Proper names of people (e.g., 'Mary,' 'Sue')

Proper names of other things (e.g., 'Fido,' 'Muffins')

Pronouns ('he,' 'she,' 'it,' 'you,' 'they,' etc.)

Noun phrases (e.g., 'her book,' 'the car,' 'this potato,' 'that desk,' 'the monster that ate Toledo')

We also have studied **predicates,** which serve to indicate properties of objects or relations that hold between objects. Predicates that take one name are called **monadic** or **one-place;** predicates that take more than one name are called **polyadic** or **many-place** (i.e., two-place, three-place, etc.). One way to find the predicates in statements is to remove names and note what remains.

PL statements that contain only names and predicates are called **atomic.** Compounds of atomic statements can be formed by using the statement connectives of SL.

EXERCISES 5.1

1. Underline the names and circle the predicates in each of the following. If you find more than one plausible answer, give them all.

   a. Mary is a student.

   b. John is sitting next to Helen.

   c. This desk is really ugly.

   d. I saw you yesterday.

   e. Today is my birthday.

   f. Her book is red.

   g. Her book really belongs to Fred.

   h. Sam took her book.

2. Which of the following can be translated as a PL atomic statement? Explain your answer in each case.

   a. John is Bill's brother.

   b. Somebody took my sandwich.

   c. Mary is related to Frank, Sue, Jane, Pete, and Roger.

   d. Thanksgiving always comes before Pearl Harbor Day.

   e. Mary is considering buying a centrifuge and so is Dan.

   f. Everybody should exercise on weekends.

3. Symbolize the following using the suggested notation.

   a. Bill hates lettuce. (*b*: 'Bill'; *H*: '_____ hates lettuce')

   b. Bill hates Sam. (*b*: 'Bill'; *H*: '_____ hates _____'; *s*: 'Sam')

   c. If Sue is in London, then she is in England. (*s*: 'Sue'; *I*: '_____ is in _____'; *l*: 'London'; *e*: 'England')

   d. Either Mary or Jane will win. (*m*: 'Mary'; *j*: 'Jane'; *W*: '_____ will win')

   e. Betty will eat cheese tonight. (*b*: 'Betty;' *E*: '_____ will eat cheese _____'; *t*: 'tonight')

4. Give a reasonably smooth English translation of each of the following, using:

   P for '_____ is a person'
   L for '_____ likes _____'
   a for 'Albert'
   b for 'Betty'
   c for 'Charlie'

   a. *Pa*

   b. *Pa ⊃ Lca*

    c. *Pa ⊃ Lac*

    d. *(Pa & Pb) ⊃ Lab*

    e. *~(Lca & Lcb)*

    f. *Lab ∨ Lba*

    g. *(Pb & Lab) ⊃ Lcb*

5. From the front page of today's newspaper, find eight examples of state-ments containing names and predicates. List your eight statements and indicate which could be considered atomic, which could be considered compounds of atomic statements, and which are neither.

5.2 QUANTIFIERS

In our discussion of names and predicates so far, it should be clear that there is an element of *generality* about predicates. For example, consider the one-place predicate:

    _____ is large.

Any name can be placed in the blank to form a statement. Thus, from this predicate, by filling in the blank with various names we can get:

    Bill is large.

    The desk is large.

    My toe is large.

    etc.

Perhaps not all the results of this filling in will make perfect sense, and some of the resulting statements will surely be false, for example, 'Tiny Tim is large'. But statements will result from this operation nevertheless.

    The use of **quantifiers** is another way of making statements from pred-icates. In English, words like 'everything,' 'something,' 'some,' 'all,' 'every,' 'any,' and 'several' serve to indicate the range of application of predicates. *Universally* quantifying the predicate '_____ is large' results in the general statement

    Everything is large.

Note that the word 'everything' does not function as a name; it does not serve to pick out a particular object.

    Clearly, a universal statement such as 'Everything is large' means that any conceivable object is large. So, anyone who asserts that everything is large is, in effect, asserting that Alan is large, Betty is large, Carlos is large,

Dorothy is large, my car is large, your teeth are large, the number .00000012 is large, and so on, for everything else.

Quantification requires special notation. For the **universal quantifier** we use the symbol ∀, which is read 'for all'. The quantifier symbol is always followed by some **individual variable,** for which we will use the letters x, y, and z, with subscripts when even more variables are needed. Remember that these three lowercase letters were explicitly reserved, so they are not used for names. When quantifiers are used, variables will also show up in the blanks of predicates. Using this notation, 'Everything is large' would be symbolized as:

∀x Lx

which would be read: 'For all x, x is large'. You should note that the choice of x as the variable here is purely arbitrary; we could have used y or z (or x_5, etc.) instead.

Quantifiers interact with SL connectives in somewhat the same way that the negation symbol does. So attaching a quantifier to a conjunction, for example, requires a set of parentheses, as in

∀x (Sx & Rx)

This PL statement is read: 'For all x, x is S and x is R'. An English statement that could be symbolized this way is 'Everything is sweet and round'.

Universal quantifiers are often joined to conditionals. So-called *universal categorical* statements like the classic[4]

All humans are mortal.

are symbolized in PL as

∀x (Hx ⊃ Mx)   (H: '_____ is human'; M: '_____ is mortal')

This PL statement can be read: 'For all x, if x is human, then x is mortal'. What this means is that for any object at all, if that thing is human, then that thing is mortal. So when we drop the universal quantifier and substitute the name of an object, for example 'Fido' (f), for the variable x, the resulting statement is

Hf ⊃ Mf

('If Fido is a human, then he or she is mortal'.) is true if the original universal statement is. Note that the universal categorical statement does *not* say that

---

[4]The logic of categorical statements as a subsystem of PL is covered in section 8.2.

everything *is* human, but only that *if* something is human, it is also mortal. Other examples of universal categorical statements that have similar PL symbolizations are

> All fish swim in the sea.
>
> All that glitters is gold.
>
> Anyone who passes the exam gets an ice cream.
>
> If something is made of iron, then it is attracted by a magnet.

Quantifiers interact with negation in several ways. A *negated* universal quantificational statement such as

> $\sim\!\forall x\, Px$

can be read: 'It is not the case that everything is a P' (or 'It is not the case that, for all x, x is P'). Since such a statement denies that everything is P, the statement requires that at least one thing not be P. A second common location for a negation is immediately following the quantifier, thus negating the quantified expression, as in

> $\forall x \sim\!Px$

This PL statement is read: 'For all x, x is *not* P'. Note the important difference between these two statements; the first, $\sim\!\forall x\, Px$, says that at least one thing is not P, whereas the second, $\forall x \sim\!Px$, says that everything is not P.

Here are several other examples of translations of statements involving negation:

Not everything is blue and soft.	$\sim\!\forall x\, (Bx\ \&\ Sx)$
Nothing is both blue and soft.	$\forall x \sim\!(Bx\ \&\ Sx)$
Not all jokes are polite.	$\sim\!\forall x\, (Jx \supset Px)$
Everything which isn't green is boring.	$\forall x(\sim\!Gx \supset Bx)$

By now it should be clear that *where* a negation occurs makes a great deal of difference. To take the last statement as an example, putting the negation first, $\sim\!\forall x\, (Gx \supset Bx)$ says, in effect, that not everything that is green is boring; putting the negation just after the quantifier, $\forall x \sim\!(Gx \supset Bx)$, says, in effect, that everything *is* green and *isn't* boring. (Remember that $\sim\!(A \supset B)$ in SL is equivalent to $A\ \&\ \sim\!B$.)

PL also makes use of a second quantifier, the **existential quantifier,** for which the symbol $\exists$ is used, followed, of course, by a variable. The existential quantifier is read: 'For some', or, alternatively, 'There is at least one _____ such that'. Thus, the statement 'Something is large' would be symbolized

∃x LX

and would be read: 'For some x, x is large' (or, 'There is at least one x such that x is large').[5] The following translations will give a good overview of the use of the existential quantifier.

Something is either red or blue.	∃x (Rx ∨ Bx)
There is a gopher in the yard.	∃x (Gx & Yx)
Something is not expensive.	∃x ~ Ex
It is not the case that something is expensive.	~∃x Ex
It is not the case that something isn't expensive.	~∃x ~ Ex

Although 'It is not the case that something isn't expensive' may seem to be an overly convoluted statement, if you think about its meaning you will find that it essentially says that everything *is* expensive. And of course, 'Everything *is* expensive' could be symbolized as ∀x Ex. What this suggests is that the two quantifiers are logically related, just as are the notions of 'all' and 'some' in English. Here, then, are two important PL equivalences that demonstrate how the two quantifiers can be interchanged:[6]

∀x Px ≡ ~∃x ~Px
∃x Px ≡ ~∀x ~Px

Saying that everything has property P (∀x Px) is thus like saying that there isn't anything that doesn't have the property (~∃x ~Px). Similarly, saying that something has property P (∃x Px) is like saying that not everything doesn't have property P (~∀x ~Px).

Summary

Before going on, you should be sure that you have the two *quantifiers* straight in your mind. The *universal* quantifier is symbolized by ∀ and is read 'For all _____'. The *existential quantifier* is symbolized by ∃ and is read 'For some _____' or 'There is at least one thing _____ such that'. Quantifiers are

---

[5]The quantifier may also be read: 'There exists an _____ such that', from which its name derives. Logicians may use different symbols for the two quantifiers:
universal quantifier: (x), $(∀x)$, $\bigwedge x$, Πx
existential quantifier: $(∃x)$, $\bigvee x$, Σx
[6]A full discussion of equivalence in PL will be found in the next chapter.

always followed by a *variable* (a place-holder for names) for which we use the lowercase letters x, y, and z, sometimes with subscripts. It is important to note that a negation preceding a quantifier, as in $\sim\forall x\ Rx$ ('Not everything is red') is quite different from a negation that follows a quantifier, as in $\exists y \sim Fy$ ('Something doesn't fly').

EXERCISES 5.2a

1. Symbolize the following, using the suggested notation: *F*: '_____ is a frog'; *G*: '_____ is green'; *E*: '_____ eats insects'

   a. Everything is green.

   b. Nothing is green.

   c. Something eats insects.

   d. All frogs are green.

   e. Some frogs eat insects.

   f. All insect eaters are frogs.

   g. No green things are insect eaters.

   h. Some insect eaters are not green.

   i. If all frogs are green, then all insect eaters are green.

2. Translate each of the following into the symbolic notation of PL. Indicate what your predicate letters represent.

   a. All those who subscribe to the *Times* are educated.

   b. No hedgehogs can read.

   c. Those who cannot read are not educated.

   d. Ducks never waltz.

   e. No officers ever decline to waltz.

   f. All my poultry are ducks.

   g. Promise-breakers are not trustworthy.

   h. Wine drinkers are very communicative.

   i. One can always trust a very communicative person.

   j. Everyone who is sane can do logic.

   k. No lunatics are fit to serve on a jury.

   l. None of your sons can do logic.

Earlier it was noted that both quantifiers behave a bit like negation in that parentheses are used to indicate to what the quantifier applies. Just as $\sim(P \supset Q)$ is different from $\sim P \supset Q$, so there is also an obvious difference between

$\forall x\ (Px \supset Sx)$

and

$\forall x\ Px \supset Sx$

The first says, 'Everything that is a P is an S'and the second says, 'If every-thing is P, then x is S'. The parentheses around $Px \supset Sx$ allow the universal quantifier to apply to the full conditional, whereas in the second case, the quantifier attaches only to the antecedent Px. And since the variable x is not a name, the consequent expression Sx ('x is an S') does not make a statement, and thus the whole of $\forall x\ Px \supset Sx$ is not a statement either! If a name (e.g., 'j') is substituted for x in the consequent, then we would have

$\forall x\ Px \supset Sj$

(i.e., 'If everything is P, then j is S'.) which *is* a PL statement. It could be the translation of 'If everything is purple, then Jim is sick', for example.

The term used to indicate to what a quantifier applies is *scope*. In the initial examples, $Px \supset Sx$ lies within the scope of the universal quantifier $\forall x$ in $\forall x\ (Px \supset Sx)$, and only Px lies within the scope of the quantifier in $\forall x\ Px \supset Sx$. The variable (in these instances, x) attached to a quantifier is officially called *the variable of quantification*, and instances of that variable in an expression are said to be *bound* by the quantifier if they lie within its scope.[7]

If we want to say 'If *anything* is P, then j is S' (e.g., 'If something is purple, then Jim is sick'), we might write it in PL as:

$\exists x\ Px \supset Sj$

that is, with an existential rather than a universal quantifier. But by changing the *scope* of quantifiers, we get startling results. For the statement

$\forall x\ (Px \supset Sj)$

('For all x, if x is P, than j is S') also says 'If anything is P, then j is S'. Thus, the equivalence holds:

$\forall x\ (Px \supset Sj) \equiv \exists x\ Px \supset Sj$

---

[7]Some accounts of PL allow for unbound, or 'free', variables. See, e.g., Elliot Mendelson, *Introduction to Mathematical Logic*, 2nd ed. (New York: D. Van Nostrand, 1979), chapter 2. As used in this text, however, all variables must be properly bound and within the scope of an appropriate quantifier.

The reason behind this equivalence is that $\exists x\ Px \supset Sj$ says that if at least one thing has the property P, then j is S. Or, in other words, take all the things that there are, if one (or more) is P, then j is S. But $\forall x\ (Px \supset Sj)$ says this too. Perhaps the easiest way to see this is to imagine the circumstances under which $\forall x\ (Px \supset Sj)$ would be *false*. Since the quantifier is universal, a single object, say with the name a, for which the statement $Pa \supset Sj$ is not true, would make the universal statement false. But the only way that $Pa \supset Sj$ could be false is if both Pa were true and Sj were false. But notice that under these conditions, $\exists x\ Px \supset Sj$ would also be false. The antecedent $\exists x\ Px$ would be true if Pa is (since something, namely a, would be true), and the consequent Sj would, of course, be false.

We will delay a bit before offering the full, formal definition of what counts as a statement in PL. But we should note at this point that any variable can be bound no more than once in a PL statement. So there is a clear *defect* in expressions like:

$$\forall x\ \exists x\ Fx$$

The problem is that the same variable, x, lies within the scope of the existential quantifier and the universal quantifier. The variable x is thus bound by two quantifiers. Such combinations are not allowed.

Summary

The *scope* of a quantifier is the portion of the expression following it to which it applies: the second occurrence of x in $\forall x\ Fx \supset Fa$ is in the scope of the universal quantifier, whereas the expression Fa is not. But if parentheses are added—to produce the statement $\forall x\ (Fx \supset Fa)$—then the whole of $Fx \supset Fa$ lies in the scope of $\forall x$. A variable is said to be *bound* if it lies within the scope of an appropriate quantifier.

EXERCISES 5.2b

1. Indicate, by means of underlining, the scope of each quantifier and the variable of the quantification in the following statements:

   a. $\forall y\ (Ty\ \&\ Fy)$

   b. $\exists x\ Gx\ \&\ Ta$

   c. $Ta\ \&\ \exists x\ Gx$

   d. $\forall x\ [Rx \supset (Tx\ \&\ Gx)]$

   e. $\forall x\ (Yx \supset {\sim}Cx)\ \&\ {\sim}\ \exists y\ (Hy\ \&\ By)$

   f. $\forall x\ [Px \supset (Tx\ \&\ \forall y\ Ry)]$

2. Symbolize the following, using the suggested notation: *M:* '_____ is a mouse'; *E:* '_____ has escaped'; *a:* 'Al'; *U:* '_____ is unhappy.'

   a. Every mouse has escaped.

   b. If any mouse has escaped, then Al is unhappy.

   c. If every mouse has escaped, then Al is unhappy.

   d. If Al is unhappy, then a mouse has escaped.

   e. If Al is unhappy, then every mouse has escaped.

So far we have discussed only quantifiers and one-place predicates. But many English statements involve polyadic predicates in combination with quantifiers, so we need to be able to represent them as well. As an example, consider

Everything is larger than something.

This statement contains *two* quantifier expressions, 'everything' and 'something', and the two-place predicate 'is larger than', for which we will use L. Since two PL quantifiers must be used, we need two variables, x and y, to indicate what we are referring to. The symbolization looks like this:

$\forall x \, \exists y \, Lxy$

which is read: 'For all x there is a y such that x is larger than y', or, in smoother English, 'Everything is larger than something'. When several quantifiers appear in the same statement, their order and the order of the variables is very important. As you can see, the following four statements are significantly different:

(1) Everything is larger than something.	$\forall x \, \exists y \, Lxy$
(2) There is something which is larger than everything.	$\exists x \, \forall y \, Lxy$
(3) There is something such that everything is larger than it.	$\exists y \, \forall x \, Lxy$
(4) Everything has something larger than it.	$\forall y \, \exists x \, Lxy$

The four statements have obvious logical connections, however. If (3) is true, then there is some particular thing such that all things are larger than that thing. Statement (1) is thus a logical consequence of (3), since, if (3) is true, then everything is larger than some one thing. The important difference between (1) and (3) is that (1) can be true without there being a particular thing such that everything is larger than it. All statement (1) requires is that for any thing, say a, there is something, say b, such that Lab ('a is larger than b'). So if, for example, it were true that Lab and Lbc and Lcd and Lde and so on for every possible name, then it would be true that everything is larger than something. But there would not necessarily be *one thing*, say *e*, such that *Lae* and *Lbe* and *Lce* and *Lde* and so on; that is, there might not be something such that everything is larger than *it*. But that is what (3) requires, as putting the existential quantifier first indicates.

A similar one-way logical relation holds between statements (2) and (4). If there is some particular thing larger than everything—as (2) states—then everything has something larger than it, as in (4). But (4) does not require that there be one such thing. For example, suppose *Lba* and *Lcb* and *Ldc* and so on are all true. Then all the things named by *a*, *b*, *c*, etc. would have something larger than them, but not necessarily the *same* thing, as statement (2) would require.

The PL notation makes all this very clear, whereas, in English, statements like 'Everything is larger than something' are ambiguous. The English statement might mean either that everything is larger than one particular thing, (3), or that everything is larger than something or other, (1). When symbolized in PL, the location of the existential quantifier is the determining factor.[8]

Sometimes two-place predicates are used with a single name or variable. So, the statement 'Everything is larger than itself' would be

$\forall x\ Lxx$

and 'Nothing is larger than itself' would be

$\sim\exists x\ Lxx$

In such cases, only a single quantifier is required even though a two-place predicate is involved.

When dealing with statements involving multiple quantifiers there will often be *overlapping* scope. Take the following as an example:

Every student takes at least one exam.

Notation: *S*: '_____ is a student'
           E: '_____ is an exam'
           T: '_____ takes _____'

Symbolization: $\forall x\ [Sx \supset \exists y\ (Ey\ \&\ Txy)]$

('For all *x*, if *x* is a student, then there is a *y* such that *y* is an exam and *x* takes *y*'.)

In this case, two variables, *x* and *y*, are required to clearly distinguish 'students' from 'exams'. You will notice that the entire expression in brackets, $[Sx \supset \exists y\ (Ey\ \&\ Txy)]$, lies within the scope of the universal quan-

---

[8]A more detailed analysis of such cases will be found in section 6.1.

tifier, whereas only the expression (*Ey* & *Txy*) is within the scope of the interior existential quantifier. So all occurrences of the variable *y* are within the scope of the existential *and* the universal quantifier. If *x* had been used for the interior existential quantifier, as well as the universal qualifier, we would confuse the references to students and exams. However, the universal quantifier of *x* is *vacuous* (has no effect on) on the occurrences of *y*. Additionally, in a statement like:

> ∀*x Pa*

even though the expression *Pa* lies within the scope of ∀*x*, the quantifier does not affect *Pa* at all since it does not contain the variable *x*. As a result, we have the following equivalence involving a vacuous quantifier:

> ∀*x Pa* ≡ *Pa*

(i.e., 'For all *x*, Al is parsimonious' is just 'Al is parsimonious').

EXERCISES 5.2c

1. Symbolize the following statements (a–k) using the suggested notation. If you believe an English statement to be ambiguous, show the various ways it might be symbolized in PL.

   G: '_____ is greater than _____'; B: '_____ is bigger than _____'

   a. Everything is greater than something.

   b. Everything is greater than everything.

   c. Something is greater than something.

   d. Something is greater than itself.

   e. Everything is greater than itself.

   f. Something is bigger than everything.

   g. Something is such that everything is bigger than it.

   h. If everything is greater than something, then something is greater than everything.

   i. Something is, and something is not, greater than everything.

   *j. If something is bigger than itself, then it is greater than itself.

   k. Something is bigger than and greater than itself.

2. Using only the following two predicates, give PL representations of the statements a–e:

   S: '_____ is a student'   L: '_____ likes _____'

   a. Some student likes a student.

   b. Some student likes every student.

c. Some student likes no student.

d. Students do not like themselves.

e. There are two students who like all students.[9]

5.3 PL STATEMENTS, INSTANCES, AND COMPONENTS

We are now ready to formulate an official definition of what counts as a PL statement. Our definition requires some additional notation and terminology, which will also be useful in chapter 6.

To indicate any individual variable letter, like x or y, we will use the bold capitals **X**, **Y**, and **Z**. And to indicate any expression at all, we will use the bold capitals **A**, **B**, and **C**, as in previous chapters. It is important to note that an *expression* might be a statement like $\forall z\ (Pz \supset Fz)$ or a string of PL symbols that is not a statement, such as $Pz \supset Fz$. Finally, the bold capital **N** (sometimes with subscripts) indicates any name whatever. We will use the general notation

A(N/X)

to indicate the result of replacing in the expression **A** every occurrence of the individual variable represented by **X** with occurrences of the name represented by **N**.

For example, if we want to specifically replace the variable x with the name a in the expression $(Gx \supset Tx)$ we might write:

$(Gx \supset Tx)\ (a/x)$

which is, of course, $Ga \supset Ta$.

Just as we did in our study of SL, we need to identify the *components* of PL statements. Quantifiers can be tricky, so we begin with them. Consider the statement: 'Everyone likes Mary', which in PL might be symbolized as:

$$\forall x\ (Px \supset Lxm)$$
(*P*: _____ is a person; *L*: _____ likes _____; *m*: Mary)

We want to insure that what we call the components of this statement have a direct bearing on its truth (or falsity) and that any component of a PL statement is itself a PL statement. So it won't do to just think of the *expressions* Px or Lxm as components of $\forall x\ (Px \supset Lxm)$, since they are not themselves PL statements (they both have variables without binding quantifiers). In-

---

[9]Because we do not have the necessary additional notation in this text, it is not possible to express statements such as 'There is a student who likes all *other* students'. See, e.g., Mendelson, *op. cit.*, pp. 79–85.

stead we will count as components of a quantificational statement all of the **substitution instances** of the quantifier, that is, all of the results of deleting the quantifier and substituting a *name* for the variable of quantification. So the substitution instances of $\forall x$ $(Px \supset Lxm)$ are:

$Pa_1 \supset La_1m$

$Pa_2 \supset La_2m$

$Pa_3 \supset La_3m$

.

.

.

$Pa_n \supset La_nm$

.

where $a_1, a_2, a_3, \ldots, a_n$, and so on are names. Note that each of the above is the result of removing the universal quantifier $\forall x$ and replacing each occurrence of the variable x with a particular name. It is important that each time this operation is conducted the same name is used to replace a variable. So, $Pa_1 \supset La_2m$ would *not* count as a substitution instance of $\forall x$ $(Px \supset Lxm)$ because the variable x has not been replaced throughout by a single name.

In addition to the list above, $\forall x$ $(Px \supset Lxm)$ has other components as well. Thus, we call the substitution instances the *immediate components* of the statement. Each of the substitution instances also has components, and these components also count as components of the original statement $\forall x$ $(Px \supset Lxm)$. The immediate components of $Pa_1 \supset La_1m$, for example, are Pa_1 and La_1m, so these also count as components of $\forall x$ $(Px \supset Lxm)$. As in SL, one finally gets to *atomic components* by repeatedly deriving the immediate components of immediate components, and so on. And it is the atomic components we are particularly interested in for the definition of truth in PL. The atomic components of $\forall x$ $(Px \supset Lxm)$ are

Pa_1	La_1m
Pa_2	La_2m
Pa_3	La_3m
.	.
.	.
Pa_n	La_nm
.	.

You may find the claim odd that, in their PL forms, the statement 'My coffee cup is green', for example, is a *component* of the statement 'Everything is green' (i.e., Ga_3 is a component of $\forall x$ Gx). After all, there is no mention of coffee cups in the general statement. What we are recognizing here is a linkage of truth-conditions: the color of my coffee cup, like the color of every other thing, is genuinely relevant to whether the statement 'Everything is green' is true or not. So, unlike SL components, which are actual constituents of statements, *PL components may contain names that are not found in the original statement*.

We assume that we have an infinity of names at our disposal, so there will clearly be an infinite number of atomic components for any quantificational statement, no matter how simple that statement may be. For example, take $\exists x\, Tx$. The result of substituting *any* name for x and removing the quantifier counts as a component of $\exists x\, Tx$. Since all of these components are atomic PL statements, e.g., Ta_1, Ta_2, Ta_3, etc., and since we can just keep going on to infinity, there is an infinite number of such atomic components. This infinity of atomic components is what makes the calculation of truth for PL statements so complicated.

Recall that any *SL* statement has the same number of atomic components as its constituent statement letters; since no SL statement is infinitely long (it wouldn't be a statement, then, since it couldn't be written), all SL statements have a finite number of atomic components, and, in most cases, the number of such components is quite small.

Now we can turn to our definition of what counts as a **PL statement:**

---

*An expression **A** will count as a PL statement if:*

1. *A is of the form $F\, N_1\, N_2\, N_3\, \ldots\, N_m$, where **F** is an m-place predicate and N_1, N_2, N_3, $\ldots$, N_m are names (note: the names in this list do not have to be different from one another),*

2. *A is of the form $\sim\!B$, where **B** is a PL statement,*

3. *A is of the form $B \vee C$, where **B** and **C** are PL statements,*

4. *A is of the form $B\, \&\, C$, where **B** and **C** are PL statements,*

5. *A is of the form $B \supset C$, where **B** and **C** are PL statements,*

6. *A is of the form $B \equiv C$, where **B** and **C** are PL statements,*

7. *A is of the form $\forall X\, B$ or $\exists X\, B$, where **X** is a variable, and, for some name **N**, $B(N/X)$ is a PL statement.*

As you can see, only two conditions—1 and 7—are different from the definition presented for SL statements in chapter 2.

Since any quantificational statement will have infinite substitution instances, there is no way to construct full grammatical trees as we did for SL statements. Condition 7 in the definition avoids this problem by using just a single instance as a test of whether a quantification counts as a statement, whereas in SL we had to examine every component. It is, therefore, important to notice that if *any* substitution instance of a quantification counts as a PL statement, then *all* such instances will count. Take our earlier example:

$\forall x\ (Px \supset Lxm)$

Using the name *a*, a substitution instance is *Pa* $\supset$ *Lam*. Since we have replaced all occurrences of the variable of quantification *x* by the name *a*, there are no unbound variables in the substitution instance; it is obviously a PL statement (since $\forall x\ (Px \supset Lxm)$ is). All the other substitution instances can be generated from *Pa* $\supset$ *Lam* by replacing the name *a* by other names. So, where **N** is a name, they *all have the form:*

$(Pa \supset Lam)\ (\mathbf{N}/a)$

Hence if one substitution instance of a quantification is a PL statement, they all are.

To see how the definition of a PL statement works, let us look at a few examples.

(1) $\forall x\ [Px \supset \exists y\ (Tx\ \&\ Fxy)]$

According to condition 7, if this is a statement, then dropping the quantifier and replacing the variable of quantification with a name should result in a statement. We will use name *a*.

$Pa \supset \exists y\ (Ta\ \&\ Fay)$

If this expression is a statement, then it must satisfy the terms of condition 5. The antecedent *Pa* and the consequent $\exists y\ (Ta\ \&\ Fay)$ must both be statements. The expression *Pa* is a statement by condition 1 (assuming that *P* is a one-place predicate), and the consequent is a statement if *Ta* & *Fab* (where name *b* is substituted for variable *y*) is a statement. Assuming that *T* is one-place and *F* is two-place, then the conjunction *Ta* & *Fab* is a statement by condition 4. Thus $\forall x\ [Px \supset \exists y\ (Tx\ \&\ Fxy)]$ is a statement.

(2) $\forall x \forall y\ Fx$

This expression may not look like a statement. But by condition 7 it is a statement as long as dropping the first quantifier and replacing the variable *x* by a name results in a statement. Again, we will use *a*.

$\forall y\ Fa$

This curious-looking expression actually counts as a statement by condition 7. It is an example of a vacuous quantification, since no occurrence of the variable y lies in the scope of $\forall y$. But according to condition 7, if we drop the quantifier and replace all occurrences of y by a name, the result should be a statement. And, indeed, the result is the statement Fa. Thus, $\forall x \forall y \, Fx$ is a statement, even though it contains a vacuous quantifier and is equivalent to $\forall x \, Fx$.

(3) $\forall y \, Gy \supset Hy$

This expression is a conditional, so both antecedent and consequent must be statements. The antecedent, $\forall y \, Gy$, clearly is a statement, by condition 7. But the consequent does not satisfy *clause 1* because Hy is not a predicate followed by a name. So, $\forall y \, Gy \supset Hy$ is *not* a statement

(4) $\forall z \, [Pz \, \& \, \exists z \, (Tz \, \& \, Rz)]$

We can see already that there will be trouble here because two quantifiers with the same variable overlap. When condition 7 is invoked and a substitution of a name—say a—is attempted, the result is:

$Pa \, \& \, \exists a \, (Ta \, \& \, Ra)$

But this expression is *not* a statement because it does not fall under one of the seven conditions that define SL statementhood. There is no provision anywhere for a quantifier followed by a name.

Official definitions, like that of PL statement given in this section, are important because they precisely define concepts that then can be invoked later on. As an example of the utility of our definition of what counts as a statement, consider the following simple rule of inference, called 'universal instantiation (UI)', that we will meet in chapter 6:

n. | $\forall X \, A$
  | .
p. | $A(N/X)$ (UI, n)

In stating this rule, we do not have to be concerned about overlapping quantifiers or variables that are not bound by a quantifier, or by other problems we have not even considered. If we assume that $\forall X \, A$ is a statement, it will not contain occurrences of unbound variables; so we can therefore be certain that $A(N/X)$ must also be a PL statement.

In PL, we also make wide use of the SL equivalence rules that we derived in chapter 4. For example, we will apply rules such as DeMorgan's laws

$\sim(A \lor B) \leftrightarrow (\sim A \, \& \, \sim B)$

to quantificational statements, in order, for example, to move from

$\forall x \, (\sim Px \, \& \, \sim Rx)$

to the logically equivalent PL statement

∀x ~(Px ∨ Rx)

But note that we will be using the **A** of the DeMorgan's laws here for *Px*, which, of course, is not a statement. So we need another concept, which we call *quasi statement*, to cover such usage. Quasi statements are like statements, but they may have unbound variables where a statement would have a name. Expressions like

Fxy
Pxy ⊃ Gx
∀x Gx & Fy

are all quasi statements. One way of thinking of them is as expressions that can be generated from statements by substituting *new* variables for names in the statement. Such generating statements for the examples above might be, respectively,

Fab
Pdf ⊃ Gd
∀x Gx & Fm

However, an expression such as ∀x Gx & Fx does *not* count as a quasi statement because there is no statement from which it can be so generated; the variable *x* cannot be substituted for *m* in ∀x Gx & Fm, for example, because *x* already occurs in ∀x Gx & Fm.

An important feature of quasi statements is that they become statements if one or more appropriate quantifiers are prefaced to them. Note that each of the quasi statements above becomes a statement when quantifiers are prefaced to each unbound variable, e.g.,

∀x ∃y Fxy
∃x ∀y (Pxy ⊃ Gx)
∃y (∀x Gx & Fy)

Note, again, that ∀x Gx & Fx also fails this test. Prefacing the quantifier ∀x to this expression does not result in a statement (since two quantifiers cannot bind the same variable).

The reverse of the quantifier preface feature also holds; eliminate one or more external quantifiers and a statement becomes a quasi statement. So, where ∀**X A** is a statement, **A** is a quasi statement.[10]

---

[10]Some authors refer to quasi statements as *open statements* because they contain unbound variables. In this terminology, the prefacing of appropriate quantifiers is sometimes said to *close* the statement. But we will insist that there is only one kind of statement and all variables

Here is a precise definition:

Quasi statement A **quasi statement** *is an expression of the form*

$A(X_1/N_1, X_2/N_2, X_3/N_3, \ldots, X_n/N_n),$ $(n \geqslant 0)$

where A is a statement and $X_1, X_2, X_3, \ldots, X_n$ *are variables that do not occur in A, and* $N_1, N_2, N_3, \ldots, N_n$ *are names.*

As will be discussed in chapter 6, all of the SL equivalence rules also hold in PL, where the letters **A, B,** and **C** with which they are expressed stand for PL statements or quasi statements.

Summary

PL statement An expression **A** will count as a PL statement if:

a. **A** is of the form **F** $N_1 \, N_2 \, N_3 \ldots N_m$, where **F** is an m-place predicate and $N_1, N_2, N_3, \ldots, N_m$ are names (note: the names in this list do not have to be different from one another),

b. **A** is of the form ~**B**, where **B** is a PL statement,

c. **A** is of the form **B** ∨ **C**, where **B** and **C** are PL statements,

d. **A** is of the form **B** & **C**, where **B** and **C** are PL statements,

e. **A** is of the form **B** ⊃ **C**, where **B** and **C** are PL statements,

f. **A** is of the form **B** ≡ **C**, where **B** and **C** are PL statements,

g. **A** is of the form ∀**X B** or ∃**X B,** where **X** is a variable and, for some name **N, B(N/X)** is a PL statement.

Quasi statement A **quasi statement** is an expression of the form

$A(X_1/N_1, X_2/N_2, X_3/N_3, \ldots, X_n/N_n),$

where **A** is a statement, $X_1, X_2, X_3, \ldots, X_n$ are variables which do not occur in **A**, and $N_1, N_2, N_3, \ldots, N_n$ are names.

Substitution instance The result of deleting a quantifier and replacing all instances of the variable of quantification with some specific name; so **A(N/X)** is the general form of a substitution instance of ∀**X A** and ∃**X A**. It is important to note that substitution instances are formed only

---

in statements must be bound by quantifiers. Technically, statements also count as quasi statements according to our definition. See exercise 5.3.7.

from quantificational PL statements, and that all substitution instances of a statement are themselves statements. In the case of a vacuous quantification, e.g., ∀x Fa, the substitution instance is just the expression (i.e., statement) following the quantifier—*Fa*.

Components In PL, the components of a statement are its immediate components, all of their immediate components, and so on. The notion of 'component' is defined as follows:

1. **A** is an immediate component of ~**A**;

2. **A** and **B** are immediate components of the statements **A** ⊃ **B**, **A** & **B**, **A** ∨ **B**, and **A** ≡ **B**;

3. For any name **N**, **A(N/X)** is an immediate component of both ∀**X A** and ∃**X A**;

4. If a statement **A** is an immediate component of statement **B**, and **B** is an immediate component of statement **C**, then **A** is a *component* of **C**.

Atomic component A statement **A** is an atomic component of a PL statement **B** if **A** is a component of **B** and **A** is a PL atomic statement.

EXERCISES 5.3

1. List the immediate components of each of the following:

    a. ∃y Fy

    b. ∃y Fy & ∀x Px

    c. Pa_2 ⊃ ∃x Px

    d. ~∀x Gx

    e. (Pa_2 ⊃ ∃x Px) ∨ ∃y Fy

    f. ∀x ∃y Gxy

2. Is it possible to list all of the atomic components of ∀x Px? Why?

3. What are the nonatomic components of a–e in exercise 5.5.1?

4. Suppose *a*, *b*, and *c* are *all* of the names available. Give a full list, under this assumption, of all of the components of each of the following:

    a. ∃y Fy

    b. ∃x Px ⊃ Pa

    c. ∀x Px ∨ ~∀x Gx

    d. ∀x (Fx ⊃ Gx)

    e. ∀x ∀y Fxy

    f. ∀x (Gx ⊃ ∃y (Hxy & Fy))

5. Determine whether the following expressions are PL statements. Cite the condition violated for any nonstatement you discover.

   a. ∀x [Pc ⊃ ∀y (Ty & Rxy)]

   b. ∃y (Px & Ty)

   c. ∀x ∀y ∀z [(Rx & Ty) ⊃ (Exyz & Gxz)]

   d. ∀x Py

   e. ∃x ∃y [Rxy & (Tz & Hx)]

   f. ∃y (Px~ & Ty)

6. Circle the quasi statements in the above.

*7. Formulate a precise rule expressing the fact that if an appropriate quantifier is prefaced to a quasi statement for each unbound variable it contains, the result is sure to be a PL statement.

6

Truth and
Consequence in PL

We are now ready to see how truth-values are determined for statements in PL. You may have already anticipated the problem; since any quantificational statement has an infinite number of components, the notions of truth, falsity, and so on are somewhat more complex than they are for SL statements. Once we have a clear sense of truth, however, we can easily adapt the familiar definitions of validity and the other logical properties and relations to PL.

6.1 TRUTH

Recall that in SL, the truth of a statement on some valuation α depends on the assignment of truth-values to its constituent statement letters. We used truth tables to conveniently keep track of these calculations. For example, an SL statement of the form **A** $\supset$ **B** is true on any valuation (or row in a truth table) that either assigns false (**F**) to **A** or true (**T**) to **B**. And, of course, SL statements that are not true on a valuation are *false* on that valuation.

The definition of truth and falsehood for PL statements is somewhat more complicated. Nevertheless, by expanding upon what is meant by a *valuation*, we can formulate a definition for PL statements that is analogous to our definition for SL statements.[1]

It is fairly obvious that a simple general statement like 'Everything is purple' is true just in case everything is, in fact, purple. So if one or more things are not purple—such as the page on which this is written—then the general statement is *not* true. To precisely formulate this intuitive sense of the truth conditions for such statements, we use the notions of *substitution instance* and *atomic component* discussed in the last chapter.

We say that the PL statement $\forall x \, Px$ (P: '___ is purple') *is true on a PL valuation* just in case every one of its substitution instances Pa_1, Pa_2, Pa_3, etc. is true on that valuation; and if any substitution instance, say, Pa_{45} (where a_{45} is the name of the page you are reading), is not true, then $\forall x \, Px$ is not true on that valuation.[2]

There are several features of our concept of a PL valuation that deserve notice. First, we will assume that each of the PL names, e.g., a_1, a_2, a_3, and so on, designates a different object. In ordinary usage, any given object, of course, can have several different names, e.g., 'George Bush', 'the forty-first President of the United States', 'the current inhabitant of the White House'. Some familiar names really do not designate any object at all, e.g., 'Sherlock Holmes'. We also will assume that no name designates more than one object; so a name like 'Bob', which is ordinarily used to designate many different people, will be assumed here to be unique. Finally, we will assume that all physical objects and most other things have names in PL, even though they do not in any actual language. PL, as we have noted, has an infinite number of names available (through the use of subscripts), so we won't run out of names very soon.[3]

Now we can proceed to a slightly richer example: the statement 'All trees lose their leaves in the fall' is true just in case each and every tree does, in fact, lose its leaves in the fall. And the statement is false if one or more trees does not lose its leaves. In PL the statement might be represented by:

$\forall x \, (Tx \supset Lx)$

(T: ___ is a tree; L: ___ loses its leaves in the fall)

---

[1]Our definitions of truth and the other semantic terms are often called 'truth-functional' or 'substitutional'. See Hugues Leblanc, *Truth-Functional Semantics* (New York: North-Holland, 1976), for a comprehensive survey. The more traditional semantics for quantificational logic in terms of domains and assignments are known as 'denotational' semantics. A full treatment will be found in, e.g., Elliot Mendelson, *Introduction to Mathematical Logic*, 2nd ed. (New York: D. Van Nostrand, 1979), chapter 2.

[2]Rigorous definitions of 'substitution instance', 'component', and the other technical terms used in this discussion are given in section 5.3.

[3]Even with an infinite number of names, there will always be unnamed things, e.g., real numbers. But because of the Loewenheim theorem and the work by Skolem (section 6.3) we can safely ignore such things as far as logical relations are concerned.

Note that the immediate components of this statement are the substitution instances:

$Ta_1 \supset La_1$
$Ta_2 \supset La_2$
$Ta_3 \supset La_3$
.
.

$Ta_n \supset La_n$
.

What $Ta_1 \supset La_1$ says is that if a_1 is a tree, then a_1 loses its leaves in the fall. Clearly this statement will have to be true if the original is to be true, where a_1 is the name of some object (but not necessarily a tree). To see this, suppose $Ta_1 \supset La_1$ were false; then a_1 is a tree (Ta_1 is true) and a_1 does not lose its leaves in the fall (La_1 is false). In this case, with a_1 a tree that does not lose its leaves, the original statement that all trees lose their leaves in the fall would clearly be false. Thus not only does $Ta_1 \supset La_1$ have to be true if the original is true, but, by the very same reasoning, so do *all* substitution instances.

You may be thinking, what about substitution instances in which the object named is *not* a tree at all, but, say, a pizza? Let a_3 be the name of some pizza; $Ta_3 \supset La_3$ still, however, says: 'If a_3 is a tree, then a_3 loses its leaves in the fall'. But we know that Ta_3 is false, since a_3 is a pizza, not a tree. What, then, is the truth-value of $Ta_3 \supset La_3$? According to the truth table for $\supset$, the statement is *true*. And so, automatically, all substitution instances of $\forall x\,(Tx \supset Lx)$ that do not involve trees are true. Such instances, consequently, don't count against the general truth or falsity of the statement. The substitution instances that do count are those in which the name substituted for the variable stands for a tree. If the statement is true of all such objects, then it is true. If not—as would be the case if $Ta_1 \supset La_1$ were false—then the statement is false.

The truth conditions for general statements like 'All trees lose their leaves in the fall' to some extent reflect the truth table for the conditional, as the discussion above indicates. This creates, as in SL, some oddities. Statements like 'Martian football players wear purple sneakers' will come out as *true* on any valuation on which there are no Martians! But the conditional is the most appropriate connective to use in the symbolization of such statements in PL, so such oddities have to be endured.[4]

We used this feature of general statements in chapter 3 during our discussion of consistency (section 3.2). We noted there that every *inconsistent*

---

[4]Other approaches that go well beyond the resources of PL are discussed in, e.g., Alan R. Anderson and Nuel Belnap, *Entailment* (Princeton, NJ: Princeton University Press, 1975).

set has a consistent kernel. One way to find a consistent kernel is to pull statements out of the set until the resulting set is consistent. But with, say, a set containing only one statement that is a contradiction, when that statement is pulled out, the resulting set is empty. So it follows that the empty set must be consistent (or else not every inconsistent set has a consistent kernel). How then could a set with no members satisfy the following definition of consistency?

> A set is consistent if all of its members are true on some valuation of all of their atomic components.

The answer is now clear; since there are no members in the empty set, the statement

> All of the members of the empty set are true on some valuation of all of their atomic components

is true. The PL form of the statement would be

∀x (Mx ⊃ Tx)

> M: '___ is a member of the empty set; T: '___ is true on a valuation to its atomic components.

Since every atomic statement of the sort Ma_1, Ma_2, Ma_3, etc. is false (on the valuation that depicts the real world), each substitution instance of the statement

$Ma_1 ⊃ Ta_1$, $Ma_2 ⊃ Ta_2$, $Ma_3 ⊃ Ta_3$,   etc.

is true. So ∀x (Mx ⊃ Tx) is true. We will see other examples of how general statements can satisfy definitions by default in chapter 8.

Let's next look at a vastly simpler case, the statement 'Something is brown', which in PL might be ∃x Bx. If this statement is to be true, then at least one thing must be brown. So, in terms of substitution instances, at least one of Ba_1, Ba_2, Ba_3, etc. must be true. Suppose a_1 is the name for 'my right loafer', an object that is, in fact, brown. Then the statement 'Something is brown' is obviously true. Does it matter whether Ba_2, Ba_3, Ba_4, etc. are also true? It doesn't, so long as Ba_1 is a true statement; with just one substitution instance true, the more general statement 'Something is brown' is true. On the other hand, if *every* substitution instance of an existential statement is false, i.e., every one of Ba_1, Ba_2, Ba_3, etc., is false, then the existential statement, ∃x Bx, is false.

Despite this complexity of calculation, we can easily state the *conditions* under which PL statements are true (and false). Our PL valuations will be assignments of truth-values true (**T**) and false (**F**) to atomic statements of PL. When single statements are being considered, PL valuations must assign truth-values to *all* of their atomic components; later on, when sets of statements are involved, valuations will encompass the atomic components of all members of the set.

Here, then, are the conditions that define **truth** for PL statements:

---

*A statement A is **true** on a valuation α that assigns truth-values to its atomic components if and only if the following conditions are met:*

1. *if the statement is atomic, it is assigned **T** on α;*
2. *if it is a ~A statement, it is not the case that A is true on α;*
3. *if it is an A ⊃ B statement, either A is not true on α or B is true on α (or both);*
4. *if it is an A & B statement, both A and B are true on α;*
5. *if it is an A ∨ B statement, either A is true on α or B is true on α (or both);*
6. *if it is an A ≡ B statement, either both A and B are true on α or neither one is true on α;*
7. *if it is an ∀X A statement, every substitution instance A(N/X), for every name N, is true on α;*
8. *if it is an ∃X A statement, at least one substitution instance A(N/X), for at least one name N, is true on α;*

And a statement is **false** on a valuation α if and only if it is not true on α.

Although tersely stated, these eight conditions completely capture the concept of truth for PL statements and reflect the common understanding of how truth and falsity interact in statements involving quantifiers. As noted in chapter 2, valuations may be thought of as ways the world might be. For example, even though it is white, the page you are reading *might* have been purple, had the publisher indulged in whimsy. Thus, on one valuation—call it α_1—the statement Pa_{45} (where a_{45} is the name of the page you are reading and P is the predicate '___ is purple') is true, and on another, say α_2, it is false. Consequently, valuation α_2 is closer, in this regard, to the way things actually are in the world than α_1. We have a right to expect that nothing impossible will show up as true on a valuation, since we think of valuations as ways the world might be. Consequently, the statement $\forall x\, Px\, \&\, {\sim}Pa_{45}$ ('Everything is purple, but the page you are reading isn't') cannot be true on any valuation. But more on this later.

EXERCISES 6.1a

1. Let valuation α be partially as follows:

Pa_1 - **T** Qa_1 - **T**
Pa_2 - **T** Qa_2 - **F**
Pa_3 - **F** Qa_3 - **T**
Pa_4 - **T** Qa_4 - **F**

Determine, whenever you can, the truth-value of each of the following on valuation α. If you think more information is needed in order to determine a truth-value, explain why.

a. $\forall x\, Px$

b. $\forall x\, Hx$

c. $\exists x\, Px$

d. $\exists x\, (Px\ \&\ Qx)$

e. $\forall x\, (Px \supset Qx)$

f. $\forall x\, (Qx \supset Px)$

g. $\forall x \sim Px$

h. $\sim\exists x\, Px$

i. $\exists x\, (Px\ \&\ Qx) \lor \sim\forall x \sim Px$

j. $Qa_3\ \&\ \forall x\, Px$

k. $\forall x\, (Px \supset \exists y\, (Hy\ \&\ Qx))$

2. Describe the conditions necessary for the truth of the following:

a. $\forall x\, (Px \supset Gx)$

b. $\forall x\, (Fx\ \&\ Gx)$

c. $\exists x\, (Fx\ \&\ Gx)$

d. $\exists x\, Fx\ \&\ \exists x\, Gx$

e. $\forall x\, Rx \supset Pa$

f. $\forall x\, (Rx \supset Pa)$

g. $\exists x\, Rx \supset Pa$

h. $\forall x\, Fx \supset \exists x\, Fx$

The determination of truth for statements involving two-place (or more) predicates can be especially tricky, yet ordinary English sentences will very often involve such forms. Let's begin with

All of her cars are green.

A PL representation might be

$\forall x ((Cx \ \& \ Bxa_1) \supset Gx)$

(a_1: 'her'; C: '___ is a car;' B: '___ belongs to ___'; G: '___ is green')

Note that there are many objects that are cars but that don't belong to her, and there are many objects that belong to her that are not cars. Furthermore, there are plenty of green things that are cars and many, many that are not. We might begin to keep track of the various substitution instances using a partial truth table, like the one below:

(1) Ca_1	Ba_1a_1	Ga_1
F	F	F

(2) Ca_2	Ba_2a_1	Ga_2
T	F	F

(3) Ca_3	Ba_3a_1	Ga_3
F	T	T

(4) Ca_4	Ba_4a_1	Ga_4
T	T	F

In case (1), the object named a_1 is not a car, is not owned by her, and is not green. This is just what we would expect since a_1 is the 'her' of the statement. In the second case, the object a_2 is a car, but neither belongs to her nor is green. The case (3) records that she owns a green object that is not a car— a book, perhaps. And in the fourth case, a_4 is a car that she owns that is not green. It is only the fourth case that gives us an answer to the question of truth here. Because we have found an object that is a car and belongs to her, but is not green, we know that the original statement is *not* true. Had we not come across this case, we would have had to keep searching.

Despite the complexity of *calculating* its truth-value, the *conditions* under which the statement $\forall x ((Cx \ \& \ Bxa_1) \supset Gx)$ is true are easy to understand: so long as every substitution instance is true on a valuation, the statement is true on that valuation. In other words, so long as every object that is both a car and owned by her is also green, the statement is true; otherwise, it is false. This is easy to say, but potentially difficult to determine in particular cases. Just think how you would try to figure out whether such a statement is true of a friend of yours. Of course if you know that she has a red car, you already know the statement to be false. But suppose the car she drives every day is green. Then you still need to figure out whether every one of her other cars is green, so you have to track down every car she owns. But how do you know that you have found them all? How do you know when to stop? In practice, this is probably not a great problem since you can usually find out how many cars a person owns.

But in the more general case, when evaluating a quantificational statement on a valuation, the problem can be immense. Since there are an infinite number of names you can substitute for the variable, you often can't be sure that a general statement like $\forall x\ ((Cx\ \&\ Bxa_1) \supset Gx)$ is true on a valuation, no matter how many instances you have already canvassed. As we will see in chapters 7 and 11, this situation has very important consequences, sometimes called the *halting problem,* when we try to automate such processes.

When two (or more) quantifiers appear in a statement, you must be especially vigilant about calculating truth-values. Take, for instance, the statement 'Everybody loves somebody'. Ordinarily, saying this would mean that every person loves at least one person, but not necessarily the same person. So Joan might love Jim and Harold might love Sue and Sue might love Jim, etc. So understood, the statement might be symbolized as:

(1) $\forall x\ \exists y\ [Px \supset (Py\ \&\ Lxy)]$

(P: '___ is a person'; L: '___ loves ___')

If, however, I mean to say that every person loves the same person (say, Harold) then I might symbolize the statement as:

(2) $\exists y\ \forall x\ [Py\ \&\ (Px \supset Lxy)]$

When I want to be very clear whether I mean (1) or (2), I should say 'Everybody loves somebody or other' in the first case, and something like 'Everybody loves the same particular person' or, even better, 'There is a person everybody loves' in the second. The conditions under which these two PL statements are true and false on valuations very clearly point out their differences, which are often obscured in casual English.

In statement (1), the substitution instances are:

$\exists y\ [Pa_1 \supset (Py\ \&\ La_1y)]$
$\exists y\ [Pa_2 \supset (Py\ \&\ La_2y)]$
$\exists y\ [Pa_3 \supset (Py\ \&\ La_3y)]$
and so on

Notice that in order for (1) to be true on a valuation, each of these instances must be true. Let's take just the first:

$\exists y\ [Pa_1 \supset (Py\ \&\ La_1y)]$

Since this is an existential quantification, it is true only if at least one sub-stitution instance is true. And, of course, *any* instance will do. Suppose the instance involves the name a_3. So considered, the statement

$Pa_1 \supset (Pa_3 \ \& \ La_1a_3)$

would thus be true (let a_1 be 'Jim' and a_3 be 'Joan'; the statement thus says 'If Jim is a person, then Joan is a person and Jim loves Joan'). So much then for the first instance. Now the second instance, $\exists y \ [Pa_2 \supset (Py \ \& \ La_2y)]$ might be true because $Pa_2 \supset (Pa_1 \ \& \ La_2a_1)$ is true. (Let a_2 be 'Sue'; the statement says 'If Sue is a person, then Jim is a person and Sue loves Jim'.) By now the point should be clear: the name substituted for the y place in each of the substitution instances of the original statement (1) can be filled in with different names. So the statement 'Everybody loves somebody' does not require that one particular person is loved by everybody.

Now look at statement (2): $\exists y \ \forall x \ [Py \ \& \ (Px \supset Lxy)]$ ('Somebody is loved by everybody'). Since it is an existential quantification (because that quan-tifier comes first), one of the following substitution instances needs to be true:

$\forall x \ [Pa_1 \ \& \ (Px \supset Lxa_1)]$
$\forall x \ [Pa_2 \ \& \ (Px \supset Lxa_2)]$
$\forall x \ [Pa_3 \ \& \ (Px \supset Lxa_3)]$
and so on

Suppose it is the second instance:

$\forall x \ [Pa_2 \ \& \ (Px \supset Lxa_2)]$

This statement says: 'Everybody loves Sue'. Its truth conditions require that all of its substitution instances are true, i.e.,

$Pa_2 \ \& \ (Pa_1 \supset La_1a_2)$
$Pa_2 \ \& \ (Pa_2 \supset La_2a_2)$
$Pa_2 \ \& \ (Pa_3 \supset La_3a_2)$
and so on

Each of these says that Sue (a_2) is a person, and if the object named is a person, then he or she loves Sue. So Jim loves Sue, and Sue loves Sue (i.e., La_2a_2), and Joan loves Sue, and so on for all others.

It is useful to compare these cases with a third, the Pollyanna statement

Somebody loves everybody.

$\exists x \ \forall y \ [Px \ \& \ (Py \supset Lxy)]$

The truth-conditions for this statement require that there be one person—say Pollyanna herself (a_1)—such that the following statement is true on some valuation:

$\forall y [Pa_1 \ \& \ (Py \supset La_1y)]$

That is, on the valuation, all of the substitution instances have to be true:

$Pa_1 \ \& \ (Pa_1 \supset La_1a_1)$
$Pa_1 \ \& \ (Pa_2 \supset La_1a_2)$
$Pa_1 \ \& \ (Pa_3 \supset La_1a_3)$
and so on

Hence Pollyanna loves herself, and, if a_2 is a person, she loves a_2, and if a_3 is a person, she loves a_3, and so on for all others, if the statement is true on the valuation. Should there be even a single object, say a_{23}, such that Pa_{23} is true (the object is a person) and Pollyanna does not love him or her, i.e., La_1a_{23} is not true, then the substitution instance

$Pa_1 \ \& \ (Pa_{23} \supset La_1a_{23})$

would thus be false. But the statement $\exists x \ \forall y [Px \ \& \ (Py \supset Lxy)]$ might still be true on that valuation, so long as it is true of some other individual, say a_4, that he or she is a person (Pa_4 is true) and all of the substitution instances of

$\forall y (Py \supset La_4y)$

are true (i.e., a_4 loves every person).

EXERCISES 6.1b

1. For each of the following, describe a valuation on which it is true.

    a. $\exists y \ \forall x \ Lxy$

    b. $\forall x \ \exists y \ Lxy$

    c. $\exists x \ \forall y \ Lxy$

    d. $\forall y \ \exists x \ Lxy$

    e. $\forall x [Px \supset \exists y (Py \ \& \ Lxy)]$

    f. $\exists y [Ry \ \& \ \forall x (Px \supset Lxy)]$

    g. $\forall x \ \forall y [(Px \ \& \ Py) \supset \exists z (Lxz \lor Lyz)]$

2. In cases a–d in exercise 1, give an English sentence that the PL statement might represent, and give an explanation in English of the truth-conditions of the sentence.

3. For each of the following, give a valuation on which it is false.

   a. ∃x Px

   b. ∀y [Ry ⊃ Py]

   c. ∀x [(Tx & Ux) ⊃ Rx]

   d. ∃z [(Pz & Tz) & Uz]

   e. ∀x [Rx ⊃ ∃y ∃z (By & Txyz)]

4. In each case in exercise 3, give an English sentence that the PL statement might represent, and describe a situation in which the sentence is false.

5. For each of the examples in exercise 1, describe a valuation on which it is false.

6.2 VALIDITY AND OTHER LOGICAL PROPERTIES AND RELATIONS IN PL

The logical properties and relations we studied in chapter 2 have exact analogues in PL. Here are the PL definitions:

Logical truth A PL statement **A** is logically true if **A** is true on every PL valuation of its atomic components.

Logical falsehood A PL statement **A** is logically false if **A** is false on every PL valuation of its atomic components.

Logical contingency A PL statement **A** is logically contingent if **A** is neither logically true nor logically false.

Logical consistency A set **S** of PL statements is logically consistent if all of the members of **S** are true on some PL valuation of their atomic components.

Logical inconsistency A set **S** of PL statements is logically inconsistent if there is no PL valuation of the atomic components of the members of **S** on which all of the statements in **S** are true.

Logical equivalence Two PL statements **A** and **B** are logically equivalent if **A** and **B** have the same truth-value on every valuation of all of the atomic components of **A** and **B**.

Logical entailment A set **S** of PL statements logically entails a PL statement **A** if **A** is true on every PL valuation, of the atomic components of the members of **S** and of **A**, on which all members of **S** are true.

Logical validity An argument whose premises are A_1, A_2, A_3, . . . , A_m, ($m \geq 1$) and whose conclusion is **B** is logically valid if the set {A_1, A_2, A_3, . . . , A_m} logically entails **B**.

These definitions are essentially those found in section 3.3, with appropriate substitutions of 'PL' for 'SL', and with the stipulation that the valuations referred to assign truth-values to the appropriate atomic components of the statements involved.

You may well wonder about our using the word 'logical' to modify each of the above terms, instead of the more restrictive 'quantificational'. We do this to reinforce a quite important point; these definitions, and indeed the whole of PL, can be considered the larger logical system of which SL is a fragment. Although we will not refer in this section to relationships that are exclusively truth-functional, we could introduce SL expressions explicitly into PL quite simply by counting statement letters as zero-place predicates. So the statement $H \supset F$, for example, would thus count as a PL statement because the statement letters H and F would be considered atomic PL statements, as predicates that do not take names. Thus, all of the familiar truth-functional principles for SL suddenly become part of PL as well; 'tautology' becomes a special case of 'logical truth', 'truth-functional consistency' becomes a special case of 'logical consistency', and so forth. For these reasons, we use the term 'logical' in the PL definitions above.

The methods of determining the presence of logical properties and relations for PL resemble those used in chapter 3 for SL but with the added complications introduced by the presence of quantifiers. When dealing with truth-functional concepts, we can always rely on algorithms such as truth tables or truth trees for a definite answer, in a finite number of steps, to the question of whether an SL statement is tautologous, for example, or whether a set entails a particular statement, and so on, for the other logical properties and relations. Here, as we shall see, matters are not so simple. As we will discuss in some detail in section 6.3 and especially in chapter 11, there can be no mechanical procedure, no general algorithm, for determining the presence of PL logical properties and relations. This startling limitation on what we and all machines can do was first proved by Alonzo Church in 1936, more than a decade before the dawn of the computer age.[5]

The least systematic procedure for showing the presence of logical properties and relations is to use descriptions of valuations. Although difficult to follow in complicated cases, demonstrations involving valuations are surprisingly easy to employ in certain subgroupings of PL statements.

The most straightforward application of this method is the presentation of an argument to show that a certain logical property or relation must be present in a specific statement or group of statements because of the nature of any valuation to the relevant atomic components. Here is an example:

---

[5]A. Church, "A Note on the *Entsheidungsproblem*," *Journal of Symbolic Logic* (1936), pp. 40–41; 101–102.

Show $\forall x\, Fx \supset Fa$ is a logical truth

> **Demonstration**   Let α be *any* valuation of the atomic components of $\forall x\, Fx$ on which it is true. Then, since Fa is an atomic component of $\forall x\, Fx$, Fa is obviously true on α. Hence, by the truth conditions for the conditional, $\forall x\, Fx \supset Fa$ is true on any valuation of its atomic components and is therefore a logical truth.

It is important to notice that the argument to establish that $\forall x\, Fx \supset Fa$ is a logical truth can easily be generalized to cover any statement of the sort $\forall X\, A \supset A(N/X)$, no matter how complex (or simple) **A** may be. So with a slight extension of the simple argument above, we have marked off a large number of PL statements as logical truths, that is, any which have the form $\forall X\, A \supset A(N/X)$.

Here is a second example, requiring a more substantial argument:

Show $\forall y\, (Fy \supset Gy)$ is equivalent to $\sim\!\exists y\, (Fy\, \&\, \sim\!Gy)$

> **Demonstration**   We want to show that on any valuation of their atomic components, both statements have the same truth-value. We can do this by pointing out that all of the substitution instances of $\forall y\, (Fy \supset Gy)$ have the form $FN \supset GN$, where **N** is a name. Now we know from SL that any statement of the form $FN \supset GN$ will have the same truth-value on any valuation as $\sim\!(FN\, \&\, \sim\!GN)$. Suppose $\forall y\, (Fy \supset Gy)$ is true on valuation α_1; then all of the substitution instances of $\forall y\, (Fy \supset Gy)$ are true on α_1, hence any statement of the form $FN \supset GN$ will be true on α_1, as will any statement of the form $\sim\!(FN\, \&\, \sim\!GN)$. But, then, there will be no statement of the form $(FN\, \&\, \sim\!GN)$ true on α_1, and hence $\exists y\, (Fy\, \&\, \sim\!Gy)$ will be *false* on α_1; hence $\sim\!\exists y\, (Fy\, \&\, \sim\!Gy)$ is *true* on α_1. On the other hand, suppose $\forall y\, (Fy \supset Gy)$ is *false* on some valuation, say α_2. Then there will be one substitution instance, say $Fa \supset Ga$, which is false on α_2. Then, $\sim\!(Fa\, \&\, \sim\!Ga)$ will also be false on α_2, and, so $Fa\, \&\, \sim\!Ga$ will be true on α_2. But, then, $\exists y\, (Fy\, \&\, \sim\!Gy)$ will be true on α_2, and so, $\sim\!\exists y\, (Fy\, \&\, \sim\!Gy)$ will be *false*. So we have shown that no matter what valuation is chosen, the two statements $\forall y\, (Fy \supset Gy)$ and $\sim\!\exists y\, (Fy\, \&\, \sim\!Gy)$ have the same truth-value; thus, they are logically equivalent.

As you may expect, such demonstrations quickly become significantly complex as additional quantifiers and polyadic predicates appear. Imagine, for example, constructing such an argument to show the equivalence between $\exists x\, [Px\, \&\, \forall y\, [Py \supset \sim\!\exists z\, (Gxyz \lor Gyxz)]]$ and $\exists x\, \forall y\, \forall z\, [Px\, \&\, [Py \supset \sim\!(Gxyz \lor Gyxz)]]$. In this situation, it would be hard not to have some nostalgia for truth tables! Presumably a demonstration of this equivalence can be produced with ingenuity and hard work; but don't worry, you will not be asked to do it.

EXERCISES 6.2

1. Construct an argument utilizing valuations to show that each of the following is a logical truth.

   a. ∀x Fx ⊃ ∃x Fx

   b. ∀x [Fx & Gx] ⊃ [∀x Fx & ∀x Gx]

   c. ∃x ∀y Lxy ⊃ ∀y ∃x Lxy

   d. [∀x Fx & ∀x Gx] ⊃ ∀x [Fx & Gx]

   e. ∃y ∀x Pxy ⊃ ∀x ∃y Pxy

   f. ∀x Fx ≡ ~∃x ~ Fx

   g. ∃x Fx ≡ ~∀x ~ Fx

   h. ∀x [Fa ⊃ Gx] ⊃ [Fa ⊃ ∀x Gx]

   i. ∀x [Fx ⊃ Ga] ⊃ [∃x Fx ⊃ Ga]

6.3 COUNTEREXAMPLES

Some questions concerning logical properties and relations can be answered by producing counterexamples in a manner analogous to that used for SL. The trick is to show the *absence* of some logical property or relation, which is often what is required, by producing a valuation that counts as a counter-example to the positive claim. So, to answer the question (negatively) whether statement **A** is a logical truth, we show that **A** is *false* on some valuation; to show that a set **S** is logically consistent, we show that the members are all true on some valuation, thus refuting the claim that the set **S** is inconsistent, and so forth. As we noticed in chapter 3, the truth tree method is essentially a systematic search for counterexamples.

Here is a catalogue of what can be shown by producing counterexamples:

1. We can show that a statement *is not logically true* by producing a valuation on which it is false.

2. We can show that a statement *is not logically false* by producing a valuation on which it is true.

3. We can thus show that a statement *is logically contingent* by showing that it is neither logically true nor logically false.

4. We can show that *a set is consistent* by producing a valuation on which all members are true.

5. We can show that *two statements are not logically equivalent* by producing a valuation on which they have different truth-values.

6. We can show that *an argument is not valid* by producing a valuation on which the premises are true and the conclusion is false.

7. We can show that *a set* **S** *does not entail a statement* **A** by showing that the set **S** ∪ {~**A**] is consistent, i.e., by producing a valuation on which all members of **S** are true and **A** is false.

The production of valuations that count as counterexamples in these seven cases is far from mechanical in PL, but there is an easy method that will often simplify the task. We begin with an argument that we want to show *invalid:*

$$\forall x \, (Rx \lor Gx)$$
$$\overline{}$$
$$\forall x \, Rx \lor \forall x \, Gx$$

We will employ what may be called *partial valuations.* These are fragments of valuations which utilize only a few of the atomic components of the statement(s) in question. Let's begin with a partial valuation involving only components containing the name a_1. The atomic components in this partial valuation are:

$$Ra_1 \qquad Ga_1$$

Now the question before us is: can we produce a counterexample to validity with just this partial valuation? To do this would require that $\forall x \, (Rx \lor Gx)$ be true on this partial valuation and $\forall x \, Rx \lor \forall x \, Gx$ be false. With only the atomic components above involved, the premise will be true if the single substitution instance $Ra_1 \lor Ga_1$ is true; and the conclusion is true if either $\forall x \, Rx$ or $\forall x \, Gx$ is true (or both are). Again, on this partial valuation, $\forall x \, Rx$ will be true if Ra_1 is, and $\forall x \, Gx$ will be true if Ga_1 is. So there is no way to produce a counterexample to the argument on this partial valuation.

Next let's try a partial valuation in which *two* names, a_1 and a_2, appear.[6] Now we have the following atomic components that receive truth-values on this partial valuation:

$$Ra_1 \qquad Ra_2 \qquad Ga_1 \qquad Ga_2$$

Can a counterexample be found in this case? Note that the premise is true on this partial valuation if *both* substitution instances, $Ra_1 \lor Ga_1$ and $Ra_2 \lor Ga_2$, are true. And the conclusion is false if both $\forall x \, Rx$ and $\forall x \, Gx$ are false. So can they be false when both $Ra_1 \lor Ga_1$ and $Ra_2 \lor Ga_2$ are true? The answer is yes, since the partial valuation might make the following truth-value assignments:

Ra_1	Ra_2	Ga_1	Ga_2
T	F	F	T

---

[6]Given our assumptions about names in PL, a_1 and a_2 are sure to be the names of different objects.

With these truth-values for the atomic components in the partial valuation, we have the following:

$Ra_1 \lor Ga_1$	$Ra_2 \lor Ga_2$	$\forall x (Rx \lor Gx)$	$\forall x\, Rx$	$\forall x\, Gx$	$\forall x\, Rx \lor \forall x\, Gx$
T	T	T	F	F	F

Thus, we have produced a counterexample to the validity of the argument on this partial valuation involving only the names a_1 and a_2.

But notice that this partial valuation can be thought of as *part* of a full valuation of *all* of the atomic components of the two statements. We can insure that the same truth-values as given above for the two statements persist in the full valuation by insisting that all of the *other* atomic components of $\forall x (Rx \lor Gx)$ are true on the full valuation. This will make $\forall x (Rx \lor Gx)$ true on the full valuation while $\forall x\, Rx \lor \forall x\, Gx$ remains false (since both $\forall x\, Rx$ and $\forall x\, Gx$ have one false substitution instance). Thus, we have produced our desired full valuation counterexample, which can be summarized as follows:

Ra_1	Ra_2	Ra_3	Ra_4	etc.	Ga_1	Ga_2	Ga_3	Ga_4	etc.
T	F	T	T	T	F	T	T	T	T

As the above illustration reveals, there are two steps in the use of partial valuation counterexamples. The first is finding an appropriate partial valuation that does the trick; the second is extending the partial valuation to a full valuation so that the essential truth-values are preserved and the full valuation is also a counterexample. Let's discuss these two issues in turn.

The Search for a Counterexample within an Appropriate Partial Valuation

In the above example we were systematic in the following sense: we began with a valuation involving a single name—a_1—and, when it proved unhelpful, we moved on to a valuation involving two names—a_1 and a_2. Since we were successful in finding a counterexample in this partial valuation, we didn't go any further, but we obviously could have if necessary. Continuing the same pattern, we would have next tried a partial valuation with three names—a_1, a_2, and a_3—and then four names, etc.

Since the truth-conditions of the statements under consideration are easily determined, it is reasonably straightforward to determine whether, for a *specific partial valuation,* a counterexample can be produced. In fact, there is even an algorithm that can be utilized. Since universal quantifications require that all substitution instances be true if the quantification is true, they are like *conjunctions.* Hence, if we have a partial valuation containing only two names—a_1 and a_2—we can use the following principle:

Statements of the sort ∀X A can be replaced by the conjunction A(a_1/X) & A(a_2/X).

Since existential quantifications require that at least one substitution instance be true if the quantification is true, they are like *disjunctions;* hence the principle (in a partial valuation of two names):

Statements of the sort ∃X A can be replaced by the disjunction A(a_1/X) ∨ A(a_2/X).[7]

To continue the above example, in a partial valuation containing two names, the original argument can be replaced as follows:

original: $\dfrac{\forall x\,(Rx \lor Gx)}{\forall x\,Rx \lor \forall x\,Gx}$

replacement: $\dfrac{(Ra_1 \lor Ga_1)\,\&\,(Ra_2 \lor Ga_2)}{(Ra_1 \,\&\, Ra_2) \lor (Ga_1 \,\&\, Ga_2)}$

Then it is a simple exercise to find a counterexample, if one exists in this partial valuation. For example, use the shortcut method and set the premise true and the conclusion false, or work out the full truth table, or do a truth tree. The values

Ra_1	Ra_2	Ga_1	Ga_2
T	F	F	T

represent one of two possible counterexamples that you will find. Can you identify the other?

Thus, *within a specific partial valuation,* where a finite number of names are involved, we can actually use truth tables or the SL truth tree method to determine whether there is a counterexample. But if we fail to produce a counterexample with a given partial valuation, we don't really know anything

---

[7] These relationships were noticed at the very outset of the development of quantificational logic. C. S. Pierce, for example, equated universal quantification to 'logical product' and existential quantification to 'logical sum'. He used the symbols Π and Σ, respectively, for the quantifiers.

about the logical status of the statement or set of statements we are studying; we can only go on to another partial valuation in which more names are found.

Imagine we are dealing with a valid argument, but don't know it. This search for a counterexample could go on indefinitely, and all we will discover at each stage is that in the given partial valuation under consideration, and all smaller ones we have tried, we have failed to find a counterexample. But for all we know, the counterexample lies in the partial valuation with just one additional name, and we go on and on and on.[8] Thus, while the method of finding a counterexample *within* a specific partial valuation is systematic, the general search for counterexamples is always potentially tedious, and in general, not algorithmic. If you are successful, you will produce a counterexample and know something; if you are unsuccessful, you will keep on looking and will not know when you should stop.

It may already be clear that the specific names involved in partial valuations, unless they occur in the original statement or statements, are irrelevant: a, b, c, etc., or a_{23}, a_{4467}, etc. will serve equally well. It is not the names but their *number* that is significant; so what we showed above was that the smallest number of names needed to produce a counterexample to the validity of the argument is two. Using names with subscripts beginning with 1, however, is the easiest way to keep track of the various partial valuations you are using.

Extending Partial Valuations to Full Valuations

It is important to note that all of the ways listed above in which counterexamples can be used actually have a common link in logical consistency, which we have discussed in earlier chapters in conjunction with truth trees. When we find a counterexample in some partial valuation, what we have actually done is shown that a certain set of statements is consistent as far as that partial valuation is concerned, i.e., that all of the statements in the set are true on that partial valuation. To make this point clear, let's go through the list again and explain how consistency comes in:

1. Showing that a statement **A** *is not logically true* is showing that set {~**A**} is logically consistent.

2. Showing that a statement **A** *is not logically false* is showing that set {**A**} is logically consistent.

3. Showing that a statement **A** *is logically contingent* is showing that both {~**A**} and {**A**} are logically consistent.

---

[8]We will later discuss subsystems of PL where we can reach a point of termination (see pp. 219–220). The general issue is related to the 'halting problem' of which we spoke earlier. We will have more to say in chapter 11.

4. Showing that *a set is consistent* is producing a valuation on which all members are true.

5. Showing that *two statements* **A** *and* **B** *are not logically equivalent* is showing that either $\{\sim$**A, B**$\}$ or $\{$**A,** $\sim$**B**$\}$ is logically consistent.

6. Showing that *an argument is not valid*, where **A**$_1$, **A**$_2$, **A**$_3$, . . . , **A**$_m$, $(m \geqslant 1)$ are the premises and **B** is the conclusion, is showing that the set $\{$**A**$_1$, **A**$_2$, **A**$_3$, . . . , **A**$_m$, $\sim$**B**$\}$ is logically consistent.

7. Showing that *a set S does not entail a statement A* is showing that the set **S** $\cup \{\sim$**A**$\}$ is consistent.

So the issue before us has two parts: can we be confident that any partial valuation can be extended to a full valuation so that the truth-values of any set of statements remain constant, and, if so, how does one do this? The answer to the first part was initially given by Leopold Loewenheim in 1915 and is known as *Loewenheim's theorem.*[9] Our version of this important logical principle is stated below:

Loewenheim's Theorem   *If there is a partial valuation on which all members of a set S are true, then S is logically consistent.*

Proof   We need to show that we can extend any given partial valuation into a full valuation by (1) maintaining the truth-value assignments to the atomic statements in the partial valuation and (2) adding truth-value assignments to those atomic statements not part of the partial valuation. We have to be careful to insure that the result counts as a valuation of all atomic components of the set of statements under consideration. So, let **S** be a set of PL statements, all of which are true on some partial valuation α_n. It should be clear that the only members of **S** we have to be concerned about are those containing quantifiers; other statements (e.g., $Ga_1 \supset Na_3$) will not change their truth-values if we extend valuation α_n to include additional atomic statements. Further, we need to insure that any component of any statement in **S** maintains its truth-value as valuation α_n is extended to a full valuation; again, we have only to worry about components containing quantifiers.

We need, then, to first consider what the full valuation will look like. Our partial valuation α_n, let us assume, makes truth-value assignments to all of the atomic components of the members of **S** for some number n of names $(n \geqslant 1)$. So, if $n = 2$, suppose the names involved are a_1 and a_2. The full valu-

---

[9]Loewenheim's original paper and a subsequent generalization and simplification by Thoralf Skolem are included in Jean van Heijenoort, *From Frege to Goedel* (Cambridge, MA: Harvard University Press, 1967).

ation—call it α—will agree with the partial valuation α_n on all truth-value assignments in α_n and will make truth-value assignments to all other atomic components of the members of **S**. The question, of course, is what those additional truth-value assignments will be.

In extending the partial valuation α_n to the full valuation α, there are two classes of components of members of **S** to consider (for our purposes here a statement counts as one of its components):

1. **Components of the sort ∀X A**

   a. Suppose ∀X **A** is true on α_n. Then in valuation α, all substitution instances—statements of the sort **A(N/X)**—should be true. Note that all of the substitution instances of ∀X **A** containing names in α_n will already be true.

   b. Suppose ∀X **A** is false on α_n. Then there is already a substitution instance of ∀X **A** that is false on α_n, and α can make any truth-value assignments to the remaining substitution instances of ∀X **A**.

2. **Components of the sort ∃X A**

   a. Suppose ∃X **A** is true on α_n. Then there is already a substitution instance—a statement of the sort **A(N/X)**—that is true on α_n. So α can make any truth-value assignments to the remaining substitution instances of ∃X **A**.

   b. Suppose ∃X **A** is false on α_n. Then in α all substitution instances of ∃X **A** should be false. Those instances containing names in α_n are, of course, already false.

And that does it! Some care will have to be taken to keep track of the various substitution instances (and *their* substitution instances, etc.), but the two classes of components cover the possibilities. Note, for example, that if a component is of the form ~∃X **A,** this case is covered under the instruction for treating false existential quantifications. Thus we have ensured that any partial valuation can be extended into a full valuation while preserving the truth-values of the members of **S**.

The strategy used in the proof above may remind you of the one we used to construct SL valuations in chapter 3 from open truth trees. Recall that a truth tree tests for consistency; a tree for a set is open if the set is consistent and closed if the set is inconsistent. In the next section, we extend truth trees to PL, and we will need to follow essentially the steps above to construct a valuation on which all the members of a set with an open tree are true. Thus, the Loewenheim theorem emerges as the basic foundation of the truth tree method for PL.

One final point: the proof above is easily adapted to support a slightly different version of the Loewenheim theorem. We have already implicitly developed the concept of the *size* of a partial valuation: the size is the number of names involved. Remembering that if any names occur in the set **S** they are automatically part of any partial valuation, we then have the following corollary to Loewenheim's theorem:

Corollary *If there is a partial valuation of size **m** (**m** ⩾ 1) on which all members of a set **S** are true, then there will be a partial valuation of size n, for any n ⩾ m, on which all members of **S** will also be true.*

The reverse of this corollary, however, does not hold. To take a simple example, the statement

$\exists x \, \exists y \, [\sim Fx \, \& \, Fy]$

while true on some partial valuations of size 2, is not true on a partial valuation of size 1, since it would then be replaced by $\sim Fa_1 \, \& \, Fa_1$. So the relationships between partial valuations in the Loewenheim theorem hold in only one direction.

Suppose you are writing a computer program to detect logical consistency and, therefore, to provide counterexamples as a way of testing claims and answering questions about logical properties and relations. Given the Loewenheim theorem, you might decide that the most efficient procedure is not to start with partial valuations of size 1 and work upward until a counterexample is found, but instead to choose a partial valuation of some arbitrary large size, say one with one thousand names, and look for counterexamples there. You would, of course, be assured of finding a counterexample on such a partial valuation *if* one exists for valuations of this size or smaller (you could use an algorithm like truth trees), but your fox-like strategy is still outfoxed by PL.

Your program will often do much more work than necessary since a vastly smaller partial valuation might have sufficed, so you are wasting time and resources. And, on the other hand, your arbitrarily large partial valuation will be too small in some cases, but you won't, of course, know which ones ahead of time. As pointed out earlier, if you fail to find a counterexample in a given partial valuation, you don't know whether to choose a larger one and try again, or to give up and declare that there probably is no counterexample, that the set you are testing isn't consistent after all.

If we restrict ourselves to a *subsystem* of PL, however, the picture brightens considerably. According to a theorem developed by Paul Bernays and Moses Schoenfinkel, when only monadic predicates are involved, we can develop algorithms for detecting the PL logical properties and relations.[10] For simplic-

---

[10]See Wilhelm Ackermann, *Solvable Cases of The Decision Problem* (Amsterdam: North-Holland, 1954), chapter 4.

ity, let's call a PL statement *monadic* if the statement contains occurrences of monadic predicates only. For example, *Fa*, $\forall x\ Tx$, and $\exists x\ [Px$ & $\forall y\ (Fy \supset Gy)]$ all count as monadic statements but $\forall x\ Gxa$ does not. Let's go on to say that *monadic PL* is that portion of PL that contains only monadic statements.

For our purposes, the Bernays-Schoenfinkel theorem can be formulated in terms of partial valuations. Here it is:

Bernays-Schoenfinkel Theorem *A set of monadic PL statements is consistent if there is a valuation of size 2^n on which all statements in the set are true, where n is the* number of different predicates occurring in members of the set.

The method that the Bernays-Schoenfinkel theorem suggests is rather unwieldy, but it does provide a mechanical way to test for all of the PL logical properties and relations involving monadic statements. We create nonquantificational statements out of our initial statements by substituting conjunctions for universal quantifications and disjunctions for existential quantifications using a valuation of size 2^n when n (monadic) predicates are involved. So if our initial set were

$$\{\exists x\ Fx, \forall x\ (Fx \supset \sim Gx), \exists x\ Gx\}$$

we would have to use $2^2\ (= 4)$ names in each of the conjunctions and disjunctions in order to provide a valuation of size 4. But from this point on we are essentially doing SL truth tables (or truth trees), which is clearly a mechanical method.

Here are the replacement statements on a partial valuation of size 4:

$$Fa_1 \vee Fa_2 \vee Fa_3 \vee Fa_4$$
$$(Fa_1 \supset \sim Ga_1)\ \&\ (Fa_2 \supset \sim Ga_2)\ \&\ (Fa_3 \supset \sim Ga_3)\ \&\ (Fa_4 \supset \sim Ga_4)$$
$$Ga_1 \vee Ga_2 \vee Ga_3 \vee Ga_4$$

It is easily discovered that there are valuations to the atomic components of the three statements on which all three statements are true, e.g.,

Fa_1	Fa_2	Fa_3	Fa_4	Ga_1	Ga_2	Ga_3	Ga_4
T	F	F	F	F	T	T	T

So, in accord with the Bernays-Schoenfinkel theorem, the set:

$$\{\exists x\ Fx, \forall x\ (Fx \supset \sim Gx), \exists x\ Gx\}$$

is logically consistent.

Summary

In this section and the last, we have discussed the logical properties and relations (see pp. 209–210).

We canvassed two methods of testing claims concerning the logical properties and relations: (1) by providing an argument couched in terms of valuations that some property or relation holds, and (2) by finding *counter-examples.* The method utilizes *partial valuations;* these assign truth-values only to atomic statements containing occurrences of a certain group of names. Except where a name occurs in a statement, the particular names involved are irrelevant. Thus, we conventionally use a_1, a_2, a_3, etc. as names and talk about *partial valuations of a certain size,* which corresponds to the number of names included. We also proved a version of Loewenheim's theorem and an important corollary:

Loewenheim's theorem *If there is a partial valuation on which all members of a set **S** are true, then **S** is logically consistent.*

Corollary *If there is a partial valuation of size m (m $\geqslant$ 1) on which all members of a set S are true, then there will be a partial valuation of size n, for any n $\geqslant$ m, on which all members of S will also be true.*

The reverse of the corollary, however, does not hold.

EXERCISES 6.3

1. For each of the following, is there a partial valuation of size 2 in which all members of the set are true? If your answer is yes, produce the valuation.

   a. $\{\forall x\,(Gx \supset\, \sim Fx),\, \exists x\, Fx\}$

   b. $\{\exists x\, Hx,\, \sim\forall x\, Hx\}$

   c. $\{\exists x\, \exists y\,(\sim Fx\, \& \, Fy)\}$

   d. $\{\forall x\, Gx \supset\, \sim Ga_1,\, \exists x\, Gx\}$

2. Using the method of counterexample, show that the following arguments are invalid.

   a. $\forall x\,(Fx \supset Hx)$
       $\forall x\,(Gx \supset Hx)$
       ———————
       $\forall x\,(Fx \supset Gx)$

   b. $\exists x\,(Fx\, \&\, Hx)$
       $\exists x\,(Hx\, \&\, Gx)$
       ———————
       $\exists x\,(Fx\, \&\, Gx)$

c. $\forall x \exists y \, Lxy$

$\overline{\exists x \forall y \, Lxy}$

d. $\forall x \exists y \, Lxy$

$\overline{\exists y \forall x \, Lxy}$

e. $\forall y \, [Py \supset \exists x \, (Gx \, \& \, Hyx)]$

$\overline{\exists x \exists y \, Hxy}$

f. $\forall x \, (Kx \supset Lx)$
$\exists x \exists y \, (Lx \, \& \, My)$

$\overline{\forall y \, (Ky \supset My)}$

3. By the method of counterexample, show that none of the following is logically true.

   a. $\exists x \, Gx \supset \forall x \, Gx$

   b. $[\exists x \, Rx \, \& \, \exists x \, Gx] \supset \exists x \, [Rx \, \& \, Gx]$

   c. $[\forall x \, Rx \supset \forall x \, Gx] \supset \forall x [Rx \, \& \, Gx]$

   d. $\exists x \, Fx \equiv Fa_1$

   e. $\forall x \exists y \, Lxy \supset \forall x \, Lxx$

   f. $[\forall x \, Fx \supset Ga] \supset \forall x [Fx \supset Ga]$

4. If any of the arguments below seems invalid to you, find a counter-example to verify your doubt.

   a. All farmers are strong; Mary is strong; therefore, Mary is a farmer.

   b. No kittens are large; some mammals are large; therefore, no kittens are mammals.

   c. Horses and cows are domesticated; some animals are domesticated; some animals are not domesticated; therefore, all horses are animals.

   d. No educators are fools; all gamblers are fools; therefore, no educators are gamblers.

   e. Only citizens are voters; not all residents are citizens; therefore, some voters are not residents.

5. Construct a proof for the corollary to Loewenheim's theorem.

7

Truth Trees and Derivations in PL

W_{e} return now to the truth trees, natural deduction derivations, and resolution derivations that we studied in chapters 3 and 4, for statement logic. All of the familiar SL rules of the systems also apply in predicate logic; other rules will be added to accomodate quantifiers. We will also discuss the **decision problem** for PL. The truth tree and resolution methods, which were algorithmic for SL, do not in general provide algorithms for determining the logical consistency of PL sets, or for any of the logical properties and relations. In chapter 11 we will study the full implications of the decision problem for PL and connect it to the theoretical limitations on computers.

7.1 TRUTH TREES AGAIN[1]

Before getting started, you should go back to section 3.4 of chapter 3 and review the SL tree rules as well as the procedure for constructing a valuation on which the members of a set with an open tree are true.

In SL, truth trees represent one of several algorithmic methods for determining logical properties and relations. In their PL role, they no longer

---

[1]The presentation of the tree rules and strategy hints in this section is derived from Hugues Leblanc and William A. Wisdom, *Deductive Logic*, 2nd ed. (New York: Allyn and Bacon, 1972), pp. 174–197.

represent an algorithm, but they are about as close as we can come to a general mechanical procedure in predicate logic. For certain subsystems of PL, as we shall see later, truth trees actually do represent an algorithmic decision procedure.

The rules for constructing SL truth trees apply in PL as well; think of the **A** and **B** of the rules as they appear in chapter 3 representing any PL statement. However, we need additional rules to handle quantifiers as they appear in the statements to be decomposed into the tree. Because there are two quantifiers, we need four additional rules; one each for the negated quantifiers and one each for the quantifiers themselves.

The first rule, for the universal quantifier, allows a substitution instance to be entered in open branches that pass through it; the rule is written as follows:[2]

Universal Quantification Rule

∀X A
·
A(N/X)

Note that the initial statement is not checked. According to this rule, we may enter a substitution instance of the quantificational statement into the tree, using any name we wish. But we do not check the initial statement because we can come back and apply the rule as many times as we wish, each time producing another substitution instance using another name. Quite clearly, the rule is justified; if a statement of the sort ∀X A is a member of a consistent set, then adding one or more substitution instances will preserve that consistency.

A closely related rule is the **negated existential quantification rule** for statements of the sort ∼∃X A (which are, of course, equivalent to statements of the sort ∀X ∼A):

Negated Existential Quantification Rule

∼∃X A
·
∼A(N/X)

---

[2]A version of this rule appears in the derivation rules of the next section under the name 'universal instantiation'.

Note once again that *the initial statement is not checked;* the rule can be invoked repeatedly on any negated existential statement. Statements of the sort ~**A(N/X)** are sure to be true on any valuation on which ~∃**X A** is true.

The next two rules also closely resemble one another; they both have restrictions on their use that are of vital importance to their correct deployment in constructing a tree. In the case of existential quantifications of the sort ∃**X A,** if they are true we know that at least one instance must also be true, but we can't be sure which one. So if a statement ∃**X A** turns up on a branch of a tree, we can safely add the instance **A(N/X)** *only if* we are sure that the name **N** has no previous occurrence on that branch, that is, only if the name **N** in the context is chosen completely arbitrarily. In using the rule, the name **N** must be *new to each and every branch in which the instance* **A(N/X)** *is entered.*

The **existential quantification rule,** then, looks like this:[3]

Existential Quantification Rule

∃X A x √
   ·
*A(N/X)

*Restriction: *the name N must be new to every branch in which the instance A(N/X) is entered.*

As an example, suppose we have the following statements in a branch of a tree:

Something is missing. (∃x Mx)

Something is not missing. (∃x ~Mx)

If we use the name *a* in a substitution instance of the first statement, according to the existential quantification rule, we enter

Ma

on the branch. But if we were to use *a again* in a substitution instance of the second statement, we would enter

~Ma

---

[3]A version of this rule, with a similar restriction, will appear in the next section under the name 'existential instantiation'.

on the branch, which, of course, closes the branch and indicates that the two initial statements are inconsistent. But both statements can easily be true; suppose my ring (*a*) is missing and my shoe (*b*) is not. The restriction avoids this sort of problem by requiring a new name for each use of the existential quantification rule.

The final rule, for negated universal quantifications, follows the same line of reasoning. If a set is consistent and a statement of the sort ~∀X **A** is a member of the set, then adding the statement ~**A**(**N**/X) will not affect the consistency of the set so long as the name **N** has not previously appeared anywhere in the set. So the same restriction applies in this case as in the previous one; the name used must be *new* to every branch into which a negated universal quantification is to be decomposed. Here, then, is the **negated universal quantification rule**:

Negated Universal Quantification Rule

~∀X A X √
    .
*~A (N/X)

*Restriction: *the name* **N** *must be new to every branch in which the instance* ~*A(N/X) is entered.*

Note that in both of these last two rules, *the initial statement is checked*; we get one shot at decomposing the statement into the tree.

You may remember that the truth trees in SL are an essentially foolproof means of detecting SL logical properties and relations. By carefully choosing which rule to apply first, the tree can be shortened or made less complicated. But even plowing through blindly, applying rules just in the order in which statements appear, always results in a finished tree that pronounces the initial set of statements inconsistent (if all branches are closed) or consistent (if one or more branch remains open). In PL, however, matters are not so simple. We can completely miss an opportunity to close a tree by misjudging when and how to apply a rule and, therefore, can find ourselves with an open tree for a logically inconsistent set, even though we have seemingly followed all the rules. So the strategy hints here are not just labor-saving devices; *they are an integral part of the tree method for PL.*

Let's begin with such a case. We want to test the simple argument: 'Everything is purple and round; therefore everything is round'. In PL notation

∀x [Px & Rx]

∀x Rx

As was our custom in chapter 3, we test an argument for validity by forming the set consisting of the premise(s) together with the negation of the conclusion, and then work out the tree for this set. So,

(1) $\forall x\,[Px\ \&\ Rx]$

(2) $\sim\!\forall x\ Rx$

———————————

(3)

We can begin by decomposing either initial statement. Each, however, will require a name in the branch that runs through the other statement and, therefore, will possibly affect the way the other statement can be decomposed. Here is what we have if we begin with statement 1, and the universal quantification rule:

(1) $\forall x\,[Px\ \&\ Rx]$

(2) $\sim\!\forall x\ Rx$

———————————

(3) $Pa_1\ \&\ Ra_1$ $\checkmark$ (from 1)

(4) Pa_1 (from 3)

(5) Ra_1 (from 3)

Next, we want to decompose statement 2 by producing $\sim\!Ra_1$ in line 6 and close the tree, thus showing that the original argument is valid. But the restriction on the negated universal quantification rule does not permit this move since a_1 already occurs in the branch (in lines 3, 4, and 5). Having started the tree as we did, the best we can do is produce a tree that looks like this:

(1) $\forall x\,[Px\ \&\ Rx]$

(2) $\sim\!\forall x\ Rx$ $\checkmark$

———————————

(3) $Pa_1\ \&\ Ra_1$ $\checkmark$ (from 1)

(4) Pa_1 (from 3)

(5) Ra_1 (from 3)

(6) $\sim\!Ra_2$ (from 2)

Such a tree is, of course, *open*, even though we have followed all of the rules. There are two ways to save the day and produce a closed tree. The first is to go back to statement 1 and again invoke the universal quantification rule, this time using the name a_2. This alternative will produce a closed tree in three more lines. A better way to proceed is to start again, this time following the first all-important strategy hint:

Strategy Hint 1 *Always decompose restricted statements first.*

Following the strategy hint produces the following closed tree:

(1) ∀x [Px & Rx]

(2) ~∀x Rx √

══════

(3) ~Ra₁   (from 2)

(4) Pa₁ & Ra₁ √   (from 1)

(5) Pa₁   (from 3)

(6) Ra₁   (from 3)
    X

A second all-important strategy emerges at this point. Given the freedom to use any name we wish in the unrestricted rules for the universal quantifier and the negated existential quantifier, it is important that in applying the unrestricted rules we use names *that already occur* before introducing any new names into the tree. Following this strategy will increase the chances of producing a closed tree early on and will keep us from missing some possible closures. Thus, the second strategy hint is

---

Strategy Hint 2 *When decomposing unrestricted statements, always use names already in the branch before introducing new names.*

The function of the rules and applications of the two strategy hints will become apparent as you work through the following examples.

Example 1   Is the following set consistent?

{Somebody ate my apple; Apples do not exist.}

Step 1   Symbolize in PL notation

∃x [Px & ∃y(Ay & Bya & Exy)], ~∃x Ax

(*P*: '__ is a person; *A*: '__ is an apple; *B*: '__ belongs to __'; *E*: '__ ate __'; *a*: 'me')

Step 2   Arrange the statements in a column; begin the tree.

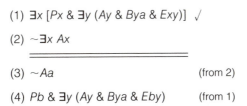

(1) ∃x [Px & ∃y (Ay & Bya & Exy)] √

(2) ~∃x Ax

—————————————

(3) ~Aa   (from 2)

(4) Pb & ∃y (Ay & Bya & Eby)   (from 1)

You will notice that both strategy hints apply to our choice of the first step. We have an existential quantifier in line 1, so strategy hint 1 tells us to decompose line 1 first. But we also have a name in line 1, so strategy hint 2 tells us to decompose line 2 to that name before any new names are introduced. Since applying the existential quantification rule to line 1 will introduce a new name (given the restriction), the best first move in this case is to decompose initial statement 2, in conjunction with strategy hint 2, to *a*, the name already in the tree. Then we go on to decompose statement 1, using the new name *b* to meet the restriction on the existential quantification rule. In general, a good way to begin a tree is to identify names that occur in the set; if names *do not* occur, use restricted rules first; if names *do* occur, use rules without restrictions and decompose to existing names.

Step 3   We haven't yet made much progress; we will have to decompose further statement 4 and, eventually, return to statement 2.

(4) Pb & ∃y (Ay & Bya & Eby) √   (from 1)

(5) Pb   (from 4)

(6) ∃y (Ay & Bya & Eby) √   (from 4)

(7) Ac & Bca & Ebc   (from 6)

We decompose statement 6 using the existential quantification rule. Since there is a restriction, we use a new name *c* for the variable *y* of quantification.

Step 4   We decompose line 7 using two applications of the conjunction rule and then take stock.

(7) Ac & Bca & Ebc √   (from 6)

(8) Ac   (from 7)

(9) Bca   (from 7)

(10) Ebc   (from 7)

Step 5   Our analysis should have revealed that our best chance of closing a branch is to go back to initial statement 2 and decompose it, following strategy hint 2 by using all of the names occurring in the tree so far (i.e., *b* and *c*), which results in

(11) ~*Ab*   (from 2)

(12) ~*Ac*   (from 2)
      X

The presence of both *Ac* (line 8) and ~*Ac* (line 12) provides the statement and its negation required by the tree rules to close the branch and, hence, the tree. Thus, the initial set is inconsistent.

Example 2   Is ∀*x* *Px* ∨ ∀*x* ~*Px* a logically true statement?

Step 1   Negate the statement and test it by means of a tree.

(1) ~[∀*x* *Px* ∨ ∀*x* ~*Px*] √
    ════════════════════════

(2) ~∀*x* *Px* √   (from 1)

(3) ~∀*x* ~*Px* √   (from 1)

(4) ~*Pa*   (from 2)

(5) ~~*Pb* √   (from 3)

(6) *Pb*   (from 5)

Note that both statements, ~∀*x* *Px* and ~∀*x* ~*Px*, that result from the decomposition of line 1 have restrictions, so they *must* be decomposed to statements with different names. Since there are no more statements to decompose or lines that can be added to the branch, and the tree is *open*, the set containing ~[∀*x* *Px* ∨ ∀*x* ~*Px*] is therefore *consistent*. So, the original statement ∀*x* *Px* ∨ ∀*x* ~*Px* is not a logical truth.

So far we have looked only at cases where the branches of the tree close or remain definitively open, as in example 2; now we will look at two different cases.

Example 3   Is the set {~∃*x* *Rx*, ∃*x* ~*Rx*} logically consistent?

Step 1   Arrange the statements in the set in a column and begin to work out the tree.

(1) $\sim\!\exists x\ Rx$

(2) $\exists x\ \sim\!Rx\ \checkmark$
====

(3) $\sim\!Ra_1$ (from 2)

Note that since $\exists x\ \sim\!Rx$ (line 2) is an existential quantification, we decompose it first (and check it) following strategy hint 1. We use a name with a subscript because of the presence of the negated existential statement in line 1 (which we can come back to); but we could have used an ordinary name as well.

(4) $\sim\!Ra_1$ (from 1)

At this point we have decomposed line 1 once and followed the advice of strategy hint 2. We now face the question of what to do next. Should we stop here? Notice that the tree rules allow us to return to line 1 over and over; here are a few examples.

(5) $\sim\!Ra_2$ (from 1)

(6) $\sim\!Ra_3$ (from 1)

(7) $\sim\!Ra_4$ (from 1)

Obviously we can go on if we wish, but to no avail. We clearly will not be able to add any statements to the branch that will result in closing the tree since all we can do is return again and again to line 1 and produce further statements of the form $\sim\!R(N/x)$. Therefore, after reaching line 4, we conclude that the set $\{\sim\!\exists x\ Rx,\ \exists x\ \sim\!Rx\}$ is logically consistent because we can see at that point that the tree will never close.

If we completely followed the decomposition rule for line 1, the construction of the tree would be an *infinite* process. Thus, in this case, the full tree cannot be worked out; however, we can *describe* the full tree. We will have more to say about infinite trees later on.

Example 4   Is the following argument logically valid?

All mad dogs have fleas.
_____

Some mad dogs have fleas.

Step 1   Symbolize the argument in PL notation.

$\forall x\ [(Mx\ \&\ Dx) \supset Fx]$
_____

$\exists x\ [(Mx\ \&\ Dx)\ \&\ Fx]$

Step 2   Arrange the premises and the negated conclusion in a column and work out the tree.

(1)   ∀x [(Mx & Dx) ⊃ Fx]

(2)   ~∃x [(Mx & Dx) & Fx]
                                       ===================

(3)   (Ma & Da) ⊃ Fa   (from 1)

(4)   ·   ~[(Ma & Da) & Fa]   (from 2)

Note that we can begin with either line 1 or line 2 since there are no restrictions on either applicable decomposition rule. We use the same name in both cases, of course.

We have eight open branches so far! If we go back to the initial statements, we will add further growth to the tree, and each of the branches will further divide and grow indefinitely as we cycle back again and again. But, as before, we can see that the tree will always be open because statements and their negations will not occur to close these branches. So even though the tree is incomplete, we can say that the set of the two initial statements is logically consistent, and, therefore, the original argument is logically invalid.

In both of the above examples, there is an obvious stopping point based on a narrow reading of strategy hint 2. Since we are not *forced* to return to unchecked statements for further decomposition, we don't, and stopping at this point in both cases leaves open branches that assure us that the tree will remain open no matter what. Now we look at a case without a natural stopping point.[4]

---

[4]The example and subsequent discussion is adapted from Richard Jeffrey, *Formal Logic: Its Scope and Limits*, 2nd ed. (New York: McGraw-Hill, 1981), p. 126f.

Example 5   Is the following set consistent?

{Everything is bigger than something or other. My toe is not bigger than itself.}

Step 1   Symbolize the statements in PL notation and arrange in a column. (Let B stand for '___ is bigger than ___' and a_1 stand for 'my toe'.)

      (1) $\forall x\, \exists y\; Bxy$

      (2) $\sim Ba_1a_1$

Step 2   Work out the tree.

      (1) $\forall x\, \exists y\; Bxy$

      (2) $\sim Ba_1a_1$

      (3) $\exists y\; Ba_1y$ √ (from 1)

      (4) Ba_1a_2 (from 3)

      (5) $\exists y\; Ba_2y$ √ (from 1)

      (6) Ba_2a_3 (from 5)

      .

      .

      .

In each line after line 3, we introduce a new name by decomposing the existential quantification in the line before. Then, following the tree rules and strategy hint 2, we go back to line 1 and decompose it with this new name, which eventually leads to yet another new name, and so on. We can see that this process will continue on and on, that there is no natural stopping point; this is a case where the tree method literally fails us. We know intuitively that the set is consistent, and inspecting the tree reveals that closure seems impossible. But in more complicated examples, this sort of inspection will not be reliable, and it isn't governed by tree rules in any case. Thus, even in this simple example, we have uncovered a limitation of the tree method for PL. Based on the truth tree method, we cannot say anything reliable about the consistency of the original set.

Let us now take stock of the various cases we have already seen so that the various possibilities within the tree method—rules and strategy hints— are clear.

Possible Outcomes of the Tree Method

Type I   Every branch of the tree closes: the set of the initial statements is therefore *logically inconsistent* (example 1).

Type II   At least one branch is *complete* and remains open (example 2). By 'complete' we mean that no more statements can be added to the branch through further decomposition of any statement through which the branch runs. In this case the set of initial statements is *logically consistent*.

Type III   At least one branch is open after the following steps (examples 3 and 4).

a. Every existential and negated universal statement on the branch is decomposed (and checked);

b. Every universal and negated existential statement is decomposed *to every name* on the branch; and

c. All other statements on the branch have been decomposed.
   Note that *only* the following types of statements can occur at this point on the branch: (1) truth-functional compound statements that are checked and decomposed, (2) universal and negated existential statements that have been decomposed to all names occurring anywhere on the branch, (3) existential and negated universal statements that are checked and decomposed, and (4) atomic statements and negated atomic statements. Even though the branch *could* continue infinitely, we can safely declare the tree to be open and the initial set of statements to be *logically consistent*.

Type IV   At least one branch is open, and nothing in the tree method tells us to stop (example 5). We may decide that the tree is not going anywhere, but the grounds of this decision will not be tree rules but ingenuity, ad hoc principles, faith, whatever.

If we properly apply the tree rules, our trees will always fall into one of these four categories. We can be assured that for every *inconsistent* set of statements there is a closed tree (Type I). However, we will have to be careful in our construction to find it, and we must follow the strategy hints. But there are consistent sets of statements that no tree will ever definitively pronounce consistent (Type IV). Thus, even though every inconsistent set has a closed tree, we may give up on a tree in the belief that it is consistent and Type IV. But if we kept going, perhaps it would turn out to be inconsistent after all.

This phenomenon is similar to the results of our search for counterexamples using partial valuations in section 6.3. In both instances we confront the limits of our methods for determining whether sets of statements are consistent or not. As we will see in chapter 11, this lack of an algorithmic procedure for determining PL consistency means that reasoning cannot be fully automated, and, hence, imposes a theoretical limit on all possible computers.[5]

It is important to note that some trees will have one branch that fits the description of Type II or Type III and other branches that are of Type IV. But only one open branch of any of the three types is required to pronounce a tree open and, hence, the set of initial statements logically consistent. Here is an example:[6]

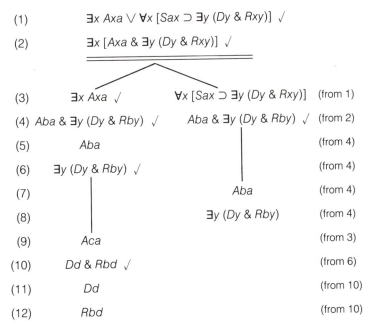

(1)	∃x Axa ∨ ∀x [Sax ⊃ ∃y (Dy & Rxy)] ✓	
(2)	∃x [Axa & ∃y (Dy & Rxy)] ✓	
(3)	∃x Axa ✓ ∀x [Sax ⊃ ∃y (Dy & Rxy)]	(from 1)
(4)	Aba & ∃y (Dy & Rby) ✓ Aba & ∃y (Dy & Rby) ✓	(from 2)
(5)	Aba	(from 4)
(6)	∃y (Dy & Rby) ✓	(from 4)
(7)	Aba	(from 4)
(8)	∃y (Dy & Rby)	(from 4)
(9)	Aca	(from 3)
(10)	Dd & Rbd ✓	(from 6)
(11)	Dd	(from 10)
(12)	Rbd	(from 10)

At this point, we have decomposed into the left branch in accord with the rules and strategy hint 2, and we can naturally stop. Note that the statements on the left branch fit the description of a Type III case. But the right branch could be further developed and will have subbranches of Type IV that go on and on. (Work out the right branch yourself.) Fortunately, as noted above, if one or more branches are Type II or III, we do not have to go any further with other branches and can declare the tree open and the set of initial statements logically consistent.

As we mentioned in section 6.3, a theorem of Bernays-Schoenfinkel provides that any set of statements in which only *monadic* predicates occur can be definitively shown to be logically consistent or inconsistent by means

---

[5]See section 11.4.
[6]From Leblanc and Wisdom, *Deductive Logic*, 194–195. The English sentences in the set are 'Either the accused has an alibi or anything he says will raise fresh doubts' and 'Some of his alibis will raise fresh doubts anyway'.

of a partial valuation no larger than 2^n, where n is the number of different predicates in the set. When this theorem is transposed into the tree method, it means that there are no trees of Type IV for sets containing only monadic predicates and that there is no need for potentially infinite branches in Type III trees either. By means of a small adjustment to the tree procedure, all branches for monadic statements are finite and contain no more than a predictable number of names. So altered, the tree method does provide an algorithm, or decision procedure, for the monadic subsystem of PL.

The tree procedure for the monadic subsystem of PL substitutes this procedure for strategy hint 2:

Monadic Procedure (*replaces strategy hint 2*) *Decompose all universal and negated existential statements into the tree by using names that already occur in open branches, passing through the statements and zero or more new names so that the total number of different names is equal to 2^n, where n is the number of different predicates in the initial statements. Check universal and negated existential statements when this decomposition has been carried out.*

Following this monadic procedure actually makes Type III trees significantly longer than they otherwise would be, since we would usually not introduce new names by decomposing universal and negated existential statements. As a result, all branches will be either closed or open and completed, and *all* statements on the tree will be either atomic or negated atomic statements or checked. Hence the trees for *monadic* PL are like SL trees, and the rules are entirely mechanical.

Summary

For easy reference, here are all of the truth tree rules together.

Truth Tree Rules

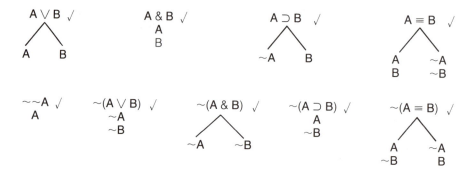

∀X A	~∃X A	∃X A ✓	~∀X A ✓
.	.	.	.
A(N/X)	~A(N/X)	A(N/X)*	~A(N/X)*

Restriction: the name **N** must be new to each and every branch in which the instance is entered.

There are two important strategy hints which are vital to the success of the tree method:

Strategy Hint 1 *Always decompose restricted statements first.*

Strategy Hint 2 *When decomposing unrestricted statements, always use names already in the branch before introducing new names.*

For the purpose of declaring the initial set of statements in a tree to be logically consistent or logically inconsistent, review the possible outcomes of the tree method properly applied (p. 234).

As we pointed out, the tree method fails to provide a general mechanized procedure for deciding on the presence and absence of the logical properties and relations for PL statements and sets of statements. Type IV cases reveal the sort of situation where the limits of the tree method are evident. But the monadic procedure permits an adaptation of the tree method which gives an algorithm for the monadic subsystem of PL.

Monadic Procedure *(replaces strategy hint 2) Decompose all universal and negated existential statements into the tree by using names that already occur in open branches, passing through the statements and zero or more new names so that the total number of different names is equal to 2^n, where n is the number of different predicates in the initial statements. Check universal and negated existential statements when this decomposition has been carried out.*

As we shall study in chapter 11, there are, in general, no *possible* means of generally mechanizing or automating the decision process for PL, which puts a very important limit on computers and computability.

EXERCISES 7.1

1. By means of the standard truth tree method, determine whether the following arguments are logically valid.

   a. ∀x Fx

      ─────

      Fa

   b. ∃x (Px & Gx)

      ─────────

      ∃x Gx

   c. ∀x (Rx ⊃ Gx)
       ∀x (Gx ⊃ Fx)

      ─────────

      ∀x (Rx ⊃ Fx)

   d. ∀x (Fx ⊃ Hx)
       ∃x (Fx & Gx)

      ─────────

      ∃x (Gx & Hx)

   e. ∀x [Fx ⊃ (Gx & Rx)]
       ∃x Gx

      ─────────────

      ∃x Rx

   f. ∀x ∃y Lxy

      ─────────

      ∃x ∃y Lxy

   g. ∀x [Px ⊃ ∃y (Ry & Lxy)]
       Pa

      ──────────────

      ∃x Lax

2. Declare by means of a truth tree whether any of the following are logically true.

   a. ∀x ∀y (Fx ⊃ Fy)

   b. ∀x (Fx ⊃ ∀y Fy)

   c. [∀x Gx ⊃ ∀x Hx] ⊃ ∀x [Gx ⊃ Hx]

   d. [∃x Gx ⊃ ∃x Hx] ⊃ ∃x [Gx & Hx]

   e. ∀x ∀y Lxy ⊃ ∃x ∀y Lxy

   f. ∀x ∃y Lxy ⊃ ∃x ∀y Lxy

   g. ∃x ∀y Lxy ⊃ ∃y ∀x Lxy

3. Determine whether the following pairs of statements are logically equivalent.

   a. ∀x Fx   and   ∀y Fy

   b. ∀x [Hx ∨ Gx]   and   ∀x Hx ∨ ∀x Gx

   c. ∀x (Gx ⊃ ~Rx) and   ~∃x (Gx & Rx)

   d. ∃x Fx ⊃ Ga and   ∀x [Fx ⊃ Ga]

4. Determine by means of truth trees whether the following arguments are logically valid or invalid.

   a. The only people who live on islands are eccentrics. Sue isn't an eccentric; therefore, she doesn't live on a island.

   b. Muskrats are lovely creatures. But salamanders are odious. Some odious creatures are unlovely. Therefore, no muskrats are odious.

   c. Bill is larger than Sue and Ellen is larger than Pete. If anything is larger than something that itself is larger than a third thing, then the first thing is larger than the third. So Bill is larger than Pete.

   d. All of Joan's books are blue. So if this book is red or yellow, then it doesn't belong to Joan.

   e. If you are arrested, you may be in for a long jail term. Only drug dealers and car thieves are arrested. Since you don't deal drugs, if you are arrested you must be a car thief.

   f. Everyone dislikes someone. So there is someone whom everyone dislikes.

5. Explain in detail why there are no Type IV trees in the monadic subsystem of PL if the monadic procedure is followed. Use the following set as an example:

$$\{∀x [Ax \ \& \ ∃y \ By], ∃x \ Rx\}$$

*7.2 PL VALUATIONS FROM OPEN TRUTH TREES

We now turn to the process of showing that a PL valuation can be constructed from any open branch of a tree of Type II or III on which all statements in the initial set are true. There are, of course, no such valuations for Type I trees since they are closed, indicating that the initial set is inconsistent. Sets that have Type IV trees are not known to be consistent or inconsistent, so no valuations can be constructed from them. The steps for constructing valuations from Type II and Type III open branches follow:

Constructing Valuations from Open Branches

   Type II trees Recall that there is an open branch that has been *completed*. The corresponding valuation to this branch assigns T to every atomic component of the initial statements that occurs unnegated on the branch and assigns **F** to *all other atomic components* of the initial statements.

   For example, here is a Type II tree that shows that the statement ∀x Px ∨ ∀x ~Px is not a logical truth (since the tree for the negation of the statement is open):

(1) $\sim[\forall x\ Px \lor \forall x \sim Px]$ $\checkmark$

═══════════════════

(2) $\sim\forall x\ Px$ $\checkmark$ (from 1)

(3) $\sim\forall x \sim Px$ $\checkmark$ (from 1)

(4) $\sim Pa_1$ (from 2)

(5) $\sim\sim Pa_2$ $\checkmark$ (from 3)

(6) Pa_2 (from 5)

To construct a valuation, we assign **T** to Pa_2 and **F** to all the other atomic components of $\forall x\ Px \lor \forall x \sim Px$, i.e., Pa_1, Pa_3, Pa_4, Pa_5, etc. Both $\forall x\ Px$ and $\forall x \sim Px$ are sure to be false on this valuation, and so the initial statement of the tree $\sim[\forall x\ Px \lor \forall x \sim Px]$ is true.

Type III trees   From an open branch that fits the Type III description, the valuation is constructed as follows:

a. Assign **T** to every atomic component of the initial statements that occurs unnegated on the branch;

b. If an atomic component **A** N_1, N_3, N_5, . . . of any initial statement is assigned **T**, then also assign **T** to all other atomic statements of the sort **A** N_2/N_1, N_4/N_3, N_6/N_5, . . . for all names N_2, N_4, N_6, . . . that do not occur in any statement on the branch; and

c. Assign **F** to all other atomic components of the initial statements.

Step (b) above is complicated, so an example of how it works may be helpful. Recall that in a Type III open branch we have stopped decomposing, even though there is at least one universal or negated existential statement in the branch to which we could return. We need our valuation to (1) assign **T** *to the appropriate atomic components* of that statement (or statements) so that it (they) will be true on the valuation, and (2) to assign **F** to all other atomic components of the initial statements. The atomic components we are interested in are precisely those that would occur unnegated on the branch were we to decompose any universal or negated existential statement to *new names*, since all existing names on the branch have already been used as strategy hint 2 requires. So take any unnegated atomic statement on such a branch, say, Ga_2a_3. This statement will be assigned **T** by the valuation, as in (a) above. Now we want also to assign the following statements **T** as well:

Ga_4a_3	Ga_2a_4
Ga_5a_3	Ga_2a_5
Ga_6a_3	Ga_2a_6
Ga_7a_3	Ga_2a_7
etc.	etc.

where $a_4, a_5, a_6, a_7, \ldots$ are all names that do not occur anywhere on the branch. The atomic statements in these lists, therefore, *would* appear on the branch as we attempted to complete it, so they must be assigned the truth-value **T** by the valuation.

As further illustration of the construction of a valuation in a Type III case, let's look again at example 3 from section 7.1:

(1) $\sim\exists x\, Rx$

(2) $\exists x \sim Rx$ √
  ⎯⎯⎯⎯

(3) $\sim Ra_1$ (from 2)

(4) $\sim Ra_1$ (from 1)

We stop at this point because there is no reason to continue; we have completely decomposed all statements that can be checked, and we decomposed the negated existential statement in line 1 to all existing names in the branch. We therefore declare the initial set to be logically consistent. To construct a valuation on which the initial statements are both true, we follow the instructions above for Type III cases, which in this case are quite straightforward. Since no unnegated atomic statements occur on the branch, we simply assign all atomic components of both initial statements **F** and call this valuation α.

It is easily verified that both $\sim\exists x\, Rx$ and $\exists x \sim Rx$ are true on α. Since Ra_1 is **F**, its negation, $\sim Ra_1$, is **T**, and so $\exists x \sim Rx$ is **T** as well on α. And since all of Ra_1, Ra_2, Ra_3, etc. are **F**, then $\sim\exists x\, Rx$ ($\equiv \forall x \sim Rx$) is **T** as well.

Here is another tree with a Type III branch:

Example 1

(1) $\exists x \sim Gx \supset \forall x\, \exists y\, Ryx$ √

(2) $\exists x\, Ka_1 x$ √

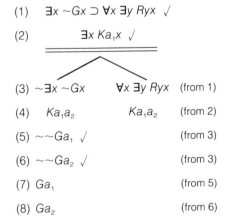

(3) $\sim\exists x \sim Gx$ $\forall x\, \exists y\, Ryx$ (from 1)

(4) $Ka_1 a_2$ $Ka_1 a_2$ (from 2)

(5) $\sim\sim Ga_1$ √   (from 3)

(6) $\sim\sim Ga_2$ √   (from 3)

(7) Ga_1 (from 5)

(8) Ga_2 (from 6)

At this point we have reached the natural stopping point on the open left branch; any further decomposition of the negated existential quantification in line 3 will bring new names into the branch; all existing names are represented in decompositions of the universal quantifications and negated existential quantifications on the branch (although not elsewhere). So we can declare the initial set logically consistent.

To construct a valuation on which both initial statements $\exists x \sim Gx \supset \forall x \exists y \, Kyx$ and $\exists x \, Ka_1x$ are true, we follow the instructions given above for Type III trees. Each of the following occurs unnegated on the branch:

$$Ka_1a_2 \qquad Ga_1 \qquad Ga_2$$

They are, therefore, assigned **T** by our valuation, which we will call α. Applying step (b) of the instructions, we also assign **T** to any other atomic component of the initial statements that would result from these atomic statements if *new* names, not in the branch, were substituted for their names. Therefore, valuation α also assigns **T** to the following:

Valuation α:

Ka_1a_3	Ka_3a_2	Ga_3
Ka_1a_4	Ka_4a_2	Ga_4
Ka_1a_5	Ka_5a_2	Ga_5
Ka_1a_6	Ka_6a_2	Ga_6
etc.	etc.	etc.

Then, in accord with step (c), α assigns **F** to all other atomic components of the initial statements. Specifically, α assigns **F** to such statements as Ka_1a_1, Ka_2a_2, and Ka_2a_1, as well as to Ra_1a_2, Ra_2a_1, etc. since in each case these do not appear unnegated on the branch and they cannot be formed from Ka_1a_2, Ga_1, or Ga_2 by substituting new names for either of the two names a_1 and a_2.

As you may have noted, the formation of valuations like α in this case will include numbers of atomic statements as **T** that are totally irrelevant to the truth of the initial statements. (Can you find some in this case?) That is perfectly acceptable; we have not promised to construct the *only* valuation that makes the initial statements true, but only to construct *a* valuation on which they are all true.

Next, we need to verify that the two initial statements in the tree above are both true on valuation α. Here are the statements again:

$$\exists x \sim Gx \supset \forall x \exists y \, Ryx \quad \text{and} \quad \exists x \, Ka_1x$$

Since all of Ga_1, Ga_2, Ga_3, etc. are **T** on α, the statement $\exists x \sim Gx$ is sure to be **F** on α, which makes the conditional $\exists x \sim Gx \supset \forall x \exists y \, Ryx$ **T** on α. In the case of the second statement, Ka_1a_2, which occurs on the branch, is assigned **T**, so $\exists x \, Ka_1x$ is therefore **T** on α as well. But note that we have successfully avoided any conflict with the restriction on the decomposition of existential quantifications because statement Ka_1a_1 is here **F** on α.

By constructing valuations from open branches of trees, we can show that an open branch of a tree may be a *counterexample*, as discussed in chapter 6, to certain claims concerning logical properties and relations. Such counterexamples can be depicted as either a full valuation or a partial valuation for some number p of names. Partial valuations come directly off open branches; the names on the branch will be the names in the partial valuation.

You can now answer the following kind of question:

Example 2 Is the following argument logically valid or invalid? If invalid, provide a counterexample that shows that the premises can be true when the conclusion is false.

All pine trees are conifers

All spruce trees are conifers

All pine trees are spruce trees.

We symbolize the argument in PL notation and construct a tree. (Let P be the predicate '_____ is a pine tree,' S be '_____ is a spruce tree' and C be '_____ is a conifer'.)

(1)	$\forall x\,[Px \supset Cx]$	
(2)	$\forall x\,[Sx \supset Cx]$	
(3)	$\sim\forall x\,[Px \supset Sx]\ \checkmark$	
(4)	$\sim[Pa_1 \supset Sa_1]\ \checkmark$	(from 3)
(5)	Pa_1	(from 4)
(6)	$\sim Sa_1$	(from 4)
(7)	$Pa_1 \supset Ca_1\ \checkmark$	(from 1)
(8)	$Sa_1 \supset Ca_1\ \checkmark$	(from 2)
(9)	$\sim Pa_1$ Ca_1	(from 7)
	X	
(10)	$\sim Sa_1$ Ca_1	(from 8)

At this point we are directed to stop, even though we could continue with further decompositions of lines 1 and 2. We have two open branches, so the initial set is consistent and, hence, the argument is invalid. We can produce a counterexample from either open branch; let's use the right one.

A partial valuation that counts as a counterexample is available from just those names occurring on the branch, i.e., a_1. So in a valuation of size 1, the following assignments will make the premises of the original argument true while the conclusion is false.

Partial valuation of size 1:

Pa_1	Sa_1	Ca_1	$\forall x\,[Px \supset Cx]$	$\forall x\,[Sx \supset Cx]$	$\forall x\,[Px \supset Sx]$
T	F	T	T	T	F

The partial valuation is constructed by following the steps in the construction of a full valuation *but just for the names that occur on the branch:* assign **T** to all unnegated atomic statements on the branch, and assign **F** to those atomic components of the initial statements that are negated on the branch.

It is easy to show that the premises are **T** on this partial valuation; since there is only one name, the universal statements have the same truth-value as the conditionals: $Pa_1 \supset Ca_1$, $Sa_1 \supset Ca_1$ and $Pa_1 \supset Sa_1$.

Since we began with an English argument, we can provide the counterexample in English as well. Take 'the tree in the quad' to be the name of the pine tree outside of the window. It is a pine tree (obviously) and a conifer, but not a spruce. This shows that *in a world consisting of just that tree,* the statements 'All pine trees are conifers' and 'All spruce trees are conifers' would be true[7], but the statement 'All pine trees are spruce trees' would be false. Obviously the argument is invalid, and this simple world shows it to be.

The full valuation that counts as a counterexample also assigns **T** to all of Pa_2, Pa_3, etc. and to all of Ca_2, Ca_3, etc. and assigns **F** to all other atomic components of the initial statements (i.e., to all of Sa_2, Sa_3, etc.). The premises are obviously **T** on the full valuation since all of their substitution instances are true. The conclusion is **F** because one of its substitution instances—$Pa_1 \supset Sa_1$—is **F**.

Summary

In this section we have studied the procedure for constructing a PL valuation from an open branch of a tree on which the members of the initial set of statements are all true. The list on pp. 239–240 summarizes how it is done for Type II and Type III open trees.

We also have pointed out that these valuations count as *counterexamples* to certain claims concerning logical properties and relations. We can provide a partial valuation as a counterexample (as in section 6.3) by dealing with

---

[7]Note that without any spruce trees, the statement 'All spruce trees are conifers' is true by default, given the PL understanding of such general statements.

just the atomic components of the initial statements occurring on the branch; a full valuation can also be described as the counterexample.

EXERCISES 7.2

For the open trees you found in exercises 7.1, construct partial valuations from an open branch, and explain how they count as counterexamples.

7.3 DERIVATIONS AGAIN[8]

Although the natural deduction system in SL has the advantage of providing a means of directly deducing a conclusion from the premises of an argument, it really is a superfluous technique. Algorithms like truth tables and truth trees make the rigors of derivations simply unnecessary for all practical purposes, except, perhaps, for sharpening logical abilities (which *is* a worthy goal). But in PL, derivations have a point, since algorithms are not available. In fact, proof techniques such as derivations are the standard means in PL of showing that one statement follows from a set of statements, or of showing that a statement is logically true (i.e., is a *theorem* of logic) because its derivation is independent of any initial assumptions. Also, two statements can be shown to be logically equivalent by means of derivations when each can be derived from the other.

Just as we used the rules for SL truth trees as a base for constructing PL trees, we can also apply to PL the derivation rules for SL, interpreting the letters **A**, **B**, **C**, etc. as any PL statement or quasi statement.[9] And of course we will make use of the derived inference rules since they make derivations much shorter. Before proceeding, you may want to go back to chapter 4 and carefully review the rules and strategies for SL derivations (the rules are listed on pp. 155–157).

We also need several new rules to allow us to deal with quantificational statements. For each quantifier we need two rules: an elimination rule and an introduction rule. We can also use the subsidiary derivations and the other now-familiar trappings of SL derivations.

Two of the new rules are quite simple: the rules for eliminating the universal quantifier and for introducing the existential quantifier.

Universal Instantiation (UI)

k. | $\forall$X A

m. | A(N/X)   (UI, k)

---

[8]The additional derivation rules for PL come from Leblanc and Wisdom.
[9]See section 5.3 for the definition of 'quasi statement'.

Existential Generalization (EG)

k. | A(N/X)

m. | ∃X A   (EG, k)

Both of these rules can be invoked at any point in a derivation and do not have restrictions. In the case of universal instantiation, we can move from a universally quantified statement to a substitution instance at will by dropping the universal quantifier and substituting a name, any name, for the variable of quantification. Here is an example of a simple derivation involving the UI rule:

Example 1   Show that *Fa* follows from ∀*x Fx*

1. | ∀*x Fx*

2. | ∀*x Fx*   (R, 1)
3. | *Fa*   (UI, 2)

It is important to remember that UI and the other three quantifier inference rules apply to *statements,* not their components. So the following use of UI in a derivation would be a mistake:

6. | ∀*x Fx* ∨ ∃*x Gx*
7. | *Fa*   (UI,6)   IMPROPER!!

The statement in line 6 is *not* a universal quantification; it is a disjunction. So UI does not apply to it.

The existential generalization rule allows us to generalize from any statement to its corresponding existential quantification. We do this by replacing *one or more occurrences* of some name in the statement by a variable and prefixing an existential quantification of that variable to the expression, so from **A(N/X)** we move to ∃**X A**. If no name **N** occurs in **A**, then the result of EG is a vacuous quantification that is equivalent to **A** itself.

A simple example of EG:

Example 2   Derive ∃*y Gyb* from *Gab*

1. | *Gab*

2. | *Gab*   (R, 1)
3. | ∃*y Gyb*   (EG, 2)

Here is another example of EG that illustrates that not every occurrence of a name must be generalized when invoking EG:

Example 3

1. | *Haa*
   |‾‾‾‾‾‾‾
2. | *Haa*   (R, 1)
3. | ∃*y Hya*   (EG, 2)

This derivation allows us to show that from 'Allen hates himself' we can derive 'Something hates Allen'. We could also have derived 'Something hates something' and 'Allen hates something'.

The very simple argument

Everything is purple and large

───────────────────────────

Something is purple

is shown valid by this derivation of the conclusion from the premise:

Example 4

1. | ∀*x* [*Px* & *Lx*]

2. | ∀*x* [*Px* & *Lx*]   (R, 1)
3. | *Pa* & *La*   (UI, 2)
4. | *Pa*   (SIMP, 3)
5. | ∃*x Px*   (EG, 4)

Care must be taken with EG not to think of it as a replacement rule. The rule applies only to statements, not to parts of statements. Thus, the following attempted use of EG is not permitted, even though the inference turns out, *in this case,* to be valid:

4. | ∀*x Fx* ⊃ *Fa*
5. | ∀*x Fx* ⊃ ∃*x Fx*   (EG, 4)   IMPROPER!!

It would be legitimate, however, to use the rule as follows:

4. | ∀*x Fx* ⊃ *Fa*
5. | ∃*y* [∀*x Fx* ⊃ *Fy*]   (EG, 4)

Here the rule is properly applied to the entire statement in line 4.

The rules for eliminating or instantiating existential quantifiers and for generalizing universal quantifiers have restrictions that must be carefully observed, as the examples on the following page illustrate.

The point of the restriction is that name **N** has to be arbitrary as far as the derivation is concerned; it cannot have a previous occurrence in the assumptions, and it cannot persist after the generalization has taken place. Recall similar restrictions on two of the quantifier tree rules. What we want to avoid here are the clearly invalid inferences like 'Bill is large; therefore, everybody is large'. But we want to allow 'Everything is purple and large; therefore, everything is purple', as in example 5.

Universal Generalization (UG)

$$
\begin{array}{ll}
1. & A_1 \\
2. & A_2 \\
& \quad \cdot \\
& \quad \cdot \\
& \quad \cdot \\
n. & A_n \\
\hline
& \quad \cdot \\
p. & B(N/X) \\
& \quad \cdot \\
q. & \forall X\, B \qquad (\text{UG, p.})
\end{array}
$$

Restriction: *N cannot occur in any of the assumptions $A_1, A_2, \ldots, A_n$ and cannot occur in $\forall X\ B$.*

Example 5

$$
\begin{array}{lll}
1. & \forall x\,[Px\ \&\ Lx] & \\
\hline
2. & \forall x\,[Px\ \&\ Lx) & (\text{R, 1}) \\
3. & Pa\ \&\ La & (\text{UI, 2}) \\
4. & Pa & (\text{SIMP, 2}) \\
5. & \forall x\, Px & (\text{UG, 4})
\end{array}
$$

Note that in line 3, the choice of the name a in conjunction with UI is purely arbitrary; the names b or a_{22} would have served equally well. Observe the way the name a functions in the following case:

Example 6

Joan likes everybody.

Everybody likes Joan.

in symbols:

$$\forall x\,[Px \supset Lax]$$

$$\forall x\,[Px \supset Lxa]$$

$$
\begin{array}{lll}
1. & \forall x\,[Px \supset Lax] & \\
\hline
2. & \forall x\,[Px \supset Lax] & (\text{R, 1}) \\
3. & Pa \supset Laa & (\text{UI, 2}) \\
4. & \forall x\,[Px \supset Lxa] & (\text{UG, 3}) \quad \text{IMPROPER!!}
\end{array}
$$

Since the name a occurs in the initial assumption of the derivation, UG in line 3 is not permitted by the restriction, nor would the following attempt to derive 'Everybody likes herself or himself' from the same assumption:

1. | $\forall x \, [Px \supset Lax]$
_____
2. | $Pa \supset Laa$ (UI, 1)
3. | $\forall x \, [Px \supset Lxx]$ (UG, 2)   IMPROPER!!

Finally, we present the restricted rule existential instantiation (EI). We need to block inferences of particular individuals from existential quantifications; we cannot allow, for example, the inference of 'Mary is smart' from 'Somebody is smart'. We know from our discussions of valuations, that if 'Somebody is smart' is true, there is at least one person who is smart, but we cannot conclude that it is Mary (or anybody else in particular). On the other hand, we need a means of moving in and out of existential quantifications so that the other derivation rules can be used. Here is the rule:

Existential Instantiation (EI)

1. | A_1
2. | A_2
   | .
   | .
   | .
n. | A_n
_____
   | .
p. | $\exists X \, B$
   | .
q. | | $B(N/X)$
   | | .
   | | _____
   | | .
r. | | C
s. | C (EI, p, q–r)

Restriction: **N** *cannot occur in any of the assumptions* $A_1, A_2, \ldots, A_n$ *and cannot occur in* $\exists X \, B$ *or* **C**.

Although we cannot just say that a particular substitution instance **B(N/X)** follows from an existential quantification $\exists x \, B$, we can say that if a statement **C** *follows from* a substitution instance, **B(N/X)**, and **C** does not contain the particular name **N**, then that statement **C** follows from the existential quantification $\exists x \, B$ itself. For example, suppose we wanted to prove that 'Somebody is happy' follows from the statement 'Somebody is rich and happy'. We might argue that *if* Mary were the person who is both rich and happy, then Mary would clearly be happy. Hence, somebody is happy.

In practice, EI is the tricky rule to use. Some planning is required so that the appropriate substitution instance is used as the assumption for a subsidiary derivation that will result in the desired statement. Here is an example:

Example 7

∃x [Gx & Rx]
———————————
∃x Gx

```
1. | ∃x [Gx & Rx]

2. | ∃x [Gx & Rx]    (R, 1)
3. | | Ga & Ra
      ——————
4. | | Ga & Ra       (R, 3)
5. | | Ga            (SIMP, 4)
6. | | ∃x Gx         (EG, 5)
7. | ∃x Gx           (EI, 2, 3–6)
```

As you can see, we create the subsidiary derivation with the assumption of the substitution instance *Ga & Ra* and then show that the desired consequence ∃x *Gx* follows from that assumption. We discharge that subsidiary derivation and return to the main derivation by means of the EI rule. Note that the justification required for the EI rule includes the line numbers of the existential quantification, and of the subsidiary derivation which has a substitution instance as an assumption and ends with the desired statement.

The EI rule is often used with other quantification rules. Note that it is the restrictions on UG that effectively block the derivation of ∀x *Fx* from ∃x *Fx*, as in the following mistaken attempt; EI is used correctly:

```
1. | ∃x Fx
     ——————
2. | ∃x Fx
3. | | Fa
      ———
4. | | Fa           (R, 3)
5. | ∀x Fx          (UG, 4)   IMPROPER!!
6. | ∀x Fx          (EI, 2, 3–5)
```

Here are a few sample derivations that show the new rules and the SL rules in action.

Example 8

All whales are mammals.

Fred isn't a mammal.
———————————
Fred isn't a whale.

```
1. | ∀x [Wx ⊃ Mx]
2. | ~Ma             (R, 1)
     ——————
3. | ∀x [Wx ⊃ Mx]    (R, 1)
4. | Wa ⊃ Ma         (UI, 3)
5. | ~Ma             (R, 2)
6. | ~Wa             (MT, 4, 5)
```

Example 9

All of Jim's friends are pacifists.

All pacifists are friends of Mary.

All of Jim's friends are friends of Mary.

1.	∀x [Fxa ⊃ Px]	
2.	∀x [Px ⊃ Fxb]	
3.	∀x [Fxa ⊃ Px]	(R, 1)
4.	Fca ⊃ Pc	(UI, 3)
5.	∀x [Px ⊃ Fxb]	(R, 2)
6.	Pc ⊃ Fcb	(UI, 5)
7.	Fca ⊃ Fcb	(HS, 4, 6)
8.	∀x [Fxa ⊃ Fxb]	(UG, 7)

To meet the restriction on the use of the UG rule, we had to instantiate both of the assumptions to the new name *c*. Had we begun with the UI rule to either of the names occurring in the assumptions, the last step would have been blocked by the restriction.

Example 10

∀x [Rx ⊃ Hx]

~∃x [Rx & ~Hx]

1.	∀x [Rx ⊃ Hx]	
2.	∃x [Rx & ~Hx]	
3.	∃x [Rx & ~Hx]	(R, 2)
4.	Ra & ~Ha	
5.	~(P & ~P)	
6.	∀x [Rx ⊃ Hx]	(R, 1)
7.	Ra ⊃ Ha	(UI, 6)
8.	Ra & ~Ha	(R, 4)
9.	Ra	(SIMP, 8)
10.	~Ha	(SIMP, 8)
11.	Ha	(MP, 7, 9)
12.	~~(P & ~P)	(IR, 5, 10, 11)
13.	P & ~P	(DN, 12)
14.	P & ~P	(EI, 3, 4–13)
15.	P	(SIMP, 13)
16.	~P	(SIMP, 13)
17.	~∃x [Rx & ~Hx]	(IR, 2, 15, 16)

To conclude to the negated statement ~∃x [Rx & ~Hx], we used a classical indirect reasoning strategy (twice!). But the twist here is that the required contradiction P and ~P was obtained by means of the EI rule and the use of a subsidiary derivation with the substitution instance Ra & $\sim Ha$ as the assumption. You may have already noted a seeming strangeness of the EI rule: when it is invoked, we are finished with the substitution instance of the original existential quantification and are concluding a statement that may have no relation to it.

Example 11

Everybody has a favorite book.

There is a book that is Susan's favorite.

(We will need the unstated premise that Susan (a) is a person.)

1. $\forall x [Px \supset \exists y (Fyx$ & $By)]$
2. Pa

3. $\forall x [Px \supset \exists y (Fyx$ & $By)]$ (R, 1)
4. Pa (R, 2)
5. $Pa \supset \exists y (Fya$ & $By)$ (UI, 3)
6. $\exists y (Fya$ & $By)$ (MP, 4, 5)
7. $\exists y (By$ & $Fya)$ (COMM&, 6)

In this case we had to instantiate line 3 to the name already in the derivation or the MP move would not have been available. This example also illustrates how the equivalence rules from SL are used in PL derivations. PL quasi statements like Fya & By in line 6 can be replaced by their equivalents by invoking the appropriate rule (here, commutativity of &).

In addition to the fairly austere set of rules already introduced, there is a variety of additional quantificational rules that are very useful in PL derivations. These quantificational equivalence rules can also be used in *equivalence derivations* in conjunction with the SL equivalence rules from chapter 4. Clearly the four quantifier inference rules—UI, UG, EI, and EG—*cannot* be used in equivalence derivations since they are nonreversible (that is one point of the restrictions on UG and EI); thus, there is no way to move in and out of quantification in such proofs. Two particular equivalence rules that are handy are the quantifier exchange rules:[10]

Quantifier Exchange (QE)

$\forall X\ A \leftrightarrow \sim\exists X \sim A$
$\exists X\ A \leftrightarrow \sim\forall X \sim A$

---

[10]Recall from our discussion in chapter 4 that the $\leftrightarrow$ symbol is not a connective; it serves to indicate that two statements are interchangeable.

We justify the inclusion of such rules by means of derivations, some of which are left as exercises.

```
1.  | ∀X A
    |―――――――
2.  | | ∃X ~A
    | |―――――――
3.  | | ∃X ~A            (R, 2)
4.  | |  | ~A(N/X)
    | |  |――――――――
5.  | |  |  | ~(B & ~B)
    | |  |  |――――――――――
6.  | |  |  | ∀X A        (R, 1)
7.  | |  |  | A(N/X)      (UI, 6)
8.  | |  |  | ~A(N/X)     (R, 4)
9.  | |  | ~~(B & ~B)     (IR, 5, 7, 8)
10. | |  | B & ~B         (DN, 9)
11. | | B & ~B            (EI, 3, 4–10)
12. | | B                 (SIMP, 11)
13. | | ~B                (SIMP, 11)
14. | ~∃X ~A              (IR, 2, 12, 13)
```

Note: the statement represented by **B** can be any statement at all so long as it doesn't contain the name **N**; we are blocked from using **A(N/X)** & **~A(N/X)** by the restriction on EI, so another statement is needed for the purpose of the IR step in line 14.

The derivation of ∀X **A** from ~∃X ~**A** is exercise 7.3.4.

Another useful set of derived equivalences are the **rules of quantificational passage,** which allow the shifting of quantifiers within a statement. These rules contain various provisos on which we will comment later.

―――――――――――

Rules of Quantificational Passage (RQP)

∀X (A ⊃ B) ↔ ∃X A ⊃ B   where **X** does not occur in **B**

∃x (A ⊃ B) ↔ ∀X A ⊃ B   where **X** does not occur in **B**

∀X (A ⊃ B) ↔ A ⊃ ∀X B   where **X** does not occur in **A**

∃X (A ⊃ B) ↔ A ⊃ ∃X B   where **X** does not occur in **A**

―――――――――――

The provisos ensure that we are not trying to pass a quantifier through an expression that contains an occurrence of the same variable of quantification. For example, in the statement

∃x Fx ⊃ ∀x Fx

we cannot shift the universal quantifier because we would then have

$\forall x \, [\exists x \, Fx \supset Fx]$

which is not a PL statement. However, if we begin with

$\exists y \, Fy \supset \forall x \, Fx$

then we could use a passage rule to obtain the equivalent statement

$\forall x \, [\exists y \, Fy \supset Fx]$

It is always possible to shift the quantifiers in a statement so that they are all outside the first set of parentheses. This usually requires repeated applications of the rules of passage. However, the *order* in which the quantifiers occur in the statement has to be carefully managed if the rules of passage are to be correctly applied. For example, in the statement above, we can shift the existential quantifier outside the parentheses as follows:

1.	$\forall x \, [\exists y \, Fy \supset Fx]$	
2.	$\forall x \, [\exists y \, Fy \supset Fx]$	(R, 1)
3.	$\exists y \, Fy \supset Fa$	(UI, 2)
4.	$\forall y \, [Fy \supset Fa]$	(RQP, 3)
5.	$\forall x \, \forall y \, [Fy \supset Fx]$	(UG, 4)

Since we can easily turn this derivation around and work it in reverse, we can show that the two statements, $\forall x \, [\exists y \, Fy \supset Fx]$ and $\forall x \, \forall y \, [Fy \supset Fx]$, are logically equivalent. Here is the other side:

1.	$\forall x \, \forall y \, [Fy \supset Fx]$	
2.	$\forall x \, \forall y \, [Fy \supset Fx]$	(R, 1)
3.	$\forall y \, [Fy \supset Fa]$	(UI, 2)
4.	$\exists y \, Fy \supset Fa$	(RQP, 3)
5.	$\forall x \, [\exists y \, Fy \supset Fx]$	(UG, 4)

But notice that we *cannot* use the rules of passage to "leapfrog" the initial universal quantifier in order to obtain $\exists y \, \forall x \, [Fy \supset Fx]$.

Sample derivations of the rules of passage are as follows; the remainder will appear as exercises:

(1) ∀X (A ⊃ B) ↔ ∃X A ⊃ B   where X does not occur in B

```
1.  | ∀X (A ⊃ B) (where X does not occur in B)
    | ‾‾‾‾‾‾‾‾‾‾‾‾‾‾‾‾
2.  | | ∃X A
    | | ‾‾‾‾‾
3.  | | ∃X A              (R, 2)
4.  | | | A(N/X)
    | | | ‾‾‾‾‾‾
5.  | | | ∀X (A ⊃ B)        (R, 1)
6.  | | | A(N/X) ⊃ B(N/X)   (UI, 5)
7.  | | | B¹¹              (MP, 5, 6)
8.  | | B                  (EI, 3, 4–7)
9.  | ∃X A ⊃ B             (CR, 2–8)
```

```
1.  | ∃X A ⊃ B    (where X does not occur in B)
    | ‾‾‾‾‾‾‾‾‾‾‾‾‾‾‾‾
2.  | | ~∀X (A ⊃ B)
    | | ‾‾‾‾‾‾‾‾‾‾‾
3.  | | ~∀X (A ⊃ B)        (R, 2)
4.  | | ~∀X (~A ∨ B)       (CE, 3)
5.  | | ~~∃X ~(~A ∨ B)     (QE, 4)
6.  | | ∃X ~(~A ∨ B)       (DN, 5)
7.  | | ∃X (~~A & ~B)      (DEM, 6)
8.  | | ∃X (A & ~B)        (DNE, 6)
9.  | | | A(N/X) & ~B
    | | | ‾‾‾‾‾‾‾‾‾‾‾
10. | | | A(N/X) & ~B      (R, 9)
11. | | | A(N/X)           (SIMP, 10)
12. | | | ∃X A             (EG, 11)
13. | | | ∃X A ⊃ B         (R, 1)
14. | | | B                (MP, 12, 13)
15. | | | ~B               (SIMP, 10)
16. | | | B & ~B           (CONJ, 14, 15)
17. | | B & ~B¹²           (EI, 8, 9–16)
18. | | B                  (SIMP, 17)
19. | | ~B                 (SIMP, 17)
20. | ~~∀X (A ⊃ B)         (IR, 2, 18, 19)
21. | ∀X (A ⊃ B)           (DN, 20)
```

---

[11]Since, by assumption, **X** does not occur in **B**, **B(N/X)** is just **B** itself.
[12]There is no occurrence of the name **N** in **B**, since **X** does not occur in **B**; so the restriction for EI is met.

(2) $\exists X (A \supset B) \leftrightarrow A \supset \exists X B$ where X does not occur in A

1.	$\exists X (A \supset B)$ (where X does not occur in A)	
2.	A	
3.	$\exists X (A \supset B)$	(R, 1)
4.	$A \supset B(N/X)$[13]	
5.	$A \supset B(N/X)$	(R, 4)
6.	A	(R, 2)
7.	$B(N/X)$	(MP, 5, 6)
8.	$\exists X B$	(EG, 7)
9.	$\exists X B$	(EI, 3, 4–8)
10.	$A \supset \exists X B$	(CR, 2–9)

1.	$A \supset \exists X B$ (where X does not occur in A)	
2.	$\exists X (A \supset B)$	
3.	$\sim\exists X (A \supset B)$	(R, 2)
4.	$\sim\sim\forall X \sim(A \supset B)$	(QE, 3)
5.	$\forall X \sim(A \supset B)$	(DN, 4)
6.	$\forall X \sim(\sim A \lor B)$	(CE, 6)
7.	$\forall X (\sim\sim A \,\&\, \sim B)$	(DEM, 6)
8.	$\forall X (A \,\&\, \sim B)$	(DNE, 7)
9.	$A \,\&\, \sim B(N/X)$	(UI, 8)
10.	$\sim B(N/X)$	(SIMP, 9)
11.	$\forall X \sim B$	(UG, 10)
12.	$\sim\sim\forall X \sim B$	(DN, 11)
13.	$\sim\exists X B$	(QE, 12)
14.	A	(SIMP, 9)
15.	$A \supset \exists X B$	(R, 1)
16.	$\exists X B$	(MP, 14, 15)
17.	$\sim\sim\exists X (A \supset B)$	(IR, 2, 16, 13)
18.	$\exists X (A \supset B)$	(DN, 17)

One final pair of equivalence rules is sometimes helpful in derivations. These allow rewriting a statement using different variables. Again a proviso is attached to each so that nonstatements do not result from the application of the rules.

Variable Rewriting Rules (VR)

$\forall X A \leftrightarrow \forall Y A(Y/X)$ *where there is no occurrence of Y in* $\forall X A$ *and* $\forall X A$ *does not lie within the scope of a quantifier of the sort* $\forall Y$ *or* $\exists Y$.

$\exists X A \leftrightarrow \exists Y A(Y/X)$ *where there is no occurrence of Y in* $\exists X A$ *and* $\exists X A$ *does not lie within the scope of a quantifier of the sort* $\forall Y$ *or* $\exists Y$.

---

[13]Since X does occur in A, $(A \supset B) (N/X)$ is sure to be the same as $A \supset B(N/X)$.

If we are just rewriting a statement like ∀x (Rx & Fx) as ∀y (Ry & Fy) then clearly the provisos are unimportant. But if we are using VR as an equivalence rule to replace a portion of a statement, then the following issue can arise:

∃x [Rx ⊃ ∀y (Gy & Pxy)]

is rewritten as

∃x [Rx ⊃ ∀x (Gx & Pxx)]

which is not a statement. But the proviso clearly blocks this move since ∀y (Gy & Pxy) contains an occurrence of the variable x.

Sometimes the use of the variable rewriting rule requires an intermediate variable. Suppose, for example, we want to rewrite

∀x ∀y [(Rx & Py) ⊃ Gxy]

as

∀y ∀x [(Ry & Px) ⊃ Gyx]

We will have to use the following steps:[14]

1.	‖	∀x ∀y [(Rx & Py) ⊃ Gxy]	
2.	‖	∀z ∀y [(Rz & Py) ⊃ Gzy]	(VR, 2)
3.	‖	∀z ∀x [(Rz & Px) ⊃ Gzx]	(VR, 3)
4.	‖	∀y ∀x [(Ry & Px) ⊃ Gyx]	(VR, 4)

The rewriting rules are commonly found in conjunction with quantifier passage rules. Using them in combination will allow all quantifiers in a statement to be brought to a position outside the parentheses. Statements having their quantifiers in this position are said to be in **prenex form**. An example is

∀y ∀x [(Ry & Px) ⊃ Gyx]

Prenex form will be important in our discussion of the resolution method in PL in the next section.

---

[14]Recall from chapter 4 that a double vertical line on the left indicates a 'reversible' equivalence derivation; only equivalence rules may be used as justifications.

Summary

Here are the natural deduction quantifier rules:

Universal Instantiation (UI)

k. | ∀X A

m. | A(N/X)   (UI, k)

Existential generalization (EG)

k. | A(N/X)

m. | ∃X A   (EG, k)

Universal generalization (UG)

1. | A₁
2. | A₂
   | .

   | .

n. | Aₙ
   | _____

   | .

p. | B(N/X)
   | .

q. | ∀X B   (UG, p.)

Restriction: **N** cannot occur in any of the assumptions **A₁, A₂, . . . , Aₙ** and cannot occur in ∀X **B**.

Existential instantiation (EI)

1. | A₁
2. | A₂
   | .

   | .

n. | Aₙ
   | _____

   | .

p. | ∃X B
   | .

q. | | B(N/X)
   | | _____

   | .

r. | | C

s. | C   (EI, p, q–r)

Restriction: **N** cannot occur in any of the assumptions **A₁, A₂, . . . , Aₙ** and cannot occur in ∃X **B** or **C**.

Quantifier exchange (QE)

∀X A ↔ ~∃X ~A
∃X A ↔ ~∀X ~A

Rules of quantificational passage (RQP)

∀X (A ⊃ B) ↔ ~∃X A ⊃ B   where X does not occur in B
∃X (A ⊃ B) ↔ ∀X A ⊃ B   where X does not occur in B
∀X (A ⊃ B) ↔ A ⊃ ∀X B   where X does not occur in A
∃X (A ⊃ B) ↔ A ⊃ ∃X B   where X does not occur in A

Variable rewriting rules (VR)

∀X A ↔ ∀Y A(Y/X)   where there is no occurrence of Y in ∀X A and ∀X A
                         does not lie within the scope of a quantifier of the sort
                         ∀Y or ∃Y.
∃X A ↔ ∃Y A(Y/X)   where there is no occurrence of Y in ∃X A and ∃X A
                         does not lie within the scope of a quantifier of the sort
                         ∀Y or ∃Y.

EXERCISES 7.3

1. Complete the following derivations by filling in the missing
   justifications.

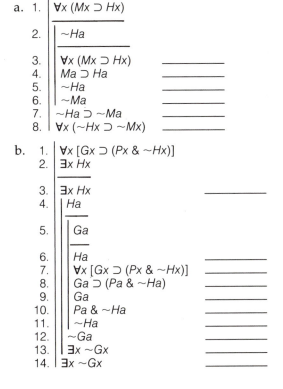

c. 1. | ∀x [Lx ⊃ ∃y (Gy & Hxy)]
----
   2. | ∀x [Lx ⊃ ∃y (Gy & Hxy)]   _____
   3. | La ⊃ ∃y [Gy & Hay]   _____
   4. | ∃y (La ⊃ [Gy & Hay])   _____
   5. | ∀x ∃y (Lx ⊃ [Gy & Hxy])   _____

d. 1. | ∀x [(Ax ∨ Cx) ⊃ Gx]
   2. | ∃x (Fx & Ax)
   3. | Fa & Aa
----
   4. | | ∀x [(Ax ∨ Cx) ⊃ Gx]   _____
   5. | | (Aa ∨ Ca) ⊃ Ga   _____
   6. | | Fa & Aa   _____
   7. | | Aa   _____
   8. | | Aa ∨ Ca   _____
   9. | | Ga   _____
   10. | | ∃x Gx   _____
   11. | ∃x (Fx & Ax)   _____
   12. | ∃x Gx   _____

2. Give a derivation of the conclusion from the premises in each valid argument in exercise 7.1.1.

3. Give a derivation of the conclusion from the premises in each valid argument in exercise 7.1.4.

4. Show by means of a derivation that ∀X A follows from ~∃X ~A.

5. Show by means of derivations that ∃X A ↔ ~∀X ~A.

6. Show by means of derivations that ∃X (A ⊃ B) ↔ ∀X A ⊃ B, where X does not occur in **B**.

7. Show by means of derivations that ∀X (A ⊃ B) ↔ A ⊃ ∀X B, where X does not occur in **A**.

8. Show by means of derivations that ∀X A ↔ ∀Y A(Y/X) where there is no occurrence of **Y** in ∀X A and ∀X A does not occur within the scope of a quantifier of the sort ∀Y or ∃Y.

9. Construct a derivation of the conclusion from the premises of each of the following arguments.

   a. All fish are slimy; therefore, nothing that is not slimy is a fish.

   b. There is a person who knows everything. If a person knows something, then he is not surprised by it. Therefore, there is a person who is not surprised by anything.

   c. Persons are wise if and only if they are educated. Therefore, if there is some person who is uneducated, then there is at least one person who is unwise.

   d. Doctors and lawyers are professionals. Some doctors overcharge. Some lawyers are crooks. Therefore, some crooks are professionals and some professionals overcharge.

   e. All horses are animals; therefore, the heads of horses are the heads of animals.

10. By means of equivalence derivations, show that the following pairs of statements are equivalent.

   a. ∀x ∀y [Px ⊃ Gy]   and   ∀x [Px ⊃ ∀y Gy]

   b. ∀x [Hx ⊃ Mx]   and   ~∃x [Hx & ~Mx]

   c. ∃x [Hx & Mx]   and   ~∀x [Hx ⊃ ~Mx]

7.4 RESOLUTION AND AUTOMATED DEDUCTION

Recall from section 4.3, that the resolution method applies the single resolution rule to statements in *clausal form*. Hence, we need to extend our conception of clausal form to cover quantifiers so that the resolution rule will be available for PL.

Much of the information in a data set consisting of a list of clauses is in the form of atomic statements and their negations. Recall that these are known as **literals.** Thus, we routinely have clauses like

   {Bab, Bcb}

In PL, as in the SL version of resolution, a clause represents the *disjunction* of its members. So the clause above, with the predicate B representing '___ is the brother of ___' and *a*, *b*, and *c* as names, is the clausal form of the statement

   Bab ∨ Bcb

(i.e., 'Either *a* is the brother of *b* or *c* is the brother of *b'*.)

PL statements without quantifiers are handled exactly like SL statements and are put into clausal form by first finding their conjunctive normal form, by means of equivalence derivations, and then converting to clausal form. Each clause, again, is a disjunction of literals, and clauses are listed in a column to indicate their conjunction.

Quantifiers, however, complicate matters somewhat. The transformation of a quantificational statement into its conjunctive normal form has several steps. The basic idea is to bring all quantifiers to a position outside the main parentheses so that the statement is in prenex form. This may require renaming variables and using the quantifier exchange rules and rules of passage. All existential quantifiers are then *eliminated*, followed by all universal quantifiers. Finally, the resulting expression is put into conjunctive normal form following the procedures from SL. Here are the steps:

1. Statements with negated quantifiers must be transformed using the quantifier exchange rules (i.e., QE):

   ~∀X A is replaced by ∃X ~A

   ~∃X A is replaced by ∀X ~A

2. Variables are relettered so that each quantifier in a statement has a different variable, using the variable rewriting rules (VR):

∀X A ↔ ∀Y A(Y/X) where there is no occurrence of Y in ∀X A and ∀X A does not lie within the scope of a quantifier of the sort ∀Y or ∃Y.

∃X A ↔ ∃Y A(Y/X) where there is no occurrence of Y in ∃X A and ∃X A does not lie within the scope of a quantifier of the sort ∀Y or ∃Y.

3. The statement is put into **prenex form**: all quantifiers are brought outside the parentheses by means of equivalence rules, especially, the rules of quantificational passage:

∀X (A ⊃ B) ↔ ∃X A ⊃ B where X does not occur in B

∃X (A ⊃B) ↔ ∀X A ⊃ B where X does not occur in B

∀X (A ⊃ B) ↔ A ⊃ ∀X B where X does not occur in A

∃X (A ⊃ B) ↔ A ⊃ ∃X B where X does not occur in A

4. Existential quantifiers *that do not occur within the scope of universal quantifiers* are instantiated to a name that does not occur in the statement (just as in the EI rule).

There are more steps, but let's pause to take stock so far. Suppose we have the PL statement

~∀x (Rx & Sx)

To put it into prenex form, we first use the quantifier exchange rules to eliminate the outside negation:

∃x ~(Rx & Sx)

Next we instantiate the existential quantifier to a new name, say *a*:

~(Ra & Sa)

Now back to the other steps.

5. Existential quantifiers *which occur within the scope of a universal quantifier* are replaced by means of a special variable called a **Skolem function.**[15]

---

[15]After Thoraf Skolem. See W. V. Quine, *Methods of Logic*, 3rd ed. (New York: Holt, Reinhart, and Winston, 1972), chapter 34. PROLOG implementations of this procedure do not require prenex form; see Quine, *Methods of Logic*, for a justification. See also, e.g., W. F. Clocksin and C. S. Mellish, *Programming in PROLOG*, 3rd ed. (New York: Springer-Verlag, 1987), chapter 10.

Consider, for example, the statement 'Everything is larger than something or other':

$\forall x \, \exists y \, Lxy$ (*L*: '_____ is larger than _____')

The reason we cannot just replace the existential quantifier, as in step 4, by instantiating it to a new name, i.e.,

$\forall x \, Lxa$

is that the result would be indistinguishable from the elimination of the existential quantifier in the statement

$\exists y \, \forall x \, Lxy$

We have gone to some lengths to insure that the order of universal and existential quantifiers is significant, so we have to protect this order even though we are eliminating quantifiers to produce PL conjunctive normal forms.

The Skolem function that is used to replace an *interior* existential quantifier is based on the universal quantification(s) in whose scope the existential quantifier occurs. Their variables of quantification will appear in the Skolem function. To represent these Skolem functions we use lowercase letters f, g, h (with subscripts if needed), and we enclose their variables in parentheses. So, in the case at hand, the existential quantifier in $\forall x \, \exists y \, Lxy$ is replaced by inserting a one-place Skolem function f for all occurrences of the variable y as follows:

$\forall x \, Lx \, f(x)$

Think of the Skolem function $f(x)$ here as meaning 'something picked out for x'. To read the expression containing the Skolem function, we would say

Every x is larger than something picked out for x.

Note that this reading preserves the idea that when, for example, name a is substituted for x, it could be the thing with name b that a is larger than, but when b is substituted for x, it is the thing named c that b is larger than, and so forth. If we had merely substituted a name, say, a, for the variable y then, of course, everything would be larger than a itself. The use of the Skolem function $f(x)$ thus preserves the distinction between $\forall x \, \exists y \, Lxy$ and $\exists y \, \forall x \, Lxy$.

To take a more complex example, suppose we have the statement

$\forall x \, \forall y \, \exists z \, Txyz$

The replacement of the interior existential quantifier will require a *two-place* Skolem function because the existential quantifier is within the scope of two universal quantifiers. We will use g for this two-place Skolem function. Thus, we have

$\forall x \, \forall y \; Txy \, g(xy)$

Here is a third example:

$\forall x \, \forall y \, \exists z \, \exists w \; [Txyz \supset (Gxw \; \& \; Hxywz)]$

Replacing the existential quantifiers with Skolem functions results in

$\forall x \, \forall y \; [Txy \, f(xy) \supset (Gx \, g(xy) \; \& \; Hxy \, g(xy) \, f(xy))]$

Note that each instance of the variable of the existential quantification is replaced by the appropriate Skolem function, and a new Skolem function is used for each existential quantification to be replaced.

By the time we have finished step 5, the statement will have *only* universal quantifiers, and all of them will be outside the main parentheses of the statement.

   6. Eliminate all universal quantifications; leave their variables of quantification in place. The result of this step is an expression without any quantifiers.

   7. Put the resulting expression into conjunctive normal form using equivalence rules.

At the end of step 7 we will have a conjunction of disjunctions. All of the disjuncts will be literals containing Skolem functions, names, and variables.

Here is an example: Put

$\forall x \; [Rx \supset \exists y \, (Py \; \& \; Txy)]$

into conjunctive normal form.

We carry out the transformation by means of an equivalence derivation (since we can go from PL conjunctive normal form back to a statement in standard form):

1.	$\forall x \; [Rx \supset \exists y \, (Py \; \& \; Txy)]$	
2.	$\forall x \, \exists y \; [Rx \supset (Py \; \& \; Txy)]$	(RQP, 1)
3.	$\forall x \; [Rx \supset (P \, f(x) \; \& \; Tx \, f(x))]$	(replace $\exists$, 2)
4.	$Rx \supset (P \, f(x) \; \& \; Tx \, f(x))$	(eliminate $\forall$, 3)
5.	$\sim Rx \lor (P \, f(x) \; \& \; Tx \, f(x))$	(CE, 4)
6.	$(\sim Rx \lor P \, f(x)) \; \& \; (\sim Rx \lor Tx \, f(x))$	(DIST, 5)

Expressions in standard form can (and will) be thought of as statements, and not quasi statements, because we assume that all variables are *tacitly* universally quantified. Tacit universal quantification may be familiar from elementary mathematics. For example, in expressions like the commutativity principle for addition,

$$(x + y) = (y + x)$$

it is assumed that the principle holds for *any* numbers x and y. The reason that such a tacit understanding is not common in treatments of PL is that, with two possible quantifiers, confusion could easily result. However, in conjunctive normal form and in clausal form, only one kind of quantification for variables is possible, since existential quantifiers are captured by means of Skolem functions or have been eliminated through replacement with names. Henceforth, then, we will assume that all variables not occurring in Skolem functions are universally quantified.

To move from the conjunctive normal form to the clausal form requires just one step:

8. As in SL, each conjunct of the conjunctive normal form statement is represented by a clause that is a set of the different disjuncts. The clauses are arranged in a list that represents their conjunction. However, for the easy application of the PL resolution rules, each clause must have distinct variables, so variable replacement is performed on the clauses to complete the transformation into PL clausal form.

    Take, as an example,

    $$(\sim Rx \lor P\, f(x))\ \&\ (\sim Rx \lor Tx\, f(x))$$

    We first form the clauses $\{\sim Rx, P\, f(x)\}$ and $\{\sim Rx, Tx\, f(x)\}$, as in SL. Then we assemble the clauses in a list and rename the variables in the second clause:

    $$\{\sim Rx, P\, f(x)\}$$
    $$\{\sim Ry, Ty\, f(y)\}$$

    When more than two clauses are listed, it is customary to use variables with subscripts (x_1, x_2, etc.). Remember, no variable may occur in more than one clause.

EXERCISES 7.4a

1. Put each of the following into conjunctive normal form:

    a. $\forall x\, (Hx \supset Mx)$

    b. $\forall x\, \forall y\, (Txy \supset Gyx)$

    c. ∃y ∀x Gyx

    d. ∀x ∃y Gyx

    e. ∃y Gy ⊃ Ga

    f. ∀x ∀y [(Fx & Fy) ⊃ ∃z ((Pzx & Pzy) ⊃ Sxy)]

    g. ∃x Gx ⊃ ∃x Fx

    h. ∀x ∃y Lxy ⊃ ∃y ∀x Lxy

    i. ∀x [Ex ⊃ ∀y (Hyx ⊃ (Ax & Hyx))]

2. Put each of the above into clausal form.

3. Construct a series of clauses that would serve as a data set about your parents, brothers and sisters, cousins, aunts, uncles, and friends (if you wish). Make all the clauses unit clauses such as {Brother Tom Jill} (i.e., Tom is the brother of Jill).

Now on to the resolution method (Res) for PL. Recall that in SL the **resolution rule** (Res) is as follows:

Let $C_1 = \{\ldots, A, \ldots\}$
Let $C_2 = \{\ldots, \sim A, \ldots\}$

| k. | C_1 |
| m. | C_2 |

p. $C_1 - \{A\} \cup C_2 - \{\sim A\}$ (Res, k, m)

This version of the rule, however, does not take into account that our literals now contain occurrences of names, variables, and Skolem functions. So an additional principle is needed.

The additional principle required for use of the resolution method in PL is the **unification principle**. Unification is essentially the application of universal instantiation and variable renaming to the literals in two clauses, in order to *unify* them under a single name or variable. Here are the three main uses of unification:

Instantiation   Consider, for example, the clauses:

    {Fa, Gy, H f(y)}   and   {~Fx, Hz}

Clearly, the resolution rule will not apply to these clauses as presented. But because *x* as a variable is understood to be universally quantified, the two literals *Fa* and *~Fx* should be thought of as being contradictory. Unification allows us to instantiate *any* variable to *any* name, which is just a version of the UI rule. So, applying unification to the second clause results in {~Fa, Hz}.

Unification can also be used on the variables that occur *in Skolem functions*. In the following case, for example,

$\{Gy, H f(y)\}$

we can use the unification rule to instantiate y to a. The result of this operation is the clause

$\{Ga, H f(a)\}$

The meaning of the instantiated Skolem function $f(a)$ is now 'the object picked out for a'. Since this is a specific object, possibly a itself, possibly some other object, we will treat instantiated Skolem functions, like $f(a)$, as *names*. Thus, if we had another clause, such as,

$\{\sim Hx\}$

we could use the unification rule to replace the variable x by $f(a)$ in order to obtain

$\{\sim H f(a)\}$

After an application of the resolution rule to the two clauses $\{Ga, H f(a)\}$ and $\{\sim H f(a)\}$, we would thus conclude:

$\{Ga\}$

Suppose, on the other hand, we had the clause

$\{H g(x)\}$

and we carried out the same unification instantiation of replacing x by $f(a)$. Then we would end up with

$\{H g(f(a))]$

Note that since $g(x)$ represents the function that picks out an object for x, the expression $g(f(a))$ is the function that picks out an object for the object picked out by the function f for object a. The expression $g(f(a))$ is an instantiated Skolem function and thus can be used as a name to replace a variable in a unification instantiation.

A situation in which such a case might arise is in *trying* to prove the validity of

$\forall y \, \exists x \, Hxy$ ('Everything has something heavier than it'.)

$\exists x \, \forall y \, Hxy$ ('Something is heavier than everything'.)

Recall that in resolution, we negate the conclusion to obtain $\sim\exists x \; \forall y \; Hxy$, which is equivalent to $\forall x \; \exists y \sim Hxy$, and then we put both the premise and the negated conclusion into clausal form and attempt to derive the empty clause.

The following clauses would result:

$\{H f(y) \, y\}$
$\{\sim Hx \, g(x)\}$

We might attempt unification by instantiating y to a in the first clause, which would result in

$\{H f(a) \, a\}$

Then if we instantiate x to $f(a)$ in the second clause, we would have

$\{\sim H f(a) \, g(f(a))\}$

But clearly, we cannot apply resolution to these two clauses, and we cannot use unification to make them similar either, since the *name a* cannot be substituted for $g(f(a))$ according to the unification rule. Thus, we have *failed* to prove the validity of the original argument.

Variable rewriting   A further use of the unification principle is to *rewrite* any variable. Recall that no variable is used in more than one clause. To use resolution in the following case

$\{Fa, Gy, H f(y)\}$
$\{\sim Gx\}$

we have to be able to rewrite the variable y in the first clause as x, or vice versa. The result will be either of the pairs

$\{Fa, Gx, H f(x)\}$ $\{\sim Gx\}$
$\{Fa, Gy, H f(y)\}$ $\{\sim Gy\}$

Note that although Skolem functions are expressions *containing* occurrences of variables, they are not variables themselves. So when we rewrite y as x in the first clause, we also rewrite $f(y)$ as $f(x)$.

Factoring   A third use of unification is to combine two literals containing the same predicate in a single clause. For example, in

$\{Fa, Gy, Gz, H f(y)\}$

factoring allows us to combine the two literals Gy and Gz by rewriting one of the variables. The result, for example, is either one of the following clauses:

$\{Fa, Gy, H f(y)\}$ or $\{Fa, Gz, H f(z)\}$

To keep track of our uses of unification, we will use the justification (U, **N/Y**) where a name **N** replaces a variable **Y**, and (U, **X/Y**) where a variable **X** replaces a variable **Y**. We count instantiated Skolem functions as names themselves. Here is a formal statement of the **unification principle**:

Unification Principle (U)

n. $\quad\{\ldots, \mathbf{A}, \ldots\}$

p. $\quad\{\ldots, \mathbf{A}, \ldots\}(\mathbf{N/Y})$ (U, **N/Y**, n)

n. $\quad\{\ldots, \mathbf{A}, \ldots\}$

p. $\quad\{\ldots, \mathbf{A}, \ldots\}(\mathbf{X/Y})$ (U, **X/Y**, n)

*(where **X** and **Y** are variables and **N** is a name)*

As a further example of how unification works, suppose we have the clauses

$\{Gxy, Hx, L f(x)\}$ and $\{\sim Gab\}$

By two applications of the unification principle, we would obtain the clause: $\{Gab, Ha, L f(a)\}$.

1. $\quad\{Gxy, Hx, L f(x)\}$
2. $\quad\{\sim Gab\}$

---
3. $\quad\{Gay, Ha, L f(a)\}$ (U, a/x, 1)
4. $\quad\{Gab, Ha, L f(a)\}$ (U, b/x, 3)

Recall from our discussion in section 4.3 that the resolution method allows us to derive clauses from an initial list of clauses, by means of repeated applications of the resolution rule. Here, of course, we will use the unification principle as well. We show that a particular statement is entailed by a set of statements by negating the statement and putting the whole group into clausal form. The clause resulting from the negating is called the **goal** of the derivation; the object is to show that the empty clause can be derived.

Let's start with a familiar example:

All humans are mortal.

Socrates is human.

_____

Socrates is mortal.

In PL notation the argument would be:

$\forall x\ (Hx \supset Mx)$

Hs

_____

Ms

To use resolution to determine whether Ms follows from $\forall x(Hx \supset Mx)$ and Hs, we first must negate the conclusion and then put the premises and the negated conclusion into clausal form.

Negated conclusion: $\sim Ms$

To put the premises and negated conclusion in clausal form:

first premise: $\forall x\ (Hx \supset Mx)$

1.	$\forall x\ (Hx \supset Mx)$	
2.	$Hx \supset Mx$	(elim $\forall$, 1)
3.	$\sim Hx \lor Mx$	(CE, 2)

clausal form: $\{\sim Hx, Mx\}$

second premise: Hs

clausal form: $\{Hs\}$

negated conclusion: $\sim Ms$

clausal form: $\{\sim Ms\}$

Then we attempt to derive the empty clause from the resulting list of clauses:

1.	$\{\sim Hx, Mx\}$	
2.	$\{Hs\}$	
3.	$\{\sim Ms\}$	
4.	$\{\sim Hs, Ms\}$	(U, s/x, 1)
5.	$\{Ms\}$	(Res, 2, 4)
6.	$\{\ \}$	(Res, 3, 5)

Since we have derived the empty clause, the original argument is clearly valid.

To see how resolution and unification can be used for the more general purpose of deriving information from data sets, suppose the following data are available concerning some family (F: '___ is the father of ___', W: '___ is female', and S: '___ is the sister of ___')

{F j b}
{F j c}
{W b}
{W c}
{~Wx, ~Wy, ~Fzx, ~Fzy, Sxy}

The first four clauses state facts, one might say, about some particular family, where j, b, and c are names (e.g., 'Joe', 'Barbara', 'Carol'). The final clause is the clausal form of what is called a *rule*; it represents a general statement about the nature of sisterhood. A more normal PL version would be:

$$\forall x \, \forall y \, [(Wx \, \& \, Wy) \supset \forall z \, ((Fzx \, \& \, Fzy) \supset Sxy)]$$

That is, 'If two females have the same father, then they are sisters'.

To put the general PL rule into clausal form (recall exercise 7.4a.1f), we first transform the statement to prenex form and then follow the steps to put it in conjunctive normal form. Here is the equivalence derivation:

1.	$\forall x \, \forall y \, [(Wx \, \& \, Wy) \supset \forall z \, ((Fzx \, \& \, Fzy) \supset Sxy)]$	
2.	$\forall x \, \forall y \, \forall z \, [(Wx \, \& \, Wy) \supset ((Fzx \, \& \, Fzy) \supset Sxy)]$	(RQP, 1)
3.	$\forall x \, \forall y \, \forall z \, [\sim(Wx \, \& \, Wy) \lor ((Fzx \, \& \, Fzy) \supset Sxy)]$	(CE, 2)
4.	$\forall x \, \forall y \, \forall z \, [(\sim Wx \lor \sim Wy) \lor ((Fzx \, \& \, Fzy) \supset Sxy)]$	(DEM, 3)
5.	$\forall x \, \forall y \, \forall z \, [(\sim Wx \lor \sim Wy) \lor (\sim(Fzx \, \& \, Fzy) \lor Sxy)]$	(CE, 4)
6.	$\forall x \, \forall y \, \forall z \, [(\sim Wx \lor \sim Wy) \lor ((\sim Fzx \lor \sim Fzy) \lor Sxy)]$	(DEM, 5)

The power of the resolution method for producing information from data in clausal form can be seen from this example. By adding the rule about sisterhood to the data set concerning parentage, we can quite easily directly derive that b and c are sisters. This derivation follows:

1.	{Wb}	
2.	{Wc}	
3.	{Fjb}	
4.	{Fjc}	
5.	{~Wx, ~Wy, ~Fzx, ~Fzy, Sxy}	
6.	{~Wb, ~Wy, ~Fzb, ~Fzy, Sby}	(U, b/x, 5)
7.	{~Wy, ~Fzb, ~Fzy, Sby}	(Res, 6, 1)
8.	{~Wc, ~Fzb, ~Fzc, Sbc}	(U, c/y, 7)
9.	{~Fzb, ~Fzc, Sbc}	(Res, 2, 8)
10.	{~Fjb, ~Fjc, Sbc}	(U, j/z, 9)
11.	{~Fjc, Sbc}	(Res, 3, 10)
12.	{Sbc}	(Res, 4, 11)

In the derivation above we used the linear resolution strategy, making exclusive use of unit resolution. Imagine that the initial clauses are part of a large data set. By working in a linear and unit strategy, we search for an application of resolution to the first clause {*Wb*} and then return to the second clause and continue. At some early point the clause {*Sbc*} emerges. Of course, with a large data set, we also need some explicit directions to halt when such a clause is derived, or else the resolution derivation might continue until all possible applications of the rule are found.

One use of resolution in PL is to answer two kinds of questions—yes/no questions and fill-in-the-blank questions—based on data sets in the form of lists of clauses.

Yes/No questions   Suppose we asked of the data set above

> Is *j* the father of *b*?

To determine the answer, we negate the statement *Fjb*, express the negation in clausal form, i.e., {~*Fjb*}, and add this clause to the data set at the top of the list. Then, by unit and linear resolution, before long the empty set is derived and we have a YES answer.

Suppose a more difficult question is asked:

> Does *c* have a sister?

Another way of asking this includes existential quantification:

> Is there an *x* such that *x* is the sister of *c*?

A negative answer is 'Nothing is the sister of *c*' (i.e., $\forall x \sim Sxc$) which in clausal form is

> {~*Sxc*}

To answer this question, we add the negative clause to our data set and try to derive the empty clause. If we add the negative clause to the bottom of the list and pursue linear resolution, the derivation is as presented above through step 12 (which becomes line 13, because we now have six initial clauses). The remaining steps are as follows:

13.	{*Sbc*}	(Res, 4, 12)
14.	{~*Sbc*}	(U, b/x, 6)
15.	{ }	(Res, 13, 14)

You are asked to do the derivation with {~*Sxc*} at the top of the list as exercise 7.4b.1.

Fill-in-the-blank questions[16]   A fill-in-the-blank question asks something like

   Who is the sister of *c*?

We can answer such questions from data sets by looking for a name to fill in the blank through resolution and unification. We first form an *answer literal* of the form ANS $X_1, X_2, X_3, \ldots$ where $X_1, X_2, X_3, \ldots$ are variables representing the blanks to be filled in. In this case, we have only one blank, and so we use the variable *x*. We take the fill-in-the-blank question to have the PL form of the quasi statement:

   Sxc?

To obtain an answer, we form a clause consisting of the *negation of the question together with the answer literal with the appropriate variable*. So we have the clause

   {~*Sxc*, ANS *x*}

This clause is then added to our data set and we try to derive the ANS literal with a name in place of the variable. Watch what happens if we just add this clause to the bottom of the twelve-step derivation above of {*Sbc*}.

12.	{*Sbc*}	(Res, 4, 11)
13.	{~*Sxc*, ANS *x*}	(added)
14.	{~*Sbc*, ANS *b*}	(U, b/x, 13)
15.	{ANS *b*}	(Res, 12, 14)

Thus we have our answer: *b* is the sister of *c*. If *c* had more than one sister, this technique would produce all answers.

EXERCISES 7.4b

1. Add the clause {~*Sxc*} to the top of the data set concerning the family of *b* and *c* and derive the empty clause by resolution and unification.

2. Use the resolution method to show the validity of the following arguments:

   a. ∀*x Fx*
      _____

      Fa

   b. ∃*x (Px & Gx)*
      _____

      ∃*x Gx*

---

[16]This material is from Genesereth and Nilsson, *Logical Foundations of Artificial Intelligence* (San Mateo, CA: Morgan Kaufmann, 1987), chapter 4.

c. $\forall x \, (Rx \supset Gx)$
   $\forall x \, (Gx \supset Fx)$
   _____
   $\forall x \, (Rx \supset Fx)$

d. $\forall x \, (Fx \supset Hx)$
   $\exists x \, (Fx \, \& \, Gx)$
   _____
   $\exists x \, (Gx \, \& \, Hx)$

e. $\forall x \, [Fx \supset (Gx \, \& \, Rx)]$
   $\exists x \, Fx$
   _____
   $\exists x \, Rx$

f. $\forall x \, \exists y \, Lxy$
   _____
   $\exists x \, \exists y \, Lxy$

g. $\forall x \, [Px \supset \exists y \, (Ry \, \& \, Lxy)]$
   Pa
   _____
   $\exists x \, Lax$

3. Put this information into clausal form, and then answer the questions using resolution derivations:

All students must take 120 credits to graduate. All students must pass freshman composition to graduate. John is a student. Mary is a student. John has not passed freshman composition. Mary has taken 120 credits. Mary has passed freshman composition. Sam has taken 120 credits.

a. Does John graduate?

b. Does Mary graduate?

c. Who has not passed freshman composition?

d. Who has taken 120 credits?

e. If Sam passes freshman composition, does Sam graduate?

II

Computing

8

Boolean Systems

To properly forge the link between logical principles and computers, we must go back in time, more than one hundred years, to the work of George Boole. Boole was one of the great pioneers of modern formal logic. His book, *The Laws of Thought* (1854), is the common ancestor of statement logic, monadic predicate logic, and the circuit designs found in every digital electronic computer.[1] The branch of mathematics known as Boolean algebra also has been developed from his work. In this chapter we will study Boole's ideas, first by roughly following his own development of the logic of sets or classes, and then by applying his system to monadic predicate logic (PL) and to statement logic (SL). With an understanding of Boolean systems we can then proceed in later chapters to study how logic is at the heart of all computers.

8.1 BOOLE'S SYSTEM

Boole begins with the simple idea of sets, or collections of things, and three basic operations on sets which, following his terminology, we will call **logical**

---

[1]The standard edition is George Boole, *An Investigation of the Laws of Thought* (New York: Dover, 1963). For a thorough study of Boole's systems, see Theodore Hailperin, *Boole's Logic and Probability*, 2nd ed. (Amsterdam: North Holland, 1986) and Harold E. Ennes, *Boolean Algebra for Computer Logic* (Indianapolis: Howard W. Sams, 1978).

addition, logical multiplication, and **complementation**. As we shall see, these are related to but are not the same as the familiar arithmetical concepts of addition, multiplication, and subtraction and have obvious ties to the connectives of statement logic. We use the following notation for Boole's operations, where A and B are sets:

Logical Addition: $A \oplus B$

Logical Multiplication: $A \cdot B$

Complementation: A'

The intended meaning of these notions is quite straightforward and may already be familiar to you from other courses. The combination of two sets is their logical addition. For example, if we add the set of dogs to the set of pigs, then we have the set of all dogs and pigs. To see this point another way, let set A be the types of cars that Frank likes best and let set B be the cars Mary likes best. Suppose Frank's favorites are the Corvette, the Ferrari, and the BMW, and Mary's are the Jaguar, the Masseratti, the BMW, and the Corvette. If we perform the logical addition $A \oplus B$ to form the set of types of cars liked best by Frank and Mary, we have the following:

$A \oplus B$ = {Ferrari, BMW, Corvette, Jaguar, Masseratti}

The order in which things in a set are listed makes no difference; we could have listed the members of $A \oplus B$ alphabetically and had the same set. The logical addition of sets differs conceptually from arithmetical addition in one crucial respect: if we add 5 to 2, for example, we would, of course, have 7. But if we logically add a set containing two objects to another set containing five objects, the result may not necessarily be a set containing seven objects. Suppose, as is the case in A and B, that two objects are members of *both* sets; then the resulting set will have only five objects as members.

The logical multiplication of two sets is the set containing *common* members of the original sets; that is, the set containing all of the things that are in both sets. In the case of Frank's favorite cars (A) and Mary's favorite cars (B),

$A \cdot B$ = {BMW, Corvette}

Boole's notions of logical addition and multiplication correspond to quite ordinary ways of talking about objects. We could easily ask, "Which types of cars do Frank and Mary like?" The right answer would, of course, be the logical addition of the set of types of cars liked by each. And to the question: "Which types of cars do they *both* like?" we would give the result of logical multiplication as the answer.

If you have already studied these ideas, you probably learned to call the logical addition of two sets the **union** and the logical multiplication the

intersection. We will stay with Boole's original terminology for reasons which become clearer later on.

Before going on to complements, we need to know another of Boole's fundamental concepts. He used the symbol **1** to stand for the set of *all* objects, which he called the **universe,** and he used the symbol **0** to stand for the **empty set**, or **nothing**.[2] (These symbols were not used by Boole to signify the numbers 1 and 0, but he had a clear analogy with arithmetic in mind, as we will see.) The idea of an empty set may seem odd, especially since we defined sets as collections of objects. How can there be a collection without any members? Boole himself doesn't have much to say about this, and perhaps there isn't much to say about nothing. But Boole's **0** is best thought of as the limiting case of the notion of a set. We immediately can see the need for **0** by considering what would happen if we consider the logical multiplication of two sets that have no members in common, say, set A {Corvette, Ferrari, BMW} and C, the set of all chickens. So what is $A \cdot C$? It can only be **0**, since set $A \cdot C$ does not have any members. This is the standard way of defining what it means for two sets X and Y to be **disjoint**, that is, not to have any common members. In Boole's system,

Sets X and Y are disjoint: $X \cdot Y = 0$

With the help of **1** and **0**, we can now define Boole's notion of *complementation*. The complement X' of a set X is the set of all things that are not members of X. So the complement of the set of dogs is the set of all things that are not dogs, or the set of non-dogs. The complement of the set of all dogs and pigs is the set of everything other than dogs and pigs, and so on. Boole devised a very graphic notation for complements. Instead of our X', he would write $1 - X$ ('1 minus X') for the complement of X.

It is probably already clear that the equal sign ($=$) in Boole's system indicates that the set on the right and the set on the left are the same; that is, that they have the same members.

EXERCISES 8.1a

1. What is the logical addition of the set of numbers from 100 to 150 and the set of numbers from 150 to 200?

2. What is the logical multiplication of the two sets mentioned in exercise 1?

3. Describe the complement of the set of cars Frank likes.

---

[2]Boole thought that these two concepts were identical. But modern set theory holds that the empty set *is* something, namely a set with no members. Boole characteristically viewed operations on sets as activities that brought new sets into creation, so he spoke of "forming" a set by the addition of two sets, and so on. For another view, see W. V. Quine, *Set Theory and Its Logic* (Cambridge, MA: Harvard University Press, 1963), chapter 1.

4. What is the complement of Boole's **0**? of his **1**?

5. Are the following true? Give an informal proof to back up your answer.

   a. $(A \cdot B)' = A' \cdot B'$

   b. $(A \oplus B)' = A' \oplus B'$

   c. $A \oplus (B \oplus C) = (B \oplus A) \oplus C$

Armed with his notions of logical addition, logical multiplication, and complementation, Boole established a number of principles. The first two are the **commutative laws** for the symbols $\cdot$ and $\oplus$:

B1. $X \oplus Y = Y \oplus X$[3]
B2. $X \cdot Y = Y \cdot X$

Because the order in which the elements of a set are listed makes no difference, a set formed by logical addition from two sets A and B can be referred to as either $A \oplus B$ or $B \oplus A$. For example, let A be {Bob, Steve, Mary} and let B be {Jim, Steve, Alice}. Putting them together by addition is the set containing all the people we named, in whatever order we wish to list them, i.e., {Alice, Bob, Jim, Mary, Steve}. Thus $\oplus$ is commutative, just as the SL statement connectives $\vee$, &, and $\equiv$ we studied in chapters 2, 3, and 4 are. Similarly, the logical multiplication of two sets can be referred to by naming either set first. Note that $A \cdot B$ would be {Steve}, and could equally be called $B \cdot A$. Thus, $\cdot$ is clearly also commutative.

Next come the **associative laws**:

B3. $X \cdot (Y \cdot Z) = (X \cdot Y) \cdot Z$
B4. $X \oplus (Y \oplus Z) = (X \oplus Y) \oplus Z$

These principles merely record the fact that logical addition and multiplication are operations on two sets at a time. So when three or more sets are involved, parentheses are officially used (as in statement logic and predicate logic) to keep things straight. As in the case of commutativity, since the order of elements in sets makes no difference, the logical addition of three sets A, B, and C could be referred to as $A \oplus (B \oplus C)$ or $B \oplus (C \oplus A)$ or $C \oplus (A \oplus B)$ or $(B \oplus A) \oplus C$ or any of the twelve possibilities. Often parentheses are dropped and $A \oplus B \oplus C$ is written, or, in the case of four sets, $A \oplus B \oplus C \oplus D$. As long as one knows how to restore the parentheses correctly, there is no particular harm in such shortcuts. Logical multiplication is associative for similar reasons, and we can safely write $A \cdot B \cdot C$ when no confusion of meaning threatens.

---

[3]In this chapter, we use the boldface capital letters **X**, **Y**, and **Z** to refer generally to sets.

The next two principles record how $\oplus$ and $\cdot$ function together; here are the **distributive laws**:

B5. $X \cdot (Y \oplus Z) = (X \cdot Y) \oplus (X \cdot Z)$
B6. $X \oplus (Y \cdot Z) = (X \oplus Y) \cdot (X \oplus Z)$

Clearly in B5 and B6, parentheses do make a difference. For example, the formulas $A \cdot (B \oplus C)$ and $(A \cdot B) \oplus C$ are not at all the same. Let's look at a specific case to get the flavor of these relationships, taking B5 first. Suppose we have three sets:

$A = \{a, b, d, f\} \qquad B = \{a, c, d\} \qquad C = \{a, b, c, e\}$

First we form $B \oplus C$, which is $\{a, c, d, e, b\}$. Then we form $A \cdot (B \oplus C)$:

$A \cdot (B \oplus C) = \{a, b, d\}$

Now let's go the other way by forming $A \cdot B$ and $A \cdot C$, and then their logical addition $(A \cdot B) \oplus (A \cdot C)$:

$A \cdot B = \{a, d\} \qquad A \cdot C = \{a, b\} \qquad (A \cdot B) \oplus (A \cdot C) = \{a, b, d\}$

Using the same sets A, B, and C, let's work through B6, $X \oplus (Y \cdot Z) = (X \oplus Y) \cdot (X \oplus Z)$, but this time in reverse order. First we form $A \oplus B$ and $A \oplus C$ and then their logical multiplication:

$A \oplus B = \{a, b, c, d, f\} \qquad A \oplus C = \{a, b, c, d, e, f\}$
$(A \oplus B) \cdot (A \oplus C) = \{a, b, c, d, f\}$

Next we want $B \cdot C$ and then $A \oplus (B \cdot C)$:

$B \cdot C = \{a, c\} \qquad A \oplus (B \cdot C) = \{a, b, c, d, f\}$

EXERCISES 8.1b

1. Give examples of Boole's principles B1–B6 using the following sets:

   a. $D = \{$Tea, Coffee, Milk$\} \qquad E = \{$Coffee, Cola, Water$\} \qquad F = \{$Juice$\}$

   b. $G = \{1, 3, 4, 5\} \qquad H = \{2\} \qquad I = \{5, 6, 2\}$

2. Give an example of each of the following using sets D and E from exercise 1a.

   a. $A \oplus A = A$

   b. $A \oplus (A \cdot B) = A \cdot (A \oplus B)$

Two simple principles that have far-reaching importance in Boole's system are the **idempotence laws** (*idempotence* means 'same power'):

B7. $X \cdot X = X$

B8. $X \oplus X = X$

Given what we have said about $\oplus$ and $\cdot$, it is clear that these principles must hold. (You have worked with B8 in exercise 8.1b.2a.) And it is also clear that their extensions must hold.

B7e. $X \cdot X \cdot X \cdot X \cdot X$ (etc.) $= X$

B8e. $X \oplus X \oplus X \oplus X$ (etc.) $= X$

We now turn to three principles involving complements. First, the **involution law**:

B9. $(X')' = X$

According to this principle, if complementation is performed twice, we return to the original set. So if we start with the set D of dogs, and then form its complement D' we have the set of non-dogs. If we then take the complement $(D')'$ of non-dogs (i.e., non-non-dogs), we have dogs again. In Boole's terms, when we subtract dogs from 1 we have $1 - D$, which represents the set of all those things that are not dogs (people, sheep, cars, toads, your fingers, etc.). Now subtract that set from 1 to get $1 - (1 - D)$ and we have the set of all non-people, non-sheep, non-cars, non-toads, etc., which is just D!

Diagrams to illustrate the principles involved in Boole's system were first developed by Boole's contemporary John Venn and are called, after him, **Venn diagrams**.[4] Sets are indicated by circles; the universe by a rectangle. A Venn diagram shows very clearly how involution works, as the figure below demonstrates. Venn diagrams are particularly useful in depicting relations in monadic predicate logic, as we will discuss in the next section.

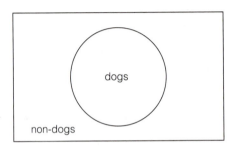

---

[4]See Martin Gardiner, *Logic Machines and Diagrams*, 2nd ed. (Chicago: University of Chicago Press, 1982), chapter 2.

Two further principles come from Boole's contemporary, Augustus DeMorgan and bear his name, **DeMorgan's laws**:

B10. $(X \oplus Y)' = X' \cdot Y'$
B11. $(X \cdot Y)' = X' \oplus Y'$

Like others you have encountered already, these principles are very similar to their SL versions in earlier chapters. The connections will be spelled out in section 8.3.

DeMorgan's laws relate all three operations to each other and indicate the **interchangeability of the operators** that characterizes Boole's system. To see how B10 and B11 work, let's use a miniature universe and let **1** be equal to the numbers from 1 though 10. So the complement of $\{1, 2, 3\}$ in this universe is $\{4, 5, 6, 7, 8, 9, 10\}$. Now let A be $\{1, 4, 7\}$ and B be $\{2, 3, 4, 8, 9\}$.

$$A \oplus B = \{1, 2, 3, 4, 7, 8, 9\}$$

The complement of a $A \oplus B$ in our miniature universe is

$$(A \oplus B)' = \{5, 6, 10\}$$

Now form the complements of A and B

$$A' = \{2, 3, 5, 6, 8, 9, 10\} \qquad B' = \{1, 5, 6, 7, 10\}$$

Their logical multiplication is

$$A' \cdot B' = \{5, 6, 10\}$$

Either $\oplus$ or $\cdot$ can be replaced by the other operator with appropriate complements. This follows from DeMorgan's laws and the involution law. For example, by the involution law, $A \oplus B$ is equal to $((A \oplus B)')'$ (i.e., the double complement). But by DeMorgan's law B10,

$$((A \oplus B)')' = (A' \cdot B')'$$

So, $A \oplus B$ equals $(A' \cdot B')'$. Although more complicated to say, the logical addition of two sets is thus the same as the complement of the logical multiplication of the complements of the two sets. By the same token, if we begin with $A \cdot B$, we can obtain $(A' \oplus B')'$; thus, logical multiplication is the same as forming the complement of the logical addition of the complements. Even though the notions of logical addition and multiplication were introduced as quite distinct operations on sets, we really need only one of them because we could get the other by means of definition through complements according to B9, B10, and B11. But it is obviously much more convenient to have both operations available.

EXERCISES 8.1c

1. Use the miniature universe of the numbers from 1 through 10 to answer the following:

    a. What is the complement of $A = \{1, 2, 3, 4\}$?

    b. What is the complement of $B = \{1, 2, 3, 4, 5, 6, 7, 8, 9\}$?

    c. Show the law of involution works for sets A and B.

    d. Show that B10 and B11 hold for A and B.

2. Give a formula using only $\oplus$ and $'$ equivalent to $(C \oplus D') \cdot E'$; eliminate any double complements.

3. Give a formula using only $\cdot$ and $'$ equivalent to $C' \oplus (C \oplus (D \cdot E))'$; eliminate any double complements.

A number of other principles hold for Boole's system. Here are the **laws of complementarity**:

B12. $X \cdot X' = 0$
B13. $X \oplus X' = 1$

One way of thinking about principle B12 is that the universe **1** is divided into two parts by any set X and its complement X'; every object will be found either in X or in X' (but not both). So the logical product of any set and its complement has to be **0**, since there can be no common members. Furthermore, when a set is logically *added* to its complement, the universe **1** results, since every object is either in X or in X'.

Finally, here are two more principles that are already clear but have not been explicitly stated:

B14. $1' = 0$ $(= 1 - 1 = 0)$
B15. $0' = 1$ $(= 1 - 0 = 1)$

When we substitute **1** and **0** for X in B7 ($X \cdot X = X$), in B8 ($X \oplus X = X$), in B12 ($X \cdot X' = 0$), and in B13 ($X \oplus X' = 1$) we get a series of formulas that are often cited as the central theorems of Boole's system.

B16. $1 \cdot 1 = 1$ (from B7)
B17. $1 \cdot 0 = 0$ (from B12)
B18. $0 \cdot 0 = 0$ (from B7)
B19. $1 \oplus 1 = 1$ (from B8)
B20. $0 \oplus 0 = 0$ (from B8)
B21. $1 \oplus 0 = 1$ (from B13)

Other important Boolean principles are these four:

B22. $X \oplus 1 = 1$

B23. $X \oplus 0 = X$

B24. $X \cdot 1 = X$

B25. $X \cdot 0 = 0$

Principles B16–B25 are interesting for two reasons. First, if one thinks of logical addition as ordinary arithmetical addition and logical multiplication as arithmetical multiplication, then, except for B19 ($1 \oplus 1 = 1$), all the principles hold exactly, as do B14 and B15 for subtraction. Replacing the Boolean operators with $+$ and $\times$ and using the numbers 0 and 1 instead of the special symbols **0** and **1**, we obtain the following list:

(1) $1 \times 1 = 1$
(2) $1 \times 0 = 0$
(3) $0 \times 0 = 0$
(4) $1 + 1 = 1$?????
(5) $0 + 0 = 0$
(6) $1 + 0 = 1$
(7) $n + 1 = 1$?????   (*n* stands for either 1 or 0)
(8) $n + 0 = n$
(9) $n \cdot 1 = n$
(10) $n \cdot 0 = 0$

As already noted, (4) and the more general (7) seem queer. But think of them this way. We are interpreting Boole's principles as formulas of the Boolean arithmetic of 0 and 1. So 0 and 1 are our *only* numbers; we have no others. Thus, by default, one might say, $n + 1$, for any n, can only equal 1, because 1 is the largest number available. With this proviso, all of Boole's principles are legitimate equalities in the Boolean arithmetic of 0 and 1 when logical addition becomes addition, logical multiplication becomes multiplication, and complementation becomes subtraction. According to Boole's own exchange principle, $X' = 1 - X$, B14 and B15 would become, respectively:

(11) $1 - 1 = 0$
(12) $1 - 0 = 1$

The interpretation of Boole's systems as the Boolean arithmetic of 0 and 1 holds for all of the principles we have discussed. Look, for example, at what happens to DeMorgan's laws (remember, either 1 or 0 can be substituted for X and for Y):

$$
\begin{array}{ll}
(X \oplus Y)' = (X' \cdot Y') & \text{Let } X = 1, Y = 1 \\
1 - (X + Y) = (1 - X) \times (1 - Y) & \\
= 1 - (1 + 1) = (1 - 1) \times (1 - 1) & \\
= \quad 1 - 1 \quad = \quad 0 \times 0 & \\
= \quad\quad 0 \quad\quad = \quad\quad 0 &
\end{array}
$$

You will be asked to carry out similar substitutions in the exercises.

We will have more to say about Boole's principles considered as Boolean arithmetic in section 8.4. Before going on, however, it should be noted that it was far from obvious that the simple operations on sets with which Boole began should also state relations between numbers. Clearly Boole uncovered some deep relationships between two very different types of things—sets, which are just collections of objects, and numbers, or at least the numbers 0 and 1. There are other important relationships in Boole's principles, as we will see in the next two sections.

Summary

Three Boolean operations, **logical multiplication** ($\cdot$), **logical addition** ($\oplus$), and **complementation** (**'**), are defined on sets. The set of all objects, or **universe**, is denoted by **1** and the **empty set** is denoted by **0**. Boolean principles show that the operations $\oplus$ and $\cdot$ obey commutative, associative, distributive, and idempotence laws (like $\vee$ and & from SL). Double complements cancel (the involution law) and DeMorgan's laws also hold. **1** is the complement of **0**, and vice versa (the complementarity laws).

The relations involving the operations and **1** and **0** are strongly reminiscent of arithmetic equations, except that $1 \oplus 1 = 1$ and $X \oplus 1 = 1$. A possible interpretation, which fits all the Boolean principles, is an arithmetic in which 0 and 1 are the only numbers available.

EXERCISES 8.1d

1. Show that principles B1–B7 are equalities using $X = 1$ and $Y = 0$.

2. Show that principles B8–B13 are equalities using $X = 0$ and $Y = 1$.

8.2 BOOLEAN MONADIC PREDICATE LOGIC

One of Boole's main concerns in the *Laws of Thought* was to clearly reveal the underlying logic of what are called *syllogisms*. The result was the beginnings of predicate logic. Boole realized that a class of common general statements—called **categorical statements**—could be represented in his system and that arguments involving such statements (syllogisms) could then be easily shown valid or invalid. Our brief review of the syllogism will provide an example of a very simple pictorial algorithm for determining the validity of this important class of arguments.

Each categorical statement in a syllogism is composed of one quantifier and two monadic predicates. Our Boolean representation of these statements uses the notion of **inequality**, which is represented by $\neq$ ('does not equal').

On the next page is a chart that shows Boolean translations for the four basic types of categorical statements. Statement types are designated as **A, E, I,** and **O,** corresponding to the first two vowels in the Latin words *affirmo* (affirm) and *nego* (negate). The *S* and *P* in the chart's PL versions are (monadic) predicates. In Boole's system they are taken to be names of sets.

Statement Type	English Form	PL	Boolean Form
A	All S are P	$\forall x\,(Sx \supset Px)$	$S \cdot P' = 0$
E	No S are P	$\forall x\,(Sx \supset\, \sim Px)$	$S \cdot P = 0$
I	Some S are P	$\exists x\,(Sx\, \& \,Px)$	$S \cdot P \neq 0$
O	Some S are not P	$\exists x\,(Sx\, \& \sim Px)$	$S \cdot P' \neq 0$

Note how Boole's system mirrors the PL interpretation of the four basic statement patterns:

1. In the case of the **A** statement, since the logical product of S and the complement P' is empty, all S's (if there are any) have to be P's.

2. In the **E** statement, the logical product of S and P is empty; so there are no S's that are P's.

3. The **I** and **O** statements in Boole's framework assert that the logical product of the two sets is *not* empty, that is, that at least one thing has both properties, belongs to both sets.

Each of the four categorical statements can also be represented by a Venn diagram, as follows. (Shaded areas are empty, unshaded areas *may* contain objects, and areas with an X in them contain objects.)

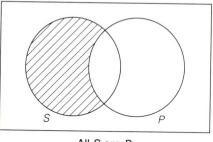

All S are P
$S \cdot P' = 0$

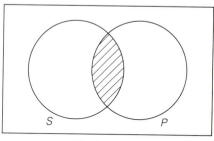

No S are P
$S \cdot P = 0$

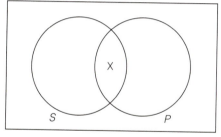

Some S are P
$S \cdot P \neq 0$

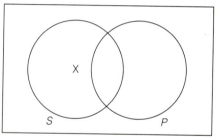

Some S are not P
$S \cdot P' \neq 0$

The Boolean principles discussed in the last section provide a means of verifying all of the possible logical relations among such categorical statements. However, to use them effectively in a formal method of derivation, we will need an inference rule as well as two additional equivalence principles, so we state these first.

Boole's Rule (B) *(a) If* $\mathbf{X} = \mathbf{Y}$ *and* $\mathbf{Z} = \mathbf{Y}$, *then* $\mathbf{X} = \mathbf{Z}$
(b) If $\mathbf{X} = \mathbf{Y}$, *then* $\mathbf{Y}$ *can replace* $\mathbf{X}$ *in any formula*

B26. $\mathbf{X} = \mathbf{Y} \iff \mathbf{X} \cdot \mathbf{Z} = \mathbf{Y} \cdot \mathbf{Z}$[5]
B27. $\mathbf{X} = \mathbf{Y} \iff \mathbf{X} \oplus \mathbf{Z} = \mathbf{Y} \oplus \mathbf{Z}$

Principles B26 and B27 immediately follow from the second part of Boole's rule. That they clearly hold for sets is easily seen. Since $\mathbf{X}$ and $\mathbf{Y}$ are the same set, there cannot be any object in $\mathbf{X} \cdot \mathbf{Z}$ that isn't in $\mathbf{Y} \cdot \mathbf{Z}$, and vice versa. Similarly, there cannot be any object in $\mathbf{X} \oplus \mathbf{Z}$ that isn't also in $\mathbf{Y} \oplus \mathbf{Z}$. So $\mathbf{X} \cdot \mathbf{Z}$ and $\mathbf{Y} \cdot \mathbf{Z}$ are the same set, as are $\mathbf{X} \oplus \mathbf{Z}$ and $\mathbf{Y} \oplus \mathbf{Z}$.

Now, on to the logic of categorical statements, Boolean style.

The application of the rule of contraposition to categorical statements, for example, may be expressed as follows:

$$\forall x \, (Sx \supset Px) \iff \forall x \, (\sim Px \subset \sim Sx)$$
$$S \cdot P' \iff P' \cdot S = 0$$

The statement $\forall x \, (\sim Px \supset \sim Sx)$ is formulated initially as $P' \cdot (S')' = \mathbf{0}$, according to the standard Boolean pattern, and then by means of the involution law (B9), the double complement is eliminated. So contraposition here becomes merely an instance of commutativity.

Boolean representation brings a welcome clarity to the expression of necessary conditions, which are often based on the contraposition principle (as noted in chapter 2). If charged batteries are a necessary condition for a working flashlight, then one might state this as 'Flashlights won't work with uncharged batteries,' or in PL,

$$\forall x \, (\sim Cx \supset \sim Wx)$$

(C: '_____ has charged batteries'; W: '_____ is a working flashlight')
In the Boolean form, the statement becomes

$$W \cdot C' = \mathbf{0}$$

---

[5]Recall from chapters 4 and 7 that the double arrow $\iff$ means that the two expressions are interchangeable.

in other words, the set consisting of working flashlights with uncharged batteries is empty.

At various points in our study of PL we noted that what we now are calling categorical statements are related to each other in significant ways. The **A**– and **O**–statements, for example, are direct opposites:

$$\forall x \, (Sx \supset Px) \equiv \sim\exists X \, (Sx \, \& \sim Px)$$

The Boolean version:

$$S \cdot P' = 0 \; \leftrightarrow \; \text{not} \, (S \cdot P' \neq 0) \quad (\text{i.e.,} \; S \cdot P' = 0)$$

Similarly, the **E** and **I** are opposites:

$$\forall x \, (Sx \supset \sim Px) \equiv \sim\exists x \, (Sx \, \& \, Px)$$

The Boolean version:

$$S \cdot P = 0 \; \leftrightarrow \; \text{not} \, (S \cdot P \neq 0) \quad (\text{i.e.,} \; S \cdot P = 0)$$

Notice that these relations are now nearly trivial consequences of the representation of categorical statements in Boole's system.

The **syllogism** is an argument consisting of two premises and a conclusion, each of which is one of the four types of categorical statement. Furthermore, the statements in a syllogism can contain no more than three different (monadic) predicates.

Turning, then, to syllogisms, let's try a few favorites.

(1) All humans are mortal.

    All Greeks are humans.

      —————————————

    All Greeks are mortal.

(H = humans; G = Greeks; M = mortals)

$H \cdot M' = 0$

$G \cdot H' = 0$

—————

$G \cdot M' = 0$

To derive the conclusion, $G \cdot M' = 0$, from the premises, we set up a derivation in much the same way we did in SL and PL. The first two lines are the premises (as assumptions), and each line thereafter is a consequence.

In addition to several of the natural deduction rules, we can appeal here to some Boolean principle or the special inference rule, Rule B. To make such derivations easier to follow, justifications cite either the property invoked, e.g. 'dist' (for distribution, B5, B6), or the particular number of the principle used if it has no familiar name.[6]

Derivation:

1.	$H \cdot M' = 0$	
2.	$G \cdot H' = 0$	
3.	$H \cdot M' = 0$	(R, 1)
4.	$G \cdot H' = 0$	(R, 2)
5.	$H \oplus (G \cdot H') = 0 \oplus H$	(B27, 4)
6.	$H \oplus (G \cdot H') = H$	(B23, 5)
7.	$(H \oplus G) \cdot (H \oplus H') = H$	(dist, 6)
8.	$(H \oplus G) \cdot 1 = H$	(compl; 7)
9.	$(H \oplus G) = H$	(B24; 8)
10.	$(H \oplus G) \cdot M' = 0$	(Rule B (b): $H \oplus G/H$; 9, 3)
11.	$(H \cdot M') \oplus (G \cdot M') = 0$	(dist; 10)
12.	$0 \oplus (G \cdot M') = 0$	(Rule B (b): $0/H \cdot M'$; 11, 3)
13.	$G \cdot M' = 0$	(B23, 12)

The two critical steps in this derivation are line 5, in which H is added to each side of the second premise by means of principle B27, $\mathbf{X} = \mathbf{Y} \leftrightarrow \mathbf{X} \oplus \mathbf{Z} = \mathbf{Y} \oplus \mathbf{Z}$, and line 12, where Rule B is used to replace $H \cdot M'$ by $\mathbf{0}$ because of the first premise.

In addition to deriving the conclusion of syllogism (1) from the premises, essentially the same reasoning will establish an extremely useful inference rule for Boole's system, which we state generally as follows:

B28. If $\mathbf{X} \cdot \mathbf{Y}' = 0$ and $\mathbf{Y} \cdot \mathbf{Z} = 0$, then $\mathbf{X} \cdot \mathbf{Z} = 0$

B28 is the Boolean analog to the rule of hypothetical syllogism that we first encountered in statement logic. To convert the above derivation into a derivation of B28, substitute $\mathbf{X}$ for G, $\mathbf{Y}$ for H, and $\mathbf{Z}$ for M'. We can thereby show that $\mathbf{X} \cdot \mathbf{Z} = 0$ follows from the premises $\mathbf{X} \cdot \mathbf{Y}' = 0$ and $\mathbf{Y} \cdot \mathbf{Z} = 0$, no matter what $\mathbf{X}$, $\mathbf{Y}$, and $\mathbf{Z}$ may be.

Here is another example:

(2) All birds can fly.

Some mammals cannot fly.

Some mammals are not birds.

$(B = $ birds; $F = $ can fly; $M = $ mammals)

$B \cdot F' = 0$

$M \cdot F' \neq 0$

$M \cdot B' \neq 0$

---

[6]The distribution law in SL was abbreviated in capital letters as DIST. However, lowercase letters are used to distinguish Boolean distribution from the SL distribution laws. But as we will see in the next section, they are, at bottom, one and the same principle.

Since we haven't developed any special principles or rules for derivations involving inequalities, we will approach such arguments by indirect reasoning; that is, we will make the additional assumption of $(M \cdot B' = 0)$ the opposite of the conclusion, in a subsidiary derivation, and show that a contradiction can be derived from the Boolean principles. Then by the same principle of indirect reasoning we used in SL and PL derivations, we can assert that the conclusion itself follows.

Derivation:
1. $B \cdot F' = 0$
2. $M \cdot F' \neq 0$

3. $M \cdot B' = 0$

4. $M \cdot B' = 0$ (R, 3)
5. $B \cdot F' = 0$ (R, 1)
6. $M \cdot F' = 0$ (B28; 4, 5)
7. $M \cdot F' \neq 0$ (R, 2)
8. $M \cdot B' \neq 0$ (IR, 3, 6, 7)

The availability of B28 saves many steps in derivations.

(3) All hagfish are slimy.

Some sea creatures are hagfish.

Some sea creatures are slimy.

H = hagfish; S = Slimy things; C = sea creatures)

$H \cdot S' = 0$

$C \cdot H \neq 0$

$C \cdot S \neq 0$

Derivation:
1. $H \cdot S' = 0$
2. $C \cdot H \neq 0$

3. $C \cdot S = 0$

4. $C \cdot S = 0$ (R, 3)
5. $H \cdot S' = 0$ (R, 1)
6. $S \cdot C = 0$ (comm; 4)
7. $H \cdot C = 0$ (B28; 5, 6)
8. $C \cdot H = 0$ (comm; 7)
9. $C \cdot H \neq 0$ (R, 2)
10. $C \cdot S \neq 0$ (IR, 3, 8, 9)

To show that a syllogism is *not* valid, we can show informally that the conclusion, in Boolean notation, can be false while the premises are assumed true. This can be done by appealing to the concepts of sets and their members, rather like the search for counterexample valuations we conducted in chapter 6. Here are a few examples:

(4) All dogs are animals.

All cats are animals.

All dogs are cats.

(D = dogs; C = cats; M = mammals)

$D \cdot A' = 0$

$C \cdot A' = 0$

$D \cdot C' = 0$

To show invalidity: Suppose $D \cdot C' \neq 0$, that is, suppose that there is an object—say, Sherlock—which is a dog but not a cat. Further suppose that both premises are true, that Sherlock, like all dogs, is an animal and all cats are animals. These suppositions are consistent. Since the conclusion can be false when the premises are true, the syllogism is *invalid*.

(5) All football fans are robust.

Some robust people like egg salad.

Some football fans like egg salad.

(F = football fan; R = robust person; E = likes egg salad)

$F \cdot R' = 0$

$R \cdot E \neq 0$

$F \cdot E \neq 0$

To show invalidity: Suppose the conclusion is false and that there is no object that is both F and E, that is, suppose $F \cdot E = 0$. Further suppose that there is some person, say Sal, who is both R and E, that is, who is robust and likes egg salad (premise 2). Just let Sal be a non-football fan, which does not conflict with the truth of the first premise. Thus, the premises can be true while the conclusion is false, and the syllogism is *invalid*.

The derivation method we have used to show that Boolean syllogisms are valid is, like all derivation methods, a *verification* technique. We are asked to *show* that a certain syllogism is valid, and we provide (if we can) a derivation of its conclusion from its premises. On the other hand, to show that a syllogism is invalid, we have constructed an informal argument based on sets and membership that shows that the premises can both be true when the conclusion is false. But we can improve on these methods; we can provide a *test* method, an algorithm, which will pronounce on the validity or invalidity of any syllogism at once.

This test method for syllogisms makes use of Venn diagrams, which consist of three overlapping circles, one for each set named by a term in the syllogism. A standard Venn diagram, for a syllogism with terms M, S, and P, is depicted below.

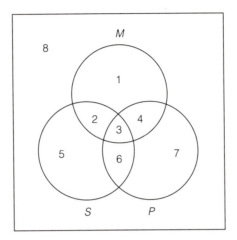

When the premises of a syllogism are represented in a Venn diagram, if the conclusion can be read off as well, the syllogism is *valid*. If the conclusion is not represented on the diagram, then the syllogism is *invalid*. The basis of the Venn diagram method is that the premises of a valid syllogism already contain all the information that is in the conclusion; therefore, representing the relations in the premises should also represent the relations in the conclusion.

The procedure is to *first* diagram universal premises and then particular premises. The diagramming proceeds by shading out regions that contain no objects and by placing an X in regions with a definite presence of objects. Because there are three circles in a Venn diagram for a syllogism, there are eight regions, each of which represents a set, as detailed in the following table:

Region	Set
1	$M \cdot S' \cdot P'$
2	$M \cdot S \cdot P'$
3	$M \cdot S \cdot P$
4	$M \cdot S' \cdot P$
5	$M' \cdot S \cdot P'$
6	$M' \cdot S \cdot P$
7	$M' \cdot S' \cdot P$
8	$M' \cdot S' \cdot P'$

In order to represent, for example, the statement $S \cdot P = 0$, regions 3 and 6 would be shaded, since the statement says there are no objects in the overlap between the S set and the P set. A slight complication enters when one has to represent a statement like $S \cdot M \neq 0$. An X is required in the overlapping area of sets S and M. But there are two regions in this overlap; regions 2 and 3. The solution is to place the X on the *line* that separates these two regions, as in the diagram below.

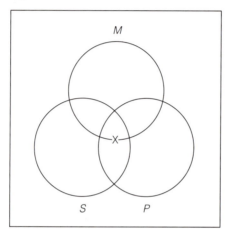

By following the rule that universal premises are diagrammed first, this situation will often not arise because one of the regions will already be shaded (as would be the case above if the other premise were $M \cdot P = 0$, for example).

Here are several syllogisms that demonstrate the Venn diagram method:

(1) No M are P $M \cdot P = 0$

    All M are S $M \cdot S' = 0$

    No S are P $S \cdot P = 0$

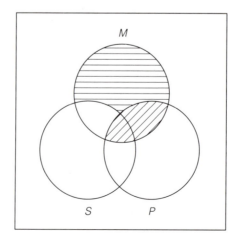

Since region 6 is not shaded, the conclusion may be false; thus, the syllogism is *invalid*.

(2) Some *M* are *P* $M \cdot P \neq 0$

    No *S* are *M* $S \cdot M = 0$

    No *S* are *P* $S \cdot P = 0$

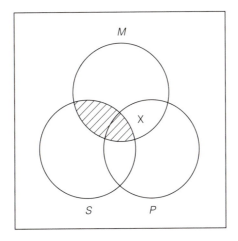

Again, the syllogism is *invalid*; region 6 is not shaded.

(3) No *M* are *P* $M \cdot P = 0$

    Some *S* are *M* $S \cdot M \neq 0$

    Some *S* are not *P* $S \cdot P' \neq 0$

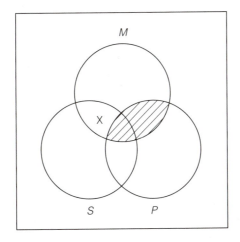

In this case, the conclusion can be read off of the diagram, so the syllogism is *valid*. Note that diagramming the universal premise ($M \cdot P = 0$) first shades region 3 so that the X required by the second premise must be placed in region 2.

(4) Some M are P $M \cdot P \neq 0$

    Some S are not M $S \cdot M' \neq 0$

    Some S are not P $S \cdot P' \neq 0$

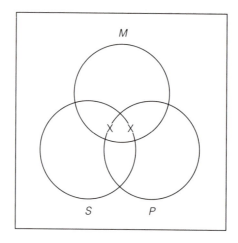

The two X's had both to be placed on lines separating regions; as a result, the conclusion cannot be read off of the diagram because an X is not found in region 2 or 5. The X on the line between 2 and 3 represents an object that could be in either region—we cannot tell—so it would be illegitimate to conclude that the object is definitely in region 2, as the conclusion would require.

In chapter 6 we noted that the monadic fragment of PL permits an algorithmic test for validity, although full PL does not. That algorithm, applied to syllogisms in either its truth table or tree form, could involve the use of up to 8 ($= 2^3$) names since each syllogism typically has three different predicates. Venn diagrams, as we have seen, provide a vastly simpler algorithm for the syllogistic part of monadic PL.

Summary

The four types of categorical statements are represented in Boole's system by means of the translations in the table on p. 000. These Boolean relations between the sets named by the predicates can be diagrammed by means of **Venn diagrams**, which use a circle for each set named by a term. Regions that are empty are indicated by shading, regions where objects definitely exist are indicated by an X.

Boolean syllogisms can be shown to be valid by means of derivations of their conclusions from their premises. Such derivations use the various Boolean principles plus the rule of inference:

Rule B *(a) If* $X = Y$ *and* $Z = Y$, *then* $X = Z$
        (b) If $X = Y$, *then* Y *can replace* X *in any formula*

Syllogisms can be shown to be invalid informally by arguments designed to demonstrate that their conclusions may be false when their premises are both true.

The **Venn diagram method**, an algorithmic method that tests Boolean syllogisms for validity, uses three overlapping circles and proceeds by diagramming the premises (universal statements first) and then determining whether the conclusion can be read off the resulting diagram. If so, the syllogism is valid (example below); if not, the syllogism is invalid.

No M are P	$M \cdot P = 0$
Some S are M	$S \cdot M \neq 0$
Some S are not P	$S \cdot P' \neq 0$

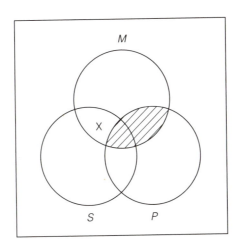

EXERCISES 8.2

1. Write the following categorical statements in Boolean notation:

   a. All football fans eat potato chips.

   b. Some fish are not tasty.

   c. No wishful thinkers need apply.

d. Only members may enter.

e. Somebody likes blue ties.

2. Give a proof using Boolean principles that each of the following is valid.

a. No sails are red.

Some fabric is red.
_____

Some fabric is not a sail.

b. Some fish are swimmers.

All swimmers are fast.
_____

Some fish are fast.

3. Show that each of the following is not valid.

a. No difficult book is entirely worthless.

Some logic books are not difficult.
_____

Some logic books are not entirely worthless.

b. Nobody who runs everyday is out of shape.

Nobody who cares about himself runs every day.
_____

Nobody who cares about himself is out of shape.

4. Test the syllogisms above by means of Venn diagrams.

8.3 BOOLEAN STATEMENT LOGIC

We have explored Boole's system as it functions in the Boolean arithmetic of 0 and 1 and in the logic of syllogisms. Next we look at using Boole's system to capture the logic of statements.

Recall the list of principles B16–B21 from section 8.1 that reveal the properties of logical addition and multiplication on the special sets **0** and **1**. They are listed below with two additional principles added by commutativity so that all possibilities are included.

$$1 \cdot 1 = 1$$
$$1 \cdot 0 = 0$$
$$0 \cdot 1 = 0$$
$$0 \cdot 0 = 0$$
$$1 \oplus 1 = 1$$
$$1 \oplus 0 = 1$$
$$0 \oplus 1 = 1$$
$$0 \oplus 0 = 0$$

These should look familiar; they are analogous to the *truth tables* for & and $\lor$ with **1** and **0** standing for the truth-values **T** and **F**, respectively.

T & T = T
T & F = F
F & T = F
F & F = F
T ∨ T = T
T ∨ F = T
F ∨ T = T
F ∨ F = F

This is a somewhat different method of presenting the truth tables for ∨ and &. What each of these equations says, in effect, is that if statements with the indicated truth-values are joined by the connective, then the resulting statement has the indicated truth-value. So, in **T & T = T**, we see that joining two true statements together by conjunction produces a true statement.

If Boole's three operations are systematically exchanged with their statement logic analogs, according to the table following, then all Boolean principles will record SL tautologies. In showing this, we will use **t** to stand for any *tautology* (for example, $A \lor \sim A$), and **f** to stand for any *logical contradiction* (for example, $A \& \sim A$).

Boolean Operation Connective	Statement Logic
logical addition ⊕	disjunction ∨
logical multiplication ·	conjunction &
complement '	negation ∼
equality =	biconditional ≡
universe 1	tautology t
empty set 0	contradiction f

Here is the list of all the Boolean principles we have discussed:

B1. $X \oplus Y = Y \oplus X$
B2. $X \cdot Y = Y \cdot X$
B3. $X \cdot (Y \cdot Z) = (X \cdot Y) \cdot Z$
B4. $X \oplus (Y \oplus Z) = (X \oplus Y) \oplus Z$
B5. $X \cdot (Y \oplus Z) = (X \cdot Y) \oplus (X \cdot Z)$
B6. $X \oplus (Y \cdot Z) = (X \oplus Y) \cdot (X \oplus Z)$
B7. $X \cdot X = X$
B8. $X \oplus X = X$
B9. $(X')' = X$
B10. $(X \oplus Y)' = X' \cdot Y'$
B11. $(X \cdot Y)' = X' \oplus Y'$
B12. $X \cdot X' = 0$
B13. $X \oplus X' = 1$

B14. $1' = 0$
B15. $0' = 1$
B16. $1 \cdot 1 = 1$
B17. $1 \cdot 0 = 0$
B18. $0 \cdot 0 = 0$
B19. $1 \oplus 1 = 1$
B20. $0 \oplus 0 = 0$
B21. $1 \oplus 0 = 1$
B22. $X \oplus 1 = 1$
B23. $X \oplus 0 = X$
B24. $X \cdot 1 = X$
B25. $X \cdot 0 = 0$
B26. $X = Y \ \leftrightarrow \ X \cdot Z = Y \cdot Z$
B27. $X = Y \ \leftrightarrow \ X \oplus Z = Y \oplus Z$
B28. If $X \cdot Y' = 0$ and $Y \cdot Z = 0$, then $X \cdot Z = 0$

In the SL versions, X, Y, and Z are statement variables: **t** is any tautology, and **f** is any logical contradiction. When these are instances of SL equivalences, the names are supplied.

T1. $X \lor Y \equiv Y \lor X$ (Commutativity)
T2. $X \& Y \equiv Y \& X$ (Commutativity)
T3. $X \& (Y \& Z) \equiv (X \& Y) \& Z$ (Associativity)
T4. $X \lor (Y \lor Z) \equiv (X \lor Y) \lor Z$ (Associativity)
T5. $X \& (Y \lor Z) \equiv (X \& Y) \lor (X \& Z)$ (Distributivity)
T6. $X \lor (Y \& Z) \equiv (X \lor Y) \& (X \lor Z)$ (Distributivity)
T7. $X \& X \equiv X$ (Idempotence &)
T8. $X \lor X \equiv X$ (Idempotence $\lor$)
T9. $\sim\sim X \equiv X$ (Double Negation)
T10. $\sim(X \lor Y) \equiv \sim X \& \sim Y$ (DeMorgan's)
T11. $\sim(X \& Y) \equiv \sim X \lor \sim Y$ (DeMorgan's)
T12. $X \& \sim X \equiv \mathbf{f}$
T13. $X \lor \sim X \equiv \mathbf{t}$
T14. $\sim \mathbf{t} \equiv \mathbf{f}$
T15. $\sim \mathbf{f} \equiv \mathbf{t}$
T16. $\mathbf{t} \& \mathbf{t} \equiv \mathbf{t}$ (Idempotence &)
T17. $\mathbf{t} \& \mathbf{f} \equiv \mathbf{f}$ (Contradiction &)
T18. $\mathbf{f} \& \mathbf{f} \equiv \mathbf{f}$ (Idempotence &)
T19. $\mathbf{t} \lor \mathbf{t} \equiv \mathbf{t}$ (Idempotence $\lor$)
T20. $\mathbf{f} \lor \mathbf{f} \equiv \mathbf{f}$ (Idempotence $\lor$)
T21. $\mathbf{t} \lor \mathbf{f} \equiv \mathbf{t}$ (Contradiction $\lor$)
T22. $X \lor \mathbf{t} \equiv \mathbf{t}$ (Tautology $\lor$)
T23. $X \lor \mathbf{f} \equiv X$ (Contradiction &)
T24. $X \& \mathbf{t} \equiv X$ (Tautology &)
T25. $X \& \mathbf{f} \equiv \mathbf{f}$
T26. $X \equiv Y \ \leftrightarrow \ X \& Z \equiv Y \& Z$
T27. $X \equiv Y \ \leftrightarrow \ X \lor Z \equiv Y \lor Z$
T28. If $X \& \sim Y \equiv \mathbf{f}$ and $Y \& Z \equiv \mathbf{f}$, then $X \& Z \equiv \mathbf{f}$

We noted in the last section that B28 was the Boolean analog of hypothetical syllogism $((X \supset Y) \& (Y \supset Z)) \supset (X \supset Z)$ expressed as a tautology, but T28 doesn't look like hypothetical syllogism at all. However, it can be seen as the same if you recall that $A \supset B$ is equivalent to $\sim(A \& \sim B)$, and $\sim f$ is equivalent to t. So T28 can be expressed as follows:

T29. If $X \supset Y \equiv t$ and $Y \supset \sim Z \equiv t$, then $X \supset \sim Z \equiv t$

which is, indeed, a version of hypothetical syllogism.

Boole did not realize that his system was, in effect, a full formal logic of statements; it was not until years later that the far-reaching implications of Boole's system were worked out by Gottlieb Frege, C. S. Pierce, Bertrand Russell, and Alfred North Whitehead, among others.[7] But as we have seen, Boole's system and statement logic are in fact two sides of the same coin. In the next section we will look at the applications of Boole's system from a slightly different point of view; in chapters 10 and 12 we will study what are perhaps the most important applications of Boolean systems: the design of electronic circuits.

Summary

In this section we discussed the connections between Boolean principles and statement logic when the Boolean operations $\oplus$, $\cdot$, and $'$ are translated as statement connectives $\vee$, $\&$, and $\sim$, respectively, and the special symbols **1** and **0** are translated as an arbitrary tautology t and an arbitrary contradiction f, respectively. All of the Boolean principles become SL tautologies under this translation.

EXERCISES 8.3

1. Verify, by means of truth tables, that the following are SL theorems:
    a. T17
    b. T18
    c. T20
    d. T22
    e. T24
    f. T26
    g. T26
    h. T27

2. State the SL version of Rule B and show that it holds as an SL rule.

---

[7]For the full story, see W. Kneale and M. Kneale, *The Development Of Logic* (Oxford: Oxford University Press, 1962).

*8.4 BOOLEAN ALGEBRA

We have studied Boole's system as relations among sets (or classes), as a representation of the Boolean arithmetic of 0 and 1, as a method of capturing the logic of categorical statements and syllogisms, and as the analog of statement logic. At a higher level of generality, Boole's system is really none of these *in itself*, although it can be interpreted in these various ways. This most general version of Boole's system is what is known as **Boolean algebra**. In this form it is an abstract, purely formal system with no specific interpretation of its components, except as they relate to each other.

A Boolean algebra, then, is any system **B** with the following components:

1. A set B of elements (we will designate these by $X, Y, Z, \ldots$).
2. An equivalence relation $\approx$ defined on the elements of B.

Note: An *equivalence relation* is any two-place relation that satisfies the following laws:
2.1 reflexivity: $\mathbf{X} \approx \mathbf{X}$
2.2 symmetry: if $\mathbf{X} \approx \mathbf{Y}$, then $\mathbf{Y} \approx \mathbf{X}$
2.3 transitivity: if $\mathbf{X} \approx \mathbf{Y}$ and $\mathbf{Y} \approx \mathbf{Z}$, then $\mathbf{X} \approx \mathbf{Z}$

3. A one-place operator ' ('inversion') defined on the elements of B so that if $\mathbf{X}$ is an element of B, so is $\mathbf{X}'$.

4. The two-place operators ∩ (called here 'meet') and ∪ (called here 'join') defined on the elements of B so that if $\mathbf{X}$ and $\mathbf{Y}$ are in B, so are $\mathbf{X} \cap \mathbf{Y}$ and $\mathbf{X} \cup \mathbf{Y}$.

5. The two designated elements of **B**: **0** and **1**.

B must satisfy the following *postulates*:[8]

P1.	$\mathbf{X} \cup \mathbf{Y} \approx \mathbf{Y} \cup \mathbf{X}$	(commutativity)
P2.	$\mathbf{X} \cap \mathbf{Y} \approx \mathbf{Y} \cap \mathbf{X}$	(commutativity)
P3.	$\mathbf{X} \cap (\mathbf{Y} \cap \mathbf{Z}) \approx (\mathbf{X} \cap \mathbf{Y}) \cap \mathbf{Z}$	(associativity)
P4.	$\mathbf{X} \cup (\mathbf{Y} \cup \mathbf{Z}) \approx (\mathbf{X} \cup \mathbf{Y}) \cup \mathbf{Z}$	(associativity)
P5.	$\mathbf{X} \cap (\mathbf{Y} \cup \mathbf{Z}) \approx (\mathbf{X} \cap \mathbf{Y}) \cup (\mathbf{X} \cap \mathbf{Z})$	(distributivity)
P6.	$\mathbf{X} \cup (\mathbf{Y} \cap \mathbf{Z}) \approx (\mathbf{X} \cup \mathbf{Y}) \cap (\mathbf{X} \cup \mathbf{Z})$	(distributivity)
P7.	$\mathbf{X} \cap \mathbf{X} \approx \mathbf{X}$	(idempotence)
P8.	$\mathbf{X} \cup \mathbf{X} \approx \mathbf{X}$	(idempotence)
P9.	$(\mathbf{X}')' \approx \mathbf{X}$	(involution)
P10.	$\mathbf{X} \cup \mathbf{0} \approx \mathbf{X}$	
P11.	$\mathbf{X} \cap \mathbf{1} \approx \mathbf{X}$	
P12.	$\mathbf{X} \cap \mathbf{X}' \approx \mathbf{0}$	(complementarity)
P13.	$\mathbf{X} \cup \mathbf{X}' \approx \mathbf{1}$	(complementarity)
P14.	$(\mathbf{X} \cup \mathbf{Y})' \approx \mathbf{X}' \cap \mathbf{Y}'$	(DeMorgan's laws)
P15.	$(\mathbf{X} \cap \mathbf{Y})' \approx \mathbf{X}' \cup \mathbf{Y}'$	(DeMorgan's laws)

---

[8]'Postulate' is another term for 'axiom'. The postulates are specified, and their consequences are called 'theorems'.

'Satisfy' here means that the equivalence relation $\approx$ on the members of set B must be defined so that each of P1 to P15 is true. For example, P13 says that for any element **X** of B, the operation join ($\cup$) between **X** and its inversion **X′** must be related by the equivalence relation $\approx$ to the designated element **1** of B.

Actually a much shorter list of postulates is all that is needed, but the short list, unfortunately, trades workability for elegance.[9] It should be noted that each of the postulates given above, except P9, has a **dual**: that is, a similar formula with $\cap$ in place of $\cup$, **0** in place of **1**, and vice versa. So P2 is the dual of P1; P3 is the dual of P4; and P12 is the dual of P13. It is an *essential* characteristic of Boolean algebras that they have this duality feature.

From these fifteen postulates, and the rule B, below, that equivalents can be freely substituted for each other, additional, now familiar, Boolean theorems can be proven.

Boole's Rule B: (a) If **X** $\approx$ **Y** and **Z** $\approx$ **Y**, then **X** $\approx$ **Z**
  (b) If **X** $\approx$ **Y**, then **Y** can replace **X** in any formula

---

For example, all of the following are theorems of any Boolean algebra:

P16. $1' \approx 0$
P17. $0' \approx 1$
P18. $X \cup (X \cap Y) \approx X$
P19. $X \cup 1 \approx 1$
P20. $X \cap 0 \approx 0$
P21. $1 \cap 1 \approx 1$
P22. $1 \cap 0 \approx 0$
P23. $0 \cap 0 \approx 0$
P24. $1 \cup 1 \approx 1$

Several sample derivations of theorems from our initial postulates are given below. These derivations, unlike those you have seen in previous sections, *do not begin with assumptions*. The first line in each case is a postulate, either one of the initial list P1–P15, or another formula that has already been derived from that group; such formulas are the *theorems* of **B**. These derivations are sometimes called *axiomatic* because they utilize axioms (postulates) as premises. But the initial axioms or postulates themselves are not derived; they are given as constituents of the system. Since the initial list of postulates P1–P15 was given in general terms, using variables **X**, **Y**, and so

---

[9]See T. Hailperin, *Boole's Logic*, chapter 1.

on, we can employ substitution instances of them. We will indicate such substitutions by citing the postulate and indicating what has been substituted for the original variable as a justification. Thus, as in the derivation of P16 that follows, P12, 1/X indicates that **1** has been substituted for **X** in P12, which yields $1 \cap 1' \approx 0$.

P16. $1' \approx 0$

Derivation:
1.	$1 \cap 1' \approx 0$	(P12, 1/X)
2.	$1' \cap 1 \approx 1'$	(P11, 1'/X)
3.	$1 \cap 1' \approx 1' \cap 1$	(P2, 1/X, 1'/Y)
4.	$1 \cap 1' \approx 1'$	(Rule B; 2, 3)
5.	$1' \approx 0$	(Rule B; 1,4)

P17. $0' \approx 1$

Derivation:
1.	$0 \cup 0' \approx 1$	(P13, 0/X)
2.	$0' \cup 0 \approx 0'$	(P10, 0'/X)
3.	$0 \cup 0' \approx 0' \cup 0$	(P1, 0/X, 0'/Y)
4.	$0 \cup 0' \approx 0'$	(Rule B; 2, 3)
5.	$0' \approx 1$	(Rule B; 1, 4)

The derivations of P16 and P17 are good illustrations of the duality property at work. Once a derivation is found for a Boolean algebra theorem, the derivation of its dual is just the dual, line by line, of the initial derivation, i.e, with the operators and constants interchanged, and, as justifications, the duals of the initial justifications in each line. So in line 1 of the derivation of P17, we used the dual P13 of the justification cited in line 1 of the original derivation (P12), and so on.

P21. $1 \cap 1 \approx 1$

Derivation: 1. $| \ 1 \cap 1 \approx 1$ (P11, 1/X)

P19. $X \cup 1 \approx 1$

Derivation:
1.	$X \cup 1 \approx X'' \cup 1''$	(P9, Rule B)
2.	$X \cup 1 \approx (X' \cap 1')'$	(P15, P9, Rule B)[10]
3.	$X \cup 1 \approx (X' \cap 0)'$	(P16, Rule B, 2)
4.	$X \cup 1 \approx (X' \cap (X \cap X'))'$	(P12, Rule b, 3)
5.	$X \cup 1 \approx (X' \cap (X' \cap X))'$	(P2, Rule B, 4)
6.	$X \cup 1 \approx ((X' \cap X') \cap X)'$	(P4, Rule B, 5)
7.	$X \cup 1 \approx (X' \cap X)'$	(P7 X'/X, Rule B, 6)
8.	$X \cup 1 \approx (X'' \cup X')$	(P15, Rule B, 7)
9.	$X \cup 1 \approx 1$	(P13, X'/X, Rule B, 8)

---

[10]Where the moves are obvious, several steps have been compressed into one.

P18. $X \cup (X \cap Y) \approx X$

Derivation:

1.	$X \cup (X \cap Y) \approx (X \cap 1) \cup (X \cap Y)$	(reflex, P11, Rule B)
2.	$X \cup (X \cap Y) \approx X \cap (1 \cup Y)$	(P5, Rule B, 1)
3.	$X \cup (X \cap Y) \approx X \cap (Y \cup 1)$	(P2, Rule B, 2)
4.	$X \cup (X \cap Y) \approx X \cap 1$	(P19Y/X, Rule B, 3)
5.	$X \cup (X \cap Y) \approx X$	(P11, Rule B, 4)

EXERCISES 8.4a

1. Give at least two examples of equivalence relations. Explain on what set the relation is defined in each case and show that each has the three essential properties 2.1–2.3 (p. 302).

2. For each of the following, give a derivation from the Boolean algebra postulates:

   $1 \cap 1 \approx 1$ $1 \cup 1 \approx 1$

   $1 \cap 0 \approx 0$ $1 \cup 0 \approx 1$

   $0 \cap 1 \approx 0$ $0 \cup 1 \approx 1$

   $0 \cap 0 \approx 0$ $0 \cup 0 \approx 0$

3. Sketch a derivation of the following version of the duality property for Boolean algebras:

   If A is a theorem of a Boolean algebra, then so is A_D, where A_D is the result of interchanging in A all occurrences of $\cup$ with $\cap$, and **0** with **1**, and vice versa.

   Hints: remember that postulates are theorems too, and that some theorems may not have any instances of $\cup$, $\cap$, **1**, or **0** (but still must be somehow covered by the derivation).

In addition to the operators $\cup$, $\cap$, $'$, and the equivalence relation $\approx$, often an additional two-place relation $<$ is found in Boolean algebras. This relation is not independent of the others, and so can be introduced by definition as follows:

Definition. $X < Y =_{def} X \cap Y \approx X$

What such a definition states is that $X < Y$ is to be thought of as shorthand in **B** for the formula $X \cap Y \approx X$. Strictly speaking, we have not introduced a new notion into **B**, but have conveniently grouped existing notions.

So defined, $<$ has a number of interesting properties:

P25. $0 < X < 1$ (i.e., $0 < X$ and $X < 1$)
P26. $X < X$
P27. If $X < Y$ and $Y < X$, then $X \approx Y$
P28. If $X < Y$ and $Y < Z$, then $X < Z$
P29. $X < Y$ if and only if $X \cup Y \approx Y$

To derive each of these, we translate back into the official symbols of **B** and then construct a derivation from the postulates and theorems. Note that derivations of P27–P29 will require assumptions, since they are 'if . . . then' statements. Two derivations follow; the remainder are left as exercises.

P27. If $X < Y$ and $Y < X$, then $X \approx Y$
$= X \approx Y$ follows from $X \cap Y \approx X$ and $Y \cap X \approx Y$

Derivation:
1.	$X \cap Y \approx X$	
2.	$Y \cap X \approx Y$	
3.	$X \cap Y \approx X$	(R, 1)
4.	$Y \cap X \approx Y$	(R, 2)
5.	$X \cap Y \approx Y$	(P2, Rule B, 4)
6.	$X \approx Y$	(Rule B; 3, 5)

P28. If $X < Y$ and $Y < Z$, then $X < Z$
$= X \cap Z \approx X$ follows from $X \cap Y \approx X$ and $Y \cap Z \approx Y$

Derivation:
1.	$X \cap Y \approx X$	
2.	$Y \cap Z \approx Y$	
3.	$X \cap Y \approx X$	(R, 1)
4.	$Y \cap Z \approx Y$	(R, 2)
5.	$X \cap (Y \cap Z) \approx X$	(3, 4; Rule B: $Y \cap Z/Y$)
6.	$(X \cap Y) \cap Z \approx X$	(P3, Rule B, 5)
7.	$X \cap Z \approx X$	(6, 3: Rule B: $X \cap Y/X$)

EXERCISES 8.4b

1. Give a derivation for:

   a. P25   b. P26   c. P29

2. Can you guess what role an operator analogous to the $<$ of Boolean algebra would play in SL, in the Boolean arithmetic of 1 and 0, and in Boole's system for sets?

All we know about the components of our Boolean algebra **B** is in the initial postulates and what follows from them. We don't know what kind of equivalence relation $\approx$ might be, nor do we know what sort of operations $\cup$ and $\cap$ are on the elements of B, other than that they comply with the postulates: they are commutative, associative etc. The two constants **0** and **1** are equally featureless, except that they are interrelated, so that $0' \approx 1$. So we cannot argue that such and such formula is a theorem because of the *nature* of **B** and its components, as we did when establishing Boole's principles on sets. This very abstractness is the strength of systems like **B**. Since we can't fall back on the intended interpretations of the symbols, we have to explore the nature of systems like **B** solely on the basis of their postulates, not on the basis of possibly erroneous intuitions. The structure that results may have (as **B** does have) numerous applications that thus reveal previously unknown relations between seemingly separate areas of knowledge. The concept of an abstract system like **B** was, at best, only dimly perceived by Boole and his contemporaries and represents an important achievement of twentieth century logic.

We defined the nature of Boolean algebras very generally as any system having the properties we have now fully specified. Now we will show that each of the following holds:

A. Statement logic (SL) is a Boolean algebra.

B. The Boolean arithmetic of 0 and 1 is a Boolean algebra.

C. The logic of the subsets of a set (a field of sets) is a Boolean algebra.

D. The logic of categorical statements and syllogisms is a part of the logic of the subsets of a set with the addition of inequalities and so is a part of a Boolean algebra with inequalities.

We have already discussed the relationship between Boole's principles and SL (section 8.3). We can now be more rigorous and state that SL is a Boolean algebra because the system SL can be viewed as a special case of **B**. To see how we might derive SL from **B**, we first define each SL symbol as a **B** symbol, as follows:

SL	B
SL Statements	elements of B
$\sim X$	X'
$X \vee Y$	$X \cup Y$
$X \,\&\, Y$	$X \cap Y$
$X \equiv Y$	$X \approx Y$
$P \,\&\, \sim P$	0
$P \vee \sim P$	1
$X \supset Y$	$X < Y$

Since **1** and **0** are designated elements of the set B, we need to equate them with specific statements from SL, so $P \vee \sim P$ and $P \,\&\, \sim P$, respectively, are utilized.

Let us say that if a formula **X** of **B** is altered by substituting SL symbols for **B** symbols in accord with the definitions just given, the result is the SL form of **X**. Next we show that $\equiv$ is an equivalence relation by proving the SL forms of 2.1–2.3 hold in SL. This is easily done. We can either derive each of the following using the natural deduction system or show that they all hold by means of truth tables (or trees).

SL 2.1 reflexivity; $X \equiv X$
SL 2.2 symmetry: if $X \equiv Y$, then $Y \equiv X$
SL 2.3 transitivity: if $X \equiv Y$ and $Y \equiv Z$, then $X \equiv Z$

Then we translate each postulate of **B** into its SL form, and show that the SL form of each of P1–P17 is a tautology. When we have done all that, we will have shown that SL is a Boolean algebra according to our original definition.

One rather pleasing consequence of all this is that the translation of the Boolean $<$ into the SL connective $\supset$ comes out exactly right. Even the somewhat paradoxical SL tautologies hold. For example, in Boolean algebra, $0 < X$, for any X. In SL terms this becomes $\mathbf{f} \supset X$, for any statement X. As we discussed in chapter 4, a contradiction entails every statement, so $\mathbf{f} \supset X$ is bound to be a tautology. (Note: the other form is $(P \ \& \sim P) \supset X$.)

To show that the Boolean arithmetic of 0 and 1 is a Boolean algebra we follow a similar strategy. First we equate the Boolean arithmetic, which we shall call **A**, with the components of **B**.

A	B
$\{0, 1\}$	elements of B
$X + Y$	$X \cup Y$
$X \times Y$	$X \cap Y$
$1 - X$	X'
$X = Y$	$X \approx Y$
0	0
1	1
$X \leqslant Y$	$X < Y$

Note $X \leqslant Y$ in Boolean arithmetic **A** means X is less than or equal to Y. When we substitute Boolean arithmetic symbols in a Boolean algebra formula, we get its *A-form*. Then we show that = (meaning 'is equal to') is an equivalence relation by showing that in Boolean arithmetic **A**:

A 2.1 reflexivity $X = X$
A 2.2 symmetry: if $X = Y$, then $Y = X$
A 2.3 transitivity: if $X = Y$ and $Y = Z$, then $X = Z$

And finally we show that the A-form of P1–P17 all hold for Boolean arithmetic (we have already discussed this point on pp. 285–286).

To show that the logic of the subsets of a set (called a **field of sets**) is a Boolean algebra is to show that a slightly modified version of what we have called Boole's system is itself a Boolean algebra.[11] The essential difference is how the special set **1** is understood. Boole himself called **1** the 'universe' or 'everything', which has a certain intuitive appeal. He then thought of his system representing the general logic of sets, of whatever size. But the problem in this attractive view is that without much fiddling it becomes paradoxical.[12] For example, how could there be a set B of the elements of the Boolean algebra if **1** is both the universe *and* a member of B? How could the universe be a member of anything? On the other hand, if we think of **1** as just *some set* (of whatever type and membership) and the variables of Boole's system (the elements of the set B) as the *subsets* of **1**, then a consistent and paradox-free interpretation of Boolean algebra is available for Boolean set theory.

Here, then, are the steps in showing that the logic of the field of sets **FS** is a Boolean algebra:

Let **1** be a set, and let **0** be the empty set:

FS	B
{1, its subsets, 0}	elements of B
$X \oplus Y$	$X \cup Y$
$X \cdot Y$	$X \cap Y$
X'	X'
$X = Y$	$X \approx Y$
0	0
1	1
$X \subset Y$	$X < Y$

Note: The formula $X \subset Y$ in the logic of a field of sets **FS** means 'X is a subset of Y.' Let the **FS** form of a formula **X** of **B** be the result of interchanging the symbols as above. Next we must show that = (now meaning 'is the same set as') is an equivalence relation as follows:

FS2.1 reflexivity: $X = X$
FS2.2 symmetry: if $X = Y$, then $Y = X$
FS2.3 transitivity: if $X = Y$ and $Y = Z$, then $X = Z$

Finally, we have to show that the **FS** form each of P1–P15 is a theorem of the logic of the field of sets. Take P11, $X \cap 1 \approx X$ as an example. In **FS** form it would be $X \cdot 1 = X$, a familiar Boolean principle. Clearly, if X is a subset of **1**, then the logical multiplication of X and **1** can only be X itself. So the **FS** form of P11 holds in a field of sets.

---

[11]See T. Hailperin, *Boole's Logic*, chapter 2.
[12]See Paul R. Halmos, *Naive Set Theory* (New York: McGraw-Hill, 1960).

The operator ⊂ in **FS** has exactly the properties of the intuitive subset relation. Each of the following holds, for example, for any set **X**:

(1) 0 ⊂ **X**
(2) **X** ⊂ 1
(3) **X** ⊂ **X**
(4) If **X** ⊂ **Y** and **Y** ⊂ **Z**, then **X** ⊂ **Z**

The standard definition of '*A* is a subset of *B*' is that any member of *A* is a member of *B*. Under this definition, the empty set **0** is a subset of every set, since it trivially satisfies the definition. Any set **X** of **a field of sets** is, of course, a subset of **1**; every set is also a subset of itself according to the definition. And the subset relation is, of course, transitive.

Boole's concept of original *complement* essentially involved his notion of a universe, **1**. So it may not be clear how the operator ' is to be interpreted in a field of sets in postulates such as P9, P12, P14, and so on, when **1** is understood as any set at all. What is needed is the concept of **relative complement,** as a way of understanding formulas such as *X'* in a field of sets. As an illustration, let **1** be the set $\{1, 2, 3, 4, 5\}$, let the other members of *B* be the 2^5 subsets of **1** (all the subsets of a set include the set itself and **0**, the empty set). Suppose *X* is $\{1,2\}$. Then *X'*, the *relative* complement of *X*, is the set of all those things in **1** which are not in *X*, i.e. $X' = \{3, 4, 5\}$. With this understanding it is easy to show that the postulates in which ' occurs are true in a field of sets.

It remains to show that Boolean monadic PL (syllogistic) is a subsystem of the logic of a field of sets with inequalities. Remember, categorical statements use only logical multiplication, complementation, equality/inequality, and the empty set **0**. These are all part of a field of sets in essentially the same sense as Boole's system originally formulates them, with the proviso that complements are understood in a relative sense. So, what should we make out of a typical categorical statement like 'All dogs are mammals'? Let the set **1** be such that both the set of dogs and the set of mammals are subsets, 'animals', for example, or 'vertebrates', or even 'objects'. Using a wide set like 'objects' allows for practically any syllogism to be formulated with subsets of the set of objects as the predicates, except of course a syllogism containing the statement 'All objects occupy space'; but then we can shift to an even wider set like 'existents', which might include abstract things like numbers, properties, and moments of time. Thus, without much fiddling, Boolean syllogistic will nicely fit into **FS** and hence into a Boolean algebra with inequalities.

Summary

This section developed Boole's system into an abstract formalism called a **Boolean algebra** and then showed that the Boolean arithmetic of 1 and 0, SL, and the logic of a field of sets **FS** are all Boolean algebras.

A Boolean algebra is any system **B** with the following components:

1. A set B of elements.

2. An equivalence relation $\approx$ defined on the elements of B.
   An *equivalence relation* is any two-place relation that satisfies the following laws:
   2.1 reflexivity: $\mathbf{X} \approx \mathbf{X}$
   2.2 symmetry: if $\mathbf{X} \approx \mathbf{Y}$, then $\mathbf{Y} \approx \mathbf{X}$
   2.3 transitivity: if $\mathbf{X} \approx \mathbf{Y}$ and $\mathbf{Y} \approx \mathbf{Z}$, then $\mathbf{X} \approx \mathbf{Z}$

3. A one-place operator ' ('inversion') defined on the elements of B so that if X is an element of B, so is X'.

4. The two-place operators $\cap$ ('meet') and $\cup$ ('join') defined on the elements of B so that if X and Y are in B, so are $X \cap Y$ and $X \cup Y$.

5. The two designated elements of B: **0** and **1**.

B must also satisfy the fifteen postulates P1–P15 listed on page 302.

EXERCISES 8.4c

1. Suppose **B** were formulated with a postulate of duality according to which if A is a theorem of **B** so is A_D, where A_D is the dual of A. How could you shorten the list of postulates P1–P15 if this rule were available?

2. Show that the **FS**-form of P2, P5, and P10 are theorems of the logic of a field of sets.

3. Show that $\leqslant$ in system **A** has the properties appropriate to the Boolean arithmetic relation 'is less than or equal to'. (Hint: First figure out what properties 'is less than or equal to' has and then show that $\leqslant$ in system **A** has them all.)

4. Why isn't Boolean syllogistic a Boolean algebra?

5. Why isn't PL a Boolean algebra?

9

Numerical Systems

*I*n this chapter we will study the fundamental properties of numerical systems, the ways in which numbers are represented. Then we turn more detailed attention to the **binary system,** which has played a crucial role in the development of computers. The circuits of any digital computer have two fundamental states: on and off.[1] Since these states exactly correspond to the binary digits **1** and **0,** electronic representation of numbers is possible by means of the binary numerical system.

In chapter 8 we studied Boolean systems, which provide a common link between statement logic, monadic predicate logic, the theory of sets, and a very restricted kind of arithmetic. In this chapter we will see that when numbers are represented in terms of the binary digits, those same Boolean principles are at work once again.[2] All of this prepares the way for our discussion of the connections between logic and computers in chapters 10, 11, and 12.

---

[1]As we will discuss in chapter 10, these states are more accurately described as high voltage and low voltage, but the point remains.

[2]In the computer world, either of the characters 1 and 0 is sometimes referred to as a *bit* of information; the term originates from the first and final two letters of *binary digit*.

9.1 NUMERICAL SYSTEMS

We all know the difference between **numerals,** which represent numbers, and the numbers themselves, although we rarely need to pay much attention to the distinction. Numerals are symbols for numbers: the Romans developed the symbols we know as **Roman numerals**—*I, IV, MCLIX,* and so forth—and the medieval Indian and Arabic world gave us our familiar **Arabic numerals**—*1, 2, 3,* etc.

In addition to the symbols themselves, numerals come in systems. We use the **decimal numerical system,** which was developed in the Middle East and Europe. Other cultures use other systems: the Maya, for example, used a base-20 numerical system; the Babylonians and other ancient people used a base-60 system. Many cultures have been limited by the lack of words or symbols for specific numbers. That one can move back and forth between different numerical systems is not a modern discovery. The traders of the ancient world brought goods from Asia and Africa to Europe and back again and had to deal not only with very different monetary systems but with different numerical systems and, hence, with different arithmetics as well.

The point that numerals represent numbers is important. Numerals are concrete things, we can write them and we have words for them; numbers, however, are abstract. Notice too that

$$3 - 1 \qquad 2^1 \qquad 147 - 145$$

are all expressions which represent the same number (two) within our familiar system. As it turns out, there may be an infinite number of ways to represent any given number while staying inside the same numerical system. Our system is called the *decimal* or *base-10* system because it uses the ten basic numerical symbols *0, 1, 2, 3, 4, 5, 6, 7, 8, 9* and works out the representation of numbers on the basis of powers of ten. By varying the number of basic symbols, we can create different numerical systems.

The representation of numbers larger than 9, in the decimal system, uses the concept of **place.** The development of this concept was a great innovation, for with a few symbols any number can be represented. Each place in the decimal system is a *power* of 10, beginning with the right-most place. For example, the number 485 can be thought of as follows in the decimal system:

4	8	5
hundreds place	tens place	ones place

What this, of course, means is that the number 485 is the sum of $400 + 80 + 5$; in other words, 4 hundreds + 8 tens + 5 ones.

The first few powers of ten are as follows:

$10^0 = 1$ (unit)
$10^1 = 10$ (ten)
$10^2 = 100$ (hundred)
$10^3 = 1000$ (thousand)
$10^4 = 10000$ (ten thousand)
$10^5 = 100000$ (hundred thousand)

The easy way to remember the powers of ten is by counting the 0's following the 1: 10^5 has five 0's, 10^2 has two 0's, and 10^0 has no 0's, and so is just 1; so powers of 10 have the same number of 0's as the exponent.

Thus, according to the decimal mode of representation, 485 can be thought of in the following way:

$$485 = (4 \times 10^2) + (8 \times 10^1) + (5 \times 10^0)$$
$$\quad\quad (400) \quad\quad\quad (80) \quad\quad\quad (5)$$

hundreds   tens   unit
place   place   place

Here is another, slightly more complicated, example:

$$10{,}974 = (1 \times 10^4) + (0 \times 10^3) + (9 \times 10^2) + (7 \times 10^1) + (4 \times 10^0)$$
$$\quad\quad (10{,}000) \quad\quad (0) \quad\quad\quad (900) \quad\quad\quad (70) \quad\quad\quad (4)$$

ten thousands   thousands   hundreds   tens   ones
place   place   place   place   place

It is possible to state a general rule for this procedure, using $a_1, a_2, a_3, \ldots,$ a_n ($n \geqslant 1$) as variables for the specific numerals in the various places in any decimal system number. If $a_3 a_2 a_1$ represents 485, then a_3 is the numeral 4; a_2 is the numeral 8; and a_1 is the numeral 5. The general rule for decimal system representation can be stated as follows:

$$a_n a_{n-1} a_{n-2} \ldots a_1 = (a_n \times 10^{n-1}) + (a_{n-1} \times 10^{n-2}) + (a_{n-2} \times 10^{n-3}) + \ldots + (a_1 \times 10^0)$$

EXERCISES 9.1a

1. Write out the following in the expanded base-10 exponent style.

   a. 1,234

   b. 56

   c. 122

   d. 1,008

   e. 23,050

2. What numbers do the following represent?

   a. $(3 \times 10^4) + (1 \times 10^3) + (0 \times 10^2) + (0 \times 10^1) + (4 \times 10^0)$

   b. $(8 \times 10^3) + (2 \times 10^2) + (9 \times 10^1) + (0 \times 10^0)$

   c. $(0 \times 10^4) + (0 \times 10^3) + (3 \times 10^2) + (0 \times 10^1) + (9 \times 10^0)$

*3. How might decimal fractions be handled in terms of exponents of 10? Rewrite the rule to cover numbers containing decimal fractions.

If you think of the odometer on a new car, when the mileage indicator gets to *9*, the next mile replaces the *9* with a *0*, and the right place on the dial starts over. But in the second place, a *1* appears, and, then, when *9* again appears in the first place, the *1* will be replaced by a *2*, and so on. This is a feature of counting in all numerical systems. After all of the basic numerals are used, there is a shift to the next place and the count in the first place begins over again. This shift to the next place is called the **carry,** and we all do this very consciously ourselves when adding lists of numbers.

To further explore how numerical systems work, let's look at the *base-8*, or *octal system*. In this system there are only eight basic numerals *0, 1, 2, 3, 4, 5, 6,* and *7.* Use of the system requires a table of the powers of 8; here are the first few entries:

$$8^0 = 1$$
$$8^1 = 8$$
$$8^2 = 64$$
$$8^3 = 512$$
$$8^4 = 4096$$
$$8^5 = 32768$$

To avoid confusion in our discussion of different numerical systems, boldface type will be used for numerals in systems other than our familiar base-10 numerical system. If there is any possibility of confusion as to which numerical system is represented, a subscript will be used, as in $\mathbf{23}_8$, which means the numeral **23** in the base-8 system.

Representation of numbers in base-8 follows the same pattern as the decimal system. To represent numbers from 0 to 7 in base-8, we use the same numeral we use in the decimal system, e.g.

$$7 = 7 \times 8^0$$

Numbers larger than 7, however, require moving to the second place and beyond; the number 8 in the base-8 system is **10**. (Recall the odometer: when we run out of numerals in the first place we go to the second place.) Beyond 7, numbers are written in terms of multiples of the powers of 8. Let's work through 36 to see how this goes:

$$36 = (4 \times 8^1) + (4 \times 8^0)$$

So we have found that 36 is (4×8^1) plus (4×8^0). In the first place, then, we will have **4** and in the second place we also have **4,** so 36, expressed in base-8, is **44.** That is,

$$44_8 = 36(\text{decimal}) = (4 \times 8^1) + (4 \times 8^0)$$

Now we will try the larger number 4,071. Obviously we need a more systematic method for expressing decimal numbers in terms of powers of 8. A simple system for accomplishing this is to first locate our number on the scale of the powers of 8 as given in the table above. Since 4,071 is between $8^3 \, (= 512)$ and $8^4 \, (= 4,096)$, the next step is to divide by the smaller of these, 8^3, and note the remainder.

$$4,071 / 512 = 7 \quad \text{remainder } 487$$

Next, repeat the same step with the remainder by dividing it by its next smallest power of 8, which is $8^2 \, (= 64)$.

$$487 / 64 = 7 \quad \text{remainder } 39$$

Next, divide the remainder by its next smaller power, which is $8^1 \, (= 8)$:

$$39 / 8 = 4 \quad \text{remainder } 7$$

Since we have reached a remainder smaller than 8, we now have all the information we need:

$$4,071 = (7 \times 8^3) + (7 \times 8^2) + (4 \times 8^1) + (7 \times 8^0)$$

So the base-8 representation of 4,071 is **7747.**

To go the other way, from base-8 to base-10, we take the base-8 expression, for example **675,** and multiply the numeral in each place by the appropriate power of 8:

$$
\begin{aligned}
675_8 &= (6 \times 8^2) + (7 \times 8^1) + (5 \times 8^0) \\
&= 384 + 56 + 5 \\
&= 445
\end{aligned}
$$

Summary

In this section, we have discussed the decimal and octal numerical systems. **Numerals** are distinct from **numbers** and are part of **representation systems.** Numerical systems are arranged around a certain **base;** the familiar system we use is the **base-10** or **decimal system.** The decimal system uses ten (Arabic) numerals and numbers larger than 9 are represented by means of **place.** In any numerical system, each place is a multiple of a power of the base; the right-most place is a multiple of the base with exponent 0, the next place is a multiple of the base with exponent 1, etc.

EXERCISES 9.1b

1. What is the base-8 representation of each of the following?

   a. 53

   b. 233

   c. 64002

2. What do these base-8 expressions equal in the decimal system?

   a. 56

   b. 112

   c. 1203

*3. What is the base-5 representation of each of the following?

   a. 23

   b. 3002

   c. 421

9.2 THE BINARY SYSTEM

The **binary,** or base-2, numerical system uses only the numerals **0** and **1,** and place values correspond to powers of 2. For reference, here is a list of some of the powers of 2:

$$2^0 = 1$$
$$2^1 = 2$$
$$2^2 = 4$$
$$2^3 = 8$$
$$2^4 = 16$$
$$2^5 = 32$$
$$2^6 = 64$$
$$2^7 = 128$$
$$2^8 = 256$$
$$2^9 = 512$$
$$2^{10} = 1028$$
$$2^{11} = 2056$$
$$2^{12} = 4112$$

To represent a number in binary notation, we express it in the now-familiar form of multiples of the powers of the base, in this case 2. The following chart is of the binary equivalents of the decimal numbers 0 to 10.

Decimal Form	Expansion in Powers of 2	Binary Form
0	0×2^0	0
1	1×2^0	1
2	$1 \times 2^1 + 0 \times 2^0$	10
3	$1 \times 2^1 + 1 \times 2^0$	11
4	$1 \times 2^2 + 0 \times 2^1 + 0 \times 2^0$	100
5	$1 \times 2^2 + 0 \times 2^1 + 1 \times 2^0$	101
6	$1 \times 2^2 + 1 \times 2^1 + 0 \times 2^0$	110
7	$1 \times 2^2 + 1 \times 2^1 + 1 \times 2^0$	111
8	$1 \times 2^3 + 0 \times 2^2 + 0 \times 2^1 + 0 \times 2^0$	1000
9	$1 \times 2^3 + 0 \times 2^2 + 0 \times 2^1 + 0 \times 2^0$	1001
10	$1 \times 2^3 + 0 \times 2^2 + 1 \times 2^1 + 0 \times 2^0$	1010

Shortcut Procedure for Converting from Decimal to Binary

There is a very simple shortcut procedure for converting decimal (whole) numbers into binary form. The trick is to divide progressively by 2 and note whether the remainder is 1 or 0. Begin with the decimal number, for example, 29. Draw a line and write the number under it on the right side, as below. Divide by 2, and write the answer (14) below and slightly to the left, write the remainder (1) above the line. Then divide the answer (14) by 2. Write the answer to this second division below and to the left, write the remainder (0) above the line. Continue until you reach 0 (Note: 1 divided by 2 = 0, remainder 1). The number above the line is the binary equivalent of the original. So the binary equivalent of 29 is **11101**.

Example

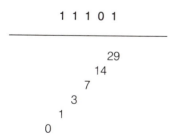

The **decimal point** in the base-10 system represents a convenient method of recording fractional amounts (which, within the base-10 system, are themselves called 'decimals'); the denominators are, of course, all powers of 10. So, for example, .01 is 1/100; .001 is 1/1000; and .34 is 34/100, or $34 \times 1/100$ or 34×10^{-2}. Similar principles are used to represent decimal fractions in the binary system. The values of the first few negative exponential powers of 2 are:

$2^{-1} = 1/2$
$2^{-2} = 1/4$
$2^{-3} = 1/8$
$2^{-4} = 1/16$
$2^{-5} = 1/32$
$2^{-6} = 1/64$

Thus, 1/2 in binary form is **.1,** which means 1×2^{-1}, and the fraction 1/4 is **.01,** which is 1×2^{-2}, or, $0 \times 2^{-1} + 1 \times 2^{-2}$.

Here is a table that gives the binary form of all of decimal fractions with 8 as denominator.

Decimal Form	Expansion in Powers of 2	Binary Form
1/8	$0 \times 2^{-1} + 0 \times 2^{-2} + 1 \times 2^{-3}$	**.001**
1/4	$0 \times 2^{-1} + 1 \times 2^{-2} + 0 \times 2^{-3}$	**.010**
3/8	$0 \times 2^{-1} + 1 \times 2^{-2} + 1 \times 2^{-3}$	**.011**
1/2	$1 \times 2^{-1} + 0 \times 2^{-2} + 0 \times 2^{-3}$	**.100**
5/8	$1 \times 2^{-1} + 0 \times 2^{-2} + 1 \times 2^{-3}$	**.101**
3/4	$1 \times 2^{-1} + 1 \times 2^{-2} + 0 \times 2^{-3}$	**.110**
7/8	$1 \times 2^{-1} + 1 \times 2^{-2} + 1 \times 2^{-3}$	**.111**

If we wanted to represent 29.25 in binary form, then, we would have the following:

$29.25 = 11101.01$

Summary

The **binary** or **base-2** numerical system uses the numerals **1** and **0**. Each place is a multiple of a power of 2, in accord with the now-familiar pattern. Fractional amounts are represented by multiples of negative powers of 2; the negative exponent indicating 1 divided by that power of 2. So 2^{-2} is equal to $1/2^2$ or 1/4. Hence **.1** binary equals 1×2^{-1}.

EXERCISES 9.2

1. Write the following decimal numbers in binary form.

a. 63

b. 671

  c. 4

  d. 982

  e. 1,309

2. Write the following binary numerals in decimal form.

  a. 101

  b. 1001100

  c. 1111

  d. 10101010

  e. 10

*3. Explain how the short-cut procedure for converting decimals into binary form works. Would a similar procedure work for converting from the decimal system into other numerical systems? Explain.

4. How might fractional amounts be represented in the octal system?

9.3 BINARY ARITHMETIC[3]

Since the binary system has only the basic numerals **1** and **0**, there are relatively few things to know about addition, subtraction, and multiplication. Here are the binary arithmetic facts:

Addition	Subtraction	Multiplication
$1 + 1 = 10$	$1 - 1 = 0$	$1 \times 1 = 1$
$1 + 0 = 1$	$1 - 0 = 1$	$1 \times 0 = 0$
$0 + 1 = 1$	$10 - 1 = 1$	$0 \times 1 = 0$
$0 + 0 = 0$	$0 - 0 = 0$	$0 \times 0 = 0$

The *binary* addition and multiplication tables are very similar to the truth tables for $\vee$ and &, and are essentially the familiar Boolean logical addition and logical multiplication operations we studied in the last chapter, except for $1 + 1 = 10$. Recall that in the Boolean arithmetic **A,** *only* the single-place symbols 1 and 0 are available, so $1 + 1 = 1$ in that system of arithmetic. But in the binary numerical system, we are able to carry to the next place, so $1 + 1$ equals **0** with a carry of **1.**

The first three entries of the subtraction table also follow Boolean principles as long as subtraction is defined as logical multiplication of the min-

---

[3]A particularly good survey is found in Thomas C. Bartee, *Digital Computer Fundamentals*, 6th ed. (New York: McGraw-Hill, 1987), chapter 2.

uend (the first number) with the Boolean complement of the subtrahend (i.e., the number to be subtracted) as follows:

Boolean	Binary Subtraction
$1 \cdot 1' = 0$	$1 - 1 = 0$
$1 \cdot 0' = 1$	$1 - 0 = 0$
$0 \cdot 0' = 0$	$0 - 0 = 0$

The final subtraction entry involves the carry digit, which is not part of the Boolean system, so there is no exact Boolean equivalent. But the formula that would be entered in that place in the Boolean table is $0 - 1 = 0$ (i.e., $0 \cdot 1' = 0$), and if the carry digit is added to the answer, we do get 1. Thus all the binary arithmetic facts can be thought of as fundamentally Boolean.

The carry digits in binary addition follow the same principles they follow in decimal addition. For example, to add the binary form of $55 + 17 + 26$,

```
    1  0  1  1  1  1        ◄──── carries
       1  1  0  1  1  1              55
       1  0  0  0  1              17
  (+)  1  1  0  1  0              26
    ─────────────────              ──
    1  1  0  0  0  1  0              98
```

The fifth column from the right, which adds four **1**'s (including the carry), may need some explanation. From the preceding column we had **1** (the carry) $+ 0 + 0 + 1$, which gave us **0** and a carry of **1**. So, in the fifth column, we have **1** (the carry) $+ 1$ (the top digit) which gives **0** with a carry of **1**. Then that **0** is added to the next **1**, which gives **1**. Then that **1** is added to the next **1**, which gives **0**, with a carry of **1**. The second carry of **1** is added to the first carry of **1**, to give a carry of **10**. The **1** of this carry falls into a new column, the **0** of this carry is added to the top digit, which yields **1**. So the carries are added just like the original digits, with further carrying to the left as necessary.

In binary subtraction, the borrowing process is essentially the same as it is in ordinary arithmetic. Here is an example of $55 - 26$:

```
       0  1              ◄──── carries
    1  1  0  1  1  1                    55
 (−)   1  1  0  1  0              (−) 26
  ─────────────────                    ──
    1  1  1  0  1                    29
```

Since $0 - 1$ is not defined in binary arithmetic, a **1** must be borrowed in the fourth column from the right, so we have $10 - 1$. This, then, makes the fifth column $0 - 1$, so another borrow from the sixth column is required. This procedure follows the rules for decimal borrowing. Recall that if a 1 is borrowed, the digit is reduced by 1. But if the digit is a 0, then it becomes a 9, and a borrow is made from the digit to the left. In the binary case, borrowing from a **0** turns it into a **1** and a **1** has to be borrowed from the digit to its left. Note what happens in the following two cases:

```
      1  0  0                    1  1  0
(−)   1  1              (−)      1  1
   ───────                    ──────────
         1                       1  1
```

Binary multiplication, on the other hand, presents no difficulties at all. The steps are exactly those of decimal multiplication. Here are two examples (the first inserts lines for the two cases of multiplying by **0**).

```
(a)                  1  1  1  0  1
      (×)            1  0  0  1
                 ─────────────────
                     1  1  1  0  1
               0  0  0  0  0
            0  0  0  0  0
         1  1  1  0  1
         ───────────────────────
         1  0  0  0  0  0  1  0  1


(b)                  1  1  1  0  1
      (×)            1  0  1  0  0
                 ─────────────────
                  1  1  1  0  1  0  0
            1  1  1  0  1
         ──────────────────────────
         1  0  0  1  0  0  0  1  0  0
```

The second example (b) shows how binary numbers with terminal **0**'s are handled in multiplication.

The procedures for binary division are also the same as in ordinary arithmetic. Here is an example.

```
                              1  0  1
         ─────────────────────────────
1  1  0  1  0 ) 1  0  0  0  0  0  1  0
               1  1  0  1  0
               ───────────────
               0  0  1  1  0  1  0
                     1  1  0  1  0
```

Summary

Binary arithmetic is simple because there are just the two numerals **1** and **0**. The addition and multiplication facts are essentially Boolean; even subtraction follows Boolean procedures. The difference is that the sum of **1** and **1** is **10** in the binary system; and in the subtraction table, **10** minus **1** equals **1**. The extra digit in each of these two cases requires that, in addition and subtraction, we keep track of carries and borrowing. Multiplication and division are essentially the same as their decimal forms.

EXERCISES 9.3

1. Add the following:

   a. 111110
      10001
      ‾‾‾‾‾‾

   b. 10101
         11
      ‾‾‾‾‾‾

   c. 100011
      111101
      ‾‾‾‾‾‾

2. Multiply the following:

   a. 1101
        11
      ‾‾‾‾‾

   b. 11001
       1001
      ‾‾‾‾‾

   c. 11001
       1100
      ‾‾‾‾‾

3. Subtract the following:

   a. 1101
        11
      ‾‾‾‾‾

   b. 11001
       1001
      ‾‾‾‾‾

   c. 11001
       1100
      ‾‾‾‾‾

4. Perform the indicated divisions:

   a. 1101/11

   b. 11001/1001

   c. 11001/1100

9.4 THE HEXADECIMAL SYSTEM[4]

Keeping track of binary digits is tedious; few people can quickly spot the difference between **100000111** and **10000111,** for example, yet the first of these

_____

[4]Material in this section is from William H. Gothmann, *Digital Electronics,* (Englewood Cliffs, NJ: Prentice-Hall, 1982), chapter 2.

Binary	Hexadecimal	Decimal
0000	0	0
0001	1	1
0010	2	2
0011	3	3
.	.	.
1001	9	9
1010	A	10
1011	B	11
1100	C	12
1101	D	13
1110	E	14
1111	F	15
1 0000	10	16
.	.	.
1 0101	15	21
1 1000	18	24
1 1001	19	25
1 1010	1A	26
.	.	.
1100 1100	CC	202

is 519 (decimal), and the second is 263. And imagine trying to use binary numerals for simple transactions, say entering your social security number into a machine. But the binary system is the coin of the realm of computer systems, as we will see in chapters 10, 11, and 12. For this reason, a very useful numerical system is the **hexadecimal, base-16** system because of the ease with which binary numerals can be *directly represented*.

As you have learned, the numbers from 0 to 15 can be represented in four binary digits **(bits), 0000** to **1111.** In a base-16 numerical system, where *each place* is occupied by numerals having values from 0 to 15, exactly four binary digits are represented by *each* hexadecimal digit. This feature is especially valuable in the computer world, where binary digit groupings tend to be standardized as four, eight, twelve, sixteen, or thirty-two. As we will see in chapters 10 and 12, the very wires in computers are grouped in this manner.

The hexadecimal system requires sixteen numerals. The first ten can be familiar Arabic numerals **0, 1, . . . , 9.** Beyond **9,** however, other symbols must be used. The capital letters **A, B, C, D, E,** and **F** are commonly used, in that order. Above is a table showing hexadecimal numbers, with binary and decimals for comparison.

Binary numerals are easy to convert to hexadecimal; each group of four binary digits receives its own hexadecimal numeral. The steps in the conversion are illustrated in the following examples:

Example 1 Convert **1010111010** to hexadecimal.

Step (a) Group the binary digits into fours, from the right:

10   1011   1010

Step (b) Assign each group the appropriate hexadecimal numeral:

2   B   A

The answer is **2BA.**

Example 2 Convert **11011110101110** to hexadecimal.

Step (a) Group the binary digits into fours, starting at the right:

11   0111   1010   1110

Step (b) Assign each group the appropriate hexadecimal numeral:

3   7   A   E

The answer is **37AE.**

Converting from hexadecimal to binary is just the reverse. Each hexadecimal digit is translated into a four-digit binary group. Here are two examples:

Example 3 Convert **4A8C** to binary.

Match each numeral with its group:

4	A	8	C
110	1010	1000	1100

The answer is **110101010001100.**

Note that hexadecimal **4** was matched with **110,** instead of **0110,** because we can ignore the initial **0.**

Example 4   Convert **FACE** to binary.

Match each numeral with its group:

F	A	C	E
1111	1010	1100	1110

The answer is **1111101011001110.**

Converting hexadecimal to decimal system numbers is done by treating each hexadecimal place as a multiple of a power of 16. Here is a table of the first few powers of 16:

$16^0 = 1$
$16^1 = 16$
$16^2 = 256$
$16^3 = 4{,}096$
$16^4 = 65{,}536$

To use the same two examples again:

Example 5   Convert **4A8C** to decimal.

$$(4 \times 16^3) + (10 \times 16^2) + (8 \times 16^1) + (12 \times 16^0)$$
$$= 16{,}384 + 2{,}560 + 128 + 12$$
$$= 19{,}084$$

Example 6   Convert **FACE** to decimal.

$$(15 \times 16^3) + (10 \times 16^2) + (12 \times 16^1) + (14 \times 16^0)$$
$$= 61{,}440 + 2560 + 192 + 14$$
$$= 64{,}206$$

Finally, to go from decimal to hexadecimal, the procedure of successive division by the base (16) is used, with the remainders converted to hexadecimal numerals (see section 9.3).

Example 7   Convert 423 to hexadecimal:

```
    1 10 7              ◄──── remainders
  _____

          423           /16
       26
      1
    0
```

The answer is **1A7.**

Example 8   Convert 72,905 to hexidecimal:

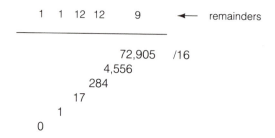

The answer is **11CC9**.

EXERCISES 9.4

1. Convert the following binary numbers to hexadecimal:
   a. 11010   c. 100001
   b. 1101111   d. 011101110111011
2. Convert the following hexadecimal numbers to binary:
   a. 14AB   c. AADD3
   b. 6A27   d. 7810D
3. Convert each of the examples in exercise 2 into decimal numbers.
4. Convert each of the following decimal numbers to hexadecimal:
   a. 5,678   c. 7,801
   b. 23   d. 623,451
*5. How would addition of hexadecimal numbers work?

*9.5 THE COMPLEMENT SYSTEM OF SUBTRACTION

In chapter 12 we will show how an electronic binary addition circuit ('a binary adder') can be built out of logic components. It is also possible to construct a subtracting circuit, but given the complexity of borrowing that binary subtraction requires, a simpler procedure is to use the addition circuit to also perform subtraction. In this section we will see how to subtract by means of adding **numerical complements.**

In any numerical system, the *complement* of a number is formed by subtracting each digit of the number from the base-minus-1 of the number system and then adding 1 to the least significant digit (i.e., right-most digit) of the result. This process is essentially the same as the Boolean complementation from chapter 8, except that in a Boolean arithmetical complement, the **1** would not be added because it is a one-digit system. But recall the *relative complement* in the Boolean theory of sets; numerical complements match that concept exactly. The complement of a decimal number is called the **10's complement** and the complement of a binary number is called the **2's complement.**

To see how all this works in the decimal system, note that we are subtracting *each digit* from 9 (the base minus 1) and then adding 1 to the result. We will use **COM** to mean the complement of a number. Here are several examples of 10's complements:

COM 4   = 6   (i.e., (9 − 4) + 1)
COM 34   = 66   (i.e., (99 − 34) + 1)
COM 117 = 883   (i.e., (999 − 117) + 1)
COM 1207 = 8793   (i.e., (9,999 − 1207) + 1)

One of the handy properties of the **COM** operation in the decimal system is that it can be performed from left to right by subtracting each digit in turn from 9 and then adding 1 to the last digit. The only complication is that the **COM** operation is always performed relative to a certain number of digits. While 004 and 4 represent the same number, their 10's complements are 996 and 6, respectively. Strictly speaking, a subscript should be attached to **COM** to indicate the number of digits involved. For example, $\text{COM}_1 \, 4 = 6$ and $\text{COM}_3 \, 4 = 996$.

We can perform complement subtraction by adding the minuend of the subtraction problem (i.e., the first number) to the COM_n of the subtrahend (i.e., the number to be subtracted from the first), where n is the number of digits in the minuend, *and then dropping the carry digit, if any.* Here are some examples in the decimal system:

Normal subtraction	10's complement subtraction
89	89
− 23	+ 77
66	166
drop the carry	= 66
114	114
− 27	+ 973
87	1087
drop the carry	= 87

(Note: because 114 has three digits, we must use $\text{COM}_3 \, 27 \, (= 973)$ rather than $\text{COM}_2 \, 27 \, (= 73)$).

Now that you have seen this procedure in action, you may be wondering how it works. Subtraction by complements takes advantage of the following principle: let M be the minuend of the subtraction problem (i.e., the first number), and let S be the subtrahend (i.e., the number to be subtracted from the first); the problem then is $M - S$. It is clear that for any number P

$$M - S = (M + (P - S)) - P$$

Now set $P = 10^n$, where n is the number of digits in the minuend (i.e., M). So $P - S$ is just the 10's complement of S, carried out to n digits. So we add M and $P - S$. Then, by subtracting P from the sum, we are just taking off the carry digit. Thus, in the first problem above, 89 minus 23: $M = 89$, $S = 23$, and $P = 100$ (i.e., 10^2). So,

$$89 - 23 = (89 + (100 - 23)) - 100$$
$$89 - 23 = (89 + 77) - 100$$
$$89 - 23 = 166 - 100$$
$$= 66$$

In the binary system we will use the 2's complement of the subtrahend (number to be subtracted). This is formed by the same rule: subtract each digit from the base-minus-1 and add **1** to the least significant digit. Since the base is 2, we subtract from **1**. In practice, the rule is very simple to use; each **1** becomes a **0**, and each **0** becomes a **1**, and a **1** is added to the result. Some examples of 2's complements are:

$$\text{COM}_4\ 1101\quad = 0011\quad (= 11)$$
$$\text{COM}_6\ 1101\quad = 110011\quad (\text{Note: } 1101 = 001101)$$
$$\text{COM}_{10}\ 110110 = 1111001010$$

When forming the 2's complement of any binary number S, we first make sure that the correct number of digits are present in S by adding **0**'s to the left so that we can form the complement for the required number of digits of the problem. When we form **COM**$_6$ **1101**, we first add two **0**'s to the left to obtain **001101**. Each **0** becomes a **1**, and vice versa, **1** is added, and the result is, as above, **110011**. As before, the **COM**$_n$ operation, for any n, can be performed from left to right.

Subtraction with 2's complements is, then, addition of the minuend and the **COM**$_n$ of the subtrahend, where n is the number of digits in the minuend, with the carry digit of the sum, if any, discarded.

Normal binary subtraction	2's complement subtraction
11011	11011
− 10100	+01100
00111	100111
drop the carry =	111
10011011	10011011
− 10100	+11101100 (Note: $n = 8$)
10000111	110000111
drop the carry =	10000111

Given the nuisance of keeping track of borrows in normal binary subtraction, the 2's complement system is obviously vastly simpler. And the complement-style subtraction has the much more important feature of allowing any adding device to become a subtracting device so long as it is connected to a circuit to form appropriate complements. In computers this means that no extra subtraction program or circuitry is required, only a means of forming complements (which is a simple problem) and then adding. As we will see in chapters 10 and 12, this is just the sort of economy that makes computers so powerful.

EXERCISES 9.5

1. Convert the following to their 10's complements:

   a. 23; $n = 2$ b. 112; $n = 3$ c. 5423; $n = 4$

2. Perform the following subtractions using 10's complements:

   a. 44 − 11   c. 13 − 9   e. 137 − 3

   b. 156 − 73   d. 2002 − 43

3. Convert the following to their 2's complements:

   a. 11; $n = 2$ c. 110011; $n = 7$

   b. 1101; $n = 4$ d. 111101; $n = 7$

4. Perform the following subtractions using 2's complements:

   a. 11011 − 11   b. 1101 − 1000   c. 1101110 − 1111

5. Explain how 2's complement subtraction works.

*6. Describe 8's complements and 8's complement subtraction in the base-8 numerical system.

10

Logical Circuits

*I*n this chapter we will study the logic properties of the circuits from which computers and all similar digital electronic devices are constructed. The grand synthesis of logic, Boolean systems, binary numerals, and computers will begin to unfold.

We begin with the logic of switches because these are easy to understand and because early computers were constructed out of thousands of electric switches, or relays. With the advent of the transistor and integrated circuitry, much more efficient electronic circuits became available, and switches gave way to gated networks, which are discussed in section 10.2. The logical properties, however, remained very similar, as we will see. Our discussion will principally focus on logical features; electronic concepts will be avoided as much as possible.

10.1 SWITCHES

A switch turns the current in a circuit on and off. So, in a very obvious way, a switch is a binary device having the two values: on and off. Here is a simple illustration of an electric circuit with a switch, a battery that supplies the current, and a light controlled by the switch. You can think of this as the circuit diagram for a flashlight.

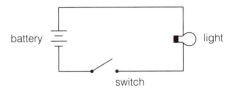

Standard symbols are used for the three components (switches are usually shown in the off or 'open' position); the lines are wires that carry the current. Assuming that everything else is normal in the circuit, the position of the switch is directly linked to the state of the light, as the following table shows.

Switch	Light
off	off
on	on

Often circuits have several switches to enable more complex control. You are probably familiar with the circuit for the interior overhead light in a car. The light can be turned on either by opening a front door or by operating the light switch on the dashboard of the car. Switches in such circuits are sometimes said to be **in parallel.** A circuit with two parallel switches is shown below.

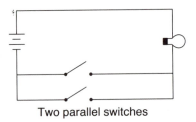

Two parallel switches

Current will flow through either switch to the light. The light will be on if the first switch is on, and it will be on if the second switch is on (and if both are on). The following table summarizes the operation of two parallel switches.

As you can see, the table is exactly the same as the truth-table for *disjunction* and the value table for Boolean logical addition, with 'on' taking the place of 'true' or **1,** and 'off' taking the place of 'false' or **0.** Thus, we can already see a connection between circuits and logic.

Remember that the car overhead light can be turned on from *three* locations: either the right or left front door and the dashboard switch. (Some

Parallel switched circuit

Switch 1	Switch 2	Light
on	on	on
on	off	on
off	on	on
off	off	off

cars have even more possibilities, but we will ignore them for now.) So the overhead light circuit consists of three switches in parallel, and the full table describing the operation of the light will have eight rows and will look like the table for $(X \lor Y) \lor Z$.

We can exploit the logical features of switches in circuits by representing the on and off conditions by means of SL sentences. For example, where X and Y are the designations for the two switches, we can represent a circuit containing two switches in parallel by means of the statement $X \lor Y$. What this representation means is that the on/off state of the circuit is given by the table for $X \lor Y$ (using on and off in place of true and false), where the X column represents the state of the X switch and the Y column represents the state of the Y switch.

It is immediately obvious that the commutative and associative rules apply to the logical representation of circuits with switches in parallel. The order of the switches makes no difference, either switch could be the top one in the above diagram; thus, $Y \lor X$ will do as well as $X \lor Y$ (commutativity). In the circuit of three parallel switches, it really doesn't matter whether the circuit is represented as $(X \lor Y) \lor Z$ or as $X \lor (Y \lor Z)$ (associativity). For simplicity, we will drop the inner parentheses in such cases, e.g., $X \lor Y \lor Z$.

Here is another circuit example from the auto world. If a car has an automatic transmission, to start the car two conditions must be met. The car must be out of gear (in either neutral or park), *and* the key must be turned to 'start'. Switches that *both* must be *on* in order for the circuit to be on are said to be **in series**. The following is a standard depiction of two series switches in a light circuit:

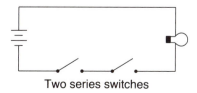

Two series switches

Notice that *both* switches must be on in order for current to flow to the light. Series switches are, then, an application of *conjunction* or Boolean logical multiplication. Using X and Y for the two switches, the table of operation is:

Series switched circuit

X	Y	Circuit
on	on	on
on	off	off
off	on	off
off	off	off

To return to the car, if the key is turned to 'start' but the shift lever is in the wrong position ('off'), then the circuit will not be on, and so the car will not start. Equally, if the key is not turned, the car won't start no matter where the shift lever is. The logical representation of two series switches in a circuit is X & Y. Once again, both commutativity and associativity hold, so when three series switches are involved, we will write X & Y & Z. Note that no matter how many switches are linked in series, all must be on for the circuit to be on. (You will be asked to draw circuits that illustrate these points in the exercises.)

You may be familiar with switches that allow a light, for example, to be completely controlled from two locations. This is a different case from the overhead light in a car; the car overhead light can be turned *on* from several locations, but can be turned *off* only if both doors are closed and the dashboard switch is off. Sitting in the driver's seat, you do not have complete control of the light; if the passenger door, for example, is open, you will have to get out and close it to shut the light off. A typical installation involving *complete* control is a stairway light controlled by switches at the bottom of the stairs and at the top.

Although we will later see that only two switches of a special kind are actually required, we will describe such circuits initially using four simple switches, two in each location. We will call the four switches X_1, X_2, Y_1, and Y_2. The basic circuit diagram, shown with all switches off, is the following:

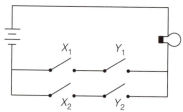

Circuit with switches at two locations

The circuit might be described as two parallel series switches. Since both X_1 and Y_1, or both X_2 and Y_2 have to be on for the current to flow through the light, the logical representation of the circuit is $(X_1 \mathbin{\&} Y_1) \vee (X_2 \mathbin{\&} Y_2)$. Since four switches are involved, the full table of possible values has sixteen lines.

X_1	X_2	Y_1	Y_2	$(X_1 \mathbin{\&} Y_1) \vee (X_2 \mathbin{\&} Y_2)$ (circuit)
on	on	on	on	on
on	on	on	off	on
on	on	off	on	on
on	on	off	off	off
on	off	on	on	on
on	off	on	off	on
on	off	off	on	off
on	off	off	off	off
off	on	on	on	on
off	on	on	off	off
off	on	off	on	on
off	on	off	off	off
off	off	on	on	off
off	off	on	off	off
off	off	off	on	off
off	off	off	off	off

Although there are sixteen possibilities for the switches, we will be interested in only *four* cases: two cases in which the circuit is on, and two in which it is off. To be able to control the light from two locations, we have to be able to turn the light on when it is turned off in the other location, and we have to be able to turn the light off when it is turned on in the other location. The trick is to be able to move the two switches at once in each location. Let's suppose that switches X_1 and X_2 are downstairs and Y_1 and Y_2 are upstairs. So by just moving X_1 and X_2, or Y_1 and Y_2, we should be able to turn the light on or off and leave the circuit in a position that will allow control in the other location. The table on the next page shows a configuration of four states that will work:

To verify that these values for the four switches will result in the light's being appropriately on or off, find the corresponding lines in the table of values. The switches in each pair move together and always have *complementary* values. (Remember from chapter 8 that complementation is negation.)

Downstairs	Upstairs	Light (circuit)
(1) X_1 = on; X_2 = off	Y_1 = on; Y_2 = off	on
(2) X_1 = on; X_2 = off	Y_1 = off; Y_2 = on	off
(3) X_1 = off; X_2 = on	Y_1 = on; Y_2 = off	off
(4) X_1 = off; X_2 = on	Y_1 = off; Y_2 = on	on

So when X_1 goes to 'on,' X_2 goes to 'off,' and so forth. Notice that starting from any of these four states, we can change either pair, and the light will have its opposite value. For example, suppose the light is off in state (2). If the upstairs switches are changed, we have state (1) with the light on, and if the downstairs switches are changed, we have state (4), with the light on. If both pairs of switches are changed simultaneously, the light remains in the state it is in, as it does when we move from state (2) to state (3).

To provide a useful means of logically describing circuits, we can use the same letter, say, X, for two switches if they both have the same value under all conditions. Where X is a switch, we can denote a switch that always has the *opposite value* as $\sim X$. So, when X is on, $\sim X$ is off, and vice versa. Since the switches in each of the pairs X_1 and X_2, and Y_1 and Y_2 are complements, a simpler analysis of the stairway light circuit is available. Note from the table that $X_1 \equiv \sim X_2$, and $Y_1 \equiv \sim Y_2$. We can represent X_1 as just X, and X_2 as $\sim X$; similarly we will let Y_1 be Y and Y_2 be $\sim Y$. This gives us the following table:

Downstairs	Upstairs	Light (circuit)
(1) X = on	Y = on	on
(2) X = on	Y = off	off
(3) X = off	Y = on	off
(4) X = off	Y = off	on

The formula represented by this table is $(X \mathbin{\&} Y) \lor (\sim X \mathbin{\&} \sim Y)$. The circuit would look like the one following. (Remember, switches are diagrammed open, even though in this case, both X and $\sim X$ cannot both be open at the same time.)

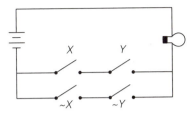

In actual practice, special switches are used that combine the complementary pairs into a single switch, called **three-way switches.** The switch itself is an arm that moves between two contacts so that it is always in a position to turn on the circuit. The standard diagram of a three-way switch depicts the arm in a neutral position (so as not to bias the switch either way), *but physically such a position is impossible:* the switch has just two positions. We will call the upper position the *positive,* and the lower the *negative,* as pictured.

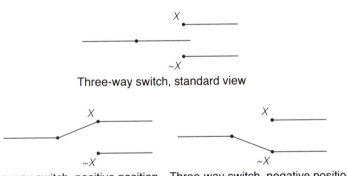

Three-way switch, standard view

Three-way switch, positive position   Three-way switch, negative position

Here is what the complete three-way switch circuit looks like:

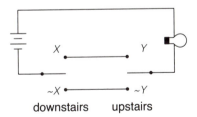

downstairs   upstairs

To further explore the workings of such a circuit, suppose you are downstairs and the light is off; here is the configuration:

Notice that by moving the X switch to the $\sim X$ position, the light will come on, and it can subsequently be turned off from either location.

Since we have already invoked negation, disjunction, and conjunction in the representation of switches and circuits, it will come as no surprise that we can graphically illustrate all of the familiar Boolean properties by means of switched-circuit diagrams. A few are below; others are found in the exercises.

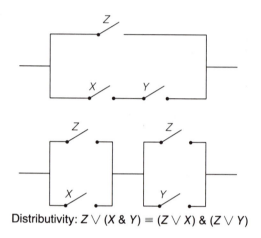

Distributivity: $Z \lor (X \ \& \ Y) \equiv (Z \lor X) \ \& \ (Z \lor Y)$

A switch in parallel with two series switches is equivalent to a series of two parallel switches, as shown above.

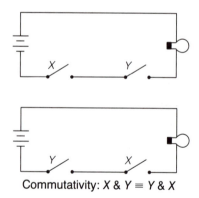

Commutativity: $X \ \& \ Y \equiv Y \ \& \ X$

Also, the order of two switches X and Y is insignificant. As we noted earlier, switches in parallel are also commutative.

When switches are linked to their complements, other basic logical principles can be represented, as the following diagrams depict:

Principle of contradiction: $X \ \& \ \sim X$

A light at the end of this circuit will always be off, because one or the other of the switches is sure to be off. On the other hand, the excluded middle, below, guarantees that the circuit will always be on. One switch will be closed in any state of the circuit.

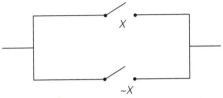

Principle of excluded middle: $X \lor \sim X$

Generally speaking, if the switches in a circuit can be represented as a *tautology*, then the circuit will be always *on*, and if a circuit can be represented by a *contradiction*, the circuit will always be *off*.

EXERCISES 10.1a

1. Use switches to design a circuit to represent each of the following:

   a. $X \lor (Y \lor Z)$

   b. $(X \& Y) \& Z$

   c. $X \lor (Y \& Z)$

   d. $X \& (Y \& Z)$

   e. $X \& (Y_1 \& ((Z_1 \& Z_2) \lor Y_2))$

2. Write the logical representation for each of the following circuits:

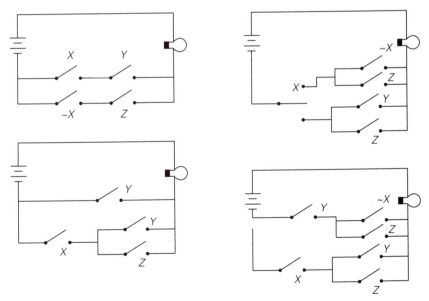

3. Give a short proof for each of the following statements:

   a. If a switch S is connected in series to a circuit that can be represented as a tautology, then the circuit will be on if and only if the switch S is on, no matter how many other switches may be involved in the circuit.
(Which logical principle is involved here?)

   b. In each of the two possible configurations (i.e., parallel and series) for connecting two equivalent switches, the circuits are the same as if a single switch were involved.
(Which logical principle is involved here?)

One of the advantages of thinking of switched circuits as having Boolean representation is that we are able to *simplify* circuits using logical principles. In practical terms, simplification means fewer materials and time and, hence, can represent significant cost reduction.

Suppose, for example, someone designed the following circuit:

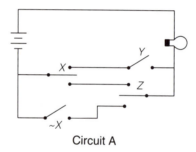

Circuit A

The initial logical representation of circuit A is

$$(X \ \& \ Y) \lor [(\sim X \ \& \ Z) \lor (\sim X \ \& \sim Z)]$$

This initial representation is read off the diagram by tracing each parallel path from the battery to the light and linking their SL representations by disjunctions. This formula obviously has a simpler form. By the law of distribution, the second disjunct, $(\sim X \ \& \ Z) \lor (\sim X \ \& \sim Z)$, is equivalent to $\sim X \ \& \ (Z \lor \sim Z)$. So the formula can be initially simplified to:

$$(X \ \& \ Y) \lor [\sim X \ \& \ (Z \lor \sim Z)]$$

But $Z \lor \sim Z$, as previously discussed, is tautologòus, and hence represents a permanently closed switch; so $\sim X \ \& \ (Z \lor \sim Z)$ is equivalent to just $\sim X$ (also by the TAUT exchange rule from chapter 4). Thus, a further simplification of the formula is possible:

$$(X \ \& \ Y) \lor \sim X$$

This reasoning shows that circuit A is thus equivalent to the following, simpler circuit:

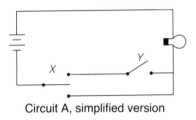

Circuit A, simplified version

The simplified version uses one three-way switch and one two-way switch while the original used two three-way switches and two two-way switches. (The original Z and ~X switches had no effect on the circuit.) Simplification has cut the materials by half.[1]

In the logical simplification of switch circuits, the goal is to eliminate as many switches as possible while retaining a logically equivalent circuit. The chain of reasoning employed invokes the exchange rules from SL such as distribution, tautology, DeMorgan's, and so forth, and takes the form of an equivalence derivation (see chapter 4, section 4.3). Finally, a circuit is drawn that is represented by the simpler formula.

As another example, we will simplify the circuit in exercises 10.1a, problem 2b.

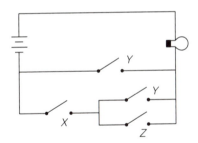

The initial representation of this circuit is $Y \lor (X \& (Y \lor Z))$. The steps in simplification are given below:

Simplify: $Y \lor (X \& (Y \lor Z))$

1.	$Y \lor (X \& (Y \lor Z))$	
2.	$(Y \lor X) \& (Y \lor (Y \lor Z))$	(DIST, 1)
3.	$(Y \lor X) \& ((Y \lor Y) \lor Z)$	(ASSC, 2)
4.	$(Y \lor X) \& (Y \lor Z)$	(TAUT, 3)
5.	$Y \lor (X \& Z)$	(DIST, 4)

---

[1] The statement $(X \& Y) \lor \sim X$ is equivalent to $Y \lor \sim X$, so a further logical simplification of the statement is also possible. But in circuits, $\sim X$ only makes sense as part of a three-way switch or by reference to another complementary switch X. So the circuit is as simple as possible.

The simplified circuit is thus:

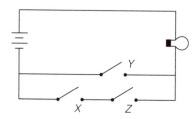

One switch is saved.

Summary

We have seen that switches in electrical circuits can be described in logical (SL or Boolean) terms. **Parallel** switches correspond to disjunctions; **series** switches correspond to conjuctions. Circuit diagrams have logical representations that can often be dramatically simplified by means of SL equivalence derivations.

EXERCISES 10.1b

1. Simplify the following and draw circuits for your simplified versions. How many switches are saved in each case?

   a. $(X \& Y) \vee (\sim X \vee \sim Y)$

   b. $(X \& Y) \vee X$

   c. $(X \& ((Y \& Z) \vee (\sim Y \& Z))) \vee (\sim X \& (Y \& Z))$

*2. Design a circuit to completely control a light from three different locations.

*3. Another version of the missionaries and cannibals problem:

   A farmer must take a dog, a goose, and a sack of corn across a river in a boat that will hold, at most, the farmer and one other thing. He has to be careful what he leaves on either shore of the river while he is crossing because, without him there, the dog will kill the goose or the goose will eat the corn.

   a. How can the crossing be accomplished without losing the goose or corn?

   b. Set up switch circuits by means of logical formulas that will turn on a light if the situation is dangerous on either shore, that is, if the dog is alone with the goose, or the goose is alone with the corn. Let F mean the farmer is on this shore and $\sim F$ that he is on the other shore, etc. One dangerous situation is $(\sim F \& G) \& (\sim D \& C)$, which means the farmer and the dog are on one shore, while the goose and corn are on the other.

c. Join the formulas together with $\vee$ and simplify.

d. Draw the simplest circuit you can for the problem.

10.2 LOGIC GATES

We now move a step closer to the circuitry of modern computers. So far, we have treated the current in our circuits simply as either on or off, and we used switches to turn these circuits on and off. But from now on, we will assume that the current is always on and that there are exactly *two* different possible on states: **high** voltage and **low** voltage (or just 'high' and 'low', for short).[2] It should come as no surprise that these two states can be thought of as Boolean values. It is customary, when discussing computer circuitry, to designate the high state as 1 and the low state as 0, and we will follow this custom. At any moment in a functioning circuit, the voltage is either 1 (high) or 0 (low), and each of these values is the complement of the other, so the vital Boolean properties of **1** and **0** are present here.[3]

We will use letters X, Y, Z, etc. to represent the states of voltage in a circuit: for example, if X is 1, then that is *high* voltage, and if Y is 0, that is *low* voltage. It is also useful to know that a current in a circuit is called a **signal** (they are either high or low) and, as previously noted, a single binary digit (1 or 0) is called a **bit.**

Computer networks are miniscule but complex circuits etched on silicon chips. One important class of these networks consists of what are called **gates.** A gate has one or more input wires and an output wire; current runs through the gate in only one direction. Depending upon its nature, a gate performs some operation on the input signal (or signals) to produce a specific output voltage. Three basic types of gates are known as **AND gates, OR gates,** and **inverter gates (I).** When computer circuits are diagrammed, each type of gate has a standard graphic representation, which is called its **logic diagram.** They are pictured below:

---

[2]The high voltage involved here is actually only about 2–5 volts.

[3]In particular, the usual Boolean equalities e.g., **X & 1** = **X,** all hold.

The wires to the left on each gate are inputs, whose values are 1 (high) or 0 (low), and the wires on the right of each gate, with the same possible values, are outputs. Once again, we find that inputs and outputs of these three gates obey the following familiar SL tables:

AND

input		output
X	Y	
1	1	1
1	0	0
0	1	0
0	0	0

OR

input		output
X	Y	
1	1	1
1	0	1
0	1	1
0	0	0

INVERTER

input	output
1	0
0	1

Given these tables, it is clear that the output of AND, OR, and inverter gates can be represented by SL formulas composed of their inputs and statement operators. Here, then, are the three gates with their logical representations:

Like switched circuits, gates and inverters can be wired together to achieve desired outputs for given inputs, and such combinations also have representations in statement logic. Here are logic diagrams of several combinations, with their respective logical formulations:

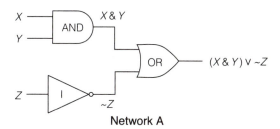

Network A

Network A has three inputs, X, Y, and Z, and its output is $(X \& Y) \lor \sim Z$. Another way of putting this is to say that this network of gates and wires obeys the following table:

NETWORK A

inputs			output
X	Y	Z	
1	1	1	1
1	1	0	1
1	0	1	0
1	0	0	1
0	1	1	0
0	1	0	1
0	0	1	0
0	0	0	1

The next two examples are even more complex:

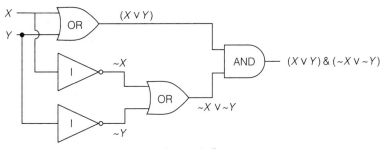

Network B

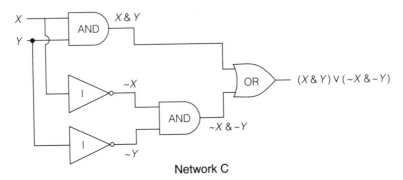

Network C

These networks illustrate that the output of one subnetwork may be an input into another; in actual computer circuitry, such networks are often very complicated. (Note: wires that connect are shown as intersecting with a node; wires that simply pass one another without connecting are shown as crossing. Only three of the four NOR gates are used.)

Gates are available with more than the two inputs we have considered so far; three, four, or more inputs are common in both AND and OR gates. Because of associativity, there is no reason to bother to arrange such inputs into groups of twos. Here are the representations of three-input gates:

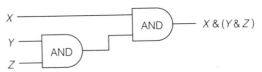

Of course, if only gates with two inputs were available, we could construct a network logically equivalent to the above three-input gates, but two gates would be required in each case, as below:

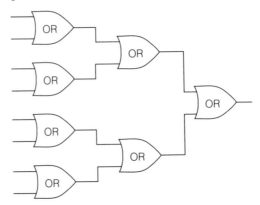

And we can string together AND or OR gates to create networks with any number of inputs. Here is an eight-input OR network:

Here is how a network of fourteen inputs consisting entirely of OR gates would normally be diagrammed:

Another common set of gates includes negated AND and OR gates, called NAND and NOR gates, respectively. Instead of using an AND or OR gate plus an inverter, these gates combine the two. They are represented as follows:

X ──┐
      │ NAND ├○── ~(X & Y) X ──┐
Y ──┘   │ NOR ○── ~(X ∨ Y)
                                    Y ──┘

Note the circles, from the inverter, which are the distinguishing visual feature of the symbols for these negated gates. For reference, the tables for NAND and NOR are below:

NAND

input		output
X	Y	
1	1	0
1	0	1
0	1	1
0	0	1

NOR

input		output
X	Y	
1	1	0
1	0	0
0	1	0
0	0	1

Because of DeMorgan's laws, each of these gates has an equivalent gate form that inverts the inputs instead of the outputs, as shown below:

NAND gate, alternative form   NOR gate, alternative form

So, the alternative NAND gate is formed by inverting the X and Y inputs of an OR gate, resulting in an output of $\sim X \lor \sim Y$, which, of course, is equivalent to $\sim(X \& Y)$. Similarly, the alternative NOR gate is formed by inverting the inputs of an AND gate, i.e., $\sim X \& \sim Y$, which is equivalent to $\sim(X \lor Y)$.

NAND and NOR gates are sometimes called **universal gates** because all logic networks can be constructed using just one of these types (recall the connectives $|$ and $\downarrow$ from chapter 2, section 2.4). Here are the logical equivalences that show that it is possible to restrict oneself to only NAND or NOR gates in designing circuits.

NAND equivalences:

1. $\sim X \equiv \sim(X \& X)$ $X \text{ NAND } X$
2. $X \& Y \equiv \sim(\sim(X \& Y) \& \sim(X \& Y))$ $(X \text{ NAND } Y) \text{ NAND } (X \text{ NAND } Y)$
3. $X \lor Y \equiv \sim(\sim(X \& X) \& \sim(Y \& Y))$ $(X \text{ NAND } X) \text{ NAND } (Y \text{ NAND } Y)$

NOR equivalences:

4. $\sim X \equiv \sim(X \lor X)$ $X \text{ NOR } X$
5. $X \& Y \equiv \sim(\sim(X \lor X) \lor \sim(Y \lor Y))$ $(X \text{ NOR } X) \text{ NOR } (Y \text{ NOR } Y)$
6. $X \lor Y \equiv \sim(\sim(X \lor Y) \lor \sim(X \lor Y))$ $(X \text{ NOR } Y) \text{ NOR } (X \text{ NOR } Y)$

Here are several illustrations of what NAND and NOR networks look like:

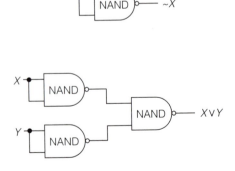

The top network shows $\sim X$ using only NAND gates; the bottom shows $X \vee Y$ using only NAND gates.

Below is a network representing $\sim X$ & Y with NOR gates:

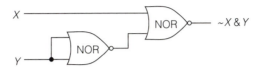

By putting Y into both inputs of a NOR gate, we obtain $\sim Y$ as output (i.e., $\sim(Y \vee Y) \equiv \sim Y$). A NOR gate with $\sim Y$ and X as inputs has $\sim X$ & Y as output, i.e., $\sim(X \vee \sim Y) \equiv (\sim X$ & $Y)$.

Another common gate is the XOR, which has the same table as exclusive disjunction. The symbol for the gate, and its table, follow:

XOR

input		output
X	Y	
1	1	0
1	0	1
0	1	1
0	0	0

Recall that the exclusive disjunction of X and Y is symbolized as either $(X \vee Y) \vee (\sim X$ & $\sim Y)$ or $\sim(X \equiv Y)$. The XOR gate is very close to binary addition (except for the first line) and will be very important later on.

So far, the only networks we have studied have had a single output for any given set of inputs. But many computer circuits are designed to have multiple outputs; we will study several such networks in section 10.5.

Summary

Logic **gates** are circuits which, in effect, perform operations on their binary input **signals** in accord with SL statement connectives. We have discussed **OR, AND, Inverter, NAND, NOR,** and **XOR** gates. Networks of such gates have logical representations and tables of values that are equivalent to the truth tables for their corresponding SL formula.

EXERCISES 10.2

1. Draw logic diagrams that have the following logical representations:

    a. $(X \lor Y) \,\&\, {\sim}X$

    b. ${\sim}(X \,\&\, Y) \,\&\, (Y \lor {\sim}X)$

    c. $X \lor (({\sim}X \,\&\, Y) \lor {\sim}(X \,\&\, {\sim}Y))$

2. Draw two different but equivalent logic diagrams for each of the following:

    a. ${\sim}(X \lor {\sim}Y)$

    b. $X \,\&\, Y$

    c. ${\sim}((X \,\&\, (X \lor {\sim}Y))$

    d. $X \equiv Y$

3. Using just NAND gates, draw a logic diagram for each of the following:

    a. ${\sim}(X \lor Y)$

    b. $X \,\&\, ({\sim}X \lor Y)$

    c. X

4. Draw logic diagrams for each of the above using only NOR gates.

*10.3 CHIPS

If you look inside any piece of electronic equipment—a pocket calculator, the microprocessor in your automatic coffee maker, or a computer—you will see what are called printed-circuit boards. These boards contain what are known as integrated circuits. On tiny silicon 'chips' are fabricated miniature circuits that contain transistors, diodes, and resistors integrated into a single package. Any given chip will usually have a number of separate circuits connected to little metal tabs or pins. The particular circuits on many chips are standardized through the electronics industry and are available from several manufacturers under a particular identifying number. On the facing page is, for example, the logic diagram for the four logic circuits on the simple 7402 IC (integrated circuit) chip.

Tabs 7 and 14 are used for the power supply connections; the other tabs are for the input and output connections to each of the NOR gates. A particular network may link together a number of gates on a single chip or gates on many of different types of chips.

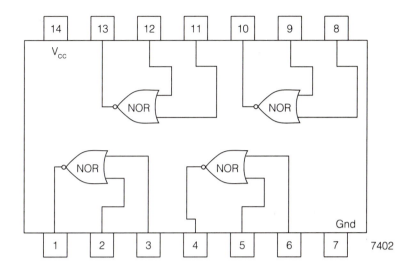

The following are representations of the logic diagram for a circuit using the 7402 chip.

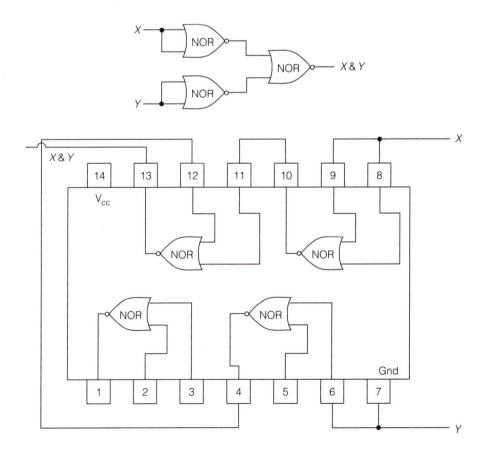

So far we have looked only at integrated circuits of comparatively simple kinds. But given the needs of the electronic industry, much more complicated circuitry is available on standard chips. The four-input binary adder, which we will discuss in chapter 12, for example, is commercially available from several manufacturers on chips with sixteen pins (e.g., 7483). The binary adder network contains thirty gates and is considered a medium-scale integrated circuit. An even more complex package is a four-input, arithmetic-logic unit that provides sixteen arithmetic and sixteen logic operations (e.g., 74181); this chip, which has sixty-four gates, is an example of a large-scale integrated circuit. Its operation will be discussed in chapter 12.

Since so many different integrated-circuit chips are commercially available, designers of electronic devices rely heavily on standard parts. But the basic work of designing circuits to perform specified operations still, finally, comes back to simple logic gates of the kind we have been discussing.

10.4 CIRCUIT SIMPLIFICATION

A designer of a computer circuit often faces the question of which network of gates will correctly transform a given set of inputs into the desired output. A useful method is to translate the desired table of inputs and output directly into an SL formula. This method always produces a correct answer, but, as we will see, the formula that results is usually much more complicated than necessary. Thus, simplifying the formula is an important second step in the circuit-design process.

The first step is a table of input and output values, the following, for example,

input		output
X	Y	
1	1	1
1	0	0
0	1	0
0	0	1

Next the **Post paraphrase** for the table is produced.[4] We create an additional column to the right of the output by writing statements that represent the conjunction of the values indicated for the inputs X and Y, as though 1 were T and 0 were F. For example, if X is 1 and Y is 0, the appropriate statement

---

[4] A more detailed version of the Post paraphrase method employed here is found in section 2.3.

would be X & $\sim Y$. The next step is to check those conjunctions in lines with 1's as outputs.

input		output	conjunction of values
X	Y		
1	1	1	X & Y ✓
1	0	0	X & $\sim Y$
0	1	0	$\sim X$ & Y
0	0	1	$\sim X$ & $\sim Y$ ✓

Then the Post paraphrase SL formula is written according to the two rules:

1. Link together by disjunction formulas that result from the conjunction of values that correspond to a 1 in the output column (i.e., those checked); ignore those next to a 0 in the output column.

2. If the output column contains no 1's, write the conjunction of the first statement letter and its negation.

Following these rules yields $(X$ & $Y) \lor (\sim X$ & $\sim Y)$, which is the Post paraphrase SL formula for the above table. (You may have noticed that the table also represents $X \equiv Y$.)

Here is another example, this time with three inputs. (Lines with 1 as the output are checked.)

input			output	conjunction of values
X	Y	Z		
1	1	1	1	X & $(Y$ & $Z)$ ✓
1	1	0	0	X & $(Y$ & $\sim Z)$
1	0	1	1	X & $(\sim Y$ & $Z)$ ✓
1	0	0	1	X & $(\sim Y$ & $\sim Z)$ ✓
0	1	1	0	$\sim X$ & $(Y$ & $Z)$
0	1	0	1	$\sim X$ & $(Y$ & $\sim Z)$ ✓
0	0	1	0	$\sim X$ & $(\sim Y$ & $Z)$
0	0	0	0	$\sim X$ & $(\sim Y$ & $\sim Z)$

The Post paraphrase for this table is

$$(X \text{ \& } (Y \text{ \& } Z)) \lor (X \text{ \& } (\sim Y \text{ \& } Z)) \lor (X \text{ \& } (\sim Y \text{ \& } \sim Z)) \lor (\sim X \text{ \& } (Y \text{ \& } \sim Z))$$

Although a network of gates could be developed directly from this SL formula, we should check to see whether there is any possible simplification, since so many gates will otherwise be required.

The simplest network would, of course, use the fewest number of gates. In logical terms, the simplest representative SL formula would have the fewest number of operators (each operator potentially being a separate gate) and statement letters, while still having the same input/output table. So the simplification problem is how to produce a logically equivalent formula with the fewest operators.

In chapter 4, we discussed the process of simplifying an SL statement by using equivalence rules to derive an *equivalent* statement. Using this process, now let's tackle the messy Post paraphrase we just produced.

Simplify: $(X$ & $(Y$ & $Z)) \lor (X$ & $(\sim Y$ & $Z)) \lor (X$ & $(\sim Y$ & $\sim Z)) \lor (\sim X$ & $(Y$ & $\sim Z))$

1.	$(X \& (Y \& Z)) \lor (X \& (\sim Y \& Z)) \lor (X \& (\sim Y \& \sim Z)) \lor (\sim X \& (Y \& \sim Z))$	
2.	$[X \lor ((Y \& Z) \& (\sim Y \& Z))] \lor (X \& (\sim Y \& \sim Z)) \lor (\sim X \& (Y \& \sim Z))$	(DIST, 1)
3.	$(X \lor ((Y \& \sim Y) \& (Z \& Z))) \lor (X \& (\sim Y \& \sim Z)) \lor (\sim X \& (Y \& \sim Z))$	(ASSC, 2)[5]
4.	$(X \lor ((Y \& \sim Y) \& Z)) \lor (X \& (\sim Y \& \sim Z)) \lor (\sim X \& (Y \& \sim Z))$	(IDEM&, 3)
5.	$[X \lor (Y \& \sim Y)] \lor (X \& (\sim Y \& \sim Z)) \lor (\sim X \& (Y \& \sim Z))$	(CON&, 4)
6.	$X \lor (X \& (\sim Y \& \sim Z)) \lor (\sim X \& (Y \& \sim Z))$	(CON\lor, 5)
7.	$X \lor [((X \& \sim Y) \& \sim Z) \lor ((\sim X \& Y) \& \sim Z)]$	(ASSC, 6)
8.	$X \lor [((X \& \sim Y) \lor (\sim X \& Y)) \& \sim Z]$	(DIST, 7)

By employing equivalence rules, we have simplified the original Post paraphrase formula to

$$X \lor [((X \& \sim Y) \lor (\sim X \& Y)) \& \sim Z]$$

This could be the formula used to design the circuit for the initial table of values. However, there is one more useful step. By inspection, a determination is made whether to use only the AND, OR, and Inverter gates or to use any of the others, i.e., NAND, NOR, or XOR. As a component of the simplified formula, $(X \& \sim Y) \lor (\sim X \& Y)$ happens to occur, which could be represented with one gate as X XOR Y. If so, then the circuit could be implemented with just three gates: OR, AND, and XOR (see exercise 10.4.3).

---

[5]Several association steps are combined in this line.

EXERCISES 10.4

1. Design simplified circuits for the following input/output tables:

a.

input		output
X	Y	
1	1	1
1	0	0
0	1	1
0	0	0

b.

input		output
X	Y	
1	1	1
1	0	1
0	1	0
0	0	1

c.

input			output
X	Y	Z	
1	1	1	1
1	1	0	0
1	0	1	1
1	0	0	1
0	1	1	0
0	1	0	0
0	0	1	0
0	0	0	0

2. Suppose the only gates available for a and b above are NAND and OR; design appropriate circuits.

3. Design a circuit for which the following statement is a representation with X, Y, and Z as inputs and which uses only AND, OR, and XOR gates.

$X \vee [((X \, \& \sim Y) \vee (\sim X \, \& \, Y)) \, \& \, Z]$

10.5 FLIPFLOPS AND REGISTERS

The activities of computers are primarily carried on by means of the logic gates we have studied. However, most computer manipulations are not simply instantaneous signals moving through circuits; they consist of **sequential** operations, carried out one after another. An essential requirement of sequential operations is **storage** of information within the circuitry of the computer. A simple means of storage is a circuit called a **flipflop;** a place where information is stored is a **register.**

In any of the networks we have looked at so far, when the input changes, the output changes according to the logical characteristics of the circuit. For example, think of a simple inverter network; when the input changes from 1 to 0, the output changes from 0 to 1 (and vice versa). This common feature of networks allows such changes to be instantly passed through the circuit. The *storage* of information, however, requires the ability to hold on to the information as the circuit changes. That is the function of the flipflop circuit.

A one-bit (i.e., one binary digit) flipflop circuit can be constructed using two NAND gates, as pictured:

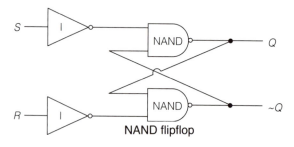

NAND flipflop

The circuit has two inputs, labeled S ('set') and R ('reset') and two outputs, marked $\sim Q$ and Q. The Q output, in effect, *stores* a single bit of information—1 or 0—and the $\sim Q$ output is always the complement of Q (unless the flipflop malfunctions).

The initial state of the flipflop is *off;* both inputs are 0. As we will see, the output of the flipflop in the off position remains whatever it was before it was turned off. If we want to store a 1 in our flipflop, we *set* the flipflop by making the S input 1 and leaving the R input at 0. If you trace along the circuit, you will see that a 1 input on S (and R left at 0), gives a 1 output on Q and 0 on $\sim Q$.

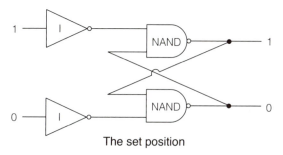

The set position

In the set position, the upper input to the upper NAND gate is 0, because of the inverter. Remember that a NAND gate has the following input/output table:

NAND

input		output
X	Y	
1	1	0
1	0	1
0	1	1
0	0	1

In the set position, the output of the upper NAND gate is therefore 1, no matter what the lower input is. That output is, of course, the value of Q in the set position. Because of the *feedback* design of the flipflop circuit, that same 1 is also the upper input of the lower NAND gate. The other input of the lower NAND gate is also 1, because of the Inverter on the R input. So the output of the lower NAND gate is therefore 0. Hence 0 is the output on the $\sim Q$ output, and 0 is the other input to the upper NAND gate.

Suppose the S input is returned to 0, called the set 'hold' position (the R remains at 0). The upper input to the upper NAND gate is now 1, but the lower input to that gate remains at 0. Thus the Q output remains at 1, and here we have the essential feature of the flipflop. The 1 is *stored*, in the sense that Q remains high, even though the S input has changed. Further changes in S do not affect Q while the flipflop is in the hold state, so long as R does not change.

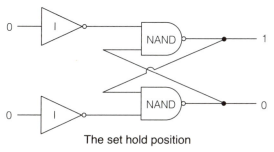

The set hold position

But now suppose we want to store a 0, and, hence, change the signal of the output Q from high to low. We need to *reset* the flipflop, by making the R input 1, and leaving the S input at 0. This makes the Q output 0, and, as the name suggests, we have **flipflopped** or **cleared** the circuit. Returning R to 0 does not affect the Q output; in the reset hold position Q stays at 0.

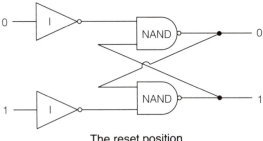

The reset position

The only combination of inputs we have not discussed is making *both S and R 1 at once.* This is an attempt to both set and reset the flipflop simultaneously; it is not possible to predict the output of the circuit in such cases. So in actual circuits, this circumstance is always avoided.

Here is a table that summarizes the operation of a flipflop. This table is unlike those presented up to now because it records a *sequence* of states; each entry depends on those that have come before:

state	input S	R	action	output Q	~Q
state 1	0	0	hold	no change	
state 2	1	0	set	1	0
state 3	0	0	hold	1	0
state 4	1	0	hold	1	0
state 5	0	1	reset	0	1
state 6	0	0	hold	0	1
state 7	1	1		unstable	

As you can see, when the inputs are both 0 (state 1), we do not know the output unless we know what the previous state of the flipflop was. Once we have set (state 2) or reset (state 5) the flipflop, we can turn it off (both inputs at 0), and it will store one bit of information at output Q. Subsequent changes in that same input will not affect the output (e.g., state 4). Once again, simultaneously setting and resetting is not valid (state 7); the flipflop could go into several possible output configurations, but we cannot predict which one.

This simple device, which is based on the truth table for a negated conjunction, is a basic form of computer 'memory'. Of course we have looked at a means of electronically storing only one bit of information, but flipflops, as we will see, can be combined so that much more information can be stored.

Flipflops themselves are, of course, components of circuits, and so are customarily symbolized as a 'block diagram', which indicates the two inputs S (set) and R (reset) and the outputs Q and $\sim Q$.

Flipflop symbol

Since one flipflop stores only a single bit of information, flipflops can be linked together to form **storage registers.** As an example, here is a four-bit register using four flipflops and some other gates and switches.

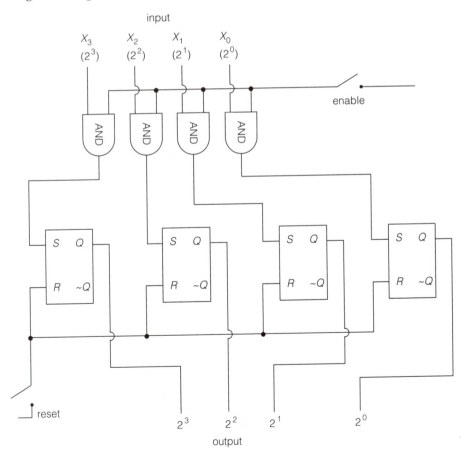

Four-bit register

Each of the inputs X_3, X_2, X_1, X_0 is a bit (1 or 0). If the information to be stored is a number, we can think of the X_3 input as the 2^3 place in a four-bit binary numeral, the X_2 as the 2^2 place, and so on. Let's assume that the network initially has 0 for each of the outputs. As long as the enable switch is off, the flipflop is in hold position. When the enable switch is on, a 1 is the input from the switch at each of the AND gates. Then the four bits of information can be stored as follows: if any input is a 1, that sets the corresponding flipflop to a 1; if the input is a 0, the flipflop stays at 0. Suppose the input is 1101 (= decimal 13), then the output is also 1101. Now suppose the enable switch is turned off, so that the right input to each of the AND gates returns to 0. The output from the circuit remains at 1101, so the register contains 1101 as its stored information.

To reset, or **clear,** the register, the reset switch is moved to the on position, sending a 1 input to the R input of each of the four flipflops. This resets the Q output in each flipflop to 0, and the output of the circuit is 0000. The register now contains 0000. The reset switch is then turned off, and the register is ready to receive new information.

Summary

Sequential operations in electronic devices require the ability to store information in the form of binary signals. A simple means of accomplishing this is the one-bit **flipflop** circuit. Because of a feedback circuit, the flipflop will hold its output value until **reset.** Several flipflops wired together can be used to form a **storage register,** where several bits of information can be stored.

EXERCISES 10.5

1. Diagram two different flipflop circuits without using NAND gates.

2. Make the necessary connections to a 7402 IC chip (see section 10.4) to form a flipflop.

11

Computability

At the most fundamental level, computer activity is very limited. As we will see in chapter 12, the central processing units of computers can only add, subtract, complement, etc., although they can perform these operations repeatedly with incredible speeds, millions of times per second. The power to do so many important and demanding tasks rests largely in the computer programs that direct the operations of the computer hardware. In this chapter we look at the algorithms that are the basis for the programs that run in computers, including the programs built into their very circuitry. In the course of our discussion we will come up against the limits of computing, and, hence, of all computers, which will provide a bridge between our discussion in chapter 7 of the *decision problem* for predicate logic and our excursions into computers themselves in chapter 12.

11.1 INSTRUCTIONS, RECURSION, AND REPRESENTATION

A number of preliminaries are required before we plunge into algorithms.

Instructions

Since algorithms are essentially sets of instructions of a certain kind, we will begin by thinking about instructions in general. Instructions are like commands. A parent instructs a child to clean up his room; an owner's manual instructs us not to switch off the computer without having saved the document displayed on the screen. We often give a *set* of instructions when we want to tell another person *how* to do something, assuming that he or she has already decided to do it. This is especially true when the activity is fairly complex, like baking a cake or playing tennis.

This standard recipe for angel food cake reveals a number of important features of instructions:[1]

A. Ingredients:

   8 egg whites
   1/4 teaspoon salt
   1 teaspoon vanilla
   1 1/4 cups sugar
   1 cup cake flour

B. To make:

   Beat the egg whites until foamy, add the salt, and beat until soft peaks form. Gradually add the sugar, beating until stiff. Sift the flour over the whites and gently fold it in. Bake in an ungreased 10-inch tube pan for 50–60 minutes, until a straw comes out clean. Frost with chocolate icing.

Now this is a fairly simple recipe from a tried and true cookbook; many thousands, perhaps millions of angel food cakes have been made according to such instructions. Yet producing a successful angel food cake remains an elusive project for many would-be cooks. Part of the problem is that the instructions contain *imprecise* terms like 'foamy', 'gradually', 'stiff', 'gently', and 'fold'. The cooking time is said to be 50–60 minutes, not an exact period such as 54.5 minutes. That a straw inserted into the cake will come out clean is also not a very precise test of doneness. Suppose after 62 minutes of baking there are damp batter particles clinging to the straw. How much longer should the cake bake before testing it again? If you say, "about an hour" you will be sure to ruin the cake; if you say "two more minutes" you probably haven't allowed enough time. But the recipe doesn't tell you how to proceed at this point. Cakes fail primarily because instructions are so imprecise about beating, soft peaks, doneness tests, and so forth. Good cooks know how to handle cake batter; novices are often hopeless, despite having the recipe in front of them.

A simpler procedure for which instructions can be given is changing a flat tire. Like the recipe for a cake, the instructions will lead a person through a series of actions, one after the other. Before reading on, you might want

---

[1]This recipe is adapted from *The Fannie Farmer Cookbook*, 12th ed., revised by Marion Cunningham with Jeri Laber (New York: Knopf, 1983), p. 520. Cooking provides numerous examples for writers on algorithms. The idea is from David Harel, *Algorithmics* (Menlo Park, CA: Addison-Wesley, 1987), ch. 1. Also see J. Shore, *The Sachertorte Algorithm and Other Antidotes to Computer Anxiety* (New York: Viking, 1985), ch. 4.

to formulate your own set of instructions for changing a tire and then compare your instructions to those given here.

One problem those giving instructions always face is how much detail to include. In tire changing, for example, can we assume that the person following the instructions knows where the trunk of the car is? Do we have to explain what a lug nut is? Or a tire iron? Or a jack? If all of the key terms and concepts have to be discussed and defined, the instructions will be quite lengthy and will be frustrating to follow by those who already are familiar with the basic notions. On the other hand, if terms are used with which a person is not familiar, then he or she will not be able to follow the instructions.

Here is a set of instructions for changing a flat tire:

1. Check the spare tire to insure that it is full of air.

2. Set the emergency brake, and block a tire on the opposite side of the car from the flat tire.

3. Remove the hubcap.

4. Loosen the lug nuts.

5. Jack up the wheel with the flat tire so that it clears the ground.

6. Remove the lug nuts, and remove the wheel.

7. Install the spare, tightening the lug nuts slightly.

8. Lower the jack, and fully tighten the lug nuts.

9. Reinstall the hubcap.

You will note that the first instruction specifies a *test:* 'check the spare'. If the spare tire passes the test and is functional, then the other instructions can be followed. If, however, the spare is also flat, then there is no point in going to the second instruction. (Did *your* tire-changing instructions include this first step?) But we should specify some other action to follow in this case. So we might add to instruction 1: '*if not*, call the garage'. The instructions additionally assume that the various tools are available and in working order, so another instruction might be inserted that prescribes a check that the jack, lugwrench, and tire iron (for the hubcap) are available. If any of these is missing, the instructions cannot be followed, and one should call the garage.

A convenient method to display instructions is by means of a **flowchart.** This is a graphic representation of a sequence of instructions that shows the relationship among the instructions and the critical nature of any tests that may be involved. Because flowcharts are so useful, a standard format has been developed for their presentation. Flowcharts are commonly read from top to bottom. Instructions and tests are kept separate, and the sequence of instructions to be followed is indicated by means of lines and arrows. Each instruction that calls for a specific *action* is usually separately written inside a *rectangle*, like this:

```
┌─────────────────────┐
│        Stir in      │
│   the baking soda.  │
└─────────────────────┘
```

The first thing that appears in a flowchart is an *oval* enclosing the word 'Start', and the final entry is an oval enclosing the word 'Stop'. In addition to instructions that call for actions, there may also be *tests* represented in the flowchart. They are in *diamonds,* and are phrased as questions that have 'yes' or 'no' answers. A separate pathway is provided for each of the two possible answers, like this:

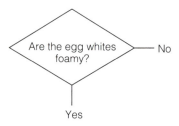

The complete flowchart for the flat-tire instructions is on the facing page.

Three tests are involved in the instructions: make sure that the appropriate tools are available, check the spare, and jack up the wheel until the tire clears the ground. In the first two, if the answer is no, then a specific action is prescribed that leads to the termination of the instructions as represented by the Stop oval. The third test, however, creates what is called a **loop.** One continues to jack the wheel up *until* the tire clears the ground. If the tire has not yet cleared the ground, the answer to the test question is no, and the flowchart sends you back to the jacking instruction (that is the loop). When the tire clears the ground, then the answer to the test question is yes, and you go on to the next instruction.

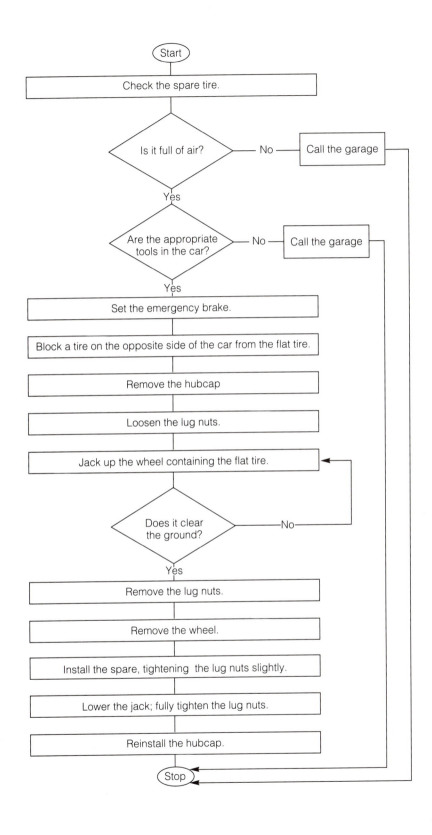

Although the use of tests and loops in flowcharts can dramatically simplify the presentation of instructions, it is important that there be a way of getting out of any loop. If we cannot exit, the loop will be *infinite* and there is no hope of ever completing the instructions. As a simple example of a potentially infinite loop, consider the following flowchart for multiplying a number *n* successively by 2 until the product exceeds 45.

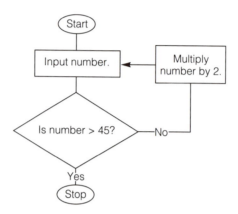

This flowchart has us begin *as an input* with some number. If that initial number is already greater than 45, then we do not multiply anything, but immediately stop; if the number is less than 45 we begin multiplying and then test the product as indicated.

But what happens if the initial number is *negative,* say −3? Then, since −3 is less than 45, we would begin multiplying by 2 and testing the products, which would be −6, −12, −24, −48, and so forth. Of course we will never reach a product that is greater than 45, so we will be caught in this loop forever! A set of instructions that cannot be completed because of an infinite loop is sometimes said *not to terminate.* We encountered such a set of instructions in the truth tree method for predicate logic in chapter 7. Recall that a truth tree with a certain kind of branch (Type IV) continued infinitely.

From this brief discussion about instructions, the following lessons emerge:

1. The purpose of instructions is to produce some *goal,* whether a cake, or a different tire on the car, or a clean room, or the preservation of information that has been entered into a computer. The instructions prescribe a series of actions, in some sequence, to accomplish the goal.

2. In framing instructions, the language used and the terms employed must be understood, or the instructions cannot be carried out. It is easy to carry out instructions in which all prescribed actions are clearly defined; varying degrees of knowledge and skill are required if the instructions contain any vague terms or fuzzy concepts (e.g., 'whip into soft peaks', 'bake between 50 and 60 minutes').

3. Instructions may make use of *tests*, at critical points. Instructions may also make use of *loops*, which direct certain actions to be repeated until some stated condition is achieved.

4. Instructions must have some termination point or else the actions may be repeated endlessly, and the goal may not ever be reached.

We also discussed the use of **flowcharts** to represent instructions. These conventionally utilize ovals to indicate the start and stop points; rectangles to indicate actions; and diamonds to indicate tests. The various nodes in a flowchart are connected by arrows to indicate the sequence that is to be followed.

EXERCISES 11.1

1. Give a set of instructions for turning on your radio, and represent these instructions by means of a flowchart. Make a list of the actions that must be performed to follow your instructions, and describe what knowledge or skill is required to use your instructions.

2. Give a set of instructions for making a stack of concrete blocks that is three feet high; include a loop in your instructions. Write a flowchart for your instructions. What actions must be performed in following your instructions? What tests are involved? How (if at all) might such instructions be formulated *without* a loop?

3. Give a complete set of instructions for moving from the desk in your room, out the door, and to the nearest window. Develop a flowchart for your instructions. Try your flowchart out on someone who either doesn't know his or her way, or at least pretends not to know. Use the simplest set of terms, concepts, and actions you can to frame your instructions.

*4. Give a set of instructions for solving the three-ring tower of Hanoi problem (see exercise 1.1.2). Provide a flowchart.

Recursion

The terms 'recursion' and 'recursive' come from the English word 'recur'. The basic idea is this: In a definition, such as that given in chapter 2 for an SL statement, there is a seeming circularity, the repeated use of the notion of 'statement'. Recall how an SL statement was defined. We said that expressions of the form $\sim$**A, A & B, A $\vee$ B, A $\supset$ B,** and **A $\equiv$ B** all are statements if **A** and **B** are statements. Now such a definition seems circular; we use the very term—statement—in the definition of that term. But as we saw through constructing statement trees, in fact the definition is not circular at all because at each level, so to speak, a different kind of statement is involved.

Take, for example, the expression $\sim[P \supset (R \vee S)]$. To satisfy the definition of statement, $\sim[P \supset (R \vee S)]$ is a statement only if $P \supset (R \vee S)$ is.

And $P \supset (R \lor S)$ is a statement only if P and $R \lor S$ are; and they are statements only if P, R, and S are. In each use of the term 'statement' in these last two sentences, the word refers to a different kind of statement. In its first use, 'statement' refers to the entire initial statement, in its second use to the immediate components, in its third use to its two components, and in its fourth use to the atomic components: the statement letters P, R, and S. At rock bottom, then, such a *recursive definition* of some infinite class **X** requires that a group of objects be initially identified as belonging to **X**. Then those things are used to determine whether other things belong, and those things determine whether other things belong, and so on up the line. In effect, the nature of a recursive definition allows for the membership of **X** to be specified in a small number of sentences. Otherwise, we would have an *infinite* chain of sentences determining the membership of **X**.

In the case of statements, this infinite chain would start with P, R, and S, for example, designated as statements (members of **X**). Then we would say that $P \& R$, $P \supset R$, $P \lor S$, $\sim R$, $\sim P$, $\sim S$, etc. are all statements, then we would say that $(P \& R) \lor P$, $\sim\sim S$, etc. are statements, and so forth, repeatedly using those things already identified as statements and adding to the class. This infinite list of sentences would clearly involve no circularity. Instead, the recursive style of expressing the definition should be viewed as a kind of shorthand for such an infinite list of sentences comprising the definition of 'statement.' Thus, when properly understood, a recursive definition does not involve circularity either.

Recursion is an important feature of algorithms as well. To give an economical statement of an algorithm, it is often useful to have a means of using the same operation over and over, but at different levels. For example, consider how you might answer the question 'How do you make a pile of thirteen stones?[2] An answer is 'Put one stone on top of a pile of 12 stones'. Notice that this answer works (recursively), provided that one is prepared to then answer the question 'How do you make a pile of twelve stones?' and so on.

The recursion in all this is more clearly revealed if the instructions are as follows, generalizing to a pile of n stones:

Instructions to make a pile of n stones

1. Put a stone on the ground.

2. Make a pile of $n - 1$ stones on top of that stone.

3. Stop.

In the next section we will study how we should further specify the instruction 'Make a pile of $n - 1$ stones'.

---

[2]The example is from Douglas R. Hofstadter, "LISP: Lists and Recursion," in *Metamagical Themas* (New York: Bantam, 1986), pp. 414–415.

The Hanoi tower problem clearly also involves recursion.[3] To transfer the n disks from peg A to B, you have to know how to transfer the $n - 1$ disks from peg A to peg C, then move the nth disk to peg B, then move the $n - 1$ disks to peg B.

As in all uses of recursion, there is a **base case,** where the chain of steps begins. In the definition of a PL statement, the base case is, of course, the atomic statement or statement letter; in the tower of Hanoi recursion, the base case is moving two disks. Any recursion must have a base case or the process will be infinite, with no way out. And that is a circle.

Representations

We have been engaged in a variety of representational systems throughout this book. We began with statement logic representation of the truth-functional form of statements. After noticing that many statements could be classified in certain categories—conjunctions, disjunctions, negations, etc.—we developed a notation for so representing the statements. Recall that by considering any statement *atomic* that could not be classified as a truth-functional compound, we were able to represent all statements in the notation of SL. The notation used was a limited vocabulary of symbols, as listed below.

Connectives: $\sim$, $\&$, $\vee$, $\supset$, and $\equiv$

Statement letters: A, B, C, etc.

Punctuation: ( )

By attaching subscripts to the capital letters, we can produce as many distinct statement letters as we might want. In this representation system we are able to write the form of *any* truth-functional statement, no matter how complex it may be.

It is important to note that all statements are finite in length. Since any speaking, writing, or other production of a statement takes *some* time, however small, the most complex statement will require some time to produce, but not an infinite amount of time. Since a finite (but potentially large) number of components are possible, a finite number of statement letters will be needed. So we have enough statement letters because we can subscript. We showed in section 2.3 that not even all five connectives are required; we can get by with negation and either conjunction or disjunction.

In SL notation, then, we can represent with a finite vocabulary of symbols all statements that *could* be produced. Since there is no limit on the number of possible statements, our finite vocabulary covers an infinite array of possible statements.

---

[3]The problem originally showed up as exercise 1.1.2 and is also found in exercise 11.1.4.

We have used other representation systems as well. For example we have used boldface capital letters, e.g., **A,** to represent any statement; boldface **N** to represent any name; in chapter 8 we used **X** to represent any set, etc. Without talking much about it, we have made use of what are called *metalanguages* when discussing SL, PL, Boolean systems, and numerical systems. The metalanguage in each case consists of characters that stand for SL statements or PL statements or their parts, and so forth.

In chapter 9 we studied various systems of numerical representation. We saw that with a vocabulary of just two symbols, *1* and *0*, it is possible to represent numbers in binary notation.[4] In later sections we will see that binary representation can be extended beyond numbers. Using an agreed-upon code, we can represent characters in binary notation, and, by extension, words, sentences, and whole libraries of books.[5] Although such strings of binary symbols will be lengthy, they will, in every case, be finite, making such representation possible. For example in chapter 12 we will study the seven-segment display used by most common calculators, digital watches, clocks, scoreboards, etc. As we will see, each character displayed has a code in binary symbols; the seven-segment code for the numeral *1*, for example, is 1100000. In addition, all of the words in this book once were stored on magnetic diskettes in the form of binary numerals, in magnetized regions corresponding to long strings of *1*'s and *0*'s.

There is no reason to limit binary representation to characters and words. Other kinds of information—sounds, diagrams, movement, light patterns, complex numerical relationships, etc.—can be put into binary form and represented by strings of binary symbols. For example, you probably know that a complete image on a color video display screen can be put into binary form, and that, at one level, it is already in that form. Each day the boundaries of what has been so represented and what hasn't are pushed back by new computer applications. For in computers only binary symbols are used at the basic level.

The ability to represent information uniformly in binary form is one of the key factors in the success of computers. The other key is the design of efficient programs that allow such information to be manipulated. We are now ready to discuss algorithms, which are the basis of all such programs.

11.2 ALGORITHMS

The feature that distinguishes algorithms from other sets of instructions is their *precision;* each step is exactly defined so that no thought is required to

---

[4]We have considered only positive natural numbers and fractions, but other numbers can be handled as well, e.g., negative numbers. It is important to note, however, that no numerical system can represent all possible numbers. See, e.g., "Infinity in Logic and Mathematics," in Paul Edwards, ed. *Encyclopedia of Philosophy,* vol. 4 (New York: Macmillan, 1972).

[5]The standard ASCII code will be found in the Appendix.

complete it and go on to the next step. This is the reason algorithmic processes are sometimes called *mechanical.* They resemble the actions of a machine rather than the typical actions of a person. Since no choices have to be made, there is no room for guesswork, ingenuity, skill, or insight. There may be some random features of algorithms, but even they proceed according to instructions rather than decisions.

In our consideration of algorithms, there are several features of the angel food cake recipe worth noticing again. First, it contains a list of ingredients, or **inputs.** We are not to start with a pound of cake flour, but exactly one cup; we are not to pour ketchup into the batter (by entailment, since ketchup isn't mentioned); and so forth. Every algorithm also has *legal inputs,* just as this recipe does; anything not initially specified as a legal input is not allowed. If a cook is successful, an angel food cake will result from the recipe. That is the recipe's goal or **output.** This, too, is a feature the cake recipe shares with algorithms: every algorithm has a specific output. Another obvious feature of recipes is that the list of instructions is **finite;** no one would hope to be able to cook otherwise. This too is an important feature of algorithms: the number of steps to carry out the instructions must be finite. The *possible* legal inputs could, however, be infinte. For example, there is no limit to the variety of SL arguments that we might test for validity using truth tables.

The cake recipe contains several **tests** that are used to determine when certain actions (beating, cooking) should cease. Algorithms often contain instructions of the **do . . . while** or **do . . . until** form; a certain operation is to be carried on until a certain stage is reached, then that operation is to halt and the next instruction is to be followed. In an algorithm, however, there cannot be any doubt as to whether the test is passed or failed; the criterion must be exact, unlike 'stiff' or 'foamy.' Suppose you wanted to make an algorithm out of the angel food cake recipe that, say, a computer-controlled robot in a large bakery could use. You would have to devise exact tests to substitute for the critical parts of the batter preparation. You might specify a precise number of minutes the egg whites are to be beaten at a specific speed, and you might work out a precise flow rate for adding the sugar (100 grams per second). Seasoned cooks will wince at the thought of the kind of cakes that might be so produced, but at least the instructions would be exact enough to be algorithmic.

Here is what we know about algorithms so far:

1. Algorithms require the specification of a set of legal inputs.

2. They contain a finite number of instructions and steps.

3. All terms must be exact, including all tests.

4. There is a specific output.

Another feature of the cake recipe you may not have noticed is that it refers to another recipe, one for chocolate icing. This feature, too, is common in algorithms. They often contain or make use of other algorithms. For example, take the instruction to add two numbers, say 432 and 679, which might be one instruction of an algorithm. Addition, of course, is recognized to be an algorithmic process. But if 'add 432 and 679' is an instruction, there is another algorithm to be unearthed. For although some human beings can add these two numbers directly, the standard technique is to add the units digits, this case producing 1 and a carry of 1, then to add the carry to the tens digits, producing another 1 and another carry of 1, and so on until the number 1,211 is reached. Thus the algorithm for adding multi-digit numbers incorporates the algorithm for adding single digits.

The angel food cake recipe doesn't actually specify which recipe for chocolate icing is to be used (several are given in the cookbook), and, in previous chapters, we have discussed several possible ways of adding 432 and 679. We could translate both numbers into binary numerals, use binary addition to produce a binary sum, and then translate back into decimal notation. Or we could add 1 to 432 over and over 679 times, or we could convert both numbers to hexadecimal notation. Notice that the cookbook author apparently isn't concerned at this point about how the chocolate icing is made, just as some algorithms do not specify how some *subalgorithm* is to be carried out. If we believe that the user of the recipe knows how to make chocolate icing, then it may not be necesary to mention the steps. Of course a full recipe would so specify, as would a *full* algorithm.

The second characteristic listed above, that algorithms must have a finite number of steps, is very important. You should notice that a small number of instructions can lead to a large number of steps, so there is reason to mention both. For example, if an instruction says that 1 is to be added repeatedly to a number, this process could go on forever. Yet such a potentially infinite number of steps stems from a *single* instruction, resulting in an **infinite loop.** Remember the essential difference between the tree method for predicate logic and for statement logic. In statement logic, we can be sure that the tree will close if the set of initial statements is inconsistent or will have open branches otherwise, and we can figure out how many steps would be required, although it is not necessary to do so. But in predicate logic, type IV trees can grow and grow.

In the course of this book you have encountered a number of algorithms and still other activities for which algorithms are easy to formulate. We will call **algorithmic** any activity or problem for which an algorithm is possible, even if we haven't ourselves been able to formulate or find an appropriate algorithm. For example, truth tables are clearly algorithmic, as we discussed in chapter 2. But a person could learn about truth tables without also learning that there is a standard, mechanical way to set up the tables and to work them out. So a beginning logic student might not yet know the algorithm, even though he or she is (dimly) aware that some algorithm may exist. Obviously, the principal proof that some activity is algorithmic is the production of an algorithm.

Here is a list of the algorithms that we have found, tried to find, or discussed at some point in previous chapters:

Chapter 1   The towers of Hanoi problem (exercise 1.1.2); the missionaries and cannibals problem (exercise 1.1.3). Note: the process of identifying arguments and their conclusions (exercise 1.2.4) is probably not algorithmic (at least not at present).[6]

Chapter 2   Constructing truth tables; determining whether an expression is an SL statement; finding Post paraphrases; translating between SL notation and Polish notation. Note: translating from ordinary English to SL notation is probably not algorithmic.

Chapter 3   Finding the truth-value of an SL statement on a valuation; testing for validity and the other logical properties and relations (truth tables and truth trees are both algorithmic). Note: the shortcut method is not an algorithm (see section 3.2).

Chapter 4   Determining validity by the resolution method; checking whether a given natural deduction derivation is correctly formulated.

Chapter 5   Determining whether an expression is a PL statement; testing an expression to determine whether it is a component of a given PL statement (but not finding all components). Note: translation from English into PL is probably not algorithmic.

Chapter 6   Determining the truth-value of a PL statement on a valuation.

Chapter 7   Testing for validity and the other logical properties and relations in monadic PL; checking whether a given natural deduction derivation is correctly formulated; determining validity by the resolution method. Testing validity in PL in general is not algorithmic, as previously noted (see section 11.4).

Chapter 8   Testing for theorems in Boolean systems; testing Boolean syllogisms for validity (see exercise 11.2a.4).

Chapter 9   Translating from one numerical system into another.

Chapter 10   Circuit simplification, in general, is not algorithmic.[7]

Before reviewing this list you may not have realized how many algorithms you have already encountered. We will return to several of these algorithms in later discussions.

---

[6]There is a significant amount of current research on computerized natural language understanding. See, for example, Terry Winograd and Fernando Flores, *Understanding Computers and Cognition* (Reading, MA: Addison-Wesley, 1987), chapter 9. A good bibliography is included.
[7]See W. V. Quine, *Methods of Logic*, 3rd ed. (New York: McGraw-Hill, 1972), pp. 66–67.

Control Instructions

In addition to the actions to be performed at each step, algorithms have **control instructions** to indicate how those steps are to be put in sequence. Here are several types of control instructions we have already encountered:

1. **Direct sequencing**   Certain steps are to be performed in order. The line numbers in an algorithm indicate the order of a direct sequence; in a flowchart, arrows are used.

2. **Branching**   The performances of some steps depend on the outcome of a test. For example, 'IF $a = b$, THEN ADD a b'. Another kind of branching sends us to some particular place in the algorithm; the instruction GOTO is used for this, followed by a line number. For example, 'IF $a > b$, THEN GOTO 3'.

3. **Bounded loops**   A step is to be performed a certain number of times; for example, 'DO n times . . . ' (where n is a number). The 'DO n times' control instruction is followed by some other instruction as in 'DO n times: POINT TO first element'.

4. **Conditional loops**   A step is to be performed *UNTIL* some condition is reached or *WHILE* some condition holds: 'ADD a b UNTIL $b \geq c$', or, 'WHILE $a > b$, ADD a b'.

Operation Instructions

All algorithms depend on a stock of **basic actions.** These are the steps that can be performed directly, without involving some other algorithm. If humans are carrying out an algorithm, the number of actions that count as basic, that need no further explanation, is potentially very large. However, these will vary from person to person. Bill may know about 'folding' and 'whipping until soft peaks form', but Sue may not. But no matter who or what is to carry it out, before an algorithm is written, a decision must be reached on what counts as a basic action and what doesn't.

Let's look at several examples of algorithms to see how various control structures are exemplified. For the sake of simplicity, we will sometimes use steps involving actions that may themselves involve algorithms (like 'add two numbers', and 'convert to binary notation'). Later on we will return to the subject of subalgorithms.

Usually the actions in an algorithm are referred to as **operations.** These are carried out on designated objects, called **operands.** To represent operations and their operands, we will use notation similar to that for predicate logic. We will write out the operation to be undertaken in capital letters, e.g., ADD, DIVIDE, CONVERT TO BINARY. The object to be operated on will be represented by a lowercase letter, like the names and individual variables from PL. So the operation of adding two numbers a and b will be written

ADD *a b*

If we want to use *s* to indicate the sum of *a* and *b* we will write:

LET *s* = ADD *a b*

We use the same conventions we did in chapter 5 regarding the order in which names of operands appear.

A major difference between predicate logic representation and algorithmic representations stems from the fact that algorithms deal with **sequence.** Throughout our discussions of SL, PL, and Boolean systems, once a letter was used to designate a statement, object, predicate, or set of statements, that designation held. The convention that in an argument, a set of statements, or a derivation all letters remain fixed in their designation is absolutely critical to the logic systems we have studied.

To underscore this point, let's consider one of the classic logical fallacies, called *equivocation,* which occurs when the meaning of a word changes in the course of an argument. For example, the equivocation fallacy would be committed if someone were to argue as follows:

Salt dissolves in water.

Harry is an old salt.

———————————

Harry dissolves in water.

Note that the logical form of the argument is only valid so long as 'salt' means the same thing in both occurrences.

In algorithms, on the other hand, we frequently need to *change* the designation of an operand. We have already seen an example in the flowchart for multiplying a positive number by 2 until the product exceeds 45. Here is that flowchart again:

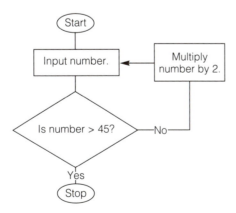

The variable that occurs in the above flowchart is the word 'number'. In its first occurrence, in the operation 'Input number', we give the variable a certain value, let's say 5. Then we test to determine whether 5 is greater than 45. Since it isn't, we then multiply 5 by 2 and go back to the 'Input number' operation. But when we return to the 'Input number' box, the variable 'number' now will designate 10. After another cycle through the loop, the variable 'number' will designate 20, and so forth.

If our task were writing out the full running of an algorithm, as we did when we constructed PL truth trees in chapter 7, then we would consider operands such as 'number' as bound *variables*, and in each cycle through the algorithm we would instantiate the variable to a different name: 5 in the first cycle, 10 in the second, 20 in the third, and so forth. This would be the same process we used when we cycled through repeated uses of the tree rules for universal quantification and negated existential quantification.

The issue here is how to represent the algorithm itself. Because algorithms are lists of instructions invoking a dynamic *sequence of operations*, not a static set of descriptive statements—like an argument—economy in representation requires that we allow the operands to change their designation as we cycle through the various steps. Therefore, we want to be able to write such instructions as

LET $m = m + 1$.

Obviously, as a *statement*, this makes no sense (or, at the least, is paradoxical). But as an *instruction* in a loop of an algorithm, it represents the operation of changing the designation of the operand (variable) m from its last value to a new value. For example, if m happens to represent the number 7, after the instruction 'LET $m = m + 1$,' m will represent 8. We can call this operation *incrementing* by 1; we could alternatively represent this operation as

INCREMENT m.

The increment instruction is important in many algorithms because it allows us to keep track of how many times a certain operation has taken place. (See the algorithm for averaging lists of numbers, below).

Here are several examples of algorithms, with commentary on how they are developed:

Algorithm 1   Add two numbers n, m, and report their sum as a binary numeral.

To begin, we must identify the steps we need to follow and their order. In this case, matters are simple; we add the numbers, and then we convert their sum to binary. We should use a reasonably clear format to indicate the steps, including the legal inputs and the output. Here, then, is the algorithm:

Legal inputs for *n* and *m*: numbers

1. START
2. INPUT *n*
3. INPUT *m*
4. LET *s* = ADD *n m*
5. LET *b* = BINARY *s* (i.e., CONVERT TO BINARY *s*)
6. OUTPUT *b*
7. STOP

The control sequence of this algorithm is entirely direct sequencing; the steps are performed one after another, in the order presribed by the line numbers.

Another example:

Algorithm 2 Find the average of the numbers *a*, *b*, *c*, *d*.

This algorithm will add the four numbers and then divide by four to obtain the desired result.

Legal inputs for *a*, *b*, *c*, *d*: numbers

1. START
2. INPUT *a*
3. INPUT *b*
4. INPUT *c*
5. INPUT *d*
6. LET *s* = ADD *a b c d*
7. LET *e* = DIVIDE *s* 4
8. OUTPUT *e*
9. STOP

We represented the operation of dividing a number *s* by 4 as 'DIVIDE *s* 4'.

Next we generalize the averaging algorithm so that the number of inputs need not be specified. The numbers to be added will constitute the **data.** The algorithm will add the first two numbers in the data, then add the next number to their sum, and so on until all numbers are added and no data remain. This is an example of a *conditional loop*. We continue carrying out steps until a certain condition is reached (no data remain); then we go on in sequence to the next step. The algorithm must also contain a provision for keeping track of how many numbers have been added so that the proper divisor can be used when the data are all in the sum.

Algorithm 3: Average a list of numbers.

1. START
2. CLEAR c
3. CLEAR s
4. DO WHILE DATA REMAIN:
   a. INPUT m
   b. LET s = SUM m s
   c. LET $c = c + 1$
5. LET d = DIVIDE s c
6. OUTPUT d
7. STOP

To keep track of how many numbers have been added, the algorithm makes use of a **counter** (the variable c). Initially the counter is *cleared*, meaning it is set to equal 0. With each increment to the counter, the number is increased by 1. When all the numbers have been added, the counter, c, then is equal to the number of numbers in the data. We also set the sum s to 0 at the outset. Then each number in turn is added to s until all the numbers are used and no data remain. The average of the list is the value of d at the conclusion of the process.

If we were constructing a physical version of this algorithm, that is, constructing a device to average lists of numbers, we might keep track of where we are in the list by means of a *pointer*. Think of the numbers in a column; each time we add a number, we move the pointer to the next number down the column until the pointer no longer points to a number. At that point, clearly, no data remain, and we would have achieved the condition of the loop and could go on to the next step (division).

The recursion in the averaging algorithm should be obvious from the manner in which variables are used. We have in line 4b: 'LET s = ADD m s', i.e.,

Let the (new) value of s be the sum of the value of m and the (old) value of s.

In a given cycle through the algorithm, we add the number that is the value in that cycle of the variable m to the sum s from the last cycle. Then we let that sum be the new value of s and go on to the next instruction. As we proceed through the algorithm, the value of the variable s thus changes as a result of step 4b in each cycle.

One way to determine whether an algorithm actually works as it is designed to do is to **trace** the algorithm for a certain set of inputs. The term 'trace' is metaphoric. Think of the loop in the averaging algorithm above as a wheel that rotates through each cycle; our trace will be a line representing the movement of the wheel through some determinate number of cycles. So let's trace the averaging algorithm for the numbers in the following list:

    23
    46
    127
    2,897
    1

This list constitutes the data for the algorithm. We move through the list from top to bottom, in effect using a pointer to determine where we are. Initially the pointer is on the first number, i.e.,

    23   ←
    46
    127
    2,897
    1

As the trace proceeds, the pointer is moved one number at a time until there are no data left, which would be the following situation:

    23
    46
    127
    2,897
    1

            ←

We can display the trace of the algorithm by means of the table on the next page, which keeps track of the values of m, s, c, and d, and the data remaining after each step.

You may wonder why we don't have a CLEAR command for the variables m and d. The reason is that the values of these variables are *set* in the various steps, so their previous values do not matter. But the variables s and c are changed by summing their present value with another number, so if they are not cleared, i.e., set to 0, at the outset, then a wrong answer may well result.

In the algorithm we do not indicate what *OUTPUT* means. A computer that runs such an algorithm in a program will have various possible output instructions, for example: 'WRITE "The average is ⟨d⟩." ' The material within double quotation marks will appear in characters on the computer screen, and whatever number is the current value of d will be written as, let us suppose, a decimal numeral in the place indicated by the corner brackets ⟨ ⟩.

Instruction	m	s	c	d	Data List	Output
START	?	?	?	?	23, 46, 127, 2,897, 1	
CLEAR s	?	0	?	?	23, 46, 127, 2,897, 1	
CLEAR c	?	0	0	?	23, 46, 127, 2,897, 1	
INPUT m	23	0	0	?	46, 127, 2,897, 1	
LET s = SUM m s	23	23	0	?	46, 127, 2,897, 1	
LET c = SUM c + 1	23	23	1	?	46, 127, 2,897, 1	
INPUT m	46	23	1	?	127, 2,897, 1	
LET s = SUM m s	46	69	1	?	127, 2,897, 1	
LET c = SUM c + 1	46	69	2	?	127, 2,897, 1	
INPUT m	127	69	2	?	2,897, 1	
LET s = SUM m s	127	196	2	?	2,897, 1	
LET c = SUM c + 1	127	196	3	?	2,897, 1	
INPUT m	2,897	196	3	?	1	
LET s = SUM m s	2,897	3,093	3	?	1	
LET c = SUM c + 1	2,897	3,093	4	?	1	
INPUT m	1	3,093	4	?	empty	
LET s = SUM m s	1	3,094	4	?	empty	
LET c = SUM c + 1	1	3,094	5	?	empty	
LET d = DIVIDE s c	1	3,094	5	618.8	empty	
OUTPUT d						618.8
STOP						

Note that if the instruction were simply: 'WRITE "The average is d,"' the sentence

> The average is d

would appear on the screen.

Algorithms often are written with other algorithms as parts. Suppose, for example, you wanted to design an algorithm that would provide the average salary of male and of female employees in some firm. The data would consist of a list of names of employees together with an indication of gender and salary. So the data might look like this:

John Jones	male	$25,000
Karen Smith	female	$31,000
Susan Smith	female	$21,000
Gertrude Ho	female	$25,000
Bill Williams	male	$20,000

We naturally want the algorithm to be general, so that it can deal with any size list and any order of males and females, including the possibility that there are no men, or no women, in the firm.

In thinking about how the algorithm might be designed, begin at the output, or goals. We want a number that represents the average of the salaries of the female employees—call it f—and we want a number that represents the average salary of the male employees—call it m. Furthermore, we want the result of the algorithm to be statements indicating what the two averages are. Each of f and m will be the output of an averaging algorithm that we already know how to design. So all we need are the steps that sends the female salaries to the female average and the male salaries to the male average. We will use tests and branches to accomplish this. Since each item in the data list has three parts—a name, the gender, and the salary—we will use the variable k for the full item, kg for the gender, and ks for the salary. So when k is

John Jones male $25,000

kg would be *male* and ks is *$25,000*. The rough design of the algorithm might look like this:

1. START
2. CLEAR m
3. CLEAR f
4. DO WHILE DATA REMAIN
 4a. INPUT k
 4b. IF kg = "male" THEN
   b1. Averaging algorithm, m
 4c. OTHERWISE
   c1. Averaging algorithm, f
5. OUTPUT
 5a. WRITE "The average of the male salaries is $\langle m \rangle$."
 5b. WRITE "The average of the female salaries is $\langle f \rangle$."
6. STOP

This algorithm will work perfectly well if the data are arranged with all three pieces: name, gender, salary. But, because of instruction 4*b*, if an item for some reason lacks a gender indication, then the algorithm will automatically consider that item a female and average the salary accordingly. The OTHERWISE instruction above creates a **default,** which means that unless an item is specified as male it is considered female. To avoid such a default, we can specify a second conditional instruction:

 4c. IF kg = "female" THEN

Since any item in the data that lacks a gender specification is faulty, we can use the OTHERWISE instruction to create a default that signals that something is wrong with the data and stops the algorithm:

4d. OTHERWISE

    d1. WRITE "Faulty data"

    d2. GOTO 6

The 'GOTO' instruction is handy because it allows us to move directly to some specific line in the algorithm.

Let's anticipate another problem. Suppose there are employees who are on unpaid leaves and their salary appears as $0 in the data. Strictly speaking, the numerical average of salaries should count such cases. But if the purpose of knowing average salaries by gender is to determine whether any gender discrimination is present in the firm, then such cases will interfere. To remove them, we can add yet another test (which would become step 4b):

IF $ks = 0$ THEN GOTO 4a

This test has the effect of throwing out any cases of individuals on leave without affecting how the algorithm proceeds in standard cases. If the condition $ks = 0$ is met, then we are told to go back to step 4a and input a new value for k. If the condition is *not* met, then we simply proceed as though the conditional were not present (this is the default condition for the conditional).

This understanding of the 'IF . . . THEN' instruction, by the way, fits exactly our earlier discussion of the SL conditional; a conditional is satisfied, or true, automatically if the antecedent is false.

Here, then, is the form of the algorithm with these additions:

1. START

2. CLEAR m

3. CLEAR f

4. DO WHILE DATA REMAIN

    4a. INPUT k

    4b. IF $ks = 0$ THEN GOTO 4a

    4c. IF $kg =$ "male" THEN

        c1. Averaging algorithm, m

    4d. IF $kg =$ "female" THEN

        d1. Averaging algorithm, f

4e. OTHERWISE

    e1. WRITE "Faulty data"

    e2. GOTO 6

5. OUTPUT

  5a. WRITE "The average of the male salaries is $$\langle m \rangle$$."

  5b. WRITE "The average of the female salaries is $$\langle f \rangle$$."

6. STOP

To produce the full algorithm we would put in the averaging algorithm in the two places indicated. Note that our counters in each subalgorithm will have to be different variables to properly keep track of the number of men and the number of women encountered. (see exercise 11.2a.3).

So far, then, we have worked with several types of **control instructions:**

Line numbers Indicate that we go through the instructions in the indicated sequence.

START Begins the algorithm.

STOP Ends the algorithm.

DO WHILE Sends us on a loop; we continue cycling until the condition is met, e.g., no data remain.

IF . . . THEN Creates a test (the antecedent) which, if met, sends us to whatever instruction follows the THEN; if the test is not met, we go on to the next line number.

IF . . . THEN . . . OTHERWISE Creates a test and gives instructions in case the test is met and in case it isn't (the OTHERWISE case).

GOTO n Sends us to line number n.

And we have worked with the following kinds of **operational instructions:**

INPUT x Give a value to the variable x from the data.

LET $x =$ Give a value to the variable x as indicated by the operation following the equals sign.

ADD $x\,y$ Add the values of x and y.

DIVIDE $x\,y$ Divide the value of x by the value of y.

CONVERT TO BINARY x Convert the decimal value of x to a binary numeral.

WRITE Display on a screen (or wherever) the characters enclosed in double quotes. Where a variable is enclosed by corner brackets, e.g., $\langle x \rangle$, the value of the variable is to be displayed.

EXERCISES 11.2a

1. Write an algorithm that tests binary numerals and prints out 'ODD' if the numeral is odd, and prints 'EVEN' if the numeral is even.

2. Write an algorithm that determines how many words occur in a given sentence.

3. Give the full algorithm for determining average salaries by gender. Provide a trace of the algorithm for at least eight items.

4. How can the Venn diagram (section 8.2) be considered an algorithm for determining the validity of syllogisms?

5. Sketch an algorithm that determines whether a column of SL statements (with various horizontal and vertical lines) counts as an SL derivation of the final statement in the column.

Now we turn to a precise formulation of some of the algorithmic procedures you have encountered in previous chapters.

The first is the construction of the basic truth table for an SL statement containing n different statement letters. Various algorithms can be found for this task, but perhaps the simplest uses binary numerals. Recall that there will be 2^n rows in such a truth table. The key idea in the algorithm is that the binary numerals for all powers of 2 consist of a 1 followed by the exponent number of zeroes. Recall that

$$2^0 (= 1) \quad = 1$$
$$2^1 (= 2) \quad = 10$$
$$2^2 (= 4) \quad = 100$$
$$2^3 (= 8) \quad = 1000$$
$$2^4 (= 16) = 10000$$
etc.

Also recall that subtracting 1 from the binary numeral for 2^n yields a binary numeral consisting of n 1's. For example, in the case of 2^4,

$$10000 - 1 = 1111.$$

If we think of 1 as **T** and 0 as **F**, the expression 1111 corresponds exactly to the truth values in the top row of the truth table for four statement letters. The subsequent rows, from the top downward, can be thought of as the result of progressively subtracting 1 from the binary numeral corresponding to the row above, with the answer expressed in four digits. So the second row of the truth table for four statement letters would thus be

$$1111 - 1 = 1110$$

The completed array of truth-values for four statement letters looks like this:

A	B	C	D
1	1	1	1
1	1	1	0
1	1	0	1
1	1	0	0
1	0	1	1
1	0	1	0
1	0	0	1
1	0	0	0
0	1	1	1
0	1	1	0
0	1	0	1
0	1	0	0
0	0	1	1
0	0	1	0
0	0	0	1
0	0	0	0

Our algorithmic procedure for creating a truth table for n statement letters, therefore, begins with the binary numeral for $2^n - 1$ and counts *down* to 0, expressing each line in n digits. It will be convenient to call the representation of a binary numeral in n digits its *n-expansion*. (So *0010* is the 4-expansion of *10*.)

Here is an algorithm producing the truth-table for n different statement letters:

1. START

2. INPUT n

3. LET $k = 2^n$

4. DO, WHILE $k > 0$

    4a. LET $k = k - 1$

    4b. CONVERT TO BINARY k

    4c. WRITE "$\langle n - \text{expansion } k \rangle$"

5. STOP

This algorithm will produce the appropriate array so long as the WRITE instruction triggers a printer that will put the *n*-expanded binary numerals in a neat column.

Another algorithmic procedure is checking whether an SL expression counts as an SL statement. A straightforward algorithm largely reduces the problem to arithmetic. The two-place connectives are replaced by $+$, negation is replaced by $-$, and all statement letters are replaced by 1. Then the appropriate addition of positive and negative numbers commences. The only problem is that we must have a scheme for dealing with parentheses. To see the problem, consider the following expression:

1. $(((A \supset B) \equiv\ \sim (C \& D)) \vee \sim F))$

If we carry out the replacement, we will have

2. $(((1\ +\ 1)\ +\ -\ (1\ +\ 1))\ +\ -1))$

This equals

3. $(((2)\ +\ -\ (2))\ +\ -1))$

To deal with the parentheses, we need to replace expressions like (n) with just n. We would then have

4. $((2\ +\ -\ 2)\ +\ -1))$

More calculation yields

5. $((0)\ +\ -1))$

More replacement of parentheses gives

6. $(0\ +\ -1))$

Calculation:

7. $(\ -\ 1))$

Parentheses replacement:

8. $-\ 1\ )$

Since the result of the calculation and parentheses replacement is not a positive or negative number, we see that the original expression was not an SL statement. As you see, the algorithm we are roughing out here assumes that the elementary rules of the arithmetic of positive and negative integers are algorithmic (which, of course, they are), but doesn't assume that such calculations will be done through parentheses. So, $-(1\ +\ 0)$ will be $-(1)$ after such calculation. We will use the operation instruction CALCULATE WITHIN PARENTHESES for such arithmetical calculations.

The algorithm to determine whether an expression is an SL statement might be formulated as follows. (Note: it is assumed that all parentheses, including outer parentheses, are in place.)

1. START

2. INPUT expression

3. IF the expression contains any non-SL symbols, THEN GOTO 8b

4. REPLACE &, ⊃, ∨, ≡, with +; and ~ with −

5. REPLACE statement letters with *1*

6. DO, WHILE number of parentheses > 1

    6a. CALCULATE WITHIN PARENTHESES

    6b. REPLACE (*n*) with *n*

    6c. IF the expression is unchanged, THEN GOTO 8b

7. IF number of parentheses = 1, THEN GOTO 8b

8. IF expression is a number, THEN

    8a. WRITE "Expression is an SL statement"

    OTHERWISE

    8b. WRITE "Expression is not an SL statement."

9. STOP

You will note that this algorithm uses the number of parentheses as a principal means of controlling the sequence of operations. In all expressions that are SL statements, the number of parentheses is even. (Remember that all SL statements have outer parentheses, even though they are usually not written.) We repeat the various 'calculate' and 'replace' operations until we have the expression with either no parentheses or just one parenthesis. However, if at any point there is more than one parenthesis but the applications of the instructions in line 6a and 6b do not change the expression, then we do not have an SL statement. Such a case would be an expression like '((,' which has two parentheses, but is obviously not a statement. If there is just one parenthesis, then the expression is not a statement, no matter what else may be the case. If there are no parentheses, then the test in line 8 is whether it is a number or some expression like *1 0* (note the space) or + +2, etc.

A related algorithm calculates the truth-value of an SL statement. To keep everything simple, we will assume that only the connectives &, ∨, and ~ are used. In this case we have as input an SL statement and a set of truth-values for the atomic statements. The algorithm makes use of the Boolean operations that correspond to the three SL connectives. We begin by replacing the statement letters by their truth-values (using *1* and *0*), and then we replace the SL connectives by their Boolean counterparts. Then calculation within parentheses takes place and the same replacement of (n) by n as in the statement testing algorithm. The truth-value of the statement will emerge when we work through to a single numeral, *1* or *0*.

Here, then, is the algorithm for determining the truth-value of an SL statement:

1. START

2. INPUT statement

3. INPUT truth-values

4. REPLACE statement letters with truth-values

5. DO WHILE number of parentheses $\geqslant 2$

   5a. CALCULATE BOOLEAN WITHIN PARENTHESES

   5b. REPLACE (*1*) by *1* and (*0*) by *0*

6. IF statement = 1, THEN

   6a. WRITE "The statement is true."

   OTHERWISE

   6b. WRITE "The statement is false."

7. STOP[8]

EXERCISES 11.2b

1. How does the algorithm that determines whether an expression is an SL statement distinguish an expression like *1 0*, which thus has too few connectives, from the numeral *10*?

2. Formulate an algorithm for checking whether an expression in Polish notation is an SL statement.

3. Formulate an algorithm for determining the truth-value of an SL statement in Polish notation.

4. Describe an algorithm that determines whether an SL statement is a tautology.

*5. Modify the algorithm that determines whether an expression is an SL statement as follows:

   a. It indicates when there are too many left parentheses.

   b. It indicates when there are too many right parentheses.

   c. It indicates when there are too many connectives.

   d. It indicates when there are too few connectives.

---

[8]These last two algorithms are modifications of those found in Morton L. Schagrin, William J. Rapaport, and Randall R. Dipert, *Logic: A Computer Approach* (New York: McGraw-Hill, 1985), chapter 5.

Sorting

One of the routine algorthmic tasks is sorting a list of items to put them into some order. You are familiar with the task of alphabetizing a list, for example, in preparing a bibliography. This is an example of sorting. A simple procedure for sorting a list of n items is by means of successive comparisons between two items on the list at a time. Suppose, for example, you want to sort the following list of five names *by length:*

Jones

William

Ho

Hart

Olivecci

One of the issues is whether the list is to be sorted so that the longest name occurs at the bottom, which is *ascending* order, or with the longest name at the top, which is *descending* order. Suppose we want the list sorted in ascending order. So the longest name should be at the bottom, and the shortest name at the top. You can probably figure out just by looking at the names, that Ho goes at the top and Olivecci goes at the bottom. But a computer requires an algorithm.

The procedure of sorting a list by comparison is called **bubblesort,** since, as we will see, items bubble up to the top of the list and down to the bottom of the list. The basic idea is that pairs of items are compared by length and the smaller is put ahead of the larger. If that is their initial order, then it is preserved; if they are out of order they are exchanged. This bubblesorting is accomplished by repeated **traversals** of the list. Here is the result of the first traversal:

Initial list	First traversal
Jones	Jones
William	Ho
Ho	Hart
Hart	William
Olivecci	Olivecci

As you can see, since *Jones* and *William* are already in order, they are left in place. But when *Ho* is compared to *William*, an exchange takes place, putting *Ho* second in the list. Next *William* (now third) is compared to *Hart* and they are exchanged, putting *Hart* third and *William* fourth. When *William* and *Olivecci* are compared, they are in the correct order.

Look now at the result of the first traversal. You can easily see that after the next traversal *Jones* will fall down below both *Ho* and *Hart* to its correct position just above *William*, so one more traversal will do it.

Initial list	First traversal	Second traversal
Jones	Jones	Ho
William	Ho	Hart
Ho	Hart	Jones
Hart	William	William
Olivecci	Olivecci	Olivecci

Notice that by starting at the top and sorting in order of the shortest to the longest name (ascending order), the largest item will find its way to the bottom of the list on the very first traversal.[9] Thus, on the second traversal we don't need to compare the bottom item with anything, and the second largest element will find its way to the bottom, etc. Consequently, the *most* traversals that a five-item list can take to completely sort the list is four. On the fourth traversal, the fourth largest item will be fourth from the bottom, so the smallest item will be on top, and the list will be sorted. Note, also, that within each traversal, four comparisons are made. So, where n items are in the list, $n - 1$ comparisons occur in each traversal, and a maximum of $n - 1$ traversals are needed to sort the list.

Of course, in formulating a general algorithm for bubblesorting, we can't take into consideration the initial order of the items in the list. Therefore, in producing an algorithm for bubblesort, we need to be prepared for the worst case and write the algorithm to make the full $n - 1$ traversals.

We can formulate an algorithm that accomplishes the bubblesort of a list of n items, as follows:

1. START

2. INPUT list

3. INPUT n

4. DO, $n - 1$ times

    4a. POINT to the first item

    4b. DO, $n - 1$ times

        b1. COMPARE item pointed to with next item

        b2. EXCHANGE items if in the wrong order

        b3. POINT to next item

---

[9]If we had started our comparisons at the bottom of the list, the smallest name would have risen to the top on the first traversal.

5. OUTPUT list

6. STOP

This bubblesort algorithm has the features of a loop within a loop. The inner loop (b1–b3) is the actual sorting on each traversal, as pairs of items are successively compared $n - 1$ times. The outer loop represents the successive $n - 1$ traversals necessary to insure that the list is fully sorted, no matter what position is initially occupied by the various items.

Although the bubblesort algorithm will produce a sorted list, it is highly **inefficient.** Some unsorted lists are closer to being sorted than others, but bubblesort treats them all alike; the same number of steps are required for a list of n items, no matter how jumbled the list may be. When we, on the other hand, are presented with a sorting problem we first look at the list to see whether it needs sorting at all. Then, if only a few items are out of order, we change their locations and declare the list sorted. But bubblesort does not stop when the list is sorted; it continues and completes its $n - 1$ traversals.

One way to improve on bubblesort is to include a test instruction that asks whether any items on the list were exchanged in the course of the last inner loop. (Recall that this same strategy was used in determining whether expressions are SL statements.) If no exchange has taken place, then the list is already sorted and the algorithm can output the sorted list and stop. Such an instruction can be substituted for line 4 as follows:

4. DO WHILE exchanges take place

Adding this refinement to bubblesort may greatly shorten its running time when it is used in a computer program. Suppose, for example, only one item is out of place in a list of 10,000 items (the telephone directory for a small city). If the full bubblesort algorithm had to be followed in this case, the number of steps would be approximately 100,000,000 (i.e.,$10,000^2$), whereas, with the additional instruction, only 19,997 steps are required. There would be two traversals: the first (9,999 steps) to change the item out of place and the second (9,998 steps), which doesn't change anything; then the algorithm outputs and stops.

Searching

Another common task is searching to *find* an item in a sorted list, like looking up someone's name in a telephone directory. The slow way to accomplish this task would be to start at the beginning of the list and compare each item in order to decide whether it is the one searched for. Suppose we are looking for the telephone number of A. Zzzyrmidgeon in a large directory that contains 1,000,000 names. Starting at the beginning of the book and working through all the names will require the full 1,000,000 steps. You, obviously, if given the task, would not do this. You would look at the last page and scan, perhaps, a column of names, say 300, before finding that A. Zzzyrmidgeon is listed.[10] What you would be doing is taking advantage of the fact that the list has already been sorted. So how can we build this more efficient procedure into an algorithm for *searching*?

A good place to start is the divide and conquer strategy. Instead of searching from the beginning of the list, we should divide the list until we come to the subsection where the item we seek is likely to be located. That is, in essence, how we use telephone books except that the list has already been divided by letter. Take the following list of numbers as an example:

2, 5, 7, 12, 34, 35, 65, 102, 167, 256, 889

Suppose we are searching for item *102*. The divide and conquer method is what is known as a **binary search,** since we continually divide by 2 until we either find the item or determine that it is not present. To put this technique into an algorithm requires a definite statement of the splitting procedure, so we must recognize that each place in a sorted list of length n has a place *index*. The indexes for the list we used above would look like this:

ITEMS: 2, 5, 7, 12, 34, 35, 65, 102, 167, 256, 889

INDEX: 1 2 3 4 5 6 7 8   9   10   11

In this example, item *2* has the index 1, and item *889* has the index 11. All divisions of lists will be the result of adding the indexes of the first and last items and dividing by 2; the result is the point at which the list is divided. For example, to divide the list above we add 1 and 11 and divide the sum (= 12) by 2, which tells us the item with index 6 is the dividing point. Since our indexes are all integers, we will have to *round up* in some cases. For example, in the next division we will have (1 + 6)/2; so we will write the rounded up integer value of the division as $|(1 + 6)/2|$ (= 4). All items larger go in one side, all small items go in the other. For our list, the first division is on the item with index $|(1 + 11)/2|$ (= 6), which is item *35*. Taking *35* out gives the following two lists:

2, 5, 7, 12, 34   65, 102, 167, 256, 889

The searched-for item is then compared to *35*, which is called the *median* of the list. The item is either equal to *35* (and the search ends) or is smaller or greater. Since *102* is greater, we then must divide again so we compute the index of the *median* of the *right* list, which is $|(7 + 11)/2|$. Note that 7 is the index of the first item *65* and 11 is the index of the last. The median of the

---

right list then has index 9 so it is item *167*. By removing the median, the two lists are now

65, 102   256, 889

Since *102* is less than the median, we next compute the index of the median of the left list, $|(7 + 8)/2| = 8$. Then the item searched for is compared to the new median; since, of course, they are equal the search ends. If they weren't equal, we would then know which item was searched for (suppose it was *65*, which is the only item less than the median *102*) or that it wasn't in the list. With a higher number of items, additional divisions and comparisons would have taken place. Note that only three comparisons were necessary to locate item *102* in the list. But the worst case in the sequential search method that begins at the first item would be eleven items, so there is a clear efficiency to the binary search procedure.

Here is the binary search algorithm for searching for the index *i* of item *m* (the searched-for item) in a sorted list of length *n*:

We will use the following variables:

L for list

f for index of the first item

j for index of the last item

i for index of the match

m for item searched for

Lmed for item that is the median in list *L*

med for index of *Lmed*

1. START
2. CLEAR *i*
3. LET $j = m$
4. LET $f = 1$
5. DO, WHILE $f \leqslant j$
   5a. LET $med = |(f + j)/2|$
   5b. IF $m > Lmed$, THEN
       b1. LET $f = med + 1$
           OTHERWISE
       b2. IF $m = Lmed$ THEN
           b2.1. LET $i = med$
           b2.2. GOTO 6
               OTHERWISE
           b2.3. LET $j = med - 1$

6. OUTPUT *i*

7. STOP

Because we have variables for both items in the list and indexes of those items, there is a surplus of symbolism in the above algorithm. Note that we have to be able to compare object *m* with items in the list. So, for example, if we are searching an alphabetical list, then the expression $m > Lmed$ would mean that word *m* comes later than the word represented by the variable *Lmed*. But the binary search algorithm has the nice property of returning the output of *0* when a searched-for item *m* is not in the list. To analyze more fully how the algorithm works, we will provide a trace for such a case. Here is a list, together with indexes:

1. Adams

2. Baker

3. Casteneda

4. Devany

5. Ebert

6. Foucout

7. Galvichelli

8. Ho

9. Irwing

10. Johnson

11. Jones

12. Karp

13. Lamchek

Suppose we want to search the list to discover where (if at all) the name Howard would be placed. The algorithm trace is as presented in the following table.

    f for index of the first item

    j for index of the last item

    i for index of the match

    m for item searched for

    Lmed for item which is the median

    med for index of *Lmed*

Notice how the algorithm directs us in splitting the original list first at the name *Galvichelli* (index 7) and, since *Howard* > *Galvichelli*, we split the list again, this time at *Jones* (index 11). Since *Howard* < *Jones*, the next split is at

Instruction	i	f	j	med	Lmed	m
START	?	?	?	?	?	Howard
CLEAR i	0	?	?	?	?	Howard
LET f = 1	0	1	?	?	?	Howard
LET j = n(13)	0	1	13	?	?	Howard
LET med = |(f + j)/2|	0	1	13	7	Galvichelli	Howard
IF m > Lmed						
THEN						
LET f = med + 1	0	8	13	7	Galvichelli	Howard
LET med = |(f + j)/2|	0	8	13	11	Jones	Howard
IF m < Lmed						
THEN						
LET j = med − 1	0	8	10	11	Jones	Howard
LET med = |(f + j)/2|	0	8	10	9	Irwing	Howard
IF m < Lmed						
THEN						
LET j = med − 1	0	8	8	9	Irwing	Howard
LET med = |(f + j)/2|	0	8	8	8	Ho	Howard
IF m > Lmed						
THEN						
LET f = med + 1	0	9*	8*	8	Ho	Howard
OUTPUT i	0					Howard
STOP						

Irwing (index 9), and since *Howard* < *Irwing*, the next split is at *Ho* (index 8). Now it is clear that the name is not in the list, since *Howard* > *Ho*, so in the next step the value of f becomes 9, while the value of j is 8 (this step is marked by asterisks). But this violates the initial DO, WHILE instruction, and so the algorithm ends with an output of $i = 0$, signifying the failure of the search to find the place of *Howard* in the list.

Later we will discuss absolute limits on computability; we will find problems no computer can possibly solve (e.g., validity in PL). But here we have been discussing another kind of limit on computers, namely practical limits imposed by inefficient algorithms. We have studied some amazing reductions in the number of steps required to run common algorithms. In one case of bubblesort, we reduced 100,000,000 steps to 19,907, in a favorable case; in our first binary search example we reduced 11 steps to 3. But it is known that a binary search in a sorted list of a billion items will require *at most* thirty comparisons, a remarkable savings of time.[11]

---

[11]Harel, *Algorithmics*, p. 126. Recall that a sequential search would have a worst case of one billion steps.

There are far worse cases: problems that are algorithmic but would take years and years of computation by the fastest computers to run their algorithms. An example you know well by this time is testing SL statements for logical properties and relations by truth-tables. Since the number of truth table cases for a statement containing n different statement letters is 2^n and we have seen that an algorithm for a single row of a truth table has a number of steps, the truth-table algorithm is horribly inefficient. To put this issue into perspective, suppose a computer can run our truth-value calculating algorithm one million times per second. Then to work through the truth-table algorithm for determining whether an SL statement with one thousand different statement letters is a tautology would take much longer than the currently estimated age of the universe!

EXERCISES 11.2c

1. Change the bubblesort algorithm so that it begins at the bottom of a list.

2. Rewrite the bubblesort algorithm so that the list will be sorted in

   a. ascending order

   b. descending order

3. Sketch an algorithm for double, two-layer sorting. Suppose the list to be sorted consists of items with two parts: a town and a state. First sort the states alphabetically, then rearrange so that the towns in each state are in alphabetical order too.

4. Try the binary search algorithm on a portion of your student telephone directory.

*5. Suppose you are searching only in alphabetical lists. Change the binary search algorithm so that the divisions will automatically take place on certain letters and indexes are not required.

11.3 TURING MACHINES

In 1936, more than ten years before the first functioning computer, the British mathematician Alan Turing published a remarkable paper.[12] Turing had been working on the problem of whether there were general algorithmic methods for determining validity, entailment, and consistency, for logical systems like predicate logic. At the time, the concept of an algorithmic method was very vague, so part of Turing's work focused on sharpening the concept itself. He hit upon using the operation of an imaginary device—the *computing*

---

[12]For the life and details of Turing's work, see Andrew Hodges, *Alan Turing: The Enigma* (New York: Simon and Schuster, 1983), esp. chs. 1 and 2; for a comprehensive account of Turing machines see J. E. Hopcraft, "Turing Machines," *Scientific American* 250 (1984), pp. 70–80. Turing's original paper is "On Computable Numbers, with an Application to the Entscheidungsproblem," included in M. Davis (ed.), *The Undecidable* (Hewlett, NY: Raven Press, 1965), pp. 116–153.

machine—to develop a precise meaning. It is important to note that even though Turing's work was to have an important role in the subsequent development of the electronic digital computer, the term 'computing' in 1936 meant only the process of arriving at the answer to some mathematical problem. So although Turing was interested in a theoretical machine capable of computation, he did not invent or first conceive of computers as we know them. Because of the importance of his work, Turing's algorithm machines quickly became known as **Turing Machines.**

Here is a description of the operation of one of these imaginary Turing machines.[13]

1. The machine consists of a **head** that *reads* (i.e., scans) symbols from and *prints* symbols on a long paper tape. This head is capable of moving across the tape in either direction.

2. The tape is divided into squares that are either blank or contain one symbol.

3. The only symbols are **1** and **0.**

4. These are the only actions that can be performed by the machine:

   a. The machine can move one square to the right.

   b. The machine can move one square to the left.

   c. The machine can read a symbol or a blank from the square it is on.

   d. The machine can erase and print a symbol on the square it is on or leave the square blank.

Our Turing machine might look like this:

Turing machine

---

[13]There are many ways of describing Turing machines. All, however, are ultimately equivalent.

To get the flavor of what a Turing machine might do, suppose a section of a tape initially has the following symbols in a series of squares:

Now imagine that the head of the Turing machine moves over the tape, reading each square and printing a symbol on it or leaving it blank. The tape afterwards looks like this:

Let us suppose what has happened is that beginning with the blank square on the far left, the Turing machine has passed over each square, moving toward the right. As the head passes over each square, the machine reads the symbol (or blank) and then erases and prints a symbol or leaves the square blank. For the sake of simplicity, we will use the term *print* for the actions of erasing a symbol, printing a symbol, or leaving the square blank. In this case, moving from left to right, the machine has left the first two **1**'s in place, and has changed the third **1** to a **0**; then it has printed two more **0**'s in succession, then a **1**, and then left the remaining squares blank as it moved along.

One way to interpret these actions of the Turing machine is to say that the *binary numeral*

111

has been replaced by the binary numeral

110001

Recall that **111** is the binary numeral for 7 and **110001** is the binary numeral for 49. So our Turing machine can be understood as having *squared* the number initially appearing on the tape.

Turing's very simple imaginary machine has proven to be an immensely powerful idea. Turing himself conjectured that if an operation can be thought of as algorithmic, then the operation can be carried out by such a machine; otherwise, the operation is nonalgorithmic. Thus, a question such as whether there is an algorithmic method for determining validity in PL becomes a question of whether PL validity can be determined by a Turing machine.

The American mathematical logician Alonzo Church also worked on the problem of defining 'mechanical' or 'algorithmic' methods in the mid-1930s.

Both Turing and Church independently came to the same conclusion: all possible definitions of what counts as a mechanical or algorithmic method or process are ultimately identical. This conclusion is known as the *Church-Turing thesis*. As a *thesis*, the claim of Church and Turing is not susceptible to rigorous proof. All that can be said is that the thesis is essentially universally accepted and that every reasonable proposal for precisely defining a mechanical or algorithmic process has been shown to be equivalent to all others.[14]

The importance of the Turing machine will become clearer as we go along; for now you should note that since all computers operate entirely on algorithms, the work of Church and Turing fundamentally connects computers and Turing machines. The limits of Turing machines, according to the Church-Turing thesis, also describe the theoretical limits of all computers.

Essentially, then, an algorithm for some operation, like raising a number n to the power of 2, is implemented by a Turing machine by formulating a set of instructions for the machine. Beginning on the first square with a symbol that is part of the binary representation of n, the machine can proceed square by square, halting when the binary representation of n^2 is on the tape.

The instructions for our Turing machine will have the machine read the symbol, if any, on the square of a tape where its read/print head is located, erase or write a symbol (i.e., 'print'), and move to the right or left. Instructions will rely on the idea that the machine at any time is in some particular internal **state** that will affect what it does next. The internal states direct the machine to act in various ways, depending upon what symbol appears on the square it is on. Recall that the first line in an algorithm is START; similarly, the initial state (for which we use A) of a Turing machine starts the machine. If there are symbols on the tape we will always assume that the read/print head is initially positioned on the left-most square that contains a symbol.

Our earlier presentation of algorithms illustrated that, unless instructed to do otherwise, instructions are completed in order, line by line. In a Turing machine, each state directs the machine to the next state. So, in each Turing machine instruction, there will be reference to an *input* state (the state the machine is in), and some input symbol is read from the square the machine is on; there will also be an *output action* of printing (putting a symbol in the square or leaving the square blank) and of moving right or left. There will be also an *output state*, the machine's state for the next instruction.

Here is a simple case. Suppose there are two possible states, A and B, the Turing machine can be in. Suppose the machine begins in the A state and either stays in the A state or goes on to the B state. We use b to indicate a blank square, R and L to indicate the possible moves—move right one

---

[14]See, for example, Daniel I. A. Cohen, *Introduction to Computer Theory* (New York: John Wiley & Sons, 1986), part 3.

square, and move left one square—and we use *H* to indicate that the machine halts; that is, upon reaching a specified input in a certain state, the machine stops all activity. This step is analogous to the STOP operation of algorithms. Obviously, without a halt state, the machine would go on indefinitely, moving one square at a time, rather like an infinite loop in an algorithm.

	Input Read	Output Print	Move	State
State A	0	0	R	A
	1	1	R	A
	b	b	L	B
State B	0	1	L	B
	1	1	L	B
	b	b	H	

What this table shows is that the Turing machine has two possible states: it can be in *A* or in *B*. If, for example, the machine is in state *A* and it is on a square with the symbol **1**, then the machine does the following:

1. prints a **1** in the square
2. moves one square to the right
3. stays in state *A* for the next step

Let's suppose the next square contains a **0**. Then the machine

4. prints a **0**
5. moves one square right
6. stays in state *A* for the next step

Then suppose the machine finds the next square blank. Then it

7. leaves the square blank
8. moves left
9. goes into state *B*

(We will return to this Turing machine later.)

As a beginning project, a simple Turing machine can be formulated that performs the operation of Boolean complementation. Beginning on the left-most digit of a string of **1**'s and **0**'s, the machine simply outputs a **1,** for a **0** input, and outputs a **0,** for a **1** input. As soon as the machine reaches a blank, it halts.

Turing machine for complementation

	Input Read	Output		
		Print	Move	State
State A	0	1	R	A
	1	0	R	A
	b	b	H	

To start the machine, we place it, as usual, on the left-most symbol. If we place it on a blank square, the machine simply halts; otherwise it runs through its program until a blank square is reached and then it halts.

We next describe a machine that detects whether numbers—expressed as binary numerals on a Turing tape—are odd or even. If a number is odd, the machine will output **1**; if the number is even, the machine will output **0**.

Turing machine for testing odd/even

	Input Read	Output		
		Print	Move	State
State A	0	0	R	A
	1	1	R	A
	b	b	L	B
State B	1	1	R	C
	0	0	R	D
State C	b	b	R	E
State D	b	b	R	F
State E	b	1	H	
State F	b	0	H	

The Turing machine is placed on the left-most digit of a string of **1**'s and **0**'s on a tape. As it runs, it stays in state A until it passes by all of the symbols and reaches a blank, which signals the end of the numeral. Then it goes into state B, moves left across one (blank) square, and reads the last digit to determine whether it is a **1**, in which case the number is odd, or a **0**, in which case the number is even. Depending on what is read, the machine goes either into state C or D and moves to the right over the blank square. Then it goes into state E or F, prints the appropriate symbol (**1** for odd and **0** for even), and halts.

In both of these Turing machines, as the machine passes over each square, a symbol or blank is read by the head, and a symbol (possibly the same one) or blank is printed. Thinking of the Turing machine in this way allows us to describe it by means of the list above of states and their various inputs and outputs; we don't need to specify an additional action of erasing a square. To erase is to *input* a symbol and *output* a blank.

You should note that the power of the Turing machine is that it deals only with symbols. These symbols could be anything: letters from the alphabet, stars, boxes, whatever. All that is required is that the head of the machine recognize the symbols (and blank squares). So the Turing machine tape in the above examples does not really contain numerals; it contains symbols that we *interpret* as (binary) numerals. In our first Turing machine, the operation just reverses the symbols; in the second, it replicates the rightmost symbol one square away.

To illustrate that the Turing machine can be thought of as working entirely at the symbolic level, here is a machine that rearranges the symbols on a tape. We looked at two of its states earlier.

Turing machine to do?

	Input Read	Output Print	Move	State
State A	0	0	R	A
	1	1	R	A
	b	b	L	B
State B	1	0	L	C
	0	1	L	D
	b	b	H	
State C	1	0	L	C
	0	1	L	D
	b	1	H	
State D	1	1	L	D
	0	0	L	D
	b	b	H	

With the machine starting on the square that is left-most in a string of symbols, the head passes the tape through until a blank square is reached. The machine moves left, and the rearrangement of symbols begins until the blank square at the left of the string is reached and the machine halts. Try a trace yourself on this machine; begin with a string of 1's and 0's and see what happens. Then try to decide what operation the machine can be thought of as performing.[15]

Universal Turing Machines

So far, our only description of any particular Turing machine is the list of instructions in the form of states and their various inputs and outputs. Each line in such a list can be represented separately as a series of five *items*, e.g., input state, input symbol, output symbol, output action, output state.

For example, the top line of the table of Turing machine instructions just depicted reads

A, 0, 0, R, A

Thus, another way of representing a Turing machine is as a list (of instructions) that looks like this:

$A,\ \mathbf{0},\ \mathbf{0},\ R,\ A$
$A,\ \mathbf{1},\ \mathbf{1},\ R,\ A$
$A,\ b,\ b,\ L,\ B$
$B,\ \mathbf{1},\ \mathbf{0},\ L,\ C$
$B,\ \mathbf{0},\ \mathbf{1},\ L,\ D$
$B,\ b,\ b,\ H,\ H$
$C,\ \mathbf{1},\ \mathbf{0},\ L,\ C$
$C,\ \mathbf{0},\ \mathbf{1},\ L,\ D$
$C,\ b,\ \mathbf{1},\ H,\ H$
$D,\ \mathbf{1},\ \mathbf{1},\ L,\ D$
$D,\ \mathbf{0},\ \mathbf{0},\ L,\ D$
$D,\ b,\ b,\ H,\ H$

(Note: in order to have exactly five entries in each line, we insert H, H as the last two items in any instruction that has a 'Halt' in it, e.g., B, b, b, H, H). This list represents the Turing machine that adds 1 to a number expressed as a binary numeral.

---

[15]Answer: incrementing a binary numeral.

It is quite easy to represent each item in any such list of Turing machine instructions by means of a code that uses binary numerals. For example, the instruction

D, 1, 1, *L,D*

might easily be expressed as follows, in standard ASCII code, which uses a block of seven binary digits for each symbol:

0100100	0001011	0001011	1100100	0100100
D	1	1	*L*	*D*

Since all Turing machine instructions expressed as a series of five items have the same form, they are also simply decoded from their ASCII representations. If all we need are 26 different state names (i.e., *A, B,* etc.) then all Turing machine instructions can be expressed by means of a 35-digit binary numeral. If we should need to represent more than 26 possible machine states in some Turing machine, we can just use several capital letters for states, e.g., *AB* or *CDEFTH,* thus increasing the number of digits in the ASCII code for any particular instruction.

Decoding an instruction begins with left digit and moves right: when we get to the ASCII code for **0** or **1**, we know what the name of the first state is, represented either by one capital letter or several. After the state name, the next seven digits are the input character (**1** or **0**), the next seven digits are the output character, the next seven are the move instruction (*L* or *R*), and so on until we reach the final seven digits, which form the last letter of the output state name. What instruction, then, is expressed in ASCII code by the following numeral?

0001100 0001011 0000011 0010101 0100100

Since each line or individual instruction of any particular Turing machine can be expressed as a binary numeral, the Turing machine itself can also be expressed as a binary numeral for all of its instructions. Just put together each and every instruction ASCII code into a string of **1**'s and **0**'s beginning with the first instruction on the left, and with the final instruction on the right, separating each particular instruction with an extra **0**, and leaving a blank square after the last instruction. We will, again, have no trouble decoding such a numeral back into the instructions, since we can begin on the left and decode one instruction at a time. The resulting numeral will be fairly large, of course, but since it is finite it still can be written.

Now imagine that we have a Turing machine, call it BIG, that has a tape on which we have written the binary numeral representing the full instructions for a second Turing machine T. Since BIG's tape (like that of any Turing machine) can be as long in both directions as we may need, we have plenty of room for such a large binary numeral. Further, suppose we have some other binary numeral on BIG's tape separated from the instruction numeral for T by a blank square. We conceive of BIG as able, because of its instructions, to simulate the operation of the second Turing machine T. BIG is started on the left of the instruction numeral for T. BIG's head reads the first instruction square by square and then proceeds across the **0** separating the first instruction from the second instruction, and so on, to the blank at the end of the instructions; then it begins to read the next numeral, which is whatever is initially on the tape of Turing machine T (i.e., the input of T). BIG's head goes back and forth, from instruction to input, until BIG has executed the instructions and produced whatever output on the tape that is appropriate for the operation of T.

If we assume that BIG's instructions are sufficiently comprehensive so that with appropriate inputs BIG can simulate the operation of any Turing machine, we have an idea of the machine Alan Turing envisioned in his 1936 paper; BIG is a *universal computing machine* that can run any algorithm in the form of a set of instructions for a Turing machine. Note that, in accord with the Church-Turing thesis, any algorithmic process can be transformed into a Turing machine, so all algorithms can run on BIG.

As we have conceived it, this Turing machine BIG—usually now called the universal Turing machine—can actually do more than simulate the operation of any Turing machine; it can simulate any actual computer that has ever or will ever be built. Suppose you own a personal computer, call it *Hal*. The universal Turing machine BIG can simulate Hal by having on its tape the complete set of instructions for the operation of Hal, including all of its programs and its circuitry. Suppose you are running a word processing program on Hal to type a term paper. Any input, like the press of a key on Hal's keyboard, can be computed by BIG just as it is done by Hal. You provide some input to Hal; some output is provided by Hal. All of this can be done by the universal Turing machine BIG. BIG can also simulate the fastest supercomputer, although a vastly larger tape will be required.

Another implication of this line of thinking is that your personal computer Hal can itself simulate any computer, even the fastest supercomputers, if you provide Hal with enough additional memory. Hal can run as a Turing machine, since all a Turing machine does is read, print (i.e., remember), and move (i.e., input the next digit). The coded Turing machine instructions for a supercomputer can be fed into Hal, thus providing the additional input. So your Hal will be chunking along, simulating a much bigger, faster supercomputer. Of course Hal will not perform at the speed of the supercomputer; Hal will be more like a glacier simulating a raging, white-water river.

Since any computer is essentially a Turing machine, the limits of Turing machines are thus the limits of computers. In the next section, we will see what these limits are.

EXERCISES 11.3

1. Write a set of instructions for a Turing machine that shortens any string of **1**'s and **0**'s by one digit, taken from the right side of the string.

2. Write a set of instructions for a Turing machine that lengthens any string of **1**'s and **0**'s by adding two digits onto the left side.

3. Write a set of instructions for a Turing machine that erases any string of digits.

4. Write a set of instructions for a Turing machine that counts the digits in a string and outputs the appropriate binary numeral. Suppose the maximum number of digits in the string is four.

5. Write a set of instructions for a Turing machine that duplicates a string of **1**'s and **0**'s by erasing the original string and writing the duplicate to the right of the position of the original.

6. Write the first five instructions for one of your Turing machines as a list of series of five objects.

7. Put the above list into ASCII code and express the list as a binary numeral. (ASCII code will be found in the Appendix.)

*8. Suppose the operation of the circuitry of your personal computer Hal can be represented as a list of instructions. Suppose you insert a program into Hal, say WIZZO. Describe a universal Turing machine like BIG that would simulate Hal running WIZZO.

11.4 THE HALTING PROBLEM

Not every Turing machine eventually *halts* when given a specific set of characters on its tape as input. For example, the simple Turing machine with the instructions

> A, b, b, R, A
>
> $A, 0, 1, L, A$
>
> $A, 1, b, R, B$
>
> B, b, b, H, H
>
> $B, 0, b, R, A$
>
> $B, 1 \ b, R, A$

will halt leaving a blank tape if the initial input is a **0** or **1**, but it will not halt if a binary numeral with more than a single digit is represented on the tape or if the tape is initially blank. In either case, it will just keep moving across the tape forever. (Note: it is assumed, as usual, that the Turing machine head is initially placed on the left-most digit of the string of characters on its tape and the initial state is A.)

Here is a Turing machine that will not halt for any binary numeral smaller than 2 (i.e., **10**):

A, b, b, R, B

A, **0, 0,** *R, B*

A, **1, 1,** *R, B*

B, **1, 1,** *R, C*

B, **0, 0,** *R, C*

B, b, b, R, B

C, **1, 1,** *R, C*

C, **0, 0,** *R, C*

C, b, b, R, D

D, b, b, H, H

D, **0,** *b, H, H*

D, **1,** *b, H, H*

On a binary numeral of two or more digits, this Turing machine reads the number and moves along the tape until it reaches a blank, and then halts. If the tape, however, is initially blank or has a single **1** or a single **0,** then the machine never halts. With a little ingenuity, it is possible to formulate a Turing machine that will halt for any range of binary numeral inputs and will not halt for others. So among *all possible* Turing machines, there will be those that will halt for any specific binary numeral input and others that will not halt for that input.

Let's return to the universal Turing machine BIG. As *its* input, we give BIG a tape on which are the characters for two binary numerals (two continuous strings of **1**'s and **0**'s); the left numeral, which we call **T**, is the coded list of instructions for some Turing machine *T* and, separated by a blank square, the right numeral (or blank tape), which we call **n,** is the numeral representing the characters (if any) on an input tape of the Turing machine *T.* BIG, as usual, is started on the left-most square of the instruction numeral **T**; BIG then simulates the operation of *T* by moving back and forth between the instructions and the *T*'s input numeral **n**. Depending on the coded instructions (numeral **T**) and the *T*'s input (numeral **n**), BIG either halts with the appropriate output of *T* given input **n,** or it doesn't halt and continues working away forever. For example, if we gave BIG as input the first set of Turing machine instructions above and the numeral **1,** then BIG would halt with its output section of the tape blank; if, on the other hand, we give BIG the same instructions together with the numeral **10,** BIG will not ever halt.

Now we will imagine a *special* universal Turing machine called BIGGER, which will simulate Turing machines in the following sense. Just as we did for BIG, we will input into BIGGER the numeral **T** (which represents the combined coded instructions of some Turing machine *T*) and an input numeral **n**. BIGGER will determine whether machine *T* will halt on inputs **T** and **n**. If *T* does halt, then BIGGER outputs a **1** on its tape; if *T* does not halt, BIGGER outputs a **0**.

We have quite a bit going on here, so let's pause to be sure that all this is clear. We have identified three distinct kinds of Turing machines:

A. Ordinary Turing machines, which run across across a tape containing a string of **1**'s and **0**'s and blank squares. This string can be thought of as a binary numeral (or blank tape) and we call it the input numeral **n**. These Turing machines will either halt on the input of a given input numeral **n**, and leave some output string of characters (or blank squares) on the tape, or they will not halt on **n**. We have designated such a Turing machine *T*, and we have called the binary numeral that represents *its* coded list of instructions **T**.

B. A universal Turing machine BIG, which simulates other Turing machines by taking their coded instructions *and* one of their input numerals as its input and running as they would, halting with some specific output or not ever halting.

C. A special universal Turing machine BIGGER, which simulates other Turing machines by taking their coded instructions *and* their input numerals as its input. BIGGER, however, outputs a **1** on its tape if the Turing machine it simulates will halt on its input numeral, and BIGGER outputs a **0** if the Turing machine never halts. In other words, BIGGER *always halts*, even though the particular Turing machine it simulates may not halt.

The following table depicts the relationship among these three kinds of Turing machines:

Turing machine	Input	Output
T	n	as appropriate to *T* and n
BIG	T n	as appropriate to *T* and n
BIGGER	T n	1 if *T* halts on n; 0 if *T* doesn't

Of course the inputs and outputs are all in the form of binary numerals on Turing machine tapes, that is, a series of squares containing **1**'s and **0**'s, and, possibly some blanks.

The *halting problem*, then, addresses the following question:

Can there be a Turing machine such as BIGGER?

That is, can there be a special Turing machine that can, in effect, determine whether any other Turing machine will halt on a given input? This is, essentially, the question Turing explored in his 1936 paper and to which he answered no. The implication of his original proof is that there are some processes that are not algorithmic because they cannot be implemented on Turing machines. As we will see in the next section, deciding questions of validity in PL is one such process.[16]

Our proof that no Turing machine can determine whether other Turing machines will halt has the form of indirect reasoning. We begin with the assumption that there is at least one such machine, like BIGGER, that can determine whether a particular Turing machine T will halt on a given input **n,** and then we show that this assumption leads to a contradiction.

The proof

1. Suppose that there is a universal Turing machine such as BIGGER, which determines whether the Turing machine T will halt on the input of **n.** If T will halt, BIGGER outputs a **1;** if T will not halt, BIGGER outputs a **0.** Note that BIGGER always halts on the input of **T** (for any Turing machine T) and **n** (representing *any* binary numeral or blank tape).

2. Further, suppose there is *another* special Turing machine called ANTI-BIGGER, which is just like BIGGER except that the particular instruction (or instructions) that has BIGGER output a **1** is (are) changed. Suppose such an instruction of BIGGER looks like this:

   C, B, 1, *H*

   The same instruction in ANTIBIGGER looks like this:

   C, b, 1, *C*

   If there are several such instructions in BIGGER, they are all altered in ANTIBIGGER. The effect of this change is that when BIGGER halts and outputs a **1,** ANTIBIGGER goes into an endless loop and does not halt at all. Note that if a Turing machine such as BIGGER exists, then a Turing machine such as ANTIBIGGER exists as well; the only difference between them is the last character in one or more instructions.

3. The operation of ANTIBIGGER can be described as follows. Its input consists of (a) a binary numeral representing the coded list of instructions from a Turing machine and (b) the binary numeral or blank tape representing an input tape in that Turing machine. Note that when the input produces an output of **1** (and a halt) in BIGGER, on the same

---

[16]See M. Davis, ed., *The Undecidable,* p. 133, for the original proof. Our version is slightly different, but follows the main lines of Turing's argument.

input ANTIBIGGER would go into an endless loop and would not halt. On the other hand, if the Turing machine doesn't halt on the input tape, then ANTIBIGGER, just like BIGGER, outputs a **0** (and halts).

4. Now for the critical step: suppose we input the following two numerals into ANTIBIGGER:

    a. the coded instructions for ANTIBIGGER

    b. the coded instructions for ANTIBIGGER

    What happens now? We have an input that consists of the coded instructions of a Turing machine and, as its input numeral, the coded instructions of the same Turing machine (note: ANTIBIGGER is a Turing machine). Of course, now we have ANTIBIGGER simulating itself, running itself as input.

5. Either ANTIBIGGER halts on the input in step 4 or it doesn't. Suppose it halts. Then the Turing machine whose coded instructions constitute its first input doesn't halt. But that Turing machine is ANTIBIGGER itself, so if ANTIBIGGER halts, then it doesn't halt, which is a contradiction. On the other hand, suppose ANTIBIGGER doesn't halt. Then the Turing machine it simulates does halt. Of course that is just ANTI-BIGGER itself. So we also have a contradiction in this case. Either way, we have a contradiction, which means that ANTIBIGGER cannot exist.

6. But ANTIBIGGER is the same sort of special universal Turing machine as the original BIGGER; they differ only in the last character of one or more instructions. *Therefore, no universal Turing machine like BIGGER can exist.*

In showing that no Turing machine like BIGGER can exist, we have isolated a task that cannot be performed by Turing machines, namely, solving the halting problem. No Turing machine can determine, in general, whether Turing machines will halt on specified inputs.

In chapter 7 we suggested in regard to predicate logic truth trees that the inability to know when to call off the search for branch-closing contradictions in type IV trees was an instance of the halting problem. And in chapter 6, when we discussed proofs of invalidity for PL arguments involving valuations of various sizes, we noted that our inability to know whether to look into a valuation of larger size for a counterexample was similarly related to the halting problem. In the next section, we discuss the relationships among these three seemingly disparate issues.

11.5 THE UNDECIDABILITY OF PREDICATE LOGIC

Alan Turing himself showed by means of the halting problem that some processes and problems cannot be implemented on Turing machines. Other researchers have added other noncomputable problems to the list. We argued in chapter 7 that one such problem is the attempt to mechanize a method of testing for the presence or absence of the logical properties and relations, such as consistency and validity, in predicate logic. This is known as the decidability problem for PL.

Decidability and Undecidability

We shall say that a logical system is **decidable** when there is a mechanical means of producing a yes or no answer to any question concerning the presence or absence of a logical property or relation. We can sharpen this definition a bit. Since all questions regarding logical properties and relations can be posed entirely in terms of the *consistency* of a set of statements, we can say that a logical system is decidable if there is a mechanical test for consistency. Given the Church-Turing thesis, the issue of decidability becomes the issue of showing that consistency can be computed by means of Turing machines.

That statement logic is decidable is easily shown. In chapters 2, 3, and 4 we discussed various mechanical or algorithmic methods for proving consistency and inconsistency: truth tables, truth trees, the resolution method.

In chapter 6, we also discussed a mechanical procedure for determining whether arguments from the monadic fragment of predicate logic (i.e., quantificational arguments with monadic predicates) are valid. The same strategy, of using valuations of size 2^n where n is the number of different monadic predicates, can be used to mechanically determine whether a set of statements is consistent or not. This property, too, can be computed by a Turing machine, so the monadic fragment of PL is also decidable.[17]

However, full predicate logic itself has been shown not to be decidable. We have already noted that neither the method of proving invalidity by producing counterexamples (chapter 6), nor the truth tree method for PL (chapter 7), nor the resolution method (chapter 7) provides a general method for determining the validity and invalidity of PL arguments. Thus none of these provides a general method for determining consistency and inconsistency either. But the failure of these three methods does not in itself rule out the existence of some other mechanical method for deciding whether a set of PL statements is consistent. To establish the undecidability of PL in our terms, we need a general proof that shows that no Turing machine can compute consistency for PL sets of statements.

Such a proof has been formulated by George Boolos and Richard Jeffrey, and we give a sketch of it here.[18] The basic strategy behind the Boolos/Jeffrey proof is to formulate a set of PL statements that describe a Turing machine

---

[17]Recall that Venn diagrams were used as a mechanical procedure for determining validity for syllogisms in section 8.2.

[18]For the full proof, see George S. Boolos and Richard C. Jeffrey, *Computability and Logic*, 2nd ed. (New York: Cambridge University Press, 1980), chapters 10 and 22.

and then show that this set can be shown consistent or inconsistent if and only if the Turing machine can handle the halting problem. Since no Turing machine can solve the halting problem, i.e., no Turing machine such as BIGGER can exist, then no Turing machine can determine the consistency or inconsistency of the set, thus showing that PL is not decidable.

The proof begins with the specification of how to formulate the members of a set of statements **T** that describe, in the notation of PL, the operation of some Turing machine T with an input of a binary numeral (or blank tape) **n**. The PL representation of T requires that we are able to use such notions as 'being in a state at a certain time' and 'a (moment of) time immediately following another (moment of) time t' so that we can say that if the machine is in a certain configuration, then in the next state it will be in some other configuration. We will also need to think of the squares on the tape of the Turing machine as being numbered, so that we can refer to the symbol on a certain square. One of the statements in **T** will be the PL representation of the following:

> If T is in state A_m at time t and is reading square number x on which symbol y occurs, then at the next time after t the machine is in state A_n reading square number z where the symbol w occurs and in all other squares, other than x, the same symbols occur at time t and the next time after t.

Other instructions for T are similarly expressed in the PL statements in **T**.

In addition to the statements representing the operation of **T**, there is one more statement that says that at certain times and on certain numbered squares there are symbols such that if the machine reads the symbol in a given state, then there is no other state, square, or symbol to be read. In other words, this statement records the conditions (if there are any) under which machine T halts given the input **n**. If, on the other hand, Turing machine T does not halt on the input of n, then this statement is an arbitrary contradiction (say $\forall x\,(Px\ \&\ \sim Px)$). Either way, we will call this halting statement H.

Let **T** be the set of PL statements that describe the operation of T, and let H be the statement that describes the halting conditions of T (if any). The proof goes to show the truth of

> **T** entails H if and only if T halts on input **n**.

Assuming that T is a Turing machine, its instructions will be consistent. Hence, **T** will be consistent. So the only conditions under which **T** will entail H is if T does halt on input **n**. For suppose T does not halt on input **n**. Then statement H is a contradiction that will not be entailed by **T**, since **T** is consistent. It follows that the following statement is also true:

> **T** $\cup$ $\{\sim H\}$ is inconsistent if and only if T halts on input **n**.

There are two direct consequences:

1. If we can determine whether a given Turing machine T halts or not on a given input **n,** then we can determine at the same time whether a given set of PL statements is inconsistent or not.

2. If we can determine whether a given set of PL statements is inconsistent or not, then we can determine whether a given Turing machine T halts or not on a given input **n.**

Put these two together and we have:

PL is decidable if and only if we can solve the halting problem.

But we cannot solve the halting problem, so PL is not decidable.

The original proof that PL is not decidable was published by Alonzo Church in 1936.[19] As noted above, Church worked independently of Alan Turing and is credited with priority in this discovery. Thus, the undecidability of PL is called **Church's theorem.** Turing's 1936 paper contains his famous proof that is the basis of the Boolos and Jeffrey argument sketched above.

Even though computers are logic machines, the work of Church and Turing shows that computers are nevertheless limited in what they can logically do. There will always be problems computers cannot solve, like determining whether a certain PL conclusion logically follows from a set of statements.

---

[19]See M. Davis, ed., *The Undecidable,* pp. 108–114.

12

Computing

Now that we have seen how logical circuits operate and have discussed algorithms and programs, we turn to actual implementations. In this chapter we will study the basic circuits for three electronic devices: a soda dispensing machine, a simple adding machine, and a logic machine (which tests statements for tautology, contradiction, etc.). Many of the fundamental operations of computers will be found in these simple devices. The final two sections of the chapter provide an overview of computers, concentrating on how programs actually run.

12.1 THE SODA MACHINE CIRCUIT

Our electronic soda machine is the common sort you have used many times.[1] You put in forty-five cents and a cup drops, ice is discharged into the cup, and the cup fills with soda. To keep things simple, only one kind of soda will be available in our machine. Even though the customer's choice of drink is limited, our machine will have several desirable features. If the machine

---

[1]The design for the soda machine is adapted from Bill R. Deem, Kenneth Muchow, and Anthony Zeppa, *Digital Computer Circuits and Concepts,* 3rd ed. (Reston, VA: Reston Publishing, 1980), pp. 191–204.

isn't working at all—if no power is connected to the machine—then coins deposited will be returned. The machine will give a limited amount of correct change, and there is a 'No Ice' button, in case the customer prefers warm soda. Coins are returned if supplies are too low to properly dispense the soda.

To capture the essential logic of the soda machine, we will think of it as a series of possible inputs leading to a number of possible outputs through a number of internal states. For example, one possible set of inputs to the machine would be the following:

1. The power is on.

2. A quarter and two dimes are deposited.

3. The 'No Ice' button is not pressed.

Assuming that everything inside the machine is normal, we should expect the following output from the machine:

1. A cup appears.

2. Ice is dispensed into the cup.

3. The cup fills with soda.

In designing our machine we want to provide for all possible situations, so we need to develop a complete list of all the possible inputs. Since we will ultimately describe the workings of the machine in binary (on/off) terms, we can think of the possible inputs as a series of states that either are *actual* (on) or are *nonactual* (off). Each such state will be designated by an appropriate symbol. To get into the spirit of this project, you might put the book aside at this moment and try to formulate your own list of every possible input state of our machine.

We want to keep our machine somewhat simple, so we will limit the coins that may be inserted and recognized by the machine. We will require that the customer deposit at least one quarter, and either (1) another quarter, (2) two dimes, (3) a dime and two nickels, or (4) four nickels. If the customer deposits any other combination, the machine will not activate. You will be asked in exercises 12.1a to think of the consequences of loosening this requirement somewhat.

Here is the full list of possible inputs:

Item	Symbol
Power	P
First quarter	Q_1
Second quarter	Q_2
First dime	D_1

Item	Symbol
Second dime	D_2
First nickel	N_1
Second nickel	N_2
Third nickel	N_3
Fourth nickel	N_4
'No Ice' button	B

This list might be thought of as the list of *recognized* inputs, since only these will cause any activity in the machine. Other inputs, such as depositing other coins or kicking the machine, are ignored.

The outputs are as follows:

Item	Symbol
Cup	K
Ice	I
Soda	S
Change	C
'No Change' light	L
Return coins	R

The 'Return coins' output is activated when the power is off, or supplies are too low to dispense a soda. The 'Change' output dispenses a nickel when two quarters are deposited and a soda is dispensed.

In addition to the input and output states, there are internal states of the machine that affect its operation. The machine has internal sensors that indicate whether there are appropriate supplies such as cups, ice, and soda. But to make change, the machine also needs to know whether it has any nickels available; if not the 'No Change' light goes on. The various internal states are these:

Item	Symbol
Nickel Sense	N_S
Soda Sense	S_S
Ice Sense	I_S
Cup Sense	K_S

The Nickel Sense (N_S) is on if there is at least one nickel available for change; since no dimes are used in making change, no dime sense is necessary. (See exercises 12.1a for some variations.) The other senses indicate whether the supplies are present in sufficient quantity for one full discharge of soda and ice into a cup.

We can write SL statements to express the conditions under which the machine functions; later we will convert these to circuit descriptions. An unnegated state symbol means that the state is actual; a negated state symbol means that it is nonactual. So the expression P & $\sim B$ means 'The power is on and the "No Ice" button is not pushed'. We would indicate the deposit of a quarter, a dime, and a nickel as Q_1 & D_1 & N_1.[2]

The machine functions properly when the outputs correspond to appropriate inputs. So we will write an expression for each possible output state that describes how it relates to appropriate inputs. The principal output, of course, is soda being dispensed into a cup. Since there should not be a cup without soda, or soda without a cup (i.e., $S \equiv K$), the expressions for soda and for cup are the same.

$$S \equiv [\![P \text{ \& } S_s \text{ \& } (I_s \vee B) \text{ \& } K_s \text{ \& } [(Q_1 \text{ \& } D_1 \text{ \& } D_2) \vee (Q_1 \text{ \& } N_1 \text{ \& } N_2 \text{ \& } N_3 \text{ \& } N_4) \\ \vee (Q_1 \text{ \& } D_1 \text{ \& } N_1 \text{ \& } N_2) \vee (Q_1 \text{ \& } Q_2 \text{ \& } N_s)]]\!]$$

This complex-looking monster says that soda will be dispensed under the following conditions:

The power is on,

AND soda is available,

AND there is ice, OR the 'No Ice' button has been pushed,

AND at least one cup is available,

AND a quarter and two dimes have been inserted,

OR a quarter and four nickels have been inserted,

OR a quarter, a dime, and two nickels have been inserted,

OR two quarters have been inserted and there is a nickel

for change.

The expression for 'Ice' would be

$$I \equiv (S \text{ \& } \sim B)$$

Ice is dispensed if soda is dispensed and the 'No Ice' button has not been pressed. Note that there is no sense of sequence in this machine; states are either on or off, and the input and internal conditions for any particular output have to be realized simultaneously. The outputs are also triggered simultaneously. You may wonder, then, how we can be sure that the cup

---

[2]For greater ease of reading expressions, parentheses are omitted in associative cases.

drops before the ice and soda are discharged. We designate this a mechanical problem, to be solved perhaps by building a small delay in the circuits to the soda and ice dispenser.

Coins are returned according to the following expression:

$$R \equiv [\sim S_s \vee (\sim I_s \,\&\, \sim B) \vee \sim K_s \vee \sim P]$$

That is, coins are returned under the following conditions:

No soda is available,

OR, no ice is available AND the 'No Ice' button has not been pushed,

OR there are no cups available,

OR the power is off.

Change of a nickel is given when a soda has been dispensed and two quarters have been deposited, i.e.,

$$C \equiv [S \,\&\, Q_1 \,\&\, Q_2 \,\&\, N_s]$$

The 'No Change' light goes on when there isn't even one nickel available, so

$$L \equiv \sim N_s$$

EXERCISES 12.1a

1. Suppose the price of a soda goes up to fifty cents, and the machine takes only quarters. How would the conditions for dispensing a soda be expressed?

2. Suppose the price of a soda is twenty-five cents, and the machine will take any combination of nickels, dimes, and quarters. What change (if any) will be required? What would the correct expressions for the soda conditions and change conditions be?

3. In the design of the soda machine, do we have to worry about someone putting in a quarter, a dime, and two nickels (which triggers the soda output) *and* getting back coins through a return?

4. Suppose the price of a soda is sixty cents. Make whatever alterations are necessary so that the machine will take any combinations of coins and will make change. Give the conditions for dispensing soda and making change.

*5. If a person puts in too few coins, or the wrong coins, or too many coins, the machine has no provision to return them. Make a list of the possible cases of this sort. Suppose a 'Coin Return' button were added. How would this addition affect the design of the machine? Are there any other modifications that would be helpful?

We can now proceed to design a circuit consisting of a network of logic gates that will connect the various input states to the appropriate output states. We will want the circuit to correspond to the following statements:

(1) $S \equiv K \equiv [\![P \mathbin{\&} S_S \mathbin{\&} (I_S \vee B) \mathbin{\&} K_S \mathbin{\&} [(Q_1 \mathbin{\&} D_1 \mathbin{\&} D_2)$
$\vee (Q_1 \mathbin{\&} N_1 \mathbin{\&} N_2 \mathbin{\&} N_3 \mathbin{\&} N_4) \vee (Q_1 \mathbin{\&} D_1 \mathbin{\&} N_1 \mathbin{\&} N_2)$
$\vee (Q_1 \mathbin{\&} Q_2 \mathbin{\&} N_S)]]\!]$

(2) $I \equiv (S \mathbin{\&} {\sim}B)$

(3) $R \equiv [{\sim}S_S \vee ({\sim}I_S \mathbin{\&} {\sim}B) \vee {\sim}K_S \vee {\sim}P]$

(4) $C \equiv [S \mathbin{\&} Q_1 \mathbin{\&} Q_2 \mathbin{\&} N_S]$

(5) $L \equiv {\sim}N_S$

and to safeguard against getting a soda and money back too,

(6) $R \equiv {\sim}S$

(Note that this last statement entails $S \equiv {\sim}R$, so if soda is dispensed, no money is returned except whatever change is due.)

The first step in designing a circuit is to simplify it as much as possible. The principal simplification available to the statement citing the conditions for S is to use the distribution law to move Q_1 out of each of the four disjuncts of $(Q_1 \mathbin{\&} D_1 \mathbin{\&} D_2) \vee (Q_1 \mathbin{\&} N_1 \mathbin{\&} N_2 \mathbin{\&} N_3 \mathbin{\&} N_4) \vee (Q_1 \mathbin{\&} D_1 \mathbin{\&} N_1 \mathbin{\&} N_2) \vee (Q_1 \mathbin{\&} Q_2 \mathbin{\&} N_S)$. Performing this step replaces the four disjuncts with the following:

$Q_1 \mathbin{\&} [(D_1 \mathbin{\&} D_2) \vee (N_1 \mathbin{\&} N_2 \mathbin{\&} N_3 \mathbin{\&} N_4) \vee (D_1 \mathbin{\&} N_1 \mathbin{\&} N_2) \vee (Q_2 \mathbin{\&} N_S)]$

The statement expressing the conditions for S then would be:

(1a) $S \equiv K \equiv [\![P \mathbin{\&} S_S \mathbin{\&} (I_S \vee B) \mathbin{\&} K_S \mathbin{\&} Q_1 \mathbin{\&} [(D_1 \mathbin{\&} D_2)$
$\vee (N_1 \mathbin{\&} N_2 \mathbin{\&} N_3 \mathbin{\&} N_4) \vee (D_1 \mathbin{\&} N_1 \mathbin{\&} N_2) \vee (Q_2 \mathbin{\&} N_S)]]\!]$

The advantage of this mode of expressing the conditions for dispensing soda is that it is clear that a quarter must be deposited in order to obtain soda from the machine.

The other significant simplification concerns the conditions for R. It turns out that we don't have to add the safeguard (6), $R \equiv {\sim}S$, because the conditions for S and R already entail this statement. The derivation is easiest in two parts, first showing that ${\sim}S$ follows from R (together with (1a) and (3) as assumptions), and then showing that R follows from ${\sim}S$. (The second part will be found in exercises 12.1b, problem 1.) Thus, in the soda machine circuit, the output corresponding to R can be represented by means of an inverter gate with S as its input (or vice versa).

1. $S \equiv [\![P \mathbin{\&} S_S \mathbin{\&} (I_S \vee B) \mathbin{\&} K_S \mathbin{\&} Q_1 \mathbin{\&} [(D_1 \mathbin{\&} D_2) \vee (N_1 \mathbin{\&} N_2 \mathbin{\&} N_3 \mathbin{\&} N_4)$
$\vee (D_1 \mathbin{\&} N_1 \mathbin{\&} N_2) \vee (Q_2 \mathbin{\&} N_S)]\!]\!]$
2. $R \equiv [\sim S_S \vee (\sim I_S \mathbin{\&} \sim B) \vee \sim K_S \vee \sim P]$

---

3. $\quad R$

---

4. $\qquad S$

---

5. $\qquad S$ (R, 4)
6. $\qquad S \equiv [\![P \mathbin{\&} S_S \mathbin{\&} (I_S \vee B) \mathbin{\&} K_S \mathbin{\&} Q_1 \mathbin{\&} [(D_1 \mathbin{\&} D_2)$ (R, 1)
$\vee (N_1 \mathbin{\&} N_2 \mathbin{\&} N_3 \mathbin{\&} N_4) \vee (D_1 \mathbin{\&} N_1 \mathbin{\&} N_2)$
$\vee (Q_2 \mathbin{\&} N_S)]\!]\!]$
7. $\qquad P \mathbin{\&} S_S \mathbin{\&} (I_S \vee B) \mathbin{\&} K_S \mathbin{\&} Q_1 \mathbin{\&} [(D_1 \mathbin{\&} D_2)$ (BW, 5, 6)
$\vee (N_1 \mathbin{\&} N_2 \mathbin{\&} N_3 \mathbin{\&} N_4) \vee (D_1 \mathbin{\&} N_1 \mathbin{\&} N_2)$
$\vee (Q_2 \mathbin{\&} N_S)]$
8. $\qquad P \mathbin{\&} S_S \mathbin{\&} (I_S \vee B) \mathbin{\&} K_S$ (SIMP, 7)
9. $\qquad S_S \mathbin{\&} (I_S \vee B) \mathbin{\&} K_S \mathbin{\&} P$ (COMM, 8)
10. $\qquad \sim\sim S_S \mathbin{\&} \sim\sim(I_S \vee B) \mathbin{\&} \sim\sim K_S \mathbin{\&} \sim\sim P$ (DNE, 9)
11. $\qquad \sim[\sim S_S \vee (\sim I_S \mathbin{\&} \sim B) \vee \sim K_S \vee \sim P]$ (DEM, 10)
12. $\qquad R$ (R, 3)
13. $\qquad R \equiv [\sim S_S \vee (\sim I_S \mathbin{\&} \sim B) \vee \sim K_S \vee \sim P]$ (R, 2)
14. $\qquad \sim S_S \vee (\sim I_S \mathbin{\&} \sim B) \vee \sim K_S \vee \sim P$ (BW, 12, 13)
15. $\qquad \sim S$ (IR, 4, 11, 14)

For the purposes of the soda machine circuit, the various symbols for the input states, internal states, and output states will now represent the usual binary signals: *1* for 'on' and *0* for 'off.' We assume the initial state of each input is *0*, and when coins are inserted, the power turned on, the 'No Ice' button pushed, etc., the appropriate inputs are active and become *1*. On the output end, to dispense a soda, the output labeled *S* must be *1*, and so on.

Here is a table showing the input, internal, and output signals in the soda machine circuit after two quarters have been inserted (and ice is desired) when the machine is in its normal state: the power is on, and the machine has ample supplies and change.

Normal State of Soda Machine After Two Quarters Inserted

Inputs	Symbol	Signal
Power	P	1
First Quarter	Q_1	1
Second Quarter	Q_2	1
First Dime	$\sim D_1$	0
Second Dime	$\sim D_2$	0
First Nickel	$\sim N_1$	0
Second Nickel	$\sim N_2$	0
Third Nickel	$\sim N_3$	0
Fourth Nickel	$\sim N_4$	0
'No Ice' button	$\sim B$	0

Internal states	Symbol	Signal
Nickel Sense	N_S	1
Soda Sense	S_S	1
Ice Sense	I_S	1
Cup Sense	K_S	1
Outputs		
Cup	K	1
Ice	I	1
Soda	S	1
Change	C	1
'No Change' light	$\sim L$	0
Return coins	$\sim R$	0

To design an appropriate circuit, we begin with the statement (1a, above) that captures the conditions for S (and K):

(1a) $S \equiv K \equiv [\![P \mathbin{\&} S_S \mathbin{\&} (I_S \vee B) \mathbin{\&} K_S \mathbin{\&} Q_1 \mathbin{\&} [(D_1 \mathbin{\&} D_2) \vee (N_1 \mathbin{\&} N_2 \mathbin{\&} N_3 \mathbin{\&} N_4)$
$\vee (D_1 \mathbin{\&} N_1 \mathbin{\&} N_2) \vee (Q_2 \mathbin{\&} N_S)]]\!]$

Each of the *disjuncts* of the expression $(D_1 \mathbin{\&} D_2) \vee (N_1 \mathbin{\&} N_2 \mathbin{\&} N_3 \mathbin{\&} N_4) \vee (D_1 \mathbin{\&} N_1 \mathbin{\&} N_2) \vee (Q_2 \mathbin{\&} N_S)$ can be represented by an AND gate, the output of which is connected as input to a four-input OR gate, as below.

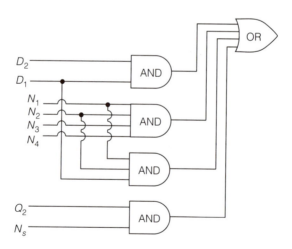

The output of that OR gate together with the remaining *conjuncts* of the above expression lead to an AND gate (note how the ice/no ice is handled by means of an OR gate and an inverter):

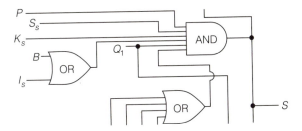

The output from the primary AND gate is of course S itself. K and R come directly from S.

The change condition requires S as an input as well as the output from the Q_2 & N_S AND gate and, of course, Q_1, as is given in statement (4):

$$C \equiv [S \ \& \ Q_1 \ \& \ Q_2 \ \& \ N_S]$$

and the 'No Change' light L is N_S inverted. The gate network looks like this:

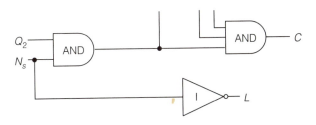

Finally, the ice dispense output I comes from an AND gate with $\sim B$ and S as inputs, as pictured below:

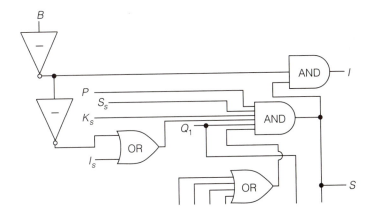

Putting these various subcircuits together yields the entire soda machine circuit:

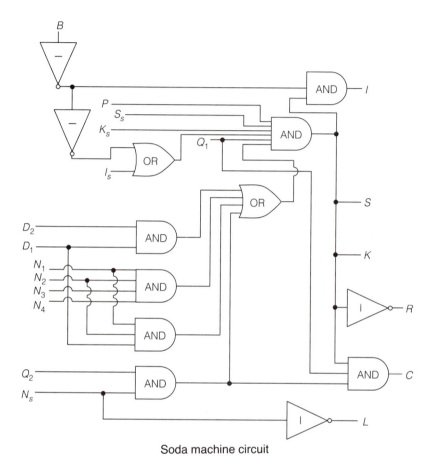

Soda machine circuit

EXERCISES 12.1b

1. Construct a derivation of R (return of coins) from $\sim S$ (no soda dispensed). (Note: Assume coins are deposited.)

2. Create a table listing the appropriate signals for the inputs, internal states, and outputs when a quarter and four nickels are inserted into the soda machine and the machine is out of cups. With reference to the circuit diagram, show that each output is as you say it should be.

3. Do the same as above, but assume that a quarter and two dimes are inserted, the 'No Ice' button is pressed, and the machine has no change but is full of other supplies.

4. How would you add a light to the soda machine that lights up when the soda is dispensed and says 'Take your soda; have a nice day'?

*5. Repeat the full machine design exercise for a candy machine that dispenses five different kinds of candy bars, three of which cost fifteen cents each and two of which cost ten cents each. Assume the machine takes nickels, dimes, and quarters and will make appropriate change.

12.2 THE ADDING MACHINE

The next device we will study is a simple adding machine, essentially an electronic calculator that performs only a single function. Like calculators you have used, our adding machine will have a keyboard on which the numbers to be added are entered, and it will have a display that shows the sum of those numbers.

If you have a calculator nearby, it may be helpful to look it over before reading on. You will notice that to enter numbers from 0 to 9, a single key is pressed; larger numbers of two or more digits require additional keystrokes. On your calculator, you first enter a number and then you indicate which function—addition, multiplication, division, etc.—you want performed; then you enter the second number and press the = (equals) key and the answer appears in the display. The calculator display will allow only a certain number of digits, usually eight. This severely limits the size of the numbers you can calculate unless the calculator has provision for so-called scientific notation, which represents numbers in terms of powers of 10: as in 4.83×10^3 for 4,830.

Pay attention to what appears in the display on your calculator when you press the various keys. Also notice what sequence you press keys in order to produce an answer to a problem. As an exercise, try solving $14 - (2 \times (3 + 5)) = ?$ Next, notice the two *clear keys* (on some models the same key is used for both). One of them, usually marked C, wipes out everything; the other, marked Cl or CE, wipes out only the number you have just entered. Try this: Enter 8 then press Cl. What happens? Next press 8 then press +. Now press Cl; what happens? Usually, the 8 continues to appear on the display in the second case, but not in the first. Now press C; the 8 should be gone forever. Many of the features of small electronic calculators will be found in the adding machine of this section and the logic machine of the next.

Our adding machine will consist of the following five components:

1. **Keyboard**   Permits entry of decimal numbers by means of keystrokes.

2. **Encoder**   Translates input of decimal numbers to binary signals.

3. **Registers**   Store binary representations of numbers.

4. **Binary adder**   Performs binary addition on inputted binary signals.

5. **Decoder/display**   Translates output of adder into a decimal display.

Even though simple, our adding machine will allow us to press keys to indicate which (decimal) numbers we want to add and will display their (decimal) sum. However, we will be restricted to a relatively small range of numbers that we can add. Our adder will be able to deal with only four bits, so the maximum sum is **1111** (binary) or 15.

Before proceeding to the circuits, recall the basic facts of binary arithmetic:

$$1 + 1 = 10$$
$$1 + 0 = 1$$
$$0 + 1 = 1$$
$$0 + 0 = 0$$

We will need a way of *carrying* digits in order to accommodate the first of these rules. An adder manages the carry by producing *two* output bits for each two input bits. One of the output bits is the sum, the other is the carry, which may be **1** or **0**. So the table for binary addition actually looks like this:

$$1 + 1 = 10$$
$$1 + 0 = 01$$
$$0 + 1 = 01$$
$$0 + 0 = 00$$

The simplest adder uses two gates, an XOR gate and an AND gate, as in the following diagram. This circuit is known as a **half-adder.** (It lacks an important input found in the full-adder circuit.)

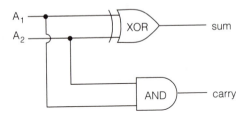

The operation of the half-adder circuit is summarized in the table below.

Half-adder

| Input | | Output | |
A_1	A_2	Carry	Sum
1	1	1	0
1	0	0	1
0	1	0	1
0	0	0	0

The carry column is, of course, just the truth table for &, and the sum column is the truth table for exclusive disjunction. Thinking of the output in binary numerical terms requires us to ignore the left-most **0**, so **01** represents binary **1**, and **00** is binary **0**.

If an XOR gate is not available, there are, of course, other ways to implement the half-adder table as a circuit. The exclusive disjunction of two statements A and B can be represented by all of the following (equivalent) SL expressions:

(1) $(A \mathbin{\&} {\sim}B) \vee ({\sim}A \mathbin{\&} B)$
(2) $(A \vee B) \mathbin{\&} {\sim}(A \mathbin{\&} B)$
(3) $(A \vee B) \mathbin{\&} ({\sim}A \vee {\sim}B)$

The first of these would require a circuit with two AND gates and an OR gate, as well as two inverters; the second requires an AND, an OR, and a NAND; and the third requires two ORs, an AND, and two inverters. You will be asked to design these circuits, as well as other possibilities, in exercise 12.2.1.

A **full-adder** circuit has a carry *input* as well as a carry output and can be implemented like this.

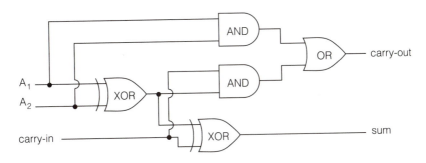

It may not be immediately obvious why a carry input is included in the full-adder. The reason is that full-adder circuits are usually linked together to form binary adders of various sizes (ours will be four bits), and the carry output from one adder becomes the carry input to another. The table that depicts the operation of the full adder is on the next page.

Notice that, in effect, a full-adder just adds three one-bit numbers in binary and gives a two-bit answer. For example, in the first row, we add $1 + 1 + 1$ to get **11**, and in the fifth row, we add $0 + 1 + 1$ to get **10**. Again, there are other possible circuit configurations for a full-adder (see exercise 12.2.2).

Full-adder

	Input		Output	
A_1	A_2	Carry-in	Carry-out	Sum
1	1	1	1	1
1	1	0	1	0
1	0	1	1	0
1	0	0	0	1
0	1	1	1	0
0	1	0	0	1
0	0	1	0	1
0	0	0	0	0

To simplify the diagram of the four-bit binary adder, we will use block diagrams for the one-bit adder circuits, as we did for flipflops in the last section. The standard block diagrams for one-bit half- and full-adders are:

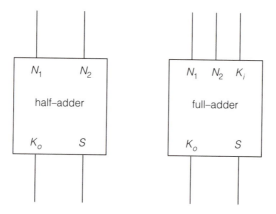

In the block diagrams N_1 and N_2 are the one-bit inputs, K_i is the carry input, K_o is the carry output, and S is the sum output.

Now the whole four-bit binary adder can be shown in block form.

The block diagram masks the fact that our four-bit adder circuit contains thirty-one gates (not counting any register circuitry). And all it will do is add numbers together that are no larger than 15 ($=$ **1111** binary)! However, to produce a useful eight-bit binary adder, we just add four additional full-adders in series to the above adder, and a sixteen-bit adder links twelve additional full-adders to the four-bit adder.

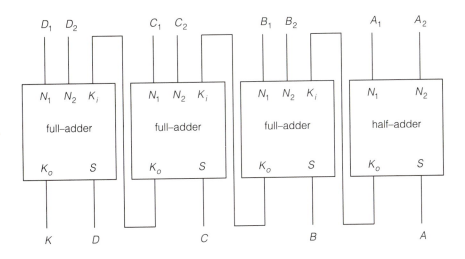

Before returning to the operation of our four-bit adder, we need to clarify the input devices: the keyboard and the encoder. The keyboard consists of a set of keys, which are actually pressure switches connected to a logic network—the encoder—that performs the required translation. Here is a diagram of the encoder circuit:

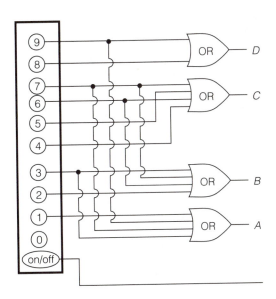

Since the gates are all OR, depressing any key sends a 1 input to some of the OR gates (remember, a 1 input to an OR gate results in a 1 output), which results in the four-bit output. The table gives the outputs for each of the gates for given decimal inputs.

Input	Output			
Keystroke	D	C	B	A
0	0	0	0	0
1	0	0	0	1
2	0	0	1	0
3	0	0	1	1
4	0	1	0	0
5	0	1	0	1
6	0	1	1	0
7	0	1	1	1
8	1	0	0	0
9	1	0	0	1

So if key 5 is depressed, a *1* input is sent to the the *A* gate and the *C* gate and these have *1*'s as output. The other gates have *0*'s as output. Using *A* as the 2^0 place, *B* as the 2^1 place, *C* as the 2^2 place, and *D* as the 2^3 place, the output of *0101* (reading *D* through *A*) exactly corresponds to the binary value **0101** of the decimal numeral 5. Thus the number 5 is represented in our adding machine by the electrical signals on the four encoder output wires.

It is important to remember that the actual physical signals in the encoder circuit are not numbers but voltages; in the above case, we have low voltage on output *D*, high voltage on output *C*, low voltage on output *B*, and high voltage on output *A*. There are no numbers or numerals in this circuit, only signals and gates. Nevertheless, we are able to *represent* numbers because of the identification of the two voltage states (high and low) with the two basic numerals (**1** and **0**) in the binary numerical system.

Now let's return to the binary adder. The binary adder circuit will have *two* sets of four-bit inputs. To keep everything straight, we will use the same letters we used for the output of the encoder, and we will think of them as standing for the same places in the binary numerical system. The first four bits (the first number to be added) we represent as D_1, C_1, B_1, and A_1, and the second four bits (the second number to be added) are D_2, C_2, B_2, and A_2.

The decoder/display takes the output from the binary adder and displays it so we can read it. To state the problem precisely, we need a means of transforming information in the form of high and low signals on the four adder output wires (say *1101*) into a form that is visible and can be understood as representing the number 13. If we could assume that everyone knew the binary numeral system, the simplest way to display *1101* (= 13) would be by means of four light bulbs used to give a four-bit binary display,

where the light being on (■) indicates **1** and the light being off (□) indicates 0. But not everybody knows or wants to know binary numerals. So our display must be in the decimal system. The solution that is familiar to everyone who has used a pocket calculator uses what are called **seven-segment displays.** These are little grids consisting of seven distinct lights with the following form:

(You might look at your calculator to see what the seven-segment display looks like.) Each individual segment of the display has a standard name, from (a) to (g). An Arabic numeral is formed when a certain number of these segments are lit. The numerals from 0 to 9 in this seven-segment form are displayed below.

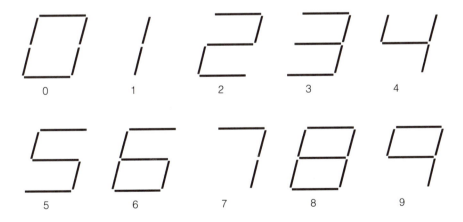

Since in the display of any particular numeral, the seven individual segment lights are either on (*1*) or off (*0*), each numeral from 0 to 9 can be represented by a seven-bit binary string of *1*'s and *0*'s. The following table gives the binary representation for the correct pattern of lighted segments for each decimal numeral.

Decimal	Binary DCBA	Seven-segment Display Pattern						
		(a)	(b)	(c)	(d)	(e)	(f)	(g)
0	0000	1	1	1	1	1	1	0
1	0001	0	1	1	0	0	0	0
2	0010	1	1	0	1	1	0	1
3	0011	1	1	1	1	0	0	1
4	0100	0	1	1	0	0	1	1
5	0101	1	0	1	1	0	1	1
6	0110	1	0	1	1	1	1	1
7	0111	1	1	1	0	0	0	0
8	1000	1	1	1	1	1	1	1
9	1001	1	1	1	0	0	1	1

On your pocket calculator there are, probably, eight of these individual seven-segment displays. A two-digit decimal number, like 14, is displayed as a 4 on the right-most display and a 1 on the display to its left. However, quite special circuitry is required to create displays of more than one digit. Calculator designers early on learned to avoid the simplistic answer of having $7 \times 8 \ (= 56)$ separate input wires to drive an eight-digit display. But we will keep things simple, since we are restricted to four bits anyway, and make use of a standard feature of most commercial seven-segment displays, namely the display of *additional symbols*.

Here are the six additional symbol outputs on a commonly used seven-segment display:[3]

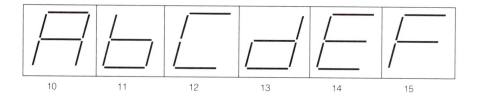

| 10 | 11 | 12 | 13 | 14 | 15 |

---

[3]These may be thought of as displays for the hexadecimal numerals from 10 to 15.

This is the table for these symbols:

Decimal	Binary DCBA	Seven-segment Display Pattern						
		(a)	(b)	(c)	(d)	(e)	(f)	(g)
10	1010	1	1	1	0	1	1	1
11	1011	0	0	1	1	1	1	1
12	1100	1	0	0	1	1	1	0
13	1101	0	1	1	1	1	0	1
14	1110	1	0	0	1	1	1	1
15	1111	1	0	0	0	1	1	1

Thus, we will be able to display answers from 0 to 15 (**0000** to **1111,** binary) on a single seven-segment display; the additional circuitry will not be necessary for our purposes here.

It is important to note that suddenly *two* kinds of binary representation are occurring. We have principally been using combinations of binary signals to represent numbers expressed as binary numerals; in four wires, for example, the signals high, high, low, high represented binary **1101** (= 13 decimal). Now we see the need to let combinations of binary signals represent other information, in this case the way decimal numerals are displayed in seven-lighted segments.

The circuitry that decodes or converts the four-bit output of the adder into the seven-bit inputs to the seven-segment displays involves, as you might expect, numerous gates. To take the particular case of the (decimal) number 4, the adder output in this instance will be the signals *0100* (reading *D* through *A*), and we need to convert these to *0110011* (reading (a) through (g)) in order to obtain the seven-segment display for the numeral 4. To get a sense of the problem, consider the circuit needed for just the segment (e), the lower left vertical segment. We can express the instances when segment (e) is *on* (i.e., *1*) by means of the Post paraphrase formula for just the portion of the above table for (e). Remember that to do this we give a separate SL expression that corresponds to each line of the table in which (e) has the value *1*, and then these expressions are joined together by means of disjunctions. We will use the four-bit output designations *D*, *C*, *B*, and *A* statement letters and, as usual, take an unnegated letter to be a *1* and a negated letter to be a *0*. Here is the relevant portion of the table, including only occurrences of (e).

Decimal	Binary DCBA	Seven-segment Display Pattern (e)
0	0000	1
2	0010	1
6	0110	1
8	1000	1
10	1010	1
14	1110	1

The six conditions under which segment (e) is on can be represented as follows:

Segment (e) is *1* when:

$\sim$D & $\sim$C & $\sim$B & $\sim$A
$\sim$D & $\sim$C & B & $\sim$A
$\sim$D & C & B & $\sim$A
D & $\sim$C & $\sim$B & $\sim$A
D & $\sim$C & B & $\sim$A
D & C & B & $\sim$A

The Post-paraphrase formula for (e) is thus

$(\sim$D & $\sim$C & $\sim$B & $\sim$A$) \lor (\sim$D & $\sim$C & B & $\sim$A$) \lor (\sim$D & C & B & $\sim$A$)$
    $\lor$ (D & $\sim$C & $\sim$B & $\sim$A$) \lor$ (D & $\sim$C & B & $\sim$A$) \lor$ (D & C & B & $\sim$A$)$

Before turning this formula into circuitry, we need to simplify it. In this case, simplification is indeed rewarding. The Post paraphrase for (e) is equivalent to

$(\sim$C $\lor$ B$)$ & $\sim$A

which, as a circuit, would look like this:

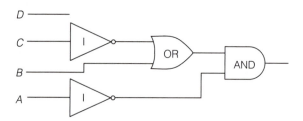

A similar procedure can be followed for each of the other segments, and, when combined, the complete circuitry needed for the decoder for a seven-segment display will result.[4]

In the operation of our adding machine, some storage will be required for the numbers as they are entered. For this purpose we provide two four-bit registers, one for each number. The first, or *keyboard*, register will store the information from the keyboard and its encoder. We can *clear* (reset) this register by pushing the 0 key. The second, or *internal*, register stores the sum of the two numbers that have been added; the display is also attached to the internal register. The internal register can be cleared by means of a special clear key marked CLEAR.

Now that we have discussed the operations of the primary components of our adding machine, we can put them all together by means of a block diagram:

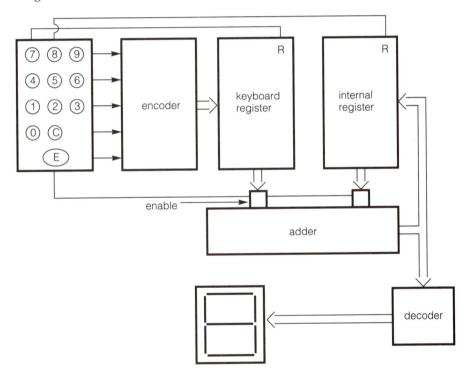

The single arrows from the keyboard to the encoder carry individual signals resulting from pressed buttons. The double arrows represent lines carrying four bits of information, except between the decoder and the display, where seven bits are conveyed. Typically such multiple lines are called

---

[4]See Thomas C. Bartee, *Digital Computer Fundamentals*, 5th ed. (New York: McGraw-Hill, 1981), p. 163, for the wiring diagram for a seven-segment display decoder.

Action	Result
press CLEAR	internal register cleared; 0 displayed
press 0	keyboard register cleared
key in number	number encoded in binary form, stored in keyboard register
press ENTER	number added to contents of internal register; sum (i.e., the number itself) stored in internal register; sum displayed
key in number	number encoded in binary form, stored in keyboard register
press ENTER	number added to contents of internal register; sum stored in internal register; sum displayed

data buses, since their function is to transport data from one place to another. Note the small boxes representing the enable switches, which the ENTER key activates, allowing information to pass from the registers into the adder. The 0 key resets the keyboard register, and the CLEAR key resets the interior register.

We can describe the operations of the adding machine at various levels of detail. At the most general level, we push a number key, press ENTER, and the number appears in the display; then we push another number key, push ENTER again, and their sum appears on the display (so long, that is, as their sum is no larger than 15). A more detailed explanation of the adding machine is given by means of the chart below, which records step by step what happens from the input stage, when the numbers to be added are keyed in, to the output stage, when their sum is displayed. As noted, one feature of the design is that the sum is stored in the internal register so that chain addition is possible; after the first sum is computed, the next number keyed in is added to the sum, and the new sum is displayed, and so on. (See table above.)

Notice that the entire control function is lodged in the ENTER key, the CLEAR key, and the 0 key; there is no stored set of instructions. The shifting of information between the two registers is accomplished through the adder. If the internal register has been cleared, then adding the contents of the two registers is just shifting the number in the keyboard register to the internal register. If a number larger than zero is in the internal register, then the sum of the numbers becomes the new contents of the internal register when the ENTER key is pressed. If no new number is keyed in, pressing ENTER again will add the number remaining in the keyboard register to the sum, store that new sum in the internal register, and display the new sum. Pressing 0 clears the keyboard register; pressing 0 and then ENTER does not affect the contents of the internal register.

Action	Result
press CLEAR	*1* signal to R input of internal register; *0000* signal through output lines to decoder; *1111110* signal to display
press 0	*1* signal to R input of keyboard register; *0000* on output lines
key in number 5	*1* signal on 5 input line to encoder; *0101* signal to keyboard register; *0101* output from keyboard register
press ENTER	*1* signal to enable on inputs to adder; *0101* input to adder; *0000* input to adder; sum (*0101*) signal to internal register; *0101* on output from internal register; *0101* signal to decoder; *1011011* signal to display
key in number 6	*1* signal on 6 input line to encoder; *0110* signal to keyboard register; *0110* output from keyboard register
press ENTER	*1* signal to enable on inputs to adder; *0110* added to *0101*; sum (*1011*) signal to internal register; *1011* signal to decoder; *0011001* signal to display

To describe the machine in even greater detail, let's work through an example and pay attention to the circuit-level activity. Suppose we want to add 5 and 6. The table above shows what happens at each step.

You may be wondering precisely what happens if we exceed the limited capacity of our adding machine, for example, by keying in two numbers whose sum exceeds the four-bit maximum (e.g., 9 plus 7). This is sometimes called the *overflow* problem. If you look back at the logic diagram for the four-bit adder, you will notice that the K output represents a fifth bit. On the five output wires from the adder, the signals *10000* will be found if 9 is added to 7. But only the D, C, B, and A outputs are connected to the display driver and, as inputs, to the internal register. So the display, in this case, will read *0* and *0000* in the internal register. Exercise 12.2.4 asks you to consider other possibilities.

EXERCISES 12.2

1. Design four different logic circuits for a one-bit half-adder.
2. Design three different logic circuits for a one-bit full-adder.
3. Design the logic circuits for the decoder for segments (b) and (g) of a seven-segment display.
4. Can you think of a modification to the design of the adding machine that will give a better solution to the overflow problem? Begin thinking

about what a better solution might include by identifying the problems the current design might cause.

*5. Try your hand at designing a simple subtraction machine.

12.3 A LOGIC MACHINE

The next step up in complexity from the very simple adding machine is to add features that even rudimentary computers and cheap pocket calculators possess: clocks, which allow operations to take place in sequence, and stored instructions for the control unit. We could just design a more sophisticated adding machine with these features, but instead we will shift our focus back to logic and create a *logic machine*. The logic machine will determine whether SL statements are tautologies or contradictions. Since the machine will be able to make these decisions for statements with up to three atomic components, the machine will also determine the validity of arguments whose premises and conclusions have no more than three atomic components and the consistency of sets whose members have no more than three atomic components.[5]

The key element in the design of the logic machine is the use of so-called **designation numbers** for SL expressions.[6] We will use three statement letters, *A*, *B*, and *C*, which can stand, as usual, for any statement. Since our interest here will be discovering tautologies and contradictions, the precise nature of the statements involved is unimportant. The idea of designation numbers arises from the standard truth table for expressions involving three statement letters.

A	B	C
T	T	T
T	T	F
T	F	T
T	F	F
F	T	T
F	T	F
F	F	T
F	F	F

---

[5]The idea of mechanized reasoning is quite old. The standard source is Martin Gardner, *Logic Machines and Diagrams*, 2nd ed. (Chicago: University of Chicago Press, 1982).
[6]See Martin Gardner, *Logic Machines*, chapter 9, and B. Girling and H. G. Moring, *Logic and Logic Design* (Aylesbury, England: International Textbook, 1973), chapter 8.

We first make the by-now familiar substitution of **1** for **T** and **0** for **F**, and then we *rotate* the table so that the vertical columns become horizontal rows of binary numerals, representing *A, B,* and *C,* as follows:

A	1 1 1 1 0 0 0 0
B	1 1 0 0 1 1 0 0
C	1 0 1 0 1 0 1 0

For this method to work, we must associate a specific binary numeral with each letter. Thus, *A* is always **11110000,** and so on.

By equating each SL statement connective with its associated Boolean operator(s), we can also assign designation numbers to any compound of *A, B,* and *C.* Here (in case you have forgotten) are the tables for each connective (the associated Boolean operator is in parentheses), with *X* and *Y* as statement variables.

Negation
(Complement)

X	~X
1	0
0	1

Conjunction
(Logical Multiplication)

X	Y	X & Y
1	1	1
1	0	0
0	1	0
0	0	0

Disjunction
(Logical Addition)

X	Y	X ∨ Y
1	1	1
1	0	1
0	1	1
0	0	0

By means of these three tables, we can, of course, express conditional and biconditional, as follows:

Conditional

X	Y	~X ∨ Y
1	1	1
1	0	0
0	1	1
0	0	1

Biconditional

X	Y	(X & Y) ∨ (~X & ~Y)
1	1	1
1	0	0
0	1	0
0	0	1

To obtain a designation number for a compound statement, we begin by writing the statement letters' designation numbers in a line and then working out the designation number for the compound using the truth table (now turned on its side).

Here is how to find the designation number for a negated statement ~*A:*

A	1	1	1	1	0	0	0	0
~*A*	0	0	0	0	1	1	1	1

A conjunction *A* & *B* would look like this:

A	1	1	1	1	0	0	0	0
B	1	1	0	0	1	1	0	0
A & *B*	1	1	0	0	0	0	0	0

Here are the designation numbers of various compounds:

~*A*	00001111
~*B*	00110011
~*C*	01010101
A & *B*	11000000
A ∨ *B*	11111100
A & *C*	10100000
~*C* ∨ *A*	11110101
A ∨ (*B* ⊃ *C*)	11111011

Under this system, a statement that is a tautology will have **11111111** as its designation number, and a statement that is a contradiction will have **00000000.** As examples,

A ⊃ (*B* ⊃ *A*)	11111111
~(*A* ∨ ~*A*)	00000000
A ≡ (*A* ∨ *A*)	11111111

Statements that are *contingent,* however, have at least one **1** and one **0** in their designation numbers.

Designing a machine that will perform such calculations of designation numbers and pronounce a statement tautologous, contradictory, or contingent requires that we have a calculator that, in effect, does Boolean arithmetic and a display that indicates when the answer consists of all **1**'s or all

0's. We will need keys for each statement letter and three operation keys for $\sim$, &, and $\vee$. The other connectives will be expressed in terms of these three. One important design question will be how the control unit will know about the groupings in complex expressions. We want to ensure, for example, that $A \vee (\sim A \,\&\, \sim A)$, which is a tautology, is not confused with $(A \vee \sim A) \,\&\, \sim A$, which is not. A simple solution is to provide a special memory register where preliminary results can be temporarily stored. Your calculator may have this kind of feature, with buttons to send numbers into memory (like M+ and M) and a button to retrieve them (like RM).

Another kind of solution is to use an alternative notation for SL expressions that can distinguish $A \vee (\sim A \,\&\, \sim A)$ from $(A \vee \sim A) \,\&\, \sim A$ without the use of parentheses. A means of doing this is sometimes called Polish notation after its originator, the Polish logician Jan Lucasiewicz.[7] In *original Polish notation*, the connectives are prefixed to their components. So, in Polish notation,

$A \,\&\, B$ is written $\&AB$,

and

$\sim A \,\&\, \sim(B \vee \sim C)$ is written $\&\sim A\sim\vee B\sim C$.

It may take a little practice to see exactly how it works, but without the use of parentheses, statements may be written without any ambiguity. This is true of mathematical expressions as well. The most common form found on calculators is *reverse Polish notation*, which places the connectives *after* their components. In reverse Polish notation

$\sim A \,\&\, \sim(B \vee \sim C)$ would be $A\sim BC\sim\vee\sim\&$.

Note that the major connective is entered last.

Our logic machine will take the special memory register route because it allows simpler circuit design, even though actual use is slightly more cumbersome than Polish notation would permit (believe it or not!). To process a statement like $\sim A \,\&\, \sim(B \vee \sim C)$, we will first have to process $\sim(B \vee \sim C)$, and then deal with the main connective.

The major components of the logic machine are essentially those of the adding machine, with slight variations, except for the addition of a **control unit**. The control unit will contain the necessary instructions to carry out three kinds of operations: complementation, Boolean addition, and Boolean multiplication. These instructions are part of the fixed memory of the control unit that is called ROM, for 'read only memory'. (We will discuss the details of control units in the next section.)

---

[7]See section 2.5 for Polish notation and various other notational systems.

Each of the three operations of the logic machine will have its own circuitry through which the control unit can send information. If the conjunction A & B is being processed, the control unit needs to send the signals *11110000* (A) and *11001100* (B) through the Boolean multiplier circuit and store the result *1100000* (the designation number of A & B) in the appropriate memory register to await the next step. To a great extent, the steps will remain under the control of the keyboard, but not entirely, as we will see.

Since in the logic machine several steps in the control unit may correspond to a single keystroke, a means to carry out *sequential* operations is needed. The solution is *clock* that sends a regular pulse through the circuits of the machine (on each tick, so to speak). Steps are taken on each pulse; the pulses themselves can be thought of as flashes of binary on and off. The faster the clock, of course, the faster the operations that are directed by the control unit.

Before moving to the details of the circuits in the logic machine, let's first review the overall operation of the machine as it processes information. Suppose, for example, that we want to know what kind of statement $A \supset$ ($\sim A$ & B) is. We first have to rewrite the statement solely in terms of the three connectives the machine recognizes, so it would become $\sim A \vee$ ($\sim A$ & B). Since the statement involves two two-place connectives, we will first have to process $\sim A$ & B and then the components of the disjunction major connective. The actions we take and the sequence of operations within the machine are listed in the chart on the next page.

Notice that there is quite a bit more going on in the logic machine than was the case in the adding machine. Part of this is due to the presence of three possible operations: complementation, Boolean addition, and Boolean multiplication. We thus have to deal with the complexity introduced by the lack of associativity when & and $\vee$ are involved in the same statement; pieces of statements have to be processed and stored in a special memory register. In the adding machine, on the other hand, the numbers in a problem of the form $n_1 + (n_2 + n_3)$ could be entered in any order, and there was no negation to worry about. In our logic machine, we no longer can use the trick of shifting data between registers by routing it through the adder circuit, since there are several possible operations.

The circuits involved in the operations of complementing, Boolean adding, and Boolean multiplying are rather simple. The basic unit the machine deals with is eight bits, since the designation numbers of all statements can be translated into eight-bit form. To complement eight bits, a simple network of inverters is required. We will call this circuit the *complementer,* and use a simple block diagram to indicate its presence in the larger circuits of the logic machine. The Boolean *adder* and *multiplier* also are of eight-bit capacity and consist of eight OR gates and eight AND gates, respectively, in parallel. Each gate has inputs from both registers.

For the sake of simplicity, the diagram below presents only a partial picture of the *multiplier* circuit, which has eight-bit inputs from each of the

Action	Result
press ~ key	a. control unit prepares to complement next entry
press *A* key	a. *A* signal to encoder b. *11110000* signal to keyboard register c. control unit sends *11110000* signal to complement circuit d. output from complementer to interior register and to decoder/display
press & key	a. control unit prepares to send contents of interior register and keyboard register to Boolean multiplier b. control unit sends contents of keyboard register to interior register
press *B* key	a. *B* signal to encoder b. *11001100* signal to keyboard register c. control unit sends outputs from keyboard register and interior register to Boolean multiplier d. output from multiplier to interior register and decoder/display
press *M* key	a. contents of interior register to memory register
(Note: At this point the machine has processsed and stored ~A & B.)	
press ~ key	same as above
press *A* key	same as above
press ∨ key	a. control unit prepares to send contents of interior register and keyboard register to Boolean adder b. control unit sends contents of keyboard register to interior register
press *RM* key	a. control unit sends contents of memory register to keyboard register b. control unit sends outputs from keyboard register and interior register to Boolean adder c. output from adder to interior register and decoder/display
press CLEAR key	a. reset keyboard and interior registers

two registers (*KR* stands for 'keyboard register'; *IR* stands for 'interior register').

Because information will be entered into and removed from the networks at various points in a sequence of operations, there are *enabling gates* at both the input and the output of the complementer, adder, and multiplier. These enabling gates are just extra AND gates on each input and output line. Only when a *1* signal is sent on the enabling line can information pass through these gates, either into or out of the network.

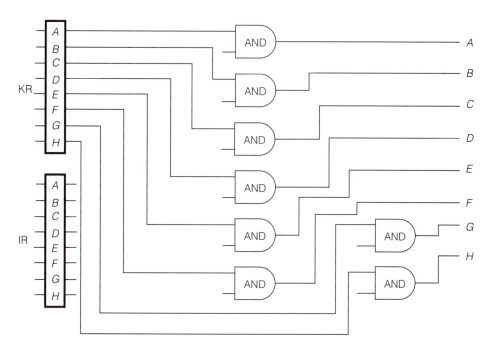

Facilitating the flow of information through the circuits of the logic machine is a *data bus*, a series of eight parallel lines through which eight bits of information, or, more simply, eight *1* or *0* signals, can move in *either direction*. This omnidirectionality is very important, because it is through the data bus that information comes to and goes from the various component networks we have described, as the machine's sequence of steps takes place. And since the very same lines are used for both input and output signals, the enable gates must be connected to the clock mentioned above to make sure the operations take place as scheduled. Here, for example, is a diagram showing how the complementer is connected to the data bus. (E_i and E_o, respectively, represent input and output enable gates.)

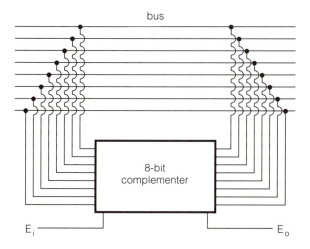

The three registers, which are also eight-bit, take their information from the data bus as well, so they too have input and output gates on each line. To move information from the keyboard register to the internal register, for example, the output of the keyboard register must be enabled (by a *1* signal through that enable line), and the input of the internal register must be enabled also. Assuming that the data bus is clear, information then flows, in effect, from one register to another.

Control over activity in the logic machine reduces to the problem of enabling input and output gates on components at the appropriate interval and storing information between steps. To complement the binary number in the keyboard register, for example, requires enabling the output of the register and the input of the complementer so that the number (in the form of signals) moves through the data bus to the complementer. Then the output of the complementer and the input of the keyboard register are enabled, and the complement comes back through the data bus and is stored in the keyboard register. Remember that information in registers is destroyed as new information enters, so the original number in the keyboard register is replaced in this operation by its complement. What permits all of this to happen are *control signals,* which can also be represented as a series of binary digits. Suppose the complementing operation on the contents of the keyboard register is the only operation we have. Then there would be four control lines, enable-input (E_i) and enable-output (E_o) on the register and enable-input and enable-output on the complementer. The following chart depicts the sequence of control signals that would then occur:

Step	Keyboard register E_i	E_o	Complementer E_i	E_o
1	0	1	1	0
2	1	0	0	1

If the control lines are set up as the table shows, *0110* as a control signal moves the contents of the keyboard register to the complementer, and *1001* moves the contents of the complementer into the register.

Let's now look at the operation of adding (in Boolean) the contents of the keyboard register and the internal register and then storing the result in the internal register. Suppose the designation number for A (**11110000**) is stored in the internal register, and the designation number for B (**11001100**) is stored in the keyboard register. The addition operation will give us the designation number for $A \vee B$ (**11111100**). Since the contents of both registers will move along the same lines in the data bus, the movement of the contents of the two registers will have to be done in sequence. The steps and control signals are as follows.

Step	Keyboard Register E_i	Keyboard Register E_o	Internal Register E_i	Internal Register E_o	Adder Side 1 E_i	Adder Side 2 E_i	Adder E_o
1	0	1	0	0	1	0	0
2	0	0	0	1	0	1	0
3	0	0	1	0	0	0	1

Since information has to be brought to the adder in two steps, one for each input side, there are three required steps in this operation. The control signals for the operation on the above table are *0100100*, *0001010*, and *0010001*.

There will be three similar steps required to multiply the contents of the two main registers and store the result in the internal register. The other operation is to move information from the internal register to the memory register (one step) and to move information from the memory register to the keyboard register (one step). Both of these actions are initiated by pressing the appropriate keys: *M* and *RM*, respectively.

Now we will tabulate all of the operational sequences in the logic machine and find their control signals. The following table uses some handy abbreviations for the enable signals to the various components. *K* is the

Address	KE_i	KE_o	IE_i	IE_o	MRE_i	MRE_o	CE_i	CE_o	$AE1_i$	$AE2_i$	AE_o	$ME1_i$	$ME2_i$	ME_o	EE_i	R
00000																
00001	0	1	1	0	0	0	0	0	0	0	0	0	0	0	0	1
00010																
00011	1	0	0	0	0	0	0	0	0	0	0	0	0	0	1	1
00100																
00101	0	1	0	0	0	0	1	0	0	0	0	0	0	0	0	0
00110	1	0	0	0	0	0	0	1	0	0	0	0	0	0	0	1
00111																
01000	0	1	0	0	0	0	0	0	1	0	0	0	0	0	0	0
01001	0	0	0	1	0	0	0	0	0	1	0	0	0	0	0	0
01011	0	0	1	0	0	0	0	0	0	0	1	0	0	0	0	1
01100																
01101	0	1	0	0	0	0	0	0	0	0	0	1	0	0	0	0
01110	0	0	0	1	0	0	0	0	0	0	0	0	1	0	0	0
01111	0	0	1	0	0	0	0	0	0	0	0	0	0	1	0	1
10000																
10001	0	0	0	1	1	0	0	0	0	0	0	0	0	0	0	1
10010																
10011	1	0	0	0	0	1	0	0	0	0	0	0	0	0	0	1

keyboard register (so KE_i is the input enable on the keyboard register), I is the internal register, MR is the memory register, C is the complementer, A is the adder, M is the multiplier, and E is the encoder circuit connected to the keys for the three statement letters. Finally, R is the counter reset, the purpose of which will be explained later. Each individual control signal has a binary designation, called its **address.** The control signals for the various operations are given in sequence.

You should have noticed that some addresses were left empty between each of the sequences of operations. These are called *beginning codes* for the operation sequences that follow them. So, **00000,** for example, is the beginning code for the operation of transferring the contents of the keyboard register to the internal register. We will have more to say about this later on.

The following chart is a summary of the control signals in the table, with their addresses:

Address	Operation
00001	Transfer contents of keyboard register to internal register; reset counter
00011	Enter encoded designation number from keyboard into keyboard register; reset counter
00101-00110	Complement contents of keyboard register; reset counter
01000-01011	Add contents of keyboard and internal registers and store in internal register; reset counter
01101-01111	Multiply contents of keyboard and internal registers and store in internal register; reset counter
10001	Transfer contents of internal register to memory register; reset counter
10011	Transfer contents of memory register to keyboard register; reset counter

The key element in performing operations in sequence is the **clock** that sends a periodic pulse (a **1** signal) through the circuits. Each step in a sequence of operations takes place during the pulse part of the cycle. After a rest (a **0** state), another pulse allows the next step to be taken, and so on. In order to keep track of where the machine is in a sequence of steps, a **counter** is required. Our counter will allow *presetting* to a specific number (five-digit binary) or being reset to **00000.** On each clock pulse, the counter (arithmetically) adds **1** to the current count. After being fully reset, the counter states are **00000, 00001, 00010,** etc. on the clock pulses. If the counter is preset, for example, to **10001,** then on the clock pulses it will move to states **10010, 10011, 10100,** and so on. Since it is a five-bit counter, when it reaches **11111** it will next go to **00000.**

The circuit for the five-bit counter is similar to the four-bit register diagrammed in section 10.5, except that it has a **ripple** feature. At each clock pulse, the following takes place: if the first flipflop (i.e., the 2^0) contains a *0*, the pulse replaces the *0* with a *1* by setting the flipflop; on the other hand, if the 2^0 flipflop contains a *1*, the pulse replaces that *1* with a *0* by resetting the flipflop, and the *1* signal is passed to the next flipflop (i.e., the 2^1), and the same process is repeated. In this manner, the clock pulse is adding (arithmetically) a 1 to the contents of the counter. When all five flipflops are *1,* the pulse causes them to all change to *0* by fully resetting.

The control unit functions by obtaining control signals, in order, from its special memory, the ROM, and implementing those signals that activate the required operations in the proper sequence. The individual control signals are found by means of their address. The ROM is a rather special kind of memory; the data at each address is permanently fixed (hence, as mentioned, the term 'read-only memory'; nothing can be later written into this memory). When a five-bit address is activated on the input lines to the ROM—which is called an **address bus**—the data stored at that address appears on the output of the ROM, which are the sixteen control lines. The signals on these lines then allow data to move around the various components of the machine. We will study the workings of control units in more detail when we turn to full-scale computers in the next section.

Suppose, for example, we want to complement the designation number currently in the keyboard register because the ~ key has been pressed. The encoder circuit produces the *beginning code* for the complement operation, which is **00100;** this is the blank address just before the complement sequence. This code is sent to the counter, and the enable line is active. This starts the counter. On the next clock pulse, this number is incremented (1 is added) by the counter, and the counter outputs *00101* to the address bus. This, of course, is the address of the first control signal for the complement operation, so the ROM outputs the sixteen-bit control signal, and the contents of the keyboard register are transferred to the complementer. On the next clock pulse, the counter increments to *00110,* which is the address of the next control sequence in the complement operation. On this control signal the contents of the complementer are transferred back to the keyboard register, and the operation is complete. Meanwhile the counter is reset to *00000* on the next clock pulse and waits for the next preset of a beginning code for its cycle.

To show how the various components of the logic machine are connected, a block diagram will be found on the next page.

The final component to be discussed is the display. There are only three conditions that any statement can be in: tautology, contingency, contradiction. So the decoder/display circuitry will be fairly simple. If a statement is

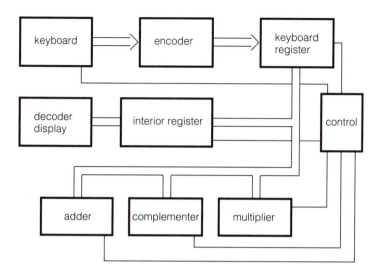

a tautology, the seven-segment display will read *1*, if it is a contradiction, the display will read *0*, and if contingent, the display will read *C*. Sample displays are below:

tautology   contradiction   contingent

As in the case of the adding machine, the decoder is directly connected to the interior register, so something will always be displayed. The table of values for the display is then as follows:

Output from Interior Register								Seven-segment Display						
1	2	3	4	5	6	7	8	(a)	(b)	(c)	(d)	(e)	(f)	(g)
1	1	1	1	1	1	1	1	0	1	1	0	0	0	0
0	0	0	0	0	0	0	0	1	1	1	1	1	1	0
otherwise . . .								1	0	0	1	1	1	0

EXERCISES 12.3

1. Explain how the logic machine could be used to determine the validity of the following arguments. Using the same basic strategy as the machine, determine their validity.

   a. $A \supset (B \supset C)$
       $B \,\&\, \sim C$
       _____

       $\sim A$

   b. $A \vee \sim B$
       $A \supset (B \supset C)$
       _____

       $B \supset C$

   c. $C \,\&\, (A \supset \sim B)$
       $\sim C \vee A$
       _____

       $\sim B$

2. How can the logic machine be used to determine whether a set of statements is consistent? Give two examples.

3. What changes in the design of the logic machine would be required to accommodate four statement letters?

4. What changes would be required in the logic machine to allow the following additional connectives?

   a. $\supset$

   b. $\equiv$

   c. $|$ (neither . . . nor)

*5. Suppose the operation processing (the complementer, adder, multiplier) could be designed with only four-bit circuits and the data bus also has a four-bit capacity. How might the design of the logic machine (for three statement letters) be altered to accommodate this restriction?

12.4 COMPUTERS

Even though our adding machine and logic machine do not even possess the capabilities and complexities of the least expensive pocket electronic calculators, they have most of the essential components of full-scale calculators and computers. Thus, they provide a useful starting point for a more general discussion of how computers function.

   Although we are all beginning to take electronic computers for granted, it is important to know that their development was the culmination of a long history of searching for ways to mechanize reasoning. Doing calculations by hand is laborious work, and the more complex the calculations the more time-consuming and error ridden the work will be. So it is not surprising to find even in the ancient world a variety of devices proposed and actually used to shorten the labor. Perhaps the best-known such device is the **abacus,** which was developed in China between 4000 and 3000 BCE. The abacus is a series of wires on which beads slide back and forth. Moving the beads holds the place of numbers, and complicated calculations can be easily carried on by a skilled abacus operator. The widespread use of the abacus was probably due to its utility in business calculations, especially as traders had to be adept at dealing with many diverse monetary systems. In the early days of electronic computers, an abacus operator was often faster than a computer because the computer data input was so slow.

But numerical computation is only part of the dream that the modern computer fulfills. Logicians as early as the thirteenth century designed and built logic machines.[8] By the nineteenth century, a number of these existed, and there was no syllogistic problem they could not handle. At the same time, an entirely separate technology produced a loom for weaving cloth that was controlled by the holes punched into a special wooden card. In this case, the problem was control or automated decision making; the pattern woven by the loom, the threads selected, and the other operations of the machine were under the control of the punched card rather than an operator.[9] Partly inspired by the success of the ability to control a loom, the English mathematician Charles Babbage together with Lady Ada Lovelace designed a mechanical device that could carry out computational programs fed into it on punched cards. The Babbage-Lovelace machine was the first real computer design, and all modern computers share design features with this nineteenth century maze of cogs, levers, wheels, and gears.

The punched paper card was the principal innovation of the American Herman Hollerith, who designed a calculating machine for the U.S. Census Bureau that was first used in the 1890 census. Prior to the development of Hollerith's machine, the compilation of census data was so slow that it was not published until many years after the census was taken and much of the utility of the information was lost. Hollerith later formed his own company to manufacture his machine; the company eventually became IBM.

Two strains of development are responsible for the development of the electronic computer in the middle of this century. First, the connection between switching circuits, statement logic, and Boolean systems was first noticed by the American logician and philosopher Charles Sanders Peirce in 1886 and worked out in detail in an historic paper by Claude Shannon in 1938.[10] Shannon's work, coupled with a growing electronics industry, permitted rapid development of the hardware capabilities for true computers.

---

[8]Gardner, *Logic Machines,* provides a thorough account of the development of logic machines.
[9]See David Harel, *Algorithmics: The Spirit of Computing* (Reading, MA: Addison-Wesley, 1987), chapter 1.
[10]The priority of Peirce is noted by Gardner, *Logic Machines,* p. 116. Shannon's paper is "A Symbolic Analysis of Relay and Switching Circuits," in *Transactions of the American Institute of Electrical Engineers,* vol. 57 (December 1938).

In the same years, there was a growing interest in the logical foundations of decision making. Fundamental work on the theory of algorithms was conducted by mathematicians and logicians such as Alan Turing, Alonzo Church, Kurt Goedel, Emil Post, and Stephen Kleene. As we discussed in chapter 11, one of the most important results of this work was a recognition of the limitations of any computer, no matter how powerful. Even before the first real computer came into operation, its limitations had, in a sense, been firmly established.

Out of the work on logic circuits, on the one hand, and algorithms, on the other, emerged more and more sophisticated equipment designed for specific purposes such as cracking codes, calculating the trajectory of artillery shells, keeping track of the positions of ships, and for carrying on business and conducting scientific research. The Second World War especially spurred on the development of such machines. But the first general purpose, electronic, digital computers that could store and implement programs first appeared in England and the United States in 1949, the EDVAC at the University of Pennsylvania and the EDSAC at Cambridge, England. And so, the computer age began.

The shift toward general purpose machines proved to be very important in the development of computers. For by designing the basic components to perform a wide variety of operations, different approaches to the same problem and entirely new applications became increasingly possible. The adding machine and the logic machine we 'constructed' in the last two sections are, by design, extremely limited special-purpose devices. They perform the tasks for which they are designed, but they can't be used for anything else. But by the early 1950s, computers were built so that their use was limited more by the imagination and ingenuity of their operators than by their design. New uses and applications are constantly being found, and, as a result of vast increases in speed and power and incredible decreases in cost, computers are simply everywhere. They have become indispensable.

The principal difference between a calculator and a true computer is the computer's ability to store its operating program instead of being under constant external control. In fact, small electronic calculators are actually hybrids because their basic operating programs are internally stored, as we saw to some extent in the case of the logic machine. But a true computer goes a step further in that new programs, new sequences of instructions, can be stored by the machine and implemented on demand. It didn't take too long in the development of computers after 1950 before storage in computers began to be called 'memory' and computers themselves became known as 'brains' and were talked about as 'intelligent.' (Alan Turing himself is partially responsible for such anthropomorphic labels.) Indeed, machine intelligence, or 'artificial intelligence', is today one of the most important fields within computer science.

The storage, or memory, capabilities of modern computers is awesome. But the important conceptual breakthrough came in the realization that *instructions* in addition to numbers could be stored. This idea was suggested in Turing's 1936 paper in which the universal Turing machine is discussed. We have already seen how this is done; instructions are coded in the same binary notation as numbers, but the computer *acts* on the instructions as it *processes* the numbers. We have also seen, in the logic machine, that although numerical processing is perhaps the most obvious use of electronic circuitry, in fact symbolic processing can be easily carried on (as Turing also anticipated). The circuits are oblivious to the differences between numbers, symbolic statements, characters, musical tones, images, or anything else that can be coded in binary form. All the computer does, in one apt phrase, is twiddle bits. And the bits are just signals through the circuitry: high voltage and low voltage.

To most users of computers, however, binary coded instructions and data are completely invisible, just as they would be to users of our adding and logic machines. Early in the development of computers it became clear that writing programs and entering data in the form of machine code was far too laborious and inefficient. On a parallel track to the continuous improvement of machine design, the development of computer program languages was also taking place. Computer languages are designed so that users can easily formulate the instructions for the routines to be performed by a computer and enter data in forms that are convenient to them instead of understandable to the machine. Hundreds of different such languages now exist; many are intended for quite specialized uses in science and industry. You are probably familar with the names of common computer 'high-level' languages such as BASIC, PASCAL, FORTRAN, C, LISP, and PROLOG.

The commands written in a high-level computer language will normally correspond to a large number of binary digits in the code understood by the machine, and many cycles of the machine operation will be involved in the execution of such commands. We saw earlier that even in our simple logic machine, a single pressing of a key brought about a number of machine cycles and the movement of binary coded data in the form of signals through the circuitry. Recall from chapter 11 that the algorithm for *averaging* a list of numbers incorporates adding a list and keeping track of how many numbers are added (by means of a counter) as well as their sum. That algorithm, which required only a few steps, is fairly similar to the one you would find in an averaging program written in a language such as BASIC or PASCAL.

Fortunately, the translation from a high-level computer language to machine code is itself performed by specialized programs called *interpreters* and *compilers*. Therefore the program can be written in a language that is reasonably easy and efficient to use, and other computer programs take care of reformulating the instructions in machine code so that the appropriate cycles and control operations take place. As a result of the development of powerful high-level computer languages, a computer programmer does not really need to know what is taking place inside the circuits, just as a person making toast does not have to understand how a toaster works.

Now let's look at the basic constituents of computers and their operations. No matter how large or small, a computer can be thought of as a system involving five major components. All information that comes into the computer comes through **input devices** and **encoders.** Computers also have a **control element,** however rudimentary it may be. This component runs the other parts of the machine, arranging the sequence of steps that are to be followed, determining where information is to be gathered and stored, and so forth. The information used in computations is stored in **memory,** which may be of varying types depending upon the nature of the machine. The computations themselves are performed by the **arithmetic-logic unit.** Normally, arithmetic-logic units are capable of a wide variety of different computations and logical manipulations. The particular calculation or operation to be performed and the source of the information for such calculations are determined by the control unit. The results of the computer computations are presented to the outside world by means of **decoders** and **output devices,** such as displays on calculators, video screens, magnetic tape, disks, punched cards, etc.

Here is a graphic representation of the major components of all computers.

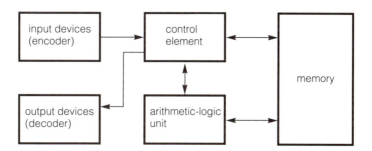

Information may enter a computer in various ways. You are probably familiar with typewriter-like keyboards connected to terminals through which information is entered. But information may also come on punch cards, paper tape, magnetic discs, or tape. Other inputs may come from light pens, optical scanners, telephone lines, voice, or hand-held devices such as joy sticks and mice. Some device, however, is always required to physically transmit the information from whatever form it has, and an encoder is required to transform the information into binary coded signals. You should notice that information goes through a double transformation as it finds its way into a computer. There is a *physical* transformation and a *symbolic* transformation. The physical change is from the original form of the information (magnetized regions, bar code, voice, keystrokes, movements of a mouse, etc.), and the symbolic change is from its current representational system (decimal numerals, letters, sounds, etc.) to binary signals.

For example, when information is entered into a personal computer by means of a mouse, the physical form of the information entered is the movement of this device, say, one inch in a certain direction. This movement is ultimately coded into binary signals that may represent the selection of two words displayed on the screen. By moving a mouse in the context of a certain computer program, a significant amount of information undergoes this transformation. As an exercise, enter some information into a computer with any input device and then give a written description of what physical form the information originally had and how the information was represented as you entered it.

Since computers often manipulate symbols as well as numerals, the use of binary representation for letters, numerals, punctuation marks, logical and mathematical symbols, and so on is very important. But there is no natural or obvious representation system, as there is for numbers as binary numerals. So agreed upon representations, or **binary codes,** have been developed that are standard in the computer industry. An example we have already used is the American Standard Code for Information Interchange or ASCII (see the Appendix).

Information, once entered, is stored in the computer memory. There are two principal regions of memory in most computers: *main* memory and *external* memory. The main memory is used to store the programs and data that the computer is currently processing; external memory is for storage of data and programs that are not in current use. Main memory can be accessed very rapidly; access to external memory, on the other hand, is much slower. Typical external memory devices are tape, magnetic disk, and optical disk. Usually programs and data are transferred from external memory to main memory prior to the execution of the program. Most of a computer's main memory is volatile; when the computer is shut off, whatever is stored is lost. The exception is what has already been referred to as 'read-only memory' or **ROM,** which is permanent. Data stored in the main memory that can be altered is usually called 'read and write memory' or **RAM.** This acronym, however, is misleading; it comes from 'random access memory,' i.e., data in storage that can be accessed directly without passing over other data first, as one has to do on a tape. Data stored as ROM is also randomly accessible, but the term RAM is used so widely that any change is unlikely.

The memory of a computer is divided into units of some fixed number of bits, called the **word** length of the memory. Common lengths are four, eight, ten, twelve, sixteen, and thirty-two bits. Other terms associated with the standard size of memory units are **byte,** which is eight bits of information (**11011010**) and **nibble,** which is four bits. Those who write about computers often visualize memory as a pile of word-length units of such and such height. The number of words is always equal to a power of 2, so memories come as units of sixteen words (2^4) or 512 words (2^9) or larger. Each individual storage location in a memory has a fixed **address.** We saw in the last section how the various instructions to the control element in the logic machine were obtained from memory by means of their addresses. The address of a memory location is fixed, but the content of that address may change (except for ROM). So a memory might be thought of, as in the following diagram, more or less like an apartment building with one apartment on each floor.

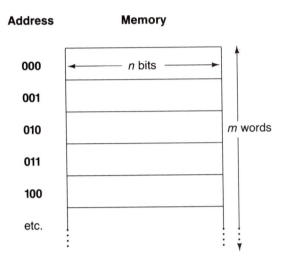

Address   **Memory**

000   ←——— *n* bits ———→

001

010   *m* words

011

100

etc.

Note, however, that the first address, **000**, is pictured at the top of the pile of memory locations. (Apartment addresses, on the other hand, begin on the bottom floor).

Programs are stored in memory as combinations of instructions and data. As far as the memory itself is concerned, instructions and data are just bits, arranged in addresses in word-length units. But a given word in memory might be the address of *another* word in memory; this possibility is the key to the ability to execute programs, to generate the next step the computer should take. It is important to remember that the address of a memory location is independent of the content at that location; addresses may even be of different lengths than the words of a memory. For example, a memory consisting of 1024 eight-bit words, or 1k words (k is short for 1,000; usually 1024 is just rounded off to 1k for simplicity), might have ten-bit addresses. So how, you may wonder, could a word of such a memory contain the address of another word? The answer lies in instructions consisting of more than just one word in a memory, as we will see in the next section.

The combination of the control element, which decodes and carries out instructions, and the arithmetic-logic unit (**ALU,** for short) is called the **central processing unit** (or **CPU**) of the computer. As a program is executed, instructions direct the control element to obtain data from various memory locations and to perform operations on that data through the arithmetic-logic unit. As discussed in previous sections, the full-adder circuit in the adding machine and the Boolean adder and multiplier of the logic machine can be thought of as simplified arithmetic-logic units. In effect, all that a computer can do is specified by the operations of the arithmetic-logic unit, the size of the memory (so that long and complex programs can be carried out), and the speed of the CPU (so that programs are executed in a reasonable amount of time). Some computers can run programs in an hour that other computers might take several lifetimes to execute.

A common, commercially available four-bit arithmetic-logic unit found in many small computers can perform a total of twenty-nine different arithmetic and logic operations. Its network diagram contains sixty-three logic gates including all control lines.[11] To indicate the range of possible actions of a standard arithmetic-logic unit, the following table lists the various *outputs* it is capable of producing. The two four-bit inputs are represented by A and B, the operators $\sim$, $\vee$, and & represent the Boolean operations of complementation, logical addition, and logical multiplication, respectively.

Logical operations	Arithmetic operations
$\sim A$	$A - 1$
$\sim(A \,\&\, B)$	$(A \,\&\, B) - 1$
$\sim A \vee B$	$(A \,\&\, \sim B) - 1$
$A \vee \sim A$	-0001
$\sim(A \vee B)$	$A + (A \vee \sim B)$
$\sim B$	$(A \,\&\, B) + (A \vee \sim B)$
$\sim[(A \vee B) \,\&\, \sim(A \,\&\, B)]$	$A - (B - 1)$
$A \vee \sim B$	$A + (A \vee B)$
$\sim A \,\&\, B$	$A + B$
$(A \vee B) \,\&\, \sim(A \,\&\, B)$	$(A \,\&\, \sim B) + (A + B)$
B	$A + A$
$A \vee B$	$(A \,\&\, B) + A$
$A \,\&\, \sim A$	$(A \,\&\, \sim B) + A$
$A \,\&\, \sim B$	
$A \,\&\, B$	
A	

This arithmetic-logic unit essentially performs only *five basic operations*. Given any two four-bit inputs, it can perform regular arithmetic addition (+) and subtraction (−), Boolean complementation ($\sim$), addition ($\vee$), and multiplication (&). Multiplication and division are handled by repeated additions and subtractions. The reason for having all these 29 possible outputs is

[11]This is the ALU of the Digital Equipment Corporation PDP-11 series, for example. See Thomas Bartee, *Computer Fundamentals*, pp. 284–285.

speed; even though a much simpler circuit could perform all of these operations, the instructions would be much more cumbersome, and programs would run more slowly.

Suppose input A is **1101** and B is **0101**. Here are some examples of what the ALU would produce as output from its possible operations:

$\sim(A \vee B)$	$= 0010$	
$A + (A \vee \sim B)$	$= 1101$	(Note: The carry bit is lost as overflow.)
$\sim B$	$= 1010$	
$(A \& B) + (A \vee \sim B)$	$= 0100$	(Note: The carry bit is lost as overflow.)
$\sim[(A \vee B) \& \sim(A \& B)]$	$= 0111$	
$A - (B - 1)$	$= 1011$	
$A \& \sim A$	$= 0000$	

It may come as a surprise that all the tasks of a modern high-speed computer can be performed by means of the above twenty-nine operations, which boil down to three logical operations plus arithmetical addition and subtraction.[12] But the power of computers derives from the ability to perform very large numbers of such operations very quickly and from the ingenuity of computer scientists and mathematicians who have reduced extremely complex problems to steps that can be performed entirely by means of these operations. We will have more to say on this topic in the next section.

The *control element*, of course, arranges for all the steps to take place in the proper order. A typical control element consists of an instruction decoder and a series of registers. The following registers are commonly available as part of the control element:

Accumulator   The register in which the output from the ALU is stored temporarily. (This function is performed by the interior register in the adding machine and the logic machine.)

Instruction register   Stores the current instruction after it is brought from memory.

Program counter   Stores the address of the next instruction to be obtained from memory. (Recall its use in the logic machine.)

Data counter   Stores the data that the current instruction requires (function of the keyboard register in logic machine and interior register of adding machine).

Instructions usually direct the control element to conduct a series of actions involving these registers and memory. However, every instruction can be broken down into a series of basic actions, each of which takes place during

---

[12]Turing machines, of course, are even simpler.

one **machine cycle.** Machine cycles are determined by a clock signal from some timing mechanism. Basic processing actions can conveniently be divided into three categories:

READ The data stored in the memory location at the address currently indicated on the program counter is brought to one of the registers.

WRITE The data stored in one of the registers is transferred to a memory location.

EXECUTE The control element directs an operation in the ALU on data stored in one or more registers.

The data moves around the CPU and to and from memory on buses—parallel lines on which signals travel. Typically there are three different buses available: the **address bus,** on which the address of the next data to be read from or written to memory is transmitted; the **data bus,** on which data move between the registers in the control element, the ALU, and memory; and the **control bus,** on which all control signals travel. The data bus is bidirectional; the others are unidirectional.

Below is a block diagram of the control element as described so far. The control bus is indicated by single lines connecting the control unit to the accumulator, the registers, the ALU, and the program counter; the other two buses are represented by double lines.

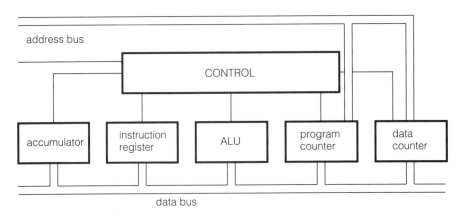

Programs, as noted, contain *sequences* of instructions. These instructions are contiguous in memory so that they may be accessed in the proper order. Individual instructions in a program are executed in cyclic fashion, as follows:

1. **Read** the instruction stored at the memory location address currently stored in the program counter and **store** it in the instruction register.

2. **Increment** (add 1 or more to) the contents of the program counter.

3. **Decode** the instruction read in step 1 and **execute** it.

4. Return to step 1.

Note that the program counter is incremented immediately after the instruction is read so that it will then contain the address of the next instruction. If individual instructions occupy several words of memory, then the program counter is incremented by that number; that is, if instructions consist of two words, then the program counter in step 2 is incremented by adding 2.

The fifth standard component of all computers is the *output device*. As is the case for input devices, output can take many forms. Information can be displayed on a cathode ray tube (CRT) on a terminal, printed, stored on magnetic or optical disks or tape, or take the form of sound, as in synthesized speech or computer-generated music. Computer output may also take the form of some *action*, such as the control of some kind of machinery. There are microprocessors in automobile engines, for example, that monitor certain functions, and their output is presented as information on the dashboard display (e.g., whether there is sufficient fuel to reach a predetermined destination). But such microprocessors also control the ratio of air to gasoline in the fuel injection system. So the output in this case takes the form of signals that become commands.

However the information comes out, it will have gone through the same double transformation: symbolic and physical. The signals from the control element to the output device are, of course, binary. They must be decoded into some other symbolic system—characters, sounds, holes—and then displayed or produced. The logic and adding machines, for example, used a seven-segment light display. Signals on seven input lines resulted in displayed decimal numerals and, in the logic machine, the letter C (contingent). High and low voltage on wires became a lighted display; binary representation became Arabic numerals or letters having specified meanings. Whatever the form the output may take, an output device containing a decoder must be connected to the control element and provided with the appropriate signals.

Summary

Here are the principal terms and concepts that have been introduced in this section.
The five major components of a computer are:

Input device/encoder

Control element

Arithmetic-logic unit (ALU)

Memory

Output device/decoder

Instruction Operation code	Machine cycle	Action
SRA(*m*)	1	Read the first word of the instruction, i.e. SRA, and store in instruction register.
	2	Read the operand, i.e. *m*, and store in the data counter.
	3	Store contents of the accumulator at address *m*.

Note: We have *m* used both as data to be stored in the data counter register and as an address at which other data is stored. This is also true of the next instruction:

LDA(*m*)	1	Read the first word of the instruction, i.e. LDA, and store in instruction register.
	2	Read the operand, i.e. *m*, and store in data counter.
	3	Store contents of memory address *m* in accumulator.
LDI(*m*)	1	Read the first word of the instruction, i.e. LDI, and store in instruction register.
	2	Read the operand, *m*, and store in accumulator.

Note: in LDA(*m*) the data at memory address *m* ends up in the accumulator, whereas in LDI(*m*), *m* itself ends up in the accumulator.

ADA(*m*)	1	Read the first word of the instruction, i.e. ADA, and store in instruction register.
	2	Read the operand, i.e. *m*, and store in data counter.

Computer memory is of two types: **external** memory, which is slow to access, and **main** memory, which is fast and contains the current program and data. Data in memory that can only be read is stored as **ROM;** data that can be read and written is stored as **RAM.** Memory is divided into units of fixed size called **words;** a word has a certain length, or number of bits (binary digits). Eight bits is a **byte;** four bits is a **nibble.**

Words are stored in memory at **addresses.** The address may contain more bits than the words. The control element contains registers and one or more **buses.** A common configuration would provide an address bus, a data bus, and a control bus. A program consists of **instructions;** each instruction contains an **instruction code** and an **operand.** An operand may be data that will be processed or may be the address of some memory location. The control element has its own **microprogram** made up of **micro-instructions** stored in a special ROM.

Instruction Operation code	Machine cycle	Action
	3	Add contents of memory address m to the contents of the accumulator, and store the sum in the accumulator.
ADI(m)	1	Read the first word of the instruction, i.e. ADI, and store in instruction register.
	2	Add the operand, m, to the contents of the accumulator and store the sum in the accumulator.
BRP(m)	1	Read the first word of the instruction, i.e. BRP, and store in instruction register.
	2	Branch: test the contents of the accumulator; if positive, read operand m and store in the program counter; if negative, do nothing.

Note: by storing m into the program counter (if the accumulator content is positive), the program 'jumps' from the current instruction to the instruction which is the content of memory address m, as in a GOTO step.

DEC(m)	1	Read the first word of the instruction, i.e. DEC, and store in instruction register.
	2	Read the operand, i.e. m, and store in data counter.
	3, 4, 5	Subtract 1 from the contents of memory location m.

*12.5 CPU INSTRUCTIONS AND PROGRAMS

This section presents a set of instructions for the control unit of a standard microprocessor.

Individual instructions consist, typically, of two parts. The first part is an **operation code,** which specifies some operation that is to be performed by the CPU. The second part is the **operand,** which may be the data that are to be processed or may be the address of some data in memory. The operation codes of instructions are, of course, binary numbers of one-word length, which are recognized as such by the control element. In describing the various instructions, however, it is customary and useful to give them three-letter names instead of referring to them in their binary coded form. A typical pattern is three capital letters followed by a lowercase letter in parentheses, e.g., *XYZ* (a). The lowercase letter represents the operand (*not* the address of the operand). The chart shows several examples of such instructions.[13] Note: the subtraction of 1 from the contents of address *m* takes three machine cycles to complete. The contents of *m* are read and transferred to the ALU, the ALU performs the subtraction, and the result is written at address *m*.

Each of the three-letter operation codes is an abbreviation for the action to be performed. Those instructions that end with I (e.g., ADI, LDI) require an *immediate* operation; the operand that follows the operation code is used itself as data. So in ADI(*m*), the operand *m* is added to the contents of the accumulator. Instructions that end in *A* (e.g., SRA, LDA) require that the operand be used as an address for the crucial portion of the operation. So in SRA(*m*), the contents of the accumulator are stored at address *m*. The first two letters usually abbreviate the particular action: SR is 'store', LD is 'load', AD is 'add', BR is 'branch' (P is 'positive,' so BRP is 'branch positive'). DEC, of course, means 'decrement.'

With these instructions, we can study a program that adds together a set of data stored in some number *n* of contiguous memory locations, beginning at some specific memory address, say *q*. To be specific, suppose there are twelve words of data to be summed, and suppose the first memory address is **0000011.** Thus we want to add together the contents of the memory locations **00000011** (decimal 3) through **00001110** (decimal 14).

The program instructions themselves also have to be in memory, so we will assign locations **00011110** (30) to **00110111** (55) to the program. Finally, we will want a memory location for the sum, which will be at address **01000000** (64), and we will need a memory location as a counter, for which address **01000001** (65) will be used. There is no particular reason for choosing these addresses. For convenience, we will refer to addresses by their decimal numerals, as given in parentheses.

The program, then, is as shown in the next chart. By running this program, the (binary) numbers stored at the designated memory locations 3 to 14 are summed, and a running total for each step will end up at the specified memory location (64). The program has a built-in loop. It first adds the last number (at address 14) to 0, stores that sum at address 64, then cycles back to the ninth step (address 38). Then it decrements the counter by 1, finds the second-to-last number (now at address 13), adds it to the contents of address 64, tests to make sure there is still another number to add, and then, since there is, loops back to the ninth step again, and so on. Eventually the counter goes to 0, after eleven steps, and the final cycle begins. As the number at address 3 is added to the contents of address 64, we have the final sum. At the BRP step (address 54) the test shows that the counter at address 65 is now 0, so the program halts. The BRP instruction could have included some signal that the test had failed (like making END appear on a screen).

---

[13]Much of the detail of the control element and the instruction set is from Henry D'Angelo, *Microcomputer Structures* (New York: Byte Books, 1981), chapter 6.

Address	Instruction	Comments
30	LDI	
31	12	
32	SRA	
33	65	The first four steps insert the number of words in memory to be summed (12) into the counter (memory address 65).
34	LDI	
35	0	
36	SRA	
37	64	These four steps insert the initial sum (0) into the sum memory location (address 64). This operation clears the sum memory location.
38	DEC	
39	65	The counter is next decreased by 1 (so 11 is now the content of address 65.
40	LDA	
41	65	
42	ADI	
43	3	
44	SRA	
45	49	The current content of the counter (11), which is stored in the accumulator register, is added to the first address of the data to be summed (3), and the result (14) is placed in memory location 49. Note that 14 is the address of the last data to be summed by the program.
46	LDA	
47	64	
48	ADA	
49	***	
50	SRA	
51	64	Next the content of address 14 (this address is stored in memory location 49) is added to the sum (the content of address 64) and stored at address 64. Note: anything could have originally been stored at address 49.
52	LDA	
53	65	
54	BRP	
55	38	The content of address 65 (currently 11) is tested to determine whether it is positive (i.e. greater than 0); since it is, the program cycles back to address 38.

By using locations in main memory for the sum (address 64) and the counter (address 65), the registers in the control element are kept free to receive and temporarily store data. As each instruction is executed, the program counter is increased by 2. The program counter is initially set to 30; the instruction at address 30 (LDI) is fetched and stored in the instruction register on the first machine cycle. On the next cycle the operand at the next address, in this case 12, is loaded (stored) in the accumulator register, and the program counter is incremented to 32. By the end of the next three machine cycles, the number 12 is stored in memory location 65 (the counter); address 65 was placed in the data counter so that 12 (in the accumulator) could be transferred to that location. The following chart shows what happens in the first ten machine cycles in running the program.

Machine cycle	Action
1	Read the operation code LDI from address 30 into the instruction register. Add to the program counter.
2	Load 12 (from the next address, i.e., 31) into the accumulator. (This is the number of numbers to be summed.)
3	Read the operation code SRA from address 32 into the instruction register. Add to the program counter.
4	Load 65 (from address 33) into the data counter. (Address 65 is the location of the counter for the program.)
5	Transfer the contents of the accumulator (i.e., 12) to the address in the data counter (i.e. 65)
6	Read the operation code LDI from address 34 into the instruction register. Add to the program counter.
7	Load 0 (from the next address, i.e. 35) into the accumulator.
8	Read the operation code SRA from address 36 into the instruction register. Add to the program counter.
9	Load 64 (from address 35) into the data counter. (Note: address 64 is the location of the running total.)
10	Transfer the content of the accumulator (0) to memory location 64 (from the data counter). (Note: clearing 64 ensures that the running total will include only the sum of the numbers to be added.)

Since the execution of each program instruction we have discussed takes from two to four machine cycles, you may wonder how all of the required control signals that permit the actions of each individual cycle are propagated. Look, for example, at cycle 7 above. Within this cycle, address 33 must be found, a signal to read its contents (**0**) must be generated, a signal to transmit **0** on the data bus must be given, a signal to store **0** in the accumulator must be given, and **0** (as a binary signal) must physically move from memory location 33 to the accumulator, thus replacing whatever may have been in the accumulator. To understand how all of this takes place, we must go to the level of the **micro-instructions** of the control element.[14]

Microinstructions allow the control element to perform the required actions to implement instructions. During any given machine cycle a number of distinct actions may have to be performed. Therefore, machine cycles are themselves divided into several *internal states*, three to five per cycle. We will refer to these internal states as T_1, T_2, T_3, etc.

As an illustration, let's study the control element activities during the execution of the ADA(14) instruction from the program. (This instruction is at addresses 48 and 49 of the first loop of the program.) The instruction says to add the contents of memory address 14 to the contents of the accumulator and store the sum in the accumulator. (See chart on the next page.)

The reason why internal state T_1 of machine cycle 3 is empty is that the control element actually overlaps machine cycles of instructions to achieve greater speed. So while the execute phase of the ADA(*m*) instruction takes place (3rd machine cycle), the read cycle of the next instruction is also being undertaken. To avoid conflict on the control bus, the execution of addition waits until the second internal state while the program counter is sending the next address (in this case 50) on the address bus. This technique of performing the end of one instruction and the beginning of the next during the same machine cycle is called the *read/execute overlap.*

The individual control signals are generated by the control element by means of the instruction decoder and are sent out on the control bus to memory, the various registers, and the ALU. The discussion of the vastly simplified control circuits of the logic machine in section 12.2 suggests how complex this aspect of the control element's function can be. But despite the number of control signals that have to be sent in the proper sequence, all that is taking place is that the *1* and *0* signals are being applied to certain lines in a predetermined order. The instructions that permit the control element to function are stored in a special micro-instruction ROM memory that is built by the manufacturer into the control element and cannot be accessed by any program. As the operation code of an instruction is decoded, an address of a location in ROM is provided, and the binary code of the appropriate control signals is supplied. This enables the specified actions of each internal state to be performed.

---

[14]The micro-instructions listed here are essentially those for the Intel Corporation 8080 microprocessor. See Andrew Veronis, *Microprocessors: Hardware and Applications* (Reston, VA: Reston Pub. Co., 1984), chapter 1. See also Rodnay Zaks, *From Chips to Systems* (Berkeley, CA: Sybex Books, 1981), chapter 2.

Machine cycle	State	Action
1	T_1	Address on program counter (48) sent to memory on the address bus.
	T_2	Memory decodes address; program counter increased by 1.
	T_3	Operation code (ADA) deposited on data bus and transferred to the instruction register.
	T_4	Operation code decoded by instruction decoder; contents of accumulator transferred to input of ALU.
2	T_1	Address on program counter (49) sent to memory on the address bus.
	T_2	Memory decodes address; program counter increased by 1.
	T_3	Content of address (14) deposited on data bus and transferred to data counter.
	T_4	Address in data counter (14) sent to memory on address bus.
	T_5	Memory decodes address, content of address sent to input of ALU.
3	T_1	
	T_2	Sum sent from ALU on data bus to accumulator.

So we have reached the end of our journey; we have moved from a first glimpse of logical form to the actual micro-instruction set of an operational CPU. The same logical principles are at work all along the way.

Appendix

AMERICAN STANDARD CODE FOR INFORMATION INTERCHANGE* (ASCII)

Alpha-numeric characters

	011	100	101
0000	0	—	P
0001	1	A	Q
0010	2	B	R
0011	3	C	S
0100	4	D	T
0101	5	E	U
0110	6	F	V
0111	7	G	W
1000	8	H	X
1001	9	I	Y
1010	—	J	Z
1011	—	K	—
1100	—	L	—
1101	—	M	—
1110	—	N	—
1111	—	O	—

Each character is represented by a unique seven digit binary numeral, determined by combining together the column code (3 digits) and the row code (4 digits).

---

*For the complete ASCII representation system, see, e.g., Thomas C. Bartee, *Digital Computer Fundamentals*, 5th ed. (New York, McGraw-Hill, 1981), p. 410.

For example, *A* is 100 (column) and 0001 (row), hence the ASCII code for *A* is 1000001. Here are some other examples:

character	ASCII
0	0110000
B	1000010
1	0110001
G	1000111
8	0111000

ASCII representations of several character strings are formed by combining the individual seven digit ASCII representations of the constituent characters. For example:

characters	ASCII
000	011000001100000110000
BIG	100001010010011000111
10	01100010110000
potato	1010000100111110101001000001101010010011 11

Answers to Selected Exercises

Section 1.1

1. b. By getting a 56 on his College Achievement exam, Bill has satisfied his foreign language requirement. He has completed his major, which means that he has fulfilled one of his all-college division requirements. He still needs to take a freshman seminar, which could also satisfy 4 credits of either his humanities or social science requirement. He would have to take 8 credit hours in the remaining division and 4 credit hours in the other division. (Suppose that Bill is a biology major. He has therefore fulfilled his natural science requirement. He takes a freshman seminar on classic literature, giving him 4 credit hours of humanities. He still needs to take 4 credit hours of humanities and 8 credit hours of social science.) He will also have to make sure that he has the 120 credit hours and a GPA of at least 2.0.

2. a. Since no hedgehogs can read, and since those who cannot read are not educated, and since those who are educated are subscribers to the *Times*, we can conclude that hedgehogs do not subscribe to the *Times*.

   c. Wine drinkers are not promise breakers. Since one can always trust a communicative person, and since wine drinkers are very communicative, one can always trust wine drinkers. One can never trust promise breakers, but since we have already established that one can always trust wine drinkers, we know that wine drinkers are not promise breakers.

   d. None of your sons can serve on a jury. Since everyone who is sane can do logic, and since none of your sons can do logic, that means that none of your sons is sane. Since none of your sons is sane, and no lunatics [also read as "no one who is not sane"] are fit to serve on a jury, none of your sons is fit to serve on a jury.

Section 1.2

1. b. Cleveland is a large city in Ohio.

   All cities in Ohio are covered by this bill.

   ———————————————————————

   Cleveland will be covered by this legislation.

   c. A statement, not an argument, because of the conditional If . . . then.

e. Sons and daughters are descendants.

Shem had descendants.

Shem had sons and daughters.

2. a. All humans are mortals.

Socrates is a human.

Socrates is a mortal.

c. All students are unhappy this week.

John is not a student.

John is happy this week.

3. a. False. A valid argument may have a false conclusion if one or more of the premises is false.

e. False. We can speak or write declarative sentences without intending to make a statement, for example, in a novel or in a play.

g. False. (See a.)

h. False. An invalid argument can still have a true conclusion. Here is an example: "Your car is tan; therefore, my car is tan (which it is!)."

Section 2.1

1. a. Truth-functional compound
Components: The keys are on the dresser; the grocery list is on the dresser.
Connective: conjunction

c. Not a truth-functional compound

e. Not a truth-functional compound

g. Truth-functional compound
Components: I will not go; he will go.
Connective: conjunction

i. Truth-functional compound
Components: Pamela will pass the test; Quincy will pass the test.
Connective: conjunction

k. Truth-functional compound
Components: The form is complete.
Connective: negation

2. a. $\sim R$ **c.** $\sim P \,\&\, \sim Q$ **e.** $P \,\&\, (\sim Q \lor R)$ **g.** $\sim (P \,\&\, Q)$

3. a. $P \lor (Q \,\&\, \sim R)$

$Q \,\&\, \sim R$

$\sim R$

$P \quad Q \quad R$

c. $\sim (Q \lor P) \,\&\, (R \lor S)$

$\sim (Q \lor P) \qquad R \lor S$

$Q \lor P$

$Q \quad P \quad R \quad S$

e. $[\sim (P \,\&\, Q) \lor S] \,\&\, [(P \,\&\, Q) \lor (S \lor (T \,\&\, S))]$

$\sim (P \,\&\, Q) \lor S \qquad (P \,\&\, Q) \lor (S \lor (T \,\&\, S))$

$\sim (P \,\&\, Q) \qquad\qquad P \,\&\, Q \quad S \lor (T \,\&\, S)$

$P \,\&\, Q \qquad\qquad\qquad\qquad T \,\&\, S$

$P \quad Q \quad S \qquad P \quad Q \quad S \quad T \quad S$

4. a.

P	Q	P & Q	~(P & Q)
T	T	T	F
T	F	F	T
F	T	F	T
F	F	F	T

c.

P	Q	P ∨ Q	~(P ∨ Q)
T	T	T	F
T	F	T	F
F	T	T	F
F	F	F	T

e.

P	Q	R	Q ∨ R	P ∨ (Q ∨ ~R)
T	T	T	T	T
T	T	F	T	T
T	F	T	T	T
T	F	F	F	T
F	T	T	T	T
F	T	F	T	T
F	F	T	T	T
F	F	F	F	F

g.

P	Q	R	Q & R	P & (Q & R)
T	T	T	T	T
T	T	F	F	F
T	F	T	F	F
T	F	F	F	F
F	T	T	T	F
F	T	F	F	F
F	F	T	F	F
F	F	F	F	F

i.

P	Q	R	Q ∨ R	P & (Q ∨ R)
T	T	T	T	T
T	T	F	T	T
T	F	T	T	T
T	F	F	F	F
F	T	T	T	F
F	T	F	T	F
F	F	T	T	F
F	F	F	F	F

k.

P	Q	R	Q & R	P ∨ (Q & R)
T	T	T	T	T
T	T	F	F	T
T	F	T	F	T
T	F	F	F	T
F	T	T	T	T
F	T	F	F	F
F	F	T	F	F
F	F	F	F	F

Section 2.2

1. a. $J \supset G$ c. $S \supset M$ e. $M \equiv S$ g. $(A \& \sim B) \supset (D \& E)$

2. a. $(P \vee Q) \supset (R \equiv S)$

c. $T \equiv \sim(Q \& (P \vee T))$

3. a. $(P \vee Q) \supset Q$

P	Q	P ∨ Q	(P ∨ Q) ⊃ Q
T	T	T	T
T	F	T	F
F	T	T	T
F	F	F	T

c. $\sim(P \supset \sim Q)$

P	Q	~Q	P ⊃ ~Q	~(P ⊃ ~Q)
T	T	F	F	T
T	F	T	T	F
F	T	F	T	F
F	F	T	T	F

e. $(P \& Q) \supset R$

P	Q	R	P & Q	(P & Q) ⊃ R
T	T	T	T	T
T	T	F	T	F
T	F	T	F	T
T	F	F	F	T
F	T	T	F	T
F	T	F	F	T
F	F	T	F	T
F	F	F	F	T

g. ~P ≡ ~Q

P	Q	~P	~Q	~P ≡ ~Q
T	T	F	F	T
T	F	F	T	F
F	T	T	F	F
F	F	T	T	T

i. P ≡ ~Q

P	Q	~Q	P ≡ ~Q
T	T	F	F
T	F	T	T
F	T	F	T
F	F	T	F

k. (P & Q) ∨ (~P & ~Q)

P & Q   ~P & ~Q

P	Q	P & Q	~P & ~Q	(P & Q) ∨ (~P & ~Q)
T	T	T	F	T
T	F	F	F	F
F	T	F	F	F
F	F	T	T	T

4. a. (1) X ⊃ C
Let **X** = the switch is closed. Let **C** = the current is flowing.

(2) ~C ⊃ ~X

(3) (A & B) ⊃ C
Let **A** = Switch A is closed. Let **B** = Switch B is closed. Let **C** = the current is flowing.

c. Having the switch(es) closed is a necessary condition for the current to be flowing.

5. a. (P ∨ Q) ⊃ (R ≡ S)

P ∨ Q   R ≡ S
P   Q   R   S

Yes, this is an SL statement.

c. T ≡ ~(Q & (P ∨ T))

~(Q & (P ∨ T))

Q & (P ∨ T)

P ∨ T

T   Q   P   T

Yes, this is an SL statement.

Section 2.3

1.

A	A ⊃ A	A	A ⊃ ~A	~(A ⊃ A)
T	T	T	F	F
F	T	F	T	F

3. 64 truth tables for 3 statement letters.
256 truth tables for 4 statement letters.

7. a. ~(~P & ~Q) b. ~[P & (~Q & R)] & ~[~(Q & ~R) & ~P]

c. ~P & (Q & ~R)

Section 2.4

1. Let P = 'Paula will speak at Commencement.'
   Let Q = 'Quincy will speak at Commencement.'
   Let T = 'Commencement will be rained out.'
   Let R = 'Robert will speak at Commencement.'
   Let S = 'Sharon will speak at Commencement.'

   a. ~P ⊃ Q
      If Paula does not speak at Commencement, then Quincy will.

   c. ~(P & ~R)
      It is not the case that Paula will speak at Commencement and Robert won't.

   e. R ⊃ (P ∨ Q)
      If Robert speaks at Commencement, then Paula or Quincy will also speak at Commencement.

   g. ~P ∨ (S & ~R)
      Paula will not speak at Commencement, or Sharon will speak and Robert won't.

2. a. T ⊃ P c. P ⊃ ~T   e. ~T ⊃ ~P (or P ⊃ T or T ∨ ~P)

   g. ((P ∨ T) & H) ⊃ R

3. a. Let W = 'The world is nasty.'   c. Let O = 'Oklahoma won.'
      Let L = 'I like it anyway.'   Let K = 'Kansas won.'
      W & L   ~Q & ~K

   e. Let P = 'Peter did it.'
      Let R = 'Ruth did it.'
      Let H = 'Helen did it.'
      [[P & (~R & ~H)] ∨ [R & (~H & ~P)]] ∨
          [[H & (~R & ~P)] ∨ [~P & (~R & ~H)]]

   g. Let S = 'You are single.'
      Let D = 'On December 31 you were unmarried.'
      Let P = 'On December 31 you were separated.'
      Let O = 'You qualify for another filing status.'
      ((D ∨ P) & ~O) ⊃ S
      NOTE: There is some ambiguity in this sentence. There should be a comma after the word *spouse* to identify the major connective in that clause.

i. Let A = 'Input A is high.'
Let B = 'Input B is high.'
Let O = 'The OR gate gives a high output.'
$((A \lor B) \supset O) \& ((\sim A \& \sim B) \supset \sim O)$

4. a. Let E = 'I get a job at home.'
Let S = 'I spend the summer at home.'
Let C = 'I have a car.'
Let J = 'I spend the summer at the Cape.'
Let P = 'My parents support me.'
Let D = 'I get a job at the Cape.'
$S \supset (E \supset C)$

$J \supset (P \lor D)$

$\sim P \& \sim C$
_____

D

Conclusion: I'll be working at the Cape this summer.

Section 2.5

1. a. *CNpq*   c. *NKpNr*   e. *CrApq*   g. *ANpKsNr*

Section 3.1

1. a. $P \lor (Q \& R)$

P	Q	R	Q & R	P ∨ (Q & R)
T	T	F	F	T

c. $\sim S \lor (Q \supset R)$

Q	R	S	~S	Q ⊃ R	~S ∨ (Q ⊃ R)
T	F	F	T	F	T

e. $P \lor [\sim P \lor (Q \supset R)]$

P	Q	R	~P ∨ (Q ⊃ R)	P ∨ [~P ∨ (Q ⊃ R)]
T	T	F	F	T

g. $[R \equiv (S \& P)] \lor Q$

P	Q	R	S	S & P	R ≡ (S & P)	[R ≡ (S & P)] ∨ Q
T	T	F	F	F	T	T

Section 3.2

1. a.

P	Q	P ⊃ ~Q	Q ⊃ ~P	P ≡ Q
T	T	F	F	T
T	F	T	T	F	←
F	T	T	T	F
F	F	T	T	T

Invalid argument.

c.

H	R	~(H ≡ R)	~H	~R
T	T	F	F	F
T	F	T	F	T
F	T	T	T	F	←
F	F	F	T	T

Invalid argument.

2. a. $P \equiv Q$

P	Q	P ≡ Q
T	T	T
T	F	F
F	T	F
F	F	T

$(P \& Q) \lor (\sim P \& \sim Q)$

P	Q	P & Q	~P & ~Q	(P & Q) ∨ (~P & ~Q)
T	T	T	F	T
T	F	F	F	F
F	T	F	F	F
F	F	F	T	T

Statements $P \equiv Q$ and $(P \& Q) \lor (\sim P \& \sim Q)$ are equivalent.

c. $P \supset Q$

P	Q	P ⊃ Q
T	T	T
T	F	F
F	T	T
F	F	T

$P \supset (P \& Q)$

P	Q	P & Q	P ⊃ (P & Q)
T	T	T	T
T	F	F	F
F	T	F	T
F	F	F	T

Statements $P \supset Q$ and $P \supset (P \& Q)$ are equivalent.

Section 3.3

1. a. Invalid argument. Counterexample: P is false, Q is either true or false, R is false, S is false.

   c. Valid argument.

   d. Invalid argument. Counter-example: Q is true, R is true.

2. a. Tautology.   c. Not a tautology.   e. Not a tautology.   g. Not a tautology.

3. a. Inconsistent.   c. Inconsistent.

5. a. If a set of statements is inconsistent, then there is no valuation on which all the members of the set are true. The conjunction of the members of the set will be false on any valuation because at least one conjunct will be false.

   c. If the set of statements $\{A_1, A_2, A_3, \ldots, A_n\}$ entails statement **B**, then on any valuation on which all of $A_1, A_2, A_3, \ldots A_n$ are true, **B** is true as well. So on any valuation on which $A_1 \& A_2 \& A_3 \& \ldots \& A_n$ is true, **B** is true; hence, $(A_1 \& A_2 \& A_3 \& \ldots \& A_n) \supset \mathbf{B}$ would also be true. And on any valuation on which $A_1 \& A_2 \& A_3 \& \ldots \& A_n$ is false, $(A_1 \& A_2 \& A_3 \& \ldots \& A_n) \supset \mathbf{B}$ is true as well. So $(A_1 \& A_2 \& A_3 \& \ldots \& A_n) \supset \mathbf{B}$ is true on every valuation.

Section 3.4

1. a. (1) $(P \vee Q) \supset {\sim}R$ √

   (2) $R \supset P$ √

   (3) $P \vee Q$ √

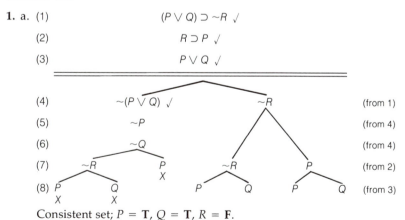

Consistent set; $P = \mathbf{T}, Q = \mathbf{T}, R = \mathbf{F}$.

c. (1) $(P \supset Q) \& (P \supset {\sim}Q)$ ✓

  (2)   P

   ═══════════════════════

  (3) $P \supset Q$ ✓   (from 1)

  (4) $P \supset {\sim}Q$ ✓   (from 1)

  (5) ${\sim}P$ Q   (from 3)
       X

  (6) ${\sim}P$ ${\sim}Q$ (from 4)
                X   X

Inconsistent set.

e. (1) $P \& {\sim}P$ ✓

  (2) $Q \& {\sim}Q$ ✓

   ═════════

  (3)   P   (from 1)

  (4) ${\sim}P$ (from 1)
      X

Inconsistent set.

3. a. (1) $P \vee Q$ ✓

    (2) ${\sim}P \& S$ ✓

    (3) ${\sim}(Q \& S)$ ✓

   ═══════════════════════

    (4) ${\sim}P$ (from 2)

    (5)   S   (from 2)

    (6) P   Q   (from 1)
       X

    (7) ${\sim}Q$ ${\sim}S$ (from 3)
             X   X

Valid argument.

c. (1) ${\sim}(P \equiv Q)$ ✓

  (2) ${\sim}P$

  (3) ${\sim}(Q \vee R)$ ✓

   ═══════════════════════

  (4) P ${\sim}P$ (from 1)

  (5) ${\sim}Q$ Q (from 1)
    X

  (6) ${\sim}Q$ (from 3)

  (7) ${\sim}R$ (from 3)
            X

Valid argument.

4. a.

(1)	$J \supset R$ ✓	
(2)	$B \supset {\sim}R$ ✓	
(3)	${\sim}(B \lor J)$ ✓	

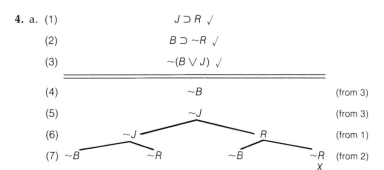

(4)	${\sim}B$	(from 3)
(5)	${\sim}J$	(from 3)
(6)	${\sim}J \qquad\qquad R$	(from 1)
(7)	${\sim}B \qquad {\sim}R \qquad {\sim}B \qquad {\sim}R$	(from 2)
	X	

Invalid argument. Counterexample: B is false, R is true, J is false.
"The jewels are not in the bank; the jewels are in his room; Jones is not the thief."

e.

(1)	${\sim}B \supset P$ ✓	
(2)	$B \supset C$ ✓	
(3)	${\sim}[{\sim}C \supset P]$ ✓	

(4)	${\sim}C$	(from 3)
(5)	${\sim}P$	(from 3)
(6)	${\sim}B \qquad\qquad C$	(from 2)
	X	
(7)	${\sim}{\sim}B \qquad P$	(from 1)
	X	
(8)	B	(from 7)
	X	

Valid argument.

5. a.

(1)	${\sim}[[P \supset [(P \lor Q) \lor Q]]$ ✓	
(2)	P	(from 1)
(3)	${\sim}[(P \lor Q) \lor Q]$ ✓	(from 1)
(4)	${\sim}(P \lor Q)$ ✓	(from 3)
(5)	${\sim}Q$	(from 3)
(6)	${\sim}P$	(from 4)
(7)	${\sim}Q$	(from 4)
	X	

Tautology.

c. (1) ~[[P ⊃ (Q ⊃ R)] ⊃ (P ⊃ Q)] √

(2)	P ⊃ (Q ⊃ R) √	(from 1)
(3)	~(P ⊃ Q) √	(from 1)
(4)	P	(from 3)
(5)	~Q	(from 3)
(6)	~P Q ⊃ R √	(from 2)
	X	
(7)	~Q R	(from 6)
	X	

Not a tautology.

7. a. For ~(**A** ∨ **B**):

A	B	~(A ∨ B)
T	T	F
T	F	F
F	T	F
F	F	T

The statement is true in one case: both ~**A** and ~**B** are true.

c. For ~(**A** ⊃ **B**):

A	B	~(A ⊃ B)
T	T	F
T	F	T
F	T	F
F	F	F

The statement is true in one case: both **A** and ~**B** are true.

For ~~**A**:

The statement is true in one case: **A** is true.

Section 3.5

1. a. Yes, John is playing.

b. No, there will not be a cut.

2. One method begins with a consistent set and adds the members of the other set one at a time, testing for consistency at each step. If adding a new member would make the combined set inconsistent, then that statement is not added, and we go on to the next. The result is sure to be consistent.

Section 4.1

1. a.

```
1.  A ⊃ B
2.  ~B
   ─────
3.  │A
    ──
4.  │A ⊃ B    (R, 1)
5.  │A        (R, 3)
6.  │B        (MP, 4, 5)
7.  │~B       (R, 2)
8.  │~A       (IR, 3, 6, 7)
```

b.

```
1.  A ⊃ B
2.  B ⊃ C
   ─────
3.  │A
    ──
4.  │A ⊃ B    (R, 1)
5.  │A        (R, 3)
6.  │B        (MP, 4, 5)
7.  │B ⊃ C    (R, 2)
8.  │C        (MP, 6, 7)
9.  A ⊃ C     (CR, 3–8)
```

d.

```
1.  P ≡ Q
2.  ~Q
   ─────
3.  │P
    ──
4.  │P        (R, 3)
5.  │P ≡ Q    (R, 1)
6.  │Q        (BW, 4, 5)
7.  │~Q       (R, 2)
8.  │~P       (IR, 3, 5, 6)
```

2. a. Derive: **(A & B) & C** from **A & (B & C)**

```
1.  │A & (B & C)
   ──────────
2.  │A & (B & C)   (R, 1)
3.  │A             (SIMP, 2)
4.  │B & C         (SIMP, 2)
5.  │B             (SIMP, 4)
6.  │C             (SIMP, 4)
7.  │A & B         (CONJ, 3, 5)
8.  │(A & B) & C   (CONJ, 6, 7)
```

c. Derive **(A ∨ B) ∨ C** from **A ∨ (B ∨ C)**

```
1.  │A ∨ (B ∨ C)
   ──────────
2.  │A ∨ (B ∨ C)       (R, 1)
3.  ││A
    ──
4.  ││A                (R, 3)
5.  ││A ∨ B            (ADD, 4)
6.  ││(A ∨ B) ∨ C      (ADD, 5)

7.  ││B ∨ C
     ─────
8.  │││B
     ──
9.  │││B               (R, 8)
10. │││A ∨ B           (ADD, 9)
11. │││(A ∨ B) ∨ C     (ADD, 10)

12. │││C
     ──
13. │││C               (R, 13)
14. │││(A ∨ B) ∨ C     (ADD, 13)
15. ││B ∨ C            (R, 7)
16. ││(A ∨ B) ∨ C      (DISJ, 2, 8–11, 12–14)
17. │(A ∨ B) ∨ C       (DISJ, 2, 3–6, 7–16)
```

Section 4.2

1. a.

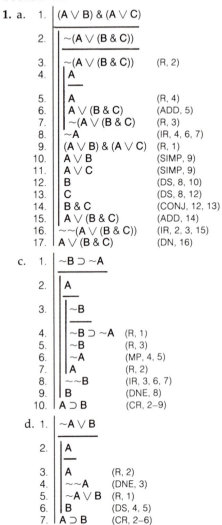

1. | (A ∨ B) & (A ∨ C)
2. || ~(A ∨ (B & C))
3. || ~(A ∨ (B & C))   (R, 2)
4. || | A
5. || | A   (R, 4)
6. || | A ∨ (B & C)   (ADD, 5)
7. || | ~(A ∨ (B & C)) (R, 3)
8. || ~A   (IR, 4, 6, 7)
9. | (A ∨ B) & (A ∨ C) (R, 1)
10. | A ∨ B   (SIMP, 9)
11. | A ∨ C   (SIMP, 9)
12. | B   (DS, 8, 10)
13. | C   (DS, 8, 12)
14. | B & C   (CONJ, 12, 13)
15. | A ∨ (B & C)   (ADD, 14)
16. | ~~(A ∨ (B & C))   (IR, 2, 3, 15)
17. | A ∨ (B & C)   (DN, 16)

c.

1. | ~B ⊃ ~A
2. || A
3. || | ~B
4. || | ~B ⊃ ~A   (R, 1)
5. || | ~B   (R, 3)
6. || | ~A   (MP, 4, 5)
7. || | A   (R, 2)
8. || ~~B   (IR, 3, 6, 7)
9. || B   (DNE, 8)
10. | A ⊃ B   (CR, 2–9)

d.

1. | ~A ∨ B
2. || A
3. || A   (R, 2)
4. || ~~A   (DNE, 3)
5. || ~A ∨ B   (R, 1)
6. || B   (DS, 4, 5)
7. | A ⊃ B   (CR, 2–6)

e. 1. | (A & B) ∨ (~A & ~B)

    2. (A & B) ∨ (~A & ~B) (R, 1)
    3. | A & B

    4. || A

    5. || A & B   (R, 3)
    6. || B   (SIMP, 5)

    7. || B

    8. || A & B   (R, 3)
    9. || A   (SIMP, 8)
    10. | A ≡ B   (BICON, 4–6, 7–9)

    11. | ~A & ~B

    12. || A

    13. ||| ~B

    14. || A   (R, 12)
    15. || ~A & ~B   (R, 11)
    16. || ~A   (SIMP, 15)
    17. || ~~B   (IR, 13, 14, 16)
    18. || B   (DNE, 17)

    19. || B

    20. ||| ~A

    21. ||| ~A   (R, 20)
    22. || B   (R, 19)
    23. ||| ~A & ~B   (R, 11)
    24. || ~B   (SIMP, 23)
    25. || ~~A   (IR, 20, 22, 24)
    26. || A   (DNE, 25)
    27. || A ≡ B   (BICON, 12–18, 19–26)
    28. | A ≡ B   (DISJ, 2, 3–10, 11–26)

h. 1. | A ∨ A

    2. A ∨ A (R, 1)
    3. | A

    4. | A   (R, 3)
    5. | A   (DISJ, 2, 3–4, 3–4)

i. 1. | ~(A ∨ B)

    2. | A

    3. | A   (R, 2)
    4. | A ∨ B   (ADD, 3)
    5. | ~(A ∨ B)   (R, 1)
    6. | ~A   (IR, 3, 4, 5)
    7. | B

    8. | B   (R, 7)
    9. | A ∨ B   (ADD, 8)
    10. | ~(A ∨ B)   (R, 1)
    11. | ~B   (IR, 8, 9, 10)
    12. | ~A & ~B   (CONJ, 6, 11)

2. a.   1.   A & A

2.   A & A   (R, 1)
3.   A   (SIMP, 2)

4.   A

5.   A   (R, 4)
6.   A & A   (CONJ, 5, 5)
7.   A ≡ (A & A)   (BICON, 1–3, 4–6)

b.   1.   A ⊃ B

2.   A

3.   A ⊃ B   (R, 1)
4.   A   (R, 2)
5.   B   (MP, 3, 4)
6.   A & B   (CONJ, 4, 5)
7.   A ⊃ (A & B)   (CR, 2–6)

8.   A ⊃ (A & B)
9.   A

10. A   (R, 9)
11. A ⊃ (A & B)   (R, 8)
12. A & B   (MP, 10, 11)
13. A   (SIMP, 12)
14. B   (SIMP, 12)
15. A ⊃ B   (CR, 9–14)
16. A ⊃ B ≡ [A ⊃ (A & B)]   (BICON, 2–7, 8–15)

d.   1.   A & (B & ~B)

2.   A & (B & ~B)   (R, 1)
3.   B & ~B   (SIMP, 2)

4.   B & ~B

5.   ~(A & (B & ~B))

6.   B & ~B   (R, 4)
7.   B   (SIMP, 6)
8.   ~B   (SIMP, 6)
9.   ~~(A & (B & ~B))   (IR, 5, 7, 8)
10. A & (B & ~B)   (DN, 9)
11. (A & (B & ~B)) ≡ (B & ~B)   (BICON, 1–3, 4–10)

4. a.   1.   P ≡ Q
2.   (P ⊃ Q) & (Q ⊃ P)   (BE, 1)
3.   (Q ⊃ P) & (P ⊃ Q)   (COM &, 2)
4.   Q ≡ P   (BE, 3)

b.   1.   ~(P & ~Q)
2.   ~P ∨ ~~Q   (DEM, 1)
3.   ~P ∨ Q   (DNE, 2)
4.   Q ∨ ~P   (COM ∨, 3)

5. c.

1.	$\sim[\sim(P \vee Q) \vee Q]$	
2.	$\sim[(\sim P \,\&\, \sim Q) \vee Q]$	(DEM, 1)
3.	$\sim[Q \vee (\sim P \,\&\, \sim Q)]$	(COM $\vee$, 2)
4.	$\sim[(Q \vee \sim P) \,\&\, (Q \vee \sim Q)]$	(DIST $\vee$/&, 3)
5.	$\sim[Q \vee \sim P]$	(TAUT &, 4)
6.	$\sim Q \,\&\, \sim\sim P$	(DEM, 5)
7.	$\sim Q \,\&\, P$	(DNE, 6)

d.

1.	$\sim\sim P \vee [P \,\&\, (Q \vee \sim Q)]$	
2.	$\sim\sim P \vee P$	(TAUT &, 1)
3.	$P \vee P$	(DNE, 2)
4.	P	(IDEM $\vee$, 3)

Section 4.3a

1. a.

1.	$P \supset Q$	
2.	$\sim P \vee Q$	(CE, 1)

b.

1.	$P \equiv Q$	
2.	$(P \supset Q) \,\&\, (Q \supset P)$	(BE, 1)
3.	$(\sim P \vee Q) \,\&\, (Q \supset P)$	(CE, 2)
4.	$(\sim P \vee Q) \,\&\, (\sim Q \vee P)$	(CE, 3)

d.

1.	$\sim(\sim P \equiv Q)$	
2.	$\sim((\sim P \,\&\, Q) \vee (P \,\&\, \sim Q))$	(BE, 1)
3.	$\sim((\sim P \,\&\, Q) \vee (P \,\&\, \sim Q))$	(DNE, 2)
4.	$(\sim(\sim P \,\&\, Q) \,\&\, (\sim(P \,\&\, Q))$	(DEM, 3)
5.	$(\sim\sim P \vee \sim Q) \,\&\, (\sim P \vee \sim\sim Q)$	(DEM, 4)
6.	$(P \vee \sim Q) \,\&\, (\sim P \vee Q)$	(DNE, 5)

2. a. $\{\sim P, Q\}$ **b.** $\{\sim P, Q\}$ **d.** $\{\sim P, Q\}$

             $\{\sim Q, P\}$ $\{P, \sim Q\}$

3. a.

1.	$P \vee (P \supset R)$	
2.	$P \vee (\sim P \vee R)$	(CE, 1)

$\{P, \sim P, R\}$

b.

1.	$\sim(P \equiv Q)$	
2.	$\sim[(P \,\&\, Q) \vee (\sim P \,\&\, \sim Q)]$	(BE, 2)
3.	$(\sim(P \,\&\, Q)) \,\&\, (\sim(\sim P \,\&\, \sim Q))$	(DEM, 2)
4.	$\sim(P \,\&\, Q) \,\&\, (\sim\sim P \vee \sim\sim Q)$	(DEM, 3)
5.	$\sim(P \,\&\, Q) \,\&\, (P \vee Q)$	(DNE, 4)
6.	$(\sim P \vee \sim Q) \,\&\, (P \vee Q)$	(DEM, 5)

$\{\sim P, \sim Q)$

$\{P, Q\}$

c.

1.	$(P \supset Q) \,\&\, (Q \supset R)$	
2.	$(\sim P \vee Q) \,\&\, (Q \supset R)$	(CE, 1)
3.	$(\sim P \vee Q) \,\&\, (\sim Q \vee R)$	(CE, 2)

$\{\sim P, Q\}$

$\{\sim Q, R\}$

Section 4.3b

1. a.

1.	$\{P, Q\}$
2.	$\{\sim P, Q\}$
3.	$\{P, \sim Q\}$
4.	$\{\sim P, \sim Q\}$
5.	$\{Q\}$ (Res, 1, 2)
6.	$\{\sim Q\}$ (Res, 3, 4)
7.	$\{\ \ \}$ (Res, 5, 6)

b.

1.	$\{P, Q\}$
2.	$\{\sim Q, \sim R\}$
3.	$\{R, \sim S\}$
4.	$\{\sim Q, S\}$
5.	$\{S\}$
6.	$\{\sim P, Q\}$
7.	$\{R\}$ (Res, 3, 5)
8.	$\{\sim Q\}$ (Res, 7, 2)
9.	$\{Q\}$ (Res, 1, 6)
10.	$\{\ \ \}$ (Res, 8, 9)

2. a. $\sim(A \lor B)$ $\sim(\sim A\ \&\ \sim B)$

$\{\sim A\}$ $\{A, B\}$

$\{\sim B\}$

1.	$\{\sim A\}$
2.	$\{\sim B\}$
3.	$\{A, B\}$
4.	$\{B\}$ (Res, 1, 3)
5.	$\{\ \ \}$ (Res, 2, 4)

c. $\sim(A\ \&\ B)$ $\sim[\sim A \lor \sim B]$

$\{\sim A, \sim B\}$ $\{A\}, \{B\}$

1.	$\{\sim A, \sim B\}$
2.	$\{A\}$
3.	$\{B\}$
4.	$\{\sim B\}$ (Res, 1, 2)
5.	$\{\ \ \}$ (Res, 3, 4)

d. $\sim A \lor \sim B$ $\sim[\sim(A\ \&\ B)]$

$\{\sim A, \sim B\}$ $\{A\}, \{B\}$

1.	$\{\sim A, \sim B\}$
2.	$\{A\}$
3.	$\{B\}$
4.	$\{\sim B\}$ (Res, 1, 2)
5.	$\{\ \ \}$ (Res, 3, 4)

3. a.

1.	$\{P, Q\}$
2.	$\{\sim Q\}$
3.	$\{\sim P\}$
4.	$\{Q\}$ (Res, 1, 3)
5.	$\{\ \ \}$ (Res, 2, 4)

b.

1.	$\{P, Q\}$
2.	$\{P, R\}$
3.	$\{\sim P\}$
4.	$\{\sim Q\}$
5.	$\{Q\}$ (Res, 1, 3)
6.	$\{\ \ \}$ (Res, 4, 5)

c.

1.	$\{P\}$
2.	$\{Q\}$
3.	$\{\sim P\}$
4.	$\{\sim Q\}$
5.	$\{\ \ \}$ (Res, 1, 3)

d.

1.	$\{P\}$
2.	$\{Q\}$
3.	$\{\sim P\}$
4.	$\{\sim Q\}$
5.	$\{\ \ \}$ (Res, 1, 3)

Section 5.1

1. b. name—John
name—Helen
predicate: . . . is sitting next to . . .

c. name—This desk
predicate: . . . is really ugly

d. name—I
   name—you
   predicate: . . . saw . . . yesterday

g. name—Her book
   name—Fred
   predicate: . . . really belongs to . . .

3. a. *Hb*   b. *Hbs*   c. *Isl* ⊃ *Ise*

4. a. Albert is a person.

   c. If Albert is a person, then Albert likes Charlie.

   e. It is not the case that Charlie likes Albert and Betty.

Section 5.2a

1. a. ∀x *Gx*   b. ~∃x *Gx*   d. ∀x (*Fx* ⊃ *Gx*)   e. ∃x (*Fx* & *Ex*)

   g. ∀x (*Gx* ⊃ ~*Ex*)   i. ∀x (*Fx* ⊃ *Gx*) ⊃ ∀x (*Ex* ⊃ *Gx*)

2. *S* = Subscribe to the *Times*   *B* = Promise breakers
   E = Are educated   *T* = Is trustworthy
   R = Can read   *V* = Wine drinkers
   H = Hedgehogs   *U* = Is very communicative
   N = Never waltz   *M* = Is sane
   D = Ducks   *L* = Can do logic
   O = Officers   *J* = Are fit to serve on a jury
   C = Ever decline to waltz   *F* = Is a son of yours
   P = My poultry

   a. ∀x (*Sx* ⊃ *Ex*)   b. ∀x (*Hx* ⊃ ~*Rx*)   c. ∀x (~*Rx* ⊃ ~*Ex*)   d. ∀x (*Dx* ⊃ ~*Wx*)

   e. ∀x (*Ox* ⊃ ~*Cx*)   f. ∀x (*Px* ⊃ *Dx*)   g. ∀x (*Bx* ⊃ ~*Tx*)   h. ∀x (*Vx* ⊃ *Ux*)

   i. ∀x (*Ux* ⊃ *Tx*)   j. ∀x (*Mx* ⊃ *Lx*)   k. ∀x (~*Mx* ⊃ ~*Jx*)   l. ∀x (*Fx* ⊃ ~*Lx*)

Section 5.2b

2. a. ∀x (*Mx* ⊃ *Ex*)   b. ∃x (*Mx* & *Ex*) ⊃ *Ua*   c. ∀x (*Mx* ⊃ *Ex*) ⊃ *Ua*

   d. *Ua* ⊃ ∃x (*Mx* & *Ex*)   e. *Ua* ⊃ ∀x (*Mx* ⊃ *Ex*)

Section 5.2c

1. a. ∀x ∃y *Gxy*   b. ∀x ∀y *Gxy*   d. ∃x *Gxx*   f. ∃x ∀y *Bxy*

   g. ∃x ∀y *Byx*   j. ∀x (*Bxx* ⊃ *Gxx*)   k. ∃x (*Bxx* & *Gxx*)

2. a. ∃x ∃y [(*Sx* & *Sy*) & *Lxy*]   c. ∃x [*Sx* & ∀y (*Sy* ⊃ ~*Lxy*)]   d. ∀x (*Sx* ⊃ ~*Lxx*)

   e. ∃x ∃y [[(*Sx* & *Sy*) & ∀z [*Sz* ⊃ (*Lxz* & *Lyz*)]]]

Section 5.3

1. a. Fa_1 b. ∃y *Fy*   f. ∃yGa_1y
   Fa_2 ∀x *Px*   ∃yGa_2y
   Fa_3 ∃yGa_3y
   etc.   etc.

4. a. *Fa*   **c.** *Pa, Pb, Pc*   **d.** *Fa* ⊃ *Ga*   **e.** *Faa, Fba, Fca*
   Fb   *Ga, Gb, Gc*   *Fb* ⊃ *Gb*   *Fab, Fac, Fbb*
   Fc   *Fc* ⊃ *Gc*   *Fbc, Fcb, Fcc*

5. a. Yes.   **c.** Yes.   **d.** No, clause *g*.   **f.** No, clause g.

Section 6.1a

1. a. False.   **d.** True.   **e.** False.   **i.** True.   **j.** False.

2. a. For any name **N**, either *PN* is false or *GN* is true.

   c. For at least one name **N**, both *FN* and *GN* are true.

   e. For some name, **N**, *RN* is false or *Pa* is true.

Section 6.1b

1. a. La_1a_2–**T**   **d.** La_2a_1–**T**   **e.** Pa_1–**T** La_1a_2–**T**
   La_2a_2–**T** La_4a_2–**T** Pa_2–**T** La_2a_2–**T**
   La_3a_2–**T** La_6a_3–**T** Pa_3–**T** La_3a_1–**T**
   La_4a_2–**T** La_8a_4–**T** Pa_4–**F**
   etc.   etc. Pa_5–**F**
                          etc.

3. a. If for every name **N**, *PN* is false.

   d. If there is no name **N** such that *PN*, *TN*, and *UN* are all true.

4. a. 'Something is purple.' (False only if there is no thing that is purple.)

   c. 'All teal umbrellas are expensive.' (False only if there is at least one cheap teal umbrella.)

   d. 'There is at least one tall peach umbrella.' (False only if no such umbrella exists.)

Section 6.2

1. a. On any valuation on which ∀*x Fx* is true, every statement of the form *FN*, where **N** is a name, is true. So ∃*x Fx* is sure to be true on such valuations as well. If ∀*x Fx* is true on a valuation, ∃*x Fx* is also true; so ∀*x Fx* ⊃ ∃*x Fx* is true on every valuation and is thus a logical truth.

   e. Suppose that ∃*y* ∀*x Pxy* is true on a valuation. Then there is a name a_m such that all statements of the sort Pa_1a_m, Pa_2a_m, Pa_3a_m, etc. are true on that valuation. So ∀*x* ∃*y Pxy* is also true on the valuation. Therefore, ∀*x* ∃*y Pxy* is true on any valuation on which ∃*y* ∀*x Pxy* is true. So ∃*y* ∀*x Pxy* ⊃ ∀*x* ∃*y Pxy* is logically true.

   i. Suppose that ∀*x* (*Fx* ⊃ *Ga*) is true on a valuation. Then for every name **N**, *FN* ⊃ *Ga* is true on that valuation. So either, for every name **N**, *FN* is false or *Ga* is true on that valuation. So either ∃*x Fx* is false or *Ga* is true on that valuation; so the conditional ∃*x Fx* ⊃ *Ga* is true on the valuation. Hence, on any valuation, if ∀*x* (*Fx* ⊃ *Ga*) is true, then so is ∃*x Fx* ⊃ *Ga*. Hence, ∀*x* (*Fx* ⊃ *Ga*) ⊃ ∃*x Fx* ⊃ *Ga* is logically true.

Section 6.3

1. a.

Fa_1	Fa_2	Ga_1	Ga_2
T	T	F	F

c.

Fa_1	Fa_2
T	F

2. a. $\forall x\,(Fx \supset Hx)$ $Fa_1 \supset Ha_1$

   $\forall x\,(Gx \supset Hx)$ $Ga_1 \supset Ha_1$

   ――――――――   ――――――――

   $\forall x\,(Fx \supset Gx)$ $Fa_1 \supset Ga_1$

Fa_1	Ga_1	Ha_1
T	F	T

b. $\exists x\,(Fx \,\&\, Hx)$ $(Fa_1 \,\&\, Ha_1) \lor (Fa_2 \,\&\, Ha_2)$

   $\exists x\,(Hx \,\&\, Gx)$ $(Ha_1 \,\&\, Ga_1) \lor (Ha_2 \,\&\, Ga_2)$

   ――――――――   ――――――――――――――――

   $\exists x\,(Fx \,\&\, Gx)$ $(Fa_1 \,\&\, Ga_1) \lor (Fa_2 \,\&\, Ga_2)$

Fa_1	Fa_2	Ga_1	Ga_2	Ha_1	Ha_2
F	T	T	F	T	T

d. $\forall x\,\exists y\,Lxy$ $(La_1a_1 \lor La_1a_2) \,\&\, (La_2a_1 \lor La_2a_2)$

   ――――――――   ――――――――――――――――――――

   $\exists y\,\forall x\,Lxy$ $(La_1a_1 \,\&\, La_2a_1) \lor (La_1a_2 \,\&\, La_2a_2)$

La_1a_1	La_1a_2	La_2a_1	La_2a_2
F	T	T	F

3. a.

Ga_1	Ga_2
T	F

f.

Fa_1	Fa_2	Ga
T	F	F

Section 7.1

1. a. (1) $\forall x\,Fx$

(2) $\sim Fa$

(3) Fa (from 1)

VALID.

c.   (1) ∀x (Rx ⊃ Gx)

    (2) ∀x (Gx ⊃ Fx)

    (3) ~∀x (Rx ⊃ Fx) √
    ════════════

    (4) ~(Ra ⊃ Fa)   (from 1)

    (5) Ra   (from 4)

    (6) ~Fa   (from 4)

    (7) Ra ⊃ Ga   √ (from 1)

    (8) Ga ⊃ Fa   √ (from 2)

    (9) ~Ga   Fa (from 8)
                  X

   (10) ~Ra   Ga (from 7)
       X   X

  VALID.

f.   (1) ∀x ∃y Lxy

    (2) ~∃x ∃y Lxy
    ══════════

    (3) ~∃y Lay   (from 2)

    (4) ∃y Lay √ (from 1)

    (5) Lab   (from 4)

    (6) ~Lab   (from 3)
        X

  VALID.

2. b. (1) ~∀x (Fx ⊃ ∀y Fy) √
      ══════════════

    (2) ~(Fa ⊃ ∀y Fy) √ (from 1)

    (3) Fa   (from 2)

    (4) ~∀y Fy √   (from 2)

    (5) ~Fb   (from 4)

  NOT LOGICALLY TRUE.

d. (1) ~[(∃x Gx ⊃ ∃x Hx) ⊃ ∃x (Gx & Hx)] √
      ═══════════════════════════

    (2)   ∃x Gx ⊃ ∃x Hx √   (from 1)

    (3)   ~∃x (Gx & Hx)   (from 1)

    (4)   ~∃x Gx   ∃x Hx √ (from 2)

    (5)   Ha   (from 4)

    (6)   ~Ga   (from 4)

    (7) ~(Ga & Ha) √   ~(Ga & Ha) √ (from 3)

    (8) ~Ga   ~Ha   ~Ga   ~Ha (from 7)

  NOT LOGICALLY TRUE.

3. b. (1)   ~[∀x (Hx ∨ Gx) ≡ (∀x Hx ∨ ∀x Gx)

(2) ∀x (Hx ∨ Gx)   ~∀x (Hx ∨ Gx)   (from 1)

(3) ~(∀x Hx ∨ ∀x Gx) ✓   (∀x Hx ∨ ∀x Gx)   (from 1)

(4) ~∀x Hx ✓   (from 3)

(5) ~∀x Gx ✓   (from 3)

(6) ~Ha   (from 4)

(7) ~Gb   (from 5)

(8)   Ha ∨ Ga ✓   (from 2)

(9)   Ha   Ga   (from 8)
         X

(10)   Hb ∨ Gb ✓   (from 2)

(11)   Hb   Gb   (from 10)

NOT EQUIVALENT.

d. (1)   ~[(∃x Fx ⊃ Ga) ≡ ∀x (Fx ⊃ Ga)]

(2)   ∃x Fx ⊃ Ga ✓   ~(∃x Fx ⊃ Ga) ✓   (from 1)

(3) ~∀x (Fx ⊃ Ga) ✓   ∀x (Fx ⊃ Ga)   (from 1)

(4)   ~∃x Fx   Ga   (from 2)

(5) ~(Fb ⊃ Ga) ✓   ~(Fb ⊃ Ga) ✓   (from 3)

(6)   ~Fb   ~Fb   (from 4)

(7)   Fb   Fb   (from 5)

(8)   ~Ga   ~Ga   (from 5)
         X   X

(9)   ∃x Fx ✓   (from 2)

(10)   ~Ga   (from 2)

(11)   Fb   (from 9)

(12)   Fb ⊃ Ga ✓   (from 3)

(13)   ~Fb   Ga   (from 11)
                      X   X

EQUIVALENT.

4. a. ∀x [Sx ⊃ Ex]

~Es
_____

~Ss

(1) ∀x [Sx ⊃ Ex]

(2) ~Es

(3) ~~Ss ✓

(4) Ss ⊃ Es ✓   (from 1)

(5) Ss ⌒ Es   (from 4)
         X

(6) Ss   (from 3)
      X

VALID.

f. ∀x ∃y ~Lxy
_____

∃y ∀x ~Lxy

(1) ∀x ∃y ~Lxy

(2) ~∃y ∀x ~Lxy

(3) ∃y ~La₁y ✓   (from 1)

(4) ~La₁a₂   (from 3)

(5) ~∀x ~Lxa₂ ✓   (from 2)

(6) ~~La₃a₂   (from 5)

(7) ∃y ~La₂y   (from 1)

(8) ∃y ~La₃y   (from 1)

(9) ~∀x ~Lxa₁   (from 2)

(10) ~∀x ~Lxa₃   (from 2)

NOT VALID. (NOTE: Type III tree.)

Section 7.2

2. b.

Fa	Fb	Fc etc.	∀x [Fx ⊃ ∀y Fy]
T	F	F	F

d.

Ga	Gb etc.	Ha	Hb etc.	(∃x Gx ⊃ ∃x Hx) ⊃ ∃x (Gx & Hx)
F	F	F	F	F

3. b.

Ga	Gb	Gc etc.	Ha	Hb	Hc etc.	∀x (Hx ∨ Gx) ≡ (∀x Hx ∨ ∀x Gx)
T	F	T	F	T	T	F

4. f.

La₁a₂	La₃a₂	La₃a₄	La₃a₅ etc.	all others
F	T	T	T	F

∀x ∃y ~Lxy	∃y ∀x ~Lxy
T	F

Section 7.3

4. 1. | $\sim\exists X \sim A$

   2. || $\sim A(N/X)$

   3. || $\sim A(N/X)$ (R, 2)
   4. || $\exists X \sim A$ (EG, 3)
   5. || $\sim\exists X \sim A$ (R, 1)
   6. | $\sim\sim A(N/X)$ (IR, 2, 4, 5)
   7. | $A(N/X)$ (DN, 6)
   8. | $\forall X\, A$ (UG, 7)

7. 1. | $\forall X\, (A \supset B)$ where X does not occur in A

   2. || A

   3. || $\forall X\, (A \supset B)$ (R, 1)
   4. || $A \supset B(N/X)$ (UI, 3) (NOTE: **N** must not occur in **A**.)
   5. || A
   6. || $B(N/X)$ (MP, 4, 5)
   7. || $\forall X\, B$ (UG, 6)
   8. | $A \supset \forall X\, B$ (CR, 2–7)

   1. | $A \supset \forall X\, B$ where X does not occur in A

   2. || A

   3. || A (R, 2)
   4. || $A \supset \forall X\, B$ (R, 1)
   5. || $\forall X\, B$ (MP, 3, 4)
   6. || $B(N/X)$ (UI, 5) (NOTE: **N** must not occur in **A**.)
   7. | $A \supset B(N/X)$ (CR, 2–6)
   8. | $\forall X\, (A \supset B)$ (UG, 7)

9. c. $\forall x\, [Px \supset (Wx \equiv Ex)]$

$\exists x\, [Px\, \&\, \sim Ex] \supset \exists x\, [Px\, \&\, \sim Wx]$

   1. | $\forall x\, [Px \supset (Wx \equiv Ex)]$

   2. || $\exists x\, [Px\, \&\, \sim Ex]$

   3. || $\exists x\, [Px\, \&\, \sim Ex]$ (R, 2)

   4. ||| $Pa\, \&\, \sim Ea$

   5. ||| $Pa\, \&\, \sim Ea$ (R, 4)
   6. ||| $\forall x\, [Px \supset (Wx \equiv Ex)]$ (R, 1)
   7. ||| $Pa \supset (Wa \equiv Ea)$ (UI, 6)
   8. ||| Pa (SIMP, 5)
   9. ||| $Wa \equiv Ea$ (MP, 7, 8)
  10. ||| $\sim Ea$ (SIMP, 5)
  11. ||| $(Wa \supset Ea)\, \&\, (Ea \supset Wa)$ (BE, 9)
  12. ||| $Wa \supset Ea$ (SIMP, 11)
  13. ||| $\sim Wa$ (MT, 10, 12)
  14. ||| $Pa\, \&\, \sim Wa$ (CONJ, 8, 13)
  15. ||| $\exists x\, [Px\, \&\, \sim Wx]$ (EG, 14)
  16. || $\exists x\, [Px\, \&\, \sim Wx]$ (EI, 3, 4–15)
  17. | $\exists x\, [Px\, \&\, \sim Ex] \supset \exists x\, [Px\, \&\, \sim Wx]$ (CR, 2–16)

e. $\forall x\ (Ex \supset Ax)$

$\forall x\ \forall y\ [(Hxy\ \&\ Ey) \supset (Hxy\ \&\ Ay)]$

1.	$\forall x\ (Ex \supset Ax)$	
2.	$Hab\ \&\ Eb$	
3.	$Hab\ \&\ Eb$	(R, 2)
4.	$\forall x\ (Ex \supset Ax)$	(R, 1)
5.	$Eb \supset Ab$	(UI, 4)
6.	Eb	(SIMP, 3)
7.	Ab	(MP, 5, 6)
8.	Hab	(SIMP, 3)
9.	$Hab\ \&\ Ab$	(CONJ, 8, 7)
10.	$(Hab\ \&\ Eb) \supset (Hab\ \&\ Ab)$	(CR, 2–9)
11.	$\forall y\ [(Hay\ \&\ Ey) \supset (Hay\ \&\ Ay)]$	(UG, 10)
12.	$\forall x\ \forall y\ [(Hxy\ \&\ Ey) \supset (Hxy\ \&\ Ay)]$	(UG, 11)

Section 7.4a

1. c. $Gf(x)x$ e. $\sim Gb \lor Ga$

f. $\sim Fx \lor \sim Fy \lor \sim Pf(x, y)x \lor \sim Pf(x, y)y \lor Sxy$

i. $(\sim Ex \lor \sim Hyx \lor Ax)\ \&\ (\sim Ex \lor \sim Hyx \lor Hyx)$

2. c. $\{Gf(x)x\}$ e. $\{\sim Gb, Ga\}$

f. $\{\sim Fx, \sim Fy, \sim Pf(x, y)x, \sim Pf(x, y)y, Sxy\}$

i. $\{\sim Ex, \sim Hyx, Ax\}$
   $\{\sim Ex, \sim Hyx, Hyx\}$

Section 7.4b

2. c.

1.	$\{\sim Rx, Gx\}$	
2.	$\{\sim Gy, Fy\}$	
3.	$\{Ra\}$	
4.	$\{\sim Fa\}$	
5.	$\{\sim Ga, Fa\}$	(U a/y, 2)
6.	$\{\sim Ga\}$	(Res, 4, 5)
7.	$\{\sim Ra, Ga\}$	(U a/x, 1)
8.	$\{\sim Ra\}$	(Res, 6, 7)
9.	$\{\ \ \}$	(Res, 3, 8)

f.

1.	$\{Lxf(x)\}$	
2.	$\{\sim Lyz\}$	
3.	$\{\sim Lyf(x)\}$	(U f(x)/z, 2)
4.	$\{\sim Lxf(x)\}$	(U x/y, 3)
5.	$\{\ \ \}$	(Res, 1, 4)

g.

1.	$\{\sim Px, Rf(x)\}$	
2.	$\{\sim Py, Lyf(y)\}$	
3.	$\{Pa\}$	
4.	$\{\sim Laz\}$	
5.	$\{\sim Pa, Laf(a)\}$	(U a/y, 2)
6.	$\{Laf(a)\}$	(Res, 3, 5)
7.	$\{\sim Laf(a)\}$	(U f(a)/z, 4)
8.	$\{\ \ \}$	(Res, 6, 7)

3. Data   **Clausal Form**

$\forall x \, [(Gx \& Sx) \supset Tx]$ $\{\sim Gx, \sim Sx, Tx\}$

$\forall x \, [(Gx \& Sx) \supset Fx]$ $\{\sim Gx, \sim Sx, Fx\}$

Sj $\{Sj\}$

Sm $\{Sm\}$

$\sim Fj$ $\{\sim Fj\}$

Tm $\{Tm\}$

Fm $\{Fm\}$

Ts $\{Ts\}$

a. The empty clause { } cannot be derived by adding $\{\sim Gj\}$ to the above clauses, so the answer is *no* based on the information given above.

c. We add $\{Fx, \mathrm{ANS}(x)\}$ to the clauses and derive $\mathrm{ANS}(j)$.

e. We add $\{Fs\}$ to the clauses, but we cannot derive $\{Gj\}$, so the answer is *no* based on the information given above.

Section 8.1a

1. The set of numbers from 100 to 200.

2. $\{150\}$

5. a. No.   Let A = pigs; B = dogs. $A \cdot B$ = empty set

$(A \cdot B)'$ = universe

A' = nonpigs

B' = nondogs

$A' \cdot B'$ = universe without dogs and pigs

c. **Yes.**   Let $A = \{1\}$ $A \oplus (B \oplus C) = \{1, 2, 3\}$

$B = \{2\}$ $B \oplus A = \{1, 2\}$

$C = \{2, 3\}$ $(B \oplus A) \oplus C = \{1, 2, 3\}$

Section 8.1b

1. a. B1: {tea, coffee, milk, cola, water} = $D \oplus E$
{tea, coffee, milk, cola, water} = $E \oplus D$

B2: {coffee} = $D \cdot E$
{coffee} = $E \cdot D$

B3: $E \cdot F = \{ \ \}$ $D \cdot E = \{coffee\}$
$D \cdot (E \cdot F) = \{ \ \}$ $(D \cdot E) \cdot F = \{ \ \}$

B4: $E \oplus F$ = {coffee, cola, water, juice}
$D \oplus (E \oplus F)$ = {tea, milk, coffee, cola, water, juice}

$D \oplus E$ = {tea, coffee, milk, cola, water}
$(D \oplus E) \oplus F$ = {tea, milk, coffee, cola, water, juice}

B5: $E \oplus F = \{\text{coffee, cola, water, juice}\}$
$D \cdot (E \oplus F) = \{\text{coffee}\}$

$D \cdot E = \{\text{coffee}\}$
$D \cdot F = \{\ \}$
$(D \cdot E) \oplus (D \cdot F) = \{\text{coffee}\}$

B6: $E \cdot F = \{\ \}$
$D \oplus (E \cdot F) = \{\text{tea, coffee, milk}\}$

$D \oplus E = \{\text{tea, coffee, milk, cola, water}\}$
$D \oplus F = \{\text{tea, coffee, milk, juice}\}$
$(D \oplus E) \cdot (D \oplus F) = \{\text{tea, coffee, milk}\}$

Section 8.1c

1. a. $\{5, 6, 7, 8, 9, 10\}$ **c.** $A' = \{5, 6, 7, 8, 9, 10\}$ **3.** $[C \cdot (C' \cdot (D \cdot E)')')']'$
$A'' = \{1, 2, 3, 4\}$

$B' = \{10\}$
$B'' = \{1, 2, 3, 4, 5, 6, 7, 8, 9\}$

Section 8.1d

1. B1: $1 \oplus 0 = 0 \oplus 1$
$1 = 1$

B2: $1 \cdot 0 = 0 \cdot 1$
$0 = 0$

B3: $1 \cdot (0 \cdot Z) = (1 \cdot 0) \cdot Z$
$1 \cdot 0 = 0 \cdot Z$
$0 = 0$

B4: $1 \oplus (0 \oplus Z) = (1 \oplus 0) \oplus Z$
$1 \oplus Z = 1 \oplus Z$

B5: $1 \cdot (0 \oplus Z) = (1 \cdot 0) \oplus (1 \cdot Z)$
$1 \cdot Z = 0 \oplus Z$
$Z = Z$

B6: $1 \oplus (0 \cdot Z) = (1 \oplus 0) \cdot (1 \oplus Z)$
$1 = 1 \cdot 1$
$1 = 1$

B7: $1 \cdot 1 = 1$ $0 \cdot 0 = 0$
$1 = 1$ $0 = 0$

Section 8.2

1. a. $F \cdot P' = O$ $F = $ football fans; $P = $ potato chip eaters

   c. $T \cdot A = O$ $T = $ wishful thinkers; $A = $ those who need apply

   e. $P \cdot L \neq O$ $P = $ persons; $L = $ those who like blue ties

2. a. $S \cdot R = O$

$F \cdot R \neq O$
_____
$F \cdot S' \neq O$

1.	$S \cdot R = O$	
2.	$F \cdot R \neq O$	
3.	$\quad F \cdot S' = O$	
4.	$\quad F \cdot S' = O$	(R, 3)
5.	$\quad S \cdot R = O$	(R, 1)
6.	$\quad F \cdot R = O$	(B28, 4, 5)
7.	$\quad F \cdot R \neq O$	(R, 2)
8.	$F \cdot S' \neq O$	(IR, 3, 6, 7)

3. b. $R \cdot O = 0$
   $C \cdot R = 0$
   _____
   $C \cdot O = 0$

R = runs every day
O = those who are out of shape
C = those who care about themselves

Suppose that the premises are true; also suppose that Jane is a person who is not a runner but is both out of shape and cares about herself. Then $C \cdot O \neq 0$; the conclusion is false and the premises are true.

Section 8.3

2. Boole's rule, SL version:

   a. If $\mathbf{A} \equiv \mathbf{B}$ and $\mathbf{C} \equiv \mathbf{B}$, then $\mathbf{A} \equiv \mathbf{C}$.

   b. If $\mathbf{A} \equiv \mathbf{B}$, then $\mathbf{B}$ can replace $\mathbf{A}$ in any statement without changing the truth-value.

   a. | 1. | $A \equiv B$ |
       | 2. | $C \equiv B$ |

3.	$A \equiv B$	(R, 1)
4.	$(A \supset B) \ \& \ (B \supset A)$	(BE, 3)
5.	$C \equiv B$	(R, 2)
6.	$(C \supset B) \ \& \ (B \supset C)$	(BE, 5)
7.	$B \supset C$	(SIMP, 6)
8.	$A \supset B$	(SIMP, 4)
9.	$A \supset C$	(HS, 8, 7)
10.	$C \supset B$	(SIMP, 6)
11.	$B \supset A$	(SIMP, 4)
12.	$C \supset A$	(HS, 10, 11)
13.	$(A \supset C) \ \& \ (C \supset A)$	(CONJ, 9, 12)
14.	$A \equiv C$	(BE, 13)

   b. If $\mathbf{A} \equiv \mathbf{B}$, $\mathbf{A}$ and $\mathbf{B}$ have the same truth-value; therefore, in any statement $\mathbf{C}$ of which $\mathbf{A}$ is a component, if $\mathbf{B}$ replaces $\mathbf{A}$, the result will have the same truth-value as $\mathbf{C}$.

Section 8.4a

1. a. 'is the same as' (the identity relation)
   Defined on the set of all objects

   (1) All things are the same as themselves.

   (2) If X is the same as Y, then Y is the same as X.

   (3) If X is the same as Y and Y as Z, then X is the same as Z.

   b. 'is equal to' (in arithmetic, $=$)
   Defined on the set of numbers

   (1) All numbers equal themselves.

   (2) If X equals Y, then Y equals X.

   (3) If X equals Y and Y equals Z, then X equals Z.

3. The duals of all of the postulates $P1$–$P18$ are also postulates (i.e., $P2$ is the dual of $P1$, etc.). So if A is derivable from some set $\{P_m, P_n, \ldots, P_z\}$ of postulates, then A_D, its dual, will be derivable by just substituting the dual for each line in the derivation.

Section 8.4b

2. $<$ is $\supset$ in SL.
$<$ is 'less than or equal to' in the Boolean arithmetic of 1 and 0.
$<$ is 'is a subset of' in Boole's system for sets.

Section 8.4c

1. We would need only $P1$, $P3$, $P5$, $P7$, $P9$, $P10$, $P12$, $P14$.

3. 'is less than or equal to' is reflexive and transitive (but not symmetrical):

   (1) $X \leqslant X$ $(X \times X = X; P7)$

   (2) If $X \leqslant Y$ and $Y \leqslant Z$, then $X \leqslant Z$.

   (If $X \times Y = X$ and $Y \times Z = Y$, then $X \times Z = X$.)

   Suppose that $X \times Y = X$ and $Y \times Z = Y$;

      then $X \times (Y \times Z) = X$ (Boole's rule (b))

      then $(X \times Y) \times Z = X$ $(P3)$

      then $X \times Z = X$ (Boole's rule (b))

   To show that $\leqslant$ is not symmetrical:

   Suppose $X \times Y = X$; let $X = 0$ and $Y = 1$, so $0 \times 1 = 0$.
   But note that $1 \times 0 = 1$ does not hold in A, so $Y \times X \neq Y$.

4. Boolean algebras do not permit inequalities.

Section 9.1a

1. a. $(1 \times 10^3) + (2 \times 10^2) + (3 \times 10^1) + (4 \times 10^0)$

   c. $(1 \times 10^2) + (2 \times 10^1) + (2 \times 10^0)$

   e. $(2 \times 10^4) + (3 \times 10^3) + (0 \times 10^2) + (5 \times 10^1) + (0 \times 10^0)$

2. a. 31,004   c. 309

Section 9.1b

2. a. $(5 \times 8^1) + (6 \times 8^0) = 46$

   c. $(1 \times 8^3) + (2 \times 8^2) + (0 \times 8^1) + (3 \times 8^0) = 643$

3. a. $(4 \times 5^1) + (3 \times 5^0)$ or 43

   c. $(3 \times 5^3) + (1 \times 5^2) + (4 \times 5^1) + (1 \times 5^0)$ or 3141

Section 9.2

1. a. **111111**   c. **100**   e. **10100011101**   **2.** a. 5   c. 15   d. 170

Section 9.3

1. a. **1001111**   c. **1100000**   **3.** a. **1010**   c. **1101**

Section 9.4

1. a. **1A**   c. **21**   d. **3BBB**

2. a. **0001 0100 1010 1011**   c. **1010 1010 1101 1101 0011**

4. b. **17**   c. **1E79**

Section 9.5

1. a. COM = 77   b. COM = 888   c. COM = 4577

3. a. **01**   c. **1001101**   d. **1000011**

4. a.   11011   c.   1101110
       + 11101   (COM$_5$ 11)   + 1110001   (COM$_7$ 1111)

       1 11000   drop carry = 11000   1 1011111   drop carry = 1011111

Section 10.1a

2. $(X \& Y) \vee (\sim X \& Z)$ $[X \& (\sim X \vee Z)] \vee [\sim X \& (Y \vee Z)]$
     $Y \vee [X \& (Y \vee Z)]$ $[Y \& (\sim X \vee Z)] \vee [X \& (Y \vee Z)]$

3. a. The logical representation of such a circuit would be $S \& (X \vee \sim X)$, which is equivalent to S, according to the principle TAUT&.

   b. The logical representations of such circuits are $S \vee S$ and $S \& S$, both of which are equivalent to S, according to the principles IDEM$\vee$ and IDEM&.

Section 10.1b

1. a. $X \vee \sim X$ (i.e., circuit always on)   b. X c. $Z \& (X \vee Y)$

Section 10.4

1. a. Y b. $\sim Y \vee X$ c. $X \& (Z \vee \sim Y)$

Section 11.1

2. Here is a set of instructions with a loop:

   1. Start.
   2. Put a block on the ground.
   3. Put a block on the pile.
   4. Is the pile 3 feet high? If yes, go to 5; if no, go to 3.
   5. Stop.

Actions: Put a block on the ground; put a block on the pile.

Test: Is the pile 3 feet high?
Here are two sets of instructions without loops, which assume that each block is .5 feet high:

   1. Start.
   2. Put a block on a pile 2.5 feet high.
   3. Stop.

Action: Put a block on a pile 2.5 feet high.

Test: None.
   1. Start.
   2. Stack six blocks on the ground.
   3. Stop.

Action: Stack six blocks on the ground.

Test: None.

Section 11.2a

1. Legal inputs for *m*: binary numerals:

  1. START

  2. DO, WHILE DATA REMAIN:
   2.1 INPUT *m*
   2.2 IF LAST CHARACTER = 0, WRITE: "⟨*m*⟩ is EVEN"
   2.3 OTHERWISE: WRITE "⟨*m*⟩ is ODD"

  3. STOP

2. Legal inputs: sentences:

  1. START   2. INPUT sentence.   3. COUNT spaces *n*

  4. LET $m = n + 1$ 5. WRITE: "The number of words is ⟨*m*⟩"   6. STOP

4. To bring out the algorithmic nature of the Venn diagram method for determining validity, it is necessary to formulate instructions for drawing Venn diagrams for syllogistic arguments and for reading them to determine whether the conclusion is represented or not.

Section 11.2b

1. The algorithm has to be able to recognize that the string *1 0* is not a number (because of the space between the numerals).

2. Legal inputs: strings of characters:

  1. START   2. INPUT string.

  3. IF string contains any non-Polish notation characters, GOTO 8.2.

  4. REPLACE E, K, A, C with +, AND N with −

  5. REPLACE statement letters with 1

  6. WHILE + remain, CALCULATE*

  7. If expression is unchanged, GOTO 8.2

  8. IF expression is a number, THEN:
   8.1 WRITE: "The expression is an SL statement."
   8.2 OTHERWISE, WRITE: "The expression is not an SL statement."

  9. STOP

*NOTE: the algorithm calculates in outfix style; i.e., $+11 = 2$.

3. Legal inputs: SL statements in Polish notation with A, K, N as connectives; truth values (1 and 0):

  1. START   2. INPUT statement   3. INPUT truth-values

  4. REPLACE statement letters by their truth values

  5. WHILE A, K, N remain, CALCULATE BOOLEAN

6. IF statement = 1, THEN:
    6.1 WRITE: "The statement is true."
    6.2 OTHERWISE, WRITE: "The statement is false."
7. STOP

Section 11.2c

1. Change line 4b, b1 to POINT at the bottom item.

2. Each item in the list has two components: a town name and a state name; e.g., Chico, California. The initial sort is on the second component, the state name. The result is a list that brings all the towns in each state together and lists the states alphabetically. Then the sort, within each state portion of the list, is done on the town names. The result is a list that might look like this:

Hot Springs, Arkansas
Atherton, California
Chico, California
Hemet, California
Newark, Delaware

Section 11.3

1. NOTE: this algorithm assumes that there is at least one symbol on the tape.

	Input	Output		
	Read	Print	Move	State
State A	1	1	R	A
	0	0	R	A
	b	b	L	B
State B	1	b	R	C
	0	b	R	C
State C	b	b	H	

3.

	Input	Output		
	Read	Print	Move	State
State A	1	b	R	A
	0	b	R	A
	b	b	H	

5.

	Input	Output		
	Read	Print	Move	State
State A	1	b	R	B
	0	b	R	B
	b	b	H	
State B	1	1	R	B
	0	0	R	B
	b	b	R	D
State C	1	1	R	C
	0	0	R	C
	b	b	R	E
State D	1	1	R	D
	0	0	R	D
	b	1	L	F
State E	1	1	R	E
	0	0	R	E
	b	0	L	F
State F	1	1	L	F
	0	0	L	F
	b	b	L	G
State G	1	1	L	G
	0	0	L	G
	b	b	R	A

Section 12.1a

1. We will need only Q_1 and Q_2 as possible coin inputs. The expression for S is now:

$P \& S_s \& (I_s \lor B) \& K_s \& (Q_1 \& Q_2)$

3. No. $S \equiv \sim R$ is entailed by the conditions for S and R (see pp. 422–23).

Section 12.1b

2.

Inputs	Signals
Power	$P = 1$
First Quarter	$Q_1 = 1$
First Nickel	$N_1 = 1$
Second Nickel	$N_2 = 1$
Third Nickel	$N_3 = 1$
Fourth Nickel	$N_4 = 1$
'No Ice' Button	$B = 0$

Internal States	
Nickel Sense	$N_s = 1$
Soda Sense	$S_s = 1$
Ice Sense	$I_s = 1$
Cup Sense	$C_s = 0$

Outputs	
Cup	$K = 0$
Ice	$I = 0$
Soda	$S = 0$
Change	$C = 0$
'No Change' Light	$L = 0$
Return Coins	$R = 1$

3.

Inputs	Signals
Power	$P = 1$
First Quarter	$Q_1 = 1$
First Dime	$D_1 = 1$
Second Dime	$D_2 = 1$
'No Ice' Button	$B = 1$

Internal States	
Nickel Sense	$N_s = 0$
Soda Sense	$S_s = 1$
Ice Sense	$I_s = 1$
Cup Sense	$C_s = 1$

Outputs	
Cup	$K = 1$
Ice	$I = 0$
Soda	$S = 1$
Change	$C = 0$
'No Change' Light	$L = 0$
Return Coins	$R = 0$

Section 12.3

1. An argument is valid if the statement $(A_1 \,\&\, A_2 \,\&\, \ldots \,\&\, A_n \,\&\, {\sim}\mathbf{B})$ is a contradiction, where $A_1, A_2, \ldots, A_n$ are the premises and $\mathbf{B}$ is the conclusion. So we form the statement that corresponds to the argument, enter it into the machine, and see whether it is pronounced a contradiction or not.

   a. Valid.   b. Valid.   c. Valid.

2. A set of statements $\{A_1, A_2, \ldots, A_n\}$ is consistent if the corresponding statement $(A_1 \,\&\, A_2 \,\&\, \ldots \,\&\, A_n)$ is not a contradiction. So enter the corresponding statement into the machine and see whether it is a contradiction or not. Note that if the corresponding statement is a contradiction, the set is inconsistent.

3. Increase the capacity of the registers, adder, multiplier, complementer, decoder, and buses to 16 bits. Adapt the encoder to use 16 character designation numbers; put a fourth statement letter on the keyboard.

Index

Pages on which terms are defined are indicated by boldface type